SPEECHES
IN WORLD
HISTORY

SPEECHES IN WORLD HISTORY

SUZANNE McINTIRE

With additional contributions by
WILLIAM E. BURNS

An imprint of Infobase Publishing

For Jud

Facts On File, Inc.
An imprint of Infobase Publishing
132 West 31st Street
New York NY 10001

Library of Congress Cataloging-in-Publication Data
Speeches in world history / [compiled by] Suzanne McIntire ; with
additional contributions by William E. Burns.
    p. cm.
 Includes bibliographical references and index.
 ISBN-13: 978-0-8160-7404-4
 ISBN-10: 0-8160-7404-6
 1. Speeches, addresses, etc. I. McIntire, Suzanne, 1951-   II. Burns,
William E., 1959-
 PN6122.S64 2008
 808.85—dc22   2008005620

Facts On File books are available at special discounts when purchased in bulk quantities
for businesses, associations, institutions, or sales promotions. Please call
our Special Sales Department in New York at (212) 967-8800 or (800) 322-8755.

You can find Facts On File on the World Wide Web at http://www.factsonfile.com

Text design by Erika K. Arroyo
Cover design by Takeshi Takahashi

Printed in the United States of America

VB FOF 10 9 8 7 6 5 4 3 2 1

This book is printed on acid-free paper and contains 30 percent postconsumer
recycled content.

Contents

THE AGE OF REVOLUTION AND EMPIRE
(1750–1900)

THE CONTEMPORARY WORLD
(1950–THE PRESENT)

List of Illustrations

Foreword

No one knows who was the first human to address his or her fellows as a group. Perhaps this person was someone organizing a hunting or gathering expedition, or urging that a clan relocate in the face of climate change or the coming of dangerous animals. Whoever it was, he or she was inaugurating a long and varied tradition of public speaking, extending through a myriad of civilizations and societies to the present day.

This book contains some of the highlights of this long human tradition. The speeches cover the time from the dawn of ancient civilization in the Middle East to the 21st century and are the work of people ranging from kings to ordinary, sometimes even anonymous, people. Some of the speakers, such as Jesus, Muhammad, and Abraham Lincoln, rank among the very greatest names in history. Others are more obscure or even unknown, but their words are often equally eloquent. By studying their words, we can learn more about speaking and also about the human condition.

Speeches in World History contains more than 200 speeches by people from all walks of life on every continent—from a Chinese ruler (Dan, duke of Zhou) who helped found the Chinese political system almost 3,000 years ago to an African woman (Wangari Maathai) who won the Nobel Peace Prize in 2004 for pioneering environmental conservation as a road to world peace. You will find significant speeches from U.S. history, little known speeches from Latin America, important addresses from the Muslim world, and speeches from the ancients on topics so timeless they are still debated today. The selections include revolutionary and patriotic addresses, eulogies, sermons, debates, trial and gallows speeches, parliamentary addresses, and incitements to battle. Most were made in response to great issues of the day—salvation and right living, war, democracy, slavery, religious and racial preju-

dice, colonialism, self-determination, women's rights, fascism and communism, nuclear proliferation, free speech, terrorism, the rights of indigenous peoples, even environmental degradation.

POLITICAL ORATORY

Politics is the area in life most strongly associated with making speeches. But not all political regimes provide a place for the orator. Dictatorships and absolute monarchies often leave little room for anyone other than the ruler himself or herself to address the public, as powerful speakers can threaten authority. Pluralistic regimes—republics and democracies that value freedom of speech—are more open to the voice of an orator. Many politicians in free societies have built their careers around their speechmaking abilities, from Cicero of Rome and Demosthenes of Athens in the ancient world to Winston Churchill, John F. Kennedy, and Barack Obama in modern times.

Political speeches vary greatly by both audience and the persuasive mission of the speaker. At times the speaker is a ruler or authority figure, giving commands to subjects and subordinates or inspiring loyalty and enthusiasm. (Kings and dictators are not the only ones to fall into this category; so do generals, such as Napoleon, who address their troops, or revolutionary leaders, such as Lenin, who inspire their followers.) Other times, the speaker addresses equals, as a member of a legislature, for example, William Pitt, who desperately tried to save Britain from fatally alienating its American colonies. A legislative speech can be organized around specific arguments and examples and conclude with a call to carry out a particular action, or it can appeal to the emotions of its hearers. Legislatures also often have specific rules about how long a speech can last and what things can and cannot be said, as is demonstrated by the elaborate codes of the British parliament and U.S. Congress that forbid members to refer to each other by name, as in the British parliamentary phrase, "The honourable member for Westminster."

Other political speakers may be addressing people outside the elite, in an attempt to gain their support. Anticolonial leaders, including Simón Bolívar and Mohandas Gandhi, have addressed the poor and oppressed in an attempt to mobilize them for violent or nonviolent action. Speakers in countries with open political systems have given speeches to ordinary people advocating particular policies or attempting to garner votes in an election. Such "campaign speeches" can outline a particular agenda, but arguments for these specific positions often play only a minor role. The real focus of many "positive" campaign speeches is persuading hearers that the speaker is a good person who shares their opinions and deserves their vote. "Negative" campaign speeches attempt to convince hearers that the speaker's opponent is unworthy of their support.

Speaking is also often part of public ceremonial occasions, as when Lincoln made his Gettysburg Address at the dedication of the memorial on the Civil War battlefield. Ceremonial addresses are very different from campaign speeches. At a ceremonial address it is considered in poor taste for a speaker to draw too much attention to him or herself or to attack political enemies. A tone of humility, as displayed by Lincoln, is often more effective than "blowing your own horn." The focus of a ceremonial speech should be on the occasion that has brought speaker and hearer together.

RELIGIOUS ORATORY

Rivaling and sometimes even eclipsing politics as a place for an orator's voice to be heard is religion. Speechmaking has been an important part of religious life for millennia. Founders of major world religions—the Buddha, Jesus, and Muhammad, to name a few—were renowned for their persuasiveness and speaking ability. The message of Judaism was never so powerfully expressed as by the voice of its prophets such as Jeremiah, who fearlessly scourged Jewish society for its failure to live up to the demands of its God. Each religion, with many others, has spawned a tradition of sermons, often integrated into services, such as the Christian Sunday sermon or the Islamic Friday *khutba*.

There are many differences of terminology between religious and political speakers. Rather than orators, religious speechmakers are preachers, and their orations are not speeches but sermons. Even so, there are many similarities in practice. Like a political speaker, a religious speaker must take his or her audience into account. Religious speakers sometimes address those who are already followers of their religion, explicating religious doctrine and law or urging hearers to greater piety. The mission of Bernard of Clairvaux and other medieval "crusade preachers" was to convince committed Christians to take the extra step of vowing to go on crusade. At other times, religious speakers address unbelievers, particularly in the early days of a religion or when it is expanding to a new area through the work of missionaries, such as the Korean Buddhist monk Musang, a seventh- and eighth-century missionary in China. In these addresses speakers must make their religious message as appealing as possible to people who do not share many of their assumptions. Once a religion is established, a parish priest or congregational rabbi might use his weekly sermons to address a community he knows intimately, building a relationship that can last for decades. A traveling revivalist such as John Wesley was, on the other hand, has the task of addressing an audience full of strangers he may never see again and must rely on themes that will move a crowd. Sometimes religious speakers claim direct inspiration from their God or gods. The enthusiastic speaker claiming divine inspiration (the term *enthusiasm* in the original Greek referred to possession by a god) has often been viewed as a threat by established religious hierarchies.

Religious speeches, like political speeches, vary in themes and tone from the emotionalism of the "revival" to the perfunctoriness of many short sermons. Some preachers appeal to the intellect, constructing their sermons as logical arguments, while others focus on the passions, relying on rhetorical appeals and variations in tone of voice to move the crowd. "Hellfire" Christian preachers use vivid depictions of the torments of the damned to frighten their hearers into repentance. Others evoke the sufferings of Jesus on the cross or the joys of heaven. Some religious speeches are reserved for special holidays or ceremonial occasions such as the Christmas and Easter sermons of Christian ministers, the Ramadan *khutbas* of Muslim preachers, or the Asarna Bucha sermons of Thai Buddhist monks. Hearers expect these sermons to focus on a well-worn set of images and ideas. Christmas sermons, for example, frequently draw on the Gospel accounts of Jesus' birth (the reason for the holiday).

Of course, given the intertwining of religion and politics throughout history, religious and political speechmaking have never been totally separate. Many political speeches include some rhetorical appeal to God, and religious idioms have greatly influenced political speakers. Candidates for election in the United States routinely refer to God and their faith in their campaign speeches. American civil rights leader Martin Luther King, Jr., an ordained minister, drew on the tradition of the African-American sermon to make fundamentally political speeches. Many preachers of the world's religious traditions have included political messages in their sermons.

FORENSIC ORATORY

The courtroom has often been an arena for speechmakers. Some of the greatest orators were also lawyers, who became as renowned for speeches made in the courtroom as in the public forum. The role of speechmaking varies greatly by legal system and by individual cases and settings. A lawyer addressing the U.S. Supreme Court, for example, will use different rhetorical tactics than a lawyer addressing a jury in a criminal trial. A legal speech can be a calm recounting of the evidence and law, or a passionate appeal meant to stir a jury or a judge. Lawyers are not the only ones to have spoken in legal settings. Some systems of law have also allowed the accused to make a statement. Even the repressive legal system of the Soviet Union allowed the dissident Natan Sharansky to speak at his trial. Persons condemned to death have even spoken immediately before their executions, maintaining their innocence or demonstrating their repentance for their crimes. King Charles I of England's moving speech from the scaffold had a great influence on hearers and subsequent readers.

Legal and political systems are intertwined, and some of the greatest political speakers from the ancient world to today have also been effective legal speakers. Cicero's speeches at trials were preserved alongside his political speeches in the Roman Senate. In the 19th century Daniel Webster, among many others, was known for his triumphs in the courtroom as well as the U.S. Congress. The skills of a trial lawyer—effective advocacy and the ability to sway hearers by combining reason with passion—are often the skills of a political speaker as well.

SPEECHMAKING AND GENDER

For most of history, the principal realms of oratory—politics, religion, and the law—have been reserved for males. Many societies defined the "public sphere" as male and relegated women to the "private," or "domestic," sphere. The outspoken man has been praised, the outspoken woman often depicted as a screeching harridan. Modesty and quiet, not oratorical talent, have been held up as the virtues for women. Because of this, there are few examples of major orations by women before the 20th century, and those rare exceptions have mostly been the speeches of queens such as Queen Elizabeth I of England. The slow opening of political and religious activism and leadership to women in the 20th century has led to a surge of women's speaking. Women such as Golda Meir of Israel, Benazir Bhutto of Pakistan, and Aung San Suu Kyi of Burma now lead republics, serve in legislatures, head political parties and movements, and make their voices heard in public assemblies, courtrooms, and religious gatherings.

THE ART OF "RHETORIC"

Since speechmaking has been so important to human society, people have studied how to do it most effectively. With its roots in ancient Greece and Rome, this study is called "rhetoric"—the science of persuasive speech. Rhetoric attracted some of the greatest minds of the ancient world, including Aristotle and Cicero, and was part of the core curriculum of ancient schools. In the Middle Ages, there was less interest in Latin rhetoric, but it was revived during the Renaissance. Renaissance "Humanists," namely, students of the ancient Greeks and Romans and their surviving texts, viewed rhetoric as one of the most precious legacies of the ancient world, and they promoted its study in the schools they founded. Rhetorical skill was intimately associated with leadership, and it was taught to the upper classes, who were expected to fill positions of authority in state, church, and private enterprise.

We owe the preservation of some of the finest speeches of the ancient Western world to their use as texts in rhetoric classes. For centuries after the issues they had originally addressed had fallen into dust, students memorized and declaimed the orations of Cicero, Demosthenes, and their peers. Rhetoricians taught the use of various "figures of speech" and different speaking styles, from the lush, wordy "Asiatic" style to the terse, unadorned "Attic" style. They instructed their pupils on which styles were appropriate for different occasions. They also taught the mechanics of speechmaking, how to speak clearly with the appropriate emphases, and how to hold their bodies and their hands most effectively. Generations of boys—rhetoric was mostly taught as a male, "public" skill—were drilled in how to speak effectively, as a skilled speaker, trained or not, could be appreciated even by those who did not agree with his position. In the modern United States and other Western societies, rhetoric and debate continue to be taught, but now to boys and girls alike.

SPOKEN AND WRITTEN SPEECHES

The experience of hearing a speech was originally evanescent. To hear and understand a speaker, you literally had to be there. Once writing had been invented, speeches did not always perish immediately after being given. Some had an afterlife that could go on for centuries or millennia. However, this afterlife was imperfect. Like other texts, speeches originally had to be copied by hand. Each manuscript copy could take hours or days of the labors of a skilled copyist. And few copyists were perfect—errors would creep in, and would then be compounded as copies of copies were made. And over the centuries many speeches, like other texts, would be lost.

Beginning in the 15th century in the Western world, and earlier in east Asia, the circulation of written texts including speeches increased vastly with the development of the printing press. Some speeches had far more impact as printed texts than they did when they were actually given. Abraham Lincoln's Gettysburg Address, coming at the end of a long day after a two-hour speech by scholar Edward Everett, attracted little notice at the time. Today, it is considered among the greatest speeches in American history.

However reproduced, the written texts of speeches come in two forms: one a prepared text that the speaker reads and the other a transcription of what the speaker said. In either case, the speaker is not necessarily the author of the speech. One of the most important questions to think about when looking at any written speech is how much the speech-as-written reflects the reality of the speech-as-spoken. Composing a speech and delivering it are different skills, often possessed by different people. Many people obligated to give speeches have no interest, energy, or time to write them. For centuries collections of sermons were sold to preachers unable or unwilling to write their own. The 20th century saw the rise of the political speechwriter profession. Few modern politicians, particularly in the United States, are suspected of writing their own speeches, at least without a lot of help. Traditionally the speechwriter is expected to be a discreet figure in the background and the speaker is treated as the author of the speech by a polite fiction. However, many speechwriters have become celebrities themselves. Theodore Sorensen, John F. Kennedy's speechwriter, and Peggy Noonan, who worked for Ronald Reagan, are two examples.

Reading a speech can be a pale shadow of hearing and seeing it delivered. A great orator is more than just the reader of a text. By putting emphasis on certain words and varying pitch and rhythm, a written speech is transformed into a spoken one. Not only is delivery important, but so is gesture, and even how speakers hold their bodies. A speaker making eye contact with his or her audience conveys a message different from one whose eyes are lifted to the heavens. Many speeches by great speakers may read as flat and lifeless, lacking the spark of live delivery, while the best-written speech will be powerless if the delivery is poor. Speakers also often improvise or deviate from written texts. Transcriptions of speeches are often "cleaned up" with mistakes, hesitations, and false starts eliminated. The gap between the speech-as-spoken and the speech-as-published goes back to the ancient world. Ancient historians like Thucydides and Sallust considered it acceptable to vastly alter speeches, or even make them up before inserting them in their histories, as the speeches they put in the mouths of historical characters were used to reinforce the main themes and analyses of their histories as a whole.

SPEECHMAKING AND TECHNOLOGY

In its origin, speechmaking was not a technology-driven activity—all the speaker needed was a voice (preferably a loud one), and perhaps an elevated place to stand. (The terms "stump speech" and "soap-box orator" refer to some primitive ways for a speaker to be elevated above the listening crowd—tree stumps and the wooden crates in which soap was shipped.) However, speechmaking, particularly in the 20th century, has been greatly influenced by the development of technology.

The 20th century saw several new technologies that affected speechmaking, including loudspeakers, sound and video recording, and broadcast technology. Loudspeakers and other amplification systems meant orators were no longer restricted to the range of the human voice. The loud, bawling speaker straining to make himself heard to a crowd of thousands became a memory. Now a speaker could address a crowd of many thousands without raising his or her voice, though it took some time for orators to learn the new skills of the microphone.

Eventually the audience did not even need to be physically present to hear a speech. Radio and television enabled speakers to address "virtual" audiences numbering in the millions. Many, many more people will hear a politician on television or the radio during the course of his or her career than will ever hear him or her in person. Because of this, orators are increasingly judged on how they come across on radio and television. American political conventions, always showcases for oratory, are now organized as television spectaculars, with the hearers physically present in the convention hall a decided afterthought. The real audience is the millions watching on television. The new technologies have also altered speechmaking styles. Radio demands an intimacy epitomized by U.S. president Franklin Delano Roosevelt's "fireside chats" while television has increasingly put a premium on short, punchy statements that can be excerpted from a speech and endlessly repeated on video (and now on Internet) sound bites.

Television, radio, and most recently the Internet have also contributed to the development of a worldwide audience. Speakers opposing tyrannical governments in their own countries such as China's Fang Lizhi, an astrophysicist who actively demanded democratic reforms, can now easily address people in other lands, hoping to gain international support for their cause. Causes not linked with a specific nation—such as fighting AIDS, banning landmines, or even Osama bin Laden's call for an international jihad—are now advocated in front of a worldwide audience as well.

The development of recording technology has also changed speechmaking. Speakers can make a speech over and over again, as speeches that are captured in sound recordings can be repeated. Tapes of a speaker can be smuggled into dictatorships, enabling him or her to gain a mass following without even setting foot in the country. Video recordings preserve not just the words of orations, but the speaker's visual presentation as well. Even so, however, an image on a screen is not the same as a live orator, and some of the immediacy of a politi-cal speech disappears when the issues it addresses are no longer relevant.

Recording technology, particularly when coupled with the rapid dissemination of audio and video files via the Internet, has also made it more difficult for political speakers. Gaffes—misstatements, slips of the tongue, and other statements that hurt rather than help the speaker—are now repeated endlessly, such as American presidential candidate Howard Dean's famous "scream" following his defeat in the Iowa caucuses in 2004. (Some have even blamed the "scream" for Dean's failure as a candidate.) It is also harder for speakers to get away with the time-honored technique of delivering different messages to different audiences. Now anything a speaker says within range of even a simple device, such as a cell phone, can instantly be sent to a worldwide audience, often one with very different concerns than the speaker's immediate audience.

All history has been described as a struggle against silence and forgetting. The words of the speakers in this collection are eloquent testimony that that struggle is worth fighting.

—William E. Burns
Instructor, George Washington University

Acknowledgments

I am very grateful to acknowledge the historians, editors, and wise advisers and assistants who helped me along the way: With his remarkable knowledge of world history, Bill Burns was a fount of information and excellent ideas. My capable editors, Claudia Schaab and Melissa Cullen-DuPont, with Alexandra Lo Re, made the entire process as pleasant as possible. My hardworking research assistant, Natalie Deibel, and photo researcher, Phinney McIntire, pitched in when time was pressing. Also providing leads and suggestions, translations, and all-around wisdom were Colin Archer, Dennis Barton, Jane Dorfman, Susan Douglas, Elaine English, Ruth Feldman, Darra Goldstein, Richard Knight, Peter Lee, Gareth Lloyd, Will McIntire, Keith Patman, Hiraku Shimoda, Richard Thornton, and the reference and interlibrary loan staff at Arlington County Libraries. Thank you all!

How to Use This Book

Arranged chronologically, *Speeches in World History* treats the development of speaking as part of the development of human society. Readers can gain fresh perspective on significant events of history, and even of our own time, by reading the words of speakers who made or witnessed the great changes of the moment.

Readers of *Speeches in World History* can become better speakers themselves by observing how the orators arranged their arguments, adapted topics to diverse audiences, and engaged hearers with powerful appeals to reason and feeling.

A wide variety of genre and geography should allow readers to find speeches of interest to them personally. The 200 selections come from 48 countries and include political addresses, gallows speeches, eulogies, sermons, debates, and the speeches of commanders before battle.

ORGANIZATION

The book is divided into six chapters based on the eras used in the National Standards for World History: Ancient World (to 550 C.E.), Expanding World (550–1450), The First Global Age (1450–1750), The Age of Revolution and Empire (1750–1900), Crisis and Achievement (1900–1950), and The Contemporary World (1950 to the present).

Each chapter includes an introductory essay setting the speeches in an overall historical context. Each speech is preceded by a fact box that lists the name of the speaker; the speaker's birth/death or reign dates; and the title, location, and date of the speech. Each also includes an introduction—providing information about the speaker, the occasion on which the address was given, and the social and political climate at the time of its delivery—and a source for the speech.

Spatial limitations have sometimes prevented the inclusion of an entire speech. In those cases, *Speeches in World History* includes excerpts covering the most important or the most famous and influential passages.

ILLUSTRATIONS

Seventy-five illustrations shed light on the speakers' personalities and historical place, from a mosaic of Alexander the Great to the very young Mohandas Gandhi in his first law office to cold-war opponents Reagan and Gorbachev raising a toast at a summit dinner.

RHETORICAL DEVICES AND FAMOUS LINES

Because so much of the beauty and power of speechmaking comes from the use of rhetorical devices, frequent sidebars use examples from the speeches to illustrate 44 different rhetorical devices, such as metaphor, parallelism, antistrophe, rhetorical question, and hyperbole. In some examples you may find more than one type of device.

Rhetorical devices are tools an orator may use to make sure he or she engages the audience. They help draw the audience's attention to the points the speaker wants to make, and even arouse emotion in the listeners. Many of these devices are commonly used in writing and even in daily speech. Others—and there are dozens of them—may require more effort to use. Do not be intimidated by their unusual names, many of them Greek. While a few rhetorical devices are invaluable to a brilliant speech (or a research paper), you would not want to use too many in one composition!

Additional sidebars present famous lines from the speeches.

APPENDIXES

The appendixes include three essays to aid students in working with speeches and speechmaking. The first, "Writing a Persuasive Speech," describes the process of choosing a topic; constructing the speech with an assertion, supporting arguments, and conclusion (peroration); and using rhetorical devices to persuade an audience of the speaker's sincerity and to arouse their emotions.

"Delivering a Great Speech" covers such concerns as practicing the speech beforehand (even using the speeches in this book for "declamation"), pacing, demeanor, and appropriate language.

"Working with Speeches as Primary Sources" offers a number of issues to consider when using a speech in historical research: the speaker's point of view and message, choice of language, the audience, the occasion, and possible bias.

At the back, readers will find a general bibliography including both print and electronic publications and a variety of indexes, including lists of speeches by title, orator, and nationality of the speaker; a list of the featured rhetorical devices; and a comprehensive index.

THE ANCIENT WORLD
(to ca. 550 C.E.)

Introduction to the Ancient World

In the period to 550 C.E. many of the great traditions and religions of civilization were built. Hinduism, Judaism, Buddhism, Greek philosophy, Confucianism, Daoism, and Christianity were all formed in this period. Although it also saw the invention, improvement and spread of many forms of writing, the spoken word remained the principal vehicle of communication. The Buddha, Confucius, Socrates, the prophets of Israel, and Jesus are all known to us not by their writings, but by their spoken words remembered and written down by their disciples.

The early history of humanity is marked by such advances as the discovery of fire and agriculture. The invention of agriculture enabled much denser populations, and eventually cities evolved, at first in the great river valleys of the Tigris and Euphrates in Mesopotamia, the Nile in Egypt, the Indus in India, and the Yangtze in China. Along with these cities arose more complex religious systems that led people to move beyond the simple hope that the gods would be favorable to them to ask questions about the right way to live. There also developed political societies, creating the demand for political leadership and the ability to articulate politics in words. The words of rulers such as China's Duke of Zhou (r. 1043–1036 B.C.E.) and King Darius of Persia (r. 521–486 B.C.E.) helped define the missions of their governments for centuries.

RELIGIOUS AND PHILOSOPHICAL SPEAKERS

One of the most important changes in human history was the rise of religions focusing on individual salvation rather than simply making sacrifices and observing rules to please the gods or God. Among the earliest of these religions of salvation was Buddhism, founded in India in the sixth century B.C.E. by Siddhartha Gautama (the word

"Buddha" is a title meaning "enlightened one"). Buddhism was the first religion to produce a body of sermons. Siddhartha Gautama, the Buddha, was known as a preacher, and his profound new message was disseminated through the spoken word. The Buddha's "Fire Sermon" and "Benares Sermon" (the latter included here) became fundamental Buddhist texts and set the pattern for legions of Buddhist preachers in the following centuries.

Public speaking was also important to the Buddha's contemporaries, the Jewish prophets in Israel. Although nowadays the word *prophet* is often used to refer to someone who predicts the future, that was only a small part of a prophet's task. Prophets such as Jeremiah, who began preaching in Jerusalem in 628 B.C.E., viewed themselves as inspired by God to proclaim His will on earth. They called the Jewish people not merely to correctly and faithfully perform ritual and sacrifice, but also to lead moral and faithful lives and to build a society pleasing to God. The prophets denounced the corruption of their own times in a way that resonated for many centuries among Jews and Christians, and their message continues to inspire to this very day.

The people of both India and Israel sought eloquence primarily in religious contexts. The first societies to break away from a fundamentally religious approach were China and Greece. At the end of the sixth century B.C.E. China produced the philosophy of Confucianism, which set forth a plan for an ideal social order without reference to the divine. Greece produced a series of intellectual innovators, *philosophers*, literally "lovers of wisdom." Greek philosophy was born in the city-states, or *polises* of Greece and its colonies in Italy and Asia Minor in the fourth century B.C.E. Greek philosophers such as Socrates sought fundamentally secular explanations of

1

the universe. Like Jeremiah and the Buddha, Socrates was known as a speaker—there are no references to written works by him. His student and greatest follower, Plato, wrote a long series of dialogues in which Socrates expounded on the truths of philosophy. The culture of Greek philosophy remained strongly oral throughout the history of the classical world. Debates between leading philosophers were major spectator events in Greek cities.

POLITICAL ELOQUENCE IN GREECE AND ROME

At the heart of the classical Greek city was the agora, a public place for speaking. The Roman republic, which followed in the footsteps of the Greek cities in many ways, called their similar space the forum. The agora and the forum became synonymous with a tradition of oratory. Many political careers were built on the ability to stand up in front of a Greek assembly or the Roman Senate or Assembly of the People and give a powerful, persuasive speech. Many Greek and Roman speakers—particularly Demosthenes of Athens (ca. 384–322 B.C.E.) and Marcus Tullius Cicero of Rome (106–43 B.C.E.)—have become legendary. Their speeches, including Demosthenes' "On the Crown" and Cicero's "First Oration against Catiline," were studied in schools and became models for orators for many centuries after.

So important was persuasive speech that the classical era produced the discipline of rhetoric, one of the major branches of the liberal arts. Elite boys were trained in it in order to participate in public affairs. Rhetoric included the study of figures of speech and how to construct a persuasive argument, as well as practical advice for speakers on how to make themselves heard and put their points across most effectively.

Another discipline that was marked by the importance of speech was the writing of history. Greek historians such as Herodotus and Thucydides of the fifth century B.C.E. included speeches as important parts of their histories. However, the speeches found in their works were not always simple transcriptions of what was actually said. The Greeks thought part of a historian's job was composing polished speeches that clearly laid out the fundamental issues at stake in historical conflicts as well as the character of the speaker. Sometimes the speeches were embellishments of the actual speeches given at the time, and sometimes they were completely fabricated by the historian. Roman historians such as Sallust, Livy, and Tacitus of the first centuries B.C.E. and C.E. inherited this practice from their Greek role models. Speaking was also important in the law. The idea of evidence was not as developed in the

ancient world as it is today, and many a case hung on which party could make the most persuasive oration. The great speakers of Greek and Roman politics were often also skilled and highly sought-after lawyers.

The city-states of Greece fought off the mighty Persian Empire in the fifth century B.C.E., but they were caught in a brutal series of wars with each other. The most important of these was the Peloponnesian War between Athens and Sparta from 431 to 404 B.C.E. As chronicled by one of Greece's greatest historians, Thucydides, the war prompted the Athenian political leader Pericles' memorable account of the greatness of Athens. However, Pericles died of disease before the war ended, and it was Sparta that carried away the victory. Several of Socrates' students became part of the group of Spartan collaborators who ruled Athens after the defeat, the "Thirty Tyrants." The Athenian democracy was restored after the overthrow of the collaborators and it was this democracy that condemned Socrates to death—an act that may have been political payback for his association with the "Tyrants."

The Spartan victory did not end the wars of the Greek cities, and after they exhausted each other they were conquered in the fourth century B.C.E. by the northern kingdom of Macedonia under Philip II and his son Alexander the Great, considered by many to be the greatest military leader in history. Alexander went on to conquer the still formidable Persian Empire and spread Greek culture and the Greek language from Egypt to northern India. It was not defeat that caused him to turn back from India, but the fact that his exhausted soldiers would no longer follow him. Soon after Alexander's death in 323 B.C.E., his empire fragmented into several kingdoms, referred to as the "Hellenistic" monarchies. The older city-states like Athens were either absorbed by the new kingdoms or found themselves politically marginalized. The change was not a good one for Greek eloquence. In the Hellenistic kingdoms a politician advanced not through public speechmaking in front of his peers or the people but through cultivating a private relationship with the monarch. Oratory became a pastime for education or public entertainment.

ROME FROM REPUBLIC TO EMPIRE

Like the city-states earlier, the Hellenistic monarchies sapped their strength through endless wars with each other. The power that would eventually sweep them away was Rome. Rome grew from a backward city on the Tiber River in Italy to an empire that encompassed the entire Mediterranean world and much more, eventually stretching from the border of Scotland to the border of Persia by the second century C.E. For centuries as it grew, Rome was a republic in which ultimate power lay in the hands of the Senate. The word "senate" literally means a gathering of old men, although the Roman Senate included many younger members of the ruling class as well. The Senate and the other important political grouping, the Assembly of the Roman People, could be swayed by eloquent speakers. Speechmaking was also important in elections and for generals such as Publius Cornelius Scipio—who fought the Carthaginian general Hannibal in the Second Punic War (218–202 B.C.E.)—when addressing their soldiers. Every Roman politician was expected to be a good speaker and every boy of the Roman elite was trained in oratory.

The great age of political oratory in Rome ended the same way it had in Greece—with the transition from a republic to a monarchy. The Roman Republic, unable to handle the transition from ruling a small city-state to vast territories in Europe, Africa, and Asia, fell after its own civil wars in the first century B.C.E. Political and military leaders including Marius, Sulla, Catiline, Cicero, Pompey, and Julius Caesar contended for power. Eventually the republic was overthrown by Julius's nephew, Augustus Caesar, who became the first Roman emperor in the year 27 B.C.E. It was no coincidence that Cicero lost his life at the hands of the new leaders of Rome. His kind of oratory would have no place in the new monarchy.

The eloquence of the new Roman Empire was only a pale shadow of the old republic's, but not all political speechmaking died out. Roman emperors such as Claudius used speeches to announce their policies, but they were addressing subjects, not peers. A first century C.E. historian of the empire, Cornelius Tacitus, continued to incorporate speeches into his histories, including the words of enemies of Rome such as Boudica, the warrior queen of the Iceni, and Caratacus, the ruler of southern Britain, as well as Roman champions such as Gnaeus Julius Agricola, his father-in-law. Flavius Josephus, a Jewish historian also of the first century C.E., did the same, incorporating the last speech of the defiant rebel and leader of the Jewish Revolt against Rome, El'azar ben Yair, in his *The Jewish War*.

THE BIRTH OF CHRISTIANITY

Almost at the same historical moment as the Roman Republic and its great tradition of public speaking was dying, another tradition of religious eloquence was being born. This was the Christian sermon. Drawing on Jewish practice, preaching goes as far back in Christianity as Jesus Christ himself, who, like the Buddha, was renowned as a persuasive preacher. His most famous utterance is the "Sermon on the Mount," which has become a prototypical sermon as well as a source of moral challenge and reflection for many generations of Christians. Christianity spread initially among the urban lower classes of the Roman cities, many of whom were illiterate (particularly women, who seem to have been attracted to the new religion more than their male contemporaries, possibly because they had less involvement in the "public" cults of official paganism). Speaking, whether to crowds in the agora or to smaller, clandestine groups during periods of persecution, was essential to spreading the Christian message.

Probably the most important event in the history of the Roman Empire after its founding was the adoption of Christianity as its official religion around the year 312. This decision, made by the Emperor Constantine, greatly increased the power and prestige of Christian bishops and priests, who were able to address far wider audiences. Preachers such as John Chrysostom in the Greek-speaking East and Ambrose of Milan in the Latin-speaking West were eventually able to defy the emperors themselves. The thoughtful, powerful sermons of Augustine of Hippo became one of the foundations of Western Christianity. Classical paganism held out stubbornly for over a century, but it eventually died out.

The adoption of Christianity may have slowed the decay of the Roman Empire, but it could not stop it. By the end of the fifth century, the Roman Empire in the west had vanished, replaced by a series of non-Roman kingdoms with little interest in polished rhetoric. The learned tradition in Latin nearly vanished, but the case was different for Greek. Before its fall, the Roman Empire had been divided into eastern and western halves, and the eastern empire with its capital at Constantinople (modern Istanbul) survived its western counterpart as the Byzantine Empire. The eastern area had been the Greek-speaking territory of the Empire, and it adopted Greek as its official language, eventually losing all familiarity with Latin. The language of Demosthenes and Socrates lived on in the words of Chrysostom and the Byzantine empress Theodora.

Speeches

DAN, DUKE OF ZHOU
(r. 1043–1036 B.C.E.)
The Shao Announcement
Luoyang, China
ca. 1036 B.C.E.

One of the five most ancient Chinese texts is the *Classic of Documents*, sometimes called *Classic of History*. It contains reports and speeches purportedly by ancient kings and other court authorities. Confucius (551–479 B.C.E.) is supposed to have edited these texts, and they were old when he worked on them. For centuries the Chinese people have studied these texts as important sources of knowledge and as models for good government. The *Classic of Documents* begins with reports from the legendary Chinese sage-kings Yao and Shun and continues through the Xia (2070–1600 B.C.E.) and Shang (or Yin, 1600–1046 B.C.E.) dynasties and the early (Western) Zhou dynasty (beginning 1045 B.C.E.). (A dynasty is a succession of rulers from a powerful family.) King Cheng was the second of the Western Zhou dynasty rulers; he reigned from 1043 to 1021 B.C.E., not long after his father, King Wu, conquered the last Shang king. King Cheng was a child when he came to power; his father's younger brother—Dan, the powerful duke of Zhou—assumed the regency for seven years until Cheng was old enough to assume the Mandate of Heaven (or *tianming*), the religious power that entitled him to rule. In the last year of his regency, as a new city, Luoyang, was being built, the duke made this speech, the Shao Announcement, describing the mandate received by a virtuous king and his heirs as long as they ruled with wisdom and benevolence. When a dynasty crumbled, possibly from corruption or cruelty, and the family was dethroned, it was said they had lost the mandate that entitled them to govern by divine right. In his speech the duke refers to the Yin, the people of the previous, defeated Shang dynasty. The duke of Zhou was one of the founding fathers of the Chinese political system; the Western Zhou dynasty he helped found would last nearly 275 years through 12 kings.

Ah! August Heaven, High God, has changed his principal son and has revoked the Mandate of this great state of Yin. When a king receives the Mandate, without limit is the grace thereof, but also without limit is the anxiety of it. Ah! How can he fail to be reverently careful!

Heaven has rejected and ended the Mandate of this great state of Yin. Thus, although Yin has many former wise kings in Heaven, when their successor kings and successor people undertook their Mandate, in the end wise and good men lived in misery. Knowing that they must care for and sustain their wives and children, they then called out in anguish to Heaven and fled to places where they could not be caught. Ah! Heaven too grieved for the people of all the lands, wanting, with affection, in giving its Mandate to employ those who are deeply committed. The king should have reverent care for his virtue.

Look at the former peoples of ancient times, the Xia. Heaven guided, indulged, and cherished them, so that they would strive to understand what Heaven favors, but by this time they have let their Mandate fall to the ground. Now look at the Yin; Heaven guided them, stayed near them, nourished them, so that they would strive to comprehend what Heaven favors; but now they have let their Mandate fall to the ground.

Now a young son succeeds to the throne; let him not, then, neglect the aged and experienced. Not only do they comprehend the virtue of our men of old—nay, more, they are sometimes able to comprehend counsels that come from Heaven.

Ah! Even though it be that the king is young, he is [Heaven's] principal son. Let him be grandly able to be in harmony with the little people. In the present time of grace, the king must not dare to be slow, but should be prudently apprehensive about what the people say.

The king will come representing the High God and himself undertake [the government here] in the midst of the lands. I, Dan, say, "Let a great city be made here; may he from this place function as the mate of August Heaven, reverently sacrificing to the higher and lower spirits. May he from this place centrally govern." When the king has a fully effective mandate, his governing of the people will then enjoy [Heaven's] grace.

Undertaking [the administration of] the Yin managers of affairs, the king should first associate them with our Zhou's managers of affairs, so as to discipline their natures, and they will day by day advance.

Let the king reverently function in his position; he cannot but be reverently careful of his virtue. We cannot fail to mirror ourselves in the Xia; also we cannot fail to mirror ourselves in the Yin. We must not presume to suppose that the Xia received the Mandate of Heaven for a fixed period of years; we must not presume to suppose that it was not going to continue. It was because they did not reverently care for their virtue that they early let their Mandate fall. We must not presume to suppose that the Yin received the Mandate of Heaven for a fixed period of years; we must not presume to suppose that it was not going to continue. It was because they did not reverently care for their virtue that they early let their Mandate fall. Now the king has succeeded them in receiving their Mandate; let us also, in regard to the mandate of these two states, continue it with like achievements; [if we do,] then the king will [truly] now begin to undertake the mandate.

Ah! It is like bearing a child: all depends on what happens when it is first born; one gives it oneself its allotment of [future] wisdom. Now as to whether Heaven is going to give an endowment of wisdom, of good fortune or bad, or an endowment of so-and-so many years, we [just] know that now we begin the undertaking of the Mandate.

Dwelling in this new city, now let the king just earnestly have reverent care for his virtue. If it is virtue that the king uses, he may pray Heaven for an enduring Mandate. As he functions as king, let him not, because the common people stray and do what is wrong, then presume to govern them by harsh capital punishments; in this way he will achieve much. In being king, let him take his position in the primacy of virtue. The little people will then pattern themselves on him throughout the world; the king will then become illustrious.

Those above and below being zealous and careful, let them say, "As we receive Heaven's Mandate, let it grandly be like the long years enjoyed by the Xia, and not fail of the years enjoyed by the Yin"—in order that [as one would wish] the king, through the little people, may receive Heaven's enduring Mandate.

Source: Zhou, Duke of. "The Shao Announcement." In *Sources of Chinese Tradition.* Vol. 1, edited by William Theodore de Bary and Irene Bloom. New York: Columbia University Press, 1999, p. 35. Copyright © 1960. Reprinted with permission of the publisher.

JEREMIAH
(ca. 640–586 B.C.E.)
"O Earth, Earth, Earth, Hear the Word"
Jerusalem
605 B.C.E.

Jeremiah was born near Jerusalem, about 640 B.C.E., during the reign of the pious King Josiah of Judah. He became one of the major prophets of the Christian Old Testament and the Hebrew Bible. He was the author of the Book of Jeremiah, and is thought to have written the Book of Lamentations. Jeremiah felt called to prophesy as a young man. Believing that the people had fallen away from God, he began to preach in 628 B.C.E. He aided King Josiah in removing idols from the temples and returning worship to the Hebrew God. He preached against immorality, false prophets, idolatry, and social injustice. After Josiah's death, King Necho II of Egypt attacked Jerusalem and took Josiah's successor, Jehoahaz (named Shallum at birth, and uninterested in upholding his father's reforms), captive. Jeremiah warned repeatedly that Jerusalem faced destruction by an angry God, and that the people of Judah must submit to their Egyptian conquerors (and the Babylonian invasion he predicted) and await God's judgment. To reinforce this message he wore a wooden oxen yoke around his neck. Jeremiah found much to protest during the calamitous reign of King Jehoiakim (another son of Josiah), which began about 609 B.C.E.; among other things, Jehoiakim allowed a return to idolatry. In the following speech Jeremiah prophesied that Jehoiakim would be buried like an ass. The king resented these speeches, and when he received a written copy of one, he burned it page by page; the prophet he threw into prison. No one listened to Jeremiah's prophecies that Babylon would capture the city (as Nebuchadnezzar II did in 598 B.C.E. and in 586, destroying the Temple). Jehoiakim's son and successor, Coniah, was taken into Babylonian exile, as Jeremiah also had predicted. Jeremiah was an unhappy man; in religious art—such as the Sistine Chapel ceiling painted by Michelangelo—he is shown sad and weeping. "Mine heart within me is broken," he said (Jeremiah 22). Today, a "jeremiad" is a long, bitter lamentation on society's ills, usually with warning of ruin. The "throne of David" refers to the revered King David of Israel, who reigned earlier, 1007 to 1005 B.C.E. Gilead was a fertile region east of the Jordan River.

Thus says the Lord: "Go down to the house of the king of Judah, and there speak this word, and say, 'Hear the word of the Lord, O king of Judah, you who sit on the throne of David, you and your servants and your people who enter these gates!'"

Thus says the Lord: "Execute judgment and righteousness, and deliver the plundered out of the hand of the oppressor. Do no wrong and do no violence to the stranger, the fatherless, or the widow, nor shed innocent blood in this place.

"For if you indeed do this thing, then shall enter the gates of this house, riding on horses and in chariots, accompanied by servants and people, kings who sit on the throne of David.

"But if you will not hear these words, I swear by Myself," says the Lord, "that this house shall become a desolation."

For thus says the Lord to the house of the king of Judah: "You are Gilead to Me, the head of Lebanon; yet I surely will make you a wilderness, cities which are not inhabited. I will prepare destroyers against you, every one with his weapons; they shall cut down your choice cedars and cast them into the fire.

"And many nations will pass by this city; and everyone will say to his neighbor, 'Why has the Lord done so to this great city?' Then they will answer, 'Because they have forsaken the covenant of the Lord their God, and worshiped other gods and served them.'"

RHETORICAL DEVICE

Apostrophe: Breaking off to address a person, or group, separate from the speaker's audience.

———

O earth, earth, earth,
hear the word of the Lord!—*Jeremiah*

O ye immortal gods, where on earth are we? In what city are we living?—*Marcus Tullius Cicero*

Lafayette, we are here. —*Charles Stanton*

Spirits of Moctezuma, Cacamatzín, Cuauhtémoc, Xicotencatl, and Caltzontzín, take pride in this august assembly, and celebrate this happy moment in which your sons have congregated to avenge your insults. —*José María Morelos*

Weep not for the dead, nor bemoan him; weep bitterly for him who goes away, for he shall return no more, nor see his native country.

For thus says the Lord concerning Shallum the son of Josiah, king of Judah, who reigned instead of Josiah his father, who went from this place: "He shall not return here anymore, but he shall die in the place where they have led him captive, and shall see this land no more.

"Woe to him who builds his house by unrighteousness and his chambers by injustice, who uses his neighbor's service without wages and gives him nothing for his work, who says, 'I will build myself a wide house with spacious chambers, and cut out windows for it, paneling it with cedar and painting it with vermilion.'

"Shall you reign because you enclose yourself in cedar? Did not your father eat and drink, and do justice and righteousness? Then it was well with him. He judged the cause of the poor and needy; then it was well. Was not this knowing Me?" says the Lord.

"Yet your eyes and your heart are for nothing but your covetousness, for shedding innocent blood, and practicing oppression and violence."

Therefore thus says the Lord concerning Jehoiakim the son of Josiah, king of Judah: "They shall not lament for him, saying, 'Alas, my brother!' or 'Alas, my sister!' They shall not lament for him, saying, 'Alas, master!' or 'Alas, his glory!'

"He shall be buried with the burial of a donkey, dragged and cast out beyond the gates of Jerusalem.

"Go up to Lebanon, and cry out, and lift up your voice in Bashan; cry from Abarim, for all your lovers are destroyed.

"I spoke to you in your prosperity, but you said, 'I will not hear.' This has been your manner from your youth, that you did not obey My voice.

"The wind shall eat up all your rulers, and your lovers shall go into captivity; surely then you will be ashamed and humiliated for all your wickedness.

"O inhabitant of Lebanon, making your nest in the cedars, how gracious will you be when pangs come upon you, like the pain of a woman in labor?

"As I live," says the Lord, "though Coniah the son of Jehoiakim, king of Judah, were the signet on My right hand, yet I would pluck you off; and I will give you into the hand of those who seek your life, and into the hand of those whose face you fear—the hand of Nebuchadnezzar king of Babylon and the hand of the Chaldeans.

"So I will cast you out, and your mother who bore you, into another country where you were not born; and there you shall die. But to the land to which they desire to return, there they shall not return.

"Is this man Coniah a despised, broken idol—a vessel in which is no pleasure? Why are they cast out, he and his descendants, and cast into a land which they do not know?"

O earth, earth, earth, hear the word of the Lord!

Thus says the Lord: "Write this man down as childless, a man who shall not prosper in his days; for none of his descendants shall prosper, sitting on the throne of David, and ruling anymore in Judah."

———

Source: Jeremiah, Chapter 22. New King James Version®. Copyright © 1982 by Thomas Nelson, Inc. Used by permission. All rights reserved.

DARIUS I
(ca. 549–486 B.C.E.)
"The Rule of One"
Media, Persia
October 522 B.C.E.

Six years after secretly murdering his brother Smerdis in order to reign unchallenged, the mad Persian king Cambyses II (son of Cyrus the Great) died. An imposter who claimed to be Smerdis pronounced himself king at Media (the portion of the Persian Empire that is now Iran). Cambyses' father-in-law detected the fraud and, with several noblemen, killed the imposter on September 29, 522 B.C.E. Among the conspirators was 29-year-old Darius, who was the son of the satrap (governor) of Parthia, and cousin to Cambyses. The seven conspirators debated how the kingdom should be ruled now that both Smerdis and Cambyses II were dead. One recommended "the rule of the many" (democracy), saying monarchs were too likely to become tyrants; instead, "raise the people to power," he said. Another suggested government only by "the best men" (oligarchy, or rule by a select group among citizens), as the people were too ignorant and unbridled. Darius took another view—rule by "the very best man in the whole state" (monarchy). The seven elected Darius as their king, although the Greek historian Herodotus, who recorded the events in *The Histories*, relates that the kingship was decided by which man's horse neighed first the following morning. (Some modern scholars think the entire imposter story may have been invented by Darius to justify his taking power.) Darius was soon known as Darius the Great. He became a conqueror of many lands and an able administrator of a vast empire, which included what is today Afghanistan, Turkey, Iraq, Israel, Jordan, Lebanon, Syria, and the Palestinian territories, in addition to parts of Pakistan, Egypt, Libya, Saudi Arabia, and the Black Sea coasts of Bulgaria, Romania, and Ukraine. His system of governing, using satraps (subordinate officials) to rule the 20 Persian provinces, was so effective that Alexander the Great later used it as well. Darius attempted to add Greece to his realm—embarking on the Persian Wars to do so—but he died without succeeding.

❧❧❧

Take these three forms of government—democracy, oligarchy, and monarchy—and let them each be at their best, I maintain that monarchy far surpasses the other two.

What government can possibly be better than that of the very best man in the whole state? The counsels of such a man are like himself, and so he governs the mass of the people to their heart's content; while at the same time his measures against evildoers are kept more secret than in other states.

Contrariwise, in oligarchies, where men vie with each other in the service of the commonwealth, fierce enmities are apt to arise between man and man, each wishing to be leader, and to carry his own measures; whence violent quarrels come, which lead to open strife, often ending in bloodshed. Then monarchy is sure to follow; and this too shows how far that rule surpasses all others.

Again, in a democracy, it is impossible but that there will be malpractices. These malpractices, however, do not lead to enmities, but to close friendships, which are formed among those engaged in them, who must hold well together to carry on their villainies. And so things go on until a man stands forth as champion of the commonalty, and puts down the evildoers. Straightway the author of so great a service is admired by all, and from being admired soon comes to be appointed king; so that here too it is plain that monarchy is the best government.

Lastly, to sum up all in a word—whence, I ask, was it that we got the freedom which we enjoy? Did democracy give it us, or oligarchy, or a monarch? As a single man recov-

Darius I the Great receives his subjects in a detail of a relief in the Treasury of the Palace at Persepolis, Persia (Iran), 491–486 B.C.E. *(SEF/Art Resource, NY)*

ered our freedom for us, my sentence is that we keep to the rule of one. Even apart from this, we ought not to change the laws of our forefathers when they work fairly, for to do so is not well.

Source: Herodotus. *The History of Herodotus.* Translated by George Rawlinson. New York: Appleton & Co., 1889, p. 395.

GAUTAMA BUDDHA
(CA. 563–483 B.C.E.)
Sermon at Benares
Benares, India
ca. 521 B.C.E.

Siddhartha Gautama was born about 563 B.C.E., a minor king's son, in a kingdom in what is now Nepal. According to tradition, even as a baby Siddhartha was destined to be a great ruler or a great holy man. Although his family wished him to become the former, he became Gautama Buddha, the wandering thinker regarded as the father of Buddhism. With five companions, Gautama set out searching for enlightenment. He joined an ascetic, or self-denying, religious group, but after living a life of such complete deprivation that he was near death, he realized asceticism would not lead to Truth. He sat beneath a fig tree and resolved not to leave until he had discovered the true path to Nirvana, a state of higher consciousness—free from human emotion and suffering. He found Nirvana in the Middle Way, between asceticism and worldliness. While meditating, Buddha (which means "Enlightened One") discovered the Four Noble Truths. These truths are: "All life is suffering; suffering is caused by desire; to eliminate suffering eliminate desire; and to eliminate desire, follow the Eightfold Path." In his Sermon at Benares, often compared to Jesus' Sermon on the Mount, Buddha was responding to his companion's greeting. The five bhikkhus (monks) had seen him approach; from his appearance they concluded he had given up the ascetic life and "become a man who lives in abundance and indulges in the pleasures of worldliness." They hailed him as a friend, not a holy man. In this address he lays out the eight paths that lead ultimately to the cessation of suffering: right view, right aspiration, right speech, right behavior, right livelihood, right effort, right thoughts, and right contemplation. Tathagata was the name Buddha used when he referred to himself; it means "one who has thus gone," and was meant to indicate his passage from being to nonbeing, in which there is no personal self. The Sermon is from the gospel *Samyutta-Nikaya,* or Connected Sayings.

Do not call the Tathagata by his name nor address him as "friend," for he is the Buddha, the Holy One. The Buddha looks with a kind heart equally on all living beings, and they therefore call him "Father." To disrespect a father is wrong; to despise him, is wicked.

The Tathagata, does not seek salvation in austerities, but neither does he for that reason indulge in worldly pleasures, nor live in abundance. The Tathagata has found the middle path.

There are two extremes, O bhikkhus, which the man who has given up the world ought not to follow—the habitual practice, on the one hand, of self-indulgence which is unworthy, vain and fit only for the worldly-minded; and the habitual practice, on the other hand, of self-mortification, which is painful, useless and unprofitable.

Neither abstinence from fish or flesh, nor going naked, nor shaving the head, nor wearing matted hair, nor dressing in a rough garment, nor covering oneself with dirt, nor sacrificing to Agni, will cleanse a man who is not free from delusions.

Reading the Vedas, making offerings to priests, or sacrifices to the gods, self-mortification by heat or cold, and many such penances performed for the sake of immortality, these do not cleanse the man who is not free from delusions.

Anger, drunkenness, obstinacy, bigotry, deception, envy, self-praise, disparaging others, superciliousness and evil intentions constitute uncleanness; not verily the eating of flesh.

A middle path, O bhikkhus, avoiding the two extremes, has been discovered by the Tathagata—a path which opens the eyes, and bestows understanding, which leads to peace of mind, to the higher wisdom, to full enlightenment, to Nirvana!

What is that middle path, O bhikkhus, avoiding these two extremes, discovered by the Tathagata—that path which opens the eyes, and bestows understanding, which leads to peace of mind, to the higher wisdom, to full enlightenment, to Nirvana?

Let me teach you, O bhikkhus, the middle path, which keeps aloof from both extremes. By suffering, the emaciated devotee produces confusion and sickly thoughts in his mind. Mortification is not conducive even to worldly knowledge; how much less to a triumph over the senses!

He who fills his lamp with water will not dispel the darkness, and he who tries to light a fire with rotten wood will fail. And how can anyone be free from self by leading a wretched life, if he does not succeed in quenching the fires of lust, if he still hankers after either worldly or heavenly pleasures. But he in whom self has become extinct is free from lust: he will desire neither worldly nor heavenly pleasures, and the satisfaction of his natural wants will not defile him. However, let him be moderate, let him eat and drink according to the needs of the body.

Sensuality is enervating: the "self-indulgent" man is a slave to pleasure to his passions, and pleasure-seeking is degrading and vulgar.

But to satisfy the necessities of life is not evil. To keep the body in good health is a duty for otherwise we shall not be able to trim the lamp of wisdom, and keep our mind strong and clear. Water surrounds the lotus-flower, but does not wet its petals.

This is the middle path, O bhikkhus, that keeps aloof from both extremes.

The spokes of the wheel are the rules of pure conduct: justice is the uniformity of their length, wisdom is the tire; modesty and thoughtfulness are the hub in which the immovable axle of truth is fixed.

He who recognizes the existence of suffering, its cause, its remedy, and its cessation has fathomed the four noble truths. He will walk in the right path.

Right views will be the torch to light his way. Right aspirations will be his guide. Right speech will be his dwelling-place on the road. His gait will be straight,

---

RHETORICAL DEVICE

Polysyndeton: Using a series of conjunctions like "and," "or," "nor" between each word or phrase. They provide formality and slow down the rush of thought.

Neither abstinence from fish or flesh, nor going naked, nor shaving the head, nor wearing matted hair, nor dressing in a rough garment, nor covering oneself with dirt, nor sacrificing to Agni, will cleanse a man who is not free from delusions. —*Gautama Buddha*

This right of the journalist is as sacred, as necessary, as imprescriptible, as the right of the legislator. —*Victor Hugo*

No realistic American can expect from a dictator's peace international generosity, or return of true independence, or world disarmament, or freedom of expression, or freedom of religion— or even good business. —*Franklin Delano Roosevelt*

for it is right behavior. His refreshments will be the right way of earning his livelihood. Right efforts will be his steps, right thoughts his breath; and right contemplation will give him the peace that follows in his footprints.

Now, this, O bhikkhus, is the noble truth concerning suffering:

Birth is attended with pain, decay is painful, disease is painful, death is painful. Union with the unpleasant is painful, painful is separation from the pleasant, and any craving that is unsatisfied, that too is painful. In brief, bodily conditions which spring from attachment are painful.

This, then, O bhikkus, is the noble truth concerning suffering.

Now this, O bhikkhus, is the noble truth concerning the origin of suffering:

Verily, it is that craving which causes the renewal of existence, accompanied by sensual delight, seeking satisfaction now here, now there, the craving for the gratification of the passions, the craving for a future life, and the craving for happiness in this life.

This, then, O bhikkhus, is the noble truth concerning the origin of suffering.

Gautama Buddha founded Buddhism in India in the sixth century B.C.E. Buddhism followed the Silk Road to China and reached Korea in 372 C.E. and Japan in 467 C.E. The Great Buddha in Kamakura, Japan, was built in 1252. *(Henry William Fu/Shutterstock)*

Now this, O bhikkhus, is the noble truth concerning the destruction of suffering:

Verily, it is the destruction, in which no passion remains, of this very thirst; it is the laying aside of, the being free from, the dwelling no longer upon this thirst.

This then, O bhikkhus, is the noble truth concerning the destruction of suffering.

Now this, O bhikkhus, is the noble truth concerning the way which leads to the destruction of sorrow. Verily! it is this noble eightfold path: that is to say:

Right views; right aspirations; right speech; right behavior; right livelihood; right effort; right thoughts; and right contemplation.

This, then, O bhikkhus, is the noble truth concerning the destruction of sorrow. By the practice of loving kindness I have attained liberation of heart, and thus I am assured that I shall never return in renewed births. I have even now attained Nirvana.

Source: Buddha. "Sermon at Benares." *The Gospel of Buddha.* Edited by Paul Carus. Chicago: Open Court Publishing Co., 1894, p. 49.

ARTEMISIA

(fifth century B.C.E.)

Advice to Xerxes I

off the island of Salamis, Greece
late September 480 B.C.E.

Darius I of Persia had been angered by the aid Greece gave to several Greek city-states that had revolted against him. He resolved to conquer Greece. In the first Persian War (492 B.C.E.), Darius's fleet foundered in storms. The Athenians repulsed Persia at Marathon in the second Persian War (490 B.C.E.). Darius's son, Xerxes, assumed leadership of a third expedition after his father's death in 486 B.C.E. The massive Persian force, with allies from many friendly states, attacked Greece in 480 B.C.E. The army under Xerxes seized Athens, but offshore the Greek fleet lay waiting nearby. Xerxes sought out advice from his navy's allied monarchs and captains. They included Artemisia, queen of Halicarnassus (which lies at the northern shore of what is now called the Bay of Gökova, in Turkey), who had supplied five of the fleet's finest triremes—war-ships powered by 50 or more oarsmen below deck—and fought the Greeks at Euboea the previous month. The Greek historian Herodotus records that Artemisia voiced concerns so boldly her friends feared for her safety from Xerxes' anger. Her candid reply pleased Xerxes; however, he followed the majority of the commanders' advice to give battle. From a throne onshore he watched the assault. Artemisia fought bravely, but she had warned that disaster would follow from engaging the Greek navy in the narrow strait, and the larger Persian fleet was indeed defeated. The Persian army had to withdraw, as the navy could no longer deliver supplies to the Peloponnese Peninsula. The Battle of Salamis is considered one of the most important in history, as the outcome preserved Greek independence and the flowering of democracy.

I was not the least brave of those who fought at Euboea, nor were my achievements there among the meanest. It is my right, therefore, O my lord, to tell you plainly what I think to be most for your advantage now. This then is my advice:

Spare your ships, and do not risk a battle, for these people are as much superior to your people in seamanship, as men to women. What so great need is there for you to incur hazard at sea? Are you not master of Athens, for which you undertook your expedition? Is not Greece subject to you? Not a soul now resists your advance. They who once resisted, were handled even as they deserved.

Now learn how I expect that affairs will go with your adversaries. If you are not over-hasty to engage with them by sea, but will keep your fleet near the land, then whether you stay as you are, or march forward towards the Peloponnese, you will easily accomplish all for which you are come here. The Greeks cannot hold out against you very long; you will soon part them asunder, and scatter them to their several homes. In the island where they lie, I hear they have no food in store; nor is it likely, if your land force begins its march towards the Peloponnese, that they will remain quietly where they are—at least such as come from that region. Of a surety they will not greatly trouble themselves to give battle on behalf of the Athenians.

On the other hand, if you are hasty to fight, I tremble lest the defeat of your sea force brings harm likewise to your land army. This, too, you should remember, O king: good masters are apt to have bad servants, and bad masters good ones. Now, as you are the best of men, your servants must needs be a sorry set. These Egyptians, Cyprians,

Cilicians, and Pamphylians, who are counted in the number of your subject-allies, of how little service are they to you!

Source: Herodotus. *The History of Herodotus.* Translated by George Rawlinson. London: John Murray, 1862, p. 258.

RHETORICAL DEVICE

Litotes: Using denial of the opposite of what you mean to create a kind of under-statement that is useful to modesty, as well as underscoring your point. (*See also* understatement)

I was not the least brave of those who fought at Euboea, nor were my achievements there among the meanest. —*Artemisia*

Our country is not flourishing. —*Václav Havel*

This war is not limited to the unfortunate territory of our country. —*Charles de Gaulle*

All this will not be finished in the first one hundred days. —*John F. Kennedy*

Peace is not a piece of paper. —*Salah Khalaf*

We are here not to fix an uncertain date in our annals, nor to draw into notice an obscure and unknown spot. —*Daniel Webster*

PERICLES
(ca. 495–429 B.C.E.)
Funeral Oration
Athens
Winter 431 B.C.E.

During a long period of peace among the warring states of ancient Greece, the great statesman Pericles led Athens in an extraordinary flowering of art, literature, architecture, and most notably, democracy. This was Athens's "Golden Age," or "Age of Pericles." He rebuilt several temples on the Acropolis that had been destroyed by Xerxes in the last Persian War (480 B.C.E.); the Parthenon is the most famous of these. He promoted a culture of tolerance and obedience to law, initiated such reforms as salaried government officials, and fostered politics in which even the poorest citizen could participate. He was a capable military leader and a magnificent orator. Although Athens and Sparta (both part of modern Greece) were allies during the Persian Wars, resentment over territory and political relations festered over the following 20 years. Sparta led the Peloponnesian League, an alliance between the small states of the Peloponnese, the large southern-most peninsula of Greece. Athens was the major power of the Hellenic (or Delian) League. Many historians blame Pericles and Athens for the start of the devastating Peloponnesian War in 431 B.C.E., as Pericles failed to deal diplomatically with the Spartans and opted for war. The Athenians also became dissatisfied with his leadership. Nevertheless, that winter the eloquent Pericles delivered the annual speech at the state funeral for all soldiers killed in that year. Rather than dwell on military glory, as was usual, the proud Pericles chose to honor the dead by praising their city, and the democracy that flourished there, for which they had given their lives. This famous eulogy was recorded (and probably embellished) by the Athenian historian Thucydides, a statesman and friend of Pericles, who was present. Many historians believe Lincoln took some inspiration from this speech while composing his own eulogy on war dead—the Gettysburg Address.

I will speak first of our ancestors, for it is right and seemly that now, when we are lamenting the dead, a tribute should be paid to their memory. There has never been a time when they did not inhabit this land, which by their valor they will have handed down from generation to generation, and we have received from them a free state. But if they were worthy of praise, still more were our fathers, who added to their inheritance, and after many a struggle transmitted to us their sons this great empire.

And we ourselves assembled here today, who are still most of us in the vigor of life, have carried the work of improvement further, and have richly endowed our city with all things, so that she is sufficient for herself both in peace and war. Of the military exploits by which our various possessions were acquired, or of the energy with which we, or our fathers, drove back the tide of war, Hellenic or Barbarian, I will not speak, for the tale would be long and is familiar to you.

But before I praise the dead, I should like to point out by what principles of action we rose to power, and under what institutions and through what manner of life our empire became great. For I conceive that such thoughts are not unsuited to the occasion, and that this numerous assembly of citizens and strangers may profitably listen to them.

Our form of government does not enter into rivalry with the institutions of others. Our government does not copy our neighbors', but is an example to them. It is true that we are called a democracy, for the administration is in the hands of the many and not of the few. But while there exists equal justice to all and alike in their private disputes, the claim of excellence is also recognized; and when a citizen is in any way distinguished,

18

he is preferred to the public service, not as a matter of privilege, but as the reward of merit. Neither is poverty an obstacle, but a man may benefit his country whatever the obscurity of his condition.

There is no exclusiveness in our public life. And in our private business we are not suspicious of one another, nor angry with our neighbor if he does what he likes; we do not put on sour looks at him which, though harmless, are not pleasant. While we are thus unconstrained in our private business, a spirit of reverence pervades our public acts; we are prevented from doing wrong by respect for the authorities and for the laws, having a particular regard to those which are ordained for the protection of the injured as well as those unwritten laws which bring upon the transgressor of them the reprobation of the general sentiment.

And we have not forgotten to provide for our weary spirits many relaxations from toil: we have regular games and sacrifices throughout the year; our homes are beautiful and elegant; and the delight which we daily feel in all these things helps to banish sorrow. Because of the greatness of our city the fruits of the whole earth flow in upon us, so that we enjoy the goods of other countries as freely as our own.

Then, again, our military training is in many respects superior to that of our adversaries. Our city is thrown open to the world, though, and we never expel a foreigner and prevent him from seeing or learning anything of which the secret if revealed to an enemy might profit him. We rely not upon management or trickery, but upon our own hearts and hands. And in the matter of education, whereas they from early youth are always undergoing laborious exercises which are to make them brave, we live at ease, and yet are equally ready to face the perils which they face. . . .

For we are lovers of the beautiful, yet simple in our tastes, and we cultivate the mind without loss of manliness. Wealth we employ, not for talk and ostentation, but when there is a real use for it. To avow poverty with us is no disgrace; the true disgrace is in doing nothing to avoid it. An Athenian citizen does not neglect the state because he takes care of his own household; and even those of us who are engaged in business have a very fair idea of politics. We alone regard a man who takes no interest in public affairs not as harmless, but as a useless character; and if few of us are originators, we are all sound judges of a policy. The great impediment to action is, in our opinion, not discussion, but the want of that knowledge which is gained by discussion. . . .

In the hour of trial Athens alone among her contemporaries is superior to the report of her. No enemy who comes against her is indignant at the reverses which he sustains at the hands of such a city; no subject complains that his masters are unworthy of him. And we shall assuredly not be without witnesses: there are mighty monuments of our power which will make us the wonder of this and of succeeding ages; we shall not need the praises of Homer or of any other panegyrist whose poetry may please for the moment, although his representation of the facts will not bear the light of day.

Much of the reason Athens was the cultural heart of the Greek world was due to the influence of the great statesman and orator Pericles. This bust of Pericles, said to be from Hadrian's Villa at Tivoli, Lazio, Italy, is now in the British Museum. *(Ablestock)*

For we have compelled every land and every sea to open a path for our valor, and have everywhere planted eternal memorials of our friendship and of our enmity. Such is the city for whose sake these men nobly fought and died; they could not bear the thought that she might be taken from them; and every one of us who survive should gladly toil on her behalf.

I have dwelt upon the greatness of Athens because I want to show you that we are contending for a higher prize than those who enjoy none of these privileges, and to establish by manifest proof the merit of these men whom I am now commemorating. Their loftiest praise has been already spoken. For in magnifying the city I have magnified them, and men like them whose virtues made her glorious. And of how few Hellenes can it be said as of them, that their deeds when weighed in the balance have been found equal to their fame! I believe that a death such as theirs has been the true measure of a man's worth; it may be the first revelation of his virtues, but is at any rate their final seal. For even those who come short in other ways may justly plead the valor with which they have fought for their country. They have blotted out the evil with the good, and have benefited the state more by their public services than they have injured her by their private actions.

None of these men were enervated by wealth or hesitated to resign the pleasures of life; none of them put off the evil day in the hope, natural to poverty, that a man, though poor, may one day become rich. But, deeming that the punishment of their enemies was sweeter than any of these things, and that they could fall in no nobler cause, they determined at the hazard of their lives to be honorably avenged, and to leave the rest. They resigned to hope their unknown chance of happiness; but in the face of death they resolved to rely upon themselves alone. And when the moment came they were minded to resist and suffer, rather than to fly and save their lives. They ran away from the word of dishonor, but on the battlefield their feet stood fast, and in an instant, at the height of their fortune, they passed away from the scene, not of their fear, but of their glory.

Such was the end of these men. They were worthy of Athens, and the living need not desire to have a more heroic spirit, although they may pray for a less fatal issue. The value of such a spirit is not to be expressed in words. Any one can discourse to you forever about the advantages of a brave defense, which you know already. But instead of listening to him I would have you day by day fix your eyes upon the greatness of Athens, until you become filled with the love of her. And when you are impressed by the spectacle of her glory, reflect that this empire has been acquired by men who knew their duty and had the courage to do it, who in the hour of conflict had the fear of dishonor always present to them, and who, if ever they failed in an enterprise, would not allow their virtues to be lost to their country, but freely gave their lives to her as the fairest offering which they could present at her feast.

The sacrifice which they collectively made was individually repaid to them; for they received again each one for himself a praise which grows not old, and the noblest of all tombs. I speak not of that in which their remains are laid, but of that in which their glory survives, and is proclaimed always and on every fitting occasion both in word and deed. For the whole earth is the tomb of famous men; not only are they commemorated by columns and inscriptions in their own country, but in foreign lands there dwells also an unwritten memorial of them, graven not on stone but in the hearts of men. Make them your examples, and, esteeming courage to be freedom and freedom to be happiness, do not weigh too nicely the perils of war.

Source: Pericles. "Funeral Oration." Translated by Benjamin Jowett. *The Universal Anthology.* Richard Garnett, ed. London: Clarke, 1899, p. 342.

SOCRATES

(469–399 B.C.E.)

The Trial Addresses

Athens

399 B.C.E.

One of the great trials of history was that of Socrates. He was one of the most influential of ancient philosophers to the growth of Western thought; he developed the Socratic Method, a way of solving problems by asking questions, which is at the heart of scientific inquiry today. In Athens, Socrates became notorious for asking irritating questions about justice, virtue, and the self to all sorts of people, most dangerously to the embarrassment of government officials. Socrates had discovered he became wise from recognizing how little he knew, while others foolishly thought they were wise when they were not. Young men of the city, including his student Plato (who would become one of the great Greek philosophers), were irresistibly attracted to his examination of their elders' shortcomings and flocked to his philosophical debates. Eager to be rid of him, Athenian leaders Anytus and Meletus accused Socrates of not honoring the state religion and corrupting Athenian youth by his teaching.

Indeed, one of Socrates' pupils had led the Council of Thirty, which briefly overthrew the fragile democracy after the Peloponnesian War (431–404 B.C.E.), and the democratic faction in power blamed Socrates for their misdeeds. Socrates was put on trial in 399 B.C.E., when he was more than 70 years of age. As always he said what he thought, provoking the court by suggesting that, far from being punished, he should receive awards for his services. He was unafraid of death and chose not to use tactics, such as bringing his children into the courtroom, that might have gained sympathy but which he felt were unworthy of an honorable man. He was convicted by a vote of about 280 to 221 (501 men sat on the jury). Here are excerpts from his speeches to the jurors (recorded, and probably embellished, by Plato, who was present). He was executed by ingesting a poisonous drink of hemlock. The account of the trial comes from Plato's *Apology* (the title refers to an older meaning of "defense").

In his defense:

I will endeavor to explain to you the origin of this name of "wise," and of this evil fame.... I will refer you to a witness who is worthy of credit, and will tell you about my wisdom—whether I have any, and of what sort—and that witness shall be the god of Delphi.

You must have known Chaerephon; he was early a friend of mine, and also a friend of yours, for he shared in the exile of the people, and returned with you. Well, Chaerephon, as you know, was very impetuous in all his doings, and he went to Delphi and boldly asked the oracle to tell him whether there was anyone wiser than I was, and the Pythian prophetess answered that there was no man wiser. Chaerephon is dead himself, but his brother, who is in court, will confirm the truth of this story.

Why do I mention this? Because I am going to explain to you why I have such an evil name. When I heard the answer, I said to myself, What can the god mean? and what is the interpretation of this riddle? for I know that I have no wisdom, small or great. What can he mean when he says that I am the wisest of men? And yet he is a god and cannot lie; that would be against his nature.

After a long consideration, I at last thought of a method of trying the question. I reflected that if I could only find a man wiser than myself, then I might go to the god with a refutation in my hand.... I went to one man after another, being not unconscious of the enmity which I provoked; and I lamented and feared this, but necessity was laid upon me—the word of God, I thought, ought to be considered first. And I said to myself, Go I must to all who appear to know, and find out the meaning of the

> The life which is unexamined is not worth living.
> *–Socrates*
>
> No evil can happen to a good man,
> either in life or after death. *–Socrates*

oracle. And I swear to you, Athenians, by the dog I swear!—for I must tell you the truth—the result of my mission was just this: I found that the men most in repute were all but the most foolish; and that some inferior men were really wiser and better. . . .

This investigation has led to my having many enemies of the worst and most dangerous kind, and has given occasion also to many calumnies. And I am called wise, for my hearers always imagine that I myself possess the wisdom which I find wanting in others. But the truth is, O men of Athens, that God only is wise; and in this oracle he means to say that the wisdom of men is little or nothing. He is not speaking of Socrates, he is only using my name as an illustration, as if he said, "He, O men, is the wisest, who, like Socrates, knows that his wisdom is in truth worth nothing."

And so I go my way, obedient to the god, and make inquisition into the wisdom of anyone, whether citizen or stranger, who appears to be wise; and if he is not wise, then in vindication of the oracle I show him that he is not wise. And this occupation quite absorbs me, and I have no time to give either to any public matter of interest or to any concern of my own, but I am in utter poverty by reason of my devotion to the god.

There is another thing: Young men of the richer classes, who have not much to do, come about me of their own accord. They like to hear the pretenders examined, and they often imitate me, and examine others themselves; there are plenty of persons, as they soon enough discover, who think that they know something but really know little or nothing. And then those who are examined by them, instead of being angry with themselves, are angry with me: This confounded Socrates, they say; this villainous misleader of youth! . . .

Someone will say: And are you not ashamed, Socrates, of a course of life which is likely to bring you to an untimely end? To him I may fairly answer: There you are mistaken. A man who is good for anything ought not to calculate the chance of living or dying; he ought only to consider whether in doing anything he is doing right or wrong—acting the part of a good man or of a bad. . . . Had Achilles any thought of death and danger? For wherever a man's place is, whether the place which he has chosen or that in which he has been placed by a commander, there he ought to remain in the hour of danger. He should not think of death or of anything, but of disgrace. . . .

Men of Athens, I honor and love you; but I shall obey God rather than you. And while I have life and strength I shall never cease from the practice and teaching of philosophy, exhorting anyone whom I meet after my manner, and convincing him, saying: O my friend, why do you who are a citizen of the great and mighty and wise city of Athens, care so much about laying up the greatest amount of money and honor and reputation, and so little about wisdom and truth and the greatest improvement of the soul, which you never regard or heed at all? Are you not ashamed of this? And if the person with whom I am arguing says: Yes, but I do care; I do not depart or let him go at once; I interrogate and examine and cross-examine him, and if I think that he has no virtue, but only says that he has, I reproach him with undervaluing the greater, and overvaluing the less.

And this I should say to everyone whom I meet, young and old, citizen and alien, but especially to the citizens, inasmuch as they are my brethren. For this is the command of God, as I would have you know; and I believe that to this day no greater good has ever happened in the state than my service to the God. For I do nothing but go about persuading you all, old and young alike, not to take thought for your persons and your properties, but first and chiefly to care about the greatest improvement of the soul.

I tell you that virtue is not given by money, but that from virtue come money and every other good of man, public as well as private. This is my teaching, and if this is the doctrine which corrupts the youth, my influence is ruinous indeed. But if anyone says that this is not my teaching, he is speaking an untruth. Wherefore, O men of Athens, I say to you, do as Anytus bids or not as Anytus bids, and either acquit me or not; but whatever you do, know that I shall never alter my ways, not even if I have to die many times.

Men of Athens, I would have you know that, if you kill such a one as I am, you will injure yourselves more than you will injure me. Meletus and Anytus will not injure me—they cannot; for it is not in the nature of things that a bad man should injure a better than himself. I do not deny that he may, perhaps, kill him, or drive him into exile, or deprive him of civil rights; and he may imagine, and others may imagine, that he is doing him a great injury. But in that I do not agree with him; for the evil of doing as Anytus is doing—of unjustly taking away another man's life—is greater far.

And now, Athenians, I am not going to argue for my own sake, as you may think, but for yours, that you may not sin against the God, or lightly reject his boon by condemning me. For if you kill me you will not easily find another like me, who, if I may use such a ludicrous figure of speech, am a sort of gadfly, given to the state by the God; and the state is like a great and noble steed who is tardy in his motions owing to his very size, and requires to be stirred into life.

I am that gadfly which God has given the state and all day long and in all places am always fastening upon you, arousing and persuading and reproaching you. And as you will not easily find another like me, I would advise you to spare me. I dare say that you may feel irritated at being suddenly awakened when you are caught napping; and you may think that if you were to strike me dead, as Anytus advises, which you easily might, then you would sleep on for the remainder of your lives, unless God in his care of you gives you another gadfly.

And that I am given to you by God is proved by this: that if I had been like other men, I should not have neglected all my own concerns, or patiently seen the neglect of them during all these years, and have been doing yours, coming to you individually, like a father or elder brother, exhorting you to regard virtue; this I say, would not be like human nature.

And had I gained anything, or if my exhortations had been paid, there would have been some sense in that. But now, as you will perceive, not even the impudence of my accusers dares to say that I have ever exacted or sought pay of anyone; they have no witness of that. And I have a witness of the truth of what I say; my poverty is a sufficient witness. . . .

To you and to God I commit my cause, to be determined by you as is best for you and me.

On his conviction:

There are many reasons why I am not grieved, O men of Athens, at the vote of condemnation. I expected it, and am only surprised that the votes are so nearly equal; for I had thought that the majority against me would have been far larger; but now, had thirty votes gone over to the other side, I should have been acquitted. . . .

And so he proposes death as the penalty. And what shall I propose on my part, O men of Athens? Clearly that which is my due. And what is that which I ought to pay or to receive? What shall be done to the man who has never had the wit to be idle during his whole life; but has been careless of what the many care about—wealth, and family interests, and military offices, and speaking in the assembly, and magistracies, and plots, and parties. . . .

Someone will say: Yes, Socrates, but cannot you hold your tongue, and then you may go [in exile] into a foreign city, and no one will interfere with you? Now I have great difficulty in making you understand my answer to this. For if I tell you that this would be a disobedience to a divine command, and therefore that I cannot hold my tongue, you will not believe that I am serious. And if I say again that the greatest good of man is daily to converse about virtue, and all that concerning which you hear me examining myself and others, and that the life which is unexamined is not worth living—that you are still less likely to believe. And yet what I say is true, although a thing of which it is hard for me to persuade you.

Moreover, I am not accustomed to think that I deserve any punishment. Had I money I might have proposed to give you what I had, and have been none the worse. But you see that I have none, and can only ask you to proportion the fine to my means. However, I think that I could afford a minae, and therefore I propose that penalty. Plato, Crito, Critobulus, and Apollodorus, my friends here, bid me say thirty minae, and they will be the sureties. Well then, say thirty minae, let that be the penalty; for that they will be ample security to you.

On being sentenced to death:
Not much time will be gained, O Athenians, in return for the evil name which you will get from the detractors of the city, who will say that you killed Socrates, a wise man; for they will call me wise even although I am not wise when they want to reproach you.

If you had waited a little while, your desire would have been fulfilled in the course of nature. For I am far advanced in years, as you may perceive, and not far from death. I am speaking now only to those of you who have condemned me to death.

And I have another thing to say to them: You think that I was convicted through deficiency of words—I mean, that if I had thought fit to leave nothing undone, nothing unsaid, I might have gained an acquittal. Not so; the deficiency which led to my conviction was not of words—certainly not. But I had not the boldness or impudence or inclination to address you as you would have liked me to address you, weeping and wailing and lamenting, and saying and doing many things which you have been accustomed to hear from others, and which, as I say, are unworthy of me.

But I thought that I ought not to do anything common or mean in the hour of danger; nor do I now repent of the manner of my defense, and I would rather die having spoken after my manner, than speak in your manner and live. For neither in war nor yet at law ought any man to use every way of escaping death. For often in battle there is no doubt that if a man will throw away his arms, and fall on his knees before his pursuers, he may escape death; and in other dangers there are other ways of escaping death, if a man is willing to say and do anything.

The difficulty, my friends, is not in avoiding death, but in avoiding unrighteousness—for that runs faster than death. I am old and move slowly, and the slower runner has overtaken me, and my accusers are keen and quick, and the faster runner, who is unrighteousness, has overtaken them. And now I depart hence condemned by you to suffer the penalty of death, and they, too, go their ways condemned by the truth to suffer the penalty of villainy and wrong; and I must abide by my award—let them abide by theirs. I suppose that these things may be regarded as fated—and I think that they are well.

And now, O men who have condemned me, I would fain prophesy to you; for I am about to die, and that is the hour in which men are gifted with prophetic power. And I prophesy to you who are my murderers, that immediately after my death punishment far heavier than you have inflicted on me will surely await you. Me you have killed because you wanted to escape the accuser, and not to give an account of your lives. But that will not be as you suppose: far otherwise.

For I say that there will be more accusers of you than there are now, accusers whom hitherto I have restrained. And as they are younger they will be more severe with you, and you will be more offended at them. For if you think that by killing men you can avoid the accuser censuring your lives, you are mistaken; that is not a way of escape

RHETORICAL DEVICE

Procatalepsis: Presenting a hearer's possible objection to the argument first, and then going on to answer it.

I may be asked, why I am so anxious to bring this subject before the British public—why I do not confine my efforts to the United States? My answer is, first, that slavery is the common enemy of mankind, and all mankind should be made acquainted with its abominable character. —*Frederick Douglass*

There are some who say that communism is the wave of the future.
Let them come to Berlin. —*John F. Kennedy*

Government rests upon force, you say. Not at all: it rests upon consent, ladies and gentlemen, and women are withdrawing their consent. —*Emmeline Pankhurst*

They are an army of impotence. You may call them an army
of safety and of guard; but they are, in truth,
an army of impotence and contempt. —*William Pitt the Elder*

Someone will say: And are you not ashamed, Socrates, of a course of life which is likely to bring you to an untimely end? To him I may fairly answer: There you are mistaken. A man who is good for anything ought not to calculate the chance of living or dying; he ought only to consider whether in doing anything he is doing right or wrong—acting the part of a good man or of a bad. —*Socrates*

which is either possible or honorable. The easiest and noblest way is not to be crushing others, but to be improving yourselves. . . .

Know this of a truth—that no evil can happen to a good man, either in life or after death. He and his are not neglected by the gods, nor has my own approaching end happened by mere chance. But I see clearly that to die and be released was better for me; and therefore the oracle gave no sign. For which reason also, I am not angry with my accusers or my condemners. They have done me no harm, although neither of them meant to do me any good, and for this I may gently blame them.

Still I have a favor to ask of them. When my sons are grown up, I would ask you, O my friends, to punish them. And I would have you trouble them, as I have troubled you, if they seem to care about riches, or anything, more than about virtue; or if they pretend to be something when they are really nothing. Then reprove them, as I have reproved you, for not caring about that for which they ought to care, and thinking that they are something when they are really nothing. And if you do this, I and my sons will have received justice at your hands.

The hour of departure has arrived, and we go our ways—I to die, and you to live. Which is better God only knows.

Source: Plato. *The Dialogues of Plato.* Translated by Benjamin Jowett. Oxford: Clarendon Press, 1875, p. 352.

DEMOSTHENES
(384–322 B.C.E.)
On the Crown
Athens

330 B.C.E.

Demosthenes, often considered the greatest orator of ancient Greece, was born in 384 B.C.E. to wealthy parents, but he was orphaned when only seven years old. As a young man, he honed his oratory in court disputing the guardians who embezzled his inheritance. He became a successful speechwriter penning lawyers' trial addresses. He took an interest in politics, and with the rise of King Philip II of Macedon (father of Alexander the Great), he found his focus. Philip had begun his campaign for empire from Pella, the capital of Macedon, seizing cities on the borders of his realm. Demosthenes recognized the danger Philip posed to Greece (or Hellas, as Greece was then called). As one of the great statesmen of Athens, he began a series of three speeches against Philip (in 351, 344, and 341 B.C.E.), called the *Philippics*. (Today any fiery, bitter speech against an individual may be termed a philippic.) Demosthenes warned the people to prepare their defense and to beware Philip's offers of peace. Despite Demosthenes' diplomatic efforts—he also

fought as a hoplite, or infantryman, in battle—Philip conquered almost all the Greek states by 338 B.C.E. Two years later, a prominent Athenian orator named Ctesiphon proposed the customary golden crown be awarded to Demosthenes for his devoted service. Aeschines, a longtime political enemy, accused Ctesiphon of falsehood in describing Demosthenes' contributions, as Demosthenes' policy toward Philip had failed. In 330 B.C.E. the matter came to a head, and Demosthenes was forced to defend Ctesiphon and himself in court. In this short excerpt from one of his finest (and very long) speeches, he details Philip's crimes, tells a story (of the fearful day Philip's army neared Athens) that proves the Athenians supported his—Demosthenes'—plan of action, and finally contends that glory goes not just to the victorious but to all brave men who do their duty. Aeschines lost the case, and he was forced into exile. The Prytanes who Demosthenes refers to are the head councilmen of Athens.

What was it fitting for the city to do, Aeschines, when she saw Philip establishing for himself a despotic sway over the Hellenes? What language should have been used, what measures proposed, by the adviser of the people at Athens? . . . When I saw that Philip himself, with whom our conflict lay, for the sake of empire and absolute power had had his eye knocked out, his collar-bone broken, his hand and his leg maimed, and was ready to resign any part of his body that Fortune chose to take from him, provided that with what remained he might live in honor and glory?

And surely no one would dare to say that it was fitting that in one bred at Pella, a place then inglorious and insignificant, there should have grown up so lofty a spirit that he aspired after the empire of Hellas, and conceived such a project in his mind; while you, who are Athenians, and who day by day in all that you hear and see behold the memorials of the gallantry of your forefathers, such baseness should be found, that you would yield up your liberty to Philip by your own deliberate offer and deed. No man would say this!

One alternative remained, and that, one which you were bound to take—that of a righteous resistance to the whole course of action by which he was doing you injury. You acted thus from the first, quite rightly and properly, while I helped by my proposals and advice during the time of my political activity. And I do not deny it. But what ought I to have done? . . .

I only ask you whether Philip, who was appropriating Euboea, and establishing it as a stronghold to command Attica; who was making an attempt upon Megara, seizing Oreus, razing the walls of Porthmus, setting up Philistides as tyrant at Oreus and Cleitarchus at Eretria, bringing the Hellespont into his own power, besieging Byzantium, destroying some of the cities of Hellas, and restoring his exiled friends to others—whether he, I say, in acting thus, was guilty of wrong, violating the truce and breaking the peace, or not? Was it fit that one of the Hellenes should arise to prevent it, or not? . . . If it was right that one should arise to prevent it, for whom could the task be more fitting than for the people of Athens? That then, was the aim of my policy; and when I saw Philip reducing all mankind to servitude, I opposed him, and without ceasing warned and exhorted you to make no surrender. . . .

Philip came with his army and seized Elateia, thinking that under no circumstances whatever should we and the Thebans join in unison after this. And though the commotion which followed in the city is known to you all, let me relate to you briefly just the bare facts.

It was evening, and one had come to the Prytanes with the news that Elateia had been taken. Upon this they rose up from supper without delay; some of them drove the occupants out of the booths in the marketplace and set fire to the wicker-work; others sent for the generals and summoned the trumpeter; and the city was full of commotion.

On the morrow, at break of day, the Prytanes summoned the Council to the Council-Chamber, while you made your way to the Assembly; and before the Council had transacted its business and passed its draft-resolution, the whole people was seated on the hill-side. And now, when the Council had arrived, and the Prytanes had reported the intelligence which they had received, and had brought forward the messenger, and he had made his statement, the herald proceeded to ask, "Who wishes to speak?" But no one came forward; and though the herald repeated the question many times, still no one rose, though all the generals were present, and all the orators, and the voice of their country was calling for some one to speak for her deliverance. For the voice of the herald, uttered in accordance with the laws, is rightly to be regarded as the common voice of our country.

And yet, if it was for those to come forward who wished for the deliverance of the city, all of you and all the other Athenians would have risen, and proceeded to the platform, for I am certain that you all wished for her deliverance. If it was for the wealthiest, the Three Hundred would have risen; and if it was for those who had both these qualifications—loyalty to the city and wealth—then those would have risen, who subsequently made those large donations; for it was loyalty and wealth that led them so to do.

But that crisis and that day called, it seems, not merely for a man of loyalty and wealth, but for one who had also followed the course of events closely from the first, and had come to a true conclusion as to the motive and the aim with which Philip was acting as he was. For no one who was unacquainted with these, and had not scrutinized them from an early period, was any the more likely, for all his loyalty and wealth, to know what should be done, or to be able to advise you.

The man who was needed was found that day in me. . . . I would have you realize that I was the only orator or politician who did not desert his post as a loyal citizen in the hour of danger, but was found there, speaking and proposing what your need required, in the midst of the terror . . . When I had spoken these words, and others in the same strain, I left the platform. All joined in commending these proposals; no one said a word in opposition; and I did not speak thus, and then fail to move a motion; nor move a motion, and then fail to serve as envoy; nor serve as envoy, and then fail to persuade the Thebans. I carried the matter through in person from beginning to end, and gave myself up unreservedly to meet the dangers which encompassed the city. . . .

Had she surrendered without a struggle those claims in defense of which our forefathers faced every imaginable peril, who would not have cast scorn upon you, Aeschines—upon you, I say; not, I trust, upon Athens nor upon me? In God's name, with what faces should we have looked upon those who came to visit the city, if events had come round to the same conclusion as they now have—if Philip had been chosen as commander and lord of all, and we had stood apart, while others carried on the struggle to prevent these things; and that, although the city had never yet in time past preferred an inglorious security to the hazardous vindication of a noble cause?

What Hellene, what foreigner, does not know, that the Thebans, and the Spartans, who were powerful still earlier, and the Persian king would all gratefully and gladly have allowed Athens to take what she liked and keep all that was her own, if she would do the bidding of another, and let another take the first place in Hellas? But this was not, it appears, the tradition of the Athenians; it was not tolerable; it was not in their nature.

From the beginning of time no one had ever yet succeeded in persuading the city to throw in her lot with those who were strong, but unrighteous in their dealings, and to enjoy the security of servitude. Throughout all time she has maintained her perilous struggle for pre-eminence, honor, and glory. And this policy you look upon as so lofty, so proper to your own national character, that, of your forefathers also, it is those who have acted thus that you praise most highly. And naturally. For who would not admire the courage of those men, who did not fear to leave their land and their city, and to embark upon their ships, that they might not do the bidding of another; who chose for their general Themistocles (who had counseled them thus), and stoned Cyrsilus to death, when he gave his voice for submission to a master's orders—and not him alone, for your wives stoned his wife also to death.

For the Athenians of that day did not look for an orator or a general who would enable them to live in happy servitude; they cared not to live at all, unless they might live in freedom. For every one of them felt that he had come into being, not for his father and his mother alone, but also for his country. And wherein lies the difference? He who thinks he was born for his parents alone awaits the death which destiny assigns him in the course of nature: but he who thinks he was born for his country also will be willing to die, that he may not see her in bondage, and will look upon the outrages and the indignities that he must needs bear in a city that is in bondage as more to be dreaded than death.

Now, were I attempting to argue that I had induced you to show a spirit worthy of your forefathers, there is not a man who might not rebuke me with good reason. But in fact, I am declaring that such principles as these are your own; I am showing that before my time the city displayed this spirit, though I claim that I, too, have had some share, as your servant, in carrying out your policy in detail.

But in denouncing the policy as a whole, in bidding you be harsh with me, as one who has brought terrors and dangers upon the city, the prosecutor, in his eagerness to deprive me of my distinction at the present moment, is trying to rob you of praises that will last throughout all time. For if you condemn the defendant on the ground that my policy was not for the best, men will think that your own judgment has been wrong, and that it was not through the unkindness of fortune that you suffered what befell you.

But it cannot, it cannot be that you were wrong, men of Athens, when you took upon you the struggle for freedom and deliverance.

No! by those who at Marathon bore the brunt of the peril—our forefathers.

No! by those who at Plataeae drew up their battle line, by those who at Salamis, by those who off Artemisium fought the fight at sea, by the many who lie in the sepulchres where the People laid them, brave men, all alike deemed worthy by their country, Aeschines, of the same honor and the same obsequies—not the successful or the victorious alone!

And she acted justly. For all these have done that which it was the duty of brave men to do; but their fortune has been that which Heaven assigned to each.

Source: Demosthenes. "On the Crown." *Public Orations of Demosthenes.* Vol. 2, translated by Arthur Wallace Pickard-Cambridge. Oxford: Clarendon Press, 1912.

ALEXANDER THE GREAT

(356–323 B.C.E.)

"To This Empire There Will Be No Boundaries"

India, now Pakistan

326 B.C.E.

One of the ancient world's most successful military commanders was Alexander the Great; he was the son of Philip II, king of Macedon, a Greek-influenced kingdom to the north. Philip built a great army to subdue the warring Greek states; his death in 336 B.C.E. left the throne, and the army, to Alexander. In 334 B.C.E. at only 20 years of age, the young Alexander crossed the Hellespont (the strait dividing Europe from Asia, today called the Dardanelles). He marched south and east to conquer the Persian-held city-states in Asia Minor (modern Turkey) and cut the difficult "Gordian Knot" at Gordium, which foretold he would lead all Asia. (The knot had tied the legendary oxcart of the Phrygian kings.) Syria, Tyre, and Gaza fell in succession, then Egypt. In Egypt he founded Alexandria and was named a deity by high priests. Turning north in 331 B.C.E., he overcame the Persian Empire in Mesopotamia, marched through Babylon (present-day Iraq), and then through Media, Hyrcania on the Caspian Sea, and east to Susiana (all in present-day Iran) by 330 B.C.E.,

defeating kings and chieftains in his path. In the mountains he campaigned three years through Bactria and the Hindu Kush (both in Afghanistan), and then turned his long-suffering army into India (modern Pakistan) in 326 B.C.E. They crossed the Hydaspes, a tributary of the Indus, and battled King Porus, whose war elephants terrified Alexander's horses and complicated his strategy. The Macedonians won but it was the rainy season and after eight years on the march the exhausted men balked at continuing into India. (They had also been offended that Alexander imitated Persian court manners and had considered demanding they prostrate themselves as if he were a god.) Alexander addressed the mutineers, urging them to cross the Hyphasis River and conquer all Asia. The men refused, and Alexander began a return trip though Persia. He died in Babylon in June 323 B.C.E., not yet 33 years old, having conquered much of the world known to him. This speech of Alexander exhorting his men to follow him was retold in the second century C.E. by the Greek historian Arrian of Nicomedia.

I observe, gentlemen, that when I would lead you on a new venture you no longer follow me with your old spirit. I have asked you to meet me that we may come to a decision together: are we, upon my advice, to go forward, or, upon yours, to turn back?

If you have any complaint to make about the results of your efforts hitherto, or about myself as your commander, there is no more to say. But let me remind you: through your courage and endurance you have gained possession of Ionia, the Hellespont, both Phrygias, Cappadocia, Paphlagonia, Lydia, Caria, Lycia, Pamphylia, Phoenicia, and Egypt.

The Greek part of Libya is now yours, together with much of Arabia, lowland Syria, Mesopotamia, Babylon, and Susia. Persia and Media with all the territories either formerly controlled by them or not are in your hands.

You have made yourselves masters of the lands beyond the Caspian Gates, beyond the Caucasus, beyond the Tanais, of Bactria, Hyrcania, and the Hyrcanian sea. We have driven the Scythians back into the desert; and Indus and Hydaspes, Acesines and Hydraotes flow now through country which is ours.

With all that accomplished, why do you hesitate to extend the power of Macedon—*your* power—to the Hyphasis and the tribes on the other side? Are you afraid that a few natives who may still be left will offer opposition? Come, come! These natives either surrender without a blow or are caught on the run—or leave their country undefended for your taking. And when we take it, we make a present of it to those who have joined us of their own free will and fight at our side.

29

Alexander the Great of Macedonia, barely out of his teens, leads his army against Darius III at Issus in southern Asia Minor (Turkey). Detail from a mosaic from Casa del Fauno, Pompeii, now in the Museo Archeologico Nazionale, Naples, Italy. *(Erich Lessing/Art Resource, NY)*

For a man who *is* a man, work, in my belief, if it is directed to noble ends, has no object beyond itself. Nonetheless, if any of you wish to know what limit may be set to this particular campaign, let me tell you that the area of country still ahead of us, from here to the Ganges and the Eastern ocean, is comparatively small. You will undoubtedly find that this ocean is connected with the Hyrcanian Sea, for the great Stream of Ocean encircles the earth. Moreover I shall prove to you, my friends, that the Indian and Persian Gulfs and the Hyrcanian Sea are all three connected and continuous. Our ships will sail round from the Persian Gulf to Libya as far as the Pillars of Hercules, whence all Libya to the eastward will soon be ours, and all Asia too, and to this empire there will be no boundaries but what God Himself has made for the whole world.

But if you turn back now, there will remain unconquered many warlike peoples between the Hyphasis and the Eastern Ocean, and many more to the northward and the Hyrcanian Sea, with the Scythians, too, not far away; so that if we withdraw now there is a danger that the territory which we do not yet securely hold may be stirred to revolt by some nation or other we have not yet forced into submission. Should that happen, all that we have done and suffered will have proved fruitless—or we shall be faced with the task of doing it over again from the beginning. Gentlemen of Macedon, and you, my friends and allies, this must not be. Stand firm; for well you know that hardship and danger are the price of glory, and that sweet is the savour of a life of courage and of deathless renown beyond the grave.

Are you not aware that if Heracles, my ancestor, had gone no further than Tiryns or Argos—or even than the Peloponnese or Thebes—he could never have won the glory which changed him from a man into a god, actual or apparent? Even Dionysus, who is a god indeed, in a sense beyond what is applicable to Heracles, faced not a few laborious tasks. Yet we have done more: we have passed beyond Nysa and we have taken the rock of Aornos which Heracles himself could not take. Come, then; add the rest of Asia to what you already possess—a small addition to the great sum of your conquests.

What great or noble work could we ourselves have achieved had we thought it enough, living at ease in Macedon, merely to guard our homes, accepting no burden beyond checking the encroachment of the Thracians on our borders, or the Illyrians and Triballians, or perhaps such Greeks as might prove a menace to our comfort?

I could not have blamed you for being the first to lose heart if I, your commander, had not shared in your exhausting marches and your perilous campaigns; it would have been natural enough if you had done all the work merely for others to reap the reward. But it is not so. You and I, gentlemen, have shared the labour and shared the danger, and the rewards are for us all.

The conquered territory belongs to you. From your ranks the governors of it are chosen. Already the greater part of its treasure passes into your hands, and when all Asia is overrun, then indeed I will go further than the mere satisfaction of our ambitions: the utmost hopes of riches or power which each one of you cherishes will be far surpassed, and whoever wishes to return home will be allowed to go, either with me or without me.

I will make those who stay the envy of those who return.

Source: Arrian. *The Campaigns of Alexander.* Translated by Aubrey de Selincourt. London: Penguin Classics, 1958, p. 292. Copyright © the Estate of Aubrey de Selincourt, 1958.

PUBLIUS CORNELIUS SCIPIO
(died 211 B.C.E.)
Against Hannibal
Placentia, Italy
November 218 B.C.E.

In the second and third centuries B.C.E. the city-state of Carthage (in what is now Tunisia) rivaled the Roman Republic for power in the Mediterranean. The two powers fought the First Punic War (264–241 B.C.E.) over Sicily; Rome won. In 219 B.C.E. the Carthaginian general Hannibal broke the treaty ending that war by attacking Saguntum, a city in Roman-held eastern Spain, setting off the Second Punic War. Hannibal marched east through France toward Italy, eluding the army that the Roman general Publius Cornelius Scipio had brought by ship to intercept him. Scipio, one of the two consuls (the two highest elected officials) of Rome, sent his legions on to Spain to fight the occupying Carthaginians, then returned to defend Italy. Hannibal continued on, and in one of the great military feats of history, crossed the Alps into northwestern Italy in early winter. Despite huge losses in the heavy snows, he arrived with 30,000 men,

6,000 horses, and 15 elephants. The Romans engaged Hannibal—the 29-year-old "furious youth" as Scipio calls him—in battle by the river Ticinus. Scipio's overconfident address to his men reveals how seriously he underestimated Hannibal. (The historian Livy has him refer in the speech to Sicilian locales of the previous war.) Defeated, Scipio was saved from death by his 19-year-old son Publius. (Publius finally overcame Hannibal 16 years later and, under the name Scipio Africanus Major, became one of the great generals of Rome.) Scipio retreated to his garrison at Placentia where, the next month, with reinforcements, he engaged Hannibal at the river Trebia. This time Hannibal deployed his elephants and, with superior military strategy, defeated the Romans again. Scipio returned to Spain to fight Carthage, and he died in battle in 211 B.C.E. Despite Scipio's defeats, Rome won the Punic Wars and Carthage was destroyed in 146 B.C.E.

⁓

Since I have offered myself voluntarily for this contest, that you might have a consul for your leader against Hannibal and the Carthaginians, a few words are required to be addressed from a new commander to soldiers unacquainted with him.

That you may not be ignorant of the nature of the war nor of the enemy, let me remind you, soldiers, that you have to fight with those whom in the former war you conquered both by land and sea; from whom you have exacted tribute for twenty years; and from whom you hold Sicily and Sardinia, taken as the prizes of victory.

In the present contest, therefore, you and they will have those feelings that are wont to belong to the victors and the vanquished. Nor are they now about to fight because they are daring, but because it is unavoidable—unless you can believe that they who declined the engagement when their forces were entire, should have now gained more confidence when two-thirds of their infantry and cavalry have been lost in the passage of the Alps, and when almost greater numbers have perished than survive.

Yes, they are few indeed (some may say,) but they are vigorous in mind and body, men whose strength and power scarce any force may withstand. On the contrary, they are but the semblances, nay, they are rather the shadows of men—being worn out with hunger, cold, dirt, and filth, and bruised and enfeebled among stones and rocks. Besides all this, their joints are frost-bitten, their sinews stiffened with the snow, their limbs withered up by the frost, their armor battered and gaping, their horses lame and powerless. With such cavalry, with such infantry, you have to fight. You will not have enemies in reality, but rather their last remains. And I fear nothing more than that when you have fought Hannibal, the Alps may appear to have conquered him.

But perhaps it was fitting that the gods themselves should, without any human aid, commence and carry forward a war with a leader and a people that violate the faith of treaties. And that we, who next to the gods have been injured, should finish the contest thus commenced and nearly completed.

I do not fear lest any one should think that I say this ostentatiously for the sake of encouraging you, while in my own mind I am differently affected. . . . I am anxious to try whether the earth has suddenly, in these twenty years, sent forth a new race of Carthaginians, or whether these are the same who fought at the islands Aegates, and whom you permitted to depart from Eryx, valued at eighteen denarii a head; and whether this Hannibal be, as he himself gives out, the rival of the expeditions of Hercules. . . .

I would, therefore, have you fight, soldiers, not only with that spirit with which you are wont to encounter other enemies, but with a certain indignation and resentment, as if you saw your slaves suddenly taking up arms against you. We might have killed them when shut up in Eryx by hunger, the most dreadful of human tortures; we might have carried over our victorious fleet to Africa, and in a few days have destroyed Carthage without any opposition. We granted pardon to their prayers; we released them from the blockade; we made peace with them when conquered; and we afterwards considered them under our protection when they were oppressed by the African war.

In return for these benefits, they come under the conduct of a furious youth to attack our country. And I wish that the contest on your side were for glory, and not for safety. It is not about the possession of Sicily and Sardinia, concerning which the dispute was formerly, but for Italy, that you must fight. Nor is there another army behind, which, if we should not conquer, can resist the enemy. Nor are there other Alps, during the passage of which fresh forces may be procured.

Here, soldiers, we must make our stand, as if we fought before the walls of Rome. Let every one consider that he defends with his arms not only his own person, but his wife and young children; nor let him only entertain domestic cares and anxieties, but at the same time let him bear in mind that the Senate and people of Rome are now anxiously regarding our efforts; and that according to what our strength and valor shall be, such henceforward will be the fortune of that city and of the Roman empire.

Source: Livy. *History of Rome.* Translated by Rev. Canon W. M. Roberts. New York: Dutton, 1924.

GAIUS MARIUS
(157–86 B.C.E.)
On Humbleness of Birth
Rome
106 B.C.E.

Gaius Marius built his noteworthy political career on his skill as one of the great professional soldiers of Rome. He served under Scipio Africanus Minor, quashing rebellion in Numantia (Spain), and he was elected a military tribune in 119 B.C.E. and praetor (highest-ranking magistrate) in 115 B.C.E. With the consul Quintus Caecilius Metellus Numidicus, he fought in North Africa against Jugurtha, the king of Numidia; Marius's military successes came in stark contrast to the cowardly, even corrupt, command of the Numidian war by previous Roman generals. He was elected consul (the Roman Republic's highest elected office) for 107 B.C.E. This command of the military gave him power to make sweeping changes in the army, previously open only to landholders. With the Marian reforms, the poorest citizens could now join, which vastly increased the army's size and in the future would make it a powerful political force for its

commanders. As he was the first in his family's history to become consul, he was considered a *novus homo* or "new man" by the Roman elite families. Privilege was so established in the Roman Senate that in 150 years, only 10 members of the plebs—the common people—became new men by being elected consul (the term of consulship was one year). For a self-made man such as Gaius Marius to have been elected consul seven times (in 107, 104–100, and 86 B.C.E.) was unprecedented. Some patricians resented this movement into the upper class from below, and groused that the rough statesman spoke no Greek and did not keep a fashionable household. Marius countered the slander that he was of low birth (and also encouraged citizens to enlist in the army) in this address to the people "recorded" by Sallust, a Roman historian (86–35 B.C.E.), in *The Jugurthine War*, Sallust's history of Rome's conflicts in Numidia.

❧

I am sensible, my fellow citizens, that the eyes of all men are turned upon me; that the just and good favor me, as my services are beneficial to the state, but that the nobility seek occasion to attack me. . . . You have commanded me to carry on the war against Jugurtha—a commission at which the nobility are highly offended.

Consider with yourselves, I pray you, whether it would be a change for the better if you were to send to this, or to any other such appointment, one of yonder crowd of nobles—a man of ancient family, of innumerable statues, and of no military experience—in order that in so important an office (and being ignorant of everything connected with it) he may exhibit hurry and trepidation and select one of the people to instruct him in his duty. For so it generally happens, that he whom you have chosen to direct, seeks another to direct him.

I know some, my fellow citizens, who, after they have been elected consuls, have begun to read the acts of their ancestors and the military precepts of the Greeks—persons who invert the order of things. For though to discharge the duties of the office is posterior, in point of time, to election, it is, in reality and practical importance, prior to it.

Compare now, my fellow citizens, me, who am a new man, with those haughty nobles. What they have but heard or read, I have witnessed or performed. What they have learned from books, I have acquired in the field; and whether deeds or words are of greater estimation, it is for you to consider. They despise my humbleness of birth; I disdain their imbecility. My condition is made an objection to me; their misconduct is a reproach to them.

The circumstance of birth, indeed, I consider as one and the same to all, but think that he who best exerts himself is the noblest. . . . If the patricians justly despise me, let them also despise their own ancestors, whose nobility, like mine, had its origin in

34

merit. They envy me the honor that I have received; let them also envy me the toils, the abstinence, and the perils by which I obtained that honor. But they, men eaten up with pride, live as if they disdained all the distinctions that you can bestow, and yet sue for those distinctions as if they had lived so as to merit them. Yet those are assuredly deceived who expect to enjoy, at the same time, things so incompatible as the pleasures of indolence and the rewards of honorable exertion.

When they speak before you, or in the senate, they occupy the greatest part of their orations in extolling their ancestors; for they suppose that, by recounting the heroic deeds of their forefathers, they render themselves more illustrious. But the reverse of this is the case; for the more glorious were the lives of their ancestors, the more scandalous is their own inaction. . . . If it be thought necessary, I can show you spears, a banner, caparisons for horses, and other military rewards, besides the scars of wounds on my breast. These are my statues; this is my nobility; honors, not left like theirs, by inheritance, but acquired amid innumerable toils and dangers.

My speech, they say, is inelegant; but that I have ever thought of little importance. Worth sufficiently displays itself; it is for my detractors to use studied language, that they may palliate base conduct by plausible words. Nor have I learned Greek; for I had no wish to acquire a tongue that adds nothing to the valor of those who teach it.

But I have gained other accomplishments, such as are of the utmost benefit to a state: I have learned to strike down an enemy; to be vigilant at my post; to fear nothing but dishonor; to bear cold and heat with equal endurance; to sleep on the ground; and to sustain at the same time hunger and fatigue. And with such rules of conduct I shall stimulate my soldiers, not treating them with rigor and myself with indulgence, nor making their toils my glory. Such a mode of commanding is at once useful to the State, and becoming to a citizen. For to coerce your troops with severity, while you yourself live at ease, is to be a tyrant, not a general.

It was by conduct such as this, my fellow citizens, that your ancestors made themselves and the republic renowned. Our nobility, relying on their forefathers' merits, though totally different from them in conduct, disparage us who emulate their virtues and demand of you every public honor as due, not to their personal merit, but to their high rank. Arrogant pretenders, and utterly unreasonable! For though their ancestors left them all that was at their disposal—their riches, their statues, and their glorious names—they left them not (nor could leave them) their virtue, which alone, of all their possessions, could neither be communicated nor received.

RHETORICAL DEVICE

Irony: Saying something to indicate the opposite of what is meant, usually as sarcasm or humor.

Heydrich was one of their great men. "One of the best Nazis,"
Hitler called him, and that, no doubt, is true. —*Wendell Willkie*

They wrote a dangerous document called
the Declaration of Independence. —*Emma Goldman*

If the patricians justly despise me, let them also despise
their own ancestors, whose nobility, like mine,
had its origin in merit. —*Gaius Marius*

They reproach me as being mean and of unpolished manners because, indeed, I have but little skill in arranging an entertainment, and keep no actor, nor give my cook higher wages than my steward—all which charges I must, indeed, acknowledge to be just; for I learned from my father, and other venerable characters, that vain indulgences belong to women and labor to men; that glory, rather than wealth, should be the object of the virtuous; and that arms and armor, not household furniture, are marks of honor.

But let the nobility, if they please, pursue what is delightful and dear to them; let them devote themselves to licentiousness and luxury; let them pass their age as they have passed their youth, in revelry and feasting, the slaves of gluttony and debauchery. But let them leave the toil and dust of the field and other such matters to us, to whom they are more grateful than banquets. This, however, they will not do; for when these most infamous of men have disgraced themselves by every species of turpitude, they proceed to claim the distinctions due to the most honorable. Thus it most unjustly happens that luxury and indolence, the most disgraceful of vices, are harmless to those who indulge in them and fatal only to the innocent commonwealth.

As I have now replied to my calumniators, as far as my own character required, though not so fully as their villainy deserved, I shall add a few more words on the state of public affairs. In the first place, my fellow citizens, be of good courage with regard to Numidia. . . . Such of you, then, as are of military age, cooperate with me and support the cause of your country; and let no discouragement, from the ill fortune of others or the arrogance of the late commanders, affect any one of you. I myself shall be with you, both on the march and in the battle, both to direct your movements and to share your dangers. I shall treat you and myself on every occasion alike; and doubtless, with the aid of the gods, all good things—victory, spoil, and glory—are ready to our hands, though even if they were doubtful or distant, it would still become every able citizen to act in defense of his country. For no man by slothful timidity has escaped the lot of mortals; nor has any parent wished for his children that they might live forever, but rather that they might act in life with virtue and honor.

I would add more, my fellow citizens, if words could give courage to the faint-hearted; to the brave I think that I have said enough.

Source: Marius, Gaius. "On Being Accused of a Low Origin." *The World's Famous Orations.* Edited by William Jennings Bryan. New York: Funk & Wagnall, 1906.

MARCUS TULLIUS CICERO
(106–43 B.C.E.)
First Oration against Catiline
Senate, Rome
November 8, 63 B.C.E.

Several of the most famous speeches from the ancient world revolve around the Catilinarian Conspiracy, an attempt to take over Rome that occurred in the first century B.C.E. The Roman Republic was then led by two consuls, or heads of state, elected yearly. In the election of 63 B.C.E., Marcus Tullius Cicero defeated Lucius Sergius Catilina (called Catiline by English-speakers), a Roman politician who had been governor of Africa. Catiline's reputation had been besmirched by false accusations, and he was furious when he lost the election. He gathered around him other disaffected politicians. Reports circulated throughout Rome that Catiline was conspiring to murder the two consuls and many of the senators, then burn the city and wage war, with the goal of taking over the government. Cicero was to be one of the first assassinated. He was an accomplished lawyer and eloquent orator and, before his election to consul, had been one of the highest-ranking magistrates, or praetors. On the morning after an attempt on his life, Cicero rose in the Senate, with Catiline present, to denounce him and expose his plan to overthrow Rome.

Catiline fled 200 miles north to his army in Etruria, where he was killed two months later by forces of the consul Antonius. Cicero delivered four famous speeches against Catiline (two in the Senate, two in the Forum to the people) in the month between discovery of the plan and execution of the conspirators. In this excerpt from the First Oration (also sometimes called the First Catilinarian), it is clear Cicero feels the occasion justifies extreme measures against Catiline (*SEE* speech by Catiline, p. 45). The "Conscript Fathers" he refers to are the senators. In 43 B.C.E., Cicero's political rival, Marcus (Mark) Antony, had Cicero declared an enemy of the state. He was captured and decapitated, his head displayed in the Forum, where it is said that Antony's wife, Fulvia, impaled his tongue with a hairpin. Cicero is considered the model of a Roman orator; he composed his speeches in a kind of meter, or rhythm, that made them exquisite to the Roman ear (this is not evident translated from the Latin, of course). His masterful speeches were studied closely for centuries, and they were memorized by schoolchildren for oratorical contests.

When, O Catiline, do you mean to cease abusing our patience? How long is that madness of yours still to mock us? When is there to be an end of that unbridled audacity of yours, swaggering about as it does now? Do not the nightly guards placed on the Palatine Hill—do not the watches posted throughout the city—does not the alarm of the people, and the union of all good men—does not the precaution taken of assembling the senate in this most defensible place—do not the looks and countenances of this venerable body here present, have any effect upon you? Do you not feel that your plans are detected? Do you not see that your conspiracy is already arrested and rendered powerless by the knowledge which every one here possesses of it? What is there that you did last night, what the night before—where is it that you were—who was there that you summoned to meet you—what design was there which was adopted by you, with which you think that any one of us is unacquainted?

Shame on the age and on its principles! The senate is aware of these things; the consul sees them; and yet this man lives. Lives! aye, he comes even into the senate. He takes a part in the public deliberations; he is watching and marking down and checking off for slaughter every individual among us. And we, gallant men that we are, think that we are doing our duty to the republic if we keep out of the way of his frenzied attacks.

You ought, O Catiline, long ago to have been led to execution by command of the consul. That destruction which you have been long plotting against us ought to have already fallen on your own head. . . .

Marcus Tullius Cicero, one of the great orators of Rome, denounces the traitor Catiline in the Roman Senate. Painting by Cesare Maccari *(Scala/Art Resource, NY)*

There was once such virtue in this republic that brave men would repress mischievous citizens with severer chastisement than the most bitter enemy. For we have a resolution of the senate, a formidable and authoritative decree against you, O Catiline. The wisdom of the republic is not at fault, nor the dignity of this senatorial body. We, we alone—I say it openly—we, the consuls, are wanting in our duty.

The senate once passed a decree that Lucius Opimius, the consul, should take care that the republic suffered no injury. Not one night elapsed. There was put to death, on some mere suspicion of disaffection, Caius Gracchus, a man whose family had borne the most unblemished reputation for many generations. There was slain Marcus Fulvius, a man of consular rank, and all his children. . . . But we, for these twenty days, have been allowing the edge of the senate's authority to grow blunt, as it were. For we are in possession of a similar decree of the senate, but we keep it locked up in its parchment—buried, I may say, in the sheath; and according to this decree you ought, O Catiline, to be put to death this instant. You live—and you live, not to lay aside, but to persist in your audacity.

I wish, O conscript fathers, to be merciful; I wish not to appear negligent amid such danger to the state; but I do now accuse myself of remissness and culpable inactivity. A camp is pitched in Italy, at the entrance of Etruria, in hostility to the republic. The number of the enemy increases every day; and yet the general of that camp, the leader of those enemies, we see within the walls—aye, and even in the senate—planning every day some internal injury to the republic. If, O Catiline, I should now order you to be arrested, to be put to death, I should, I suppose, have to fear lest all good men should say that I had acted tardily, rather than that any one should affirm that I acted cruelly. But yet this, which ought to have been done long since, I have good reason for not doing as yet. I will put you to death, then, when there shall be not one person possible to be found so wicked, so abandoned, so like yourself, as not to allow that it has been rightly done. As long as one person exists who can dare to defend you, you shall live; but you shall live as you do now, surrounded by my many and trusty guards, so that you shall not be able to stir one finger against the republic. Many eyes and ears shall still observe and watch you, as they have hitherto done, though you shall not perceive them.

For what is there, O Catiline, that you can still expect, if night is not able to veil your nefarious meetings in darkness, and if private houses can not conceal the voice of your conspiracy within their walls—if everything is seen and displayed? . . .

O ye immortal gods, where on earth are we? in what city are we living? what constitution is ours? There are here—here in our body, O conscript fathers, in this the most holy and dignified assembly of the whole world, men who meditate my death, and the death of all of us, and the destruction of this city, and of the whole world. I, the consul, see them; I ask them their opinion about the republic, and I do not yet attack, even by words, those who ought to be put to death by the sword. You were, then, O Catiline, at Lecca's that night. You divided Italy into sections. You settled where every one was to go; you fixed whom you were to leave at Rome, whom you were to take with you. You portioned out the divisions of the city for conflagration; you undertook that you yourself would at once leave the city, and said that there was then only this to delay you—that I was still alive. Two Roman knights were found to deliver you from this anxiety, and to promise that very night, before daybreak, to slay me in my bed. All this I knew almost before your meeting had broken up. I strengthened and fortified my house with a stronger guard; I refused admittance, when they came, to those whom you sent in the morning to salute me, and of whom I had foretold to many eminent men that they would come to me at that time.

As, then, this is the case, O Catiline, continue as you have begun. Leave the city at least; the gates are open; depart. That Manlian camp of yours has been waiting too long for you as its general. And lead forth with you all your friends, or at least as many as you can; purge the city of your presence. You will deliver me from a great fear, when there is a wall between you and me. Among us you can dwell no longer—I will not bear it, I will not permit it, I will not tolerate it. . . .

With these omens, O Catiline, be gone to your impious and nefarious war, to the great safety of the republic, to your own misfortune and injury, and to the destruction of those who have joined themselves to you in every wickedness and atrocity. Then do you, O Jupiter, who were consecrated by Romulus with the same auspices as this city, whom we rightly call the stay of this city and empire, repel this man and his companions from your altars and from the other temples—from the houses and walls of the city—from the lives and fortunes of all the citizens; and overwhelm all the enemies of good men, the foes of the republic, the robbers of Italy, men bound together by a treaty and infamous alliance of crimes, dead and alive, with eternal punishments.

RHETORICAL DEVICE

Hyperbole: Exaggerating for emphasis. Enormously effective, this should be used only rarely as it is easily overdone.

We behold nothing but unpunished wickedness.
—*St. Bernard of Clairvaux*

There is being created a world of masters and slaves in the image of Germany herself.
—*Edouard Daladier*

There are here—here in our body, O conscript fathers, in this the most holy and dignified assembly of the whole world, men who meditate my death, and the death of all of us, and the destruction of this city, and of the whole world. —*Marcus Tullius Cicero*

The last hopes of mankind, therefore, rest with us. —*Daniel Webster*

Source: Cicero. "First Oration against Catiline." *Select Orations of Marcus Tullius Cicero.* Translated by C. D. Yonge. Philadelphia: David McKay, 1896, p. 3.

JULIUS CAESAR
(100–44 B.C.E.)
"The Alternative of Exile"
Senate, Rome
December 5, 63 B.C.E.

Although his family was no longer wealthy, Gaius Julius Caesar came from aristocratic heritage, his family roots extending back in time to the Trojan hero Aeneas (and purportedly through Aeneas to the goddess Venus). He was noted as a superb orator even as a young man. He had been a military tribune and was elected head of the state religion in 63 B.C.E., the year of the Catilinarian Conspiracy, when politician Lucius Sergius Catilina (or Catiline) attempted to take over the Roman Senate by force. Caesar was a rival of the consul Cicero (one of the two heads of state) in politics. Cicero came from the *optimates,* the traditionalist faction; they were the party of those with political heritage (with a family member who had once been consul) and who wished to retain powers for the Senate. Caesar (along with Catiline) was a member of the *populares,* or "populists," party of the late Roman Republic, who felt the populace should hold the balance of power. On December 5, 63 B.C.E., the Senate debated what punishment to award the conspirators (including Publius Cornelius Lentulus, who had been consul in 71 B.C.E.), with opinion strongly in favor of death. Although there was suspicion that Caesar might have conspired in the plot with Catiline, Caesar swayed the Senate briefly, arguing against executing the five. As the historian Sallust relates, Caesar asked for mercy and protested setting bad precedent by condemning them without a trial. Then Cicero delivered his Fourth Oration against Catiline and the senators settled on death. (*SEE* Cicero's First Oration, p. 37.) In coming years, Julius Caesar would be elected consul, conquer Gaul (modern France, Belgium, northern Italy, and parts of Switzerland, Germany, and the Netherlands), invade Britain, start a civil war, and become Egyptian queen Cleopatra's lover. He would be appointed dictator in 44 B.C.E. in the last years of the Roman Republic (it would shortly become the Roman Empire).

❦

Fathers of the Senate, all men who deliberate upon difficult questions ought to be free from hatred and friendship, anger and pity. When these feelings stand in the way the mind cannot easily discern the truth, and no mortal man has ever served at the same time his passions and his best interests. When you apply your intellect, it prevails; if passion possesses you, it holds sway, and the mind is impotent.

I might mention many occasions, Fathers of the Senate, when kings and peoples under the influence of wrath or pity have made errors of judgment; but I prefer to remind you of times when our forefathers, resisting the dictates of passion, have acted justly and in order. In the Macedonian war (which we waged with king Perses), the great and glorious community of the Rhodians, which owed its growth to the support of the Roman people, was unfaithful to us and hostile. But after the war was over and the question of the Rhodians was under discussion, our ancestors let them go unpunished for fear that some might say that the wealth of the Rhodians—rather than resentment for the wrong they had done—had led to the declaration of war.

So, too, in all the Punic wars; although the Carthaginians both in time of peace and in the course of truces had often done many abominable deeds, the Romans never retaliated when they had the opportunity but they inquired rather what conduct would be consistent with their dignity than how far the law would allow them to go in taking vengeance on their enemies. You likewise, Fathers of the Senate, must beware of letting the guilt of Publius Lentulus and the rest have more weight with you than your own dignity, and of taking more thought for your anger than for your good name. If a punishment commensurate with their crimes can be found, I favour a departure from

Julius Caesar—military hero, orator, and statesman—became dictator in the Roman Republic's last days, as it transitioned to empire. *(Photo by Amra Pasic)*

precedent; but if the enormity of their guilt surpasses all men's imagination, I should advise limiting ourselves to such penalties as the law has established.

The greater number of those who have expressed their opinions before me have deplored the lot of the commonwealth in finished and noble phrases. They have dwelt upon the horrors of war, the wretched fate of the conquered, the rape of maidens and boys, children torn from their parents' arms, matrons subjected to the will of the victors, temples and homes pillaged, bloodshed and fire; in short, arms and corpses everywhere, gore and grief.

But, O ye immortal gods! what was the purpose of such speeches? Was it to make you detest the conspiracy? You think that a man who has not been affected by a crime so monstrous and so cruel will be fired by a speech! Nay, not so.

No mortal man thinks his own wrongs unimportant; many, indeed, are wont to resent them more than is right. But not all men, Fathers of the Senate, are allowed the same freedom of action. If the humble, who pass their lives in obscurity, commit any offence through anger, it is known to few; their fame and fortune are alike. But the actions of those who hold great power, and pass their lives in a lofty station, are known to all the world. So it comes to pass that in the highest position there is the least freedom of action. There, neither partiality nor dislike is in place, and anger least of all; for what in others is called wrath, this in a ruler is termed insolence and cruelty. . . .

But, you may say, who will complain of a decree which is passed against traitors to their country? Time, I answer, the lapse of years, and Fortune, whose caprice rules the nations. Whatever befalls these prisoners will be well deserved. But you, Fathers of the Senate, are called upon to consider how your action will affect other criminals. All bad precedents have originated in cases which were good. But when the control of the government falls into the hands of men who are incompetent or bad, your new precedent is transferred from those who well deserve and merit such punishment to the undeserving and blameless.

The Lacedaemonians, after they had conquered the Athenians, set over them thirty men to carry on their government. These men began at first by putting to death without a trial the most wicked and generally hated citizens, whereat the people rejoiced greatly and declared that it was well done. But afterwards their licence gradually increased, and the tyrants slew good and bad alike at pleasure and intimidated the rest. Thus the nation was reduced to slavery and had to pay a heavy penalty for its foolish rejoicing. . . .

For my own part, I fear nothing of that kind for Marcus Tullius or for our times, but in a great commonwealth there are many different natures. It is possible that at another time, when someone else is consul and is likewise in command of an army, some falsehood may be believed to be true. When the consul, with this precedent before him, shall draw the sword in obedience to the senate's decree, who shall limit or restrain him?

Our ancestors, Fathers of the Senate, were never lacking either in wisdom or courage, and yet pride did not keep them from adopting foreign institutions, provided they were honorable. They took their offensive and defensive weapons from the Samnites, the badges of their magistrates for the most part from the Etruscans. In fine, whatever they found suitable among allies or foes, they put in practice at home with the greatest enthusiasm, preferring to imitate rather than envy the successful.

But in that same age, following the usage of Greece, they applied the scourge to citizens and inflicted the supreme penalty upon those found guilty. Afterwards, when the state reached maturity and because of its large population factions prevailed; when the blameless began to be oppressed and other wrongs of that kind were perpetrated; then they devised the Porcian law and other laws, which allowed the condemned the alternative of exile. This seems to me, Fathers of the Senate, a particularly cogent reason why we should not adopt a new policy. Surely there was greater merit and wisdom in those men, who from slight resources created this mighty empire, than in us, who can barely hold what they gloriously won.

Do I then recommend that the prisoners be allowed to depart and swell Catiline's force? By no means! This, rather, is my advice: that their goods be confiscated and that they themselves be kept imprisoned in the strongest of the free towns; further, that no one hereafter shall refer their case to the senate or bring it before the people, under pain of being considered by the senate to have designs against the welfare of the state and the common safety.

Source: Sallust. *Sallust.* Translated by J. C. Rolfe. Loeb Classical Library. New York: Putnam, 1921.

MARCUS PORCIUS CATO
(95–46 B.C.E.)
"Foes Are within Our Walls"
Senate, Rome
December 5, 63 B.C.E.

Marcus Porcius Cato, called Cato the Younger, was a Stoic philosopher and politician who lived simply and approached political life with a determination to root out wrongs and corruption wherever he found them. He was considered one of the most honest men of his time. (His great-grandfather, Cato the Elder, had been consul, the highest elective office in the government, in 195 B.C.E.) In 63 B.C.E., Cato the Younger was a senator and tribune and a member of the *optimates,* the conservative or traditionalist faction in government. He was allied with Marcus Tullius Cicero, also an *optimate* and one of the two consuls of the Roman Republic. After Cicero had exposed the conspiracy of Catiline to overthrow the government in 63 B.C.E., Catiline escaped from Rome. The remaining five conspira-

tors in the city were rounded up, and the Senate met to debate what should be done with them. Julius Caesar argued for leniency—the usual punishment of sending the plotters into exile (*SEE* Caesar's speech, p. 40). Cato called for execution, less as punishment, he said, than as a means of removing future danger to the state. In his speech, he characteristically took the opportunity to deplore what he felt was the loss of virtue in Rome. Executing Roman citizens without trial was extremely unusual, but the Senate voted for death, which Cicero, as consul, approved. They were strangled that day. Cato continued in his opposition to Julius Caesar, and in the civil war that followed he sided with the general Pompey in an attempt to remove Caesar from power. They were defeated, in 46 B.C.E., and Cato committed suicide.

My feelings are very different, Fathers of the Senate, when I turn my mind to the plot and the danger we are in, and when I reflect upon the recommendations of some of our number. The speakers appear to me to have dwelt upon the punishment of these men who have plotted warfare upon their country, parents, altars, and hearths. But the situation warns us rather to take precautions against them than to argue about what we are to do with them. For in the case of other offences you may proceed against them after they have been committed. With this, unless you take measures to forestall it, in vain will you appeal to the laws when once it has been consummated. Once a city has been taken nothing is left to the vanquished.

Nay, in the name of the immortal gods I call upon you, who have always valued your houses, villas, statues, and paintings more highly than your country. If you wish to retain the treasures to which you cling, of whatsoever kind they may be, if you even wish to provide peace for the enjoyment of your pleasures, wake up at last and lay hold of the reins of state. Here is no question of revenues or the wrongs of our allies; our lives and liberties are at stake. Oftentimes, Fathers of the Senate, I have spoken at great length before this body; I have often deplored the extravagance and greed of our citizens, and in that way I have made many men my enemies. . . .

Now, however, the question before us is not whether our morals are good or bad, nor how great or glorious the empire of the Roman people is, but whether all that we have, however we regard it, is to be ours, or with ourselves is to belong to the enemy.

At this point (save the mark!) someone hints at gentleness and long-suffering! But in very truth we have long since lost the true names for things. It is precisely because squandering the goods of others is called generosity, and recklessness in wrongdoing is called courage, that the republic is reduced to extremities. Let these men by all means, since such is the fashion of the time, be liberal at the expense of our allies; let them be merciful to plunderers of the treasury; but let them not be prodigal of our blood, and in sparing a few scoundrels bring ruin upon all good men.

In fine and finished phrases did Gaius Caesar a moment ago before this body speak of life and death, regarding as false, I presume, the tales which are told of the Lower World, where they say that the wicked take a different path from the good, and dwell in regions that are gloomy, desolate, unsightly, and full of fears. Therefore he recommended that the goods of the prisoners be confiscated, and that they themselves be imprisoned in the free towns, doubtless through fear that if they remained in Rome the adherents of the plot or a hired mob would rescue them by force. As if, indeed, there were base and criminal men only in our city and not all over Italy, or as if audacity had not greatest strength where the power to resist it is weakest! Therefore, this advice is utterly futile if Caesar fears danger from the conspirators; but if amid such general fear he alone has none, I have the more reason to fear for you and for myself.

Be assured, then, that when you decide the fate of Publius Lentulus and the rest, you will at the same time be passing judgment on Catiline's army and all the conspirators. The more vigorous your action, the less will be their courage. But if they detect the slightest weakness on your part, they will all be here immediately, filled with reckless daring.

Do not suppose that it was by arms that our forefathers raised our country from obscurity to greatness. If that were so, we should have a much fairer state than theirs, since we have a greater number of citizens and allies than they possessed, to say nothing of arms and horses. But there were other qualities which made them great, which we do not possess at all: efficiency at home, a just rule abroad, in counsel an independent spirit free from guilt or passion. In place of these we have extravagance and greed, public poverty and private opulence. We extol wealth and foster idleness. We make no distinction between good men and bad, and ambition appropriates all the prizes of merit. And no wonder! When each of you schemes for his own private interests, when you are slaves to pleasure in your homes and to money or influence here, the natural result is an attack upon the defenseless republic.

But I let that pass. Citizens of the highest rank have conspired to fire their native city. They stir up to war the Gauls, bitterest enemies of the Roman people. The leader of the enemy with his army is upon us. Do you even now hesitate and doubtfully ask yourselves what is to be done with foemen taken within your walls? . . .

In the days of our forefathers Titus Manlius Torquatus, while warring with the Gauls, ordered the execution of his own son, because he had fought against the enemy contrary to orders, and the gallant young man paid the penalty for too great valor with his life. Do you hesitate what punishment to inflict upon the most ruthless traitors? . . .

Fathers of the Senate, if (Heaven help us!) there were any room for error I should be quite willing to let you learn wisdom by experience, since you scorn my advice. But as it is, we are beset on every side. Catiline with his army is at our throats. Other foes are within our walls, aye, in the very heart of Rome. Neither preparations nor plans can be kept secret; therefore the more need of haste.

This, then, is my recommendation: whereas our country has been subjected to the greatest peril through the abominable plot of wicked citizens, and whereas they have been proven guilty by the testimony of Titus Volturcius and the envoys of the Allobroges, and have confessed that they have planned murder, arson, and other fearful and cruel crimes against their fellow citizens and their country, let those who have confessed be treated as though they had been caught red-handed in capital offences, and be punished after the manner of our forefathers.

Source: Sallust. *Sallust.* Translated by J. C. Rolfe. Loeb Classical Library. New York: Putnam, 1921.

CATILINE

(108–62 B.C.E.)

To His Soldiers

Pistoria, Italy

January 62 B.C.E.

Lucius Sergius Catilina, or Catiline, came from a distinguished old Roman family whose glory had faded. He had commanded troops in several wars and been a governor of Africa. When he returned to Rome to run for election as one of the two consuls (the highest elective office in the government), his candidacy was ended by accusations that he had abused his power as governor, despite the fact that he was acquitted of the charges. He ran again on a platform that favored ordinary citizens and the poor—he was popular among the people—and was defeated in 63 B.C.E. by his more conservative political enemy, Marcus Tullius Cicero. Catiline began to conspire with other failed politicians to achieve his ends through force. The details of Catiline's conspiracy—to murder enemies in the Senate, burn Rome, and overthrow the government—were laid out by Cicero in his Orations against Catiline, delivered in the Senate (*SEE*

Cicero's First Oration, p. 37). After enduring the first of these *philippics* (denunciatory speeches), and observing how the senators shunned him, Catiline rushed out of the city to the army that a confederate had raised for him in Etruria, north of Rome. Shortly after, the Senate formerly declared him an enemy of the people. The five conspirators left in Rome (including Publius Cornelius Lentulus, previously a consul, who betrayed the conspiracy with naive scheming) were discovered—when they were executed, many of Catiline's troops deserted him. What was left of his forces, about 3,000 men, advanced to meet the army of the consul Antonius at Pistoria. After preparing his troops for battle with this speech, Catiline bravely fought in front with his men, rather than remaining at the rear as was usual for a general, and he died falling among the bodies of the enemy. The source is *The Conspiracy of Catiline*, by the Roman historian Sallust.

❧

I am well aware, soldiers, that words cannot inspire courage; and that a spiritless army cannot be rendered active, or a timid army valiant, by the speech of its commander. Whatever courage is in the heart of a man, whether from nature or from habit, so much will be shown by him in the field. And on him whom neither glory nor danger can move, exhortation is bestowed in vain, for the terror in his breast stops his ears.

I have called you together, however, to give you a few instructions, and to explain to you, at the same time, my reasons for the course which I have adopted. You all know, soldiers, how severe a penalty the inactivity and cowardice of Lentulus has brought upon himself and us; and how, while waiting for reinforcements from the city, I was unable to march into Gaul. In what situation our affairs now are, you all understand as well as myself. Two armies of the enemy, one on the side of Rome, and the other on that of Gaul, oppose our progress, while the want of grain, and of other necessaries, prevents us from remaining, however strongly we may desire to remain, in our present position. Whithersoever we would go, we must open a passage with our swords.

I conjure you, therefore, to maintain a brave and resolute spirit, and to remember, when you advance to battle, that on your own right hands depend riches, honor, and glory, with the enjoyment of your liberty and of your country.

If we conquer, all will be safe, we shall have provisions in abundance, and the colonies and corporate towns will open their gates to us. But if we lose the victory through want of courage, those same places will turn against us, for neither place nor friend will protect him whom his arms have not protected. Besides, soldiers, the same exigency does not press upon our adversaries, as presses upon us; we fight for our country, for our liberty, for our life. They contend for what but little concerns them, the power of a small party. Attack them, therefore, with so much the greater confidence, and call to mind your achievements of old.

We might, with the utmost ignominy, have passed the rest of our days in exile. Some of you, after losing your property, might have waited at Rome for assistance from others. But because such a life, to men of spirit, was disgusting and unendurable, you resolved upon your present course. If you wish to quit it, you must exert all your resolution, for none but conquerors have exchanged war for peace. To hope for safety in flight, when you have turned away from the enemy the arms by which the body is defended, is indeed madness. In battle, those who are most afraid are always in most danger, but courage is equivalent to a rampart.

When I contemplate you, soldiers, and when I consider your past exploits, a strong hope of victory animates me. Your spirit, your age, your valor, give me confidence, to say nothing of necessity, which makes even cowards brave. To prevent the numbers of the enemy from surrounding us, our confined situation is sufficient.

But should Fortune be unjust to your valor, take care not to lose your lives unavenged. Take care not to be taken and butchered like cattle, rather than, fighting like men, to leave to your enemies a bloody and mournful victory.

Source: Sallust. *The Conspiracy of Catiline.* Translated by Rev. John Selby Watson. New York: Harper, 1867.

HORTENSIA
(first century B.C.E.)
"When Have There Not Been Wars?"
Forum, Rome
42 B.C.E.

Hortensia was the daughter of a noted Roman orator and wealthy consul, Quintus Hortensius. She had natural speaking ability and studied the great Greek orators. When the women of Rome needed a spokesperson, they naturally turned to her. As the Roman Republic decayed in the first century B.C.E. (the transition to empire occurred about 27 B.C.E. when Octavian became emperor), civil war was frequent—there were no fewer than 10 civil wars in that time. From 49 to 45 B.C.E., the political rivals Pompey and Julius Caesar warred, and when Caesar was murdered in 44 B.C.E., another costly civil war followed: Octavian and Mark Antony (a Roman general and consul) led armies against those of Caesar's assassins, Brutus and Cassius. One way of paying for these wars was by seizing the property of proscribed persons. Proscription was the condemning to death of a person without trial, often to settle political scores, with his or her property forfeited to the state. Anyone could kill the "public enemy" on sight. A rash of proscriptions occurred in 43 B.C.E. (the orator Cicero was among them). The following year, the government had to raise still more funds, and it voted to tax Rome's 1,400 wealthiest women. This infuriated the women, who had few political rights to justify taxing them (they couldn't vote or take part in the Senate). Fulvia, the wife of Mark Antony, one of the three triumvirs at the head of government, rebuffed them so they moved on to the Forum. In her speech—related by Greek historian Appian in his *Civil Wars*—Hortensia refers to the Oppian Law, a time after the wars against Carthage in the second and third centuries B.C.E. when the treasury was depleted and women had been restricted in how much wealth they could possess. The men of the Forum were outraged at their audacity in addressing men in public, but the watching crowd supported the women. The law was soon changed to tax only the wealthiest 400 women, and to compel men to loan money to the state.

As befitted women of our rank addressing a petition to you, we had recourse to the ladies of your households. But having been treated as did not befit us, at the hands of Fulvia, we have been driven by her to the forum.

You have already deprived us of our fathers, our sons, our husbands, and our brothers, whom you accused of having wronged you; if you take away our property also, you reduce us to a condition unbecoming our birth, our manners, our sex. If we have done you wrong, as you say our husbands have, proscribe us as you do them. But if we women have not voted any of you public enemies, have not torn down your houses, destroyed your army, or led another one against you; if we have not hindered you in obtaining offices and honors—why do we share the penalty when we did not share the guilt?

Why should we pay taxes when we have no part in the honors, the commands, the state-craft, for which you contend against each other with such harmful results? "Because this is a time of war," do you say? When have there not been wars, and when have taxes ever been imposed on women, who are exempted by their sex among all mankind?

Our mothers did once rise superior to their sex and made contributions when you were in danger of losing the whole empire and the city itself through the conflict with the Carthaginians. But then they contributed voluntarily, not from their landed property, their fields, their dowries, or their houses (without which life is not possible to free women) but only from their own jewelry—and even these not according to the fixed valuation. Not under fear of informers or accusers, not by force and violence, but what they themselves were willing to give.

What alarm is there now for the empire or the country? Let war with the Gauls or the Parthians come, and we shall not be inferior to our mothers in zeal for the common safety; but for civil wars may we never contribute, nor ever assist you against each other!

We did not contribute to Caesar or to Pompey. Neither Marius nor Cinna imposed taxes upon us. Nor did Sulla, who held despotic power in the state, do so. Whereas you say that you are re-establishing the commonwealth!

Source: Appian. *Civil Wars.* 4.32–34. Translated by Horace White. Loeb Classical Library. Cambridge, Mass.: Harvard University Press, 1913.

JESUS OF NAZARETH
(ca. 4 B.C.E.–ca. 33 C.E.)
The Sermon on the Mount
Galilee, Israel
28 to 30 C.E.

Jesus of Nazareth was born about 4 B.C.E. and lived most of his life in Nazareth, a town in Galilee (now in Israel). (In the Christian religion, Jesus is the son of God.) He was a carpenter who probably had apprenticed with his father. After his Jordan River baptism at about age 30 by John the Baptist, Jesus became a traveling teacher throughout the villages and countryside along the Sea of Galilee. He was followed everywhere by crowds of ordinary people interested in his teachings. He probably spoke in Aramaic, though he knew Hebrew and a little Greek. At one location he withdrew to a higher spot on the hillside, and to his disciples he delivered his most famous address on living a moral life, the Sermon on the Mount. It is the longest speech attributed to Jesus in the Bible, and contains the introductory eight Beatitudes ("Blessed are the poor in spirit") and the Lord's Prayer ("Our Father, who art in Heaven"), which are regular elements of many Christian worship services. The King James Version of the Bible, produced in 1611, contains the best-known English-language translation of the Sermon. For hundreds of years such passages from the Bible were the few written works with which the common person was acquainted, and the Bible was often the only book a family might own. The sermon's beauty will be familiar to many readers, who will recognize in it phrases, expressions, and whole passages incorporated now into hundreds of other works of literature, even movies, Broadway plays, and rock songs. Many great people, including nonviolent social activists Mohandas Gandhi and Martin Luther King, Jr., credited the Sermon on the Mount as having a major influence on their lives and thought. This text is from the New Testament Gospel of Matthew in the New King James Version of the Bible.

Blessed are the poor in spirit, for theirs is the kingdom of heaven.

Blessed are those who mourn, for they shall be comforted.

Blessed are the meek, for they shall inherit the earth.

Blessed are those who hunger and thirst for righteousness, for they shall be filled.

Blessed are the merciful, for they shall obtain mercy.

Blessed are the pure in heart, for they shall see God.

Blessed are the peacemakers, for they shall be called sons of God.

Blessed are those who are persecuted for righteousness' sake, for theirs is the kingdom of heaven.

Blessed are you when they revile and persecute you, and say all kinds of evil against you falsely for My sake. Rejoice and be exceedingly glad, for great is your reward in heaven, for so they persecuted the prophets who were before you.

You are the salt of the earth; but if the salt loses its flavor, how shall it be seasoned? It is then good for nothing but to be thrown out and trampled underfoot by men.

You are the light of the world. A city that is set on a hill cannot be hidden. Nor do they light a lamp and put it under a basket, but on a lampstand, and it gives light to all who are in the house. Let your light so shine before men, that they may see your good works and glorify your Father in heaven.

Do not think that I came to destroy the Law or the Prophets. I did not come to destroy but to fulfill. For assuredly, I say to you, till heaven and earth pass away, one jot or one tittle will by no means pass from the law till all is fulfilled. Whoever therefore breaks one of the least of these commandments, and teaches men so, shall be called

> Blessed are the poor in spirit, for theirs is the kingdom of heaven. —*Jesus of Nazareth*
>
> You are the light of the world.
> —*Jesus of Nazareth*

least in the kingdom of heaven; but whoever does and teaches them, he shall be called great in the kingdom of heaven. For I say to you, that unless your righteousness exceeds the righteousness of the scribes and Pharisees, you will by no means enter the kingdom of heaven.

You have heard that it was said to those of old, "You shall not murder, and whoever murders will be in danger of the judgment."

But I say to you that whoever is angry with his brother without a cause shall be in danger of the judgment. And whoever says to his brother, "Raca!" shall be in danger of the council. But whoever says, "You fool!" shall be in danger of hell fire. Therefore if you bring your gift to the altar, and there remember that your brother has something against you, leave your gift there before the altar, and go your way. First be reconciled to your brother, and then come and offer your gift. Agree with your adversary quickly, while you are on the way with him, lest your adversary deliver you to the judge, the judge hand you over to the officer, and you be thrown into prison. Assuredly, I say to you, you will by no means get out of there till you have paid the last penny.

You have heard that it was said to those of old, "You shall not commit adultery." But I say to you that whoever looks at a woman to lust for her has already committed adultery with her in his heart. If your right eye causes you to sin, pluck it out and cast it from you; for it is more profitable for you that one of your members perish, than for your whole body to be cast into hell. And if your right hand causes you to sin, cut it off and cast it from you; for it is more profitable for you that one of your members perish, than for your whole body to be cast into hell.

Furthermore it has been said, "Whoever divorces his wife, let him give her a certificate of divorce." But I say to you that whoever divorces his wife for any reason except sexual immorality causes her to commit adultery; and whoever marries a woman who is divorced commits adultery.

Again you have heard that it was said to those of old, "You shall not swear falsely, but shall perform your oaths to the Lord." But I say to you, do not swear at all: neither by heaven, for it is God's throne; nor by the earth, for it is His footstool; nor by Jerusalem, for it is the city of the great King. Nor shall you swear by your head, because you cannot make one hair white or black. But let your "Yes" be "Yes," and your "No," "No." For whatever is more than these is from the evil one.

You have heard that it was said, "An eye for an eye and a tooth for a tooth." But I tell you not to resist an evil person. But whoever slaps you on your right cheek, turn the other to him also. If anyone wants to sue you and take away your tunic, let him have your cloak also. And whoever compels you to go one mile, go with him two. Give to him who asks you, and from him who wants to borrow from you, do not turn away.

You have heard that it was said, "You shall love your neighbor and hate your enemy." But I say to you, love your enemies, bless those who curse you, do good to those who hate you, and pray for those who spitefully use you and persecute you, that you may be sons of your Father in heaven; for He makes His sun rise on the evil and on the good, and sends rain on the just and on the unjust.

For if you love those who love you, what reward have you? Do not even the tax collectors do the same? And if you greet your brethren only, what do you do more than others? Do not even the tax collectors do so? Therefore you shall be perfect, just as your Father in heaven is perfect.

Take heed that you do not do your charitable deeds before men, to be seen by them. Otherwise you have no reward from your Father in heaven. Therefore, when you do a charitable deed, do not sound a trumpet before you as the hypocrites do in the synagogues and in the streets, that they may have glory from men. Assuredly, I say to you, they have their reward. But when you do a charitable deed, do not let your left hand know what your right hand is doing, that your charitable deed may be in secret; and your Father who sees in secret will Himself reward you openly.

And when you pray, you shall not be like the hypocrites. For they love to pray standing in the synagogues and on the corners of the streets, that they may be seen by men. Assuredly, I say to you, they have their reward. But you, when you pray, go into your room, and when you have shut your door, pray to your Father who is in the secret place, and your Father who sees in secret will reward you openly. And when you pray, do not use vain repetitions as the heathen do. For they think that they will be heard for their many words.

Therefore do not be like them. For your Father knows the things you have need of before you ask Him. In this manner, therefore, pray: Our Father in heaven, hallowed be Your name. Your kingdom come. Your will be done on earth as it is in heaven. Give us this day our daily bread. And forgive us our debts, as we forgive our debtors. And do not lead us into temptation, but deliver us from the evil one. For Yours is the kingdom and the power and the glory forever. Amen.

For if you forgive men their trespasses, your heavenly Father will also forgive you. But if you do not forgive men their trespasses, neither will your Father forgive your trespasses.

Moreover, when you fast, do not be like the hypocrites, with a sad countenance. For they disfigure their faces that they may appear to men to be fasting. Assuredly, I say to you, they have their reward. But you, when you fast, anoint your head and wash your face, so that you do not appear to men to be fasting, but to your Father who is in the secret place; and your Father who sees in secret will reward you openly.

Do not lay up for yourselves treasures on earth, where moth and rust destroy and where thieves break in and steal; but lay up for yourselves treasures in heaven, where neither moth nor rust destroys and where thieves do not break in and steal. For where your treasure is, there your heart will be also.

The lamp of the body is the eye. If therefore your eye is good, your whole body will be full of light. But if your eye is bad, your whole body will be full of darkness. If therefore the light that is in you is darkness, how great is that darkness!

No one can serve two masters; for either he will hate the one and love the other, or else he will be loyal to the one and despise the other. You cannot serve God and mammon.

Therefore I say to you, do not worry about your life, what you will eat or what you will drink; nor about your body, what you will put on. Is not life more than food and the body more than clothing? Look at the birds of the air, for they neither sow nor reap nor gather into barns; yet your heavenly Father feeds them. Are you not of more value than they? Which of you by worrying can add one cubit to his stature?

So why do you worry about clothing? Consider the lilies of the field, how they grow: they neither toil nor spin; and yet I say to you that even Solomon in all his glory was not arrayed like one of these. Now if God so clothes the grass of the field, which today is, and tomorrow is thrown into the oven, will He not much more clothe you, O you of little faith?

Therefore do not worry, saying, "What shall we eat?" or "What shall we drink?" or "What shall we wear?" For after all these things the Gentiles seek. For your heavenly Father knows that you need all these things. But seek first the kingdom of God and His righteousness, and all these things shall be added to you. Therefore do not worry about tomorrow, for tomorrow will worry about its own things. Sufficient for the day is its own trouble.

Judge not, that you be not judged. For with what judgment you judge, you will be judged; and with the measure you use, it will be measured back to you. And why do you look at the speck in your brother's eye, but do not consider the plank in your own eye?

Or how can you say to your brother, "Let me remove the speck from your eye"; and look, a plank is in your own eye? Hypocrite! First remove the plank from your own eye, and then you will see clearly to remove the speck from your brother's eye.

Do not give what is holy to the dogs; nor cast your pearls before swine, lest they trample them under their feet, and turn and tear you in pieces.

Ask, and it will be given to you; seek, and you will find; knock, and it will be opened to you. For everyone who asks receives, and he who seeks finds, and to him who knocks it will be opened. Or what man is there among you who, if his son asks for bread, will give him a stone? Or if he asks for a fish, will he give him a serpent? If you then, being evil, know how to give good gifts to your children, how much more will your Father who is in heaven give good things to those who ask Him! Therefore, whatever you want men to do to you, do also to them, for this is the Law and the Prophets.

Enter by the narrow gate; for wide is the gate and broad is the way that leads to destruction, and there are many who go in by it. Because narrow is the gate and difficult is the way which leads to life, and there are few who find it.

Beware of false prophets, who come to you in sheep's clothing, but inwardly they are ravenous wolves. You will know them by their fruits. Do men gather grapes from thornbushes or figs from thistles? Even so, every good tree bears good fruit, but a bad tree bears bad fruit. A good tree cannot bear bad fruit, nor can a bad tree bear good fruit. Every tree that does not bear good fruit is cut down and thrown into the fire. Therefore by their fruits you will know them.

Not everyone who says to Me, "Lord, Lord," shall enter the kingdom of heaven, but he who does the will of My Father in heaven. Many will say to Me in that day, "Lord, Lord, have we not prophesied in Your name, cast out demons in Your name, and done many wonders in Your name?" And then I will declare to them, "I never knew you; depart from Me, you who practice lawlessness!"

Therefore whoever hears these sayings of Mine, and does them, I will liken him to a wise man who built his house on the rock: and the rain descended, the floods came, and the winds blew and beat on that house; and it did not fall, for it was founded on the rock.

But everyone who hears these sayings of Mine, and does not do them, will be like a foolish man who built his house on the sand: and the rain descended, the floods came, and the winds blew and beat on that house; and it fell. And great was its fall.

Source: Jesus. Sermon on the Mount. Gospel of Matthew. New King James Version®. Copyright © 1982 by Thomas Nelson, Inc. Used by permission. All rights reserved.

CLAUDIUS I
(10 B.C.E.–54 C.E.)
"United under Our Name"
Rome
48 C.E.

As Rome's empire grew ever larger, its colonies began seeking representation in government. Claudius I, the fourth emperor of Rome, ruled from 41 to 54 C.E., after succeeding the assassinated despot Caligula. Claudius was the nephew of the emperor Tiberius (r. 14–37 C.E.), and he inherited an age of peace and prosperity. He had not been destined for the throne, as he was ill with a palsy that made him physically weak, but he was an intelligent man interested in history. He sent an army to invade Britain and added provinces at the edges of the empire. The extensive system of Roman roads made travel easier than it had ever been, and robust commerce brought more contact between Rome and its citizens. Like American colonists without a say in the British parliament, petitioners from far-flung provinces asked for public office. Roman senators grumbled at the idea of allowing foreigners to take Senate seats. In this speech, recorded by Roman historian Tacitus in *The Annals*, Claudius answers them with a history of how Rome had always admitted the best the empire had to offer. He points to the Aequi, the Julii, Coruncanii, and Porcii, and other tribes absorbed in Rome's earliest years; he singles out Narbon Gaul (Gallia Narbonensis), which became a colony in 118 B.C.E. Though he didn't say so in his address, he had himself been born in Gaul (now France). The Senate acquiesced and the Aedui—a Gallic tribe who befriended Julius Caesar 100 years earlier—received the right to send senators to Rome.

My ancestors, the most ancient of whom was made at once a citizen and a noble of Rome, encourage me to govern by the same policy of transferring to this city all conspicuous merit, wherever found. And indeed I know, as facts, that the Julii came from Alba, the Coruncanii from Camerium, the Porcii from Tusculum, and not to inquire too minutely into the past, that new members have been brought into the Senate from Etruria and Lucania and the whole of Italy, that Italy itself was at last extended to the Alps, to the end that not only single persons but entire countries and tribes might be united under our name.

We had unshaken peace at home; we prospered in all our foreign relations, in the days when Italy beyond the Po was admitted to share our citizenship, and when, enrolling in our ranks the most vigorous of the provincials, under color of settling our legions throughout the world, we recruited our exhausted empire. Are we sorry that the Balbi came to us from Spain, and other men not less illustrious from Narbon Gaul? Their descendants are still among us, and do not yield to us in patriotism.

What was the ruin of Sparta and Athens, but this, that mighty as they were in war, they spurned from them as aliens those whom they had conquered? Our founder Romulus, on the other hand, was so wise that he fought as enemies and then hailed as fellow-citizens several nations on the very same day. Strangers have reigned over us. That freedmen's sons should be entrusted with public offices is not, as many wrongly think, a sudden innovation, but was a common practice in the old commonwealth.

But, it will be said, we have fought with the Senones. I suppose then that the Volsci and Aequi never stood in array against us. Our city was taken by the Gauls. Well, we also gave hostages to the Etruscans, and passed under the yoke of the Samnites. On the whole, if you review all our wars, never has one been finished in a shorter time than that with the Gauls. Thenceforth they have preserved an unbroken and loyal peace. United as they now are with us by manners, education, and intermarriage, let them bring us their gold and their wealth rather than enjoy it in isolation.

Everything, Senators, which we now hold to be of the highest antiquity, was once new. Plebeian magistrates came after patrician; Latin magistrates after plebeian; magistrates of other Italian peoples after Latin. This practice too will establish itself, and what we are this day justifying by precedents, will be itself a precedent.

Source: Tacitus. *Annals.* Book 11. Translated by Alfred John Church and William Brodribb. New York: Random House, 1942.

CARATACUS
(first century C.E.)
To Emperor Claudius
Rome
51 C.E.

Restrained by chains, the captured Caratacus, king of the Catuvellauni tribe of Britons, addresses Emperor Claudius I in Rome. *(Ablestock)*

Roman general Julius Caesar had invaded Britain in 54 B.C.E., but it was the four legions and auxiliary troops sent by Emperor Claudius I in 43 C.E. that would secure the Roman conquest and make much of Britain into a province of Rome. (*SEE* Claudius's speech, p. 53.) Britain was not a unified commonwealth then, as it is today, but a land of small tribes and kingdoms. In the south ruled Caratacus, one of the last great tribal chieftains. He was the son of Cunobelinus, who had been king of the powerful Catuvellauni tribe in the island's southeast region. The Roman historian Cornelius Tacitus relates how, after warring with the Romans for many years, Caratacus took on General Publius Ostorius Scapula in 51 C.E. in present-day Wales. Caratacus's army of Britons was drawn from local tribes, the Silures and the Ordovices. Ostorius defeated Caratacus's troops, but Caratacus himself escaped to the Brigantes, a realm to the north. Unfortunately the Brigantine queen did not give him shelter, but instead delivered him to the Romans. As was done with defeated kings, Ostorius brought Caratacus to Rome in chains. Along with his wife and brothers and the treasures of war, the captured chieftain was exhibited before the people in a grand parade. On reaching the seat of the Emperor Claudius, the unbowed and fearless Caratacus made this speech, whereupon Claudius pardoned him and his family and had them released. But Caratacus never returned to Britain; he was said to have admired Rome too much to leave.

Had my moderation in prosperity been equal to my noble birth and fortune, I should have entered this city as your friend rather than as your captive. And you would not have disdained to receive, under a treaty of peace, a king descended from illustrious ancestors and ruling many nations.

My present lot is as glorious to you as it is degrading to myself. I had men and horses, arms and wealth. What wonder if I parted with them reluctantly? If you Romans choose to lord it over the world, does it follow that the world is to accept slavery?

Were I to have been at once delivered up as a prisoner, neither my fall nor your triumph would have become famous. My punishment would be followed by oblivion, whereas, if you save my life, I shall be an everlasting memorial of your clemency.

Source: Tacitus. *Complete Works of Tacitus.* Translated by Alfred John Church and William Brodribb. New York: Modern Library, 1942.

BOUDICA
(died 60 C.E.)
"A Woman's Resolve"
East Anglia, Britain
60 C.E.

In his book *The Annals*, the Roman historian Tacitus told of Boudica (or Boadicea), the red-haired warrior queen of the Iceni, a Celtic tribe of ancient southeast Britain. She was the wife of Prasutagus, a "client king" who, after the conquest of Britain in 43 C.E., continued ruling only by permission of Rome. The status of "client state" allowed the tribe to remain otherwise independent. At his death in 59 C.E., Prasutagus left his wealth to be divided between his two daughters and the emperor, Nero, hoping to safeguard his family. The Romans, however, did not permit inheritance by women, and client states customarily became a possession of the Roman Empire after the death of the client king. The Romans flogged the queen, raped her daughters, and seized her possessions. The Iceni people were already restive; they resented the soldiers in their towns and the taxes they were forced to pay. The absence of the Roman governor, Gaius Suetonius Paulinus (he was in Wales, subduing the druids), emboldened them. Boudica raised a great army of Britons among the Iceni and other tribes. They proceeded to sack three Roman towns: Verulamium (now St. Albans), Londinium (London), and Camulodunum (Colchester), and massacred a Roman legion. Suetonius's return from Wales with his legionaries posed her greatest test. On the eve of battle, she rode in a chariot among her army, encouraging her thousands of troops with this address. The battle was furious, but after the vastly outnumbered Romans triumphed she killed herself with poison. Suetonius's victory ensured that Britain would remain Rome's possession.

Queen of the Iceni tribe of Britons, Boudica rides among her troops as they mass for battle against the Romans in 60 C.E. *(Ablestock)*

It is not as a woman descended from noble ancestry, but as one of the people that I am avenging lost freedom, my scourged body, the outraged chastity of my daughters. Roman lust has gone so far that not our very persons, nor even age or virginity, are left unpolluted.

But heaven is on the side of a righteous vengeance. A legion which dared to fight has perished; the rest are hiding themselves in their camp, or are thinking anxiously of flight. They will not sustain even the din and the shout of so many thousands, much less our charge and our blows.

If you weigh well the strength of the armies, and the causes of the war, you will see that in this battle you must conquer or die. This is a woman's resolve; as for men, they may live and be slaves.

Source: Tacitus. *Annals.* Book 14. Translated by Alfred John Church and William Brodribb. New York: Random House, 1942.

EL'AZAR BEN YAIR
(died 73 C.E.)
Speech at Masada
Masada, Judaea (today Israel)

73 C.E.

At the time of the Great Jewish Revolt in 66 C.E., the Roman Empire had ruled Judaea (modern-day Israel) since 63 B.C.E. For more than 100 years, the Romans had imposed their laws and taxes on the Jewish population. Although relations were tense throughout Judaea's years as a Roman client kingdom (a kingdom able to rule with permission of Rome), with Nero's accession to the throne on the death of Roman emperor Claudius in 54 C.E., the embers of Jewish discontent became a raging conflagration. To bolster the imperial finances, Nero ordered his governor in Judaea to confiscate the treasure contained in the Jews' Temple at Jerusalem. Incensed that their Temple had been despoiled by pagans, as well as their lives burdened by taxation, many Jews revolted. The Roman army eventually reconquered Jerusalem and burned the Temple in 70 C.E. Fleeing for their lives, the remaining rebels and their families retreated to the cliff-top fortress of Masada. For three years the 960 men, women, and children endured a siege by Rome's Tenth Legion, only to discover in early May 73 C.E. that their last line of defense had been breached and their destruction was imminent. It was then that El'azar ben Yair, the leader of the rebels, exhorted the people at Masada to commit suicide rather than face the slavery, rape, and murder that would accompany the Romans' assault. Ben Yair's fateful words were followed almost to the letter; when the Romans ascended the cliff the next morning they were met with eerie silence. As recorded by Flavius Josephus, a famous Jewish general turned Roman citizen and historian (who heard the story from two women who hid themselves during the suicide), the story of Masada and its fanatical defenders has come to symbolize Jewish resistance and bravery in face of insurmountable odds.

❧

My loyal followers, long ago we resolved to serve neither the Romans nor anyone else but only God, who alone is the true and righteous Lord of men; now the time has come that bids us prove our determination by our deeds.

At such a time we must not disgrace ourselves; hitherto we have never submitted to slavery, even when it brought no danger with it; we must not choose slavery now, and with it penalties that will mean the end of everything if we fall alive into the hands of the Romans. For we were the first of all to revolt, and shall be the last to break off the struggle. And I think it is God who has given us this privilege, that we can die nobly and as free men, unlike others who were unexpectedly defeated.

In our case it is evident that daybreak will end our resistance, but we are free to choose an honorable death with our loved ones. This our enemies cannot prevent, however earnestly they may pray to take us alive; nor can we defeat them in battle.

Let our wives die unabused, our children without knowledge of slavery; after that, let us do each other an ungrudging kindness, preserving our freedom as a glorious winding-sheet. But first let our possessions and the whole fortress go up in flames; it will be a bitter blow to the Romans, that I know, to find our persons beyond their reach and nothing left for them to loot. One thing only let us spare—our store of food: It will bear witness when we are dead to the fact that we perished not through want but because, as we resolved at the beginning, we chose death rather than slavery.

If only we had all died before seeing the Sacred City utterly destroyed by enemy hands, the Holy Sanctuary so impiously uprooted! But since an honorable ambition deluded us into thinking that perhaps we should succeed in avenging her of her enemies, and now all hope has fled, abandoning us to our fate, let us at once choose death with honor and do the kindest thing we can for ourselves, our wives, and our children, while it is still possible to show ourselves any kindness. After all, we were born to die, we and those we brought into the world: this even the luckiest must face.

But outrage, slavery, and the sight of our wives led away to shame with our children—these are not evils to which man is subject by the laws of nature: men undergo them through their own cowardice if they have a chance to forestall them by death and will not take it. We are very proud of our courage, so we revolted from Rome. Now in the final stages they have offered to spare our lives and we have turned the offer down. Is anyone too blind to see how furious they will be if they take us alive? Pity the young whose bodies are strong enough to survive prolonged torture; pity the not-so-young whose old frames would break under such ill-usage. A man will see his wife violently carried off; he will hear the voice of his child crying "Daddy!" when his own hands are fettered.

Come! While our hands are free and can hold a sword, let them do a noble service! Let us die unenslaved by our enemies, and leave this world as free men in company with our wives and children.

Source: El'azar ben Yair. "At Masada." *Classics of Jewish Literature.* Edited by Leo Lieberman and Arthur Beringause. New York: Philosophical Library, 1987, p. 9. Reprinted by permission of Philosophical Library, New York.

"Britain Is Explored and Subdued"
Caledonia, now Scotland
84 C.E.

As the Roman governor of Gaul, Julius Caesar first sought to conquer Britain in 55 B.C.E.; Roman emperor Claudius I launched a second invasion nearly 100 years later. In 70 C.E. Emperor Vespasian sent Gnaeus Julius Agricola to command one of the original four legions Claudius had sent to subdue Britain, and not long afterward Vespasian made Agricola governor. Agricola was born in Narbonne Gaul (today's south of France) in 40 C.E. He knew Britain; he had served under Gaius Suetonius Paulinus, whose Second Legion quashed the Iceni warrior queen Boudica's revolt against Rome. (*See* Boudica's speech, p. 56.) Roman commanders were succeeding in Britain in part because the tribes rarely banded together to fight the Roman Empire, and could be defeated one at a time. Early Roman campaigns had targeted Wales and southern Britain. Later operations focused on the north of the island, possibly even Ireland. From the historian Cornelius Tacitus (who was Agricola's son-in-law) comes this soldierly pep-talk given by Agricola as his troops were about to fight the larger Caledonian force gathered at Mt. Graupius, Caledonia (now Scotland). Tacitus also gives Calcagus, the Caledonian chieftain, a speech in which he condemns the Romans with this famous line: "To robbery, slaughter, plunder they give the false name of 'empire' and where they make a desert, they call it peace." While Calcagus may have escaped, the conquest of Caledonia secured Britain for Rome. Agricola's triumphs against the various tribes of Britain (including Scotland and Wales)—and his achievement in building forts and garrisons the length of the island—stirred the jealousy of Emperor Domitian, Vespasian's son. Domitian ordered him to return the next year to Rome to an unwanted retirement. He died eight years later.

~~~

It is now the eighth year, my fellow-soldiers, in which, under the high auspices of the Roman Empire, you have been conquering Britain through your valor and perseverance. In so many expeditions, in so many battles, whether you have been required to exert your courage against the enemy or your patient labors against the nature of the country itself, neither have I been dissatisfied with my soldiers nor you with your general.

In this mutual confidence we have proceeded beyond the limits of former commanders and former armies, and are now become acquainted with the extremity of the island, not by uncertain rumor, but by actual possession with our arms and encampments. Britain is explored and subdued. How often during a march, when embarrassed by mountains, bogs, and rivers, have I heard the bravest among you exclaim: "When shall we find the enemy? When shall we be led to the field of battle?"

At length they are unearthed from their retreats; your desires and your valor have now free scope; and every circumstance is equally propitious to the victor and ruinous to the vanquished. For the greater our glory in having marched over vast tracts of land, penetrated forests, and crossed arms of the sea, while advancing toward the foe, the greater will be our danger and difficulty if we should attempt a retreat. We are inferior to our enemies in knowledge of the country, and less able to command supplies of provisions; but we have arms in our hands, and in these we have everything.

For myself, it has long been a principle that a retreating general or army is never safe. Not only, then, are we to reflect that death with honor is preferable to life with ignominy, but to remember that security and glory are seated in the same place. Even to fall in this extremest verge of earth and of nature cannot be considered an inglorious fate.

If unknown nations or unproved troops were drawn up against you, I would exhort you by the examples of other armies. As it is, remember your own honors, question your own eyes. These are they who, last year, attacking by surprise a single legion amid the obscurity of night, were put to flight by a shout—the greatest runaways of all the Britons, and therefore the longest survivors. As, when penetrating woods and thickets, the fiercest animals boldly rush upon the hunters, while the weak and timorous flee at their mere shouts, so the bravest of the Britons have long since fallen. The remaining number consists solely of the cowardly and spiritless, whom you at length see within your reach, not because they have stood their ground, but because they have been over-taken. Torpid with fear, their bodies are fixed and chained down in yonder field, which to you will speedily be the scene of a glorious and memorable victory.

Here bring your toils and services to a conclusion; close with one great day a struggle of fifty years; and convince your countrymen that to the army ought not to be imputed either the protraction of the war or the causes of the rebellion.

Source: Tacitus. *Agricola.* Edited by Guy Carleton Lee. *The World's Orators.* New York: Putnam, 1900, p. 260.

ST. JOHN CHRYSOSTOM
(ca. 349–407)
On Sanctuary in the Church
Constantinople
399

Saint John Chrysostom was born in the Mediterranean seacoast city of Antioch (now Antakya, in
modern Turkey) in 349. Antioch was an important
trading center under the Roman Empire, and after the
Emperor Constantine made Christianity the empire's
official religion in 323, it became an important seat of
the early Christian church as well. The city was one
of Christianity's original three patriarchates, or headquarters of the patriarch (archbishop). In Antioch John
Chrysostom first studied classical literature and rhetoric, and he then advanced to theology. He became a
committed Christian, and began preaching in 386 in
a voice so eloquent he received the name Chrysostom,
which meant "golden mouth." Chrysostom is known
for eight sermons he gave around this time that were
meant to stop his flock in Antioch from attending Jewish worship services; he denounced Jews in belittling
terms and attributed responsibility for Jesus' death to
them. (The sermons were exploited over the centuries,
as recently as the Nazi era, to justify anti-Semitism.)
He was an ascetic, living simply and avoiding worldly
pleasures, whose concern for the poor and ability to
relate Christian teachings to the lives of his congregation made him extremely popular. In 398 Chrysostom
became Patriarch of Constantinople, an assignment
he did not relish. He disliked the state officials' lavish displays of finery and the corruption he witnessed
among the clergy. In the year 399 Eutropius, an official
known for his greed, fell out of favor with the emperor
and feared he would be killed. Although Eutropius had
previously tried to eliminate the church as a traditional
place of sanctuary for the persecuted, he fled for asylum
to Chrysostom's church. Hundreds of people watched
the spectacle, as the patriarch addressed himself alternately to the quaking Eutropius and the congregation.
Eutropius later was captured elsewhere and executed.

"Vanity of vanities, all is vanity"—it is always seasonable to utter this but more especially at the present time. Where are now the brilliant surroundings of your consulship?
Where are the gleaming torches? Where is the dancing, and the noise of dancers' feet,
and the banquets and the festivals? Where are the garlands and the curtains of the
theatre? Where is the applause which greeted you in the city, where the acclamation in
the hippodrome and the flatteries of spectators? They are gone—all gone: a wind has
blown upon the tree shattering down all its leaves, and showing it to us quite bare, and
shaken from its very root. . . . And inasmuch as deceitful things, and maskings and pre-
tence seem to many to be realities, it behooves each one every day both at supper and at
breakfast, and in social assemblies, to say to his neighbor and to hear his neighbor say
in return, "Vanity of vanities, all is vanity."

Was I not continually telling you that wealth was a runaway? But you would not
heed me. Did I not tell you that it was an unthankful servant? But you would not be
persuaded. Behold, actual experience has now proved that it is not only a runaway, and
ungrateful servant, but also a murderous one, for it is this which has caused you now
to fear and tremble.

Did I not say to you when you continually rebuked me for speaking the truth, "I
love you better than they do who flatter you?" "I who reprove you care more for you
than they who pay you court?" Did I not add to these words by saying that the wounds
of friends were more to be relied upon than the voluntary kisses of enemies? If you had
submitted to my wounds, their kisses would not have wrought you this destruction: for
my wounds work health, but their kisses have produced an incurable disease.

61

Where are now your cup-bearers? Where are they who cleared the way for you in the market place, and sounded your praises endlessly in the ears of all? They have fled, they have disowned your friendship, they are providing for their own safety by means of your distress. But I do not act thus, nay in your misfortune I do not abandon you, and now when you are fallen I protect and tend you. And the Church which you treated as an enemy has opened her bosom and received you into it; whereas the theatres which you courted, and about which you were oftentimes indignant with me have betrayed and ruined you. . . .

And I say these things now not as trampling upon one who is prostrate, but from a desire to make those who are still standing more secure; not by way of irritating the sores of one who has been wounded, but rather to preserve those who have not yet been wounded in sound health; not by way of sinking one who is tossed by the waves, but as instructing those who are sailing with a favorable breeze, so that they may not become overwhelmed. . . .

For who was more exalted than this man? Did he not surpass the whole world in wealth? Had he not climbed to the very pinnacle of distinction? Did not all tremble and fear before him? Yet lo! he has become more wretched than the prisoner, more pitiable than the menial slave, more indigent than the beggar wasting away with hunger, having every day a vision of sharpened swords and of the criminal's grave, and the public executioner leading him out to his death. . . .

But indeed what need is there of any words from me, when he himself has clearly depicted this for us as in a visible image? For yesterday when they came to him from the royal court intending to drag him away by force, and he ran for refuge to the holy furniture, his face was then, as it is now, no better than the countenance of one dead: and the chattering of his teeth, and the quaking and quivering of his whole body, and his faltering voice, and stammering tongue, and in fact his whole general appearance were suggestive of one whose soul was petrified.

RHETORICAL DEVICE

Sententia: Using a wise maxim that applies to the situation, sometimes ending the speech.

I am here also because the slave owners do not want me to be here. . . . I have adopted a maxim laid down by Napoleon, never to occupy ground which the enemy would like me to occupy. —*Frederick Douglass*

I hope to be pardoned, Sir, for my zeal upon this occasion.
It is an old and wise caution that when our neighbor's house
is on fire we ought to take care of our own. —*Andrew Hamilton*

Magnanimity in politics is not seldom the truest wisdom; and
a great empire and little minds go ill together. —*Edmund Burke*

"Vanity of vanities, all is vanity"—it is always seasonable to utter this but more
especially at the present time. —*St. John Chrysostom*

Now I say these things not by way of reproaching him, or insulting his misfortune, but from a desire to soften your minds towards him, and to induce you to compassion, and to persuade you to be contented with the punishment which has already been inflicted. For since there are many inhuman persons amongst us who are inclined, perhaps, to find fault with me for having admitted him to the sanctuary, I parade his sufferings from a desire to soften their hardheartedness by my narrative.

For tell me, beloved brother, wherefore are you indignant with me? You say it is because he who continually made war upon the Church has taken refuge within it. Yet surely we ought in the highest degree to glorify God, for permitting him to be placed in such a great strait as to experience both the power and the loving kindness of the Church: Her power in that he has suffered this great vicissitude in consequence of the attacks which he made upon her. Her loving kindness in that she whom he attacked now casts her shield in front of him and has received him under her wings, and placed him in all security. Not resenting any of her former injuries, but most lovingly opening her bosom to him. For this is more glorious than any kind of trophy, this is a brilliant victory, this puts both Gentiles and Jews to shame. This displays the bright aspect of the Church: in that having received her enemy as a captive, she spares him, and when all have despised him in his desolation, she alone like an affectionate mother has concealed him under her cloak, opposing both the wrath of the king, and the rage of the people, and their overwhelming hatred. . . .

But, you say, he cut off the right of refuge here by his ordinances and various kinds of laws. Yes! yet now he has learned by experience what it was he did, and he himself by his own deeds has been the first to break the law, and has become a spectacle to the whole world, and silent though he is, he utters from thence a warning voice to all, saying, "do not such things as I have done, that you suffer not such things as I suffer." . . .

Has he inflicted great wrongs and insults on you? I will not deny it. Yet this is the season not for judgment but for mercy; not for requiring an account, but for showing loving kindness; not for investigating claims but for conceding them; not for verdicts and vengeance, but for mercy and favor. Let no one then be irritated or vexed, but let us rather beseech the merciful God to grant him a respite from death, and to rescue him from this impending destruction, so that he may put off his transgression. And let us unite to approach the merciful Emperor, beseeching him for the sake of the Church, for the sake of the altar, to concede the life of one man as an offering to the Holy Table. . . .

Let us rescue the captive, the fugitive, the suppliant from danger that we ourselves may obtain the future blessings by the favor and mercy of our Lord Jesus Christ, to whom be glory and power, now and for ever, world without end. Amen.

Source: Schaff, Philip, ed. *A Select Library of the Nicene and Post-Nicene Fathers of the Christian Church.* Buffalo, N.Y.: Christian Literature Co., 1886.

ST. AUGUSTINE OF HIPPO
(354–430)
Sermon on the Happy Life
Carthage
413–414

Augustine of Hippo was a Berber, born in Roman Africa in what is now Algeria. His mother, Monica, was a devout Christian later canonized as a saint by the church. As a teenager, Augustine was interested in philosophy. He read Roman philosophers and orators such as Marcus Tullius Cicero (SEE the speech by Cicero, p. 37), and he left home to study rhetoric (persuasive speaking) in Carthage. Carthage was a center of Christianity, an important Roman city on the Mediterranean seacoast (now in Tunisia) where numerous synods, or church councils, were held to discuss religious issues. There he founded a school of rhetoric, took a mistress for many years, and became a follower of Manichaeism, a Persian religion popular at that time. From 376 he taught school in Rome and then Milan, but he was not in Milan long before he had a spiritual reawakening to Christianity. He returned to North Africa in 388 to become a priest in Hippo Regius. The port city of Hippo had been the home of ancient Numidian kings; in the fourth and fifth centuries under the Romans it was called Hippo Regius. (Today Hippo lies in Algeria; its modern name is Annaba.) There Augustine put his talent in rhetoric to use; he preached hundreds of sermons coaxing the people to Christianity, and he served as bishop of Hippo for 30 years. He wrote prolifically as a philosopher and theologian, introducing the thinking of classical Rome to Christian reasoning; for that reason he is called the "Christian Plato." In this sermon (on Acts 17:18–34) given in Carthage, Augustine refers to the missionary visit of Paul the Apostle to Athens around 51 C.E., several centuries earlier. Saint Paul had visited the Areopagus, an Athenian court, where he debated the followers of two branches of Greek philosophy, the Epicureans and the Stoics, on the source of the happy life.

❧

I AM SURE you noticed, as I did, when the Acts of the Apostle were read aloud, that Paul addressed the Athenians and was called a sower of words by those who mocked the truth. Thus he was called by his mockers, but he is not to be rejected by the believers. For he was in truth more than a sower of words; he was a reaper of virtue. Even I, a man of insignificant stature and of an excellence in no way comparable with his, am allowed to sow in the fields of God; for I sow the words of God in your hearts and await a rich harvest in the growth of virtue. . . .

Paul spoke at Athens. Through their achievements in literature and learning, the Athenians enjoyed great renown. This country was the home of the great philosophers. Their vast and diverse learning expanded through the other countries of Greece and then through the entire world. . . .

If you recall the reading, you will recall it said that some of the Stoic and Epicurean philosophers entered into debate with the Apostle. I have no doubt that many of you do not know who these Stoic and Epicurean philosophers are or were, what they thought, what they viewed as the truth, and what they pursued in their philosophies. And yet, since I am speaking in Carthage, there surely are many of you who do know this. . . .

First of all, take note of the pursuit common to all philosophers, in which they have five divisions and categories of thought. All philosophers have made a common effort to attain the happy life in study, in seeking, in discourse, and in life itself. This is the single object of philosophy. I would say, however, that the philosophers have this in common with us: if I were to ask of you why you believe in Christ and why you have become Christians, everyone would answer truthfully by saying, "For the happy life." Therefore the pursuit of the happy life is a goal common to philosophers and Christians.

The question, however, and the distinction between us is where such a pleasing thing as the happy life is to be found. After all, I believe that every man seeks the happy life, desires the happy life, craves, yearns for, and pursues the happy life.

It seems then that I may not have said enough by asserting that Christians and philosophers have the pursuit of the happy life in common. I should have said that they have this in common with all men, be they good or bad. For the good man is good that he may be happy, and the evil man would not be so were it not for the hope that this is the way to a happy life. With the good man it is apparent that he is good that he may attain the happy life. With the evil man, however, some may doubt whether he too seeks the happy life. But if I were to draw apart the evil men from the good and ask them, "Do you wish to be happy?" none of them would answer "No." . . .

The subject of our inquiry is what it is that makes life happy. Imagine before your eyes the Epicureans, the Stoics, and the Apostle. I could just as well have said the Epicureans, Stoics, and Christians. Let us first ask the Epicureans what it is that renders life happy. "The pleasures of the body," they will answer. I urge you to believe that they claim this, for there are those present who can judge my words. Not having read their writings, you may not know that this is the belief of the Epicureans. But there are those present who have read their works.

Saint Augustine of Hippo, a father of the early Christian Church. Painting by Lippo Memmi (1285–1361), Pushkin Museum, Moscow *(Ablestock)*

Let us return, however, to questioning the philosophers. What does the Epicurean say it is that renders life happy? He will answer, "The pleasure of the body." What does the Stoic say it is that renders life happy? He will answer, "Steadfastness of spirit." May your love of God bear with me: we are Christians, and we are passing judgment on the philosophers. Learn now why only these two schools were brought forward for debate with the Apostle. The entire range of man's nature is encompassed in the body and the soul. It is in one of these two, namely the body, that the Epicureans find the happy life, while the Stoics find the happy life in the spirit. . . .

In the belief that there is no life after death and that they have nothing save that which delights the flesh, the Epicureans say, "Let us eat and drink, for tomorrow we shall die." . . .

With the Stoics, however, we shall have no mean contention. Whenever asked what it is to which they attribute the happy life, they will answer that it is to be found not in the pleasures of the body, but in steadfastness of the spirit. What of the Apostle? Did he assent to this? If he did so, then let us also assent. But he did not. The Scripture rebukes those who trust in their own strength. By attributing the supreme good for man to the body, the Epicurean puts his hope in himself. The Stoic, however, who attributes the supreme good for man to the soul, assigns it to a better portion of man. But he too puts his hope in himself. Neither the Stoic nor the Epicurean, however, is anything more than a man. *Cursed be the man that trusteth in man.*

RHETORICAL DEVICE

Metaphor: Using a word that normally means one thing to designate another, and thus making a comparison. *(See the related* simile.*)*

For the whole earth is the tomb of famous men. —*Pericles*

I am going to my cold and silent grave. My lamp of life is nearly extinguished; my race is run; the grave opens to receive me, and I sink into its bosom!
—*Robert Emmet*

A glory has departed and the sun that warmed and brightened our lives has set and we shiver in the cold and dark.
—*Jawaharlal Nehru, speaking of the death of Mahatma Gandhi*

I sow the words of God in your hearts and await a rich harvest in the growth of virtue. —*Saint Augustine of Hippo*

It is, in other words, time for a national oil change. That is apparent to anyone who has looked at our national dipstick. —*Al Gore*

What are we to decide? Arraigned before us are three men: an Epicurean, a Stoic, and a Christian. Let us question each of them what it is that renders life happy. The Epicurean will answer: "The delights of the body"; the Stoic will answer: "Steadfastness of spirit"; and the Christian will answer: "The gift of God."

Thus, my brothers, the Epicurean and the Stoic have debated with the Apostle as though before our very eyes, and in their debate they have shown us what to reject and what to accept. Steadfastness of spirit is of course a commendable thing, for it engenders sound judgment of good and evil; it confers justice upon each man; it restrains the passions; and it gives courage to bear hardship with equanimity. This is a great and commendable thing. The Stoic should praise it as highly as he can, but let him tell us whence he has his steadfastness of spirit. It is not your steadfastness of spirit that makes you happy, but He who gave it to you, He who inspired in you both the will to crave it and the power to apply it. . . .

The philosophers have taught themselves the ways of error. Some have said one thing and others have said something else. But the way was hidden from them, for *"God resists the proud."* Had it not come to us, it would lie hidden also from us. Thus the Lord said, *"I am the way."* Idle traveler, you do not even wish to find the way, and the way comes to you. You were asking where you should go: *"I am the way."* You were asking where you should go: *"I am the truth and the life."* You will not lose your way when you go through Him and to Him.

This is the teaching of the Christians, in no way comparable and in every way preferable to the teachings of the philosophers, whether it is matched against the baseness of the Epicureans or the arrogance of the Stoics.

Source: St. Augustine. "On Acts 17:18–34 [P.L. 150]." *Selected Sermons of St. Augustine.* Translated by Quincy Howe. New York: Holt, Rinehart & Winston, 1966, p. 89.

THEODORA
(ca. 500–548)
"Purple Is the Noblest Shroud"
Constantinople
January 18, 532

Theodora was the wife of Justinian I, emperor in the early years of the Eastern Roman Empire (also called the Byzantine Empire). She was the daughter of the keeper of trained bears for the Blues, one of the teams at the Hippodrome (an immense racetrack and entertainment complex) in Constantinople. After her father's death, she became an actress and the courtesan of a provincial governor. She met Justinian, who was a military commander and the most influential adviser and adopted son of his uncle, Emperor Justin I. Impressed with her strong-willed nature, Justinian married Theodora in 523; this was possible because sometime earlier, Justin had passed a law permitting marriages between men of senatorial rank and the lower classes. On his uncle's death in 527 Justinian became emperor, and he allowed Theodora to rule jointly with him, which was unusual for the time. Never forgetting her lowly background, Empress Theodora spoke out on behalf of protection for women, including rights relating to divorce, property, and rape. Five years after Justinian and Theodora became co-emperors, the Nika riots began at the Hippodrome, where the unruly population was accustomed to staging political demonstrations along with watching chariot racing. People were angry over taxes and other issues they had no means of correcting under the empire. The mob took up the chant "Nika!" meaning "Win!" in Greek. Very quickly the riot engulfed the racetrack. Flames spread across the city; after five days thousands of people were dead. Justinian and Theodora were trapped within the besieged palace, which lay next to the Hippodrome. To the other side of the palace was the opportunity of escape: by sea to Thrace. The Byzantine historian Procopius relates how the empress rebuffed any idea of fleeing the revolt, preferring, she said, a death shroud of purple. (Purple was an expensive dye, usually reserved for royalty.) With his formidable wife beside him, Justinian quickly ordered his most loyal generals to dispense with the rebels. Their troops lay siege to the Hippodrome, where they killed 30,000 rioters and quelled the revolt. Today Theodora is a saint in the Eastern Orthodox Church.

A detail of Byzantine empress Theodora and her court, from a mosaic in S. Vitale, Ravenna, Italy. *(Scala/Art Resource, NY)*

My lords, the present occasion is too serious to allow me to follow the convention that a woman should not speak in a man's council. Those whose interests are threatened by extreme danger should think only of the wisest course of action, not of conventions.

In my opinion, in the present crisis if ever, flight is not the right course, even if it should bring us to safety. It is impossible for a person, having been born into this world, not to die, but for one who has reigned it is intolerable to be a fugitive. May I never be

> The royal purple is the noblest shroud. —*Theodora*

deprived of this purple robe, and may I never see the day when those who meet me do not call me empress.

If you wish to save yourself, my lord, there is no difficulty. We are rich; over there is the sea, and yonder are the ships. Yet reflect for a moment whether, once you have escaped to a place of security, you would not gladly exchange such safety for death.

As for me, I agree with the adage that the royal purple is the noblest shroud.

Source: Theodora. *Women at the Podium: Memorable Speeches in History.* Edited by Michele S. Nix. New York: HarperCollins, 2000, p. 53.

THE EXPANDING WORLD
(CA. 550–1450)

Introduction to the Expanding World

The period from 550 to 1450 was marked by the expansion of religions, including the already established religions of Christianity and Buddhism as well as Islam, which originated in this period. The rise of religions, as well as trade networks such as the Silk Road, which linked China to the Mediterranean through Central Asia, helped bring different peoples and civilizations into more direct contact, sometimes friendly, sometimes hostile.

THE POST-ROMAN WEST

After the fall of the Western Roman Empire in the fifth century the Catholic Church with its headquarters in Rome survived as the most important centralized force in the West. The bishop of Rome was revered as the head of the church throughout western Europe and Italy. The most successful of the new kingdoms that followed the fall of the western Roman Empire in the fifth century were the Franks of modern France and the Anglo-Saxons of England. In the East, the Roman Empire survived with the capital of both state and church at Constantinople. This Greek-speaking empire eventually became known as the Byzantine Empire, or Byzantium, in the 19th century.

The study of rhetoric and speaking declined in the West with the loss of classical culture: Although it persisted in the Greek-speaking East, in the West the elaborate Greek and Roman system of rhetorical training and education fell into disuse with the fall of the Roman Empire, and the system of education that followed would be governed by the church and its needs. The flight away from the city to the country, which had began in the late Roman Empire (in both the East and the West), would also end the culture of public debate and rhetorical exhibition in the forum, and make it more difficult to get together an audience for any form of speaking.

THE RISE OF ISLAM

The most dramatic and significant event of the early Middle Ages was the rapid rise of the new religion and society of Islam, an Arabic word referring to "submission to God." Islam originated in the city of Mecca in the Arabian Peninsula in the seventh century. Meccans had been exposed to Christianity and Judaism for centuries prior but the city retained its own distinctive religious culture, as well as serving as a pilgrimage center for worshipers of Arabia's gods. The founder of Islam, a merchant named Muhammad, claimed to be receiving revelations from God. He and his followers met great resistance from Mecca's traditional rulers, who forced him to relocate to the city of Medina in 622. (This is the Hegira, an Arabic word for flight, and the beginning date of the Islamic calendar.) From Medina Muhammad and his followers waged war against the Meccans, eventually returning in triumph to the city and establishing the first Islamic state in 629.

In the decades following Muhammad's death in 632, his followers defeated some of the most powerful empires of the time and under the Umayyad dynasty established an Islamic state, or caliphate, stretching from the borders of France to the borders of China. The first caliph (a term meaning "successor," given to the head of the Muslim community) was one of Muhammad's most trusted followers, Abu Bakr. The caliphate defeated the strongest powers of the eastern Mediterranean, the longtime rivals Byzantium and Persia. Persia was destroyed as a kingdom, and Byzantium expelled from the Middle East. In 711 Moorish general Tariq ibn Ziyad took Islam into Europe, leading an Islamic army that destroyed the Visigothic kingdom of Spain, and eventually brought nearly all of modern Spain and Portugal under the new faith. Islamic expansion in western Europe was eventually halted by

Charles Martel, a ruler of the Frankish Carolingian dynasty, at the battle of Tours in 732. Martel's grandson, Charles the Great or "Charlemagne," would later establish the largest European empire since the fall of Rome.

In the early days of the Islamic empire, a relatively small Muslim elite ruled over a vast non-Muslim population. However, the establishment of the empire was ultimately followed by the conversion of most of its population to the Islamic religion. Although it took centuries for the majority of the population of the Middle East to become Muslim, the results of the cultural revolution of Islamization have endured. Islam was accompanied by Arabic, the language of the Quran, Islam's holy book, and the earliest traditions of Muhammad and his companions. (Muslims have historically been reluctant to translate their holy book from its original language, unlike Christians.) Islamic preaching took the form of the *khutba*, the sermon delivered at the mosque, before midday prayer on Friday (the holiest day of the week for Muslims) and on other special occasions. It remains an important part of Islamic life.

The unity of the caliphate proved transitory. Like the Roman Empire before it, it was too large to administer effectively as a centralized state. Under the Abbasids, who had gained power in 750, rival caliphates were formed in Spain and Egypt. The Abbasid caliphs also followed the Romans in using foreigners, usually Turks from Central Asia, as soldiers. By the 10th century, the line of Abbasid caliphs in Baghdad continued, but real power lay in the hands of local warlords, many of Turkish origin.

THE MAKING OF CHRISTIAN EUROPE

Although it did not spread with the rapidity of Islam, Christianity in both its Greek and its Latin forms was also moving into new territories. Missionaries sent from Rome and Ireland won the Anglo-Saxons of Britain to Christianity. The Roman missionaries initially landed in the kingdom of Kent in 597, where they were welcomed by King Aethelberht (r. 560–616). In the following centuries, Germany, Scandinavia, Hungary, and East Central Europe fell to Latin Christianity. Greek Christian churches looking to Constantinople as the center of their faith were established in the Balkans and Russia, and Greek or "Orthodox" Christianity became an important part of the identity of many Slavic peoples.

For most of the Middle Ages in Christian Europe, by far the most important form of public speaking was preaching. The feudal kingdoms of Europe had little room for public deliberation—kings and lords took advice, or did not, in council. Eloquence also played little role in the legal system, which was based mostly on oath-taking. There may have been public debate in the trade-based city-states such as Venice and Genoa that emerged in northern Italy in the 10th century, but little record survives. A few secular orations, such as "Before the Battle of Hastings," William of Normandy's 1066 address to his troops during his conquest of England, were preserved in histories. Preachers such as England's Wulfstan II (d. 1023), however, addressed crowned kings as well as thousands of ordinary people, and their words often shaped great events. Since the clergy comprised the majority of the literate population of the Middle Ages, sermons were also far more likely to be written down than were secular orations.

Preaching helped inspire a new movement that began at the end of the 11th century—the Crusades. An adaptation of the old idea of holy war, the Crusades were initially directed at the Muslim forces that had placed the Christian empire of Byzantium on the defensive. The Crusades—"wars for the cross"—began with a sermon by Pope Urban II at a meeting of French leaders at Clermont in 1095. Urban inspired thousands to "take the cross" and vow to journey to the Holy Land. Over the next two centuries thousands of crusade sermons would be preached by humble clerics as well as by star preachers such as the Cistercian monk Bernard of Clairvaux (who was later recognized by the church as St. Bernard of Clairvaux). Preachers appealed to the horror Christians felt at the Christian holy places being under the possession of the Muslims and the hopes of many that crusading would lead God to remit their sins.

The First Crusade was the most successful, taking advantage of Islamic political fragmentation to capture the holy city of Jerusalem. However, to hold Jerusalem and defend the other territorial acquisitions the crusaders made required constant reinforcement from Europe. Thus preaching crusade was an ongoing process, lasting for centuries even after the Crusades themselves had ended. Over time, the concept of "crusade" also broadened. Crusades would be directed against Muslims in Spain and Portugal, against the Lithuanian pagans in Europe's northeast, against heretics, and eventually against the political enemies of the papacy such as the Holy Roman Emperor Frederick II (1212–50; crowned 1220) as well as other temporal rulers. The Fourth Crusade, in 1204, would even be aimed at the Christian city of Constantinople. The taking of the city with massacres and looting would poison relations between Eastern and Western Christians for centuries. The most successful of the Crusades within Europe itself would be the Spanish and Portuguese *Reconquista,* of which one significant event was the fall of the Islamic city of Lisbon to a Christian army in 1147. This loss of focus on the Middle East, however, contributed to the crusaders being ultimately driven out of the Holy Land. The last crusader stronghold fell in 1291, less than two centuries after the First Crusade. Europe's preachers took the opportunity to remind their listeners that the catastrophe was a punishment for the sins of Christendom and to urge, in vain, the setting out of yet another crusader army.

Beginning in the 11th century, the cities of Europe had begun to grow. Medieval society, although still heavily rural, was increasingly influenced by the concentrations of population in the cities. The greatest symbol of this transformation are the mighty cathedrals built in this period. The new cities also provided audiences for preaching, but the existing parish and monastic churches were not altogether adequate to serve the new populations. In the 13th century, effective urban preaching was particularly associated with a new clerical group, the friars. The two main orders of friars, or "mendicants," were informally known as the Franciscans, founded by Italian mystic Francis of Assisi and the Dominicans, named after their founder, the Spanish priest Dominic. Both founders were recognized as saints by the church. The official name of the Dominicans was, and remains, the "Order of Preachers" and, like its Franciscan rivals, the order would produce numerous eloquent preachers throughout its long history.

The later Middle Ages were marked by increasingly violent class conflicts, particularly after the economic crisis following the devastating "Black Death" epidemic of 1347, which killed between one-third and one-half of the population of Europe. Major rebellions of peasants and the poor, led by commoners such as John Ball, racked England and France, and sometimes they resulted in the expression of strikingly modern ideas of equality. Oral communication and speechmaking were particularly important to these movements, as the vast mass of the peasantry was illiterate.

THE SPREAD OF BUDDHISM

Buddhism lost ground to both Hinduism and Islam in its heartland of India during this period. By the end of the Middle Ages, Indian Buddhism had all but disappeared. However, at the same time it was spreading through a great portion of East Asia. The spread of Buddhism through East Asia was less dramatic than the rise of Islam and Christianity, but it had similar cultural effects. Buddhism had already reached China by the end of the Later Han dynasty (25–220 C.E.), but became an important religious force during the Tang dynasty (618–907). Buddhist monks and preachers became a common sight in China's cities, although never again would Buddhism be as intellectually and culturally dominant in China as it was during the Tang period.

From China the religion spread to countries such as Japan, Korea, and Vietnam that looked to China as their cultural leader. Like European Christianity, Buddhism was carried by monks such as Musang and welcomed by rulers such as Emperor Kotoku of Japan (r. 645–654). However, Buddhism lacked Christianity or Islam's central organization and standardization. There was no "Buddhist pope" or group of authorities maintaining standard doctrine and practice. Nor did any sacred Buddhist text have the authoritative status of the Bible or the Quran. Different forms of Buddhism developed through its contact with East Asian culture. Chan Buddhism, which emphasized the sudden attainment of enlightenment through disciplined meditation, originated in China (in the seventh century) but flowered in Japan (in the late 12th century), where it became known as Zen. In the 13th century the Japanese monk Nichiren, who, like the European friars, addressed his message to the growing population of the cities, devised a form of Buddhism based on a text known as the *Lotus Sutra.* Nichiren's Buddhism was deeply intertwined with Japanese identity.

This period, which saw the expansion and confrontation of many cultural, political, and religious traditions, set the stage for ever-increasing cultural interaction in the following centuries.

Speeches

ÆTHELBERHT OF KENT
(died 616)
Welcome to Augustine
Isle of Thanet, Kent
597

Æthelberht of Kent became king in 590 C.E. of one of Britain's numerous early Anglo-Saxon kingdoms. King Æthelberht's wife, Bertha, daughter of a Frankish king, was a Christian. She restored an old church that had gone out of use, and she made it her chapel. She was the only Christian in Kent, because the Romans had taken their religion with them when they had finally left Britain more than a century earlier. In Rome, Pope Gregory I (r. 590–604) decided to convert the English kingdoms to Christianity. In 596 he dispatched Augustine, a trusted monk, as a missionary with about 40 monks to accompany him. Augustine acquired interpreters

Outdoors, where he believed he would be safe from the visitors' magic, King Æthelberht of Kent receives Augustine, a missionary sent by Pope Gregory I in 597. *(Ablestock)*

as they passed through the land of the Franks (today's France). In spring of the next year, they landed on the Isle of Thanet, off the coast of Kent in the southeast of England, and sent for the king. Aethelberht was careful to greet the missionaries outside, rather than indoors, believing that might provide some protection against the strangers' magic. The monks carried a silver cross and a painting of Jesus, and they approached singing and praying. Æthelberht made Augustine a short welcoming speech, as recorded by the Venerable Bede, an English monk who wrote the first history of England in 730 C.E. The king eventually agreed to be baptized, and he became the first Christian king of Anglo-Saxon Britain; he was later recognized as a saint. Augustine built a monastery in Canterbury, the old Roman fortress-town that was the largest town in Kent, and rebuilt Bertha's small church. Augustine soon after became the first archbishop of Canterbury. In 2003, Rowan Williams became the 104th archbishop of Canterbury; he is the head of the Anglican Communion.

Your words and promises are very fair, but as they are new to us, and of uncertain import, I cannot approve of them so far as to forsake that which I have so long followed with the whole English nation.

But because you are come from far into my kingdom, and, as I conceive, are desirous to impart to us those things which you believe to be true, and most beneficial, we will not molest you, but give you favorable entertainment, and take care to supply you with your necessary sustenance.

Nor do we forbid you to preach and gain as many as you can to your religion.

Source: Bede, *Ecclesiastical History of the English People.* Translated by J. A. Giles. Edited by James Harvey Robinson. *Readings in European History,* Vol. 1. Boston: Ginn & Co. 1904, p. 99.

MUHAMMAD
(570–632)
The Farewell Sermon
Mt. Arafat, near Mecca
February 632

The Prophet Muhammad was born in 570 in Mecca, a town near the Red Sea in what is now central Saudi Arabia. He was a merchant. When he was 40, he went on a retreat into the countryside and had revelations from God. The revelations included verses of the Quran (or Koran), the holy book of Islam. He felt called to preach, but Mecca held an important polytheistic (having many gods) pagan shrine—the Kaaba—and the townspeople did not welcome his teachings that there was only one God, Allah. Because of persecution, Muhammad fled his native city north to Medina in 622 C.E. The Islamic calendar begins in this year, the year of the Hegira, or Flight. In Medina, Muhammad built a great community of faith from the numerous tribes. (Muslims believe not that he founded Islam, but that he restored the true religion of the earlier prophets of Judaism and Christianity, and was in fact the last prophet.) For several years, his forces battled the pagan Meccans, as he extended his influence throughout Arabia. In 630 he conquered Mecca and converted the Kaaba to an Islamic shrine and the pagan pilgrimage to an Islamic ritual. The people of Mecca became Muslims. Two years later, in the spring, Muhammad and many followers left Medina to perform the first hajj, or pilgrimage, to Mecca's holy sites. As he died shortly after, this became known as the farewell pilgrimage. Accompanied by a great crowd, the Prophet proceeded to a sacred site on a hill just outside Mecca, Mt. Arafat, where he delivered his farewell sermon. This important address prescribed a moral life and underscored the brotherhood of all Muslims, and today it exists in several different versions. All Muslims aspire to complete the Hajj—as the Prophet mentions in his speech—and during which the pilgrims must spend time in contemplation on Mt. Arafat. Many also travel to Medina to visit the Prophet's Tomb.

O People, lend me an attentive ear, for I know not whether, after this year, I shall ever be amongst you again. Therefore listen to what I am saying to you carefully and take these words to those who could not be present here today.

O People, just as you regard this month, this day, this city as sacred, so regard the life and property of every Muslim as a sacred trust. Return the goods entrusted to you to their rightful owners. Hurt no one so that no one may hurt you. Remember that you will indeed meet your lord, and that he will indeed reckon your deeds. Allah has forbidden you to take usury (interest), therefore all interest obligation shall henceforth be waived. Your capital is yours to keep. You will neither inflict nor suffer any inequity . . .

Beware of Satan, for your safety of your religion. He has lost all hope that he will ever be able to lead you astray in big things, so beware of following him in small things.

O People, it is true that you have certain rights with regard to your women, but they also have rights over you. Remember that you have taken them as your wives only under Allah's trust and with His permission. If they abide by your right then to them belongs the right to be fed and clothed in kindness. Do treat your women well and be kind to them for they are your partners and committed helpers. And it is your right that they do not make friends with any one of whom you do not approve, as well as never to be unchaste.

O People, listen to me in earnest, worship Allah, say your five daily prayers (Salah), fast during the month of Ramadan, and give your wealth in Zakat. Perform Hajj if you can afford to.

All mankind is from Adam and Eve—an Arab has no superiority over a non-Arab nor a non-Arab has any superiority over an Arab. Also a white has no superiority over a black nor a black has any superiority over a white, except by piety and good action.

Learn that every Muslim is a brother to every Muslim and that the Muslims constitute one brotherhood. Nothing shall be legitimate to a Muslim which belongs to a fellow Muslim unless it was given freely and willingly.

Do not therefore do injustice to yourselves. Remember, one day you will appear before Allah and answer for your deeds. So beware, do not stray from the path of righteousness after I am gone.

O People, no prophet or apostle will come after me and no new faith will be born. Reason well, therefore, O People, and understand my words which I convey to you. I leave behind me two things, the Qur'an and my example, the Sunnah, and if you follow these you will never go astray.

All those who listen to me shall pass on my words to others and those to others again; and may the last ones understand my words better than those who listen to me directly.

Be my witness, O Allah, that I have conveyed your message to your people.

Source: Muhammad. "Prophet Muhammad's Last Sermon." *Authentic Islamic Literature.* Available online. URL: http://www.quraan.com/index.aspx?tabindex=4&tabid=11&bid=16&cid=1. Accessed on December 15, 2007.

All mankind is from Adam and Eve—an Arab has no superiority over
a non-Arab nor a non-Arab has any superiority over an Arab. Also a white has
no superiority over a black nor a black has any superiority over a white,
except by piety and good action. —*Muhammad*

ABU BAKR
(ca. 573–634)
Upon Succeeding the Prophet Muhammad
Medina, now Saudi Arabia
632 C.E.

Abu Bakr, the father of the prophet Muhammad's wife Aisha, became Muhammad's successor on his death on June 8, 632. He was called "al-Saddiq," meaning "the faithful" or "truthful." He was a close companion of Muhammad, and one of the first to accept him as the Prophet. (SEE Muhammad's Farewell Sermon, page 79.) Abu Bakr accompanied the Prophet alone on the flight from Mecca, and in Medina he fought with Muhammad in the battles against the Meccans. On the day that Muhammad died, conflict arose over whether the Muslims from Mecca or from the tribes of Medina should choose the successor. The two groups met in Medina. To quickly settle the dispute, Abu Bakr was selected, although some went along unwillingly. Those who were unhappy with the choice felt that Muhammad's young cousin (and son-in-law) Ali ibn Abi Talib had a better right to the succession because he carried the same bloodline and was the first male after Muhammad to accept Islam. Ali's faction did not swear allegiance to Abu Bakr. (Ali eventually became the fourth of the four "Rightly-Guided Caliphs" revered by Sunni Muslims, but disagreements over his right to the original succession caused a split in Islam, with his followers forming the Shia branch, and the greater majority following Sunni Islam.) As successor, Abu Bakr was the first of the four Rightly-Guided Caliphs who had personally known Muhammad. While he governed for only two years before he died in 634, Abu Bakr is esteemed among Sunni Muslims as one of the founding fathers of Islam. The following speech to the people, on his succession, reveals the respect he gave to law and to the consent of the governed,

his willingness to accept advice, and his commitment to God and the Prophet.

Abu Bakr and Muhammad's son-in-law, Ali ibn Abi Talib, accompany Muhammad (traditionally shown without detail) on a journey. Painting from the book *Life of the Prophet*, 1594 *(The New York Public Library/Art Resource, NY)*

Behold! I have been charged with the responsibilities of government.

I am not the best among you. I shall need all the advice and help that you can give.

If I act well, you must support me. If I make a mistake, advise me.

To tell the truth to him who is given the responsibility to rule is dutiful allegiance. To hide it would be treason.

The strong and the weak are equal in my eyes, and I want to mete out justice to both.

As I obey God and His Prophet, you must obey me. If I disobey the Laws of God and the Prophet, I forfeit my right to your obedience.

Arise for your prayer. God have mercy upon you.

Source: Allana, Gulam, ed. *A Rosary of Islamic Readings.* Karachi: National Publishing House, 1973, p. 9.

EMPEROR KOTOKU
(596?–654)
On the White Pheasant
Asuka, Japan
650

Early Japanese culture was heavily influenced by China, by way of the Korean Peninsula. Buddhism arrived in Japan in the sixth century, when Emperor Kotoku's capital was in Asuka, near present-day Nara. Kotoku's Taika Reform, proclaimed in 646 in an attempt to model Japanese government in the centralized Chinese manner, brought all land under the ownership of the emperor and demanded allegiance of clans and warlords. It also instituted new systems of taxation and land use. Japanese people studied the Chinese language and Chinese arts, literature, and religion. In the year 650, an official from the province of Anato brought Emperor Kotoku a rare white pheasant found on Mount Onoyama. Historians from the Paekche of Korea searched their records and found that white pheasants had indeed been seen in China, in 68 C.E. during the reign of Ming Ti of the Han dynasty, and also during the earlier Chou (or Zhou) dynasty. The bird was a lucky omen for Japan. Buddhist monks suggested that the emperor should announce a general amnesty to celebrate with the people. The head priest observed that the creature signified the reign of a sage and humane ruler and also, "when a Ruler is of frugal habits, white pheasants are made to come forth on the hills." A few days later the white pheasant, which had been allowed the run of the palace garden, was carried grandly in a litter (a covered and curtained couch) to the emperor's hall by the Imperial Chieftain and his escort. There the court guards were arrayed for the most ceremonial of occasions. The great ministers and certain princes and lords took turns conveying the pheasant's litter and placed it before Kotoku and the crown prince. One among the great ministers congratulated the emperor, saying the pheasant was a sign he would rule for 10,000 years. In reply, Kotoku made this address, adding at the end that falcons, as predators posing a threat to pheasants, were to be kept away.

When a sage Ruler appears in the world and rules the Empire, Heaven is responsive to him, and manifests favorable omens. In ancient times, during the reign of Cheng-wang of the Chou Dynasty, a ruler of the Western land, and again in the time of Ming Ti of the Han Dynasty, white pheasants were seen.

In this Our Land of Japan, during the reign of the Emperor Homuda, a white crow made its nest in the Palace. In the time of the Emperor O-sazaki, a Dragon-horse appeared in the West. This shows that from ancient times until now, there have been many cases of auspicious omens appearing in response to virtuous rulers. What we call phoenixes, unicorns, white pheasants, white crows, and such like birds and beasts, even including herbs and trees, in short all things having the property of significant response, are favorable omens and auspicious signs produced by Heaven and Earth.

Now that wise and enlightened sovereigns should obtain such auspicious omens is meet and proper. But why should We, who are so empty and shallow, have this good fortune? It is no doubt wholly due to Our Assistants, the Ministers, Imperial Chieftains, Deity Chieftains, Court Chieftains, and Local Chieftains, each of whom, with the utmost loyalty, conforms to the regulations that are made. For this reason, let all, from the Ministers down to the functionaries, with pure hearts reverence the gods of Heaven and Earth, and one and all accepting the glad omen, make the Empire to flourish.

The provinces and districts in the four quarters having been placed in our charge by Heaven, We exercise supreme rule over the Empire. Now in the province of Anato, ruled over by Our divine ancestors, this auspicious omen has appeared. For this reason We proclaim a general amnesty throughout the Empire, and begin a new year-period, to be called Haku-chi, White Pheasant. Moreover, We prohibit the flying of falcons within the limits of the province of Anato.

Source: Nihongi: Chronicles of Japan from the Earliest Times to A.D. *697.* Translated by W. G. Aston. First published in the *Transactions and Proceedings of the Japan Society.* London: Kegan Paul, 1896.

TARIQ IBN ZIYAD
(died 720)
Before the Battle of Guadalete
Gibraltar
April 30, 711 C.E.

By 711 C.E. Islam had spread through North Africa, across what are now Libya, Tunisia, Algeria, and Morocco. In that year, Tariq ibn Ziyad, the governor of Tangier (today a seaport of Morocco), led an army of Muslim Berbers across the Strait of Gibraltar (the narrow seaway connecting the Mediterranean with the Atlantic) in the first phase of the Muslim conquest of Spain and Portugal. Tariq and his army had been sent by the Muslim governor of North Africa, Musa ibn Nusayr. According to what is probably legend, Musa had promised to aid Count Julian of Ceuta, a Christian, against Roderick, the last Visigothic king of Spain, as Roderick had impregnated Julian's daughter during the time that she was sent to his court for education. (The port city of Ceuta in Morocco faces Gibraltar across the strait.) More likely, an ambitious Julian hoped to form an alliance against Roderick and invade his territory. Julian provided the vessels in which Tariq's 1,700 men crossed the Strait of Hercules (Strait of Gibral-

tar) to launch the invasion. On landing, Tariq burned the ships so his troops could not lose heart and flee the Visigoths. In mid-July, with 7,000 men and Julian's army alongside them, he defeated the larger force of King Roderick in a three-day battle west of Gibraltar by the river Guadalete. Roderick was killed. Tariq was named the governor of Al-Andalus (the Muslim-held portion of the Iberian Peninsula) that year, although he returned to North Africa just one year later. By 718 most of the Iberian Peninsula had been conquered. The Moors (Muslim Berbers and Arabs of North Africa) ruled Portugal until the arrival of the Christian crusaders from Western Europe in the 12th century, and they remained a force in Spain for nearly eight centuries. The name Gibraltar results from centuries of corruption of "Jebel Tariq," meaning Mountain of Tariq. Tariq's address to his soldiers upon landing was included by Al-Maqqari, an Arab historian of the early 1600s, in his chronicle *The Breath of Perfumes.*

Oh my people, whither would you flee? Behind you is the sea, before you, the enemy. You have left now only the hope of your courage and your constancy.

Remember that in this country you are more unfortunate than the orphan seated at the table of the avaricious master. Your enemy is before you, protected by an innumerable army; he has men in abundance. But you, as your only aid, have your own swords and, as your only chance for life, such chance as you can snatch from the hands of your enemy. If the absolute want to which you are reduced is prolonged ever so little, if you delay to seize immediate success, your good fortune will vanish, and your enemies, whom your very presence has filled with fear, will take courage.

Put far from you the disgrace from which you flee in dreams, and attack this monarch who has left his strongly fortified city to meet you. Here is a splendid opportunity to defeat him, if you will consent to expose yourselves freely to death. Do not believe that I desire to incite you to face dangers which I shall refuse to share with you. In the attack I myself will be in the fore, where the chance of life is always least.

Remember that if you suffer a few moments in patience, you will afterward enjoy supreme delight. Do not imagine that your fate can be separated from mine, and rest assured that if you fall, I shall perish with you, or avenge you.

You have heard that in this country there are a large number of ravishingly beautiful Greek maidens, their graceful forms are draped in sumptuous gowns on which gleam pearls, coral, and purest gold, and they live in the palaces of royal kings.

RHETORICAL DEVICE

Zeugma: Using one word, usually a verb, to govern or connect two or more other words.

It was we, the people; not we, the white male citizens;
nor we, the male citizens; but we, the whole people,
who formed the Union. —*Susan B. Anthony*

We have seen that the law was not the same for a white and
for a black, accommodating for the first,
cruel and inhuman for the other. —*Patrice Lumumba*

Behind you is the sea, before you, the enemy. —*Tariq ibn Ziyad*

Where cruelty exists, the law does not. —*Alberto Mora*

Let both sides join in creating a new endeavor . . . where the strong are just and
the weak secure and the peace preserved. —*John F. Kennedy*

The Commander of True Believers, Alwalid, son of Abdalmelik, has chosen you for this attack from among all his Arab warriors, and he promises that you shall become his comrades and shall hold the rank of kings in this country. Such is his confidence in your intrepidity. The one fruit which he desires to obtain from your bravery is that the word of God shall be exalted in this country, and that the true religion shall be established here.

The spoils will belong to yourselves.

Remember that I place myself in the front of this glorious charge which I exhort you to make. At the moment when the two armies meet hand to hand, you will see me, never doubt it, seeking out this Roderick, tyrant of his people, challenging him to combat, if God is willing. If I perish after this, I will have had at least the satisfaction of delivering you, and you will easily find among you an experienced hero, to whom you can confidently give the task of directing you.

But should I fall before I reach to Roderick, redouble your ardor, force yourselves to the attack and achieve the conquest of this country, in depriving him of life. With him dead, his soldiers will no longer defy you.

Source: Horne, Charles, ed. *The Sacred Books and Early Literature of the East.* Vol. 6. New York: Parke, Austin, Lipscomb, 1917, p. 241.

MUSANG
(680–762)
Preaching the Dharma
Chengdu (Ch'eng-tu), China
ca. 728–762

The early Chan master Musang was born in Silla, one of the Three Kingdoms of Korea, in 680 C.E. He was reputed to be a son of the king, Sŏngdŏk. Silla, allied with Tang China, had just conquered the kingdom of Paekche in the Korean Peninsula's southwest, and the kingdom of Koguryo in the north. This ushered in a period of stability in which religious orders thrived. Buddhism had arrived in Korea in about 372 from China, and it had been Silla's official religion from about 527; Korean thinkers made reciprocal contributions to Chinese Buddhism (and also introduced it to Japan). (*SEE* Buddha's sermon, page 13) The anonymous source *Lidai fabao ji* (*Record of the Triratna under Successive Dynasties*) of about 774 C.E. states that Musang shaved his head and journeyed to China "to search for a teacher and seek the Path," a search he undertook in 728. In China, Chan Buddhism was flourishing under the Tang dynasty, one of the golden ages of Chinese civilization. Chan, a form of Mahayana Buddhism, emphasized enlightenment achieved through meditation, often through a master-disciple relationship. (In Japanese, this practice is called Zen; in Korean, Sŏn.) In China, Musang was called Wuxiang, or Monk Kim. He studied meditation with a Chan master (or *dhyana* master, a teacher of the practice of seated meditation) in Chengdu, and he became a patriarch of the Buddhist Meditation School. Musang became the abbot first of Jingzhong Monastery in Chengdu, and later of Dashengzi Monastery, which he helped to build; he had several important disciples and may also have influenced the Buddhism of Tibetan monks traveling through China. "No-recollection is the discipline, no-thought is the meditation, and no-forgetfulness is the wisdom," he said. The *Record of the Triratna* also records that at the beginning and end of each year Musang "set up the Platform of the Path, and preached the dharma [truthful doctrine] from the pulpit," to monastics and lay people.

First, softly invoke the name of the Buddha. With all your breath meditate on the Buddha. Then stop the voice and stop thinking. The absence of memory, the absence of thought, and the absence of delusion: the first is *sīla* [morality]; the second, *samādhi* [concentration]; and the third, *prajñā* [wisdom]. These three phrases furnish absolute control over good and evil passions and influences.

With the absence of thought, the mind is like a bright mirror that reflects all phenomena. The rise of thought is like the back of a mirror that cannot reflect anything.

To know clearly birth and death—and to know them without interruption—is to see the Buddha. It is like a story of two men who went together to another country. Their father sent them a letter with instructions. One son obtained the letter, finished it, and followed his father's teachings without breaking the discipline. Another did the same, but he went against his father's teachings and committed many evil deeds. All living beings are like this. One who relies on the absence of thought is like an obedient son. One who is set on words is like a disobedient son.

To use another parable, when one man was drunk and lying about, his mother went and called him, "Let's go home." But the drunken son was bewildered and railed against his own mother. Likewise, all living beings, drunk with ignorance, do not believe that by looking into their own nature they can become buddhas.

Source: Lee, Peter H., and William Theodore de Bary. *Sources of Korean Tradition.* Vol. 1. New York: Columbia University Press, 1997, p. 121. Copyright © 1997 Columbia University Press. Reprinted with permission of the publisher.

WULFSTAN II
(died 1023)
Sermon of the Wolf to the English
York, England
1014

Wulfstan II was made bishop of London in the last years of the first millennium, and he became archbishop of York in 1002. He is known for his sermons, which he wrote in the common language of his time (now called Old English), rather than in Latin. His most famous sermon is *Sermo Lupi ad Anglos,* which means "Sermon of the Wolf to the English" (he used Wolf as a pen name). The times were difficult in southeast England. The people had been beset by Danish and Norwegian invaders (Vikings) for 30 years and famine had devastated the countryside. These Vikings had arrived with an enormous fleet in 991, led by the Norwegian Olaf Tryggvason (king of Norway, r. 995–ca. 1000), who intended to retake the Danelaw, the vast section of England held by Vikings in the ninth century. Olaf and his raiders attacked London and ravaged large areas of southeast England. The English king Æthelred (called the Unready, or more accurately, the Ill-Counselled, r. 978–1016) was betrayed by several treacherous aides and was forced several times to purchase peace with large sums of gold and silver. The Vikings also demanded the payment of tributes. In response, King Æthelred ordered massacres of the Danes living in England, but this only brought further depredations by Danish commander Sweyn Haraldsson. Sweyn succeeded in forcing out Æthelred—who fled to Normandy (northern France)—and made himself king of England in 1013. All this misfortune, murder, and famine, coming as it did at the millennium's end, was believed by Wulfstan to be a punishment from God for sin. Wulfstan's sermon admonished the English to reform their ways or face the "hellish torment" prepared for them, and it was intended to be delivered to the people from the pulpit in churches across the countryside.

Dear men, understand that this is true: the world is in haste and it approaches the end, and because it is ever worldly, the longer it lasts, the worse it becomes; and so it must necessarily greatly worsen before the coming of Antichrist because of the sins of the people, and indeed it will become then fearful and terrible throughout the world.

Understand also completely that the devil has deceived this people too much, and that there has been little faith among men, though they speak fair words, and too many crimes have gone unchecked in the land. . . .

Alas for the wretchedness and alas for the great humiliation which the English now endure wholly through the anger of God! Often two Vikings, or sometimes three, drive the muster of the Christian men from coast to coast out from the midst of this nation huddled together, as a great shame to us all, if we could really and rightly perceive it, but all the insulting which we often endure we requite by honouring those who insult us. We pay them continually, and they humiliate us daily. They ravage and they burn, plunder and steal and carry off to their fleet. And lo! what other thing is clear and evident in all these events if not the anger of God?

Also it is no marvel although misfortune befall us, because we know full well that for many years now men have too often not cared what they did in word or deed. But this nation has become, as it may appear, very corrupted by manifold sins and by many crimes, by murder and evil deeds, by avarice and greed, by stealing and robbery, by the barter of men and pagan abuses, by betrayals and trickeries, by attacks on kinsmen and manslaughters, by violation of holy orders and breaches of divine law, by incest and various fornications.

And also widely, as we said before, by the breaking of oaths and of pledges and by various lies many more than there should be are lost and perjured, and the disregarding of church feasts and fasts happens widely time and again. And also there are in the land degenerate apostates and cruel persecutors of the church and fierce tyrants, altogether too many, and everywhere despisers of divine laws and Christian customs, and foolish mockers everywhere in the nation, very often of those things which God's messengers command and most of all of those things which should always by right pertain to God's law.

And therefore it has now become far and wide as a very evil custom, that men are now more ashamed for good deeds than for evil deeds; because too often one spurns good deeds with derision and reviles godfearing men altogether too much, and most of all one reproves and treats with scorn altogether too often those who love the right and have an awe of God in any matter. . . .

Here are murderers and slayers of kin and killers of priests and persecutors of monasteries; and here are perjurers and contrivers of murder; and here are harlots and child murderers and many foul adulterous whoremongers; and here are wizards and witches; and here are plunderers and robbers and thieves and, to speak most briefly, a countless number of all crimes and foul deeds. And it does not shame us at all in respect of that, but it greatly puts us to shame that we begin the penance as the books teach, and that is evident in this wretched sinful people. Alas, many may easily think of much besides this which one man alone might not quickly examine, so wretchedly it happens now all the time widely throughout this nation. And indeed let each one earnestly examine himself, and let him not delay all too long.

But lo! in the name of God let us do as is needful for us, protect ourselves as we may most earnestly, lest we all perish together.

There was a chronicler called Gildas in the time of the Britons who wrote about their misdeeds, how they by their sins angered God so excessively that at last he allowed the army of Englishmen to conquer their homeland to destroy entirely the seasoned strength of the Britons. And that happened as he foretold, by the plundering by powerful men and the covetousness of ill-gotten gains, by the lawlessness of the people and by bad judgments in legal cases, by the slackness of bishops, and by the base cowardice of God's messengers who all too often kept silent about the truth and mumbled with their jaws where they should have called out. Also by the foul pride of the people and by gluttony and by manifold sins they destroyed their native land and themselves perished.

But let us do as there is need for us to do, be warned by such things. . . . And let us love God and follow God's laws and very earnestly perform that which we (or those who were our sponsors at baptism), promised when we received baptism. And let us order our words and deeds rightly and earnestly cleanse our thoughts, and carefully honour oath and pledge, and maintain some loyalty among us without evil practice. And let us often reflect on the great judgment to which we all shall come, and earnestly save ourselves from the surging fire of hellish torment, and earn for ourselves the glories and the joys which God has prepared for those who do his will in the world. May God help us, Amen.

Source: Wulfstan II. "The Sermon of the Wolf to the English." Translated by M. C. Seymour. *The Anglo-Saxon World*. Edited by Kevin Crossley-Holland. Suffolk: Boydell, 1982, p. 265.

WILLIAM THE CONQUEROR
(ca. 1028–1087)
Before the Battle of Hastings
Senlac Hill, East Sussex, England
October 14, 1066

William the Conqueror was born about 1028 in Normandy, in the area of northern France still called by that name; he was only seven when he became Duke William II of Normandy, succeeding his father, Duke Robert II of Normandy, in 1035. When he conquered England in 1066, he also became King William I of England. England had been settled since the fifth century by people from the Angle and Saxon tribes (of Germany) and the Jutes (of Denmark). Across the English Channel, the Normans were recently descended from Viking roots in Scandinavia. After warring against the Franks of France, they lived in Normandy (the name comes from "Northman"), opposite England's south coast. The two lands had growing relations. In the 11th century English kings had married Norman nobility. The second-to-last Anglo-Saxon king, Edward the Confessor (r. 1042–1066), had a Norman mother, Emma, the daughter of Duke Richard I of Normandy (r. 996–1026/7). Emma was the aunt of Duke William. In fact, King Edward had spent his youth exiled in Normandy to escape Viking depredations from the invasion of 1013. He had no direct heir. On Edward's death in January 1066, Harold Godwinson, the powerful Anglo-Saxon earl of Wessex, was crowned King Harold II of England. In Normandy, Duke William was enraged, as he claimed King Edward—his cousin—had promised him the English throne and Harold had sworn his support. William launched his invasion in late September; on October 14 his army met Harold's on Senlac Hill near the town of Hastings. Harold was killed and his army defeated. The Battle of Hastings became the first stage of the Norman conquest of England and the end of the age of Anglo-Saxon dominance. The Normans brought the customs of fealty, land ownership, and labor of the European feudal system to England and added a large vocabulary to the English language. Henry of Huntingdon, an English historian writing in the 12th century, related a speech he said William gave to his five squadrons of cavalrymen before the Battle of Hastings.

What I have to say to you, Normans, the bravest of nations, does not spring from any doubt of your valor or uncertainty of victory, which never by any chance or obstacle escaped your efforts. If, indeed, once only you had failed of conquering, it might be necessary to inflame your courage by exhortation. But how little does the inherent spirit of your race require to be roused! . . .

Did not Rollo, my ancestor, the founder of our nation, with your progenitors, conquer at Paris the king of the Franks in the heart of his dominions? Nor could he obtain any respite until he humbly offered possession of the country—which from you is called Normandy—with the hand of his daughter.

Did not your fathers take prisoner the king of the French, and detain him at Rouen till he restored Normandy to your Duke Richard, then a boy; with this stipulation, that in every conference between the King of France and the Duke of Normandy, the duke should have his sword by his side, while the king should not be allowed so much as a dagger? This concession your fathers compelled the great king to submit to, as binding forever.

Did not the same duke lead your fathers to Mirmande, at the foot of the Alps, and enforce submission from the lord of the town, his son-in-law, to his own wife, the duke's daughter? Nor was it enough to conquer mortals; for he overcame the devil himself, with whom he wrestled, and cast down and bound him, leaving him a shameful spectacle to angels.

But why do I go back to former times? When you, in our own time, engaged the French at Mortemer, did not the French prefer flight to battle, and use their spurs instead of their swords; while—Ralph, the French commander, being slain—you reaped the fruits of victory, the honor and the spoil, as natural results of your wonted success?

Ah! Let any one of the English whom our predecessors, both Danes and Norwegians, have defeated in a hundred battles, come forth and show that the race of Rollo ever suffered a defeat from his time until now, and I will submit and retreat.

Is it not shameful then, that a people accustomed to be conquered, a people ignorant of the art of war, a people not even in possession of arrows, should make a show of being arrayed in order of battle against you, most valiant? Is it not a shame that this King Harold, perjured as he was in your presence, should dare to show his face to you?

It is a wonder to me that you have been allowed to see those who by a horrible crime beheaded your relations and Alfred my kinsman, and that their own accursed heads are still on their shoulders.

Raise then your standards, my brave men, and set no bounds to your merited rage. Let the lightning of your glory flash, and the thunders of your onset be heard from east to west, and be the avengers of the noble blood that has been spilled.

Source: Henry of Huntingdon. *The Chronicle of Henry of Huntingdon.* Translated by Thomas Forester. London: Henry Bohn, 1853, p. 210.

POPE URBAN II
(1042–1099)
Calling for a Crusade to the Holy Land
Clermont, France
November 27, 1095

Pope Urban II was born Odo of Lagery in 1042 in France to a noble family. He rose through the ranks of clergy until he was elected pope in 1088. He took the name Urban II. In March 1095 an ambassador from the Byzantine emperor Alexius I requested assistance against the Muslim Seljuk Turks, who had seized much of Asia Minor (Turkey). The Byzantine Empire had an historical relationship with Rome, the seat of the popes, as it was Christian and had succeeded the eastern branch of the Roman Empire. At the next church council, Urban II would preach a sermon with far-reaching effects for centuries. Even today, the word "crusade" evokes a millennium of resentment from Arabs and Muslims of the Middle East. At the time of Urban's reign, Muslim caliphs had held the Holy Lands since the seventh-century birth of Islam. There had been little persecution of Christians until 1010, when the caliph Hakim destroyed the Church of the Holy Sepulcher, which tradition said was built on the site of Jesus' burial. The

seizure of Jerusalem by Seljuk Turks in 1071 increased religious tension. Then, at the Council of Clermont, Pope Urban II preached his call for an army of pilgrims to reclaim Jerusalem, promising forgiveness of sins as their reward. The crowd cried, "Deus vult!" ("God wills it!"), which he assigned as their battle cry. The crusaders overwhelmed Constantinople, seized Antioch, and entered Jerusalem in 1099. They killed nearly the entire population of the city, Jews and Christians as well as Muslims. Jerusalem was taken, but Urban II died before receiving word. He had set in motion the first of eight major crusades and many minor ones, and the only crusade that achieved its goal. In addition, the crusaders had established four Latin Kingdoms, or crusader states, on the eastern shore of the Mediterranean: Edessa, Antioch, Tripoli, and Jerusalem. There are five versions of Urban's great speech recorded by different chroniclers. Here is the account recorded by Robert the Monk (or Robert of Reims) from the *Historia Hierosolymitana*.

Oh, race of Franks, race from across the mountains, race beloved and chosen by God (as is clear from many of your works), set apart from all other nations by the situation of your country, as well as by your Catholic faith and the honor which you render to the holy Church: to you our discourse is addressed, and for you our exhortations are intended. We wish you to know what a grievous cause has led us to your country, for it is the imminent peril threatening you and all the faithful which has brought us hither.

From the confines of Jerusalem and from the city of Constantinople a grievous report has gone forth and has repeatedly been brought to our ears; namely, that a race from the kingdom of the Persians, an accursed race, a race wholly alienated from God, "a generation that set not their heart aright and whose spirit was not steadfast with God," has violently invaded the lands of those Christians and has depopulated them by pillage and fire. They have led away a part of the captives into their own country, and a part have they have killed by cruel tortures. They have either destroyed the churches of God or appropriated them for the rites of their own religion. They destroy the altars, after having defiled them with their uncleanness. . . . The kingdom of the Greeks is now dismembered by them and has been deprived of territory so vast in extent that it could not be traversed in two months' time.

On whom, therefore, rests the labor of avenging these wrongs and of recovering this territory, if not upon you—you, upon whom, above all other nations, God has conferred remarkable glory in arms, great courage, bodily activity, and strength to humble the heads of those who resist you? Let the deeds of your ancestors encourage you and incite your minds to manly achievements—the glory and greatness of King Charlemagne, and of his son Louis, and of your other monarchs, who have destroyed the kingdoms of the Turks and have extended the sway of the holy Church over lands previously possessed by the pagan.

Let the holy sepulcher of our Lord and Savior, which is possessed by the unclean nations, especially arouse you, and the holy places which are now treated with ignominy and irreverently polluted with the filth of the unclean. Oh, most valiant soldiers and descendants of invincible ancestors, do not degenerate, but recall the valor of your progenitors.

But if you are hindered by love of children, parents, or wife, remember what the Lord says in the Gospel, "He that loveth father or mother more than me is not worthy of me." "Every one that hath forsaken houses, or brethren, or sisters, or father, or mother, or wife, or children, or lands, for my name's sake, shall receive an hundredfold, and shall inherit everlasting life." Let none of your possessions restrain you, nor solicitude for your family affairs. For this land which you inhabit, shut in on all sides by the seas and surrounded by the mountain peaks, is too narrow for your large population; nor does it abound in wealth; and it furnishes scarcely food enough for its cultivators. Hence it is that you murder and devour one another, that you wage war, and that very many among you perish in civil strife.

Let hatred therefore depart from among you; let your quarrels end; let wars cease; and let all dissensions and controversies slumber. Enter upon the road to the Holy Sepulcher. Wrest that land from the wicked race, and subject it to yourselves. That land which, as the Scripture says, "floweth with milk and honey" was given by God into the power of the children of Israel. Jerusalem is the center of the earth; the land is fruitful above all others, like another paradise of delights. This spot the Redeemer of mankind has made illustrious by His advent, has beautified by His sojourn, has consecrated by His passion, has redeemed by His death, has glorified by His burial.

This royal city, however, situated at the center of the earth, is now held captive by the enemies of Christ and is subjected, by those who do not know God, to the worship of the heathen. She seeks, therefore, and desires to be liberated, and ceases not to implore you to come to her aid. From you especially she asks succor, because as we have already said, God has conferred upon you above all other nations great glory in arms. Accordingly, undertake this journey eagerly for the remission of your sins, with the assurance of the reward of imperishable glory in the kingdom of heaven. [Here the crowd cried, "God wills it!"]

Most beloved brethren, today is manifest in you what the Lord says in the Gospel, "Where two or three are gathered together in my name, there am I in the midst of them." For unless God had been present in your spirits, all of you would not have uttered the same cry; since, although the cry issued from numerous mouths, yet the origin of the cry was one. Therefore I say to you that God, who implanted this in your breasts, has drawn it forth from you. Let that then be your war cry in battle, because it is given to you by God. When an armed attack is made upon the enemy, let this one cry be raised by all the soldiers of God: "It is the will of God! It is the will of God!"

And we neither command nor advise that the old or those incapable of bearing arms, undertake this journey. Nor ought women to set out at all without their husbands, or brother, or legal guardians. For such are more of a hindrance than aid, more of a burden than an advantage. Let the rich aid the needy, and according to their wealth let them take with them experienced soldiers. The priests and other clerks, whether secular or regular, are not to go without the consent of their bishop; for this journey would profit them nothing if they went without permission. Also, it is not fitting that laymen should enter upon the pilgrimage without the blessing of their priests.

Whoever, therefore, shall determine upon this holy pilgrimage, and shall make his vow to God to that effect, and shall offer himself to him for sacrifice, as a living victim, holy and acceptable to God, shall wear the sign of the cross of the Lord on his forehead or on his breast. When, indeed, he shall return from his journey, having fulfilled his vow, let him place the cross on his back between his shoulders. Thus shall ye, indeed, by this twofold action, fulfill the precept of the Lord, as He commands in the Gospel, "He that taketh not his cross, and followeth after me, is not worthy of me."

Source: Ogg, Frederic Austin, ed. *Source Book of Medieval History.* New York: American Book Co., 1908.

ST. BERNARD OF CLAIRVAUX
(1090–1153)
Calling for a Second Crusade
Vézelay, France
March 31, 1146

Like Pope Urban II (*SEE* Urban's speech page 92), Bernard of Clairvaux was born in France to parents of nobility. He became the first abbot of the Cistercian abbey at Clairvaux when he was just 25 years old. He had a persuasive personality and an unusual willingness, for a clergyman, to assert himself in public affairs. The advice of the eloquent abbot was sought by the politically powerful, and his influence came to rival that of the popes. The Cistercian order expanded under him, and it received prominence when a monk who had previously served at Clairvaux was elected pope in 1145— Pope Eugene III. The pope found himself unwelcome in Rome because of political unrest, and he returned to live near Clairvaux; he was a great friend of Bernard. Just a year or two earlier, the Turks had seized Edessa, one of several crusader states (portions of the Holy Lands held by crusaders since the First Crusade, 1095–99). Pope Eugene III convinced Bernard to preach a new crusade,

and the abbot delivered his great sermon on Palm Sunday, 1146. He was enormously successful at attracting participants—even King Louis VII (r. 1137–80) and his wife, Eleanor of Aquitaine, signed on. Bernard set out on a speaking campaign in France and Germany; this Second Crusade was to be better organized and properly led. He was successful in enlisting Holy Roman Emperor Conrad III of Germany to command alongside Louis. Ordinary people also departed on crusade in great numbers—poor nobles, farmers with failed crops, but mostly people seeking spiritual gain and forgiveness of sin. The crusade was a disastrous failure; this time, previously disorganized Muslim leaders had united forces in face of the common threat posed by the Turks and crusaders. Although Louis and Conrad got as far as Jerusalem, the Seljuk Turks substantially defeated their troops in Asia Minor. With much of their armies destroyed, the kings limped home three years after Bernard's call.

You cannot but know that we live in a period of chastisement and ruin; the enemy of mankind has caused the breath of corruption to fly over all regions. We behold nothing but unpunished wickedness. The laws of men or the laws of religion have no longer sufficient power to check depravity of manners and the triumph of the wicked. The demon of heresy has taken possession of the chair of truth, and God has sent forth His malediction upon His sanctuary.

Oh, ye who listen to me, hasten then to appease the anger of Heaven, but no longer implore His goodness by vain complaints. Clothe not yourselves in sackcloth, but cover yourselves with your impenetrable bucklers; the din of arms, the dangers, the labors, the fatigues of war are the penances that God now imposes upon you. Hasten then to expiate your sins by victories over the infidels, and let the deliverance of holy places be the reward of your repentance.

If it were announced to you that the enemy had invaded your cities, your castles, your lands; had ravished your wives and your daughters, and profaned your temples— which among you would not fly to arms? Well, then, all these calamities, and calamities still greater, have fallen upon your brethren, upon the family of Jesus Christ, which is yours.

Why do you hesitate to repair so many evils—to revenge so many outrages? Will you allow the infidels to contemplate in peace the ravages they have committed on Christian people? Remember that their triumph will be a subject for grief to all ages and an eternal opprobrium upon the generation that has endured it. Yes, the living God has

Saint Bernard preaches a Second Crusade in France to an audience that includes King Louis VII and his queen, Eleanor of Aquitaine. The year is 1146. Painting by Emile Signol *(Snark/Art Resource, NY)*

charged me to announce to you that He will punish them who shall not have defended Him against His enemies.

Fly then to arms. Let a holy rage animate you in the fight, and let the Christian world resound with these words of the prophet, "Cursed be he who does not stain his sword with blood!" If the Lord calls you to the defense of His heritage, think not that His hand has lost its power. Could He not send twelve legions of angels or breathe one word and all His enemies would crumble away into dust? But God has considered the sons of men, to open for them the road to His mercy. His goodness has caused to dawn for you a day of safety by calling on you to avenge His glory and His name.

Christian warriors, He who gave His life for you, today demands yours in return. These are combats worthy of you, combats in which it is glorious to conquer and advantageous to die. Illustrious knights, generous defenders of the Cross, remember the example of your fathers who conquered Jerusalem, and whose names are inscribed in Heaven. Abandon then the things that perish, to gather unfading palms, and conquer a Kingdom which has no end.

Source: Michaud, Joseph-Francois and William Robson. *The History of the Crusades.* Vol. 1 London: George Routledge and Sons, 1881, p. 333.

MOORISH ELDER OF LISBON
(ca. 12th century)
"This City Is Ours"
Lisbon, Portugal
June 30, 1147

On May 23, 1147, a fleet of 164 ships sailed from England for the Holy Land (which generally refers to Israel and the historical geographic region of Palestine), carrying English, Flemish, and Norman crusaders on the only successful expedition of the Second Crusade. They were likely seafarers of the lower classes, as the English nobility had shown little enthusiasm for the Crusades; England was prosperous then, and members of the upper class were most likely to have been faced with some kind of difficulty at home before being tempted to take the cross. The fleet stopped in Oporto to offer aid to Alfonso I, the first king of Portugal, in capturing Lisbon. (The Moors—Muslim Arabs and Berbers of North Africa—had conquered Lisbon more than 350 years earlier during the Muslim invasion of Europe.) An unsuccessful attack on Lisbon by other crusaders had taken place five years previously, in 1142. On June 30, 1147, with a force of almost 13,000 men behind them, the archbishop of Braga and bishop of Oporto, both Portuguese Christians, met on the besieged city's walls with the Muslim chief elders of Lisbon and the commander of the city fortress. The archbishop offered peace and safety, and the right to practice their religion, if Lisbon surrendered, but destruction if they resisted. A Moorish elder, his name unrecorded, rebuffed the invaders' offer. The elder's speech was recorded by Osbernus, the chronicler of *De Expugnatione Lyxbonensi* (*The Conquest of Lisbon*), who scholars believe was a priest with the crusaders. On July 1 the assault began, and the city was captured by October 23. The crusaders spent the winter in Lisbon, and they continued on to Jerusalem the next February.

I perceive that you have your words very well under control. You are not transported by your speech, nor has it carried you further than you meant to go. It has been directed to a single end, namely to the taking of our city.

But I cannot wonder enough concerning you, for while a single forest or a district suffices for many elephants and lions, neither the land nor the sea is enough for you. Verily, it is not the want of possessions but ambition of the mind which drives you on.

As to what you have advanced above concerning the lot assigned to each, truly you interfere with our destiny. Labeling your ambition zeal for righteousness, you misrepresent vices as virtues. For your greed has already grown to such proportions that base deeds not only please you but even delight you; and now the opportunity of effecting a cure has almost passed, for the consummate wrongness of your greed has almost exceeded the bounds of natural measure.

You adjudge us to exile and destitution in order that you may become famous. This kind of vainglorious boasting is defined as crass ambition. But your greed, when it has grown beyond measure, has always been smothered in itself and dwindled away. How many times now within our memory have you come with pilgrims and barbarians to subdue us and drive us hence? But do your possessions give you no pleasure at all, or have you incurred some blame at home, that you are so often on the move? Surely your frequent going and coming is proof of an innate mental instability, for he who is unable to arrest the flight of the body cannot control the mind.

Not yet have we decided to hand over our city unconditionally to you or to remain in it and become your subjects. Not yet has our magnanimity advanced to the point where we would give up certainties for uncertainties. For in large affairs, decisions must be made with largeness of view.

This city did indeed, as I believe, once belong to your people; but now it is ours. In the future it will perhaps be yours. But this shall be in accordance with divine favor. While God willed, we have held it; when he shall have willed otherwise, we shall no longer hold it. For there is no wall which is impregnable against the arbitrament of his will. Therefore, let us be content with whatsoever shall please God, who has so often saved our blood from your hands. And for this reason, and rightly, we cease not to marvel at him and his powers, namely because he cannot be conquered, and because he may hold all evil under his feet, and because—than which reason nothing can be more extraordinary—he overcomes misfortunes, sorrows, and injuries for us.

But get you hence, for entry into the city lies not open to you except through trial of the sword. For your threats and the tumults of barbarians, whose strength we know better than their language, are not highly valued among us. And as for the calamities and the unconquerable ills which you promise, they depend upon the future, if and when they ever come to pass; and it is surely senseless to be too anxious about the future and voluntarily to invite nothing but miseries upon oneself. . . .

But why should I delay you longer? Do what you can. We will do what the divine will determines.

Source: David, Charles Wendell, ed and trans. *De expugnatione Lyxbonensi (The Conquest of Lisbon)*. New York: Columbia University Press, 1936, p. 121. Copyright © 1936, Columbia University Press. Reprinted with permission of the publisher.

ST. FRANCIS OF ASSISI
(CA. 1182–1226)
Sermon to the Birds
near Assisi, Italy
1214

St. Francis was born in Assisi, a small town in Italy, about 1182. As a young man from a privileged background, he enjoyed friendship and merriment. At the age of 20, Francis became a soldier. He was captured in his first battle (with the neighboring town of Perugia) and was imprisoned for a year. After his release, he became increasingly conscious of the poor and disadvantaged. Visions and mystical experiences—and a pilgrimage to Rome in 1206—led him to take a vow of poverty and devotion to others. When his family objected to his choice of occupation, he gave up even his family. He set out on the road to preach, barefoot and poorly dressed, to bring others to God and to repentance for sins. His way of life attempted to imitate Christ's, and his example drew many to join him. In 1209, with the permission of Pope Innocent III, he founded the Franciscans, a Roman Catholic religious order that has traditionally ministered to the poor. His order grew rapidly, and he established Franciscan houses in other countries of western Europe. The Catholic Church named him a saint just two years after his death in 1226; he is today one of the best loved of all Christian saints. Often shown in drawings with animals, St. Francis is remembered for his joyous love of nature, speaking of "Brother Hare" and "Sister Lark." In Greccio, near Assisi, he set up the first nativity scene using live animals for the town's Christmas celebrants. In 1214 St. Francis set out on a preaching tour through Umbria, the region around Assisi. While passing through a meadow, his companions saw him stop to preach to the birds. This famous little sermon makes allusions to Jesus' Sermon on the Mount: "Consider the birds of the air; they neither sow nor reap nor gather into barns, and yet your heavenly Father feeds them."

Saint Francis preaches to the birds, in a painting by Giotto di Bondone (1266–1336). *(Réunion des Musées Nationaux/Art Resource, NY)*

My little sisters the birds, you are much obliged to God your creator, and always and in every place you ought to praise Him, because He has given you liberty to fly wherever you will and has clothed you with twofold and threefold raiment. Moreover, He preserved your seed in Noah's Ark that your race might not be destroyed.

Again, you are obliged to Him for the element of the air which He has appointed for you. Furthermore, you sow not neither do you reap, yet God feeds you and gives you rivers and fountains from which to drink. He gives you mountains and valleys for your refuge, and high trees in which to build your nests. And, since you know neither how to sew or to spin, God clothes you and your little ones; so, clearly your Creator loves you, seeing that He gives you so many benefits.

Guard yourselves, therefore, you little sisters the birds, from the sin of ingratitude and be ever mindful to give praise to God.

Source: Ugolino, di Monte Santa Maria. *The Little Flowers of St. Francis of Assisi.* Edited by W. Heywood. New York: Vintage, 1998.

NICHIREN
(1222–1282)
"My Life Is the *Lotus Sutra*"
Kamakura, Japan
September 12, 1271

Nichiren, founder of modern Nichiren Buddhism (a branch of Japanese Buddhism), became a monk at age 16. He took the name Nichiren, meaning "sun" and "lotus." (The lotus is a sacred flower representing purity in Buddhism.) After much study, he came to believe the *Lotus Sutra*—purportedly one of Gautama Buddha's final scriptures—was the true form of Buddhism, and he provoked controversy by insisting other branches of the faith should be abandoned by the government. He believed that only through the *Lotus Sutra* would the Japanese achieve the Buddhist aim of alleviating suffering and also protect themselves from calamities such as the threat of Mongol invasions. (In the 1200s under Kublai Khan the Mongol Empire was expanding rapidly, and Japan was forced to repel invasions, as Nichiren predicted, in 1274 and 1281.) He submitted three treatises on the "correct form of Buddhism" to the authorities, denouncing the government for supporting heretics. The first, titled *Establishment of the Legitimate Teaching for the Security of the Country*, was written in 1260. "Woe, woe!" he wrote. "Thousands of people have been enchanted and led astray, so they wander in Buddhism as men without a guide." Religious authorities reacted strongly; he was briefly exiled within Japan and nearly murdered by hostile officials. In 1271 he delivered his second "remonstration," and was condemned to death by the authorities. Soldiers put him upon a horse and were leading him through Kamakura (a city in present-day Kanagawa, south of Tokyo) to the beach for execution, when they passed the shrine of Hachiman—god of war, guardian of samurai, and protector of Japan. Nichiren called to Hachiman to watch over him, like all the Buddhas and gods of heaven and earth who, he believed, had promised to preserve those who labored on behalf of the *Lotus Sutra*. At the moment of execution, so it was said, a great blaze of light shattered the executioner's sword and scattered the terrified men, sparing Nichiren's life. When his third remonstrance was ignored, Nichiren went into exile voluntarily in 1274, writing and teaching until his death. In his speech, Nichiren refers to the Buddhist monk Dengyō Daishi (767–822), also called Saichō, and to Lord Shakyamuni, another name for Guatama Buddha, the founder of Buddhism.

* * *

O Hachiman! Are you in truth a Divine Being?

When the Great Master Dengyo preached on the Lotus Sutra, did you not do homage to him by laying at his feet a gown of purple color?

I now say to you that I am the only one whose life is the Lotus Sutra. There is no fault in me whatsoever; I am proclaiming the Truth, for the sole purpose of saving the people who dwell in the land from sinking into the deepest of hells on account of degrading the Lotus.

If it came to pass that this land were subjugated by the Mongols, would you, O Hachiman, alone with the Sun Goddess, be in safety? Let me now say to you that when our Lord Shakyamuni preached the Lotus, all the Buddhas gathered together from ten quarters, like unto a sun and a sun, a moon and a moon, stars and stars, mirrors and mirrors, and were ranged face to face with one another. And with hosts of heaven within their midst, deities and saints of India, China, and Japan present in the congregation, all of them vowed to watch over those who should labor to perpetuate the Lotus Sutra.

Now you should come hither and fulfill what you have sworn. Why do you not come to fulfill your promise? When I, Nichiren, this night shall have been beheaded and shall have passed away to the Paradise of Vulture Peak, I shall declare to Our Lord Shakya-muni that you, Hachiman, and the Sun Goddess have not fulfilled the vows. Therefore if you are afraid, tarry not, but do your duty!

Source: Tsunoda, Ryusaku, William Theodore de Bary, and Donald Keene, eds. *Sources of Japanese Tradition.* New York: Columbia University Press, 1958, p. 226.

JOHN BALL
(died 1381)
"All Men by Nature Were Created Alike"
Blackheath, London, England
June 12, 1381

John Ball was a dissident English clergyman excommunicated in 1376 for advocating social reform. He was an itinerant, or traveling, priest, influenced by John Wycliffe—another activist priest at odds with the Roman Catholic Church. At this time the pope wielded considerable power over England—demanding payments of tribute in 1365, for example. Through English church politics, Wycliffe advocated loosening the Roman church's hold over the spiritual and daily life of the English people. Because he wrote that the church should give up its land and valuables to return to simpler roots, he became unpopular with the English clergy as well. Both men's pleas for reform contributed to the Peasants' Revolt (also called Wat Tyler's Revolt) of 1381. This peasant rebellion had its origin in the Black Death (a plague that killed about one-third of the population of Europe from 1347 to 1352), which left labor scarce and wages rising. When King Richard II imposed new taxes, as well as laws to hold down wages, peasants and tradesmen were enraged. In 1381 John Ball joined the revolt when rebels, led by Wat Tyler, released him from the archbishop of Canterbury's prison in Kent, where he had been confined for preaching after his excommunication. On the march to London, Ball addressed the rebels at Blackheath commons, near Greenwich, advocating social equality and urging destruction of the ruling classes of royalty, clergy, and wealthy landowners. He began with a witty epigram that is quoted to this day ("delved" and "span" refer to digging and spinning), as recorded by the English historian and monk Thomas Walsingham, who lived during the time. Thousands of people sacked the city's prison and the homes of the elite; among the dead was the despised archbishop of Canterbury, Simon of Sudbury. However, the revolt ultimately failed. One month later, after a trial, Ball was hanged, drawn, and quartered—the punishment for high treason.

When Adam delved and Eve span, who was then the gentleman? —*John Ball*

When Adam delved and Eve span, who was then the gentleman?

From the beginning, all men by nature were created alike, and our bondage or servitude came in by the unjust oppression of naughty men. For if God would have had any bondmen from the beginning, he would have appointed who should be bond and who free.

And therefore I exhort you to consider that now the time is come, appointed to us by God, in which you may (if you will) cast off the yoke of bondage, and recover liberty.

I counsel you therefore well to bethink yourselves, and to take good hearts unto you, that after the manner of a good husband that tills his ground and rids it of such evil weeds as choke and destroy the good corn, you may destroy first the great lords of the realm, and after, the judges and lawyers and questmongers, and all other who have undertaken to be against the commons.

For so shall you procure peace and surety to yourselves in time to come. And by dispatching out of the way the great men, there shall be an equality in liberty, and no difference in degrees of nobility, but a like dignity and equal authority in all things brought in among you.

Source: Rhys, Ernest, ed. *British Historical and Political Orations from the 12th to the 20th Century.* NY: E. P. Dutton, 1915, p. 4.

THE FIRST GLOBAL AGE
(1450–1750)

Introduction to the First Global Age

The period 1450 to 1750 was marked by numerous cultural changes, including the invention of printing, and by the expansion of the Western domination over the rest of the world that would continue into the 21st century.

HUMANISM AND THE EUROPEAN RENAISSANCE

Secular oratory began to return to European culture in the late 14th and 15th centuries. A movement called humanism (which positions human beings and their worth, along with their capacity for self-realization through reason, at the center of the universe, rather than God or other qualities of nature) revived the study of Latin and Greek classics. Although the movement started with the study of old Latin texts, humanists were soon led to an interest in the ancient Greeks who had so influenced the Romans. There was little knowledge of the Greek language in western Europe at the time, but classical Greek had been preserved in the Byzantine Empire. Byzantium was slowly disintegrating under the remorseless pressure of the Ottoman Turks, who took the last Byzantine city, Constantinople, in 1453. The final decades of Byzantium were marked by a succession of Greek intellectuals migrating to western Europe, bringing Greek manuscripts and knowledge of the classical Greek language to a European populace hungry for them. By the end of the 15th century, humanist intellectuals such as Italian philosopher Giovanni Pico della Mirandola were displaying a mastery of Greek as well as Latin sources.

Rhetorical and oratorical texts were particularly interesting to humanists. One of the great triumphs of the movement was the rediscovery of the classic Latin rhetoric textbook *Institutio oratoria* (*Oratorical Institute*) by Marcus Fabius Quintilianus, and no ancient figure was more revered than the Roman orator Marcus Tullius Cicero. Humanistic rhetorical studies were particularly suited to the city-states of northern Italy, such as Florence, Milan, and Venice. These cities, which had many similarities in their organization to the cities of classical Greece and Rome, had revived the ancient tradition of public debate. Politicians such as Florence's statesman and ruler Lorenzo de' Medici (r. 1478–92) used their oratorical skills to advance their careers. Humanists also drafted letters and orations and went on embassies (diplomatic missions) for their cities' rulers.

The humanism and art of the Renaissance did not meet with the approval of all, and preaching retained a powerful presence alongside the new secular oratory. The Florentine Dominican friar Girolamo Savonarola (1452–98) raised his formidable voice to urge a reformation of Florentine morals, even encouraging mass burnings of those material goods that ministered to a luxurious and worldly way of life, including paintings and sculptures, that he called "bonfires of the vanities."

THE PRINTING PRESS

European culture was transformed by the invention of the printing press in the early 1450s and its spread over the following decades. From its origins in the German city of Mainz, printing crossed into every European country west of Russia by the end of the century. Literally millions of printed texts poured from Europe's presses. Printing provided a far vaster amount of reading material and contributed to a literacy rate that would continue to increase steadily. The press also introduced the new issue of "freedom of the press," which would be debated for centuries.

Printing not only multiplied texts, but it also "fixed" them—while hand copying always introduced changes for all but the briefest documents, printing offered the possibility of producing hundreds or thousands of identical copies. The ease of copying printed texts also made it much more difficult for a printed text, than for a manuscript text, to be lost or suppressed. The humanist resurgence, embodied in printed books, would be a permanent addition to European culture. Printing and literacy also vastly expanded the audience a writer could address. This would affect speeches and sermons as much as any other genre. Speeches would henceforth have a second life in print, one in which they might well reach many more readers than hearers.

THE DISCOVERY OF AMERICA AND THE BEGINNINGS OF EUROPEAN IMPERIALISM

In retrospect, the early 16th century can be clearly seen as the beginning of the great age of European expansion. However, Europeans at the time were more likely to see it as a great age of European contraction. The Ottoman Turks continued their expansion on the European continent and in the Mediterranean for centuries after the fall of Constantinople. In the first few decades following Genoese sailor and navigator Christopher Columbus's "discovery" of America in 1492, more books were written and published in Europe about the Turks than about the New World.

Motivations for the European exploration and conquest of much of the rest of the world included greed for wealth, love of glory, and religious zeal. For many, the early phases of European conquest were a continuation of the Crusades or of the reconquest of Spain and Portugal from the Muslims that was completed in 1492. Even Columbus suggested that one use of the wealth he promised to acquire would be to launch a great crusade to Jerusalem.

European expansion in the 15th and 16th centuries included the Portuguese circumnavigation of Africa and establishment of bases in the Indian Ocean, but the most dramatic events were the Spanish conquests in the Americas. One of the most notable Spanish conquests was that of the Aztec Empire of Mexico by a small force led by the conquistador Hernán Cortés in 1519. Another was that of the Inca Empire of Peru by a force under conquistador Francisco Pizarro in 1532. Both conquests were ruthless and bloody, and they led to the creation of new Spanish provinces in the Americas. "Conquistadors" like Cortés and Pizarro justified their actions by claiming that they were spreading the true Catholic religion in areas previously the domain of Satan. Cortés, an arrogant and ambitious man, could

also humbly welcome the friars whose task it was to reclaim Native Americans from the devil. The precious metals and other sources of wealth in the colonies enriched the Spanish crown and contributed to Spanish predominance in Europe, while the conquerors and their followers thought of themselves as illustrious heroes like Caesar or Alexander. Influenced by the ancient historians and humanism, the early chroniclers included the speeches of both Spaniards and natives such as the Aztec ruler Moctezuma in their histories.

By the 17th century the French and English had joined the hunt for colonies, focusing on North America under leaders such as Englishman John Winthrop, who would become the first governor of the Massachusetts Bay colony in 1629, and Joseph-Antoine de la Barre, who would become governor of New France (present-day Quebec) in 1682. French and English settlers in North America faced native societies that were very different from those in Mexico and Peru. They were not centrally organized monarchies run from the top down, but societies based on discussion and consensus, with a strong tradition of persuasive speech. Europeans allied with native tribes such as the Iroquois, or competed with other European powers for their support. This required diplomacy and speechmaking from both Native Americans and Europeans. Those European diplomats and interpreters who learned Native languages were impressed with the eloquence of Native speakers such as Powhatan, chief of the Powhatan Confederacy, and Garangula, chief of the Onondaga.

RELIGIOUS REFORMATION

Within Europe itself, the most important cultural change of the 16th century was religious reformation, both Protestant and Catholic. The Protestant break with the Roman Catholic Church began with the German monk Martin Luther in the early 16th century and spread through northern Europe. The new Protestant churches, whether Lutheran, Calvinist, Anglican, or one of the many smaller sects, eliminated much of the pageantry and ritual of Catholicism. What was left was the sermon. Preaching took the place of the Catholic mass to become the central experience of Protestant services. Protestantism was advanced by a host of eloquent preachers, from leaders such as Luther and John Calvin to numerous anonymous pastors. The tradition of Protestant preaching would find many heirs in the following centuries, such as John Wesley, who founded Methodism in 1738.

The Catholic Church did not passively accept the loss of much of Europe but fought back vigorously. The church had its own rich tradition of preaching to draw on, and it would not easily allow itself to be excelled. New religious orders founded in the period, such as the Jesuits in 1536, would lay great emphasis on communicating the Catholic message through sermons. Protestantism wasn't the only challenge the church faced. The expanding European empires, led by the Catholic kingdoms of Portugal and Spain, opened up previously unknown or unexplored continents to Catholic missionaries. By the mid-16th century, the Catholic missionary effort extended to every inhabited continent except Australia, then unknown to Europeans. Scorching denunciations of sin in the tradition of Savonarola continued to be issued on both sides of the Atlantic. Cruelties inflicted on Native Americans were denounced by a succession of Catholic preachers including António de Montesinos, Bartolomé de Las Casas, and António Vieira, although the effect they had on actual practices was limited.

The Catholic Reformation, also known as the "Counter-Reformation," narrowed the limits of permissible speech in the Catholic world. Catholic doctrine was standardized and aggressively reasserted at the Council of Trent from 1545 to 1563. The Roman Inquisition (established in 1540 on the model of the earlier Spanish Inquisition of 1481) helped enforce the new, dogmatic model of Catholic belief. The "Index of Forbidden Books," established in 1557, was a list, in theory binding on all Catholics, of the books they were banned from owning or reading. The most celebrated victim of the Catholic Reformation was the Italian scientist Galileo Galilei. Galileo's belief in the "Copernican" theory, that the Earth orbits the Sun rather than the other way around, was defined as heretical by the church due to its perceived contradiction of the Bible. Despite the fact that Galileo recanted under pressure from the Inquisition, he was treated by Protestants, and even some Catholics, as a martyr to intellectual freedom.

THE WARS OF RELIGION AND THE ENGLISH CIVIL WAR

Protestants and Catholics did not compete only through preaching and writing. From the beginnings of the Reformation, different religious factions engaged in armed conflict in the "wars of religion." These included the French civil wars from 1562 to 1598, the Spanish Armada against England in 1588, the Dutch war of independence against Spain from 1568 to 1684, and the greatest and bloodiest of all, the Thirty Years' War that began in Germany and lasted from 1618 to 1648.

The opening of religious debate caused by the Reformation and the rise of the printing press led to a new kind of politics in which political issues were discussed openly in speeches and pamphlets. The degree to which this changed politics varied by the extent of power wielded by censorships in different countries and by differences in political institutions. One of the places where it had the most dramatic effect was England, which combined an erratic censorship with an already existing parliament. Unlike other European parliaments the English parliament was growing rather than diminishing in power. Even rulers like Elizabeth I of England (r. 1558–1603) and her successor James I (r. 1603–25) felt the need to justify themselves before their people.

Conflicts between crown and people in England and its sister kingdoms of Scotland and Ireland eventually led to a series of wars referred to as the English Civil War or the War of the Three Kingdoms beginning in 1642. Religious and political issues were combined in these wars, in which Puritans (reformed Protestants who resisted the "high church" practices of the Protestant Church of England) allied themselves with the English parliament and the Scottish Calvinist radicals known as Covenanters. The king, Charles I (r. 1625–49), Protestant himself, led a group combining English and Scottish royalists and Catholics in an uneasy alliance with Irish Catholics. Both sides used pamphlets and speeches to sway the undecided. In fact, for many of the speeches and sermons of the civil war period, the point was less that they be delivered than that they be printed. Censorship broke down almost completely during the war, and the rival parliamentary presses in London and royalist presses in Oxford spewed forth a plethora of pamphlets and newspapers. Radicals like Thomas Rainborow, part of the Leveler movement to end the monarchy and give voting rights, religious freedom, and political equality to all men (not just high-born men) put forth radical new ideas of democracy. Although the Parliamentarians placed much more emphasis on persuasion than did the Royalists, who appealed to simple loyalty, one of the most influential speeches of all was that made by Charles I at his execution by the victorious Parliamentarians in 1649. By keeping the flames of loyalty alive, it contributed to the later "Restoration" to the throne of his son Charles II in 1660.

By the second half of the 17th century, most of the wars of religion were over, and Europe had settled down as a place where Protestant and Catholic states were willing to live together, if not necessarily to tolerate dissent within their own societies. Despite the sufferings of Galileo, who was accused of heresy and was forced on his knees to renounce his beliefs, science continued to develop, and by the 18th century secularization was well under way. New challenges to tradition emerged in America, as speakers such as lawyer Andrew Hamilton drew on the legacy of the Reformation and the English Civil War to call for increased freedom.

Speeches

LORENZO DE' MEDICI
(1449–1492)
On the Pazzi Conspiracy
Florence, Italy

May 1478

Scholar, poet, and musician, brilliant "Lorenzo the Magnificent" ruled the Florentine Republic—the center of the early Italian Renaissance—from the time he was 20 in 1469. The Renaissance, a period of rapid cultural change and flowering of literature, arts, and humanist philosophy, began in Italy in the 1400s and had spread through Europe by the 1600s. Lorenzo de' Medici came from a prosperous family of bankers, whose clients included the Roman Catholic popes; Medici wealth made possible his calling as a patron of the arts. Among the illustrious artists he supported were Italians Michelangelo, Botticelli, and Leonardo da Vinci. Medici was a popular politician and diplomat, as he was tolerant and clever in his dealings with people. Although the Medici family rarely had an official title in the running of the city, they ruled Florence for many decades. Other banking families, such as the Pazzi and Salviati, grew jealous of Medici power. One rival even emerged in the figure of Pope Sixtus IV, who hoped to expand the territory of the Papal States, in part by defeating the Medici and putting

his own nephew, Girolamo Riario, in power in Florence. On April 26, 1478, members of the Pazzi and Salviati families, including the Archbishop of Pisa, with the connivance of Pope Sixtus, attempted to take over the city-state. This event is known as the Pazzi Conspiracy. While Lorenzo and his younger brother, Giuliano de' Medici, were attending mass in the Duomo, Florence's cathedral, assassins stabbed Giuliano to death and wounded Lorenzo, who escaped. The archbishop and his party, having gone to the palace to take control, were seized by guards and hanged from upper windows. The Pazzi were hunted down by angry citizens and their property confiscated. Meanwhile, frustrated in his ambitions, Sixtus served Florence with an interdict (a form of excommunication that can be placed upon a city). With his own army, and that of traditional papal ally, King Ferdinand I of Naples, the pope prepared to attack Florence. Lorenzo assembled the town fathers and offered to leave the city if it would help save it, as reported by the Florentine Niccolò Machiavelli in his *History of Florence*.

Most excellent signors, and you, magnificent citizens, I know not whether I have more occasion to weep with you for the events which have recently occurred, or to rejoice in the circumstances with which they have been attended.

Certainly, when I think with what virulence of united deceit and hatred I have been attacked, and my brother murdered, I cannot but mourn and grieve from my heart, from my very soul. Yet when I consider with what promptitude, anxiety, love, and unanimity of the whole city my brother has been avenged and myself defended, I am not only compelled to rejoice, but feel myself honored and exalted; for if experience has shown me that I had more enemies than I apprehended, it has also proved that I possess more warm and resolute friends than I could ever have hoped for.

I must therefore grieve with you for the injuries others have suffered, and rejoice in the attachment you have exhibited toward myself; but I feel more aggrieved by the injuries committed, since they are so unusual, so unexampled, and (as I trust you believe) so undeserved on our part. Think, magnificent citizens, to what a dreadful point ill fortune has reduced our family, when among friends, amidst our own relatives, nay, in God's holy temple, we have found our greatest foes. Those who are in danger turn to their friends for assistance; they call upon their relatives for aid; but we found ours armed, and resolved on our destruction. Those who are persecuted, either from public or private motives, flee for refuge to the altars. But where others are safe, we are assassinated; where parricides and assassins are secure, the Medici find their murderers.

But God, who has not hitherto abandoned our house, again saved us, and has undertaken the defense of our just cause. What injury have we done to justify so intense desire of our destruction? Certainly those who have shown themselves so much our enemies, never received any private wrong from us; for, had we wished to injure them, they would not have had an opportunity of injuring us. If they attribute public grievances to ourselves (supposing any had been done to them), they do the greater injustices to you, to this palace, to the majesty of this government, by assuming that on our account you would act unfairly to any of your citizens. And such a supposition, as we all know, is contradicted by every view of the circumstances; for we, had we been able, and you, had we wished it, would never have contributed to so abominable a design.

Whoever inquires into the truth of these matters, will find that our family has always been exalted by you, and from this sole cause, that we have endeavored by kindness, liberality, and beneficence, to do good to all; and if we have honored strangers, when did we ever injure our relatives? If our enemies' conduct has been adopted, to gratify their desire for power (as would seem to be the case from their having taken possession of the palace and brought an armed force into the piazza), the infamous, ambitious, and detestable motive is at once disclosed. If they were actuated by envy and hatred of our authority, they offend you rather than us; for from you we have derived all the influence we possess. Certainly usurped power deserves to be detested; but not distinctions conceded for acts of kindness, generosity, and magnificence. And you all know that our family never attained any rank to which this palace and your united consent did not raise it.

Cosmo, my grandfather, did not return from exile with arms and violence, but by your unanimous desire and approbation. It was not my father, old and infirm, who defended the government against so many enemies, but yourselves by your authority and benevolence defended him; neither could I, after his death, being then a boy, have maintained the position of my house except by your favor and advice. Nor should we ever be able to conduct the affairs of this republic, if you did not contribute to our support. Therefore, I know not the reason of their hatred toward us, or what just cause they have of envy. Let them direct their enmity against their own ancestors, who, by their pride and avarice, lost the reputation which ours, by very opposite conduct, were enabled to acquire.

But let it be granted we have greatly injured them, and that they are justified in seeking our ruin; why do they come and take possession of the palace? Why enter into league with the pope and the king, against the liberties of this republic? Why break the long-continued peace of Italy? They have no excuse for this; they ought to confine their vengeance to those who do them wrong, and not confound private animosities with public grievances.

Hence it is that since their defeat our misfortune is the greater; for on their account the pope and the king make war upon us, and this war, they say, is directed against my family and myself. And would to God that this were true; then the remedy would be sure and unfailing, for I would not be so base a citizen as to prefer my own safety to yours. I would at once resolve to ensure your security, even though my own destruction were the immediate and inevitable consequence.

But as the wrongs committed by princes are usually concealed under some less offensive covering, they have adopted this plea to hide their more abominable purpose. If, however, you think otherwise, I am in your hands; it is with you to do with me what you please. You are my fathers, my protectors, and whatever you command me to do I will perform most willingly. Nor will I ever refuse, when you find occasion to require it, to close the war with my own blood which was commenced with that of my brother.

Source: Machiavelli, Niccolò. *History of Florence.* Edited by Charles W. Colby. New York: Colonial Press, 1901.

GIOVANNI PICO DELLA MIRANDOLA
(1463–1494)
"Oration on the Dignity of Man"
Rome, Italy
1486

Giovanni Pico della Mirandola was a Renaissance humanist, a prodigious thinker who turned to classical texts to study science and philosophy in an attempt to reconcile Christian beliefs with the thought of Plato and Aristotle. As a child, Pico studied ancient languages, and as a brilliant young man of 14, he entered the university to study church law and, later, philosophy. He joined the court of wealthy scholar and art patron Lorenzo de' Medici in Florence (SEE Lorenzo de' Medici's speech, page 113) and by 23 had written a treatise he called the *900 Theses*. To accompany it, he wrote "Oration on the Dignity of Man." This would become one of the most important documents—the "Manifesto"—of the Italian Renaissance, and a defining moment in Western civilization. Pico wrote his "Oration" with the intention of addressing a council of scholars in Rome, who would debate the merits of his *900 Theses*. Pope Innocent VIII investigated the *The-*

ses for heresy and would not permit the debate. Pico was imprisoned for several years and died mysteriously soon after, in 1494. The address was never delivered as Pico envisioned. In the oration's opening paragraphs, Pico imagines God speaking to man—to Adam, precisely—giving humankind free will to "fashion yourself in the form you may prefer." He has God say that, from a point in the world's middle, "it will be in your power to descend to the lower, brutish forms of life; [or] you will be able, through your own decision, to rise again to the superior orders whose life is divine." This new idea of man's power to determine his own path to perfection broke with Christian tradition that held man was born sinful. With other humanists, Pico believed in a dignified, not corrupt, man, who could reach his own highest aims—even become one with God—by choosing a life of contemplation and discipline instead of sensual pursuits.

Most esteemed Fathers, I have read in the ancient writings of the Arabians that Abdala the Saracen on being asked what, on this stage, so to say, of the world, seemed to him most evocative of wonder, replied that there was nothing to be seen more marvelous than man. And that celebrated exclamation of Hermes Trismegistus, "What a great miracle is man, Asclepius!" confirms this opinion.

And still, as I reflected upon the basis assigned for these estimations, I was not fully persuaded by the diverse reasons advanced for the pre-eminence of human nature; that man is the intermediary between creatures, that he is the familiar of the gods above him as he is the lord of the beings beneath him; that, by the acuteness of his senses, the inquiry of his reason and the light of his intelligence, he is the interpreter of nature, set midway between the timeless unchanging and the flux of time; the living union (as the Persians say), the very marriage hymn of the world, and by David's testimony but little lower than the angels.

These reasons are all, without question, of great weight; nevertheless, they do not touch the principal reasons, those, that is to say, which justify man's unique right for such unbounded admiration. Why, I asked, should we not admire the angels themselves and the beatific choirs more?

At long last, however, I feel that I have come to some understanding of why man is the most fortunate of living things and, consequently, deserving of all admiration; of what may be the condition in the hierarchy of beings assigned to him, which draws upon him the envy, not of the brutes alone, but of the astral beings and of the very intelligences which dwell beyond the confines of the world. A thing surpassing belief and smiting the soul with wonder. Still, how could it be otherwise? For it is on this ground that man is, with complete justice, considered and called a great miracle and a being worthy of all admiration.

Hear then, oh Fathers, precisely what this condition of man is; and in the name of your humanity, grant me your benign audition as I pursue this theme.

God the Father, the Mightiest Architect, had already raised, according to the precepts of His hidden wisdom, this world we see, the cosmic dwelling of divinity, a temple most august. He had already adorned the supercelestial region with Intelligences, infused the heavenly globes with the life of immortal souls and set the fermenting dung-heap of the inferior world teeming with every form of animal life. But when this work was done, the Divine Artificer still longed for some creature which might comprehend the meaning of so vast an achievement, which might be moved with love at its beauty and smitten with awe at its grandeur.

When, consequently, all else had been completed (as both Moses and Timaeus testify), in the very last place, He bethought Himself of bringing forth man. Truth was, however, that there remained no archetype according to which He might fashion a new offspring, nor in His treasure-houses the wherewithal to endow a new son with a fitting inheritance, nor any place, among the seats of the universe, where this new creature might dispose himself to contemplate the world. All space was already filled; all things had been distributed in the highest, the middle and the lowest orders. Still, it was not in the nature of the power of the Father to fail in this last creative élan; nor was it in the nature of that supreme Wisdom to hesitate through lack of counsel in so crucial a matter; nor, finally, in the nature of His beneficent love to compel the creature destined to praise the divine generosity in all other things to find it wanting in himself.

At last, the Supreme Maker decreed that this creature, to whom He could give nothing wholly his own, should have a share in the particular endowment of every other creature. Taking man, therefore, this creature of indeterminate image, He set him in the middle of the world and thus spoke to him:

"We have given you, O Adam, no visage proper to yourself, nor endowment properly your own, in order that whatever place, whatever form, whatever gifts you may, with premeditation, select, these same you may have and possess through your own judgment and decision. The nature of all other creatures is defined and restricted within laws which We have laid down.

"You, by contrast, impeded by no such restrictions, may, by your own free will, to whose custody We have assigned you, trace for yourself the lineaments of your own nature. I have placed you at the very center of the world, so that from that vantage point you may with greater ease glance round about you on all that the world contains. We have made you a creature neither of heaven nor of earth, neither mortal nor immortal, in order that you may, as the free and proud shaper of your own being, fashion yourself in the form you may prefer. It will be in your power to descend to the lower, brutish forms of life; you will be able, through your own decision, to rise again to the superior orders whose life is divine."

We have made you a creature neither of heaven nor of earth,
neither mortal nor immortal, in order that you may,
as the free and proud shaper of your own being, fashion yourself
in the form you may prefer. —*Pico della Mirandola*

Oh unsurpassed generosity of God the Father, Oh wondrous and unsurpassable felicity of man, to whom it is granted to have what he chooses, to be what he wills to be! The brutes, from the moment of their birth, bring with them, as Lucilius says, "from their mother's womb" all that they will ever possess. The highest spiritual beings were, from the very moment of creation, or soon thereafter, fixed in the mode of being which would be theirs through measureless eternities.

But upon man, at the moment of his creation, God bestowed seeds pregnant with all possibilities, the germs of every form of life. Whichever of these a man shall cultivate, the same will mature and bear fruit in him. If vegetative, he will become a plant; if sensual, he will become brutish; if rational, he will reveal himself a heavenly being; if intellectual, he will be an angel and the son of God. And if, dissatisfied with the lot of all creatures, he should recollect himself into the center of his own unity, he will there become one spirit with God, in the solitary darkness of the Father, Who is set above all things, himself transcend all creatures.

Who then will not look with awe upon this our chameleon, or who, at least, will look with greater admiration on any other being? . . .

It is not the bark that makes the tree, but its insensitive and unresponsive nature; nor the hide which makes the beast of burden, but its brute and sensual soul; nor the orbicular form which makes the heavens, but their harmonious order. Finally, it is not freedom from a body, but its spiritual intelligence, which makes the angel.

If you see a man dedicated to his stomach, crawling on the ground, you see a plant and not a man; or if you see a man bedazzled by the empty forms of the imagination, as by the wiles of Calypso, and through their alluring solicitations made a slave to his own senses, you see a brute and not a man. If, however, you see a philosopher, judging and distinguishing all things according to the rule of reason, him shall you hold in veneration, for he is a creature of heaven and not of earth; if, finally, a pure contemplator, unmindful of the body, wholly withdrawn into the inner chambers of the mind, here indeed is neither a creature of earth nor a heavenly creature, but some higher divinity, clothed in human flesh.

Who then will not look with wonder upon man, upon man who, not without reason in the sacred Mosaic and Christian writings, is designated sometimes by the term "all flesh" and sometimes by the term "every creature," because he molds, fashions and transforms himself into the likeness of all flesh and assumes the characteristic power of every form of life? This is why Evantes the Persian in his exposition of the Chaldean theology, writes that man has no inborn and proper semblance, but many which are extraneous and adventitious: whence the Chaldean saying: "Enosh hu shinnujim vekammah tebhaoth haj"—"man is a living creature of varied, multiform and ever-changing nature."

A central figure of the Italian Rennaissance, Giovanni Pico della Mirandola undertook to refashion the concept of man as a creature capable of reaching for perfection. The Catholic Church saw heresy in his ideas and imprisoned him. Painting by unknown 16th-century artist, Palazzo Pitti, Florence *(Scala/Art Resource, NY)*

But what is the purpose of all this? That we may understand—since we have been born into this condition of being what we choose to be—that we ought to be sure above all else that it may never be said against us that, born to a high position, we failed to appreciate it, but fell instead to the estate of brutes and uncomprehending beasts of burden; and that the saying of Aspah the Prophet, "You are all Gods and sons of the Most High," might rather be true; and finally that we may not, through abuse of the generosity of a most indulgent Father, pervert the free option which he has given us from a saving to a damning gift.

Let a certain saving ambition invade our souls so that, impatient of mediocrity, we pant after the highest things and (since, if we will, we can) bend all our efforts to their attainment. Let us disdain things of earth, hold as little worth even the astral orders and, putting behind us all the things of this world, hasten to that court beyond the world, closest to the most exalted Godhead. There, as the sacred mysteries tell us, the Seraphim, Cherubim and Thrones occupy the first places; but, unable to yield to them, and impatient of any second place, let us emulate their dignity and glory. And, if we will it, we shall be inferior to them in nothing.

Source: Pico della Mirandola, Giovanni. *Oration on the Dignity of Man.* Translated by A. Robert Caponigri. Washington, D. C.: Regnery Publishing, 1996.

GIROLAMO SAVONAROLA

(1452–1498)

"Let Me Be Persecuted"

Florence, Italy

Spring 1497

Girolamo Savonarola was born in 1452 in northern Italy. He joined the Dominican order and soon began writing condemnations of the lax morals of Renaissance clergy. As a religious reformer, he set the stage for Martin Luther's coming challenge to the Catholic Church (in 1521), which would start the Protestant Reformation. Savonarola arrived in Florence in 1491 to head the Dominican house there. The ascetic monk found the secular pope, Alexander VI of the powerful Italian Borgia family, particularly corrupt. Among other transgressions, Pope Alexander held lavish parties with dancing, enriched the Borgia family, and appeared openly with his four children (he was obliged under church tradition to remain celibate). Savonarola's popular jeremiads (long speeches or sermons of complaint) urging clerical reform—and a return to goodness and charity—infuriated Alexander. Shortly after the ruler of Florence, Lorenzo de' Medici (r. 1469–92), died in 1492, leaving his son Piero to manage Florence, King Charles VIII of France (r. 1483–98) marched on Italy with territorial ambitions. In the views of many, Piero capitulated too easily, and angry Florentines drove the Medici family from the city. In the Medici's absence, Savonarola emerged as one of the city's most extraordinary leaders. His followers assembled thousands of young boys, dressed in white smocks, who marched in procession to sermons and brought "sinful" objects such as mirrors, playing cards, wigs, and even paintings, to throw on Savonarola's "bonfires of the vanities." Defiant citizens rioted in the streets and an epidemic of plague roiled the city. During Lent (in spring, the 40 days before Easter) of 1497, Savonarola's sermons were attended by the loyal Florentine notary, Lorenzo Violi, who recorded these fragments. (On occasion, Savonarola refers to himself as The Friar.) The pope, angered by Savonarola's words, excommunicated him just weeks later. When Savonarola would not quit preaching, the Florentine fathers condemned him to death. He was hanged and burned at the stake the next year.

The Church has been ruined by wealth. Would you say then, O Friar, that the Church should have no temporal wealth? Nay, it would be heresy to say this, for we cannot believe that St. Sylvester would have accepted riches for the Church, or St. Gregory confirmed her in possession of them, had it been unlawful so to do; and for this reason we submit ourselves to the Church of Rome.

Oh, but which is best, that she have riches or have them not? This is a serious question, for we all see that for the sake of wealth she has been led to do evil, and of this I need give you no proof. We will therefore reply, but in no absolute sense, even as the mariner who does not absolutely wish to cast his riches into the sea, but only seeks to escape danger, and will say that the Church would be better without riches, since she could thus be drawn nearer to God. Wherefore I say to my friars, "Seek to adhere to poverty, for when riches enter among you, death too comes in.". . .

Whoever has usurped any ecclesiastical property, let him restore it to the Church of Christ, if there be any good pastors; if not, let him give it to the poor without regard to the canonical law. You, O canonist, may say what you will, but my chief canon shall ever be that of charity. I bid you take this for your rule, that no canon can be opposed to charity and conscience, for, if so, it is a false canon. . . .

What is all this war stirred against me? What is its cause? Only because I have discovered the corruption of the wicked. . . . But I will do, even as Frà Jacopone in Consistory, who on being bidden to preach in a certain way, looked round and repeated three times, "I marvel that the earth does not split and engulf you on account of your sins."

119

The earth teems with bloodshed, yet the priests take no heed; rather by their evil example they bring spiritual death upon all. They have withdrawn from God, and their piety consists in spending their nights with harlots, and all their days in chattering in choirs; and the altar is made a place of traffic for the clergy. They say that God hath no care of the world, that all comes by chance, nor do they believe that Christ is present in the sacrament. . . .

Come here you ribald Church. The Lord says: I gave you beautiful vestments, but you have made idols of them. You have dedicated the sacred vessels to vainglory, the sacraments to simony; you have become a shameless harlot in your lusts; you are lower than a beast, you are a monster of abomination. Once, you felt shame for your sins, but now you are shameless. Once, anointed priests called their sons nephews; but now they speak no more of their nephews, but always and everywhere of their sons.

Everywhere you have made a public place and raised a house of ill fame. And what does the harlot? She sits on the throne of Solomon, and solicits all the world. He that has gold is made welcome and may do as he will, but he that seeks to do good is driven forth. O Lord, my Lord, they will allow no good to be done! And thus, O prostitute Church, you have displayed your foulness to the whole world, and stink unto Heaven. You have multiplied your fornications in Italy, in France, in Spain, and all other parts.

Behold, I will put forth My hand, says the Lord, I will smite you, you infamous wretch. My sword shall fall on your children, on your house of shame, on your harlots, on your palaces, and my justice shall be made known. Earth and heaven, the angels, the good and the wicked, all shall accuse you, and no man shall be with you. I will give you into your enemy's hand. . . .

O priests and friars, you, whose evil example has entombed this people in the sepulcher of ceremonial. I tell you this sepulcher shall be burst asunder, for Christ will revive His Church in His spirit. Think you that St. Francis, St. Dominic, and the other saints have forgotten their creed, and no longer intercede for it? We must all pray for its renovation.

Write to France and to Germany; write everywhere to this effect: That Friar you know of, bids you all seek the Lord and implore His coming. Haste you at full speed, O you messengers! Think you that we alone are good? That there be no servants of God in other places? Jesus Christ has many servants, and great numbers of them, concealed in Germany, France and Spain, are now bewailing this evil.

In all cities and strong places, in all manors and convents, there be some inspired with this fire of zeal. They send to whisper somewhat in my ear, and I reply—Remain concealed until you hear the summons—*Lazare, veni foras!* I am here, because the Lord appointed me to this place, and I await His call, but then will I send forth a mighty

Impassioned Catholic preacher Girolamo Savonarola fatally risked his own excommunication and death by fervently denouncing sin and papal corruption. After a painting by Fra Bartolomeo, ca. 1498 *(Museo di San Marco, Florence)*

RHETORICAL DEVICE

Climax: Arranging phrases or sentences in the order of growing importance, to arrive at a finish.

Come here to this gate! Mr. Gorbachev, open this gate!
Mr. Gorbachev, tear down this wall! —*Ronald Reagan*

You have become a shameless harlot in your lusts; you are lower
than a beast, you are a monster of abomination. —*Savonarola*

Where is America going, and who will unite her and be her guide?
Alone and as one people she is rising. Alone she is fighting.
Alone she will win. —*José Martí*

Whatever happens, the flame of the French resistance must not be extinguished
and will not be extinguished. —*Charles de Gaulle*

---

cry that shall resound throughout Christendom, and make the corpse of the Church to tremble even as trembled the body of Lazarus at the voice of our Lord.

Many of you say that excommunications will be decreed; but I repeat to you that more than excommunication is intended. For my part, I beseech You, O Lord, that it may come quickly. What, have you no fear? Not I, for they seek to excommunicate me because I do no evil. Bear this excommunication aloft on a lance and open the gates to it. I will reply unto it, and if I do not amaze you, then you may say what you will. I shall make so many faces turn pale, that they will seem to you a multitude; and I will send forth a shout that will cause the world to tremble and shake.

I know well that there be one in Rome that strives against me without cease. But that man is not moved by religious zeal, but only hates me because he is ever crawling after great lords and potentates. Others say: The Friar has yielded, he has sent one of his friends to Rome. I can tell you that folks there hold not these views; and that if I wished to play the part of a flatterer, I should not now be in Florence, nor clad in a tattered robe, and would be able to escape my present danger.

But I seek none of these things, O Lord; I seek only Your cross. Let me be persecuted. I ask this grace of You. Let me not die in my bed, but let me give my blood for You, even as You gave Yours for me. . . . Meanwhile doubt not, my children, for the Lord will certainly lend us His aid.

Source: Villari, Pasquale. *The Life and Times of Girolamo Savonarola.* Translated by Linda Villari. New York: Scribner, 1888.

ANTÓNIO DE MONTESINOS
(died 1540)
"Are They Not Men?"
Santo Domingo, Española
December 1511

Dominican friars arrived about 1510 to minister to the Spanish colony on Española (or Hispaniola, now Haiti and the Dominican Republic). The colony had grown rapidly after Christopher Columbus's first visit to the island in 1492, and the priests were aghast to discover the cruelty and semi-slavery directed at the native people of the Indies. The *encomienda* system, established by Spain in 1493, allowed up to 300 Indians per conquistador, or *encomendero,* to be used for forced labor as long as they were indoctrinated into Christian teachings. Several hundred thousand native people had perished from disease and mistreatment in less than 20 years. In 1511 on the fourth Sunday in Advent, Catholic preacher António de Montesinos climbed to the pulpit to rebuke his parishioners for their conduct and became one of the first Europeans to speak up for the people of the New World. This ser-mon so moved the conscience of one hearer, Bartolomé de Las Casas (*SEE* Las Casas's sermon, page 132), that he gave up his Indian serfs and returned to Spain to plead the cause of the Indians with the king with some success. Las Casas wrote a prodigious account of the time, *History of the Indies,* and included the story of António de Montesinos's sermon. He noted that Diego Columbus (son of Christopher Columbus) was in the audience that Sunday—Columbus had just been appointed Admiral of the Indies—and he described Montesinos as the liveliest and most accomplished speaker among the Dominicans. His "talent lay in a certain sternness when reproaching faults," Las Casas reported. Montesinos's opening line is from St. John the Baptist, who said, "I am the voice of one cry-ing in the wilderness," when asked his name by the Pharisees.

❧

I am the voice of one crying in the wilderness.

In order to make your sins known to you I have mounted this pulpit, I who am the voice of Christ crying in the wilderness of this island. And therefore it behooves you to listen to me, not with indifference but with all your heart and senses. For this voice will be the strangest, the harshest and hardest, the most terrifying that you ever heard or expected to hear.

This voice declares that you are in mortal sin, and live and die therein by reason of the cruelty and tyranny that you practice on these innocent people.

Tell me, by what right or justice do you hold these Indians in such cruel and hor-rible slavery? By what right do you wage such detestable wars on these people who lived mildly and peacefully in their own lands, where you have consumed infinite numbers of them with unheard of murders and desolations?

Why do you so greatly oppress and fatigue them, not giving them enough to eat or caring for them when they fall ill from excessive labors, so that they die or rather are slain by you, so that you may extract and acquire gold every day?

And what care do you take that they receive religious instruction and come to know their God and creator, or that they be baptized, hear mass, or observe holidays and Sundays?

Are they not men?

Do they not have rational souls? Are you not bound to love them as you love yourselves?

How can you lie in such profound and lethargic slumber?

Be sure that in your present state you can no more be saved than the Moors or Turks who do not have and do not want the faith of Jesus Christ.

Source: de Montesinos, António. "Sermon of Father Montesinos." *Readings in Latin American Civilization.* Edited by Benjamin Keen. Cambridge: Riverside Press, 1955, p. 88.

MOCTEZUMA II
(ca. 1466–1520)
Welcoming Hernán Cortés to Mexico
Tenochtitlán, or City of Mexico
November 8, 1519

Where Mexico City now stands once lay Tenochtitlán, the flourishing capital city of the Aztecs (or Mexicas) on Lake Texcoco. A quarter of a million people inhabited this island metropolis, which was crossed by canals and linked to the lakeshore by causeways (raised road ways across wet ground or water). Moctezuma II, the last great king (r. 1502–20), ruled while the Aztec Empire was at a peak of wealth and power. Then in 1519 Hernán Cortés arrived on the Yucatán coast with 600 conquistadores, looking for gold. As he marched inland, Cortés picked up allies from those cities and regions, such as Cempoala and Tlaxcala, that were oppressed by the Aztecs. Earlier historians have said that Moctezuma unfortunately assumed Cortés was the god Quetzalcoatl returning from the East (as supposedly had been foretold by Aztec lore), and he sent envoys to present gold finery to the god Cortés was presumed to be. Present-day historians, however, attribute that idea to Spanish influence and mythologizing. In any case, the Aztec king dressed in his finest,

and with nobles in attendance, met the Spaniard with fabulous gold necklaces and a speech of welcome. Cortés replied, "We have come to your house in Mexico as friends. There is nothing to fear." The Aztec king was soon imprisoned by Cortés, and murdered eight months later. The conquistadores laid siege, plundering, burning, and killing, until the ruined Tenochtitlán surrendered on August 13, 1521. There are two versions of Moctezuma's speech welcoming Cortés, one from Cortés's *Letters of Cortés to Charles V,* the other from the *Florentine Codex,* a native account. There are many reasons why the speeches seem so different. The conversation between Moctezuma and Cortés required two translators: a native woman who translated Moctezuma's Nahuatl language into Mayan, and a Spaniard who spoke Mayan fluently. Cortés recorded his version shortly after, while the Mexican account was written down (assisted by a Spanish priest) 35 years later by elderly natives who had been present at the conquest.

Moctezuma's speech from the *Florentine Codex*

Our lord, you are weary. The journey has tired you, but now you have arrived on the earth. You have come to your city, Mexico. You have come here to sit on your throne, to sit under its canopy.

The kings who have gone before, your representatives, guarded it and preserved it for your coming. The kings Itzcoatl, Motecuhzoma the Elder, Axayacatl, Tizoc and Ahuitzol ruled for you in the City of Mexico. The people were protected by their swords and sheltered by their shields.

Do the kings know the destiny of those they left behind, their posterity? If only they are watching! If only they can see what I see!

No, it is not a dream. I am not walking in my sleep. I am not seeing you in my dreams. . . . I have seen you at last! I have met you face to face! I was in agony for five days, for ten days, with my eyes fixed on the Region of the Mystery. And now you have come out of the clouds and mists to sit on your throne again.

This was foretold by the kings who governed your city, and now it has taken place. You have come back to us; you have come down from the sky. Rest now, and take possession of your royal houses. Welcome to your land, my lords!

Moctezuma greets Hernán Cortés with a gold necklace, in a miniature from the *History of the Indians,* by Diego Durán, 1579 *(Bridgeman-Giraudon/Art Resource, NY)*

Moctezuma's speech from Cortés, *Letters of Cortés*

We have known for a long time, from the chronicles of our forefathers, that neither I, nor those who inhabit this country, are descendants from the aborigines of it, but from strangers who came to it from very distant parts.

And we also hold that our race was brought to these parts by a lord, whose vassals they all were, and who returned to his native country, and had many descendants, and had built towns where they were living. When, therefore, he wished to take them away with him they would not go, nor still less receive him as their ruler, so he departed.

And we have always held that those who descended from him would come to subjugate this country and us, as his vassals. And according to the direction from which you say you come, which is where the sun rises, and from what you tell us of your great lord, or king, who has sent you here, we believe, and hold for certain, that he is our rightful sovereign, especially as you tell us that since many days he has had news of us.

Hence you may be sure that we shall obey you, and hold you as the representative of this great lord of whom you speak, and that in this there will be no lack or deception; and throughout the whole country you may command at your will (I speak of what I possess in my dominions), because you will be obeyed, and recognized, and all we possess is at your disposal.

Since you are in your rightful place, and in your own homes, rejoice and rest, free from all the trouble of the journey and wars which you have had, for I am well aware of all that has happened to you between Puntunchan and here, and I know very well that the people of Cempoal and Tascaltecal have told you many evil things respecting me.

Do not believe more than you see with your own eyes, especially from those who are my enemies, and were my vassals, yet rebelled against me on your coming (as they say), in order to help you. I know they have told you also that I have houses with walls of gold, and that the furniture of my halls, and other things of my service, were also of gold, and that I am, or make myself, a god, and many other things. The houses you have seen are of lime and stone and earth.

Look at me, and see that I am flesh and bones, the same as you, and everybody, and that I am mortal and tangible. Look how they have lied to you! It is true indeed that I have some things of gold, which have been left to me by my forefathers. All that I possess, you may have whenever you wish.

I shall now go to other houses where I live; but you will be provided here with everything necessary for you and your people, and you shall suffer no annoyance, for you are in your own house and country.

Sources: Cortés, Hernán. *Five Letters of Relation to the Emperor Charles V.* Translated by Francis Augustus MacNutt. Cleveland: A. H. Clark, 1908.

Leon-Portilla, Miguel. *Broken Spears: The Aztec Account of the Conquest of Mexico.* Boston: Beacon Press, 1962, p. 64. Copyright © 1962, 1990 by Miguel Leon-Portilla. Reprinted by permission of Beacon Press, Boston.

MARTIN LUTHER
(1483–1546)
"I Stand Here and Can Say No More"
Worms, Germany
April 18, 1521

Martin Luther was 22 when he felt called to enter a monastery. Two years later he became a priest, and shortly afterward began teaching theology at the University of Wittenberg. In October 1517 he set off the Protestant Reformation by posting on a church door The Ninety-five Theses, or arguments, against the Roman Catholic Church. He hoped to reform church doctrine, especially those teachings that declared that individuals could have no personal relationship with God except through the help of priests, and that permitted the sale of indulgences, or pardons for sin. (At the time, Pope Leo X [r. 1513–21] was raising money to rebuild Rome's Basilica of St. Peter by selling such pardons.) Luther also rejected the pope's authority over Germany. The theses were rapidly distributed throughout Europe. A papal bull (pope's proclamation, or edict) was issued in 1520 that Luther must recant or face excommunication, but he publicly burned the papers in defiance. Not surprisingly, Pope Leo excommunicated him as a heretic on January 3, 1521. Luther was called for questioning by Holy Roman Emperor Charles V before the Diet (a legislative assembly) at Worms (a city in southern Germany). He was asked whether he still maintained the truth of his writings, and he replied with this speech. A controversy exists over whether Luther actually said, "I stand here and can say no more." The diet's final decision—the Edict of Worms—ruled that Luther was a heretic whose writings were henceforth banned and who could be killed as an outlaw. A supporter, Prince Frederick III, hid Luther for a year in Wartburg Castle to protect him. There he kept himself busy translating the Bible from Latin into German, the first translation of the Bible into the everyday language of a people. He escaped serious punishment and went on to spread the gospel of Protestantism.

***

Most serene Emperor, and you illustrious princes and gracious lords—

I this day appear before you in all humility, according to your command, and I implore your majesty and your august highnesses, by the mercies of God, to listen with favor to the defense of a cause which I am well assured is just and right. I ask pardon, if by reason of my ignorance, I am wanting in the manners that befit a court, for I have not been brought up in king's palaces, but in the seclusion of a cloister.

Two questions were yesterday put to me by his imperial majesty; the first, whether I was the author of the books whose titles were read; the second, whether I wished to revoke or defend the doctrine I have taught. I answered the first, and I adhere to that answer.

As to the second, I have composed writings on very different subjects. In some I have discussed Faith and Good Works, in a spirit at once so pure, clear, and Christian, that even my adversaries themselves, far from finding anything to censure, confess that these writings are profitable, and deserve to be perused by devout persons. The pope's bull, violent as it is, acknowledges this. What, then, should I be doing if I were now to retract these writings? Wretched man! I alone, of all men living, should be abandoning truths approved by the unanimous voice of friends and enemies, and opposing doctrines that the whole world glories in confessing!

I have composed, secondly, certain works against popery, wherein I have attacked such as by false doctrines, irregular lives, and scandalous examples, afflict the Christian world, and ruin the bodies and souls of men. And is not this confirmed by the grief of all who fear God? Is it not manifest that the laws and human doctrines of

> I stand here and can say no more. —*Martin Luther*

the popes entangle, vex, and distress the consciences of the faithful, while the crying and endless extortions of Rome engulf the property and wealth of Christendom, and more particularly of this illustrious nation?

If I were to revoke what I have written on that subject, what should I do . . . but strengthen this tyranny, and open a wider door to so many and flagrant impieties? Bearing down all resistance with fresh fury, we should behold these proud men swell, foam, and rage more than ever! And not merely would the yoke which now weighs down Christians be made more grinding by my retraction—it would thereby become, so to speak, lawful—for, by my retraction, it would receive confirmation from your most serene majesty, and all the states of the Empire. Great God! I should thus be like to an infamous cloak, used to hide and cover over every kind of malice and tyranny.

In the third and last place, I have written some books against private individuals, who had undertaken to defend the tyranny of Rome by destroying the faith. I freely confess that I may have attacked such persons with more violence than was consistent with my profession as an ecclesiastic. I do not think of myself as a saint; but neither can I retract these books, because I should, by so doing, sanction the impieties of my opponents, and they would thence take occasion to crush God's people with still more cruelty.

Yet, as I am a mere man, and not God, I will defend myself after the example of Jesus Christ, who said: "If I have spoken evil, bear witness against me." How much more should I, who am but dust and ashes, and so prone to error, desire that every one should bring forward what he can against my doctrine.

Therefore, most serene Emperor, and you illustrious princes, and all, whether high or low, who hear me, I implore you by the mercies of God to prove to me by the writings of the prophets and apostles that I am in error. As soon as I shall be convinced, I will instantly retract all my errors, and will myself be the first to seize my writings, and commit them to the flames.

What I have just said I think will clearly show that I have well considered and weighed the dangers to which I am exposing myself. But far from being dismayed by them, I rejoice exceedingly to see the Gospel this day, as of old, a cause of disturbance and disagreement. It is the character and destiny of God's word. "I came not to send peace unto the earth, but a sword," said Jesus Christ. God is wonderful and awful in His counsels. Let us have a care, lest in our endeavors to arrest discords, we be bound to fight against the holy word of God and bring down upon our heads a frightful deluge of inextricable dangers, present disaster, and everlasting desolations. . . .

Let us have a care lest the reign of the young and noble prince, the Emperor Charles, on whom, next to God, we build so many hopes, should not only commence, but continue and terminate its course under the most fatal auspices. I might cite examples drawn from the oracles of God. I might speak of Pharaohs, of kings of Babylon, or of Israel, who were never more contributing to their own ruin than when, by measures in appearances most prudent, they thought to establish their authority! "God removeth the mountains and they know not."

In speaking thus, I do not suppose that such noble princes have need of my poor judgment; but I wish to acquit myself of a duty that Germany has a right to expect from her children. And so commending myself to your august majesty, and your most serene highnesses, I beseech you in all humility, not to permit the hatred of my enemies to rain upon me an indignation I have not deserved.

Since your most serene majesty and your high mightinesses require of me a simple, clear and direct answer, I will give one, and it is this: I cannot submit my faith either to the pope or to the council, because it is as clear as noonday that they have fallen into error and even into glaring inconsistency with themselves.

If, then, I am not convinced by proof from Holy Scripture, or by cogent reasons, if I am not satisfied by the very text I have cited, and if my judgment is not in this way brought into subjection to God's word, I neither can nor will retract anything, for it can not be right for a Christian to speak against his conscience.

I stand here and can say no more. God help me. Amen.

Source: Bryan, William Jennings, ed. *The World's Famous Orations.* New York: Funk & Wagnall, 1906.

HERNÁN CORTÉS
(1485–1547)
"These Shabbily Dressed Men"
Mexico City, Mexico

June 1524

Hernán Cortés was born in 1485 in Medellín, Spain. He arrived in the Indies in 1503, in the first wave of Spanish colonists, and worked as a notary, governor's secretary, and even town mayor in Hispaniola (now Haiti and the Dominican Republic) and Cuba. In 1519 Cuba's governor, Diego Velázquez de Cuéllar, assigned Cortés to lead an expedition of 11 ships to explore Mexico. With more than 500 men, horses, and a cannon onboard, Cortés set sail. Contrary to Cuéllar's last-minute instructions to abort the mission, Cortés marched to Tenochtitlán, Moctezuma's Aztec capital, attracting Indian allies among the Aztecs' enemies. Cortés and his men seized the city in 1521, preparing the way for the conquest of all Mexico (SEE Moctezuma's speeches, page 124). Cortés immediately sent to Spain for missionaries. Holy Roman Emperor Charles V (and king of Spain, as Charles I; r. 1516–56) was happy to oblige, as the Catholic Church, the power behind the throne in retaking Spain from the Muslims (the Reconquista had only concluded 30 years earlier), would enable Spain to spread its influence in the New World. The reception of the first contingent of 12 priests was witnessed by Juan de Villagomez, one of the few Spaniards in Mexico City just after the conquest. Villagomez shared the story with Gerónimo de Mendieta, a Franciscan friar who wrote his *Ecclesiastical History of the Indians* in 1595. The "Twelve Apostles," as Mendieta called them, arrived on the coast in May 1524; it took the barefooted men, dressed in simple coarse robes, a month to reach the city. Overjoyed, Cortés commanded that all nearby Indian chiefs attend the reception. The Indians were amazed by the friars' threadbare clothes in contrast to the showy attire of the conquistadores, and they whispered to each other, "Poor, poor." They copied Cortés and the Spanish captains in kneeling and kissing the arrivals' hands, but they "stood as if stunned by this unusual event." Cortés realized he had to do more to explain who these paupers were.

Hernán Cortés, conqueror of Mexico and the Aztecs. Engraving by George Vertue in 1724 after a painting by Titian *(Ablestock)*

Do not marvel that I, who am captain general, governor, and lieutenant of the Emperor of the World, should render obedience and submission to these shabbily dressed men who have come to us from Spain. For the power that governors enjoy . . . extends only to the bodies and estates of men, which are the outward and visible part that is perishable and corruptible on this earth.

But the dominion that these men wield is over men's immortal souls, each of which has greater worth and price than all the gold or silver or precious stones in the world, or than the heavens themselves. For God has endowed them with power to guide men's souls to heaven to enjoy eternal glory, if they will accept their aid.

But if they reject it, they are damned and must go to Hell to suffer eternal torments, as happened to all your forebears for lack of ministers to teach them knowledge of the God who created us. . . .

And so that the same may not happen to you, and lest through ignorance you go where your fathers and grandfathers went before you, these priests of God, whom you call *teopixques,* have come to show you the way of salvation. Regard them, therefore, with much esteem and reverence as the guides of your souls, messengers of the most high God, and your spiritual fathers.

Listen to their teachings and heed their advice and commands, and see to it that all the rest obey them, for such is my will and that of the Emperor our Lord, and of God himself . . . who sent them to this land.

Source: Keen, Benjamin, ed. *Readings in Latin American Civilization.* Cambridge: Riverside Press, 1955, p. 140.

BARTOLOMÉ DE LAS CASAS
(1474–1566)
The Valladolid Debate
Valladolid, Spain
August 1550

In 1502 Bartolomé de Las Casas sailed to Hispaniola (now Haiti and the Dominican Republic) on Nicolas de Ovando's expedition to colonize the island. Spain had established the *encomienda*, a feudal system in which colonists could summon gangs of Indians for slave labor in exchange for maintaining order and converting them to Christianity. In practice, the Indians were ruthlessly exploited, dying in appalling numbers from famine, overwork, and disease. Upon witnessing this indefensible treatment of the Indians, Las Casas was radicalized. He became a priest, and in 1511 he heard the Dominican friar António de Montesinos give a sermon (*SEE* Montesinos's sermon, page 122) admonishing the colonists for their actions. Las Casas joined the Dominicans in 1522. On repeated trips to Spain, he defended the Indians before King Charles I (r. 1516–56) and received the title "Protector of the Indians." In 1542 Las Casas published *A Short Account of the Destruction of the Indies*, an influential book detailing the horrors of the Spanish conquest. He persuaded King Charles to impose the "New Laws" to gradually abolish the *encomienda* system. The king, concerned about the growing power of the *encomenderos* (conquistadores holding *encomiendas*) and the division in his court (Las Casas had even been accused of treason), requested that Las Casas publicly debate the issue with Spanish humanist thinker Juan Ginés de Sepúlveda. The days-long debate would determine the morality of Spain's conflicts with the Indians. Sepúlveda—he had never been to the Americas—argued on the colonists' behalf that the idolatrous Indians were "slaves by nature" who required masters to mold them into Christians. The 76-year-old Las Casas—the "Apostle of the Indies"—countered that they were free people capable of enlightenment and that the pope (and thus Spain) had no authority to require anyone to become Christian. The 14 theologians and scholars serving as judges never submitted a collective decision for this extraordinary debate, but Las Casas appeared to have won as he continued to publish widely. This is from the early part of *Defense against the Persecutors and Slanderers of the Peoples of the New World Discovered across the Seas*. (He refers at one point to Diodorus, a Greek historian of the first century B.C.E.)

THEY who teach, either in word or in writing, that the natives of the New World, whom we commonly call Indians, ought to be conquered and subjugated by war before the gospel is proclaimed and preached to them so that, after they have finally been subjugated, they may be instructed and hear the word of God, make two disgraceful mistakes.

First, in connection with divine and human law they abuse God's words and do violence to the Scriptures, to papal decrees, and to the teaching handed down from the holy fathers. And they go wrong again by quoting histories that are nothing but sheer fables and shameless nonsense. . . .

Who is there possessed of only a sound mind, not to say a little knowledge of theology, who has dared to pronounce a judgment and opinion so un-Christian that it spawns so many cruel wars, so many massacres, so many bereavements, and so many deplorable evils? Do we not have Christ's words: "See that you never despise any of these little ones," "Alas for the man who provides obstacles," "He who is not with me is against me; and he who does not gather with me scatters," and "Each day has trouble enough of its own"?

Who is so godless that he would want to incite men who are savage, ambitious, proud, greedy, uncontrolled, and everlastingly lazy to pillage their brothers and destroy their souls as well as their possessions, even though war is never lawful except when it is waged because of unavoidable necessity?

And so what man of sound mind will approve a war against men who are harmless, ignorant, gentle, temperate, unarmed, and destitute of every human defense? For the results of such a war are very surely the loss of the souls of that people who perish without knowing God and without the support of the sacraments, and, for the survivors, hatred and loathing of the Christian religion. Hence the purpose God intends, and for the attainment of which he suffered so much, may be frustrated by the evil and cruelty that our men wreak on them with inhuman barbarity.

What will these people think of Christ, the true God of the Christians, when they see Christians venting their rage against them with so many massacres, so much bloodshed without any just cause, at any rate without any just cause that they know of (nor can one even be imagined), and without any fault committed on their [the Indians] part against the Christians?

What good can come from these military campaigns that would, in the eyes of God, who evaluates all things with unutterable love, compensate for so many evils, so many injuries, and so many unaccustomed misfortunes? Furthermore, how will that nation love us, how will they become our friends (which is necessary if they are to accept our religion), when children see themselves deprived of parents, wives of husbands, and fathers of children and friends? When they see those they love wounded, imprisoned, plundered, and reduced from an immense number to a few? When they see their rulers stripped of their authority, crushed, and afflicted with a wretched slavery? All these things flow necessarily from war.

Who is there who would want the gospel preached to himself in such a fashion? Does not this negative precept apply to all men in general: "See that you do not do to another what you would not have done to you by another"? And the same for the affirmative command: "So always treat others as you would like them to treat you." This is

---

RHETORICAL DEVICE

Enumeratio: Listing the results, the parts, or the causes for a complete explanation.

_____

Our policy is directed not against any country or doctrine but against hunger, poverty, desperation, and chaos. —*George C. Marshall*

And so what man of sound mind will approve a war against men who are harmless, ignorant, gentle, temperate, unarmed, and destitute of every human defense? —*Bartolomé de Las Casas*

It was not we who started the war. It was they, the aristocrats, the military caste, the priesthood, the scions of the nobility, the fascists and degenerates, who forced the war upon us. —*Dolores Ibárruri*

How else is the world to take America seriously, when democracy at home is daily being outraged, free speech suppressed, peaceable assemblies broken up by overbearing and brutal gangsters in uniform; when free press is curtailed and every independent opinion gagged. —*Emma Goldman*

something that every man knows, grasps, and understands by the natural light that has been imparted to our minds.

It is obvious from all this that they who teach that these gentlest of sheep must be tamed by ravening wolves in a savage war before they are to be fed with the word of God are wrong about matters that are totally clear and are opposed to the natural law. Moreover, they commit an ungodly error when they say that these wars are just if they are waged as they should be. They mean, I suppose, if they are waged with restraint, by killing only those who have to be killed in order to subjugate the rest. . . .

I shall show how wrong they are in fact, with great harm to their own souls. For the Creator of every being has not so despised these peoples of the New World that he willed them to lack reason and made them like brute animals, so that they should be called barbarians, savages, wild men, and brutes, as they [Sepúlveda et al.] think or imagine. On the contrary, they [the Indians] are of such gentleness and decency that they are, more than the other nations of the entire world, supremely fitted and prepared to abandon the worship of idols and to accept, province by province and people by people, the word of God and the preaching of the truth. . . .

Long before they had heard the word Spaniard they had properly organized states, wisely ordered by excellent laws, religion, and custom. They cultivated friendship and, bound together in common fellowship, lived in populous cities in which they wisely administered the affairs of both peace and war justly and equitably, truly governed by laws that at very many points surpass ours, and could have won the admiration of the sages of Athens. . . .

I call the Spaniards who plunder that unhappy people torturers. Do you think that the Romans, once they had subjugated the wild and barbaric peoples of Spain, could with secure right divide all of you among themselves, handing over so many head of both males and females as allotments to individuals? And do you then conclude that the Romans could have stripped your rulers of their authority and consigned all of you, after you had been deprived of your liberty, to wretched labors, especially in searching for gold and silver lodes and mining and refining the metals? And if the Romans finally did that, as is evident from Diodorus, [would you not judge] that you also have the right to defend your freedom, indeed your very life, by war?

Sepúlveda, would you have permitted Saint James to evangelize your own people of Córdoba in that way? For God's sake and man's faith in him, is this the way to impose the yoke of Christ on Christian men? Is this the way to remove wild barbarism from the minds of barbarians? Is it not, rather, to act like thieves, cut-throats, and cruel plunderers and to drive the gentlest of people headlong into despair?

The Indian race is not that barbaric, nor are they dull witted or stupid, but they are easy to teach and very talented in learning all the liberal arts, and very ready to accept, honor, and observe the Christian religion and correct their sins (as experience has taught) once priests have introduced them to the sacred mysteries and taught them the word of God.

Source: de Las Casas, Bartolomé. *In Defense of the Indians.* Translated by Stafford Poole. DeKalb: Northern Illinois University Press, 1974, p. 25. Copyright © 1974 Northern Illinois University Press. Used by permission of the publisher.

ELIZABETH I
(1533–1603)
"The Heart and Stomach of a King"
Tilbury, England
August 9, 1588

The daughter of Henry VIII (r. 1509–47) and his executed queen, Anne Boleyn, Elizabeth I ruled England for 45 long years (from 1558 to 1603) and gave her name to the Elizabethan age. She was called the "Virgin Queen;" it was during her reign that English mariner Walter Raleigh explored the North American coast and named it Virginia. Elizabeth kept England out of war for three decades, but English attacks on Spanish ships and tensions between Protestant England and Catholic Spain (over aid England was giving Dutch rebels), brought the two countries to war. In 1588 King Philip II of Spain sent his great Armada—130 ships carrying 18,000 soldiers—to invade England. Philip had also ordered his general, Alessandro Farnese, the duke of Parma, to ready his larger army from the Spanish-held Netherlands to be conveyed across the English Channel to fight. Despite the considerable danger to herself—the Armada had been sighted off the coast three weeks earlier and sea battles were underway—in August the queen traveled to Tilbury, where the river Thames meets the sea, to cheer on her troops awaiting the invasion. (The Span-

> I have the heart and stomach of a king.
> —*Queen Elizabeth I*

iards were expected to take advantage of the Thames to reach London.) She is traditionally described as riding among her soldiers in a splendid white dress and armored breastplate. She reviewed a battle exercise, then spoke to them directly, demolishing any idea that the army was at a disadvantage led by a woman. Officers and soldiers kneeled to listen. When she swore "on the word of a prince," she was referring to herself. Riding beside her was Robert Dudley, earl of Leicester, the lieutenant general who would take her place in battle (and of whom she said no "prince" ever commanded a better subject). Parma and his troops never reached England. The Spanish Armada was defeated by England's navy, partly under the command of Sir Francis Drake, but war with Spain continued until after Elizabeth's death in 1603.

My loving people, we have been persuaded by some that are careful of our safety, to take heed how we commit ourselves to armed multitudes, for fear of treachery. But I assure you, I do not desire to live to distrust my faithful and loving people.

Let tyrants fear—I have always so behaved myself that, under God, I have placed my chiefest strength and safeguard in the loyal hearts and good will of my subjects.

And therefore I am come amongst you, as you see at this time, not as for my recreation or sport, but being resolved, in the midst and heat of the battle, to live or die amongst you all; to lay down, for my God, and for my kingdom, and for my people, my honor and my blood, even in the dust.

I know I have but the body of a weak and feeble woman. But I have the heart and stomach of a king, and of a king of England, too; and think foul scorn that Parma or Spain, or any prince of Europe, should dare to invade the borders of my realm, to which, rather than any dishonor should grow by me, I myself will take up arms. I myself will be your general, judge, and rewarder of every one of your virtues in the field.

I know already, by your forwardness, that you have deserved rewards and crowns; and we do assure you, on the word of a prince, they shall be duly paid you. In the meantime my lieutenant general shall be in my stead, than whom never prince commanded a more noble and worthy subject.

Not doubting by your obedience to my general, by your concord in the camp, and by your valor in the field, we shall shortly have a famous victory over these enemies of my God, of my kingdom, and of my people.

Source: Hume, David. *The History of England.* Vol. 4. Boston: Phillips, Samson, 1854, p. 545.

JAMES I
(1566–1625)
"Kings Are Justly Called Gods"
Parliament, London
March 21, 1609

Before James I became king of England and Ireland in 1603, he was James VI, king of Scotland. His mother, the Catholic Mary Queen of Scots, had been executed in 1587 by Queen Elizabeth I of England (a Protestant and Mary's first cousin), after a long imprisonment (*SEE* speech by Elizabeth, page 135). James had ruled Scotland for more than 20 years when Elizabeth died without any heirs. As Elizabeth's oldest blood relative, he became king of England. James took a moderate policy toward Catholics in Protestant England, and he was distrusted by both sides. However, during his reign the King James Version of the Bible was translated by scholars and became the Bible of choice for several hundred years. James is known in the United States especially for giving his name to the first permanent English settlement in America—Jamestown, Virginia, in 1607. But before acceding to the English throne in 1603, he had written a treatise on the divine right of kings, laying out his theory that kings take their authority from God rather than from the people. He maintained that he had the right of "royal prerogative" to enact laws without the consent of Parliament, although he also agreed that power must be tempered by God's guidance and a concern for law and tradition and the welfare of the people. In this speech to Parliament in 1609, he defends his right to absolute power. He explains his beliefs that kings have the same authority over their subjects that fathers have over their children, and that it is treason to question a king's actions. James increasingly ruled without regard for the advice of counselors—two years later he used the royal prerogative to dissolve Parliament and rule without it. Ironically, his son, King Charles I (r. 1625–49), inherited James's belief in his own supremacy (although not his moderation) and was beheaded by his subjects as a tyrant (*SEE* Charles's speech, p. 148).

The state of monarchy is the supremest thing upon earth. For kings are not only God's lieutenants upon earth, and sit upon God's throne, but even by God himself they are called gods. . . .

Kings are justly called gods, for that they exercise a manner or resemblance of divine power upon earth. For if you will consider the attributes to God, you shall see how they agree in the person of a king. God hath power to create, or destroy, make or unmake at his pleasure, to give life or send death, to judge all, and to be judged nor accountable to none. To raise low things, and to make high things low at his pleasure, and to God are both soul and body due. And the like power have Kings: they make and unmake their subjects; they have power of raising, and casting down, of life and of death, judges over all their subjects, and in all causes, and yet accountable to none but God only.

They have power to exalt low things, and abase high things, and make of their subjects like men at the chess—a pawn to take a bishop or a knight, and to cry up or down any of their subjects, as they do their money. And to the king is due both the affection of the soul, and the service of the body of his subjects. . . .

As for the father of a family, they had of old under the law of nature, *patriam potestatem* [fatherly power], which was *potestatem vitae et necis* [power of life and death] over their children or family (I mean such fathers of families as were the lineal heirs of those families whereof kings did originally come). For kings had their first original from them, who planted and spread themselves in colonies throughout the world.

Now a father may dispose of his inheritance to his children at his pleasure, even disinherit the eldest upon just occasions and prefer the youngest, according to his liking; make them beggars or rich at his pleasure; restrain or banish out of his presence as he finds them give cause of offence, or restore them in favor again with the penitent sinner. So may the king deal with his subjects. . . .

A king governing in a settled kingdom leaves to be a king and degenerates into a tyrant as soon as he leaves off to rule according to his laws. In which case the king's conscience may speak unto him, as the poor widow said to Philip of Macedon; either govern according to your law, *aut ne Rex sis* [or you will not be king]. And though no Christian man ought to allow rebellion of people against their prince, yet doth God never leave kings unpunished when they transgress these limits. For in that same psalm where God saith to kings, *vos dii estis* [you are gods], he immediately thereafter concludes, "But ye shall die like men."

The higher we are placed, the greater shall our fall be. *Ut casus sic dolor* [with chance comes grief] the taller the trees be, the more in danger of the wind; and the tempest beats forest upon the highest mountains. Therefore all kings that are not tyrants, or perjured, will be glad to bound themselves within the limits of their laws. And they that persuade them the contrary, are vipers, and pests, both against them and the commonwealth. For it is a great difference between a king's government in a settled state, and what kings in their original power might do *in individuo vago* [as a free individual]. As for my part, I thank God I have ever given good proof, that I never had intention to the contrary. And I am sure to go to my grave with that reputation and comfort, that never king was in all his time more careful to have his laws duly observed, and himself to govern thereafter, than I.

I conclude then this point touching the power of kings with this axiom of divinity, that as to dispute what God may do is blasphemy, but *quid vult Deus* [what God wants], that divines may lawfully and do ordinarily dispute and discuss; for to dispute *a posse ad esse* [from "maybe" to "is"] is both against logic and divinity: So is it sedition in subjects to dispute what a king may do in the height of his power. But just kings will ever be willing to declare what they will do, if they will not incur the curse of God.

I will not be content that my power be disputed upon, but I shall ever be willing to make the reason appear of all my doings, and rule my actions according to my laws.

Source: Wooten, David. *Divine Right and Democracy: An Anthology of Political Writings in Stuart England.* London: Penguin Books, 1986, p. 107.

POWHATAN
(ca. 1547–1618)
To Captain John Smith
Werowocomoco, Virginia
1609

The first English colonists arrived at Jamestown, Virginia, on May 14, 1607. It was the first venture for the Virginia Company, which had been chartered by King James I (r. England and Ireland, 1603–25) to settle North America. They found building homes and finding food in the New World difficult. Captain John Smith provided the discipline necessary to grow food and secure the settlement, but those who survived the first winters partly owed their lives to help they received from the many tribes of the Powhatan Confederacy. However, the settlers took lands that the Indians considered theirs, and disputes arose over trading for food and weapons. While exploring for food in 1607, Smith had encountered the Powhatan Confederacy's chief Wahunsonacock (called Powhatan by the colonists). Smith was captured and nearly executed before the chief's 13-year-old daughter, Pocahontas, intervened. The captain's skill at diplomacy smoothed relations with the Indians for more than a year but, early in 1609, Powhatan summoned Smith to his home at Werowocomoco (today Wicomico, Virginia). Smith took a well-armed party; he was suspicious of Powhatan's intention, as Powhatan had twice planned to kill him. They discussed trading for corn while Smith tried to keep secret that the settlement was out of food. Powhatan, who was about 62, warned the 29-year-old Captain John Smith about abusing the Indians' friendship, but Smith refused to send away their weapons as Powhatan asked, wary of another massacre. Smith left the colony later that year for England, and he never returned to Jamestown. The winter that followed this speech of warning was called "the starving time;" not even a fifth of the 500 settlers survived. After Powhatan's death in 1618, conflicts continued, and in 30 years' time the tribe had been nearly annihilated.

I am now grown old, and must soon die; and the succession must descend, in order, to my brothers, Opitchapan, Opekankanough, and Catataugh, and then to my two sisters, and their two daughters. I wish their experience was equal to mine; and that your love to us might not be less than ours to you.

Why should you take by force that from us which you can have by love? Why should you destroy us, who have provided you with food? What can you get by war?

We can hide our provisions, and fly into the woods; and then you must consequently famish by wronging your friends.

What is the cause of your jealousy? You see us unarmed, and willing to supply your wants, if you will come in a friendly manner, and not with swords and guns, as to invade an enemy.

I am not so simple, as not to know it is better to eat good meat, lie well, and sleep quietly with my women and children; to laugh and be merry with the English; and, being their friend, to have copper, hatchets, and whatever else I want, than to fly from all, to lie cold in the woods, feed upon acorns, roots, and such trash, and to be so hunted that I cannot rest, eat, or sleep.

In such circumstances, my men must watch, and if a twig should but break, all would cry out, "Here comes Captain Smith"; and so, in this miserable manner, to end my miserable life. And Captain Smith, this might be soon your fate too, through your rashness and unadvisedness.

Chief Wahunsonacock of the Powhatan Confederacy was called Powhatan by Captain John Smith's party of settlers in Jamestown, Virginia. Engraving from John Smith's *Generall Historie of Virginia*, 1624 *(Ablestock)*

I, therefore, exhort you to peaceable councils. And, above all, I insist that the guns and swords, the cause of all our jealousy and uneasiness, be removed and sent away.

Source: Drake, Samuel Gardner. *Book of the Indians.* Boston: Antiquarian Bookstore, 1833, p. 13.

JOHN WINTHROP
(1588–1649)
"We Shall Be as a City upon a Hill"
Flagship *Arbella,* off the coast of England

March 1630

Puritans (who were called *Dissenters* at the time) were radical Protestants unhappy with the practice of religion in early 17th-century England. Not satisfied with the Protestant English church's break with Roman Catholicism, they felt Catholic influence still permeated church ritual and religious texts, and that kings and politics still held too much authority. Many families wanted to start a new life in the New World, free of the corrupting influence of the Church of England. To do this, the Puritans obtained a charter from King Charles I (r. 1625–49) for an American colony. On April 7, 1630, the Massachusetts Bay Company's fleet of ships took sail from England with almost 1,000 Puritan immigrants seeking religious freedom. They landed in Salem on June 12, and soon settled the area where the city of Boston now stands. On board the flagship *Arbella* was

John Winthrop, a prosperous, well-educated London lawyer and devout Puritan. He had with him half his family and several servants, and the rest followed the next year. He would be elected governor of the Massachusetts Bay colony 12 times and become one of the first notable Americans. His son and grandson, both named John Winthrop, would also be colonial governors. As the *Arbella* was preparing for the voyage, Winthrop gathered the passengers for a long sermon, "A Model of Christian Charity," at the end of which he set forth the ideals by which they would build an exemplary community worthy of the world's praise. The sermon quotes from Jesus' Sermon on the Mount (SEE the sermon, page 49), and has itself been quoted many times. The "city upon a hill" was a theme favored by U.S. presidents John F. Kennedy and Ronald Reagan in their speech-making.

Thus stands the case between God and us.

We are entered into a Covenant with Him for this work. We have taken out a commission. The Lord hath given us leave to draw our own articles. We have professed to enterprise these and those ends, upon these and those accounts. We have hereupon besought of Him favor and blessing. Now if the Lord shall please to hear us, and bring us in peace to the place we desire, then hath he ratified this Covenant and sealed our commission, and will expect a strict performance of the articles contained in it.

But if we shall neglect the observation of these articles which are the ends we have propounded, and, dissembling with our God, shall fail to embrace this present world and prosecute our carnal intentions, seeking great things for ourselves and our posterity, the Lord will surely break out in wrath against us; be revenged of such a (sinful) people, and make us know the price of the breach of such a Covenant.

Now the only way to avoid this shipwreck, and to provide for our posterity, is to follow the counsel of Micah, to do justly, to love mercy, to walk humbly with our God. For this end we must be knit together, in this work, as one man. We must entertain each other in brotherly affection. We must be willing to abridge ourselves of our superfluities, for the supply of other's necessities. We must uphold a familiar commerce together in all meekness, gentleness, patience, and liberality. We must delight in each other; make other's condition our own; rejoice together, mourn together, labor and suffer together, always having before our eyes our commission and community in the work, as members of the same body. So shall we keep the unity of the spirit in the bond of peace.

The Lord will be our God and delight to dwell among us, as his own people, and will command a blessing upon us in all our ways. So that we shall see much more of his wisdom, power, goodness and truth, than formerly we have been acquainted with.

> We shall find that the God of Israel is among us, when ten of us
> shall be able to resist a thousand of our enemies; when he shall make us
> a praise and a glory, that men shall say of succeeding plantations,
> "The Lord make it like that of New England." For we must consider
> that we shall be as a city upon a hill. —*John Winthrop*

We shall find that the God of Israel is among us, when ten of us shall be able to resist a thousand of our enemies; when he shall make us a praise and a glory, that men shall say of succeeding plantations, "The Lord make it like that of New England." For we must consider that we shall be as a city upon a hill.

The eyes of all people are upon us. So that if we deal falsely with our God in this work we have undertaken, and so cause him to withdraw his present help from us, we shall be made a story and a by-word throughout the world. We shall open the mouths of enemies to speak evil of the ways of God, and all professors for God's sake. We shall shame the faces of many of God's worthy servants, and cause their prayers to be turned into curses upon us till we be consumed out of the good land whither we are a-going.

I shall shut this discourse with that exhortation of Moses, that faithful servant of the Lord, in his last farewell to Israel (Deut. 30).

Beloved, there is now set before us life and good, death and evil, in that we are commanded this day to love the Lord our God, and to love one another, to walk in his ways and to keep his Commandments and his Ordinance and his Laws, and the articles of our Covenant with him, that we may live and be multiplied, and that the Lord our God may bless us in the land whither we go to possess it. But if our hearts shall turn away so that we will not obey, but shall be seduced, and worship and serve other Gods, our pleasure and profits, and serve them; it is propounded unto us this day, we shall surely perish out of the good land whither we pass over this vast sea to possess it.

Therefore let us choose life that we and our seed may live, by obeying His voice and cleaving to Him, for He is our life and our prosperity.

Source: Stedman, Edmund Clarence, and Ellen Mackay Hutchinson. *A Library of American Literature,* Vol. 1. New York: Charles Webster, 1889, p. 306.

GALILEO GALILEI
(1564–1642)
Abjuration before the Roman Inquisition
Rome
June 22, 1633

Galileo Galilei was born in 1564 in Pisa, in northern Italy. A brilliant student, he became a university professor teaching mathematics, geometry, and astronomy. He discovered several laws of motion, and he constructed a revolutionary telescope that allowed him to be the first to see the craters of Earth's Moon and the moons of Jupiter. Galileo was 36 in 1600 when Italian philosopher Giordano Bruno was burned at the stake for teaching a "blasphemous" Copernican theory of an infinite and changing universe. The church upheld Aristotle's view that the heavens were unchanging and Earth was the center of the universe. Nevertheless, Galileo persevered in scientific studies that he felt demonstrated the truth of the Earth's motion around the Sun, and in 1613 he began to publish astronomical observations that clashed with church doctrine. In 1616 he was ordered by Pope Paul V (r. 1605–21) through the Jesuit cardinal Robert Bellarmine (the chief Inquisitor at Giordano Bru-no's trial), to stop promoting his theory of a heliocentric, or Sun-centered, universe. With only a few supporters among the clergy Galileo bravely moved ahead, publishing a book, *Dialogue of the Two Principal Systems of the World*, in 1632. The next year, Galileo was accused of heresy for writing the book, due to its discussion of the earth's movement. The charges required him to present himself in Rome. A sick old man at the age of 70, he traveled on a litter (a carrying chair) to Rome, where the Roman Inquisition examined him. (The Inquisition was a permanent body of high officials whose job included defending the faith from heretics; their investigations were often religious persecutions resulting in torture and death.) Shown the instruments of torture and faced with death, Galileo was forced on his knees to abjure, or renounce, his beliefs. After delivering this speech, he received a sentence of house arrest for life; at home, he continued to write in secret.

❧

I, Galileo Galilei, son of the late Vincenzo Galilei, of Florence, aged seventy years, being brought personally to judgment and kneeling before your Most Eminent and Most Reverend Lords Cardinals, General Inquisitors of the universal Christian republic against heretical depravity, having before my eyes the Holy Gospels, which I touch with my own hands, swear that I have always believed, and now believe, and with the help of God will in future believe, every article which the Holy Catholic and Apostolic Church of Rome holds, teaches, and preaches.

But because I have been enjoined by this Holy Office altogether to abandon the false opinion which maintains that the sun is the centre and immovable, and forbidden to hold, defend, or teach the said false doctrine in any manner, and after it hath been signified to me that the said doctrine is repugnant with the Holy Scripture, I have written and printed a book, in which I treat of the same doctrine now condemned, and adduce reasons with great force in support of the same, without giving any solution, and therefore have been judged grievously suspected of heresy.

That is to say, that I held and believed that the sun is the centre of the universe and is immovable, and that the earth is not the centre and is movable.

Willing, therefore, to remove from the minds of your Eminences, and of every Catholic Christian, this vehement suspicion rightfully entertained toward me, with a sincere heart and unfeigned faith I abjure, curse, and detest the said errors and heresies, and generally every other error and sect contrary to the Holy Church.

And I swear that I will never more in future say or assert anything verbally, or in writing, which may give rise to a similar suspicion of me. But if I shall know any heretic,

Galileo Galilei answers charges of heresy before the Roman Inquisition in 1633. Painting by Joseph Robert-Fleury *(Réunion des Musées Nationaux/Art Resource, NY)*

or anyone suspected of heresy, that I will denounce him to this Holy Office, or to the Inquisitor or Ordinary of the place where I may be.

I swear, moreover, and promise, that I will fulfill and observe fully, all the penances which have been or shall be laid on me by this Holy Office. But if it shall happen that I violate any of my said promises, oaths, and protestations (which God avert!), I subject myself to all the pains and punishments which have been decreed and promulgated by the sacred canons, and other general and particular constitutions against delinquents of this description.

So, may God help me, and his Holy Gospels, which I touch with my own hands. I, the above-named Galileo Galilei, have abjured, sworn, promised, and bound myself as above, and in witness thereof with my own hand have subscribed this present writing of my abjuration, which I have recited word for word.

Source: Fahie, John Joseph. *Galileo, His Life and Work.* New York: James Pott & Co., 1903, p. 319.

"All Law Lies in the People"
Putney, England
October 29, 1647

Early in his reign (1625–49), King Charles I of England precipitated conflict with Parliament by denying Parliament's power and privileges. He did not summon a Parliament at all between 1629 and 1640. His Protestant subjects believed him overly sympathetic to Catholicism, at a time when many felt even the Protestant Church of England was too "popish." These reforming Protestants were called Puritans. Finding himself in need of money to pay his military in 1640, Charles was forced to summon a Parliament. When this new Parliament passed laws that restricted Charles's power in 1642, he sent his army into Parliament's very building, which resulted in the start of the English Civil War (1642–51). Charles's Royalists banded with Church of England supporters, collectively called "Cavaliers," to battle Parliamentarians allied with Puritan "Roundheads," who opposed Charles I. Thomas Rainborow was a colonel in the New Model Army, one of several armies raised by Parliament, and the only one with professional soldiers. Oliver Cromwell, a Puritan Member of Parliament, served as lieutenant-general of the horse in this army; Rainborow's men were foot soldiers, devoted Puritans who hoped to end the monarchy and establish a republic. After Charles surrendered in 1646, it was unclear how power would be shared and what rights the common people would receive. Rainborow, a Member of Parliament since early 1647, was a Leveler, that is, a member of a movement calling for an end to the monarchy and the grant of voting rights, religious freedom, and political equality to all men (not just high-born men). The Levelers drew up an *Agreement of the People* calling for a Parliament elected by the people. The Army's leading radicals, such as Thomas Rainborow, were required by their more moderate leaders, such as Henry Ireton, a general and member of Parliament, to gather near London in October 1647 at what came to be called the Putney Debates. On the second day of the debates, Rainborow spoke, expressing his belief that each man had the right to a say in government. These views, while fundamental to later political liberties, were rejected as impractical. Rainborow was murdered by Royalists the next year.

⁂

I think that the poorest he that is in England hath a life to live, as the greatest he; and therefore truly, sir, I think it's clear, that every man that is to live under a government ought first by his own consent to put himself under that government.

And I do think that the poorest man in England is not at all bound in a strict sense to that government that he hath not had a voice to put himself under; and I am confident that, when I have heard the reasons against it, something will be said to answer those reasons, insomuch that I should doubt whether he was an Englishman or no, that should doubt of these things. . . .

I do very much care whether there be a king or no king, lords or no lords, property or no property; and I think, if we do not all take care, we shall all have none of these very shortly. But as to this present business, I do hear nothing at all that can convince me, why any man that is born in England ought not to have his voice in election of burgesses.

It is said that if a man have not a permanent interest, he can have no claim; and that we must be no freer than the laws will let us be, and that there is no law in any chronicle will let us be freer than that we now enjoy. Something was said to this yesterday.

I do think that the main cause why Almighty God gave men reason, it was that they should make use of that reason, and that they should improve it for that end and purpose that God gave it them. And truly, I think that half a loaf is better than none if a man be hungry (this gift of reason without other property may seem a small thing), yet I think there is nothing that God hath given a man that any one else can take from him.

And therefore I say, that either it must be the Law of God or the law of man that must prohibit the meanest man in the kingdom to have this benefit as well as the greatest.

I do not find anything in the Law of God, that a lord shall choose twenty burgesses, and a gentleman but two, or a poor man shall choose none: I find no such thing in the Law of Nature, nor in the Law of Nations.

But I do find that all Englishmen must be subject to English laws, and I do verily believe that there is no man but will say that the foundation of all law lies in the people, and if it lie in the people, I am to seek for this exemption.

Source: Rainborow, Thomas. "The Putney Debates." University of Essex. Available online. URL: http://courses.essex.ac.uk/cs/cs101/putney.htm. Accessed on September 30, 2007.

CHARLES I
(1600–1649)
From the Scaffold
London, England
January 30, 1649

Like his father, James I, who lived from 1566 to 1625, Charles I was king of England, Scotland, and Ireland (r. 1625–49). James had bequeathed Charles with a fatal belief in the divine right of kings (*SEE* James's speech, page 137). Charles accepted no challenge to his actions, believing that as God's anointed monarch, to oppose him was to oppose God. His Roman Catholic sympathies and Catholic wife, Henrietta Maria of France, did not endear him to Protestants, as it was a time of unrest against "high church" practices in the Protestant Church of England. Protestants who resisted such "popery" were called Puritans; they led a growing movement against the king. Parliament had less power in the 1600s than it possesses in England today—Charles could dissolve Parliament and rule without it, as he did from 1629 to 1640. Needing funds to pay his military in a conflict with Scottish Presbyterians, however, he was forced to call a new Parliament. The new members of Parliament were openly hostile, crafting laws to prevent him from dissolving Parliament or raising taxes without their consent. Furious, the king sent his army into the House of Commons, causing Parliament to break with him soon after. The English Civil War followed in 1642; England divided into Royalists (and Church of England "Cavaliers") against Parliamentarians (and Puritan "Roundheads"). The Parliamentarians planned to abolish the monarchy and declare a republic. Oliver Cromwell, Puritan Member of Parliament, raised an army and became the able commander of the Parliamentarians. After Charles's defeat, a court convicted him for making war against Parliament. The next day Charles was executed on a high platform, while the common people were kept at a distance so few could hear him speak. Contrary to what the republicans expected, the beheading of the "martyr king" became a broad reproach against critics of the monarchy, and the deed cemented the monarchy's power in England. The Church of England established January 30 as a feast day in remembrance.

I shall be very little heard of anybody here; I shall therefore speak a word unto you here. Indeed I could hold my peace very well, if I did not think that holding my peace would make some men think that I did submit to the guilt as well as to the punishment. But I think it is my duty to God first, and to my country, for to clear myself both as an honest man, a good king, and a good Christian.

I shall begin first with my innocence. In truth, I think it not very needful for me to insist long upon this, for all the world knows that I never did begin a war with the two Houses of Parliament. And I call God to witness—to whom I must shortly make an account—that I never did intend for to encroach upon their privileges. They began upon me: it is the militia they began upon. They contest that the militia was mine, but they thought it fit to have it from me. And to be short, if anybody will look to the dates of the commissions—of their commissions and mine—and likewise to the declarations, will see clearly that they began these unhappy troubles, not I.

So that as to the guilt of these enormous crimes that are laid against me, I hope in God that God will clear me of it, I will not; I am in charity. God forbid that I should lay it upon the two Houses of Parliament. There is no necessity of [doing so] either. I hope they are free of this guilt, for I do believe that ill instruments between them and me have been the chief cause of all this bloodshed, so that by way of speaking, as I find myself clear of this, I hope and pray God that they may too.

Yet for all this, God forbid that I should be so ill a Christian as not to say that God's judgments are just upon me. Many times he does pay justice by an unjust sentence;

that is ordinary. I will only say this, that an unjust sentence that I suffered for to take effect, is punished now by an unjust sentence upon me. That is, so far as I have said, to show you that I am an innocent man.

Now for to show you that I am a good Christian. I hope there is a good man that will bear me witness that I have forgiven all the world and even those in particular that have been the chief causes of my death. Who they are, God knows; I do not desire to know. I pray God forgive them. But this is not all—my charity must go further. I wish that they may repent, for indeed they have committed a great sin in that particular. I pray God with St. Stephen that this be not laid to their charge—nay not only so, but that they may take the right way to the peace of the kingdom, for my charity commands me not only to forgive particular men, but my charity commands me to endeavor to the last gasp the peace of the kingdom. So, sirs, I do wish with all my soul, and I do hope there is some here will carry it further, that they may endeavor the peace of the kingdom.

Now, sirs, I must show you both how you are out of the way, and I will put you in the way. First you are out of the way, for certainly all the way you have ever had yet—as I could find by anything—is in the way of conquest. Certainly this is an ill way. For conquest, sirs, in my opinion is never just, except there be a good just cause, either for the matter of wrong or just title. And then if you go beyond it, the first quarrel that you have to it, that makes it unjust at the end that was just at the first. But if it be only a matter of conquest, then it is a great robbery; as a pirate said to Alexander the Great that he was a great robber, he was but a petty robber. And so, sirs, I do think the way that you are in is much out of the way.

Charles I, king of England, was not recognized as an orator, but his brave speech on the scaffold helped perpetuate his memory as the "Martyr King." Painting by Daniel Mytens *(Ablestock)*

Now, sirs, for to put you in the way. Believe it, you will never do right, nor God will never prosper you, until you give God His due, the King his due—that is, my successor—and the people their due. I am as much for them as any of you. You must give God his due by regulating rightly His Church (according to His Scripture) which is now out of order. For to set you in a way particularly, now I cannot; but only this: a national synod freely called, freely debating among themselves, must settle this, when that every opinion is freely and clearly heard.

For the King, indeed I will not [at that point a gentleman touched the ax, and the king said]—Hurt not the Ax that may hurt me—For the King, the laws of the land will clearly instruct you in that. Therefore, because it concerns my own particular, I only give you a touch of it.

For the people—and truly I desire their liberty and freedom as much as anybody whomsoever—but I must tell you that their liberty and their freedom consists in having of government those laws by which their life and their goods may be most their own. It is not for having a share in government, sirs; that is nothing pertaining to them. A subject and a sovereign are clean different things. And therefore until they do that—I mean, that you do put the people in that liberty as I say—certainly they will never enjoy themselves.

Sirs, it was for this that now I am come here. If I would have given way to an arbitrary way for to have all laws changed according to the power of the sword, I need not have come here. And therefore I tell you—and I pray God it be not laid to your charge—that I am the martyr of the people.

In truth, sirs, I shall not hold you much longer, for I will only say this to you, that in truth I could have desired some little time longer because that I would have put this that I have said in a little more order and a little better digested than I have done. And therefore I hope you will excuse me.

I have delivered my conscience. I pray God that you do take those courses that are best for the good of the kingdom and your own salvations.

[Here Dr. Juxon, Bishop of London, spoke: Will Your Majesty, though it may be very well known Your Majesty's affections to religion, yet it may be expected that you should say somewhat for the world's satisfaction.]

I thank you very heartily, my lord, for that I had almost forgotten it. In truth, sirs, my conscience in religion, I think is very well known to all the world. And therefore I declare before you all that I die a Christian according to the profession of the Church of England as I found it left me by my father. And this honest man I think will witness it. Sirs, excuse me for this same. I have a good cause, and I have a gracious God. I will say no more.

I go from a corruptible to an incorruptible crown, where no disturbance can be, no disturbance in the world.

Source: Fellowes, W. D. *Historical Sketches of Charles the First.* London, John Murray, 1828, p. 161.

ANTÓNIO VIEIRA
(1608–1697)
"The Sins of Maranhão"
Maranhão, Brazil
First Sunday in Lent, 1653

António Vieira was born in Lisbon, but he was taken to the Portuguese colony of Bahia, in Brazil, by his parents and educated there. He took vows as a Jesuit (a member of the Roman Catholic Society of Jesus devoted to missionary and educational work) and taught rhetoric—the writing and delivery of speeches and sermons. He would become one of the Portuguese language's literary greats. Like António de Montesinos of Spain (SEE Montesinos's sermon, page 122), Vieira was a priest who championed the cause of native peoples of the New World. He returned from Brazil to Lisbon in 1640, part of a delegation to the coronation of King John IV (r. 1640–56). Vieira's brilliant oratory and fine writing won for him assignments as a courtier (a royal court attendant), and later as a diplomat to countries in western Europe. But after 13 years away, he wished to return to Brazil. In 1653, he arrived in Maranhão, a poor Portuguese colony in northern Brazil. Reinvigorated by a return to missionary life, he found on his arrival that enslavement of the Indians was well established in the settlement. Expensive African slaves were out of the reach of the poor tobacco and cotton farmers, who had only to seize native peoples from the interior to find labor for their fields and houses. Vieira summoned all the brilliant oratory he had mastered, and Sunday after Sunday he castigated the white slave-owning class in scorching sermons. He proposed that they could keep as slaves only Indians acquired in a just war or rescued from cannibals. Other Indians were to be paid.) These harangues so angered the colonists that Vieira was sent back to Portugal in 1661, along with 30 other Jesuit priests forced out of Maranhão for their activism. At home and in Rome he continued his advocacy for the Indians and for the Jews of Portugal, despite two years imprisonment at the hands of the Portuguese Inquisition. Twenty years later he was permitted to return to Brazil, and he died there in 1697.

At what a different price the devil today buys souls compared to what he offered for them previously! There is no market in the world where the devil can get them more cheaply than right here in our own land.

In the Gospel, he offered all the kingdoms of the world for one soul; in Maranhão the devil does not need to offer one-tenth as much for all the souls. It is not necessary to offer worlds, nor kingdoms; it is not necessary to offer cities, nor towns, nor villages. All he has to do is offer a couple of Tapuya Indians and at once he is adored on both knees.

What a cheap market! An Indian for a soul! That Indian will be your slave for the few days that he lives; and your soul will be a slave for eternity, as long as God is God. This is the contract that the devil makes with you. Not only do you accept it but you pay him money on top of it. . . .

Do you know, Christians, do you know, nobles and people of Maranhão, what is the fast which God requires of you this Lent? It is that you loosen the bands of injustice, and that you set those free whom you hold captives, and whom you oppress. These are the sins of Maranhão; these are what God commands me to announce: "Show my people their transgression." Christians, God commands me to undeceive you, and I undeceive you on the part of God. You are all in mortal sin! You are all living and dying in a state of condemnation, and you are all going straight to Hell! Many are already there, and you also will soon be there with them, except you change your lives. . . .

Every man who holds another unjustly in servitude, being able to release him, is certainly in a state of condemnation. All men, or almost all men in Maranhão, hold oth-

RHETORICAL DEVICE

Antimetabole: The second half of a sentence or expression that uses the parts of the first in reverse order.

When there are many men without honor, there are always others who bear in themselves the honor of many men. —*Fidel Castro, quoting José Martí*

We say that if America has entered the war to make the world safe for democracy, she must first make democracy safe in America. —*Emma Goldman*

Christians, God commands me to undeceive you, and
I undeceive you on the part of God. —*Antonio Vieira*

We must remember that the peoples do not belong to the governments
but that the governments belong to the peoples. —*Bernard Baruch*

Let us never negotiate out of fear.
But let us never fear to negotiate. —*John F. Kennedy*

ers unjustly in servitude; all, therefore, or almost all, are in a state of condemnation. You will tell me, that even if it were thus, they did not think of it, nor know it, and that their good faith would save them. I deny it! . . . They ought to have thought of it and to have known it. Some are condemned for certainty, others for doubt, others for ignorance. They who were certain are condemned for not making restitution; they who were in doubt are condemned for not examining; they who were in ignorance are condemned for not knowing what it was their duty to know.

Oh, if these graves could open, and some of those who have died in this miserable state might appear among us, how certain it is that you would read this truth clearly by the light of their devouring flames. Would you know why God does not permit them to appear to you? For the reason which Abraham gave to the rich man when he besought that Lazarus might be sent to his brethren: "They have Moses and the Prophets; it is not necessary that one should come from Hell to tell them the truth."

My brethren, if there be any who doubt upon this matter, here are the laws, here are the lawyers, let the question be asked. You have three religious orders in the state, and among them so many subjects of such virtue and such learning. Ask them, examine the matter, inform yourselves. But religious orders are not necessary; go to Turkey, go to Hell, for there can neither be Turk so beturked in Turkey, nor Devil so bedevilled in Hell, as to affirm that a free man may be a slave.

But you will say to me, this people, this country, this government cannot be supported without Indians. Who is to bring us a pitcher of water or a bundle of wood? Who is to plant our manioc? Must our wives do it? Must our children do it? In the first place, as you will presently see, these are not the straits in which I would place you. But if necessity and conscience require it, then I reply, yes! and I repeat it, yes! You and your wives and your children ought to do it. We ought to support ourselves with our own hands; for better is it to be supported by the sweat of one's own brow than by another's blood.

Oh, you riches of Maranhão! What if these mantles and cloaks were to be wrung? They would drip blood. . . .

Let us give this remedy to the country in which we live, let us give this honor to the Portuguese nation, let us give this example to Christendom, let us give this fame to the world! Let the world know, let the heretics and the heathen know, that God was not deceived when he chose the Portuguese for conquerors and preachers of his holy name. Let the world know that there is still truth, that there is still the fear of God, that there is still a soul, that there is still a conscience, and that interest is not the absolute and universal lord of all.

Source: Burns, E. Bradford, ed. *A Documentary History of Brazil.* New York: Knopf, 1966, p. 83.

JOSEPH-ANTOINE DE LA BARRE
(1622–1688)
Address to the Five Nations
near present-day Oswego, New York, United States
September 5, 1684

Joseph-Antoine de La Barre became governor of New France (today's Quebec) in 1682. The French were officially at peace with the Iroquois Confederacy, also called the Five Nations, a powerful confederation of tribes that occupied a large territory in what is now New York State. The Five Nations were the Mohawks, Oneidas, Onondagas, Cayugas, and Senecas. It was an uncertain peace, however, as the English—enemies of France—were the Iroquois' allies. France had made the Hurons (enemies of the Iroquois) their allies in the fur trade, the most all-encompassing commercial venture in the region. In 1683 the French and Iroquois Wars (intermittently 1640s–98) erupted again, once more over domination of the fur trade. The next year, French governor de La Barre readied his ships and sailed from Fort Cataraqui (also called Ft. Frontenac), near what is now Kingston, Ontario, at the head of the St. Lawrence River. He crossed Lake Ontario and set up camp at Anse de la Famine, near what is now Oswego, New York. Many of his men fell seriously ill and were in no shape to fight the Iroquois. De La Barre decided to bluff his way through this difficulty. He sent his interpreter, Charles Le Moyne, whom the Indians called Ohguesse, to call the chiefs of the Five Nations to council. Garangula, the Onondaga tribe's great orator, brought 30 warriors. The warriors formed a semicircle about him; de La Barre's men completed the circle. Within the ring, de La Barre began to speak. He intended to terrify the Indians with threats of war. He complained about mistreatment of French traders and his Indian allies, and about friendly acts done for the British. At important points in his address, de La Barre presented beaded wampum belts to emphasize his sincerity. (*See* the reply by Garangula, page 156.)

The king, my master, being informed that the Five Nations have often infringed the peace, has ordered me to come hither with a guard, and to send Ohguesse to the Onondagas, to bring the chief sachems to my camp. The intention of the great king is that you and I may smoke the calumet of peace together, but on this condition, that you promise me, in the name of the Senecas, Cayugas, Onondagas, and Mohawks, to give entire satisfaction and reparation to his subjects and for the future never to molest them.

The Senecas, Cayugas, Onondagas, Oneidas, and Mohawks have robbed and abused all the traders that were passing to the Illinois and Miamies, and other Indian nations, the children of my king. They have acted, on these occasions, contrary to the treaty of peace with my predecessor. I am ordered, therefore, to demand satisfaction; and to tell them, that in case of refusal or their plundering us any more, that I have express orders to declare war.

This belt confirms my words.

The warriors of the Five nations have conducted the English into the lakes, which belong to the king, my master, and brought the English among the nations that are his children to destroy the trade of his subjects, and withdraw these nations from him. They have carried the English thither, notwithstanding the prohibition of the late Governor of New York, who foresaw the risk that both they and you would run. I am willing to forget those things; but if ever the like should happen for the future, I have express orders to declare war against you.

This belt confirms my words.

Your warriors have made several barbarous incursions on the Illinois and the Miamies. They have massacred men, women, and children; they have made many of these nations prisoners, who thought themselves safe in their villages in time of peace. These people, who are my king's children, must not be your slaves. You must give them their liberty, and send them back into their own country. If the Five Nations shall refuse to do this, I have express orders to declare war against them.

This belt confirms my words.

This is what I have to say to Garangula, that he may carry to the Senecas, Onondagas, Oneidas, Cayugas, and Mohawks, the declaration which the king, my master, has commanded me to make. He does not wish them to force him to send a great army to Cadarackui Fort, to begin a war, which must be fatal to them. He would be sorry that this fort, that was the work of peace, should become the prison of your warriors. We must endeavor on both sides to prevent such misfortunes. The French, who are the brethren and friends of the Five Nations, will never trouble their repose, provided that the satisfaction which I demand be given, and that the treaties of peace be hereafter observed. I shall be extremely grieved if my words do not produce the effect which I expect from them; for then I shall be obliged to join with the Governor of New York, who is commanded by his master to assist me, and burn the castles of the Five Nations, and destroy you.

This belt confirms my words.

Source: Butler, Frederick. *A Complete History of the United States of America.* Hartford, 1821, p. 92.

GARANGULA
(17th century)
"Do Not Choke the Tree of Peace"
near present-day Oswego, New York, United States
September 5, 1684

The English translation of *Grand Gueule* is Big Mouth, the name this Onondaga chief received from the French because he was such an impressive speaker. The Indians pronounced his French nickname as one word, "Garangula." His native name was Otreouti. The English governor of New York, Thomas Dongan (called Corlear by the Indians), had previously warned Garangula that the Onondagas were subjects of the English king. Garangula would not hear of it, as the Iroquois saw themselves only as allies, not subjects. The Onondagas were said to have replied, "You say we are subjects to the King of England and the Duke of York. We say we are brethren, and take care of ourselves." In 1684 the aged Garangula met in what is now northern New York State with the French governor of New France (Quebec), Joseph-Antoine de La Barre, whom the Indians called Yonnondio. Disruptions to the important fur trade—and attacks by the Iroquois—had angered the French; de La Barre had crossed Lake Ontario with plans to make war on the powerful Five Nations of the Iroquois Confederacy, who were allied with the English. (The Five Nations were the Mohawks, Oneidas, Onondagas, Cayugas, and Senecas). De La Barre called together a council of chiefs, and he addressed them through his interpreter (SEE de La Barre's speech, page 154). Garangula then revealed he knew the Frenchmen (camped at nearby Anse de la Famine) were too sick to fight, and he mocked their pretense of going to war. He cautioned both governors to preserve the peace. At the end of each portion of his address, Garangula presented beaded wampum belts, as was customary, to make the speech official. De la Barre returned to Quebec the next day.

❦

Yonnondio, I honor you, and the warriors that are with me likewise honor you. Your interpreter has finished your speech. I now begin mine. My words make haste to reach your ears; hearken to them.

Yonnondio, you must have believed, when you left Quebec, that the sun had burnt up all the forests which render our country inaccessible to the French, or that the lakes had so far overflowed the banks that they had surrounded our castles, and that it was impossible for us to get out of them.

Yes, Yonnondio, surely you must have dreamt so; and the curiosity of seeing so great a wonder has brought you so far. Now you are undeceived, since I and the warriors here present are come to assure you that the Senecas, Cayugas, Onondagas, Oneidas, and Mohawks are yet alive. I thank you in their name for bringing back into their country the calumet which your predecessor received from their hands. It was happy for you that you left under ground that murdering hatchet which has been so often dyed in the blood of the French.

Hear, Yonnondio, I do not sleep; I have my eyes open, and the sun which enlightens me, discovers to me a great captain at the head of a company of soldiers, who speaks as if he were dreaming. He says that he only came to the lake to smoke on the great calumet with the Onondagas. But Garangula says that he sees the contrary; that it was to knock them on the head if sickness had not weakened the arms of the French.

I see Yonnondio raving in a camp of sick men, whose lives the Great Spirit has saved by inflicting this sickness on them. Hear, Yonnondio, our women had taken their clubs, our children and old men had carried their bows and arrows into the heart of your camp, if our warriors had not disarmed them, and kept them back, when your messenger Ohguesse came to our castles. It is done, and I have said it.

Hear, Yonnondio, we plundered none of the French but those that carried guns, powder, and ball to the Twightwies and Chictaghicks, because those arms might have cost us our lives. Herein we follow the example of the Jesuits, who stoveall the kegs of rum brought to our castles, lest the drunken Indians should knock them on the head. Our warriors have not beaver enough to pay for all these arms that they have taken; and our old men are not afraid of the war.

This belt preserves my words.

We carried the English into our lakes to trade there with the Utawawas and Quatoghies as the Andirondacks brought the French to our castles to carry on a trade, which the English say is theirs. We are born free. We neither depend on Yonnondio nor Corlear. We may go where we please, and carry with us whom we please. If your allies be your slaves, use them as such. Command them to receive no other but your people.

This belt preserves my words.

We knocked the Twightwies and Chictaghicks on the head because they had cut down the trees of peace which were the limits of our country. They had hunted beavers on our land. They had acted contrary to the customs of all Indians; for they left none of the beavers alive: they killed both male and female. They brought the Satanas into the country to take part with them, after they had concerted ill designs against us. We have done less than either the English or French, that have usurped the lands of so many Indian nations, and chased them from their own country.

This belt preserves my words.

Hear, Yonnondio, what I say is the voice of all the Five Nations: hear what they answer. Open your ears to what they speak. The Senecas, Cayugas, Onondagas, Oneidas, and Mohawks say, that when they buried the hatchet at Cadarackui (in the presence of your predecessor) in the middle of the fort, they planted the tree of peace in the same place, to be there carefully preserved, that in a place of a retreat for soldiers, that fort might be a rendezvous for merchants; that in place of arms and ammunition of war, beavers and merchandize should only enter there.

Hear, Yonnondio, take care for the future, that so great a number of soldiers as appear there, do not choke the tree of peace planted in so small a fort. It will be a great loss if after it had so easily taken root you should stop its growth, and prevent its covering your country and ours with its branches. I assure you, in the name of the Five Nations, that our warriors shall dance to the calumet of peace under its leaves, and shall remain quiet on their mats, and shall never dig up the hatchet till their brother Yonnondio, or Corlear, shall, either jointly or separately, endeavor to attack the country which the Great Spirit has given to our ancestors.

This belt preserves my words; and this other, the authority which the Five Nations have given me.

Source: Butler, Frederick. *A Complete History of the United States of America.* Hartford, 1821, p. 93.

ANDREW HAMILTON
(1676–1741)
In Defense of Freedom of the Press
New York City
August 4, 1735

Scottish-born Andrew Hamilton was attorney general in Pennsylvania from 1717 to 1724, served twice as speaker of the Pennsylvania House of Representatives, and was the British colonies most celebrated trial lawyer. In 1735 he defended John Peter Zenger—a German immigrant and printer arrested for publishing articles critical of William Cosby, the much disliked royal governor of the colony of New York. Zenger had already run afoul of the tyrannical Cosby by printing a dissenting pamphlet for a New York Supreme Court justice in 1733. The only existing New York newspaper at the time, the *New York Gazette,* was under the governor's influence. However, on November 5, 1733, the first issue of a new weekly paper, the *New York Weekly Journal,* was printed and published by Zenger. This paper, written by Cosby's political enemies, contained unsigned stories detailing the governor's interference in an election, among other criticisms, and editorialized on the importance of liberty of the press. Cosby ordered the *Journal* burned in October 1734. On November 17, Zenger was arrested and charged with "seditious libels" (writings critical of the government intended to provoke its downfall) that were "inflaming minds with contempt of His Majesty's government." Zenger was thrown in jail until his trial. Because Cosby had Zenger's local lawyers disbarred, the eloquent Hamilton came all the way from Philadelphia to take the difficult case, working for free. His brilliant defense before the duplicitous governor's handpicked judges persuaded the jury that the published articles were true and thus not libelous. Hamilton had challenged the unpopular libel laws under which Zenger was charged, and defended not only Zenger but also the freedom of the press. Zenger's subsequent acquittal set an important precedent for press freedom in the colonies, and for the principle that no one can be accused of libel for writing the truth.

***

May it please Your Honor, I agree with Mr. Attorney that government is a sacred thing, but I differ widely from him when he would insinuate that the just complaints of a number of men who suffer under a bad administration is libeling that administration. Had I believed that to be law, I should not have given the Court the trouble of hearing anything that I could say in this cause. . . .

There is heresy in law as well as in religion, and both have changed very much. We well know that it is not two centuries ago that a man would have been burned as a heretic for owning such opinions in matters of religion as are publicly written and printed at this day. . . . From which I think it is pretty clear that in New York a man may make very free with his God, but he must take a special care what he says of his governor.

It is agreed upon by all men that this is a reign of liberty. While men keep within the bounds of truth I hope they may with safety both speak and write their sentiments of the conduct of men in power, I mean of that part of their conduct only which affects the liberty or property of the people under their administration. Were this to be denied, then the next step may make them slaves; for what notions can be entertained of slavery beyond that of suffering the greatest injuries and oppressions without the liberty of complaining, or if they do, to be destroyed, body and estate, for so doing?

It is said and insisted on by Mr. Attorney that government is a sacred thing; that it is to be supported and reverenced; that it is government that protects our persons and estates, prevents treasons, murders, robberies, riots, and all the train of evils that overturns kingdoms and states and ruins particular persons. And if those in the administration, especially the supreme magistrate, must have all their conduct censured by private

158

men, government cannot subsist. This is called a licentiousness not to be tolerated. It is said that it brings the rulers of the people into contempt, and their authority not to be regarded, and so in the end the laws cannot be put into execution.

These, I say, and such as these, are the general topics insisted upon by men in power and their advocates. But I wish it might be considered at the same time how often it has happened that the abuse of power has been the primary cause of these evils, and that it was the injustice and oppression of these great men that has commonly brought them into contempt with the people. The craft and art of such men is great, and who that is the least acquainted with history or law can be ignorant of the specious pretenses that have often been made use of by men in power to introduce arbitrary rule, and to destroy the liberties of a free people? . . .

If a libel is understood in the large and unlimited sense urged by Mr. Attorney, there is scarce a writing I know that may not be called a libel, or scarce a person safe from being called to an account as a libeler. For Moses, meek as he was, libeled Cain; and who is it that has not libeled the Devil? . . .

Gentlemen: The danger is great in proportion to the mischief that may happen through our too great credulity. A proper confidence in a court is commendable, but as the verdict, whatever it is, will be yours, you ought to refer no part of your duty to the discretion of other persons. If you should be of the opinion that there is no falsehood in Mr. Zenger's papers, you will, nay pardon me for the expression, you ought, to say so—because you do not know whether others—I mean the Court—may be of that opinion. It is your right to do so, and there is much depending upon your resolution as well as upon your integrity.

The loss of liberty, to a generous mind, is worse than death. And yet we know that there have been those in all ages who for the sake of preferment, or some imaginary honor, have freely lent a helping hand to oppress, nay to destroy, their country.

This brings to my mind that saying of the immortal Brutus when he looked upon the creatures of Caesar, who were very great men but by no means good men. "You Romans," said Brutus, "if yet I may call you so, consider what you are doing. Remember that you are assisting Caesar to forge those very chains that one day he will make you yourselves wear." This is what every man who values freedom ought to consider. He should act by judgment and not by affection or self-interest; for where those prevail, no ties of either country or kindred are regarded; as upon the other hand, the man who loves his country prefers its liberty to all other considerations, well knowing that without liberty life is a misery. . . .

Power may justly be compared to a great river. While kept within its due bounds it is both beautiful and useful. But when it overflows its banks, it is then too impetuous to be stemmed; it bears down all before it, and brings destruction and desolation wherever it comes. If, then, this is the nature of power, let us at least do our duty, and like wise men who value freedom use our utmost care to support liberty, the only bulwark against lawless power, which in all ages has sacrificed to its wild lust and boundless ambition the blood of the best men that ever lived.

I hope to be pardoned, Sir, for my zeal upon this occasion. It is an old and wise caution that when our neighbor's house is on fire we ought to take care of our own. For though—blessed be God I live in a government where liberty is well understood and freely enjoyed, yet experience has shown us all—I am sure it has to me—that a bad precedent in one government is soon set up for an authority in another. And therefore I cannot but think it my, and every honest man's, that while we pay all due obedience to men in authority we ought at the same time to be upon our guard against power wherever we apprehend that it may affect ourselves or our fellow subjects.

I am truly very unequal to such an undertaking on many accounts. You see that I labor under the weight of many years, and am bowed down with great infirmities of body. Yet, old and weak as I am, I should think it my duty, if required, to go to the utmost part of the land where my services could be of any use in assisting to quench the flame of prosecutions upon informations, set on foot by the government, to deprive a people of the right of remonstrating (and complaining, too) of the arbitrary attempts of men in power.

Men who injure and oppress the people under their administration provoke them to cry out and complain, and then make that very complaint the foundation for new oppressions and prosecutions. I wish I could say that there were no instances of this kind.

But to conclude: The question before the Court and you, Gentlemen of the Jury, is not of small or private concern. It is not the cause of one poor printer, nor of New York alone, which you are now trying. No! It may in its consequence affect every free man that lives under a British government on the main of America. It is the best cause. It is the cause of liberty.

And I make no doubt but your upright conduct this day will not only entitle you to the love and esteem of your fellow citizens, but every man who prefers freedom to a life of slavery will bless and honor you as men who have baffled the attempt of tyranny, and by an impartial and uncorrupt verdict have laid a noble foundation for securing to ourselves, our posterity, and our neighbors, that to which nature and the laws of our country have given us a right to liberty of both exposing and opposing arbitrary power (in these parts of the world at least) by speaking and writing truth.

Source: Chandler, Peleg Whitman. *American Criminal Trials.* Vol. I. Boston: Charles Little & James Brown, 1841, p. 162.

JOHN WESLEY
(1703–1791)
"The New Birth"
Great Britain
1740

John Wesley, the founder of Methodism (a revival in the 18th-century Church of England stressing conversion and personal holiness), was the 15th child of a Church of England minister, Samuel Wesley, and his wife, Susannah. Devout from his youth, Wesley found the Protestant Church of England unsatisfying. Many ministers were worldly and uninterested in holiness, and the dominant preaching tradition focused on morality and the "reasonableness" of religion. At Oxford, Wesley became the leader of a small ascetic (self-denying) group known as the "Holy Club" or "Methodists," which included his brother Charles Wesley, a great hymn-writer, and another famous English preacher, George Whitefield. In 1735 Wesley went on a preaching trip to Georgia, then a British colony, but his preaching against the slave trade led to opposition, and he returned to Britain. Shortly afterward, he began the "field-preaching" that would bring him fame. In the economically dynamic Britain of the 18th century, many rapidly growing communities lacked parish churches, and Church of England clergy were often reluctant to minister to the poor and uneducated. Wesley preached daily in open fields and halls to coal-miners and other poor workers and their families. Traveling preachers were viewed with suspicion; he faced opposition, sometimes violent, from church and state officials who opposed preaching outside the church authority structure, as well as from ordinary people who disliked his call for renouncing sin. Although Wesley never formally broke from the Church of England, he was a great organizer and built his own institutions outside of it. After his death, that organization became the Methodist Church. Wesley's preaching focused not on church doctrines, but on the need for conversion. His sermons appealed to the emotions rather than to the intellect—his was a "religion of the heart." The emphasis on being "born again" still influences contemporary evangelical Christianity. This excerpt is from "The New Birth," a sermon he preached more than 60 times across England.

Before a child is born into the world he has eyes, but sees not; he has ears, but does not hear. He has a very imperfect use of any other sense. He has no knowledge of any of the things of the world, or any natural understanding. To that manner of existence which he then has, we do not even give the name of life. It is then only when a man is born, that we say he begins to live.

For as soon as he is born, be begins to see the light, and the various objects with which he is encompassed. His ears are then opened, and he hears the sounds which successively strike upon them. At the same time, all the other organs of sense begin to be exercised upon their proper objects. He likewise breathes, and lives in a manner wholly different from what he did before.

How exactly doth the parallel hold in all these instances! While a man is in a mere natural state, before he is born of God, he has, in a spiritual sense, eyes and sees not; a thick impenetrable veil lies upon them. He has ears, but hears not; he is utterly deaf to what he is most of all concerned to hear. His other spiritual senses are all locked up: He is in the same condition as if he had them not. Hence he has no knowledge of God; no intercourse with him; he is not at all acquainted with him. He has no true knowledge of the things of God, either of spiritual or eternal things; therefore, though he is a living man, he is a dead Christian. . . .

From hence it manifestly appears, what is the nature of the new birth. It is that great change which God works in the soul when he brings it into life, when he raises it from the death of sin to the life of righteousness. It is the change wrought in the whole

In an engraving after a portrait by Nathaniel Hone (ca. 1766), John Wesley challenges the Church of England by preaching in the open air. He became the founder of Methodism. *(Ablestock)*

soul by the almighty Spirit of God when it is "created anew in Christ Jesus;" when it is "renewed after the image of God, in righteousness and true holiness;" when the love of the world is changed into the love of God: pride into humility; passion into meekness; hatred, envy, malice, into a sincere, tender, disinterested love for all mankind. In a word, it is that change whereby the earthly, sensual, devilish mind is turned into the "mind which was in Christ Jesus." This is the nature of the new birth: "So is every one that is born of the Spirit.". . .

But "without holiness no man shall see the Lord," shall see the face of God in glory. Of consequence, the new birth is absolutely necessary in order to eternal salvation. Men may indeed flatter themselves (so desperately wicked and so deceitful is the heart of man!) that they may live in their sins till they come to the last gasp, and yet afterwards live with God; and thousands do really believe, that they have found a broad way which leadeth not to destruction.

"What danger," say they, "can a woman be in that is so harmless and so virtuous? What fear is there that so honest a man, one of so strict morality, should miss of heaven; especially if, over and above all this, they constantly attend on church and sacrament?" One of these will ask with all assurance, "What! Shall not I do as well as my neighbors?" Yes as well as your unholy neighbors; as well as your neighbors that die in their sins! For you will all drop into the pit together, into the nethermost hell! You will all lie together in the lake of fire; "the lake of fire burning with brimstone." Then, at length, you will see (but God grant you may see it before!) the necessity of holiness in order to glory; and, consequently, of the new birth, since none can be holy, except he be born again. . . .

But perhaps the sinner himself, to whom in real charity we say, "You must be born again," has been taught to say, "I defy your new doctrine; I need not be born again: I was born again when I was baptized. What! Would you have me deny my baptism?"

I answer, First, there is nothing under heaven which can excuse a lie; otherwise I should say to an open sinner, If you have been baptized, do not own it. For how highly does this aggravate your guilt! How will it increase your damnation! Was you devoted to God at eight days old, and have you been all these years devoting yourself to the devil? Was you, even before you had the use of reason, consecrated to God the Father, the Son, and the Holy Ghost? And have you, ever since you had the use of it, been flying in the face of God, and consecrating yourself to Satan?

Does the abomination of desolation—the love of the word, pride, anger, lust, foolish desire, and a whole train of vile affections—stand where it ought not? Have you set up all the accursed things in that soul which was once a temple of the Holy Ghost; set apart for an "habitation of God, through the Spirit;" yea, solemnly given up to him? And do you glory in this, that you once belonged to God? O be ashamed! Blush! Hide yourself in the earth! Never boast more of what ought to fill you with confusion, to make you ashamed before God and man!

I answer, Secondly, you have already denied your baptism; and that in the most effectual manner. You have denied it a thousand and a thousand times; and you do so still, day by day. For in your baptism you renounced the devil and all his works. Whenever, therefore, you give place to him again, whenever you do any of the works of the devil, then you deny your baptism. Therefore you deny it by every willful sin; by every act of uncleanness, drunkenness, or revenge; by every obscene or profane word; by every oath that comes out of your mouth. Every time you profane the day of the Lord, you thereby deny your baptism; yea, every time you do any thing to another which you would not he should do to you.

I answer, Thirdly, be you baptized or unbaptized, "you must be born again;" otherwise it is not possible you should be inwardly holy; and without inward as well as outward holiness, you cannot be happy, even in this world, much less in the world to come. Do you say, "Nay, but I do no harm to any man; I am honest and just in all my dealings. I do not curse, or take the Lord's name in vain; I do not profane the Lord's day. I am no drunkard; I do not slander my neighbor, nor live in any willful sin?" If this be so, it were much to be wished that all men went as far as you do. But you must go farther yet, or you cannot be saved: Still, "you must be born again."

Do you add, "I do go farther yet; for I not only do no harm, but do all the good I can?" I doubt that fact; I fear you have had a thousand opportunities of doing good which you have suffered to pass by unimproved, and for which therefore you are accountable to God. But if you had improved them all, if you really had done all the good you possibly could to all men, yet this does not at all alter the case; still, "you must be born again." Without this, nothing will do any good to your poor, sinful, polluted soul.

"Nay, but I constantly attend all the ordinances of God: I keep to my church and sacrament." It is well you do: But all this will not keep you from hell, except you be born again. Go to church twice a day; go to the Lord's table every week; say ever so many prayers in private; hear ever so many good sermons; read ever so many good books; still, "you must be born again:" None of these things will stand in the place of the new birth; no, nor any thing under heaven.

Let this therefore, if you have not already experienced this inward work of God, be your continual prayer: "Lord, add this to all thy blessings—let me be born again! Deny whatever thou pleasest, but deny not this; let me be 'born from above!' Take away whatsoever seemeth thee good—reputation, fortune, friends, health—only give me this, to be born of the Spirit, to be received among the children of God! Let me be born, 'not of corruptible seed, but incorruptible, by the word of God, which liveth and abideth for ever;" and then let me daily 'grow in grace, and in the knowledge of our Lord and Savior Jesus Christ!'"

Source: Emory, John. *The Works of the Reverend John Wesley.* Vol. 1. New York: Mason & Lane, 1840, p. 402.

THE AGE OF
REVOLUTION AND EMPIRE
(1750–1900)

Introduction to the Age of Revolution and Empire

The period from 1750 to 1900 was an age of revolution in both politics and economics. The political revolutions began in the late 18th century with the American Revolution (1775–83), the French Revolution of 1789, the Haitian Revolution (1791–1804), and the Latin American revolutions. A second wave of political revolutions included the French Revolution of 1830 and the European revolutions of 1848. The economic revolution was the Industrial Revolution that began in England in the late 18th century and in the 19th century spread through the British Isles, continental Europe, and the United States. Industrialism also contributed to the building of the great European empires of the 19th century.

THE AMERICAN REVOLUTION

The American Revolution was caused by differences between a British government that was increasingly centralizing its empire and the leaders of the American colonies, seeking to preserve and enhance their freedom of action. The conflict led to war and ultimately independence for America. The revolution was controversial on both shores of the Atlantic. Some revolutionary leaders, such as Boston's Samuel Adams, were "rabble-rousers" who used their oratorical skills to mobilize popular sentiment in favor of confrontation. Many Americans, known as "loyalists," wished to remain part of the British Empire, while particularly early in the conflict many Britons were sympathetic to the American cause. Former prime minister William Pitt (the Elder, 1708–78) was an exceptionally eloquent champion of the American cause in the British parliament. The debate on independence was also lively in America. The rhetoric of the American revolution, marked by ringing exclamations such as that attributed to the Virginia statesman Patrick Henry, who declared, "Give me liberty or give me death!," would echo through the centuries in America and elsewhere.

After the colonies and their European allies had won the war against Great Britain in 1783, Americans needed to shape a new political order. The original arrangement proved unsatisfactory, and after a convention in 1787, the U.S. Constitution and Bill of Rights were adopted. The first president of the newly created United States of America, the revolutionary general George Washington, would become one of the most admired figures of the age.

REVOLUTIONS IN FRANCE AND HAITI

In this period, one revolution commonly led to another. French aid had been vital in winning American freedom, but the war greatly added to the French government's financial burden. French people were also excited by the new American republic and wondered if some of its features could be duplicated on French soil. An attempt to reform French government and finances led to the outbreak of the great French revolution of 1789. The revolution became more radical in the following years. While revolutionaries had originally boasted of their loyalty to the king, eventually the revolutionary authorities executed King Louis XVI (r. 1774–92) and his queen, Marie Antoinette (r. 1774–92). France found itself at war with half of Europe as the National Assembly resounded with the words of such orators and statesmen as the comte de Mirabeau, Maximilien Robespierre, and Georges-Jacques Danton.

The revolutionary armies defended France from its neighbors, but the strengthening of the military eventually led to the fall of the Republic. The oratory of the French Republic, like its political culture, died a temporary death when the successful general Napoleon Bonaparte overthrew the government to eventually rule

France as "Emperor Napoleon" in 1804. Like many authoritarian politicians, Napoleon detested "talking-shops" and reduced France's surviving parliamentary institutions to rubber stamps. Napoleon himself was a gifted speaker, but only when addressing soldiers or followers. His addresses on the eve of battle became classics. Napoleon's defeat at Waterloo in 1815 was followed by the restoration of the French royal family, but the culture of the revolution remained strong. Further revolutions followed in 1830 and in 1848.

The French Revolution also contributed to the Haitian Revolution, when the slaves on the French island colony of Saint-Domingue rose in the name of freedom (1791–1804). The revolution's leader, Toussaint Louverture, was an ex-slave. Toussaint Louverture overcame opposition both on and off the island to overthrow the French planters and free the enslaved. He eventually secured the abolition of slavery in the French empire as a price for Saint-Domingue's remaining French. When Napoleon attempted to restore slavery in the French Caribbean and reconquer Saint-Domingue to restore direct French rule, he captured and imprisoned Toussaint. However, the freed slaves defeated his armies and made their country independent under the name of "Haiti." The Haitian rebels also helped bring the issue of slavery and its abolition to the top of the international agenda.

REVOLUTION IN LATIN AMERICA AND IRELAND

The wars of the French Revolution and Napoleon led to a need for European empires to concentrate their resources in Europe itself. The weakening of imperial control, and the spread of the ideals of the French Revolution, led to a series of revolutions in imperial possessions. The revolutions in British-controlled Ireland were unsuccessful, but eloquent leaders such as Robert Emmet left a legacy to subsequent Irish nationalists. The greatest revolutionary changes occurred in Latin America when a wave of revolutionary movements swept all of the Spanish possessions on the American mainland—an empire that had been built over the course of three centuries—in the space of a few years. Spanish rule was overthrown and new governments established under the leadership and inspiring words of men such as Miguel Hidalgo and José María Morelos of Mexico and Simón Bolívar of Venezuela. Brazil also established its independence from Portugal, but by peaceful means.

"REPUBLICAN" POLITICAL CULTURE

Most of the political revolutions of the 18th and 19th centuries were in support of republicanism—the Americans relatively quickly (after eight years by 1783), the

French after a long 40-year struggle that only ended in 1870. Numerous other nations abolished the hereditary rule of kings and emperors. Even countries that retained a monarchy, such as Great Britain, moved steadily in the direction of limiting monarchical power via a written or unwritten constitution. The post-revolutionary world was awash in popular assemblies, and the career of politician proved attractive to many middle and upper-class men. These new assemblies—the U.S. Congress and state legislatures, the French National Assembly, the German Reichstag, and a host of others—joined older institutions such as the British parliament as showcases for oratory. Eloquent speakers such as America's New Hampshire lawyer Daniel Webster made outstanding political careers for themselves.

Even in societies in which politics was relatively peaceful, causes such as Catholic emancipation in Ireland or the abolition of slavery in the British Empire and the United States required bringing the pressure of mass organization to bear on the political elite. The rise of mass politics brought new challenges for orators. Political orators found it as important to be able to address crowds at a public meeting as to speak to small groups of their peers in parliamentary chambers. The audience for speeches, at least in written form, was also increased by the rise of the periodical press. Reports of speeches and debates were a staple for many newspapers.

SLAVERY AND ABOLITION

One of the most important political causes in the 19th century was the "abolitionist" movement, which worked for the abolition first of the international slave trade and then of slavery itself. The roots of the movement lay in Great Britain, the preeminent slave-trading nation of the 18th century. Under the leadership of Member of Parliament William Wilberforce, the abolitionist movement pioneered many forms of political activism. Speeches in Parliament were coordinated with addresses to crowds in the country together with petitioning, boycott campaigns, and pamphleteering. Slaveowners in the British Caribbean fiercely resisted abolition for many years. Important milestones included the abolition of the British slave trade in 1807 and the abolition of slavery itself in the British Empire in 1834.

The struggle in America was even more dramatic, as abolitionists faced the might of the southern planters, whose economy was increasingly dependent on slavery in the 19th century. Speakers such as the ex-slave Frederick Douglass denounced slavery throughout the northern states. Eventually, slavery led to the secession of most of the southern, slaveholding states from the United States. In the great Civil War that followed from 1861 to 1865, the Union was led by Abraham Lincoln, considered by many to be America's greatest president, and certainly its most eloquent. Lincoln's Gettysburg Address, given at the dedication of a cemetery for the Union dead, is one of the most famous speeches in American history. Union victory in the Civil War led to the end of slavery in America.

INDUSTRY AND EMPIRE

The "industrial revolution" is a phrase invented long after what it describes. Beginning in late 18th-century England, artificial power, most notably the steam engine, began to usurp the place of natural power—human and animal muscle, wind and water. Many technological processes, beginning with textiles, were mechanized. Constant technological innovation became a part of life, and production zoomed to previously unheard-of levels.

Industrialism brought with it a host of new social issues. The new cities it created were crowded, dirty, filled with bad housing and vulnerable to sweeping epidemics. Workers and employers were locked into an economic and political conflict that often became violent. Established agricultural elites and the new industrial ones had different and often clashing economic interests.

Industrialism also contributed to the growing power of the West over other societies. Of course, Western empires were long-established at the beginning of the period, but the late 19th century saw European imperialism reach its height. The basis of 19th-century imperialism lay in the technological and organizational advantage of European nations. Britain, France, Germany, Belgium, Russia, and other European powers possessed more rapid firing and accurate guns, and better ships and transportation than did the indigenous societies of Asia and Africa. Europeans won most, although not all, of the wars. Colonial wars were often fought with much savagery and with genocidal and near genocidal brutality, particularly as they came to be defined as racial wars or as wars of civilization against barbarism. The partition of Africa between various colonial powers in the late 19th century—the "scramble for Africa"—was particularly violent, and the words of African leaders like Machemba and Wobogo could do little to stop the European onslaught.

NEW SOCIAL MOVEMENTS— SOCIALISM, NATIONALISM, SUFFRAGISM

The political impulse of democratization and the new problems created by industrialization eventually led to the birth of a new political movement—socialism. Socialism is difficult to define, and many people have called and still call themselves socialists. It is basically a belief that economic exploitation can and should be abolished. Socialism in the European tradition essentially emerged from two sources: revolutionary and Utopian. Revolutionary socialists hoped and worked for the destruction of the power of governments and economic elites. Their tradition ultimately stemmed from the more democratic side of the French Revolution. The other tradition was "Utopian" socialism. Utopian socialists wanted to build new institutions such as communes. These institutions would be economically just, and their examples would spread through existing society. By the late 19th century, however, socialism lost much of its revolutionary and utopian zeal, and many Socialist parties devoted their energies to electoral politics.

Socialism was not the only, or in many places even the most important, revolutionary force of 19th-century Europe. There emerged in many countries a new emphasis on ethnic identity and a belief that an ethnicity, or "nation," should be politically independent and united. In some politically fragmented European territories such as Germany and Italy, a long struggle to establish a united state took place. In other territories where a nation found itself under foreign rule, such as Poland, then governed by Russia, the struggle was to throw off the "foreign yoke." The Habsburg Empire in south-central and eastern Europe was particularly known for the cutthroat politics of its numerous nationalities (Vienna, Budapest, and Prague were its major centers of power) and inspirational leadership came from nationalists such as Hungary's liberal statesman Louis Kossuth.

Women were another subjugated element among the population that began to assert itself. Denied voting and other political rights in the new republics and democracies, women—and a few male allies such as English philosopher and Member of Parliament John Stuart Mill—began to speak out. They demanded a better deal for themselves, not just on the vote but on other issues such as control over property and access to higher education and the professions. The vote, or "suffrage," was the centerpiece of the movement, however, which was often called "suffragism." Leaders such as Lucy Stone and Susan B. Anthony in the United States made strong arguments for their cause, but they won only limited progress on securing the vote until the 20th century.

Speeches

MINAVAVANA, CHIPPEWA CHIEF
(died 1770)
"You Know That His Enemies Are Ours"
Ft. Michilimackinac, now Michigan, United States
Mid-September 1761

The French and Indian War (1754–63) was fought in North America between France and Britain, with the aid of Indians on both sides. It was fought over the ambitions of two European countries for territorial domination in the New World, and the fears British Protestant colonists harbored of French Catholic rule. It was also one of several wars around the globe (between 1756 and 1763) known collectively as the Seven Years' War. These wars would make Britain a great colonial power and leave France without most of its colonial possessions. (The British colonists' success would also give them the first taste of independence from the mother country.) In 1760 Britain seized Montreal and Quebec, and the French surrendered. The capture of New France—now Canada—dismayed the Great Lakes Indian tribes friendly to the French. They hoped France would retake the region. The next year, with 60 painted and armed warriors at his side, Mackinac Chippewa (Ojibwa) Chief Minavavana (or Menehwehna) angrily addressed a terrified white man in Ft. Michilimackinac, a former French trading post (in present-day Michigan). That man was Alexander Henry, a 22-year-old English adventurer from New Jersey, dressed as a Frenchman, who had ventured to Mackinac to trade for furs. Minavavana and his men had discovered Henry paddling his canoe on a nearby waterway; they were not fooled by the disguise. Luck was with Henry—he had enough goods to make a satisfactory present, and lived to record this speech in an account of his travels. Two years later Minavavana captured Fort Michilimakinac during the war called Pontiac's Rebellion (1763–64), until it was retaken by the British. He was killed in 1770 in a British attack.

Englishman! It is to you that I speak, and I demand your attention.

Englishman! You know that the French king is our father. He promised to be such; and we, in return, promised to be his children. This promise we have kept.

Englishman! It is you that have made war with this our father. You are his enemy. And how then could you have the boldness to venture among us, his children? You know that his enemies are ours.

Englishman! We are informed that our father, the king of France, is old and infirm, and that being fatigued with making war on your nation, he is fallen asleep. During his sleep, you have taken advantage of him, and possessed yourselves of Canada. But his nap is almost at an end. I think I hear him already stirring, and inquiring for his children, the Indians. And when he does awake, what must become of you? He will destroy you utterly!

Englishman! Although you have conquered the French, you have not yet conquered us. We are not your slaves. These lakes, these woods and mountains were left to us by our ancestors. They are our inheritance, and we will part with them to none. Your nation supposes that we, like the white people, cannot live without bread, and pork, and beef. But you ought to know that He—the Great Spirit and Master of Life—has provided food for us in these broad lakes and upon these mountains.

Englishman! Our father, the king of France, employed our young men to make war upon your nation. In this warfare, many of them have been killed; and it is our custom to retaliate, until such time as the spirits of the slain are satisfied. Now the spirits of the slain are to be satisfied in either of two ways. The first is by the spilling of the blood of the nation by which they fell; the other, by covering the bodies of the dead, and thus allaying the resentment of their relations. This is done by making presents.

RHETORICAL DEVICE

Antonomasia: Substituting an epithet or title for a person's name.

Cuba, what would have become of you had you let your Apostle die?
—*Fidel Castro, speaking of José Martí, apostle of Cuban independence*

Englishman! Although you have conquered the French, you have
not yet conquered us. We are not your slaves. —*Minavavana, speaking to
Alexander Henry, English adventurer and trader*

Our beloved leader, Bapu as we called him, the Father of the Nation,
is no more. —*Jawaharlal Nehru, speaking of Mahatma Gandhi*

Englishman! Your king has never sent us any presents, nor entered into any treaty with us. Wherefore he and we are still at war; and, until he does these things, we must consider that we have no other father, nor friend, among the white men than the king of France.

But, for you, we have taken into consideration that you have ventured your life among us, in the expectation that we should not molest you. You do not come armed, with an intention to make war. You come in peace, to trade with us and supply us with necessaries, of which we are much in want. We shall regard you, therefore, as a brother; and you may sleep tranquilly, without fear of the Chippewas.

As a token of our friendship, we present you with this pipe to smoke.

Source: Henry, Alexander. *Alexander Henry's Travels and Adventures in the Years 1760–1776.*
Edited by Milo Milton Quaife. Chicago: Lakeside Press, 1921, p. 43.

WILLIAM PITT THE ELDER
(1708–1778)
Toward Repealing the Stamp Act
House of Commons, London, England
January 14, 1766

William Pitt (the Elder) entered the British parliament in 1735 and was immediately recognized for his magnificent oratory. He had a long, illustrious career. Under King George II, he was the brilliant manager of the Seven Years' War (1756–63), laying the foundation for Britain's empire, but his genius for foreign policy went unappreciated by the next king, George III, who came to the throne in 1760. England was in considerable debt from the French and Indian War (1754–63), and Parliament saw a solution in taxing the colonies to obtain funds. The Stamp Act of 1765 was intended in particular to help pay for the garrisons of English troops guarding the colonies. The act required tax stamps to be bought and attached to all legal papers including wills or deeds, newspapers, pamphlets, advertisements, and even playing cards sold in the colonies. Colonial reaction was swift. Delegates from nine colonies formed the Stamp Act Congress, which met in October 1765 in New York City. The congress declared that as the colonists were not represented in Parliament, they were being taxed without their consent. Colonists who opposed the tax refused to buy the stamps; some even broke into a tax agent's home and hung his effigy (a representation of his image) from a tree. Throughout the colonies, protest groups formed calling themselves the Sons of Liberty—Patrick Henry, Paul Revere, John Hancock, and Sam Adams all joined. In the British parliament, William Pitt was among the few Englishmen who understood the Americans' position. In January, he rose to object to taxing the colonies without representation. When one of the Stamp Act's promoters suggested that Pitt was stirring up the colonists to rebellion, he stood again to deliver this speech. Parliament repealed the Stamp Act two months later.

Gentlemen, Sir, I have been charged with giving birth to sedition in America.

They have spoken their sentiments with freedom against this unhappy act, and that freedom has become their crime. Sorry I am to hear the liberty of speech in this house imputed as a crime. But the imputation shall not discourage me. It is a liberty I mean to exercise. No gentleman ought to be afraid to exercise it. It is a liberty by which the gentleman who calumniates it might have profited; he ought to have desisted from his project.

The gentleman tells us America is obstinate; America is almost in open rebellion. I rejoice that America has resisted. Three millions of people, so dead to all the feelings of liberty as voluntarily to submit to be slaves, would have been fit instruments to make slaves of the rest.

I come not here armed at all points, with law cases and acts of parliament, with the statute book doubled down in dog's-ears, to defend the cause of liberty: If I had, I myself would have cited the two cases of Chester and Durham. I would have cited them to show that even under former arbitrary reigns, parliaments were ashamed of taxing a people without their consent, and allowed them representatives. Why did the gentleman confine himself to Chester and Durham? He might have taken a higher example in Wales; Wales, that never was taxed by parliament till it was incorporated. I would not debate a particular point of law with the gentleman. I know his abilities. I have been obliged to his diligent researches. But, for the defense of liberty, upon a general principle, upon a constitutional principle, it is a ground on which I stand firm—on which I dare meet any man.

Member of the British parliament William Pitt (the Elder) was elevated to the earldom of Chatham in 1766, a reward from King George III to his minister of war. Pitt's son, also named William Pitt and nicknamed "the Younger," followed his father into Parliament to become prime minister in 1783 at only 24 years of age. Engraving by John Keyse Sherwin (1751–90) *(Library of Congress)*

The gentleman tells us of many who are taxed, and are not represented—the India Company, merchants, stockholders, manufacturers. Surely many of these are represented in other capacities, as owners of land, or as freemen of boroughs. It is a misfortune that more are not equally represented. But they are all inhabitants and, as such, are they not virtually represented? Many have it in their option to be actually represented. They have connections with those that elect, and they have influence over them. The gentleman mentioned the stockholders: I hope he does not reckon the debts of the nation as a part of the national estate.

Since the accession of King William, many ministers, some of great, others of more moderate abilities, have taken the lead of government. None of these thought, or ever dreamed, of robbing the colonies of their constitutional rights. That was reserved to mark the era of the late administration. Not that there were wanting some, when I had the honour to serve his majesty, to propose to me to burn my fingers with an American stamp act. With the enemy at their back, with our bayonets at their breasts, in the day of their distress, perhaps the Americans would have submitted to the imposition; but it would have been taking an ungenerous, an unjust advantage. The gentleman boasts of his bounties to America! Are not those bounties intended finally for the benefit of this kingdom? If not, he has misapplied the national treasures!

I am no courtier of America. I stand up for this kingdom. I maintain that the parliament has a right to bind, to restrain America. Our legislative power over the colonies is sovereign and supreme. When it ceases to be sovereign and supreme, I would advise every gentleman to sell his lands, if he can, and embark for that country. When two countries are connected together, like England and her colonies, without being incorporated, the one must necessarily govern. The greater must rule the less. But she must so rule it as not to contradict the fundamental principles that are common to both.

If the gentleman does not understand the difference between external and internal taxes, I cannot help it. There is a plain distinction between taxes levied for the purpose of raising a revenue, and duties imposed for the regulation of trade, for the accommodation of the subject; although, in the consequences, some revenue might incidentally arise from the latter.

The gentleman asks, when were the colonies emancipated? But I desire to know, when were they made slaves? But I dwell not upon words. When I had the honour of serving his Majesty, I availed myself of the means of information which I derived from my office; I speak, therefore, from knowledge. My materials were good; I was at pains to collect, to digest, to consider them; and I will be bold to affirm, that the profits to Great Britain from the trade of the colonies, through all its branches, is two millions a year.

This is the fund that carried you triumphantly through the last war. . . . You owe this to America: this is the price America pays you for her protection. . . .

The gentleman must not wonder he was not contradicted when, as minister, he asserted the right of parliament to tax America. I know not how it is, but there is a modesty in this House which does not choose to contradict a minister. I wish gentlemen would get the better of this modesty. . . .

A great deal has been said withoutdoors of the power, of the strength, of America. It is a topic that ought to be cautiously meddled with. In a good cause, on a sound bottom, the force of this country can crush America to atoms. I know the valour of your troops. I know the skill of your officers. There is not a company of foot that has served in America out of which you may not pick a man of sufficient knowledge and experience to make him governor of a colony there. But on this ground, on the Stamp Act, when so many here will think a crying injustice, I am one who will lift up my hands against it.

In such a cause, your success would be hazardous. America, if she fell, would fall like a strong man. She would embrace the pillars of the state, and pull down the constitution along with her. Is this your boasted peace—not to sheathe the sword in its scabbard, but to sheathe it in the bowels of your countrymen? Will you quarrel with yourselves, now the whole House of Bourbon is united against you? . . .

The Americans have not acted in all things with prudence and temper. They have been wronged; they have been driven to madness by injustice. Will you punish them for the madness you have occasioned? Rather let prudence and temper come first from this side. I will undertake for America, that she will follow the example. There are two lines in a ballad of Prior's, of a man's behaviour to his wife, so applicable to you and your colonies, that I cannot help repeating them:

Be to her faults a little blind

Be to her virtues very kind.

Upon the whole, I will beg leave to tell the House what is my opinion. It is that the Stamp Act be repealed absolutely, totally, and immediately; that the reason for the repeal be assigned, because it was founded on an erroneous principle. At the same time, let the sovereign authority of this country over the colonies be asserted in as strong terms as can be devised, and be made to extend to every point of legislation whatsoever; that we may bind their trade, confine their manufactures, and exercise every power whatsoever, except that of taking money from their pockets without their consent.

Source: Miller, Marion Mills. *Great Debates in American History.* Vol. 1. New York: Current Literature Publishing Co., 1913, p. 45.

WILLIAM PITT THE ELDER
(1708–1778)
"Justice to America"
House of Commons, London, England
January 20, 1775

William Pitt became earl of Chatham and prime minister (for two years) in 1766 after successful service as minister of war conducting Britain's victorious Seven Years' War (1756–63). He was a friend of the American colonies, one whose advice regarding the colonies King George III (r. 1760–1820) unwisely rejected. The eloquent Pitt denounced the Stamp Act in 1766, and for years he begged Parliament to retract the harsh measures exacted against the Americans. His speeches reflect his admiration and respect for the statesmen of the colonies. As tension grew in the colonies, British troops were massed in New York and in Boston (under General George Gage) to counter civil disorder. The soldiers were increasingly housed in private homes, to the anger of citizens. In January 1775, because he did not have the ear of King George III, Pitt was forced to deliver his advice to the king through a speech to Parliament. When Pitt mentions "a person of undoubted respect and authenticity," but does not refer to him by name, he is speaking of American colonist Benjamin Franklin, publisher, scientist, inventor, and diplomat. He also mentions "violent and oppressive acts" that he recommends Parliament rescind. These were the Intolerable Acts enacted by Parliament in 1774; they included the Boston Port Act, which closed the port to all ships until Massachusetts paid for the destroyed tea and lost customs revenue from the Boston Tea Party the year before. (The Boston Tea Party was the result of the Tea Act, in which Britain granted the East India Company a monopoly on all tea exported to the colonies.) The Intolerable Acts were repealed three years into the American Revolutionary War (1775–83) but, as Pitt had predicted, the moment of opportunity was lost. Pitt's motion in this speech to remove the English troops from Boston lost by a vote of 18 to 68. George III did not heed Pitt's counsel. The American Revolution began on April 19 at Lexington and Concord three months after this speech was delivered.

As I have not the honor of access to his Majesty, I will endeavor to transmit to him, through the constitutional channel of this House, my ideas of America, to rescue him from the misadvice of his present ministers. . . .

I hope I am not premature in submitting to you my present motion: "That a humble address be presented to His Majesty humbly to desire and beseech His Majesty that, in order to open the way towards a happy settlement of the dangerous troubles in America, by beginning to allay ferments and soften animosities there; and, above all, for preventing in the meantime any sudden and fatal catastrophe at Boston, now suffering under the daily irritation of an army before their eyes posted in their town: it may graciously please His Majesty that immediate orders be dispatched to General Gage for removing His Majesty's forces from the town of Boston."

I wish, my Lords, not to lose a day in this urgent, pressing crisis. An hour now lost in allaying ferments in America may produce years of calamity. For my own part, I will not desert, for a moment, the conduct of this weighty business, from the first to the last, unless nailed to my bed by the extremity of sickness. I will give it unremitted attention. I will knock at the door of this sleeping and confounded ministry, and will rouse them to a sense of their danger.

When I state the importance of the colonies to this country, and the magnitude of danger hanging over this country from the present plan of misadministration practiced against them, I desire not to be understood to argue for a reciprocity of indulgence between England and America. I contend not for indulgence, but justice to America;

and I shall ever contend that the Americans justly owe obedience to us in a limited degree—they owe obedience to our ordinances of trade and navigation; but let the line be skillfully drawn between the objects of those ordinances and their private internal property. Let the sacredness of their property remain inviolate. Let it be taxable only by their own consent, given in their provincial assemblies, else it will cease to be property. . . .

When I urge this measure of recalling the troops from Boston, I urge it on this pressing principle, that it is necessarily preparatory to the restoration of your peace and the establishment of your prosperity. It will then appear that you are disposed to treat amicably and equitably; and to consider, revise, and repeal, if it should be found necessary (as I affirm it will), those violent acts and declarations which have disseminated confusion throughout your empire.

Resistance to your acts was necessary, as it was just; and your vain declarations of the omnipotence of Parliament, and your imperious doctrines of the necessity of submission, will be found equally impotent to convince or to enslave your fellow-subjects in America, who feel that tyranny, whether ambitioned by an individual part of the Legislature, or the bodies who compose it, is equally intolerable to British subjects.

The means of enforcing this thraldom are found to be as ridiculous and weak in practice as they are unjust in principle. Indeed, I cannot but feel the most anxious sensibility for the situation of General Gage, and the troops under his command, thinking him, as I do, a man of humanity and understanding; and entertaining, as I ever will, the highest respect, the warmest love for the British troops. Their situation is truly unworthy; penned up—pining in inglorious inactivity. They are an army of impotence. You may call them an army of safety and of guard; but they are, in truth, an army of impotence and contempt. And, to make the folly equal to the disgrace, they are an army of irritation and vexation.

I therefore urge and conjure your Lordships immediately to adopt this conciliating measure. I will pledge myself for its immediately producing conciliatory effects, by its being thus well timed; but if you delay till your vain hope shall be accomplished of triumphantly dictating reconciliation, you delay forever. . . .

But his Majesty is advised that the union in America cannot last. Ministers have more eyes than I, and should have more ears; but with all the information I have been able to procure, I can pronounce it a union solid, permanent, and effectual. . . . Of this spirit of independence, animating the nation of America, I have the most authentic information. It is not new among them. It is, and has ever been, their established principle, their confirmed persuasion. It is their nature and their doctrine.

I remember, some years ago, when the repeal of the Stamp Act was in agitation, conversing in a friendly confidence with a person of undoubted respect and authenticity, on that subject, and he assured me with a certainty which his judgment and opportunity gave him, that these were the prevalent and steady principles of America—that you might destroy their towns, and cut them off from the superfluities, perhaps the conveniences of life, but that they were prepared to despise your power, and would not lament their loss, while they have—what, my Lords?—their woods and their liberty. The name of my authority, if I am called upon, will authenticate the opinion irrefragably. . . .

But it is not repealing this act of Parliament, it is not repealing a piece of parchment, that can restore America to our bosom. You must repeal her fears and her resentments, and you may then hope for her love and gratitude. But now, insulted with an armed force posted at Boston, irritated with a hostile array before her eyes, her concessions, if you could force them, would be suspicious and insecure. . . .

When your Lordships look at the papers transmitted us from America—when you consider their decency, firmness, and wisdom, you cannot but respect their cause, and wish to make it your own. For myself, I must declare and avow, that in all my reading and observation, and it has been my favorite study—I have read Thucydides, and have studied and admired the master-states of the world—that for solidity of reasoning, force of sagacity, and wisdom of conclusion, under such a complication of difficult circumstances, no nation or body of men can stand in preference to the general Congress at Philadelphia.

I trust it is obvious to your Lordships that all attempts to impose servitude upon such men, to establish despotism over such a mighty continental nation, must be vain, must be fatal. We shall be forced ultimately to retract; let us retract while we can, not when we must. I say we must necessarily undo these violent, oppressive acts. They must be repealed. You will repeal them. I pledge myself for it, that you will, in the end, repeal them. I stake my reputation on it. I will consent to be taken for an idiot if they are not finally repealed. Avoid, then, this humiliating, disgraceful necessity. With a dignity becoming your exalted situation, make the first advances to concord, to peace, and happiness; for that is your true dignity, to act with prudence and justice. . . .

Every motive, therefore, of justice and of policy, of dignity and of prudence, urges you to allay the ferment in America by a removal of your troops from Boston, by a repeal of your acts of Parliament, and by demonstration of amicable dispositions toward your colonies. On the other hand, every danger and every hazard impend to deter you from perseverance in your present ruinous measures. Foreign war hanging over your heads by a slight and brittle thread; France and Spain watching your conduct, and waiting for the maturity of your errors, with a vigilant eye to America and the temper of your colonies, more than to their own concerns, be they what they may.

To conclude, my Lords, if the ministers thus persevere in misadvising and misleading the King, I will not say that they can alienate the affections of his subjects from his crown, but I will affirm that they will make the crown not worth his wearing.

I will not say that the King is betrayed, but I will pronounce that the kingdom is undone.

Source: Scotland, Andrew, ed. *The Power of Eloquence: A Treasury of British Speech.* London: Cassell, 1961, p. 17.

EDMUND BURKE
(1729–1797)
On Conciliation with America
House of Commons, London, England
March 22, 1775

A native of Ireland, Edmund Burke was the child of a Protestant father and Roman Catholic mother. (Burke took after his father's religious influences and was himself Protestant.) Burke's interest in philosophical debate showed itself early—he started a debating club at Dublin's Trinity College that still exists today. After receiving his degree, Burke moved to London where he entered the House of Commons in 1765. (The House of Commons was and remains the lower house of Parliament, composed of democratically elected members. The upper house, the House of Lords, was composed of appointed hereditary peers, or nobles.) As a Protestant, unlike most of his Catholic countrymen, Burke was permitted to serve in Parliament. Because his mother, however, was a Roman Catholic, Burke fought against persecution of Catholics by the British authorities in Ireland whenever the opportunity arose. Like William Pitt the Elder, Burke was a supporter of the American colonies, and though he held that Brit-ain had the right in theory to tax the colonies, he felt it was unwise to do so. He delivered his maiden, or first, speech for repealing the Stamp Act of 1765, by which King George III (r. 1760–1820) and Parliament had imposed heavy taxes on the American colonists without giving them representation in Parliament. After the Boston Tea Party's destruction of taxed tea on December 16, 1773, Burke again argued in vain against collecting taxes in America. Now, only four weeks before the start of the American Revolution (1775–83), Burke rose to plead for conciliation with the colonies in his most eloquent and famous speech. To explain the colonists' "fierce spirit of liberty," he highlights their descent from Englishmen, their Protestant religion, the institution of slavery in the South, their education in the law, and the 3,000 miles separating them from England. (He also uses the expression *sursum corda*, which means "lift up your hearts.") Burke's resolution for conciliation with America failed in the vote.

We are called upon again to attend to America; to attend to the whole of it together. And to review the subject with an unusual degree of care and calmness. . . .

America, gentlemen say, is a noble object. It is an object well worth fighting for. Certainly it is, if fighting a people be the best way of gaining them. . . .

First, sir, permit me to observe, that the use of force alone is but temporary. It may subdue for a moment, but it does not remove the necessity of subduing again; and a nation is not governed which is perpetually to be conquered.

My next objection is its uncertainty. Terror is not always the effect of force; and an armament is not a victory. If you do not succeed, you are without resource; for, conciliation failing, force remains; but, force failing, no further hope of reconciliation is left. Power and authority are sometimes bought by kindness but they can never be begged as alms by an impoverished and defeated violence.

A further objection to force is, that you impair the object by your very endeavors to preserve it. The thing you fought for is not the thing which you recover; but depreciated, sunk, wasted, and consumed in the contest. Nothing less will content me than whole America. I do not choose to consume its strength along with our own, because in all parts it is the British strength that I consume. I do not choose to be caught by a foreign enemy at the end of this exhausting conflict, and still less in the midst of it. I may escape; but I can make no insurance against such an event. Let me add, that I do not choose wholly to break the American spirit, because it is the spirit that has made the country. . . .

> Magnanimity in politics is not seldom the truest wisdom; and a great empire and little minds go ill together. —*Edmund Burke*

These, sir, are my reasons for not entertaining that high opinion of untried force, by which many gentlemen, for whose sentiments in other particulars I have great respect, seem to be so greatly captivated.

But there is still behind a third consideration concerning this object, which serves to determine my opinion on the sort of policy which ought to be pursued in the management of America, even more than its population and its commerce—I mean its temper and character. In this character of the Americans a love of freedom is the predominating feature, which marks and distinguishes the whole. And, as an ardent is always a jealous affection, your Colonies become suspicious, restive, and untractable whenever they see the least attempt to wrest from them by force, or shuffle from them by chicane, what they think the only advantage worth living for.

This fierce spirit of liberty is stronger in the English Colonies, probably, than in any other people of the earth, and this from a variety of powerful causes, which, to understand the true temper of their minds, and the direction which this spirit takes, it will not be amiss to lay open somewhat more largely.

The people of the Colonies are descendants of Englishmen. England, sir, is a nation which still, I hope, respects, and formerly adored her freedom. The Colonists emigrated from you when this part of your character was most predominant; and they took this bias and direction the moment they parted from your hands. They are, therefore, not only devoted to liberty, but to liberty according to English ideas and on English principles. . . .

Religion, always a principle of energy, in this new people is no way worn out or impaired; and their mode of professing it is also one main cause of this free spirit. The people are Protestants; and of that kind which is the most averse to all implicit submission of mind and opinion. This is a persuasion not only favorable to liberty, but built upon it. I do not think, sir, that the reason of this averseness in the dissenting churches from all that looks like absolute government, is so much to be sought in their religious tenets, as in their history.

Everyone knows that the Roman Catholic religion is at least coeval with most of the governments where it prevails; that it has generally gone hand in hand with them; and received great favor and every kind of support from authority. The Church of England, too, was formed from her cradle under the nursing care of regular government. But the dissenting interests have sprung up in direct opposition to all the ordinary powers of the world, and could justify that opposition only on a strong claim to natural liberty. Their very existence depended on the powerful and unremitted assertion of that claim. All Protestantism, even the most cold and passive, is a kind of dissent. . . .

In Virginia and the Carolinas they have a vast multitude of slaves. Where this is the case in any part of the world, those who are free are by far the most proud and jealous of their freedom. Freedom is to them not only an enjoyment, but a kind of rank and privilege. Not seeing there that freedom—as in countries where it is a common blessing, and as broad and general as the air—may be united with much abject toil, with great misery, with all the exterior of servitude, liberty looks, among them, like something that is more noble and liberal. I do not mean, sir, to command the superior morality of this sentiment, which has at least as much pride as virtue in it; but I cannot alter the nature of man. The fact is so; and these people of the southern Colonies are much more strongly, and with a higher and more stubborn spirit, attached to liberty than those to the northward.

Permit me, sir, to add another circumstance in our Colonies, which contributes no mean part toward the growth and effect of this untractable spirit—I mean their education. In no country perhaps in the world is the law so general a study. The profession itself is numerous and powerful; and in most provinces it takes the lead. The greater number of the deputies sent to Congress were lawyers. But all who read, and most do read, endeavor to obtain some smattering in that science. I have been told by an eminent bookseller, that in no branch of his business, after tracts of popular devotion, were so many books as those on the law exported to the Plantations. The Colonists have now fallen into the way of printing them for their own use. I hear that they have sold nearly as many of Blackstone's Commentaries in America as in England. . . .

The last cause of this disobedient spirit in the Colonies is hardly less powerful than the rest, as it is not merely moral, but laid deep in the natural constitution of things. Three thousand miles of ocean lie between you and them. No contrivance can prevent the effect of this distance in weakening government. Seas roll and months pass between the order and the execution; and the want of a speedy explanation of a single point is enough to defeat the whole system. . . .

Then, sir, from these six capital sources of descent, of form of government, of religion in the northern Provinces, of manners in the southern, of education, of the remoteness of situation from the first mover of government—from all these causes a fierce spirit of liberty has grown up. It has grown with the growth of the people in your Colonies, and increased with the increase of their wealth; a spirit that, unhappily meeting with an exercise of power in England, which however lawful is not reconcilable to any ideas of liberty, much less with theirs, has kindled this flame that is ready to consume us. . . .

In this situation, let us seriously and coolly ponder. What is it we have got by all our menaces, which have been many and ferocious? What advantage have we derived from the penal laws we have passed, and which, for the time, have been severe and numerous? What advances have we made toward our object by the sending of a force which, by land and sea, is no contemptible strength? Has the disorder abated? . . .

If we mean to conciliate and concede, let us see of what nature the concessions ought to be. To ascertain the nature of our concession, we must look at their complaint. The Colonies complain that they have not the characteristic mark and seal of British freedom. They complain that they are taxed in Parliament in which they are not represented. If you mean to satisfy them at all, you must satisfy them with regard to this complaint. If you mean to please any people, you must give them the boon which they ask; not what you may think better for them, but of a kind totally different. . . .

My hold of the Colonies is in the close affection which grows from common names, from kindred blood, from similar privileges, and equal protection. These are ties which, though light as air, are as strong as links of iron. Let the Colonies always keep the idea of their civil rights associated with your government; they will cling and grapple to you, and no force under heaven will be of power to tear them from their allegiance. But let it be once understood that your government may be one thing, and their privileges another; that these two things may exist without any mutual relation; the cement is gone; the cohesion is loosened; and everything hastens to decay and dissolution.

As long as you have the wisdom to keep the sovereign authority of this country as the sanctuary of liberty, the sacred temple consecrated to our common faith; wherever the chosen race and sons of England worship Freedom, they will turn their faces toward you. The more they multiply, the more friends you will have. The more ardently they love liberty, the more perfect will be their obedience. Slavery they can have anywhere. It is a weed that grows in every soil. They may have it from Spain; they may have it from Prussia; but, until you become lost to all feeling of your true interest and your natural dignity, freedom they can have from none but you. . . .

Magnanimity in politics is not seldom the truest wisdom; and a great empire and little minds go ill together. If we are conscious of our situation, and glow with zeal to fill our place as becomes our station and ourselves, we ought to auspicate all our public proceeding on America with the old warning of the Church, *sursum corda!*

We ought to elevate our minds to the greatness of that trust to which the order of Providence has called us. By adverting to the dignity of this high calling, our ancestors have turned a savage wilderness into a glorious empire, and have made the most extensive and the only honorable conquests not by destroying, but by promoting, the wealth, the number, the happiness of the human race.

Let us get an American revenue as we have got an American empire. English privileges have made it all that it is; English privileges alone will make it all that it can be.

Source: Scotland, Andrew, ed. *The Power of Eloquence: A Treasury of British Speech.* London: Cassell, 1961, p. 48.

As Edmund Burke noted in his 1775 address to Parliament (*SEE* Burke's speech, page 181), many of the radicals among American colonists were lawyers or studied law as a pastime. Patrick Henry was born in 1736 in Hanover, Virginia. He had little opportunity to attend school and was largely self-taught. As a trial lawyer he was known for his magnificent oratory, even more so for denouncing the 1765 Stamp Act (which imposed taxes on the colonists) in the Virginia legislature and for asserting the rights of the colonies in the Continental Congress (an inter-colonial assembly formed in 1774). At the Second Virginia Convention in 1775, Henry introduced resolutions urging Virginia to arm the militia and prepare to defend itself against the British. Future U.S. presidents George Washington and Thomas Jefferson were attending, as well as Benjamin Harrison, Richard Henry Lee, and other noted Virginians. The convention was held in Richmond's St. John's Church; it was full, with people listening in at the windows. Henry addressed himself to Peyton Randolph, president of the convention (and also of the Continental Congress). He referred to a small group of men who had just spoken against his resolutions, urging caution and patience; they included Richard Bland, Benjamin Harrison, and Edmund Pendleton, all delegates to the Continental Congress. This illustrious speech made members of the audience "sick with excitement" and when Henry finished the famous last words, he sank back into his seat thrusting an imaginary dagger into his body. The audience leaped up, shouting, "To arms!" When the vote was taken, the resolutions passed. He was elected governor of Virginia in 1776 and again in 1784. Mistrustful of the federal Constitution, feeling that it might endanger the rights of the states, Henry helped shepherd the addition of the first 10 amendments, the Bill of Rights, to the U.S. Constitution in 1791. Patrick Henry's celebrated Revolutionary War speech, however, is only an approximation of what Henry actually said, as it was first written down by his biographer, William Wirt, 40 years afterward. In the next century, the motto "Liberty or Death" would be taken up by African-American abolitionists—among them minister Henry Highland Garnet in his "Call to Rebellion" address—agitating for freedom for American slaves.

Mr. President: No man thinks more highly than I do of the patriotism, as well as abilities, of the very worthy gentlemen who have just addressed the House. But different men often see the same subject in different lights; and, therefore, I hope that it will not be thought disrespectful to those gentlemen, if, entertaining as I do opinions of a character very opposite to theirs, I shall speak forth my sentiments freely and without reserve.

This is no time for ceremony. The question before the House is one of awful moment to this country. For my own part I consider it as nothing less than a question of freedom or slavery; and in proportion to the magnitude of the subject ought to be the freedom of the debate. It is only in this way that we can hope to arrive at truth, and fulfill the great responsibility which we hold to God and our country. Should I keep back my opinions at such a time, through fear of giving offense, I should consider myself as guilty of treason towards my country, and of an act of disloyalty towards the majesty of heaven, which I revere above all earthly kings.

Mr. President, it is natural to man to indulge in the illusions of hope. We are apt to shut our eyes against a painful truth, and listen to the song of that siren, till she transforms us into beasts. Is this the part of wise men, engaged in a great and arduous struggle for liberty? Are we disposed to be of the number of those who, having eyes, see not, and having ears, hear not, the things which so nearly concern their temporal salvation? For my part, whatever anguish of spirit it may cost, I am willing to know the whole truth—to know the worst and to provide for it.

I have but one lamp by which my feet are guided; and that is the lamp of experience. I know of no way of judging of the future but by the past. And judging by the past, I wish to know what there has been in the conduct of the British ministry for the last ten years, to justify those hopes with which gentlemen have been pleased to solace themselves and the House?

Is it that insidious smile with which our petition has been lately received? Trust it not, sir; it will prove a snare to your feet. Suffer not yourselves to be betrayed with a kiss. Ask yourselves how this gracious reception of our petition comports with these warlike preparations which cover our waters and darken our land. Are fleets and armies necessary to a work of love and reconciliation? Have we shown ourselves so unwilling to be reconciled that force must be called in to win back our love? Let us not deceive ourselves, sir. These are the implements of war and subjugation—the last arguments to which kings resort.

I ask gentlemen, sir, what means this martial array, if its purpose be not to force us to submission? Can gentlemen assign any other possible motives for it? Has Great Britain any enemy, in this quarter of the world, to call for all this accumulation of navies and armies?

No, sir, she has none. They are meant for us; they can be meant for no other. They are sent over to bind and rivet upon us those chains which the British ministry have been so long forging. And what have we to oppose to them? Shall we try argument? Sir, we have been trying that for the last ten years. Have we anything new to offer on the subject? Nothing.

We have held the subject up in every light of which it is capable; but it has been all in vain. Shall we resort to entreaty and humble supplication? What terms shall we find which have not been already exhausted? Let us not, I beseech you, sir, deceive ourselves longer.

Sir, we have done everything that could be done to avert the storm which is now coming on. We have petitioned; we have remonstrated; we have supplicated; we have prostrated ourselves before the throne, and have implored its interposition to arrest the tyrannical hands of the ministry and Parliament.

Our petitions have been slighted; our remonstrances have produced additional violence and insult; our supplications have been disregarded; and we have been spurned, with contempt, from the foot of the throne. In vain, after these things, may we indulge the fond hope of peace and reconciliation. There is no longer any room for hope.

If we wish to be free—if we mean to preserve inviolate those inestimable privileges for which we have been so long contending—if we mean not basely to abandon the noble struggle in which we have been so long engaged, and which we have pledged

Patrick Henry, famous for his 1775 address to the Second Virginia Convention, also gave an earlier notable speech in 1765, in debating the Virginia Resolutions regarding the Stamp Act. Referring to Brutus, one of Julius Caesar's assassins, and Oliver Cromwell, whose revolt led to the execution of King Charles I, Henry cried at the close of his address, "Caesar had his Brutus, Charles the First his Cromwell, and George the Third may profit by their example!" He was interrupted by shouts of "Treason! Treason!" He later apologized, saying he remained King George's loyal subject. *(Library of Congress, Prints and Photographs Division [LC-USZ62-102566])*

RHETORICAL DEVICE

Allusion: A reference to a notable event or person. Allusion can help paint a picture explaining the topic, and reward hearers who recognize the reference.

Had Achilles any thought of death or danger? For wherever a man's place is, whether the place which he has chosen or that in which he has been placed by a commander, there he ought to remain in the hour of danger. —*Socrates, an allusion to the Greek hero of the Trojan War*

Suffer not yourselves to be betrayed with a kiss. Ask yourselves how this gracious reception of our petition comports with these warlike preparations which cover our waters and darken our land. —*Patrick Henry, a biblical allusion to Judas' betrayal of Jesus with a kiss*

America, if she fell, would fall like a strong man. She would embrace the pillars of the state, and pull down the constitution along with her. —*William Pitt the Elder, a biblical allusion to Samson*

---

ourselves never to abandon until the glorious object of our contest shall be obtained, we must fight! I repeat it, sir, we must fight! An appeal to arms and to the God of Hosts is all that is left us!

They tell us, sir, that we are weak—unable to cope with so formidable an adversary. But when shall we be stronger? Will it be the next week, or the next year? Will it be when we are totally disarmed, and when a British guard shall be stationed in every house? Shall we gather strength by irresolution and inaction? Shall we acquire the means of effectual resistance, by lying supinely on our backs, and hugging the delusive phantom of hope, until our enemies shall have bound us hand and foot?

Sir, we are not weak, if we make a proper use of the means which the God of nature hath placed in our power. Three millions of people, armed in the holy cause of liberty, and in such a country as that which we possess, are invincible by any force which our enemy can send against us. Besides, sir, we shall not fight our battles alone. There is a just God who presides over the destinies of nations, and who will raise up friends to fight our battles for us.

The battle, sir, is not to the strong alone; it is to the vigilant, the active, the brave. Besides, sir, we have no election. If we were base enough to desire it, it is now too late to retire from the contest. There is no retreat but in submission and slavery! Our chains are forged! Their clanking may be heard on the plains of Boston! The war is inevitable—and let it come! I repeat it, sir, let it come!

It is in vain, sir, to extenuate the matter. Gentlemen may cry, "Peace! Peace!" but there is no peace. The war is actually begun! The next gale that sweeps from the north will bring to our ears the clash of resounding arms! Our brethren are already in the field! Why stand we here idle? What is it that gentlemen wish? What would they have? Is life so dear, or peace so sweet, as to be purchased at the price of chains and slavery? Forbid it, Almighty God! I know not what course others may take; but as for me, give me liberty, or give me death!

Source: Tyler, Moses Coit. *Patrick Henry.* Boston: Houghton, Mifflin, 1887, p. 123.

SAMUEL ADAMS
(1722–1803)
"No Other Alternative Than Independence"
Philadelphia, Pennsylvania, United States
August 1, 1776

Samuel Adams was born in 1722 in Boston, Massachusetts. He was an excellent writer, who studied theology with the idea of being a preacher, but later moved on to politics. Even before the 1765 Stamp Act imposed taxes on the colonists, he was one of the first to question whether the British parliament had the right to tax the American colonies without their consent. Together with another rebel from Massachusetts, James Otis, he organized the Stamp Act Congress to discuss how the colonies might unite against British tyranny. Later that year he was elected a member of the Massachusetts legislature. With the wealthy Boston merchant John Hancock, Adams organized the Boston Tea Party in December 1773 to protest the British tax on tea. During this incident, colonists broke open the chests of tea being imported by the East India Company and threw £10,000 worth of tea into the Boston harbor. Again with John Hancock, he formed the radical patriot group Sons of Liberty, which played a central role in resistance to the Stamp Act. For these seditious activities both Adams and Hancock were wanted under a British warrant of arrest. The impassioned fury of Adams's writing and speeches drove the American colonists along the road to revolution. In 1776, the year after the American Revolutionary War broke out in the Massachusetts towns of Lexington and Concord, Massachusetts sent Adams as a delegate to the Second Continental Congress in Philadelphia, Pennsylvania. The congress consisted of representatives from each colony who met to air grievances against the British and to oversee formation of the Continental army. On August 1, a month after the Continental Congress adopted the revolutionary Declaration of Independence (on July 4, 1776), and the day before they fixed their signatures to the historic document, Adams rose from his seat in the State House and, in excited, lofty speech, assured the delegates of his confidence in their ability to win the war (which they would, in 1783). After the war, Adams served in the Massachusetts senate and was elected governor.

Countrymen and Brethren: I would gladly have declined an honor to which I find myself unequal. I have not the calmness and impartiality which the infinite importance of this occasion demands. I will not deny the charge of my enemies, that resentment for the accumulated injuries of our country, and an ardor for her glory, rising to enthusiasm, may deprive me of that accuracy of judgment and expression which men of cooler passions may possess. Let me beseech you, then, to hear me with caution, to examine your prejudice, and to correct the mistakes into which I may be hurried by my zeal. . . .

No man had once a greater veneration for Englishmen than I entertained. They were dear to me as branches of the same parental trunk, and partakers of the same religion and laws. I still view with respect the remains of the constitution as I would a lifeless body, which had once been animated by a great and heroic soul.

But when I am aroused by the din of arms; when I behold legions of foreign assassins, paid by Englishmen to imbrue their hands in our blood; when I tread over the uncoffined bodies of my countrymen, neighbors, and friends; when I see the locks of a venerable father torn by savage hands, and a feeble mother, clasping her infants to her bosom, and on her knees imploring their lives from her own slaves, whom Englishmen have allured to treachery and murder; when I behold my country, once the seat of industry, peace, and plenty, changed by Englishmen to a theatre of blood and misery, Heaven forgive me, if I cannot root out those passions which it as implanted in my bosom, and detest submission to a people who have either ceased to be human, or have not virtue enough to feel their own wretchedness and servitude!

Men who content themselves with the semblance of truth, and a display of words, talk much of our obligations to Great Britain for protection. Had she a single eye to our advantage? A nation of shopkeepers are very seldom so disinterested. Let us not be so amused with words; the extension of her commerce was her object. When she defended our coasts, she fought for her customers, and convoyed our ships loaded with wealth, which we had acquired for her by our industry. She has treated us as beasts of burthen, whom the lordly masters cherish that they may carry a greater load. Let us inquire also against whom she has protected us? Against her own enemies with whom we had no quarrel, or only on her account, and against whom we always readily exerted our wealth and strength when they were required. . . .

Did the protection we received annul our rights as men, and lay us under an obligation of being miserable? Who among you, my countrymen, that is a father, would claim authority to make your child a slave because you had nourished him in infancy? Tis a strange species of generosity which requires a return infinitely more valuable than anything it could have bestowed; that demands as a reward for a defense of our property a surrender of those inestimable privileges, to the arbitrary will of vindictive tyrants, which alone give value to that very property. . . .

Courage, then, my countrymen, our contest is not only whether we ourselves shall be free, but whether there shall be left to mankind an asylum on earth for civil and religious liberty. Dismissing, therefore, the justice of our cause, as incontestable, the only question is, What is best for us to pursue in our present circumstances?

The doctrine of dependence on Great Britain is, I believe, generally exploded; but as I would attend to the honest weakness of the simplest of men, you will pardon me if I offer a few words on that subject.

We are now on this continent, to the astonishment of the world, three millions of souls united in one cause. We have large armies, well disciplined and appointed, with commanders inferior to none in military skill, and superior in activity and zeal. We are furnished with arsenals and stores beyond our most sanguine expectations, and foreign nations are waiting to crown our success by their alliances. There are instances of, I would say, an almost astonishing Providence in our favor; our success has staggered

RHETORICAL DEVICE

Onomatopoeia: Choosing words that sound like the thing being described provide rich language for speeches.

But when I am aroused by the din of arms . . . —*Samuel Adams*

Our chains are forged! Their clanking may be heard on
the plains of Boston! —*Patrick Henry*

I see, out of the very midst of this great assemblage, rise the bleeding
image of Hungary, looking to you with anxiety whether . . .
there be in the thunder of your huzzas a trumpet-call
of resurrection. —*Louis Kossuth*

our enemies, and almost given faith to infidels; so we may truly say it is not our own arm which has saved us.

The hand of heaven appears to have led us on to be, perhaps, humble instruments and means in the great Providential dispensation which is completing. We have fled from the political Sodom; let us not look back, lest we perish and become a monument of infamy and derision to the world. For can we ever expect more unanimity and a better preparation for defense; more infatuation of counsel among our enemies, and more valor and zeal among ourselves? The same force and resistance which are sufficient to procure us our liberties will secure us a glorious independence and support us in the dignity of free, imperial States.

We cannot suppose that our opposition has made a corrupt and dissipated nation more friendly to America, or created in them a greater respect for the rights of mankind. We can therefore expect a restoration and establishment of our privileges, and a compensation for the injuries we have received from their want of power, from their fears, and not from their virtues. The unanimity and valor which will effect an honorable peace can render a future contest for our liberties unnecessary. He who has strength to chain down the wolf is a madman if he let him loose without drawing his teeth and paring his nails. . . .

Other nations have received their laws from conquerors; some are indebted for a constitution to the suffering of their ancestors through revolving centuries. The people of this country, alone, have formally and deliberately chosen a government for themselves, and with open and uninfluenced consent bound themselves into a social compact. Here no man proclaims his birth or wealth as a title to honorable distinction, or to sanctify ignorance and vice with the name of hereditary authority. He who has most zeal and ability to promote public felicity, let him be the servant of the public. . . .

We have no other alternative than independence, or the most ignominious and galling servitude. The legions of our enemies thicken on our plains; desolation and death mark their bloody career, whilst the mangled corpses of our countrymen seem to cry out to us as a voice from heaven. . . . Our Union is now complete; our constitution composed, established, and approved. You are now the guardians of your own liberties. We may justly address you, as the decemviri did the Romans, and say, "Nothing that we propose can pass into a law without your consent. Be yourselves, O Americans, the authors of those laws on which your happiness depends."

You have now in the field armies sufficient to repel the whole force of your enemies and their base and mercenary auxiliaries. The hearts of your soldiers beat high with the spirit of freedom; they are animated with the justice of their cause, and while they grasp their swords can look up to Heaven for assistance.

Your adversaries are composed of wretches who laugh at the rights of humanity, who turn religion into derision, and would, for higher wages, direct their swords against their leaders or their country. Go on, then, in your generous enterprise with gratitude to Heaven for past success, and confidence of it in the future. For my own part, I ask no greater blessing than to share with you the common danger and common glory. If I have a wish dearer to my soul than that my ashes may be mingled with those of a Warren and Montgomery, it is that these American States may never cease to be free and independent.

Source: Wells, William V. *The Life and Public Services of Samuel Adams.* Vol. 3. Boston: Little, Brown, 1875, p. 407.

WILLIAM PITT THE ELDER
(1708–1778)
"You Cannot Conquer America"
House of Lords, London, England
November 18, 1777

William Pitt the Elder's health had long been poor; he suffered from gout (a painful disease of the joints) and a mental illness, probably depression, that periodically robbed him of years of service in Parliament. Although brilliant, he had not been a success as British prime minister (from 1766 to 1768), as he had been unable to assemble a cohesive cabinet. Hugely popular with the people for expanding Britain's empire, he was called the "Great Commoner," although accepting a peerage, or aristocratic rank—as earl of Chatham—in 1766 cost him some of that support. Pitt, with the younger Irish-born British statesman Edmund Burke and a small group of supporters, had long petitioned Parliament to change its harsh position toward the American colonies. Pitt was in no way in favor of independence for America; it had been his work of many years to keep the colonies for Britain's empire. But the colonies had united and declared independence on July 4, 1776, and by November 1777 the

Americans' Continental Army was putting up an unexpected defense. As the conflict ground on, Parliament was shocked to discover that American statesman Benjamin Franklin (along with American diplomats Silas Deane and Arthur Lee) was in Paris as the U.S. ambassador, and France—Britain's historical enemy—was showing signs of entering into an alliance with the United States. Still unafraid to criticize King George III (r. 1760–1820) over his mismanagement of the colonies, the 70-year-old Pitt, "old and weak," as he said of himself, rose to speak. This is one of Pitt's greatest speeches. He opened with congratulation to the king on the birth of a daughter, Princess Sophia. But, as he continues in this excerpt, he could not indulge in congratulations on the conduct of the war in the colonies. He criticizes hiring Hessian mercenaries, and barbarically using Indians to fight the colonists, Britain's own people. Pitt's resolution to cease hostilities lost in the vote, 97 to 24.

❦

This, my lords, is a perilous and tremendous moment! It is not a time for adulation. The smoothness of flattery cannot now avail—cannot save us in this rugged and awful crisis. It is now necessary to instruct the Throne in the language of truth. We must dispel the illusion and the darkness which envelop it, and display, in its full danger and true colors, the ruin that is brought to our doors. . . .

France, my lords, has insulted you. She has encouraged and sustained America; and, whether America be wrong or right, the dignity of this country ought to spurn at the officious insult of French interference. The ministers and ambassadors of those who are called rebels and enemies are in Paris; in Paris they transact the reciprocal interests of America and France. Can there be a more mortifying insult? Can even our ministers sustain a more humiliating disgrace? Do they dare to resent it? Do they presume even to hint a vindication of their honor, and the dignity of the State, by requiring the dismission of the plenipotentiaries of America? Such is the degradation to which they have reduced the glories of England!

The people whom they affect to call contemptible rebels, but whose growing power has at last obtained the name of enemies; the people with whom they have engaged this country in war, and against whom they now command our implicit support in every measure of desperate hostility—this people, despised as rebels, or acknowledged as enemies, are abetted against you, supplied with every military store, their interests consulted, and their ambassadors entertained, by your inveterate enemy! And our ministers dare not interpose with dignity or effect. Is this the honor of a great kingdom? . . .

> My lords, you cannot conquer America.
> —*William Pitt the Elder*

My lords, this ruinous and ignominious situation, where we cannot act with success, nor suffer with honor, calls upon us to remonstrate in the strongest and loudest language of truth, to rescue the ear of majesty from the delusions which surround it. The desperate state of our arms abroad is in part known. No man thinks more highly of them than I do. I love and honor the English troops. I know their virtues and their valor. I know they can achieve any thing except impossibilities, and I know that the conquest of English America is an impossibility.

You cannot, I venture to say it, you CANNOT conquer America. Your armies in the last war effected every thing that could be effected; and what was it? It cost a numerous army, under the command of a most able general, now a noble lord in this House, a long and laborious campaign, to expel five thousand Frenchmen from French America. My lords, you cannot conquer America. What is your present situation there? We do not know the worst; but we know that in three campaigns we have done nothing and suffered much. Besides the sufferings, perhaps total loss of the Northern force, the best-appointed army that ever took the field, commanded by Sir William Howe, has retired from the American lines. He was obliged to relinquish his attempt, and with great delay and danger to adopt a new and distant plan of operations. We shall soon know, and in any event have reason to lament, what may have happened since.

As to conquest, therefore, my lords, I repeat, it is impossible. You may swell every expense and every effort still more extravagantly; pile and accumulate every assistance you can buy or borrow; traffic and barter with every little pitiful German prince that sells and sends his subjects to the shambles of a foreign prince. Your efforts are for ever vain and impotent—doubly so from this mercenary aid on which you rely; for it irritates to an incurable resentment the minds of your enemies, to overrun them with the mercenary sons of rapine and plunder, devoting them and their possessions to the rapacity of hireling cruelty!

If I were an American, as I am an Englishman, while a foreign troop was landed in my country, I never would lay down my arms—never—never—never! . . .

The independent views of America have been stated and asserted as the foundation of this address. My lords, no man wishes for the due dependence of America on this country more than I do. To preserve it, and not confirm that state of independence into which your measures hitherto have driven them, is the object which we ought to unite in attaining. . . .

My lords, I have submitted to you, with the freedom and truth which I think my duty, my sentiments on your present awful situation. I have laid before you the ruin of your power, the disgrace of your reputation, the pollution of your discipline, the contamination of your morals, the complication of calamities, foreign and domestic, that overwhelm your sinking country. Your dearest interests, your own liberties, the Constitution itself totters to the foundation. All this disgraceful danger, this multitude of misery, is the monstrous offspring of this unnatural war. We have been deceived and deluded too long. Let us now stop short. . . .

I shall, therefore, my lords, propose to you an amendment of the address to his majesty, to be inserted immediately after the two first paragraphs of congratulation on the birth of a princess, to recommend an immediate cessation of hostilities, and the commencement of a treaty to restore peace and liberty to America, strength and happiness to England, security and permanent prosperity to both countries. This, my lords, is yet in our power; and let not the wisdom and justice of your lordships neglect the happy, and, perhaps, the only opportunity.

Source: Celebrated Speeches of Chatham, Burke & Erskine. Philadelphia: Biddle, 1845, p. 34.

BENJAMIN FRANKLIN
(1706–1790)
To the Constitutional Convention
Philadelphia, Pennsylvania, United States
September 17, 1787

Benjamin Franklin was born in Boston, Massachusetts, the youngest son in a large family. He learned the printing trade with his older brother, then struck out on his own for Philadelphia, where he would make his fame and fortune. A scientist, inventor, printer, postmaster, diplomat, and commonsense philosopher, Franklin proved to be a Founding Father of the United States and a great statesman of the Revolutionary War. In Philadelphia, he started the first lending library, published a newspaper, the *Pennsylvania Gazette,* and the yearly *Poor Richard's Almanack,* founded the American Philosophical Society, and set aside time to experiment with electricity. He entered politics, and by 1764 was Speaker of Pennsylvania's House of Representatives. In that year he was sent to London to conduct business for the colony. He opposed the Stamp Act of 1765, then under discussion in Parliament, and traveled to Paris where the French made much of his scientific discoveries and he made many friends. On his return to America in 1775, the American Revolutionary War against Britain (1775–83) had begun. Franklin helped draft the Declaration of Independence for the Second Continen-

tal Congress (the colonial assembly that served as the national government) and was one of its signers. During the war he was the young country's indispensable minister to France, where he obtained military aid and political alliance. At the war's end in 1783, the United States floundered with its relatively powerless government. A Constitutional Convention was organized on May 25, 1787, in the Pennsylvania State House (now called Independence Hall) to draw up a blueprint for a strong national government; Pennsylvania sent Franklin as a delegate. The writing of the Constitution took months of debate and compromise in Philadelphia's hot summer and was not finished until the fall of that year. On September 17, Franklin urged the delegates to sign, arguing that though the document might have faults there was not likely to be another better. The frail elder statesman, then in his eighties, asked James Wilson, another Pennsylvania delegate, to read his address. The Constitution was then sent to the 13 states for ratification; in December, Delaware was the first to vote to approve the document. The Constitution was ratified on June 21, 1788, and went into effect on March 4, 1789.

I confess that I do not entirely approve of this Constitution at present; but, sir, I am not sure I shall never approve it, for, having lived long, I have experienced many instances of being obliged, by better information or fuller consideration, to change opinions even on important subjects, which I once thought right, but found to be otherwise. It is therefore that, the older I grow, the more apt I am to doubt my own judgment of others.

Most men indeed, as well as most sects in religion, think themselves in possession of all truth, and that wherever others differ from them, it is so far error. Steele, a Protestant, in a dedication, tells the Pope that the only difference between our two churches in their opinions of the certainty of their doctrine is, the Romish Church is infallible, and the Church of England is never in the wrong. But, though many private persons think almost as highly of their own infallibility as of that of their sect, few express it so naturally as a certain French lady, who, in a little dispute with her sister, said: "But I meet with nobody but myself that is always in the right."

In these sentiments, sir, I agree to this Constitution, with all its faults—if they are such—because I think a general government necessary for us, and there is no form of government but what may be a blessing to the people, if well administered. And I believe, further, that this is likely to be well administered for a course of years, and can only end in despotism, as other forms have done before it, when the people shall become so corrupted as to need despotic government, being incapable of any other.

I doubt, too, whether any other convention we can obtain may be able to make a better Constitution; for, when you assemble a number of men, to have the advantage of their joint wisdom, you inevitably assemble with those men all their prejudices, their passions, their errors of opinion, their local interests, and their selfish views. From such an assembly can a perfect production be expected?

It therefore astonishes me, sir, to find this system approaching so near to perfection as it does; and I think it will astonish our enemies, who are waiting with confidence to hear that our counsels are confounded like those of the builders of Babel, and that our States are on the point of separation, only to meet hereafter for the purpose of cutting one another's throats. Thus I consent, sir, to this Constitution, because I expect no better, and because I am not sure that it is not the best.

The opinions I have had of its errors I sacrifice to the public good. I have never whispered a syllable of them abroad. Within these walls they were born, and here they shall die. If every one of us, in returning to our constituents, were to report the objections he has had to it, and endeavor to gain partisans in support of them, we might prevent its being generally received, and thereby lose all the salutary effects and great advantages resulting naturally in our favor among foreign nations, as well as among ourselves, from our real or apparent unanimity.

Much of the strength and efficiency of any government, in procuring and securing happiness to the people, depends on opinion, on the general opinion of the goodness of that government, as well as of the wisdom and integrity of its governors. I hope, therefore, for our own sakes, as a part of the people, and for the sake of our posterity, that we shall act heartily and unanimously in recommending this Constitution wherever our influence may extend, and turn our future thoughts and endeavors to the means of having it well administered.

On the whole, sir, I cannot help expressing a wish that every member of the convention who may still have objections to it, would, with me, on this occasion, doubt a little of his own infallibility, and, to make manifest our unanimity, put his name to this instrument.

Source: Franklin, Benjamin. *Autobiography and Other Writings.* Edited by Ormond Seavey. New York: Oxford University Press, 1998.

WILLIAM WILBERFORCE
(1759–1833)
"The Number of Deaths Speaks for Itself"
House of Commons, London, England
May 12, 1789

English abolitionist and statesman William Wilberforce studied at Cambridge University, where he became close friends with William Pitt "the Younger" (son of the renowned William Pitt, Earl of Chatham [1708–78]). Wilberforce was elected to Parliament in 1780 at the early age of 21. Spiritual as a youngster, five years later he had a religious reawakening and began to devote his energies to the young anti-slavery movement. With a large group of Quakers and several prominent evangelical Protestants (including Thomas Clarkson, who wrote numerous important essays against slavery), he helped found the Committee for the Abolition of the Slave Trade. As a member of the committee, Wilberforce became the movement's valuable link to Parliament, where he was widely respected as a man of conscience and great eloquence. His close relationship with William Pitt, the prime minister, also assisted him in bringing slavery to the public's attention. He was years ahead of the American anti-slavery movement when, as a member of the House of Commons, he addressed the House in 1789 on the horrors of the African slave trade. Two years later he presented a bill in Parliament to end the slave trade, but it was defeated. Undaunted, he introduced an anti-slavery bill almost every year in the House of Commons, and the Slave Trade Act was finally passed in 1807, which abolished the British slave trade. The United States followed the next year with a ban on importing slaves into the country, although permitting slavery itself to continue. Slavery itself was abolished throughout the British Empire in 1834.

***

In opening, concerning the nature of the slave trade, I need only observe that it is found by experience to be just such as every man who uses his reason would infallibly conclude it to be. For my own part, so clearly am I convinced of the mischiefs inseparable from it, that I should hardly want any further evidence than my own mind would furnish by the most simple deductions. Facts, however, are now laid before the House.

A report has been made by his Majesty's privy council, which, I trust, every gentleman has read, and which ascertains the slave trade to be just such in practice as we know, from theory, it to be. What should we suppose must naturally be the consequence of our carrying on a slave trade with Africa? With a country vast in its extent, not utterly barbarous, but civilized in a very small degree? Does any one suppose a slave trade would help their civilization? Is it not plain that she must suffer from it? That civilization must be checked; that her barbarous manners must be made more barbarous; and that the happiness of her millions of inhabitants must be prejudiced with her intercourse with Britain? Does not every one see that a slave trade carried on around her coasts must carry violence and desolation to her very center? . . .

I must speak of the transit of the slaves in the West Indies. This I confess, in my own opinion, is the most wretched part of the whole subject. So much misery condensed in so little room is more than the human imagination had ever before conceived.

I will not accuse the Liverpool merchants. I will allow them, nay, I will believe them to be men of humanity. And I will therefore believe, if it were not for the multitude of these wretched objects, if it were not for the enormous magnitude and extent of the evil which distracts their attention from individual cases and makes them think generally, and therefore less feelingly, on the subject, they would never have persisted in the trade. I verily believe therefore, if the wretchedness of any one of the many hundred Negroes

RHETORICAL DEVICE

Expletive: Placing a word or short phrase (such as *indeed, in fact, without doubt, in short, to tell the truth, of course, I think*) at the beginning or interrupting the sentence to emphasize the nearby words.

Puerto Rico, we know, is not a republic. —*Luis Muñoz Marín*

As soon as ever I had arrived thus far in my investigation of the slave trade, I confess to you, sir, so enormous, so dreadful, so irremediable did its wickedness appear that my own mind was completely made up for the abolition. —*William Wilberforce*

I have organized for you an administration of justice and finance; in short, I have given you a government. —*Simón Bolívar*

When some extremists ask the Palestinians to give up this sublime objective, this, in fact, means asking them to renounce their identity and every hope for the future. —*Anwar Sadat*

stowed in each ship could be brought before their view, and remain within the sight of the African merchant, that there is no one among them whose heart would bear it.

Let anyone imagine to himself six or seven hundred of these wretches chained two and two, surrounded with every object that is nauseous and disgusting, diseased, and struggling under every kind of wretchedness! How can we bear to think of such a scene as this? One would think it had been determined to heap upon them all the varieties of bodily pain for the purpose of blunting the feelings of the mind. And yet, in this very point (to show the power of human prejudice), the situation of the slaves has been described by Mr. Norris, one of the Liverpool delegates, in a manner which I am sure will convince the House how interest can draw a film over the eyes so thick that total blindness could do no more; and how it is our duty therefore to trust not to the reasonings of interested men, or to their way of coloring a transaction.

"Their apartments," says Mr. Norris, "are fitted up as much for their advantage as circumstances will admit. The right ankle of one, indeed, is connected with the left ankle of another by a small iron fetter, and if they are turbulent, by another on their wrists. They have several meals a day; some of their own country provisions, with the best sauces of African cookery; and by way of variety, another meal of pulse, etc., according to European taste. After breakfast they have water to wash themselves, while their apartments are perfumed with frankincense and lime juice. Before dinner, they are amused after the manner of their country. The song and dance are promoted," and, as if the whole were really a scene of pleasure and dissipation, it is added that games of chance are furnished. "The men play and sing, while the women and girls make fanciful ornaments with beads, which they are plentifully supplied with."

Such is the sort of strain in which the Liverpool delegates, and particularly Mr. Norris, gave evidence before the privy council. What will the House think when, by the concurring testimony of other witnesses, the true history is laid open. The slaves, who are sometimes described as rejoicing at their captivity, are so wrung with misery at leaving their country that it is the constant practice to set sail at night, lest they should be sensible of their departure. The pulse which Mr. Norris talks of are horse beans; and the scantiness, both of water and provision, was suggested by the very legislature of Jamaica, in the report of their committee, to be a subject that called for the interference of Parliament.

Mr. Norris talks of frankincense and lime juice; when the surgeons tell you the slaves are stowed so close that there is not room to tread among them; and when you have it in evidence from Sir George Younge that even in a ship which wanted two hundred of her complement, the stench was intolerable.

The song and the dance are promoted, says Mr. Norris. It had been more fair, perhaps, if he had explained that word "promoted." The truth is that for the sake of exercise these miserable wretches, loaded with chains, oppressed with disease and wretchedness, are forced to dance by the terror of the lash, and sometimes by the actual use of it. "I," says one of the other evidences, "was employed to dance the men, while another person danced the women." Such, then is the meaning of the word "promoted;" and it may be observed too, with respect to food, that an instrument

Leading abolitionist William Wilberforce was a deeply religious member of the British parliament. His tireless anti-slavery campaign led to the Slave Trade Act of 1807. Engraving from 1814 *(Ablestock)*

is sometimes carried out, in order to force them to eat, which is the same sort of proof how much they enjoy themselves in that instance also.

As to their singing, what shall we say when we are told that their songs are songs of lamentation upon their departure which, while they sing, are always in tears, insomuch that one captain (more humane as I should conceive him, therefore, than the rest) threatened one of the women with a flogging, because the mournfulness of her song was too painful for his feelings.

In order, however, not to trust too much to any sort of description, I will call the attention of the House to one species of evidence which is absolutely infallible. Death, at least, is a sure ground of evidence, and the proportion of deaths will not only confirm, but if possible will even aggravate our suspicion of their misery in the transit.

It will be found, upon an average of all the ships of which evidence has been given at the privy council, that, exclusive of those who perish before they sail, not less than twelve and one half per cent perish in the passage. Besides these, the Jamaica report tells you that not less than four and one half per cent die on shore before the day of sale, which is only a week or two from the time of landing. One third more die in the seasoning, and this in a country exactly like their own, where they are healthy and happy, as some of the evidences would pretend. The diseases, however, which they contract on shipboard, the astringent washes which are to hide their wounds, and the mischievous tricks used to make them up for sale, are, as the Jamaica report says (a most precious and valuable report, which I shall often have to advert to), one principle cause of this mortality.

Upon the whole, however, here is a mortality of about fifty per cent, and this among Negroes who are not bought unless quite healthy at first, and unless (as the phrase is with cattle) they are sound in wind and limb. How then can the House refuse its belief to the multiplied testimonies, before the privy council, of the savage treatment of the Negroes in the middle passage? Nay, indeed, what need is there of any evidence? The number of deaths speaks for itself, and makes all such inquiry superfluous. As soon as ever I had arrived thus far in my investigation of the slave trade, I confess to you, sir, so enormous, so dreadful, so irremediable did its wickedness appear that my own mind was completely made up for the abolition.

A trade founded in iniquity, and carried on as this was, must be abolished, let the policy be what it might—let the consequences be what they would, I from this time determined that I would never rest till I had effected its abolition.

Source: Cobbett, William, John Wright, and T. C. Hansard. *The Parliamentary History of England.* Vol. 28. London: Longman, Hurst, Rees, 1816, p. 42.

William Pitt the Younger received his nickname to distinguish him from his father, William Pitt, earl of Chatham (1708–78)—the prime minister and parliamentarian who attempted so valiantly to alter Britain's actions toward the American colonies. As a teenager, he was there on April 7, 1778, in the House of Lords when the elder Pitt, aged and in poor health, gave the last great speech of his life and collapsed (he died one month later). Born late in his father's life, Pitt followed his footsteps into the House of Commons. His election in 1781 made him, at 22, a particularly youthful member of Parliament like his close friend from Cambridge University, William Wilberforce. Pitt was a brilliant speaker, like his father, and gained attention for speeches appealing for peace with the Americans. Although he had been a poor student in school, he quickly rose through the ranks and just one year later was appointed chancellor of the exchequer, a position similar to secretary of the treasury. In another quick year, at the age of 24, George III (r. 1760–1820) named Pitt prime minister. Many people, especially those who disliked the king, made fun of the idea of a prime minister so young, but over time Pitt gained their respect, particularly for bringing the nation out of the debt incurred during the American Revolutionary War (1775–83). He served as prime minister for nearly 20 years, spread over two terms. In 1792, while Pitt was prime minister, his lifelong friend Wilberforce, a devout abolitionist, persuaded him to denounce slavery in the House of Commons. Although Pitt worked hard to pass a bill ending British participation in the slave trade, he died before the Slave Trade Act was passed in 1807 (slavery itself was abolished in the British Empire in 1834). Here is an excerpt from Pitt's great antislavery address.

But now, sir, I come to Africa. That is the ground on which I rest, and here it is that I say my right honorable friends do not carry their principles to their full extent.

Why ought the slave trade to be abolished? Because it is incurable injustice.

How much stronger, then, is the argument for immediate than gradual abolition? By allowing it to continue even for one hour, do not my right honorable friends weaken—do not they desert—their own argument of its injustice? If on the ground of injustice it ought to be abolished at last, why ought it not now? Why is injustice to be suffered to remain for a single hour?

From what I hear without doors, it is evident that there is a general conviction entertained of its being far from just; and from that very conviction of its injustice, some men have been led, I fear, to the supposition that the slave trade never could have been permitted to begin but from some strong and irresistible necessity—a necessity, however, which, if it was fancied to exist at first, I have shown cannot be thought by any man whatever to exist now.

This plea of necessity, thus presumed, and presumed, as I suspect, from the circumstance of injustice itself, has caused a sort of acquiescence in the continuance of this evil. Men have been led to place it among the rank of those necessary evils which were supposed to be the lot of human creatures, and to be permitted to fall upon some countries or individuals, rather than upon others, by that being whose ways are inscrutable to us, and whose dispensations, it is conceived, we ought not to look into.

The origin of evil is indeed a subject beyond the reach of human understandings; and the permission of it by the Supreme Being is a subject into which it belongs not to us to enquire. But where the evil in question is a moral evil which a man can scrutinize, and where that moral evil has its origin with ourselves, let us not imagine that we can clear our consciences by this general, not to say irreligious and impious, way of laying aside the question. . . .

I know of no evil that ever has existed, nor can imagine any evil to exist, worse than the tearing of seventy or eighty thousand persons annually from their native land, by a combination of the most civilized nations, inhabiting the most enlightened part of the globe, but more especially under the sanction of the laws of that nation which calls herself the most free and the most happy of them all. Even if these miserable beings were proved guilty of every crime before you take them off (of which however not a single proof is adduced), ought we to take upon ourselves the office of executioners? And even if we condescend so far, still can we be justified in taking them, unless we have clear proof that they are criminals?

But if we go much farther—if we ourselves tempt them to sell their fellow creatures to us, we may rest assured that they will take care to provide by every method, by kidnapping, by village breaking, by unjust wars, by iniquitous condemnations, by rendering Africa a scene of bloodshed and misery, a supply of victims increasing in proportion to our demand. Can we then hesitate in deciding whether the wars in Africa are their wars or ours? . . .

There was a time, sir, which it may be fit sometimes to revive in the remembrance of our countrymen, when even human sacrifices are said to have been offered in this island. But I would peculiarly observe on this day, for it is a case precisely in point, that the very practice of the slave trade once prevailed among us. Slaves, as we may read in Henry's history of Great Britain, were formerly an established article of our exports. "Great numbers," he says, "were exported like cattle, from the British coast, and were to be seen exposed for sale in the Roman market."

It does not distinctly appear by what means they were procured; but there was unquestionably no small resemblance, in the particular point, between the case of our ancestors and that of the present wretched natives of Africa. For the historian tells you that "adultery, witchcraft, and debt were probably some of the chief sources of supplying the Roman market with British slaves—that prisoners taken in war were added to the number—and that there might be among them some unfortunate gamesters who, after having lost all their goods, at length staked themselves, their wives, and their children."

Every one of these sources of slavery has been stated, and almost precisely in the same terms, to be at this hour a source of slavery in Africa. And these circumstances, sir, with a solitary instance or two of human sacrifices, furnish the alleged proofs that Africa labors under a natural incapacity for civilization; that it is enthusiasm and fanaticism to think that she can ever enjoy the knowledge and the morals of Europe; that Providence never intended her to rise above a state of barbarism; that Providence has irrevocably doomed her to be only a nursery for slaves for us free and civilized Europeans.

Allow of this principle, as applied to Africa, and I should be glad to know why it might not also have been applied to ancient and uncivilized Britain. Why might not some Roman senator, reasoning on the principles of some honorable gentlemen, and pointing to British barbarians, have predicted with equal boldness, "There is a people that will never rise to civilization—there is a people destined never to be free—a people without the understanding necessary for the attainment of useful arts; depressed by the hand of nature below the level of the human species; and created to form a supply of slaves for the rest of the world." Might not this have been said, according to the principles which we now hear stated, in all respects as fairly and as truly of Britain herself at that period of her history, as it can now be said by us of the inhabitants of Africa? . . .

If, then, we feel that this perpetual confinement in the fetters of brutal ignorance would have been the greatest calamity which could have befallen us; if we view with gratitude and exultation the contrast between the peculiar blessings we enjoy and the wretchedness of the ancient inhabitants of Britain; if we shudder to think of the misery which would still have overwhelmed us, had Great Britain continued to the present times to be the mart for slaves to the more civilized nations of the world, through some cruel policy of theirs, God forbid that we should any longer subject Africa to the same dreadful scourge, and preclude the light of knowledge, which has reached every other quarter of the globe, from having access to her coasts!

I trust we shall no longer continue this commerce, to the destruction of every improvement on that wide continent, and shall not consider ourselves as conferring too great a boon, in restoring its inhabitants to the rank of human beings. I trust we shall not think ourselves too liberal if, by abolishing the slave trade, we give them the same common chance of civilization with other parts of the world. . . .

I shall oppose to the utmost every proposition which in any way may tend either to prevent or even to postpone for an hour the total abolition of the slave trade: a measure which, on all the various grounds which I have stated, we are bound, by the most pressing and indispensable duty, to adopt.

Source: Goodrich, Chauncey A., ed. *Select British Eloquence.* New York: Harper & Bros, 1853, p. 586.

GEORGES-JACQUES DANTON
(1759–1794)
"Always to Dare!"
Paris, France
September 2, 1792

By 1789, the unpopularity of the French monarchy reached a boiling point. Wars and taxation had impoverished and starved the common people of France, while King Louis XVI (r. 1774–92) and his wife, Marie Antoinette (r. 1774–92), spent lavishly on an extravagant lifestyle. Prices were high for food while jobs were scarce. The French people resented the clergy, too, for owning too much land and being allied with the throne. When an assembly of the people tried to convene on June 20, 1789, the king attempted to prevent the gathering by closing the meeting hall under the pretext of preparing for a royal meeting. They reconvened on an indoor tennis court and made plans to draw up a constitution. On July 14, an angry mob stormed an infamous prison in Paris, the Bastille, to seize weapons and ammunition kept there; the French Revolution, and a long period of political instability (1789–99) had begun. The aristocratic privilege of the *ancien régime*, or Old Regime, with power in the hands of an absolute monarch, was over. King Louis was deposed in 1791. A National Assembly formed from the vast Third Estate (the commoners), jettisoning the old three-tiered Estates General legislative body that gave most power to the First Estate (nobility) and Second Estate (clergy). Outside the country, monarchs across Europe debated whether to intervene, as France seemed interested in sending revolution abroad and the lives of the king and his family appeared threatened. War broke out between France and Austria (allied with Prussia) in April 1792 (Austria's Emperor Leopold II was Marie Antoinette's brother). Georges-Jacques Danton, a radical lawyer, became a minister of justice in the temporary French government. As the foreign armies approached Paris from the direction of Verdun in northeast France, Danton made this valiant speech of encouragement. In the bloody chaos that followed, Parisian revolutionaries massacred hundreds of French royalists and clergy; and within weeks the Prussians and Austrians withdrew from France. Shortly afterward, Danton became a member of the National Convention and voted for the execution of King Louis. He was one of the leading revolutionists caught between rival factions during the Reign of Terror (August 1793–July 1794), when under Maximilien de Robespierre, another French revolutionary put in charge of the newly formed Committee of Public Safety, as many as 20,000 people lost their lives to execution and imprisonment. Danton, accused of treason and corruption and found guilty by Robespierre's tribunal, died in April 1794 on the guillotine.

⁓⟳⁓

It is a satisfaction for the ministers of a free people to announce to them that their country will be saved. All are stirred, all are enthused, all burn to enter the combat.

You know that Verdun is not yet in the power of our enemies and that its garrison swears to immolate the first who breathes a proposition of surrender.

One portion of our people will guard our frontiers; another will dig and arm the entrenchments; the third with pikes will defend the interior of our cities. Paris will second these great efforts.

The commissioners of the Commune will solemnly proclaim to the citizens the invitation to arm and march to the defense of the country. At such a moment you can proclaim that the capital deserves the esteem of all France. At such a moment this National Assembly becomes a veritable committee of war.

We ask that you concur with us in directing this sublime movement of the people, by naming commissioners to second and assist all these great measures. We ask that anyone refusing to give personal service or to furnish arms shall meet the punishment of death. We ask that proper instructions be given to the citizens to direct their movements. We ask that carriers be sent to all the departments to notify them of the decrees that you proclaim here.

> To conquer we have to dare, to dare again, always to dare! —*Georges-Jacques Danton*

The tocsin we shall sound is not the alarm signal of danger; it orders the charge on the enemies of France.

To conquer we have to dare, to dare again, always to dare! And France will be saved!

Source: Brewer, David J., ed. *World's Best Orations from the Earliest Period to the Present Time.* Vol 5. Chicago: Ferd. P. Kaiser, 1899, p. 1,625.

MAXIMILIEN DE ROBESPIERRE
(1758–1794)
"Louis Must Perish because Our Country Must Live!"
Paris, France
December 3, 1792

After a long period of growing resentment against the monarchy, the French people took matters into their own hands in 1789. In that year two significant events occurred: the unpopular King Louis XVI (r. 1774–92) attempted to prevent an assembly of the common people from meeting to discuss their grievances against the nobility and clergy; and insurrectionists, or rebels, stormed the Bastille (a Paris prison) in search of weapons. A newly organized National Assembly (made up of townspeople and some liberal nobles and churchmen) gave power to the common man for the first time on June 17, 1789, when delegates swore to continue meeting until they had written a constitution for France. The assembly revoked the privileges of the nobles and the Catholic Church, both of which were allied with the throne, and set up a National Convention to produce the new constitution. One of the convention's first acts was to try Louis XVI—captured with his family in June 1791 while trying to escape—for treason. One delegate was Maximilien de Robespierre,

a lawyer and orator who was a committed revolutionary patriot and a friend of Georges-Jacques Danton, also a French delegate (later enmity between them would cause Robespierre to agree to Danton's death in April 1794). (*See* Danton's speech, page 202.) In this ringing address, Robespierre calls for the king's execution; he can be heard thinking through, with much sarcasm, the justification for condemning the king without a trial. Louis was beheaded by guillotine on January 21, 1793 (his wife, Marie Antoinette, was beheaded on October 16 of that year). This was followed by the year-long Reign of Terror (August 1793–July 1794), unleashed by Robespierre's Committee of Public Safety, in which many thousands of royalist sympathizers and persons inconvenient to the revolutionaries—even Danton, who was accused of treason and corruption—were executed, frequently after hasty, unfair trials, or even without trials. The tyrannical Robespierre was guillotined two years later by his own National Convention, who had grown fearful themselves of becoming victims of the Terror.

⁓⋈⁓

What is the conduct prescribed by sound policy to cement the republic? It is to engrave deeply into all hearts a contempt for royalty, and to strike terror into the partisans of the king. To place his crime before the world as a problem, his cause as the object of the most imposing discussion that ever existed, to place an immeasurable space between the memory of what he was and the title of a citizen, is the very way to make him most dangerous to liberty.

Louis XVI was king, and the republic is established. The question is solved by this single fact. Louis is dethroned by his crimes, he conspired against the republic; either he is condemned or the republic is not acquitted. To propose the trial of Louis XVI is to question the Revolution. If he may be tried, he may be acquitted; if he may be acquitted, he may be innocent. But if he be innocent, what becomes of the Revolution? If he be innocent, what are we but his calumniators? The coalition is just; his imprisonment is a crime; all the patriots are guilty; and the great cause which for so many centuries has been debated between crime and virtue, between liberty and tyranny, is finally decided in favor of crime and despotism!

Citizens, beware! You are misled by false notions. The majestic movements of a great people, the sublime impulses of virtue present themselves as the eruption of a volcano, and as the overthrow of political society. When a nation is forced to recur to the right of insurrection, it returns to its original state. How can the tyrant appeal to the social compact? He has destroyed it! What laws replace it? Those of nature: the people's

RHETORICAL DEVICE

Parallelism: This device gives the sentences or parts of a sentence similar form and balance that creates an ear-catching pattern and conveys that the ideas are of equal importance.

What they have but heard or read,
I have witnessed or performed. —*Gaius Marius*

Nothing is so difficult to build and
nothing so easy to destroy as peace. —*Johannes Rau*

To propose the trial of Louis XVI is to question the Revolution.
If he may be tried, he may be acquitted; if he may be acquitted,
he may be innocent. —*Maximilien Robespierre*

He who has not heard, has not wanted to hear; he who does not know, has not
wanted to know; he who has forgotten has sought to forget. —*Ernst Toller*

My fellow countrymen, today the guns are silent. A great tragedy has ended.
A great victory has been won. —*Douglas MacArthur*

safety. The right to punish the tyrant or to dethrone him is the same thing. Insurrection is the trial of the tyrant; his sentence is his fall from power. His punishment is exacted by the liberty of the people. The people dart their thunderbolts, that is, their sentence; they do not condemn kings, they suppress them—thrust them back again into nothingness.

In what republic was the right of punishing a tyrant ever deemed a question? Was Tarquin tried? What would have been said in Rome of anyone had undertaken his defense? Yet we demand advocates for Louis! They hope to gain the cause; otherwise we are only acting an absurd farce in the face of Europe. And we dare to talk of a republic! Ah! We are so pitiful for oppressors because we are pitiless towards the oppressed!

Two months since, and who would have imagined there could be a question here of the inviolability of kings? Yet today a member of the National Convention, Citizen Pétion, brings the question before you as though it were one for serious deliberation! Oh crime! Oh shame!

Maximilien de Robespierre was a deputy to the National Convention during the French Revolution of 1789–99. He ushered in a Reign of Terror after condeming King Louis XVI to the guillotine and also became its victim. *(Ablestock)*

The tribune of the French people has echoed the panegyric of Louis XVI. Louis combats us from the depths of his prison, and you ask if he be guilty, and if he may be treated as an enemy. Will you allow the Constitution to be invoked in his favor? If so, the Constitution condemns you; it forbids you to overturn it. Go, then, to the feet of the tyrant and implore his pardon and clemency.

But there is another difficulty. To what punishment shall we condemn him? The punishment of death is too cruel, says one. No, says another, life is more cruel still, and we must condemn him to live. Advocates, is it from pity or from cruelty you wish to annul the punishment of crimes? For myself I abhor the penalty of death; I neither love nor hate Louis; I hate nothing but his crimes. I demanded the abolition of capital punishment in the Constituent Assembly, and it is not my fault if the first principles of reason have appeared moral and judicial heresies. But you who never thought this mercy should be exercised in favor of those whose offences are pardonable, by what fatality are you reminded of your humanity to plead the cause of the greatest of criminals? You ask an exception from the punishment of death for him who alone could render it legitimate.

A dethroned king in the very heart of a republic not yet cemented! A king whose very name draws foreign wars on the nation! Neither prison nor exile can make his an innocent existence. It is with regret I pronounce the fatal truth. Louis must perish rather than a hundred thousand virtuous citizens. Louis must perish because our country must live!

Source: Hazeltine, Mayo, ed. *Famous Orations.* New York: Collier & Son, 1903, p. 117.

CHARLES JAMES FOX
(1749–1806)
"The Principle Which Gives Life to Liberty"
London, England
November 25, 1795

Charles James Fox became a member of Parliament when he was only 19 years old. In rapid succession, he took high posts in the Admiralty and Treasury, his eloquence speeding him on the road to power. In 1782 he became foreign secretary. King George III (r. 1760–1820) disliked Fox intensely, in part for his vociferous opposition to the war against the American colonies. Fox was a "liberal" of the time, a minister who supported the French Revolution (1789–99), opposed discrimination against Catholics, and who helped bring a bill to end slavery before the House in 1806, two months before he died. When the French Revolution erupted in 1789, kings and monarchists all over Europe grew uneasy. Prime Minister William Pitt (the Younger), an advocate of the monarchy and an enemy of Fox, took steps to prevent changes to Parliament—including suspending habeas corpus (which stated that a person must be present in court), in order to try rebels in their absence if necessary. On January 21, 1793, France executed King Louis XVI, and Britain (with other European monarchies) went to war against France. In Britain, taxes had to be raised to pay for the conflict and the poor had difficulty affording food. Two years later, King George was traveling in a carriage to speak in Parliament when he was assailed by tens of thousands of protesters calling for him to get rid of Pitt and his taxes, some even yelling, "No king, no war, no famine, no Pitt." In response, Pitt introduced repressive sedition laws, which prohibited large public meetings and political speeches, and made it treasonable to refer with contempt to the king or government. In the House of Commons, Fox spoke up in characteristic resistance to these curtailments of civil liberties and for freedom of speech and the press. Like most educated men of the time, Fox knew Latin intimately, and he peppers his speech with quotations from the ancient Roman poets Virgil and Horace and the historian Tacitus. He also refers to an *imprimatur*, meaning official approval to print, and to a *dicatur*, meaning official approval to speak.

***

Our government is valuable, because it is free. What, I beg gentlemen to ask themselves, are the fundamental parts of a free government? I know there is a difference of opinion upon this subject. My own opinion is, that freedom does not depend upon the executive government, nor upon the administration of justice, nor upon any one particular or distinct part, nor even upon forms so much as it does on the general freedom of speech and of writing.

With regard to freedom of speech, the bill before the House is a direct attack upon that freedom. No man dreads the use of a universal proposition more than I do myself. I must nevertheless say, that speech ought to be completely free, without any restraint whatever, in any government pretending to be free.

By being completely free, I do not mean that a person should not be liable to punishment for abusing that freedom, but I mean freedom in the first instance. The press is so at present, and I rejoice it is so; what I mean is, that any man may write and print what he pleases, although he is liable to be punished, if he abuses that freedom; this I call perfect freedom in the first instance.

If this is necessary with regard to the press, it is still more so with regard to speech. An *imprimatur* has been talked of, and it will be dreadful enough; but a *dicatur* will be still more horrible. No man has been daring enough to say, that the press should not be free: but the bill before them does not, indeed, punish a man for speaking, it prevents him from speaking.

> **RHETORICAL DEVICES**
>
> **Parade of Horribles:** Listing a series of possible dreadful events gives emphasis to the speaker's prediction. *(See its relative,* hyperbole*)*
>
> ---
>
> So take away the freedom of speech or of writing, and the foundation of all your freedom is gone. You will then fall, and be degraded and despised by all the world for your weakness and your folly, in not taking care of that which conducted you to all your fame, your greatness, your opulence, and prosperity. —*Charles James Fox*
>
> My lords. . . . I have laid before you the ruin of your power, the disgrace of your reputation, the pollution of your discipline, the contamination of your morals, the complication of calamities, foreign and domestic, that overwhelm your sinking country. —*William Pitt the Elder*

For my own part, I never heard of any danger arising to a free state from the freedom of the press, or freedom of speech; so far from it, I am perfectly clear that a free state cannot exist without both. The honourable and learned gentleman has said, will we not preserve the remainder by giving up this liberty? I admit that, by passing of the bill, the people will have lost a great deal. A great deal! Aye, all that is worth preserving. For you will have lost the spirit, the fire, the freedom, the boldness, the energy of the British character, and with them its best virtue.

I say, it is not the written law of the constitution of England, it is not the law that is to be found in books, that has constituted the true principle of freedom in any country, at any time. No! it is the energy, the boldness of a man's mind, which prompts him to speak, not in private, but in large and popular assemblies, that constitutes, that creates, in a state, the spirit of freedom. This is the principle which gives life to liberty; without, the human character is a stranger to freedom. If you suffer the liberty of speech to be wrested from you, you will then have lost the freedom, the energy, the boldness of the British character.

It has been said, that the right honourable gentleman rose to his present eminence by the influence of popular favour, and that he is now kicking away the ladder by which he mounted to power. Whether such was the mode by which the right honourable gentleman attained his present situation I am a little inclined to question; but I can have no doubt that if this bill shall pass, England herself will have thrown away that ladder, by which she has risen to wealth (but that is the last consideration), to honour, to happiness, and to fame.

Along with energy of thinking and liberty of speech, she will forfeit the comforts of her situation, and the dignity of her character, those blessings which they have secured to her at home, and the rank by which she has been distinguished among the nations. These were the sources of her splendour, and the foundation of her greatness—*Sic fortis Etruria crevit, scilicet et rerum facta est pulcherrima Roma* ["Thus Etruria grew strong, and Rome became the most glorious thing on earth"].

We need only appeal to the example of that great city whose prosperity the poet has thus recorded. In Rome, when the liberty of speech was gone, along with it vanished all that had constituted her the mistress of the world. I doubt not but in the days of Augustus there were persons who perceived no symptoms of decay, who exulted even in their fancied prosperity, when they contemplated the increasing opulence and splendid edifices of that grand metropolis, and who even deemed that they possessed their ancient liberty, because they still retained those titles of offices which had existed under the republic.

What fine panegyrics were then pronounced on the prosperity of the empire!—*Tum tutus bos prata perambulat* ["For safe the herds range field and fen"]. This was flattery to Augustus: to that great destroyer of the liberties of mankind, as much an enemy to freedom, as any of the detestable tyrants who succeeded him. So with us, we are to be flattered with an account of the form of our government, by King, Lords, and Commons—. . . *Eadem magistratuum vocabular* ["At home all was quiet; the titles of the magistrates were unchanged"].

There were some then, as there are now, who said that the energy of Rome was not gone; while they felt their vanity gratified in viewing their city; which had been converted from brick into marble. They did not reflect that they had lost that spirit of manly independence which animated the Romans of better times, and that the beauty and splendour of their city served only to conceal the symptoms of rottenness and decay.

So if this bill passes you may for a time retain your institution of juries and the forms of your free Constitution, but the substance is gone, the foundation is undermined;—your fall is certain and your destruction inevitable.

As a tree that is injured at the root and the bark taken off, the branches may live for a while, some sort of blossom may still remain; but it will soon wither, decay, and perish: so take away the freedom of speech or of writing, and the foundation of all your freedom is gone. You will then fall, and be degraded and despised by all the world for your weakness and your folly, in not taking care of that which conducted you to all your fame, your greatness, your opulence, and prosperity. . . .

Let us put a stop to the madness of this bill; for if you pass it, you will take away the foundation of the liberty of the people of England, and then farewell to any happiness in this country!

Source: Fox, Charles James. *Speeches of the Right Honourable Charles James Fox in the House of Commons.* Vol. 6. London: Longman, 1815, p. 45.

NAPOLEON BONAPARTE
(1769–1821)
To His Soldiers on Entering Milan
Milan, Italy
May 15, 1796

Napoleon Bonaparte was born on the French island of Corsica to an Italian family. He attended a French military school as a boy and joined the army as a teenager. In 1795, as a relatively young brigadier-general, he led revolutionary forces defending the National Convention, assembled at the Tuileries Palace, from royalist defenders of the monarchy. (The National Convention had been set up by Maximelien de Robespierre in 1792 to produce the new constitution). The next year as commander in chief of the French "Army of Italy," Napoleon marched his troops over the Apennine Mountains and across Italy. They crossed the rivers Po, Tessino, and Adda, defeating the Sardinian army and ousting the Austrian occupiers of Milan in mid-May 1796. His flattering short speeches to his devoted troops—he speaks of himself as one of them—reflect his genius in addressing his army; his men called him "the little corporal" in affection. The Italians welcomed him, hoping he would unite the tiny kingdoms and republics then under foreign domination, and his success made him the toast of Europe. The French Revolutionary Wars of 1792–1802 (fought against European powers such as Austria, Prussia, Russia, and Great Britain, who were concerned about the export of revolution from France) at first were waged to defend the Revolution, and only later to gain conquests for empire. Napoleon next led an expedition against the British in Egypt (in 1798) and the Ottoman Empire in Syria (in 1799). Back in France, political unrest led to a coup that installed him as First Consul, or head of government, in November 1799. Napoleon proclaimed himself emperor of France in 1804 and king of Italy the next year. By 1808 he controlled much of Europe, but he made the fatal mistake of invading Russia; his army crippled, foreign armies marching on France forced him to abdicate, or give up the throne, in 1814. Britain exiled Napoleon to the remote island of St. Helena in the South Atlantic Ocean, where he died in 1821.

Soldiers! You have precipitated yourselves like a torrent from the Apennines. You have overwhelmed or swept before you all that opposed your march. Piedmont, delivered from Austrian oppression, has returned to her natural sentiments of peace and friendship toward France. Milan is yours, and over all Lombardy floats the flag of the Republic.

To your generosity only do the Dukes of Parma and of Modena now owe their political existence. The army which proudly threatened you finds no remaining barrier of defense against your courage. The Po, the Ticino, the Adda, could not stop you a single day. Those vaunted ramparts of Italy proved insufficient; you traversed them as rapidly as you did the Apennines.

Successes so numerous and brilliant have carried joy to the heart of your country! Your representatives have decreed a festival, to be celebrated in all the communes of the Republic, in honor of your victories. There will your fathers, mothers, wives, sisters, all who hold you dear, rejoice over your triumphs, and boast that you belong to them.

Yes, soldiers, you have done much; but much still remains for you to do. Shall it be said of us that we knew how to conquer, but not to profit by victory? Shall posterity reproach us with having found a Capua in Lombardy? Nay, fellow soldiers! I see you already eager to cry "To arms!" Inaction fatigues you! And days lost to glory are to you days lost to happiness.

Let us, then, be gone! We have yet many forced marches to make, enemies to vanquish, laurels to gather, and injuries to avenge! Let those who have sharpened the daggers of civil war in France, who have basely assassinated our ministers, who have burned our vessels at Toulon—let them now tremble! The hour of vengeance has struck!

But let not the people be disquieted. We are the friends of every people: and more especially of the descendants of the Brutuses, the Scipios, and other great men to whom we look as bright exemplars. To reestablish the Capitol; to place there with honor the statues of the heroes who made it memorable; to rouse the Roman people, unnerved by many centuries of oppression—such will be some of the fruits of our victories. They will constitute an epoch for posterity.

To you, soldiers, will belong the immortal honor of redeeming the fairest portion of Europe. The French people, free and respected by the whole world, shall give to Europe a glorious peace, which shall indemnify it for all the sacrifices which it has borne the last six years. Then, by your own firesides you shall repose; and your fellow citizens, when they point out any one of you, shall say: "He belonged to the army of Italy!"

Source: Bryan, William Jennings, ed. *The World's Famous Orations.* Vol. 7. New York: Funk & Wagnall, 1906.

GEORGE WASHINGTON
(1732–1799)
"Observe Good Faith and Justice to All Nations"
Philadelphia, Pennsylvania, United States
September 17, 1796

As a young man in colonial Virginia, George Washington worked as a surveyor before serving in the Virginia Regiment in the French and Indian War (1754–63). He led the Continental Army to victory as commander in chief through many reversals during the Revolutionary War (1775–83). After presiding over the 1787 Constitutional Convention, which wrote the young country's first constitution, Washington served two terms as the first president of the United States, from 1789 to 1797. He was a competent executive, and he did not permit the office of president to take on any flavor of monarchy. The enormously popular Revolutionary War general and president has been called the "Father of His Country" for more than 200 years. Before retiring to his home at Mt. Vernon, Virginia, Washington delivered to Congress a Farewell Address in which he offered, from his experience, advice on the path a young country should follow. This Farewell Address in later years became a guidebook of political wisdom and continues to be quoted widely. In the early part of the speech, Washington declines to run for president a third time and gives profuse thanks for honors bestowed on him. He expresses concern that Americans should see themselves as one people, not residents of regions of the country, and he confesses himself profoundly uneasy with political parties. He counsels his hearers to avoid public debt and, like a good father, to respect morality and religion. But foremost is the need for the United States to make its own way in the world and remain free from entanglements in its interaction with foreign governments. At the time he spoke, Britain and France were at war once again, and Washington was desperate to ensure that the young country would not be drawn in.

Observe good faith and justice toward all nations; cultivate peace and harmony with all. Religion and morality enjoin this conduct, and can it be that good policy does not equally enjoin it? It will be worthy of a free, enlightened, and, at no distant period, a great nation, to give to mankind the magnanimous and novel example of a people always guided by an exalted justice and benevolence. Who can doubt that, in the course of time and things, the fruits of such a plan would richly repay any temporary advantages which might be lost by a steady adherence to it? Can it be that providence has not connected the permanent felicity of a nation with its virtue? The experiment, at least, is recommended by every sentiment which ennobles human nature. Alas! is it rendered impossible by its vices?

In the execution of such a plan nothing is more essential than that permanent, inveterate antipathies against particular nations and passionate attachments for others should be excluded, and that, in place of them, just and amicable feelings toward all should be cultivated. The nation which indulges toward another an habitual hatred or an habitual fondness is in some degree a slave. It is a slave to its animosity or to its affection, either of which is sufficient to lead it astray from its duty and its interest. Antipathy in one nation against another disposes each more readily to offer insult and injury, to lay hold of slight causes of umbrage, and to be haughty and intractable, when accidental or trifling occasions of dispute occur. Hence, frequent collisions; obstinate, envenomed, and bloody contests. The nation, prompted by ill will and resentment, sometimes impels to war the government, contrary to the best calculations of policy. The government sometimes participates in the national propensity, and adopts through passion what reason would reject; at other times it makes the animosity of the nation subservient to projects of hostility instigated by pride, ambition, and other sinister and pernicious motives. The peace often, sometimes perhaps the liberty, of nations has been the victim.

So, likewise, a passionate attachment of one nation for another produces a variety of evils. Sympathy for the favorite nation, facilitating the illusion of an imaginary common interest in cases where no real common interest exists, and infusing into one the enmities of the other, betrays the former into a participation in the quarrels and wars of the latter, without adequate inducement or justification. It leads also to concessions to the favorite nation of privileges denied to others, which is apt doubly to injure the nation making the concessions by unnecessarily parting with what ought to have been retained, and by exciting jealousy, ill will, and a disposition to retaliate, in the parties from whom equal privileges are withheld. And it gives to ambitious, corrupted, or deluded citizens (who devote themselves to the favorite nation) facility to betray or sacrifice the interests of their own country without odium, sometimes even with popularity; gilding with the appearances of a virtuous sense of obligation, a commendable deference for public opinion, or a laudable zeal for public good, the base or foolish compliances of ambition, corruption, or infatuation.

As avenues to foreign influence in innumerable ways, such attachments are particularly alarming to the truly enlightened and independent patriot. How many opportunities do they afford to tamper with domestic factions, to practice the arts of seduction, to mislead public opinion, to influence or awe the public councils! Such an attachment of a small or weak toward a great and powerful nation dooms the former to be the satellite of the latter.

Against the insidious wiles of foreign influence (I conjure you to believe me, fellow citizens), the jealousy of a free people ought to be constantly awake, since history and experience prove that foreign influence is one of the most baneful foes of republican government. But that jealousy, to be useful, must be impartial, else it becomes the instrument of the very influence to be avoided, instead of a defense against it. Excessive partiality for one foreign nation and excessive dislike of another cause those whom they actuate to see danger only on one side, and serve to veil and even second the arts of influence on the other. Real patriots, who may resist the intrigues of the favorite, are liable to become suspected and odious; while its tools and dupes usurp the applause and confidence of the people, to surrender their interests.

The great rule of conduct for us, in regard to foreign nations, is, in extending our commercial relations, to have with them as little political connection as possible. So far as we have already formed engagements, let them be fulfilled with perfect good faith. Here let us stop.

Europe has a set of primary interests which to us have none, or a very remote, relation. Hence she must be engaged in frequent controversies, the causes of which are essentially foreign to our concerns. Hence, therefore, it must be unwise in us to implicate ourselves, by artificial ties, in the ordinary vicissitudes of her politics or the ordinary combinations and collisions of her friendships or enmities.

Our detached and distant situation invites and enables us to pursue a different course. If we remain one people, under an efficient government the period is not far off when we may defy material injury from external annoyance; when we may take such an attitude as will cause the neutrality we may at any time resolve upon to be scrupulously respected; when belligerent nations, under the impossibility of making acquisitions upon us, will not lightly hazard the giving us provocation; when we may choose peace or war, as our interest, guided by justice, shall counsel.

Why forego the advantages of so peculiar a situation? Why quit our own to stand upon foreign ground? Why, by interweaving our destiny with that of any part of Europe,

> Observe good faith and justice towards all nations. Cultivate peace and harmony with all.
> —*George Washington*

entangle our peace and prosperity in the toils of European ambition, rivalship, interest, humor, or caprice?

It is our true policy to steer clear of permanent alliances with any portion of the foreign world—so far, I mean, as we are now at liberty to do it; for let me not be understood as capable of patronizing infidelity to existing engagements. I hold the maxim no less applicable to public than to private affairs, that honesty is always the best policy. I repeat it, therefore, let those engagements be observed in their genuine sense. But, in my opinion, it is unnecessary and would be unwise to extend them.

Taking care always to keep ourselves, by suitable establishments, on a respectable defensive posture, we may safely trust to temporary alliances for extraordinary emergencies.

Harmony, and a liberal intercourse with all nations are recommended by policy, humanity, and interest. But even our commercial policy should hold an equal and impartial hand; neither seeking nor granting exclusive favors or preferences; consulting the natural course of things; diffusing and diversifying by gentle means the streams of commerce, but forcing nothing; establishing, with powers so disposed, in order to give trade a stable course, to define the rights of our merchants, and to enable the government to support them, conventional rules of intercourse, the best that present circumstances and mutual opinion will permit, but temporary, and liable to be from time to time abandoned or varied, as experience and circumstances shall dictate; constantly keeping in view that it is folly in one nation to look for disinterested favors from another; that it must pay with a portion of its independence for whatever it may accept under that character; that, by such acceptance, it may place itself in the condition of having given equivalents for nominal favors, and yet of being reproached with ingratitude for not giving more. There can be no greater error than to expect or calculate upon real favors from nation to nation. It is an illusion which experience must cure, which a just pride ought to discard.

In offering to you, my countrymen, these counsels of an old and affectionate friend, I dare not hope they will make the strong and lasting impression I could wish; that they will control the usual current of the passions, or prevent our nation from running the course which has hitherto marked the destiny of nations. But if I may even flatter myself that they may be productive of some partial benefit, some occasional good; that they may now and then recur to moderate the fury of party spirit, to warn against the mischiefs of foreign intrigue, to guard against the impostures of pretended patriotism: this hope will be a full recompense for the solicitude for your welfare by which they have been dictated.

Source: Washington, George. "The Farewell Address." University of Virginia. Available online. http://gwpapers.virginia.edu/documents/farewell/transcript.html. Accessed December 14, 2007.

TOUSSAINT LOUVERTURE
(1743–1803)
"A Land of Slavery Purified by Fire"
Ravine-à-Couleuvres, Haiti
February 23, 1802

François-Dominique Toussaint was born about 1743 in Saint-Domingue, a French colony on the island of Hispaniola that would later become Haiti. His father was an enslaved African chief. Toussaint's French master allowed his slave some schooling, and he eventually became an accomplished manager on the plantation, earning his freedom in 1774. The French Revolution's astounding message of freedom, equality, and brotherhood in 1789 changed the political climate on the island—very soon the first slave rebellions broke out. In 1791 the slaves revolted in Saint-Domingue in one of history's few successful slave insurrections. Toussaint, after spiriting the family of his former master to safety along with his own, formed an army led by black generals. He added *Louverture* to his name (sometimes written L' Ouverture), meaning "the opening." They fought first against their French colonial masters, then a British invasion in 1793 (the British hoped to prevent the spread of revolution to their colony, Jamaica), and lastly against a French expedition sent in 1802 by Napoleon, whom Toussaint refers to as the Consul. (Napoleon had been installed as First Consul, or head of government, in 1799.) Toussaint abolished slavery, outlawed racial distinctions, and gave everyone the same rights; he took control even of Santo Domingo, the side of the island under Spanish rule. Toussaint was a lion-hearted man who fought at the head of his troops; while preparing to battle General de Rochambeau's French forces, Toussaint addressed his soldiers in words that recall Patrick Henry urging Virginia to arms in March 1775 (SEE Henry's speech, p. 185). Although Haitian forces succeeded in routing the French, Toussaint was captured in 1803. Imprisoned in France, he did not live out the year, but in 1804 Haiti was the first country in Latin America to win its freedom. Chastened by defeat in the Caribbean, Napoleon gave up his New World plans—he sold the Louisiana Territory to the United States. And it was the beginning of the end for slavery in the New World.

François-Dominique Toussaint took the name Louverture and successfully led an army of slaves against the European colonizers of Saint-Domingue (now Haiti) in 1791. *(Schomburg Center/Art Resource, NY)*

❦

You are going to fight against men who have neither faith, law, nor religion. They promise you liberty; they intend your servitude. Why have so many ships traversed the ocean, if not to throw you again into chains? They disdain to recognize in you submissive children, and if you are not their slaves, you are rebels.

215

The mother-country, misled by the Consul, is no longer anything for you but a step-mother . . . Uncover your breasts, you will see them branded by the iron of slavery.

During ten years, what have you not undertaken for liberty? Your masters slain or put to flight; the English humiliated by defeat; discord extinguished, a land of slavery purified by fire and evolving more beautiful than ever under liberty. These are your labors and these the fruits of your labors. And the foe wishes to snatch both out of your hands. . . .

Their bones will be scattered among these mountains and rocks and tossed about by the waves of the sea. Never more will they behold their native land, . . . and liberty will reign over their tomb.

Source: James, C. L. R. *The Black Jacobins: Toussaint L'Ouverture and the San Domingo Revolution.* New York: Vintage, 1963, p. 307.

ROBERT EMMET

(1778–1803)

"My Country Was My Idol"

Dublin, Ireland

September 19, 1803

The American Revolution (1775–83) and French Revolution (1789–99) were not long past when 25-year-old Robert Emmet ventured an uprising against the severely repressive British rule of Ireland. He was a Protestant university student with a reputation for oratory and love of his country when he joined a patriotic group, the Society of United Irishmen. The United Irishmen had been organized by nationalists in 1791 to reform the anti-Catholic Irish Parliament (which labored under the thumb of the British parliament) and to give representation to Catholics, as well as Protestants. The society had been forced to go into hiding when France and Britain declared war on each other in 1793 and Parliament had responded with new laws to punish treason against the British crown. The United Irishmen, exiled in France, turned to France for assistance in their determination to obtain independence from Britain. In May 1798 insurrection erupted in Ireland, but aid from France arrived too late and Britain was able to quash the uprising. In 1802 Britain abolished the Irish parliament, adding Irish representatives to the British parliament. Back from exile in Paris, Robert Emmet hoped to succeed with a second uprising. In July 1803 he set his plot into motion, but the poorly planned rebellion failed. Although Emmet escaped, he was caught a month later while visiting his fiancée, Sarah Curran. He was tried for treason; unknown to him, his lawyer was an informer in the pay of the British. Asked if he had anything to say why he should not be sentenced to death, the eloquent Emmet delivered this impassioned speech, or allocution, from the dock. The next day, September 20, the young hero was hanged and his body spirited away by the authorities.

My lords, I am asked what have I to say why sentence of death should not be pronounced on me according to law. I have nothing to say that can alter your predetermination, nor that it will become me to say with any view to the mitigation of that sentence which you are here to pronounce, and I must abide by. But I have that to say which interests me more than life, and which you have labored to destroy. I have much to say why my reputation should be rescued from the load of false accusation and calumny which has been heaped upon it.

I do not imagine that, seated where you are, your minds can be so free from prejudice as to receive the least impression from what I am going to utter. I have no hopes that I can anchor my character in the breast of a court constituted and trammeled as this is. I only wish, and it is the utmost I expect, that your lordships may suffer it to float down your memories untainted by the foul breath of prejudice, until it finds some more hospitable harbor to shelter it from the storm by which it is at present buffeted.

Was I only to suffer death after being adjudged guilty by your tribunal, I should bow in silence, and meet the fate that awaits me without a murmur. But the sentence of law which delivers my body to the executioner, will, through the ministry of that law, labor in its own vindication to consign my character to obloquy—for there must be guilt somewhere: whether in the sentence of the court or in the catastrophe, posterity must determine. A man in my situation, my lords, has not only to encounter the difficulties of fortune, and the force of power over minds which it has corrupted or subjugated, but the difficulties of established prejudice.

The man dies, but his memory lives. That mine may not perish, that it may live in the respect of my countrymen, I seize upon this opportunity to vindicate myself from some of the charges alleged against me. . . .

> Let no man write my epitaph. —*Robert Emmet*

I appeal to the immaculate God—I swear by the throne of Heaven, before which I must shortly appear—by the blood of the murdered patriots who have gone before me—that my conduct has been through all this peril and all my purposes, governed only by the convictions which I have uttered, and by no other view, than that of their cure, and the emancipation of my country from the super-inhuman oppression under which she has so long and too patiently travailed; and that I confidently and assuredly hope that, wild and chimerical as it may appear, there is still union and strength in Ireland to accomplish this noble enterprise. . . . If there is a true Irishman present, let my last words cheer him in the hour of his affliction. . . .

I am charged with being an emissary of France! An emissary of France! And for what end? It is alleged that I wished to sell the independence of my country! And for what end? Was this the object of my ambition? And is this the mode by which a tribunal of justice reconciles contradictions? No, I am no emissary; and my ambition was to hold a place among the deliverers of my country—not in power, nor in profit, but in the glory of the achievement!

Sell my country's independence to France! And for what? Was it for a change of masters? No! But for ambition! O my country, was it personal ambition that could influence me? Had it been the soul of my actions, could I not by my education and fortune, by the rank and consideration of my family, have placed myself among the proudest of my oppressors?

My country was my idol; to it I sacrificed every selfish, every endearing sentiment; and for it, I now offer up my life. O God! No, my lord; I acted as an Irishman, determined on delivering my country from the yoke of a foreign and unrelenting tyranny. . . . I wished to place her independence beyond the reach of any power on earth. I wished to exalt her to that proud station in the world which Providence had destined her to fill.

Connection with France was indeed intended, but only as far as mutual interest would sanction or require. Were they to assume any authority inconsistent with the purest independence, it would be the signal for their destruction; we sought aid, and we sought it, as we had assurances we should obtain it—as auxiliaries in war and allies in peace.

RHETORICAL DEVICE

Antithesis: Here the speaker juxtaposes two contrasting ideas or images (in a balanced or parallel fashion) to make an important point clear.

North America was born of the plow, Spanish America
of the bulldog. —*José Martí*

I am no courtier of America. I stand up for this kingdom. —*William Pitt the Elder*

The man dies, but his memory lives. —*Robert Emmet*

We gave them corn and meat; they gave us poison in return. —*Red Jacket*

Were the French to come as invaders or enemies, uninvited by the wishes of the people, I should oppose them to the utmost of my strength. Yes, my countrymen, I should advise you to meet them on the beach, with a sword in one hand, and a torch in the other; I would meet them with all the destructive fury of war; and I would animate my countrymen to immolate them in their boats, before they had contaminated the soil of my country. . . .

But it was not as an enemy that the succors of France were to land. I looked indeed for the assistance of France; but I wished to prove to France and to the world that Irishmen deserved to be assisted!—that they were indignant at slavery, and ready to assert the independence and liberty of their country.

I wished to procure for my country the guarantee which Washington procured for America. To procure an aid which, by its example, would be as important as its valor, disciplined, gallant, pregnant with science and experience; which would perceive the good, and polish the rough points of our character. They would come to us as strangers, and leave us as friends, after sharing in our perils and elevating our destiny. These were my objects—

Irish nationalist Robert Emmet exemplifies the tradition of stirring Irish oratory. *(Library of Congress)*

not to receive new taskmasters, but to expel old tyrants; these were my views, and these only became Irishmen. It was for these ends I sought aid from France, because France, even as an enemy, could not be more implacable than the enemy already in the bosom of my country. . . .

Let no man dare, when I am dead, to charge me with dishonor. Let no man attaint my memory by believing that I could have engaged in any cause but that of my country's liberty and independence, or that I could have become the pliant minion of power in the oppression or the miseries of my countrymen. . . .

Be yet patient! I have but a few words more to say. I am going to my cold and silent grave. My lamp of life is nearly extinguished; my race is run; the grave opens to receive me, and I sink into its bosom! I have but one request to ask at my departure from this world—it is the charity of its silence!

Let no man write my epitaph: for as no man who knows my motives dare now vindicate them, let not prejudice or ignorance asperse them. Let them and me repose in obscurity and peace, and my tomb remain uninscribed, until other times, and other men, can do justice to my character. When my country takes her place among the nations of the earth, then, and not till then, let my epitaph be written. I have done.

Source: Cruikshank, George. *History of the Irish Rebellion in 1798 . . . and Emmet's Insurrection in 1803.* London: George Bell and Sons, 1894, p. 427.

RED JACKET
(ca. 1758–1830)
"We Never Quarrel about Religion"
Buffalo, New York, United States
Summer 1805

Red Jacket of the Seneca tribe was born Otetiani in the Finger Lakes region of upstate New York. When he became a chief he received the name Segoyewatha, which means "he keeps them awake"—a reference to his skill as a public speaker. In fact, he was one of the greatest Native American orators, and he was as proud of his speaking ability as he was of being a warrior. Native Americans at that time had no written language. Their governments relied on oral persuasion; fluency in speech was a sign of spiritual power, and without spiritual power a man could not become chief. Red Jacket liked to wear a red coat he received during the Revolutionary War when the Senecas had allied themselves with the British. Later his portrait was painted wearing an immense silver peace medal George Washington gave him in 1792 when he led a delegation of chiefs to Philadelphia to discuss peace between the Six Nations (Mohawks, Oneidas, Onondagas, Cayugas, Senecas, and Tuscaroras) and the United States. He honored this new allegiance, fighting with the Americans against the British in the War of 1812. Red Jacket otherwise shunned the customs of whites and promoted the traditional way of life for his people. Constantly pressured by white land speculators, the "medal chief" proved his skill at negotiating with U.S. Indian commissioners in the Canandaigua Treaty of 1794, which fixed the boundaries of Seneca lands. In 1805, Reverend Cram, a Boston missionary of the Moravian Church, arrived to request permission to preach to the Senecas, likely with the ultimate goal of converting the tribe to Christianity. At a conference of chiefs at Buffalo Creek, Red Jacket used clear logic and diplomacy to defend the Native Americans' religion and rebuff outsiders who would force their unwanted religion on his people.

Friend and Brother, it was the will of the Great Spirit that we should meet together this day. He orders all things and has given us a fine day for our council. He has taken His garment from before the sun and caused it to shine with brightness upon us. Our eyes are opened that we see clearly; our ears are unstopped that we have been able to hear distinctly the words you have spoken. For all these favors we thank the Great Spirit, and Him only.

Brother, this council fire was kindled by you. It was at your request that we came together at this time. We have listened with attention to what you have said. You requested us to speak our minds freely. This gives us great joy; for we now consider that we stand upright before you and can speak what we think. All have heard your voice and all speak to you now as one man. Our minds are agreed.

Brother, you say you want an answer to your talk before you leave this place. It is right you should have one, as you are a great distance from home and we do not wish to detain you. But first we will look back a little and tell you what our fathers have told us and what we have heard from the white people.

Brother, listen to what we say. There was a time when our forefathers owned this great island. Their seats extended from the rising to the setting sun. The Great Spirit had made it for the use of Indians. He had created the buffalo, the deer, and other animals for food. He had made the bear and the beaver. Their skins served us for clothing. He had scattered them over the country and taught us how to take them. He had caused the earth to produce corn for bread. All this He had done for His red children because He loved them. If we had some disputes about our hunting ground they were generally settled without the shedding of much blood.

But an evil day came upon us. Your forefathers crossed the great water and landed on this island. Their numbers were small. They found friends and not enemies. They told us they had fled from their own country for fear of wicked men and had come here to enjoy their religion. They asked for a small seat. We took pity on them, granted their request, and they sat down among us. We gave them corn and meat; they gave us poison in return.

The white people, brother, had now found our country. Tidings were carried back and more came among us. Yet we did not fear them. We took them to be friends. They called us brothers. We believed them and gave them a larger seat. At length their numbers had greatly increased. They wanted more land; they wanted our country. Our eyes were opened and our minds became uneasy. Wars took place. Indians were hired to fight against Indians, and many of our people were destroyed. They also brought strong liquor among us. It was strong and powerful, and has slain thousands.

Red Jacket, or Segoyewatha, Seneca chief, wears the George Washington peace medal given him on a diplomatic mission to Philadelphia in 1792. From a painting by Charles Bird King *(Library of Congress)*

Brother, our seats were once large and yours were small. You have now become a great people, and we have scarcely a place left to spread our blankets. You have got our country, but are not satisfied; you want to force your religion upon us.

Brother, continue to listen. You say that you are sent to instruct us how to worship the Great Spirit agreeably to His mind; and, if we do not take hold of the religion which you white people teach we shall be unhappy hereafter. You say that you are right and we are lost. How do we know this to be true? We understand that your religion is written in a Book. If it was intended for us, as well as you, why has not the Great Spirit given to us, and not only to us, but why did He not give to our forefathers the knowledge of that Book, with the means of understanding it rightly. We only know what you tell us about it. How shall we know when to believe, being so often deceived by the white people?

Brother, you say there is but one way to worship and serve the Great Spirit. If there is but one religion, why do you white people differ so much about it? Why not all agreed, as you can all read the Book?

Brother, we do not understand these things. We are told that your religion was given to your forefathers and has been handed down from father to son. We also have a religion which was given to our forefathers and has been handed down to us, their children. We worship in that way. It teaches us to be thankful for all the favors we receive, to love each other, and to be united. We never quarrel about religion.

Brother, the Great Spirit has made us all, but He has made a great difference between His white and His red children. He has given us different complexions and different customs. To you He has given the arts. To these He has not opened our eyes. We know these things to be true. Since He has made so great a difference between us in other things, why may we not conclude that He has given us a different religion accord-

> Brother, we do not wish to destroy your religion or take it from you. We only want to enjoy our own.
> —*Red Jacket*

ing to our understanding? The Great Spirit does right. He knows what is best for His children; we are satisfied.

Brother, we do not wish to destroy your religion or take it from you. We only want to enjoy our own.

Brother, you say you have not come to get our land or our money, but to enlighten our minds. I will now tell you that I have been at your meetings and saw you collect money from the meeting. I cannot tell what this money was intended for, but suppose that it was for your minister; and, if we should conform to your way of thinking, perhaps you may want some from us.

Brother, we are told that you have been preaching to the white people in this place. These people are our neighbors. We are acquainted with them. We will wait a little while and see what effect your preaching has upon them. If we find it does them good, makes them honest, and less disposed to cheat Indians, we will then consider again of what you have said.

Brother, you have now heard our answer to your talk, and this is all we have to say at present. As we are going to part, we will come and take you by the hand, and hope the Great Spirit will protect you on your journey and return you safe to your friends.

Source: Moquin, Wayne, ed. *Great Documents in American Indian History.* New York: Da Capo Press, 1973, p. 31.

MIGUEL HIDALGO
(1753–1811)
The Cry of Dolores
Dolores, Mexico
September 16, 1810

French emperor Napoleon's invasion of Spain in 1808 ignited rebellion across Spain's empire in the Americas. In Mexico, Father Miguel Hidalgo, a criollo (Spanish, but born in America) priest, ministered to his downtrodden Indian and mestizo (mixed-race) parishioners in tiny impoverished Dolores. He was a humanitarian concerned with improving the plight of the poor; he established orchards and tradesmen's workshops for potters, weavers, and blacksmiths. After reading about the French Revolution, which occurred just 20 years earlier (1789–99), Hidalgo plotted with local revolutionists to rebel against Spanish colonial rule and its many indignities, including the tribute tax paid by Indians to the king. They were betrayed, but warned in the night, the 57-year-old Hidalgo forged ahead. When the villagers found no one in church for early Sunday Mass, they assembled before his house. He met them with the Grito de Dolores (Cry of Dolores), which proclaimed the people's desire for a true "patria," or fatherland, and began the Mexican War of Independence. His untrained peasant army grew to 80,000 men and seized a number of cities before defeat in March 1811 by Spanish troops. Hidalgo was excommunicated by the Inquisition, and he was executed on July 30, 1811. The little town that had benefited from his kindness renamed itself Dolores Hidalgo after Mexico achieved independence in 1821 (exactly 300 years after Moctezuma's Aztec Empire fell at the hands of Hernán Cortés [SEE Moctezuma's speech, page 124]). Hidalgo's Grito is recited in Independence Day celebrations today, with the ringing of Dolores's church bell, which has been moved to the National Palace in Mexico City. The exact words of the speech are not known. Some have him crying, "Death to bad government! Death to the Spaniards!" This version is by Juan de Aldama, a co-conspirator of Hidalgo who was present that morning.

RHETORICAL DEVICE

Exergasia: Repeating the same idea using other words, as a way of amplifying the idea.

The moment of our freedom has arrived.
The hour of our liberty has struck. —*Miguel Hidalgo*

You are not alone. We are with you. The whole world is with you. —*Jean Chrétien*

Among us you can dwell no longer—I will not bear it, I will not permit it,
I will not tolerate it. —*Marcus Tullius Cicero*

Long ago we made a tryst with destiny, and now the time comes
when we shall redeem our pledge, not wholly or in full measure,
but very substantially. —*Jawaharlal Nehru*

What is more, my comrades are neither dead nor forgotten;
they live today, more than ever. . . . —*Fidel Castro*

Beneath the banner of the Virgin of Guadalupe, Father Miguel Hidalgo leads his Mexican peasant army against Spanish forces in the months before his capture and execution in 1811. Painting by Juan O'Gorman. *(Schalkwijk/Art Resource, NY)*

My friends and countrymen: Neither the king nor tributes exist for us any longer. We have borne this shameful tax, which only suits slaves, for three centuries as a sign of tyranny and servitude—a terrible stain which we shall know how to wash away with our efforts.

The moment of our freedom has arrived. The hour of our liberty has struck; and if you recognize its great value, you will help me defend it from the ambitious grasp of the tyrants.

Only a few hours remain before you see me at the head of the men who take pride in being free. I invite you to fulfill this obligation. And so without a patria nor liberty we shall always be at a great distance from true happiness.

It has been imperative to take this step as now you know, and to begin this has been necessary. The cause is holy and God will protect it. The arrangements are hastily being made and for that reason I will not have the satisfaction of talking to you any longer.

Long live, then, the Virgin of Guadalupe!

Long live America for which we are going to fight!

Source: Hamill, Hugh M., Jr. *The Hidalgo Revolt: Prelude to Mexican Independence.* Gainesville: University of Florida Press, 1966, p. 121.

JOSÉ MARÍA MORELOS
(1765–1815)
"Spirits of Moctezuma . . . Take Pride"
Chilpancingo, Mexico
September 14, 1813

José María Morelos was a mixed-race Roman Catholic priest of humble origins, born in 1765 in Valladolid (now Morelia) in south-central Mexico. To the northeast in Dolores, another priest was serving a different parish, namely Father Miguel Hidalgo, who had been Morelos's mentor in their seminary. On September 16, 1810, Hidalgo set off the Mexican War of Independence from Spain with his rallying speech, the "Cry of Dolores" (SEE Hidalgo's speech, page 223). After several successful attacks against the wealthy Spanish landowners and authorities in neighboring cities, Hidalgo's enormous peasant army reached Valladolid and secured it in October 1810. Hearing of the army's approach, José María Morelos sought out Hidalgo, who encouraged him to form a revolutionary army in southwestern Mexico. When Hidalgo was caught and executed the next year, Morelos took over leadership of the independence movement. He was a natural military commander; in three campaigns his army of 10,000 seized a number of towns, including Oaxaca and Acapulco, from Spanish control. In the fall of 1813, representatives from the newly freed areas of Mexico assembled at a small town near Acapulco to form the Congress of Chilpancingo. They elected Morelos as commander in chief. After declaring Anahuac (the Aztecs's Valley of Mexico) free of Spain, the abolition of slavery, and government by representatives of the people, he addressed the delegates, invoking the sites of battles, the names of executed leaders, and the spirits of Aztec rulers. For two months the delegates worked to draw up a national constitution for Mexico. By December, however, Morelos's army was in retreat from Spanish forces. He was captured two years later, excommunicated by the church, tried for treason, and shot on December 22, 1815.

Our enemies have been obliged to reveal to us certain important truths; we were not ignorant of them, but the despotism of the government under whose yoke we have been oppressed attempted to hide them from us. They are: that sovereignty resides essentially in the people; that having been transmitted to monarchs, by their absence, death, or captivity, it falls back on the people; that they are free to reorganize their political institutions in any way which is agreeable to them; and that no people have the right to subjugate another. . . .

These oppressed people, similar to the Israelites who worked for Pharaoh, are tired of suffering, and they lift their hands to the sky, and make their clamoring heard before the throne of the Eternal. Taking pity on their misfortunes, He opens His mouth and decrees that Anahuac should be free. In the town of Dolores this voice was heard, and it was like a thunderbolt. . . .

Spirits of Las Cruces, of Aculco, Guanajuato, Calderon, Zitácuaro, and Cuautla! Spirits of Hidalgo and Allende should be witness to our flood of tears! You, who govern this august assembly, accept the most solemn pledge which we make to you today—that we shall die or save the country. But we do not undertake or execute anything for our own welfare if we do not decide beforehand to protect religion and its institutions, to conserve properties, to respect the rights of the people, to forget our mutual misunderstandings, and to work incessantly for fulfilling these sacred objectives. . . .

Spirits of Moctezuma, Cacamatzín, Cuauhtémoc, Xicotencatl, and Caltzontzín, take pride in this august assembly, and celebrate this happy moment in which your sons have congregated to avenge your insults. After August 12, 1521, comes September

8, 1813. The first date tightened the chains of our slavery in Mexico-Tenochtitlán; the second one broke them forever in the town of Chilpancingo. . . .

We are therefore going to restore the Mexican empire, and improve the government. We are going to be the spectacle of the cultured nations which will observe us. Finally, we are going to be free and independent.

Source: Timmons, Wilbert H. *Morelos of Mexico.* El Paso: Texas Western College Press, 1963, p. 118.

SIMÓN BOLÍVAR
(1783–1830)
"The Illustrious Name of Liberator"
Caracas, Venezuela
January 2, 1814

Simón Bolívar, revolutionary hero and statesman of Venezuela, liberated not only his own country from Spain but five others in South and Central America as well. He was born in 1783 to a wealthy family in Caracas, Venezuela, which had been a Spanish colony for nearly 300 years. As a teenager he left for Spain to continue his schooling, and at the age of 22 he vowed to devote himself to freeing Venezuela. Five years later, when revolution broke out, he would have the opportunity. After French emperor Napoleon Bonaparte invaded Spain and set his older brother, Joseph Bonaparte, on the Spanish throne in June 1808, the uncertain times provided ripe opportunity for revolution in South America. Venezuelan patriot Francisco de Miranda (who had aided the colonists in the American Revolution (1775–83) and then participated in the French Revolution (1789–99)) declared independence in 1810, and Bolívar joined his dictatorship. Miranda's rebel army was defeated by Venezuelan royalists and Spanish forces in 1812 (with the surprise aid of a devastating earthquake), and Bolívar took refuge in neighboring Colombia. With Miranda imprisoned in Spain, Bolívar took control of the resistance from his exile in Colombia. On August 6, 1813, he reentered Caracas leading rebel troops after months of battling royalists loyal to Spain. He gave this address before the Caracas Assembly after being proclaimed Liberator of Venezuela (although final independence came later in 1821). Bolívar's vision was never limited to one country—his aim was for freedom and republican government for all South America. The wars for independence that he led also brought independence to Colombia (1819), Panama (1821), Ecuador (1822), Peru (1824), and Bolivia (1825), which is named after Bolívar. All these countries eventually proclaimed him *El Libertador*—"The Liberator."

HATRED OF TYRANNY banished me from Venezuela when I saw my country enchained for the second time; but love of liberty overcame every obstacle in the path which I took to redeem my country from the cruelties and tortures of the Spaniard and brought me back from the distant banks of the Magdalena.

My armies, repeatedly triumphant, have everywhere taken possession and have destroyed the powerful foe. Your chains now shackle your oppressors. The Spanish blood that tinges the battlefield has avenged your slain countrymen.

I have not given you freedom; for this you are indebted to my fellow-soldiers. Behold their noble wounds, which still bleed; recall to mind those who have perished in battle. My glory has been in the leading of these brave soldiers.

Neither vanity nor lust for power inspired me in this enterprise. The flame of freedom lighted this sacred fire within me, and the sight of my fellow-citizens suffering the ignominy of death on the scaffold, or languishing in chains, compelled me to take up the sword against the enemy. The justice of our cause united the most valorous soldiers under my banners, and a just Providence accorded us victory.

My desire to save you from anarchy and to destroy the enemies who were endeavoring to sustain the oppressors forced me to accept and retain the sovereign power. I have given you laws; I have organized for you an administration of justice and finance; in short, I have given you a government.

Citizens, I am not your sovereign. Your representatives must make your laws; the national treasury is not the property of him who governs you. Every administration of your interests must render you an account of his stewardship. Judge impartially for yourselves whether I have used the elements of power for my own advancement, or whether I have devoted my life, my thoughts, my every moment to make of you a nation by augmenting your resources or, rather, by creating them.

I yearn for the moment when I can transfer this power to the representatives which you will choose. I sincerely trust, Gentlemen, that you will exempt me from an office which not a few of you could hold with distinction. Grant me the one honor to which I aspire—that of continuing to fight your enemies; for I shall never sheathe my sword so long as my country's freedom is not absolutely assured. . . .

Compatriots, you honor me with the illustrious name of Liberator. The officers and soldiers of the army are the true liberators; it is they who have earned the gratitude of the nation. You know well the authors of your restoration—those valorous soldiers and their dauntless commanders . . . whose courage and prowess are immortalized in Niquitao, Barquisimeto, Bárbula, Las Trincheras, and Araure.

Compatriots, I have not come to oppress you with my victorious arms. I have come to bring you the rule of law. I have come with the intention of safeguarding your most sacred rights. Military despotism cannot insure the happiness of a people, nor can the supreme command conferred upon me be of more than temporary advantage to the Republic.

A victorious soldier earns no right to rule his country. He is not the arbiter of her laws or government; he is the defender of her freedom. His glories must blend with those of the Republic, and his ambition must be satisfied with contributing to the happiness of his country.

I have vigorously defended your interests on the field of honor, and I promise that I shall uphold them to the last day of my life. Your honor, your glory will be ever dear to my heart; but the weight of authority burdens me. I beg you to relieve me from a task which is beyond my strength. Choose your representatives, your statesmen, and a just government; and be assured that the armies that have saved the Republic will forever protect Venezuela's liberty and national honor. . . .

Citizens, you urge in vain that I continue to exercise indefinitely the authority that I possess! The popular assemblies throughout Venezuela cannot convene without danger. I am aware of this situation, my Countrymen, and I will comply with my own feelings in choosing the law which circumstances impose upon me; but, I will act as the trustee of supreme authority only until this danger ceases. Thereafter, no human power shall make me take up the sceptre of despotism that necessity now thrusts into my hands. I promise you that it shall not oppress you, but that it shall pass into the hands of your representatives the moment they can be assembled.

I shall not usurp an authority that is not mine. I proclaim to all the people: No one can hold your sovereignty except by violent and unlawful means. Flee from that country where one man exercises all the power, for it is a land of slaves. You call me Liberator of the Republic; I shall never be her oppressor. . . . I am a plain citizen who prefers the freedom, glory, and well-being of his fellow-citizens to personal aggrandizement.

Accept, then, my sincerest expressions of heartfelt gratitude for the spontaneous acclaim with which you have named me your dictator. And, in taking leave of you, I promise that the general will of the people shall ever be my supreme law, and that the people's will shall guide me in all my actions, even as the object of my efforts shall be your glory and your freedom.

Source: Bierck, Harold A., ed. *Selected Writings of Bolivar.* Translated by Lewis Bertrand. New York: Banco de Venezuela/Colonial Press, 1951.

DANIEL WEBSTER
(1782–1852)
The Bunker Hill Oration
Charlestown, Massachusetts, United States
June 17, 1825

As a young man, Daniel Webster devoted himself to a classical pastime, the study of speech making. He never achieved his ambition of being elected U.S. president—he ran for the office three times—but he was a preeminent American statesman widely considered the greatest orator of his day. He opened a law practice in New Hampshire and entered politics as a federalist, having a fervent interest in strong national government. In 1812 he was elected to the U.S. House of Representatives, and in 1827 to the U.S. Senate, partly on the strength of his growing reputation as an orator. In 1825, as a congressman, he had delivered at Bunker Hill one of his peerless platform performances. The year marked the 50th anniversary of the American Revolution (1775–83). The Marquis de Lafayette had come from France for a celebratory tour of the United States and had been lionized at every stop. Lafayette—and other people young at the time of the Revolution—served as an honored guest at the laying of the cornerstone for the Bunker Hill Monument in Charlestown, Massachusetts, just outside Boston. Webster gave this famous address, memorializing the brave but losing engagement of American forces against the British in the Battle of Bunker Hill. This bloody battle took place on June 17, 1775 (not long after the battles at Lexington and Concord that marked the start of the Revolution), as American troops attempted to prevent the British from extending their occupation of Boston to Charlestown. In later years, Webster became U.S. secretary of state under the ninth U.S. president, William Henry Harrison. He labored always to keep the northern and southern states in the Union, and supported, under much criticism, the Compromise of 1850 intended to prevent civil war. Webster died in 1852, after losing his third attempt at the presidency.

We are among the sepulchers of our fathers. We are on ground distinguished by their valor, their constancy, and the shedding of their blood. We are here not to fix an uncertain date in our annals, nor to draw into notice an obscure and unknown spot. If our humble purpose had never been conceived, if we ourselves had never been born, the 17th of June, 1775, would have been a day on which all subsequent history would have poured its light, and the eminence where we stand a point of attraction to the eyes of successive generations.

But we are Americans. We live in what may be called the early age of this great continent; and we know that our posterity, through all time, are here to enjoy and suffer the allotments of humanity. We see before us a probable train of great events; we know that our own fortunes have been happily cast; and it is natural, therefore, that we should be moved by the contemplation of occurrences which have guided our destiny before many of us were born, and settled the condition in which we should pass that portion of our existence which God allows to men on earth. . . .

The great event in the history of the continent, which we are now met here to commemorate, that prodigy of modern times, at once the wonder and the blessing of the world, is the American Revolution. In a day of extraordinary prosperity and happiness, of high national honor, distinction, and power, we are brought together in this place by our love of country, by our admiration of exalted character, by our gratitude for signal services and patriotic devotion. . . .

The great wheel of political revolution began to move in America. Here its rotation was guarded, regular, and safe. Transferred to the other continent, from unfortunate but natural causes, it received an irregular and violent impulse; it whirled along with a fearful celerity; till at length, like the chariot-wheels in the races of antiquity, it took fire from the rapidity of its own motion, and blazed onward, spreading conflagration and terror around.

We learn from the result of this experiment how fortunate was our own condition, and how admirably the character of our people was calculated for setting the great example of popular governments. The possession of power did not turn the heads of the American people, for they had long been in the habit of exercising a great degree of self-control. Although the paramount authority of the parent state existed over them, yet a large field of legislation had always been open to our Colonial assemblies. They were accustomed to representative bodies and the forms of free government; they understood the doctrine of the division of power among different branches, and the necessity of checks on each.

The character of our countrymen, moreover, was sober, moral, and religious; and there was little in the change to shock their feelings of justice and humanity, or even to disturb an honest prejudice. We had no domestic throne to overturn, no privileged orders to cast down, no violent changes of property to encounter. In the American Revolution, no man sought or wished for more than to defend and enjoy his own. None hoped for plunder or for spoil. Rapacity was unknown to it; the axe was not among the instruments of its accomplishment; and we all know that it could not have lived a single day under any well-founded imputation of possessing a tendency adverse to the Christian religion. . . .

The people have begun, in all forms of government, to think, and to reason, on affairs of state. Regarding government as an institution for the public good, they demand a knowledge of its operations, and a participation in its exercise. A call for the representative system, wherever it is not enjoyed, and where there is already intelligence enough to estimate its value, is perseveringly made. Where men may speak out, they demand it; where the bayonet is at their throats, they pray for it . . .

And, now, let us indulge an honest exultation in the conviction of the benefit which the example of our country has produced, and is likely to produce, on human freedom and human happiness. Let us endeavor to comprehend in all its magnitude, and to feel in all its importance, the part assigned to us in the great drama of human affairs. We are placed at the head of the system of representative and popular governments. Thus far our example shows that such governments are compatible, not only with respectability and power, but with repose, with peace, with security of personal rights, with good laws, and a just administration.

We are not propagandists. Wherever other systems are preferred, either as being thought better in themselves, or as better suited to existing conditions, we leave the preference to be enjoyed. Our history hitherto proves, however, that the popular form is practicable, and

With Henry Clay and John Calhoun, Daniel Webster formed the "Great Triumvirate" of statesmen and orators in the U.S. Senate from about 1830 to 1850. Webster's impressive bearing and flowing oratory made him a powerful figure in Congress and as secretary of state. *(Library of Congress)*

that with wisdom and knowledge men may govern themselves; and the duty incumbent on us is to preserve the consistency of this cheering example and take care that nothing may weaken its authority with the world. If, in our case, the representative system ultimately fail, popular governments must be pronounced impossible. No combination of circumstances more favorable to the experiment can ever be expected to occur. The last hopes of mankind, therefore, rest with us; and if it should be proclaimed, that our example had become an argument against the experiment, the knell of popular liberty would be sounded throughout the earth.

These are excitements to duty; but they are not suggestions of doubt. Our history and our condition, all that is gone before us and all that surrounds us, authorize the belief that popular governments, though subject to occasional variations, in form perhaps not always for the better, may yet in their general character be as durable and permanent as other systems. We know, indeed, that in our country any other is impossible. The principle of free government adheres to American soil. It is bedded in it, immovable as its mountains.

And let the sacred obligations which have devolved on this generation and on us sink deep into our hearts. Those who established our liberty and our government are daily dropping from among us. The great trust now descends to new hands. Let us apply ourselves to that which is presented to us as our appropriate object. We can win no laurels in a war for independence. Earlier and worthier hands have gathered them all. Nor are there places for us by the side of Solon, and Alfred, and other founders of states. Our fathers have filled them. But there remains to us a great duty of defense and preservation; and there is opened to us also a noble pursuit to which the spirit of the times strongly invites us.

Our proper business is improvement. Let our age be the age of improvement. In a day of peace, let us advance the arts of peace and the works of peace. Let us develop the resources of our land, call forth its powers, build up its institutions, promote all its great interests, and see whether we also, in our day and generation, may not perform something worthy to be remembered. Let us cultivate a true spirit of union and harmony.

In pursuing the great objects which our condition points out to us, let us act under a settled conviction, and an habitual feeling, that these twenty-four states are one country. Let our conception be enlarged to the circle of our duties. Let us extend our ideas over the whole of the vast field in which we are called to act. Let our object be our country, our whole country, and nothing but our country. And, by the blessing of God, may that country itself become a vast and splendid monument, not of oppression and terror, but of wisdom, of peace, and of liberty, upon which the world may gaze with admiration forever.

Source: Whipple, Edwin Percy, ed. *The Great Speeches and Orations of Daniel Webster.* New York: Little, Brown, 1914, p. 124.

DANIEL O'CONNELL
(1775–1847)
"Justice for Ireland"
House of Commons, London, England
February 4, 1836

Daniel O'Connell was born a Catholic in 1775 in the southwestern corner of Ireland. At that time, Protestant England dominated almost all aspects of life in largely Catholic Ireland. Under a draconian system sometimes called the Protestant Ascendancy, Catholics could not own land, could not join the military or attend university, could not serve as judges, and could not serve in Parliament. (Catholics in England and Scotland lived under similar restrictions.) O'Connell became a successful lawyer in Dublin, but he remained aloof from the United Irishmen's independence movement, which he felt resorted too easily to violence. Even after the Act of Union in 1800, which joined mostly Protestant Great Britain to unwilling Ireland (and abolished the Irish parliament), O'Connell preferred political solutions. He began to campaign for Catholic Emancipation—the abolishing of laws restricting the rights of Catholics. He organized the powerful Catholic Association, which helped Catholics run for public office. O'Connell himself won election to the British House of Commons in 1828, which forced the government's hand in passing the Catholic Emancipation Act of 1829. This act gave Catholics the right to take seats in the House of Commons, and O'Connell soon began to be called "The Liberator." He next set his sights on repealing the Act of Union. He organized immense "meetings," which tens of thousands of people attended, until the British government suppressed them. He was arrested and jailed for three months in 1843 for sedition (rebelling against lawful authority). In this speech in Parliament, O'Connell is asking whether Ireland will get the same relief from prejudicial laws that Catholics in Scotland and England had just received.

The question is one in the highest degree interesting to the people of Ireland. It is, whether we mean to do justice to that country—whether we mean to continue the injustice which has been already done to it, or to hold out the hope that it will be treated in the same manner as England and Scotland. That is the question. We know what "lip service" is; we do not want that. There are some men who will even declare that they are willing to refuse justice to Ireland; while there are others who, though they are ashamed to say so, are ready to consummate the iniquity, and they do so.

England never did do justice to Ireland—she never did. What we have got of it we have extorted from men opposed to us on principle—against which principle they have made us such concessions as we have obtained from them. . . .

Years are coming over me, but my heart is as young and as ready as ever in the service of my country, of which I glory in being the pensionary and the hired advocate. I stand in a situation in which no man ever stood yet—the faithful friend of my country—its servant—its stave, if you will—I speak its sentiments by turns to you and to itself. I require no £20,000,000 on behalf of Ireland—I ask you only for justice: will you—can you—I will not say dare you refuse, because that would make you turn the other way. I implore you, as English gentlemen, to take this matter into consideration now, because you never had such an opportunity of conciliating. Experience makes fools wise; you are not fools, but you have yet to be convinced. . . .

I may be laughed and sneered at by those who talk of my power; but what has created it but the injustice that has been done in Ireland? That is the end and the means of the magic, if you please—the groundwork of my influence in Ireland. If you refuse justice to that country, it is a melancholy consideration to me to think that you are adding substantially to that power and influence, while you are wounding my country

---

RHETORICAL DEVICE

Epanalepsis: Giving emphasis to the beginning of a sentence or clause by repeating it at the end.

———————————————————

England never did do justice to Ireland—she never did. —*Daniel O'Connell*

The dream we dream is a realistic dream. —*Luis Muñoz Marín*

Judge not, that you not be judged. —*Jesus of Nazareth*

The K.A.U. is you, and you are the K.A.U. —*Jomo Kenyatta*

---

to its very heart's core; weakening that throne, the monarch who sits upon which, you say you respect; severing that union which, you say, is bound together by the tightest links, and withholding that justice from Ireland which she will not cease to seek till it is obtained.

Every man must admit that the course I am taking is the legitimate and proper course—I defy any man to say it is not. Condemn me elsewhere as much as you please, but this you must admit.

You may taunt the ministry with having coalesced me, you may raise the vulgar cry of "Irishman and Papist" against me, you may send out men called ministers of God to slander and calumniate me; they may assume whatever garb they please, but the question comes into this narrow compass. I demand, I respectfully insist: on equal justice for Ireland, on the same principle by which it has been administered to Scotland and England.

I will not take less. Refuse me that if you can.

Source: Hazeltine, Mayo, ed. *Famous Orations.* Vol. 5. New York: Collier & Son, 1903, p. 120.

FREDERICK DOUGLASS
(1818–1895)
Against Slavery
Moorfields, England
May 22, 1846

In 1838 at the age of 21, Frederick Bailey escaped from slavery in Maryland to New Bedford, Massachusetts, where he found work on the waterfront. There he took a new name: Frederick Douglass. He began speaking against slavery in his church, attracting the attention of white abolitionists with his powerful voice and commanding platform presence. The famous abolitionist orator William Lloyd Garrison of the Massachusetts Anti-Slavery Society soon recognized Douglass's incomparable talent, and Douglass became one of their most important speakers, traveling the Northeast delivering addresses in large and small towns. With his many evident accomplishments, some questioned whether he had ever truly been a slave, and he felt obliged to publish an autobiography, *Narrative of the Life of Frederick Douglass.* The book was a popular success (even translated into French and German), but it provided enough detail on his life that Douglass feared slavecatchers might find him; he sailed to England in 1845 to avoid recapture. He made fast friends among British antislavery societies, delivering speeches throughout Britain, sometimes sharing the stage with brilliant orators like Daniel O'Connell (*SEE* his speech, page 233) and John Bright (*SEE* his speech, page 243) to enlist support abroad against slavery in the United States. In this 1848 address, Douglass spoke for three hours to nearly 3,000 people packed into a church hall; the enthusiastic audience punctuated his talk alternately with cries of horror and "Hear, hear!" After British supporters purchased his freedom for 150 pounds in 1847, he returned to America. In Rochester, New York, and later in Washington, D.C., he pursued a passionate calling as an abolitionist speaker, edited an antislavery newspaper, became a confidant of President Abraham Lincoln, and was appointed minister to Haiti. But long before that time, he had transcended his birth in slavery and lack of formal education to become one of the greatest orators in U.S. history.

❦

I feel exceedingly glad of the opportunity now afforded me of presenting the claims of my brethren in bonds in the United States to so many in London and from various parts of Britain, who have assembled here on the present occasion. I have nothing to commend me to your consideration in the way of learning, nothing in the way of education, to entitle me to your attention; and you are aware that slavery is a very bad school for rearing teachers of morality and religion.

Twenty-one years of my life have been spent in slavery, personal slavery, surrounded by degrading influences such as can exist nowhere beyond the pale of slavery; and it will not be strange, if under such circumstances, I should betray in what I have to say to you a deficiency of that refinement which is seldom or ever found, except among persons that have experienced superior advantages to those which I have enjoyed. . . .

An attempt has been made in this country to establish the conviction that the free states of the Union have nothing whatever to do with the maintenance and perpetuity of slavery in the southern states, and many persons coming from the United States have represented themselves as coming from the free states, and have shirked all responsibility in regard to slavery on this ground.

Now, I am here to maintain that slavery is not only a matter belonging to the states south of the line, but is an American institution—a United States institution—a system that derives its support as well from the non-slave-holding states, as they are called, as from the slave-holding states. The slave-holding states, to be sure, enjoy all the profits of slavery—the institution exists upon their soil; but if I were going to give the exact

As a slave boy of 13, Frederick Douglass bought a copy of the children's book of oratory his young white friends used in school. He studied the book at every opportunity, and 10 years after his small purchase, he embarked on a life-long calling as an abolitionist and civil rights speaker. *(Library of Congress)*

position of the northern and southern states it would be simply this—the slave states are the slave-holding states, while the non-slave states are the slavery-upholding states. . . .

The will and the wishes of the master are the law of the slave. He is as much a piece of property as a horse. If he is fed, he is fed because he is property. If he is clothed, it is with a view to the increase of his value as property. Whatever of comfort is necessary to him for his body or soul, that is inconsistent with his being property, is carefully wrested from him, not only by public opinion, but by the law of the country. He is carefully deprived of everything that tends in the slightest degree to detract from his value as property.

He is deprived of education. God has given him an intellect—the slave holder declares it shall not be cultivated. If his moral perception leads him in a course contrary to his value as property, the slave holder declares he shall not exercise it. The marriage institution cannot exist among slaves, and one-sixth of the population of democratic America is denied its privileges by the law of the land. What is to be thought of a nation boasting of its liberty, boasting of its humanity, boasting of its Christianity, boasting of its love of justice and purity, and yet having within its own borders three millions of persons denied by law the right of marriage?—what must be the condition of that people? . . .

This is American slavery—no marriage—no education—the light of the Gospel shut out from the dark mind of the bondman—and he forbidden by law to learn to read. If a mother shall teach her children to read, the law in Louisiana proclaims that she may be hanged by the neck. If the father attempt to give his son a knowledge of letters, he may be punished by the whip in one instance, and in another be killed, at the discretion of the court. Three millions of people shut out from the light of knowledge! It is easy for you to conceive the evil that must result from such a state of things.

I now come to the physical evils of slavery. I do not wish to dwell at length upon these, but it seems right to speak of them, not so much to influence your minds on this question, as to let the slave holders of America know that the curtain which conceals their crimes is being lifted abroad; that we are opening the dark cell, and leading the people into the horrible recesses of what they are pleased to call their domestic institution.

We want them to know that a knowledge of their whippings, their scourgings, their brandings, their chainings, is not confined to their plantations, but that some negro of theirs has broken loose from his chains—has burst through the dark incrustation of slavery, and is now exposing their deeds of deep damnation to the gaze of the Christian people of England.

The slave holders resort to all kinds of cruelty. If I were disposed, I have matter enough to interest you on this question for five or six evenings, but I will not dwell at length upon these cruelties. Suffice it to say, that all the peculiar modes of torture that were resorted to in the West India Islands, are resorted to, I believe, even more frequently, in the United States of America. Starvation, the bloody whip, the chain, the gag, the thumb-screw, cat-hauling, the cat-o'-nine-tails, the dungeon, the bloodhound, are all in requisition to keep the slave in his condition as a slave. . . . The bloodhound is regularly trained in the United States, and advertisements are to be found in the southern papers of the Union, from persons advertising themselves as bloodhound trainers, and offering to hunt down slaves at fifteen dollars a piece, recommending their hounds as the fleetest in the neighbourhood, never known to fail.

Advertisements are from time to time inserted, stating that slaves have escaped with iron collars about their necks, with bands of iron about their feet, marked with the lash, branded with red hot irons, the initials of their master's name burned into their flesh; and the masters advertise the fact of their being thus branded with their own signature, thereby proving to the world, that, however daring it may appear to non-slave holders, such practices are not regarded as discreditable or daring among the slave holders themselves. . . .

I may be asked, why I am so anxious to bring this subject before the British public—why I do not confine my efforts to the United States? My answer is, first, that slavery is the common enemy of mankind, and all mankind should be made acquainted with its abominable character. My next answer is, that the slave is a man, and, as such, is entitled to your sympathy as a brother. All the feelings, all the susceptibilities, all the capacities, which you have, he has. He is a part of the human family. He has been the prey—the common prey—of Christendom for the last 300 years, and it is but right, it is but just, it is but proper, that his wrongs should be known throughout the world.

I have another reason for bringing this matter before the British public, and it is this, slavery is a system of wrong, so blinding to all around, so hardening to the heart, so corrupting to the morals, so deleterious to religion, so sapping to all the principles of justice in its immediate vicinity, that the community surrounding it lack the moral stamina necessary to its removal.

RHETORICAL DEVICE

Understatement: Deemphasizing an idea for effect, and sometimes to be tactful. (*See also* litotes)

Here then is work for us to do. —*Frederick Douglass, referring to the campaign to end slavery*

I want to avoid violence. —*Mahatma Gandhi, speaking of his campaign of civil disobedience*

Hostilities exist. —*Franklin D. Roosevelt, speaking after Japan's attack on Pearl Harbor*

We wanted to go to the moon, so we went there. —*Muhammad Yunus*

It is a system of such gigantic evil, so strong, so overwhelming in its power, that no one nation is equal to its removal. It requires the humanity of Christianity, the morality of the world, to remove it. Hence I call upon the people of Britain to look at this matter, and to exert the influence I am about to show they possess, for the removal of slavery from America. I can appeal to them, as strongly by their regard for the slave holder as for the slave, to labour in this cause.

I am here because you have an influence on America that no other nation can have. You have been drawn together by the power of steam to a marvellous extent; the distance between London and Boston is now reduced to some 12 or 14 days, so that the denunciations against slavery uttered in London this week, may be heard in a fortnight in the streets of Boston, and reverberating amidst the hills of Massachusetts. There is nothing said here against slavery, that will not be recorded in the United States.

I am here also, because the slave holders do not want me to be here; they would rather that I was not here. I have adopted a maxim laid down by Napoleon, never to occupy ground which the enemy would like me to occupy. The slave holders would much rather have me, if I will denounce slavery, denounce it in the northern states, where their friends and supporters are, who will stand by and mob me for denouncing it. . . .

The slave holders felt that when slavery was denounced among themselves, it was not so bad, but let one of the slaves get loose, let him summon the people of Britain, and make known to them the conduct of the slave holders towards their slaves, and it cuts them to the quick, and produces a sensation such as would be produced by nothing else. The power I exert now is something like the power that is exerted by the man at the end of the lever; my influence now is just in proportion to the distance that I am from the United States. . . .

I expose slavery in this country, because to expose it is to kill it. Slavery is one of those monsters of darkness to whom the light of truth is death. Expose slavery, and it dies. Light is to slavery what the heat of the sun is to the root of a tree, it must die under it. . . .

I want the slave holder surrounded, as by a wall of anti-slavery fire, so that he may see the condemnation of himself and his system glaring down in letters of light.

I want him to feel that he has no sympathy in England, Scotland, or Ireland; that he has none in Canada, none in Mexico, none among the poor wild Indians; that the voice of the civilized, aye, and savage world, is against him.

I would have condemnation blaze down upon him in every direction, till, stunned and overwhelmed with shame and confusion, he is compelled to let go the grasp he holds upon the persons of his victims, and restore them to their long-lost rights. Here, then, is work for us all to do.

Source: Douglass, Frederick. *The Frederick Douglass Papers.* Edited by John Blassingame. Vol. 1. New Haven, Conn.: Yale University Press, 1979, p. 269.

VICTOR HUGO
(1802–1885)
Against Capital Punishment
Paris, France
June 11, 1851

Victor Hugo was born in 1802, shortly after the French Revolution (1789–99) and during the reign of Napoleon Bonaparte (1769–1821), a time of great turmoil in France. He began publishing poetry at an early age, and during a long life he wrote an abundance of plays and novels as well, among them *The Hunchback of Notre Dame* and *Les Misérables*. With his works' emphasis on the emotional and spiritual aspects of life and the freedom of the individual, Hugo was one of the most important artists and intellectuals of the 19th-century Romantic movement. Concerned over social injustice, he wrote and campaigned in particular against the death penalty, publishing a novel in his twenties called *The Last Day of a Man Condemned to Death*, and a paper titled *Essay on Capital Punishment*. "The scaf-

fold," he wrote, "is the only edifice which revolutions do not demolish." In 1851 his eldest son, Charles, age 25, was arrested for writing critically about the death sentence that an executed man, named Montcharmant, had received. At Charles's trial, Hugo spoke spiritedly in his son's defense, but Charles was fined and sent to prison for six months. Hugo was passionately committed to republican France, and when Napoleon III restored the monarchy—the Second Empire—with himself as emperor in 1852, Hugo spoke out fearlessly against him. Hugo was forced to flee the country, and he spent 18 years in exile living in Guernsey, one of the Channel Islands belonging to Britain. He wrote *Les Misérables* while there. When he returned to France in 1870, nearly 70 years old, the public heaped him with adoration.

Gentlemen of the jury, if there is a culprit here, it is not my son—it is myself—it is I! I, who for these last twenty-five years have opposed capital punishment—have contended for the inviolability of human life—have committed this crime, for which my son is now arraigned.

Here I denounce myself, Mr. Advocate General! I have committed it under all aggravated circumstance—deliberately, repeatedly, tenaciously. Yes, this old and absurd *lex talionis*—this law of blood for blood—I have combated all my life, all my life, gentlemen of the jury! And, while I have breath, I will continue to combat it, by all my efforts as a writer, by all my words and all my votes as a legislator! I declare it before the crucifix; before that victim of the penalty of death, who sees and hears us; before that gibbet to which, two thousand years ago, for the eternal instruction of the generations, the human law nailed the Divine!

In all that my son has written on the subject of capital punishment—and for writing and publishing which he is now before you on trial—in all that he has written, he has merely proclaimed the sentiments with which, from his infancy, I have inspired him.

Gentlemen jurors, the right to criticize a law, and to criticize it severely—especially a penal law—is placed beside the duty of amelioration, like a torch beside the work under the artisan's hand. This right of the journalist is as sacred, as necessary, as imprescriptible, as the right of the legislator.

What are the circumstances? A man, a convict, a sentenced wretch, is dragged on a certain morning to one of our public squares. There he finds the scaffold! He shudders, he struggles, he refuses to die. He is young yet—only twenty-nine. Ah! I know what you will say—"He is a murderer!" But hear me.

Two officers seize him. His hands, his feet, are tied. He throws off the two officers. A frightful struggle ensues. His feet, bound as they are, become entangled in the ladder.

RHETORICAL DEVICE

Personification: Giving human abilities or qualities to an inanimate object or abstraction, for reasons of beautiful and metaphoric language, but also to awaken interest and make concepts more real to the hearer.

The Angel of Death has been abroad throughout the land;
you may almost hear the beating of his wings. —*John Bright*

Bolívar appears with his cohort of luminaries. Even the volcanoes acclaim him and publish him to the world, their flanks shaking and thundering. —*José Martí*

The guillotine, though vanquished, remains standing. There it frowns all day in the midst of a sickened population. —*Victor Hugo*

He uses the scaffold against the scaffold! The struggle is prolonged. Horror seizes on the crowd. The officers, sweat and shame on their brows, pale, panting, terrified, despairing, despairing with I know not what horrible despair—shrinking under that public reprobation which ought to have visited the penalty and spared the passive instrument, the executioner—the officers strive savagely. The victim clings to the scaffold and shrieks for pardon. His clothes are torn, his shoulders bloody; still he resists.

At length, after three-quarters of an hour of this monstrous effort, of this spectacle without a name, of this agony—agony for all, be it understood, agony for the assembled spectators as well as for the condemned man—after this age of anguish, gentlemen of the jury, they take back the poor wretch to his prison.

The people breathe again. The people, naturally merciful, hope that the man will be spared. But no—the guillotine, though vanquished, remains standing. There it frowns all day in the midst of a sickened population. And at night, the officers, reinforced, drag forth the wretch again, so bound that he is but an inert weight. They drag him forth, haggard, bloody, weeping, pleading, howling for life, calling upon God, calling upon his father and mother—for like a very child had this man become in the prospect of death—they drag him forth to execution.

He is hoisted on to the scaffold, and his head falls! And then through every conscience runs a shudder.

Source: Bryan, William Jennings, ed. *The World's Famous Orations.* Vol. 7. New York: Funk & Wagnall, 1906, p. 193.

LOUIS KOSSUTH
(1802–1894)
"Become the Lafayettes of Hungary"
New York City
December 6, 1851

Hungary had been governed by Austria for more than 150 years when fiery journalist and orator Louis Kossuth led a popular rebellion against the Austrian Empire. He was born in Hungary in 1802 to a well-to-do family. He studied law and took a job at the Austrian-dominated Hungarian National Diet (or General Assembly). Because he was an excellent writer he began covering the debates in the Diet, but he was imprisoned for three years for reporting on the proceedings of the Hungarian regional assemblies, which was forbidden. (The Diet was dissolved in 1836 but allowed to reopen three years later.) In 1841 Kossuth took the job of top editor for a newspaper, the liberal *Pesti Hirlap*; he tried through impassioned articles on reform to encourage a revival of the Hungarian national identity. He was elected to the newly opened Diet in 1847 and, with his powers of eloquence and natural fervor, quickly worked himself into a position of authority. A year later the opportunity for independence came when revolution, beginning in Sicily and France, erupted across Europe. Kossuth became the celebrated hero of the Hungarian revolution, but because he championed the Magyar ethnic group (with which he identified) over the Croats, Serbs, Romanians, Slovaks, and other minority groups, he ultimately failed to unite the people. He declared independence for Hungary in 1849 and became president, but only four months later—with Russia's aid—Austria crushed the revolt. Kossuth escaped to Turkey. He was detained there until an American warship, the USS *Mississippi*, liberated him and brought him to New York. His plea for aid delivered in this speech was warmly received in the United States, where thousands of people turned out to see him, but it brought little real assistance to Hungary.

***

Let me, before I go to work, have some hours of rest upon this soil of freedom, your happy home. Freedom and home; what heavenly music in those two words! Alas! I have no home, and the freedom of my people is downtrodden. . . .

When I look over these thousands of thousands before me, the happy inheritance of yonder freedom for which your fathers fought and bled—and when I turn to you, citizens, to bow before the majesty of the United States, and to thank the people of New York for their generous share in my liberation, and for the unparalleled honor of this reception—I see, out of the very midst of this great assemblage, rise the bleeding image of Hungary, looking to you with anxiety whether there be in the luster of your eyes a ray of hope for her; whether there be in the thunder of your huzzas a trumpet-call of resurrection. . . .

Gentlemen, I have to thank the people, Congress, and government of the United States for my liberation from captivity. Human tongue has no words to express the bliss which I felt, when I—the downtrodden Hungary's wandering chief—saw the glorious flag of the Stripes and Stars fluttering over my head.

When I first bowed before it with deep respect—when I saw around me the gallant officers and the crew of the *Mississippi* frigate—the most of them the worthiest representatives of true American principles, American greatness, American generosity—and to think that it was not a mere chance which cast the Star-spangled Banner around me, but that it was your protecting will—to know that the United States of America, conscious of their glorious calling, as well as of their power, declared, by this unparalleled act, to be resolved to become the protectors of human rights—to see a powerful vessel of America coming to far Asia to break the chains by which the mightiest despots of

Europe fettered the activity of an exiled Magyar, whose very name disturbed the proud security of their sleep—to feel restored by such a protection, and, in such a way, to freedom, and by freedom to activity; you may be well aware of what I have felt, and still feel, at the remembrance of this proud moment of my life.

Others spoke—you acted; and I was free! . . .

I came not to your glorious shores to enjoy a happy rest—I came not with the intention to gather triumphs of personal distinction, but because a humble petitioner, in my country's name, as its freely chosen constitutional chief, humbly to entreat your generous aid.

And then it is to this aim that I will devote every moment of my time, with the more assiduity, with the more restlessness, as every moment may bring a report of events which may call me to hasten to my place on the battle-field, where the great, and I hope, the last battle will be fought between liberty and despotism—a moment marked by the finger of God to be so near that every hour of delay of your generous aid may prove fatally disastrous to oppressed humanity.

And, thus having stated my position to be that of a humble petitioner in the name of my oppressed country, let me respectfully ask: Do you not regret to have bestowed upon me the high honor of this glorious reception, unparalleled in history?

I say unparalleled in history, though I know that your fathers have welcomed Lafayette in a similar way; but Lafayette had mighty claims to your country's gratitude. He had fought in your ranks for your freedom and independence; and, what was still more, in the hour of your need he was the link of your friendly connection with France—a connection the results of which were two French fleets of more than thirty-eight men-of-war and three thousand gallant men, who fought side by side with you against Cornwallis, before Yorktown; the precious gift of twenty-four thousands muskets; a loan of nineteen millions of dollars; and even the preliminary treaties of your glorious peace negotiated at Paris by your immortal Franklin.

I hope the people of the United States, now itself in the happy condition to aid those who are in need of aid, as itself was once in need, will kindly remember these facts; and you, citizens of New York, you will yourselves become the Lafayettes of Hungary.

Lafayette had great claims to your love and sympathy, but I have none. I came a humble petitioner, with no other claims than those which the oppressed have to the sympathy of freemen who have the power to help, with the claim which the unfortunate has to the happy, and the downtrodden has to the protection of eternal justice and of human rights. In a word, I have no other claims than those which the oppressed principle of freedom has to the aid of victorious liberty.

Source: Headley, P. C. *The Life of Louis Kossuth.* Auburn: Derby and Miller, 1852, p. 247.

JOHN BRIGHT
(1811–1889)
"The Angel of Death"
House of Commons, London, England
February 23, 1855

John Bright was born a Quaker in 1811. As a Nonconformist (member of a religious group other than the Church of England), he was never afraid to take a stand against popular ideas. He represented the city of Manchester in Parliament, where he was known for legislation favoring business interests. But he also had a side to him that detested what he felt was unchristian, such as capital punishment and the flogging of soldiers, and most importantly, unjust wars. He lost his seat in the House of Commons in taking a position against the disastrous Crimean War, which was popular with the public as well as parliamentarians. The Crimean war began in late 1853, between Russia and an alliance composed of France, Britain, Sardinia, and the Ottoman Empire. Conflict had begun between France and Russia, each appealing to the Ottomans over who had authority as protector of Christianity in the Holy Lands, then held by the Ottoman Empire.

Britain, always concerned over the imperial ambitions of Russia and the Ottomans in fearing that one would gain dominance in the Mediterranean, was drawn in. When France won the dispute by a show of saber rattling, Tsar Nicholas I (r. 1825–55) marched troops into Ottoman principalities. The war began in the Crimea, a Russian peninsula on the Black Sea, whose major city was Sevastopol, where the Russian fleet was headquartered. Four thousand British soldiers died in combat, while another 18,000 wounded men died needlessly from neglect and unsanitary conditions; their plight would make British nurse and social reformer Florence Nightingale famous for taking a cadre of nurses to serve in the war zone. In this context, Bright made his most celebrated, although fruitless, address to the 70-year-old prime minister, Lord Palmerston (1855–65), which left the entire House of Commons moved beyond words.

The fact is that we are at war with the greatest military power, probably, of the world, and that we are carrying on our operations at a distance of 3,000 miles from home, and in the neighborhood of the strongest fortifications of that great military empire. . . .

I shall not say one word here about the state of the army in the Crimea, or one word about its numbers or its condition. Every Member of this House, every inhabitant of this country, has been sufficiently harrowed with details regarding it. To my solemn belief, thousands—nay, scores of thousands of persons—have retired to rest, night after night, whose slumbers have been disturbed or whose dreams have been based upon the sufferings and agonies of our soldiers in the Crimea.

I should like to ask the noble Lord at the head of the Government—although I am not sure if he will feel that he can or ought to answer the question—whether the noble Lord the Member for London has power, after discussions have commenced, and as soon as there shall be established good grounds for believing that the negotiations for peace will prove successful, to enter into any armistice?

I know not, Sir, who it is that says "No, no," but I should like to see any man get up and say that the destruction of 200,000 human lives lost on all sides during the course of this unhappy conflict is not a sufficient sacrifice. You are not pretending to conquer territory. You are not pretending to hold fortified or unfortified towns. You have offered terms of peace which, as I understand them, I do not say are not moderate. And breathes there a man in this House or in this country whose appetite for blood is so insatiable that, even when terms of peace have been offered and accepted, he pines for that assault in which of Russian, Turk, French and English, as sure as one man dies, 20,000 corpses will strew the streets of Sebastopol? . . .

243

> The Angel of Death has been abroad throughout the land; you may almost hear the beating of his wings. —*John Bright*

I cannot but notice, in speaking to Gentlemen who sit on either side of this House, or in speaking to any one I meet between this House and any of those localities we frequent when this House is up—I cannot, I say, but notice that an uneasy feeling exists as to the news which may arrive by the very next mail from the East.

I do not suppose that your troops are to be beaten in actual conflict with the foe, or that they will be driven into the sea; but I am certain that many homes in England in which there now exists a fond hope that the distant one may return—many such homes may be rendered desolate when the next mail shall arrive.

The Angel of Death has been abroad throughout the land; you may almost hear the beating of his wings. There is no one, as when the first-born were slain of old, to sprinkle with blood the lintel and the two side-posts of our doors, that he may spare and pass on. He takes his victims from the castle of the noble, the mansion of the wealthy, and the cottage of the poor and the lowly, and it is on behalf of all these classes that I make this solemn appeal.

I tell the noble Lord, that if he be ready honestly and frankly to endeavor, by the negotiations about to be opened at Vienna, to put an end to this war, no word of mine, no vote of mine, will be given to shake his power for one single moment, or to change his position in this House. I am sure that the noble Lord is not inaccessible to appeals made to him from honest motives and with no unfriendly feeling.

The noble Lord has been for more than forty years a Member of this House. Before I was born, he sat upon the Treasury bench, and he has spent his life in the service of his country. He is no longer young, and his life has extended almost to the term allotted to man.

I would ask, I would entreat the noble Lord to take a course which, when he looks back upon his whole political career—whatever he may therein find to be pleased with, whatever to regret—cannot but be a source of gratification to him. By adopting that course he would have the satisfaction of reflecting that, having obtained the object of his laudable ambition—having become the foremost subject of the Crown, the director of, it may be, the destinies of his country, and the presiding genius in her councils—he had achieved a still higher and nobler ambition: that he had returned the sword to the scabbard—that at his word torrents of blood had ceased to flow—that he had restored tranquility to Europe, and saved this country from the indescribable calamities of war.

Source: Bright, John. *Speeches on the Public Affairs of the Last Twenty Years.* London: Camden Hotten, 1869, p. 47.

LUCY STONE
(1818–1893)
"A Disappointed Woman"
Cincinnati, Ohio, United States
October 17, 1855

Lucy Stone was born in Massachusetts to a large farming family. She was one of the first American women to attend college (Oberlin College in Oberlin, Ohio), which she paid for herself by teaching and performing other jobs as her family (and society) did not approve of higher education for women. She was a superb orator and began lecturing on women's rights and for the abolition of slavery almost as soon as she graduated from college. She married the abolitionist Henry Blackwell in May 1855; another first for her was to keep her maiden name after marriage—she called herself Mrs. Stone. This was so unusual for the time that, for decades, women who kept their own names after marriage were called "Lucy Stoners." Blackwell was an unusually progressive-minded man—he had already given speeches for women's rights before they married, and he supported Stone's activism all her life. Shortly after their wedding day the couple published a protest against the marriage laws, which they felt discriminated against women. A few months later, at the 1855 National Women's Rights Convention in Cincinnati, Ohio, she cleverly took the lead from a male speaker who had just referred to the women's rights movement as being the work of "a few disappointed women." A leader in both the abolitionist and the women's suffrage movements, she founded the American Equal Rights Association in 1866 with suffragists Susan B. Anthony, Elizabeth Cady Stanton, and Frederick Douglass. Different ideas of how best to demand equal rights for blacks and women led to a split in that organization; accordingly, she founded in 1869, with her husband, the American Woman Suffrage Association (AWSA), which continued to agitate for the rights of American blacks. She also edited AWSA's magazine, *Woman's Journal*.

The last speaker alluded to this movement as being that of a few disappointed women.

From the first years to which my memory stretches, I have been a disappointed woman. When with my brothers, I reached forth after the sources of knowledge, I was reproved with "It isn't fit for you; it doesn't belong to women." Then there was but one college in the world where women were admitted, and that was in Brazil. I would have found my way there, but by the time I was prepared to go, one was opened in the young State of Ohio—the first in the United States where women and Negroes could enjoy opportunities with white men.

I was disappointed when I came to seek a profession worthy an immortal being—every employment was closed to me, except those of the teacher, the seamstress, and the housekeeper. In education, in marriage, in religion, in everything, disappointment is the lot of woman. It shall be the business of my life to deepen this disappointment in every woman's heart until she bows down to it no longer. I wish that women, instead of being walking show-cases, instead of begging of their fathers and brothers the latest and gayest new bonnet, would ask of them their rights.

The question of Woman's Rights is a practical one. The notion has prevailed that it was only a ephemeral idea; that it was but women claiming the right to smoke cigars in the streets, and to frequent bar-rooms. Others have supposed it a question of comparative intellect; others still, of sphere. Too much has already been said and written about woman's sphere. Trace all the doctrines to their source and they will be found to have no basis except in the usages and prejudices of the age. This is seen in the fact that what is tolerated in woman in one country is not tolerated in another. In this country, women may hold prayer-meetings, etc., but in Mohammedan countries it is written upon their mosques, "Women and dogs, and other impure animals, are not permitted to enter."

Wendell Phillips says, "The best and greatest thing one is capable of doing, that is his sphere." I have confidence in the Father that when He gives us the capacity to do anything, He does not make a blunder. Leave women, then, to find their sphere. And do not tell us before we are born even, that our province is to cook dinners, darn stockings, and sew on buttons.

> In education, in marriage, in religion, in everything, disappointment is the lot of woman. —*Lucy Stone*

We are told woman has all the rights she wants; and even women, I am ashamed to say, tell us so. They mistake the politeness of men for rights—seats, while men stand in this hall tonight, and their adulations, but these are mere courtesies. We want rights. The flour merchant, the house builder, and the postman charge us no less on account of our sex; but when we endeavor to earn money to pay all these, then, indeed, we find the difference.

Man, if he have energy, may hew out for himself a path where no mortal has ever trod, held back by nothing but what is in himself; the world is all before him, where to choose; and we are glad for your, brothers, men, that is so. But the same society that drives forth the young man, keeps woman at home—a dependent—working little cats on worsted, and little dogs on punctured paper; but if she goes heartily and bravely to give herself to some worthy purpose, she is out of her sphere and she loses caste.

Women working in tailor-shops are paid one-third as much as men. Some one in Philadelphia has stated that women make fine shirts for twelve and a half cents apiece; that no women can make more than nine a week, and the sum thus earned, after deducting rent, fuel, etc., leaves her just three and a half cents a day for bread. Is it a wonder that women are driven to prostitution? Female teachers in New York are paid fifty dollars a year, and for every such situation there are five hundred applicants. I know not what you believe of God, but I believe He gave yearnings and longings to be filled, and that He did not mean all our time should be devoted to feeding and clothing the body.

The present condition of woman causes a horrible perversion of the marriage relation. It is asked of a lady, "Has she married well?" "Oh, yes, her husband is rich." Woman must marry for a home, and you men are the sufferers by this; for a woman who loathes you may marry you because you have the means to get money which she can not have. But

Lucy Stone played a central role as journalist and orator in the women's rights movement in the United States. She also never let enthusiasm for her original cause blind her to injustices leveled at black Americans. *(Library of Congress)*

when woman can enter the lists with you and make money for herself, she will marry you only for deep and earnest affection.

I am detaining you too long, many of you standing, that I ought to apologize, but women have been wronged so long that I may wrong you a little. . . . I have seen a woman at manual labor turning out chair-legs in a cabinet-shop, with a dress short enough not to drag in the shavings. I wish other women would imitate her in this. It made her hands harder and broader, it is true, but I think a hand with a dollar and a quarter a day in it, better than one with a crossed ninepence. . . .

The widening of woman's sphere is to improve her lot. Let us do it, and if the world scoff, let it scoff—if it sneer, let it sneer.

Source: Stanton, Elizabeth Cady, Susan B. Anthony, and Matilda Joslyn Gage. *History of Woman Suffrage.* Vol. 1. Rochester, N.Y.: Charles Mann, 1889, p. 165.

DAVID LIVINGSTONE
(1813–1873)
"Commerce and Christianity"
Cambridge, England
December 4, 1857

David Livingstone, Scottish missionary doctor and explorer, began his 33-year-long mission in 1840 in the south of Africa. As a child he had enjoyed hiking the countryside around his Lanarkshire home, and in Africa he would travel the length and breadth of the continent as no European had before—he was the first European to visit the great waterfall that he named Victoria Falls (after Victoria, queen of Great Britain and Ireland 1837–1901). Early in his mission to South Africa he trekked through the interior to the west coast (to Luanda, Angola) and then across to the east coast (where the Zambezi River flows through Mozambique). He kept a journal on the geography and people, as he had always been interested in the natural world. He was pained by the slavery he found in Africa, and he hoped that encouraging more missionaries to come work there would help end the practice. He returned home to Britain briefly in 1857, where he spoke on his travels and discoveries to excited audiences at Cambridge University. His address inspired new interest in the mysterious continent with its uncharted interior and, in 20 years, the European "scramble" for territorial claims in Africa began. In the meantime, Livingstone left his missionary work behind and found funding from the British government for scientific expeditions, first along the Zambezi River and later to discover the source of the Nile. When he was not heard from for some time, American reporter Henry Morton Stanley of the *New York Herald* set out to find him. When he did locate the old missionary on Lake Tanganyika (bordering present-day Tanzania and the Democratic Republic of the Congo), in 1871, Stanley is said to have greeted him with "Dr. Livingstone, I presume." Livingstone died in what is now Zambia in 1873.

David Livingstone returned home to Britain in 1857 to share the news of his explorations in Africa and the opportunities he felt awaited missionaries. (*Engraving from* Missionary Travels and Researches in South Africa *by David Livingstone, London, 1857*) (*Ablestock*)

If you look at the map of Africa, you will discover the shortness of the coastline, which is in consequence of the absence of deep indentations of the sea. This is one reason why the interior of Africa has remained so long unknown to the rest of the world. Another reason is the unhealthiness of the coast, which seems to have reacted upon the disposition of the people, for they are very unkindly, and opposed to Europeans passing through their country.

In the southern part of Africa lies the great Kalahari desert, not so called as being a mere sandy plain, devoid of vegetation—such a desert I never saw until I got between Suez and Cairo. . . .

My object in going into the country south of the desert was to instruct the natives in a knowledge of Christianity, but many circumstances prevented my living amongst them more than seven years, amongst which were considerations arising out of the slave system carried on by the Dutch Boers. I resolved to go into the country beyond, and soon found that for the purposes of commerce, it was necessary to have a path to the sea. I might have gone on instructing the natives in religion, but as civilization and Christianity must go on together, I was obliged to find a path to the sea, in order that I should not sink to the level of the natives.

The chief was overjoyed at the suggestion, and furnished me with twenty-seven men, and canoes and provisions, and presents for the tribes through whose country we had to pass. We might have taken a shorter path to the sea than that to the north, and then to the west, by which we went; but along the country by the shorter route there is an insect called the tsetse, whose bite is fatal to horses, oxen, and dogs, but not to men or donkeys. [Laughter.] You seem to think there is a connection between the two. . . .

There was a desire in the various villages through which we passed to have intercourse with us, and kindness and hospitality were shown us; but when we got near the Portuguese settlement of Angola the case was changed, and payment was demanded for everything. But I had nothing to pay with. Now the people had been in the habit of trading with the slavers, and so they said I might give one of my men in payment for what I wanted. When I showed them that I could not do this, they looked upon me as an interloper and I was sometimes in danger of being murdered.

As we neared the coast, the name of England was recognized, and we got on with ease. Upon one occasion, when I was passing through the parts visited by slave-traders, a chief who wished to show me some kindness offered me a slave-girl. Upon explaining that I had a little girl of my own, whom I should not like my own chief to give to a black man, the chief thought I was displeased with the size of the girl and sent me one a head taller. By this and other means I convinced my men of my opposition to the principle of slavery, and when we arrived at Loanda I took them on board a British vessel, where I took a pride in showing them that those countrymen of mine and those guns were there for the purpose of putting down the slave-trade. They were convinced from what they saw of the honesty of Englishmen's intentions, and the hearty reception they met with from the sailors made them say to me, "We see they are your countrymen, for they have hearts like you." . . .

I had gone towards the coast for the purpose of finding a direct path to the sea, but on going through the country we found forests so dense that the sun had not much influence on the ground, which was covered with yellow mosses, and all the trees with white lichens. Amongst these forests were little streams, each having its source in a bog; in fact nearly all the rivers in that country commence in bogs. Finding it impossible to travel here in a wheel conveyance, I left my wagon behind, and I believe it is standing in perfect safety, where I last saw it, at the present moment. The only other means of conveyance we had was ox-back, by no means a comfortable mode of traveling. I therefore came back to discover another route to the coast by means of the river Zambesi. . . .

There is a large central district containing a large lake formed by the course of the Zambesi, to explore which would be well worthy of the attention of any individual wishing to distinguish himself.

Having got down amongst the people in the middle of the country, and having made known to my friend the chief my desire to have a path for civilization and commerce on the east, he again furnished me with means to pursue my researches eastward. And to show how disposed the natives were to aid me in my expedition, I had 114 men to accompany me to the east. . . .

In a commercial point of view, communication with this country is desirable. Angola is wonderfully fertile, producing every kind of tropical plant in rank luxuriance. Passing on to the valley of Quango, the stalk of the grass was as thick as a quill, and towered above my head, although I was mounted on my ox. Cotton is produced in great abundance, though merely woven into common cloth. Bananas and pineapples grow in great luxuriance; but the people having no maritime communication, these advantages are almost lost. The country on the other side is not quite so fertile, but in addition to indigo, cotton, and sugar-cane, produces a fibrous substance, which I am assured is stronger than flax.

The Zambesi has not been thought much of as a river by Europeans, not appearing very large at its mouth; but on going up it for about seventy miles, it is enormous. The first three hundred miles might be navigated without obstacle, then there is a rapid, and near it a coal-field of large extent.... In going back to that country my object is to open up traffic along the banks of the Zambesi, and also to preach the Gospel. The natives of Central Africa are very desirous of trading, but their only traffic is at present in slaves, of which the poorer people have an unmitigated horror. It is therefore most desirable to encourage the former principle, and thus open a way for the consumption of free productions, and the introduction of Christianity and commerce.

By encouraging the native propensity for trade, the advantages that might be derived in a commercial point of view are incalculable; nor should we lose sight of the inestimable blessings it is in our power to bestow upon the unenlightened African, by giving him the light of Christianity. Those two pioneers of civilization—Christianity and commerce—should ever be inseparable; and Englishmen should be warned by the fruits of neglecting that principle as exemplified in the result of the management of Indian affairs. By trading with Africa, also, we should at length be independent of slave labor, and thus discountenance practices so obnoxious to every Englishman.

Though the natives are not absolutely anxious to receive the Gospel, they are open to Christian influences. Among the Bechuanas the Gospel was well received. These people think it a crime to shed a tear, but I have seen some of them weep at the recollection of their sins when God had opened their hearts to Christianity and repentance. It is true that missionaries have difficulties to encounter, but what great enterprise was ever accomplished without difficulty? It is deplorable to think that one of the noblest of our missionary societies, the Church Missionary Society, is compelled to send to Germany for missionaries, whilst other societies are amply supplied. Let this stain be wiped off. The sort of men who are wanted for missionaries are such as I see before me—men of education, standing, enterprise, zeal, and piety....

I beg to direct your attention to Africa. I know that in a few years I shall be cut off in that country, which is now open. Do not let it be shut again! I go back to Africa to try to make an open path for commerce and Christianity—do you carry out the work which I have begun. I leave it with you!

Source: Livingstone, David. *Dr. Livingstone's Cambridge Lectures.* Edited by Rev. William Monk. Cambridge: Deighton, Bell and Co., 1858, p. 1.

THOMAS HENRY HUXLEY
(1825–1895)
"An Ape for His Grandfather"
Oxford, England
June 30, 1860

Charles Darwin published his revolutionary book *On the Origin of Species* in 1859, which contained a detailed argument for evolution through natural selection (the mechanism by which traits favoring a species' survival and reproduction become more common over time, sometimes resulting in new species). It was quickly attacked by clergy opposed to the theory of evolution, especially the astounding idea of man's descent from apes. The next year, a young British biologist named Thomas Henry Huxley saved the new science from ridicule when he participated in a debate between several Darwinians and Samuel Wilberforce, the bishop of Oxford (son of abolitionist William Wilberforce), who had no scientific learning. It was a "clash between Science and the Church." With many clergymen in the crowd at the Oxford University Museum, Wilberforce particularly directed his sarcasms at Huxley, asking whether it was through his grandfather or his grandmother that he was descended from a monkey? The question, while witty, was Wilberforce's mistake. Huxley rose to speak, and an admiring observer of Huxley's retort wrote later, "He was not ashamed to have a monkey for his ancestor, but he would be ashamed to be connected with a man who used great gifts to obscure the truth." Huxley received the nickname "Darwin's bulldog" for defending Darwin's theory of evolution. He was the son of a poor math teacher who could afford only a few years of schooling for him. Huxley never let that hold him back; he taught himself Latin, Greek, and German, became an expert on anatomy, and studied medicine. His research as a naturalist while he served as ship doctor on a scientific voyage, earned him attention from the scientific community, and he became a university professor of natural history (the study of living things in their ecosystems). For the rest of his life he devoted himself to the study of vertebrate evolution (the evolution of animals with backbones), especially that of humans.

❧

I asserted—and I repeat—that a man has no reason to be ashamed of having an ape for his grandfather.

If there were an ancestor whom I should feel shame in recalling it would rather be a man—a man of restless and versatile intellect—who, not content with an equivocal success in his own sphere of activity, plunges into scientific questions with which he has no real acquaintance, only to obscure them by an aimless rhetoric, and distract the attention of his hearers from the real point at issue by eloquent digressions and skilled appeals to religious prejudice.

Source: Huxley, Leonard. *Life and Letters of Thomas Henry Huxley.* Vol. 1. New York: D. Appleton, 1916, p. 199.

JOHN BRIGHT
(1811–1889)
Against American Slavery
Birmingham, England
December 18, 1862

As a teenage member of a temperance (anti-alcohol) society, earnest young Englishman John Bright discovered he had a gift for public speaking. He made his considerable reputation as an orator over free trade issues, at first fighting the corn laws, which were government subsidies for grain. He was elected to Parliament in 1843, shortly before the escaped American slave Frederick Douglass arrived on his celebrated speaking tour of Britain in 1845. Bright was a Quaker, a member of the first religious denomination to organize against slavery in Great Britain (the Committee for the Abolition of the Slave Trade was founded in 1787 largely by Quakers). Slavery had been entirely abolished in the British Empire in 1834, and slaves could not be imported into the United States after 1810. But within the United States, slavery was still alive and served as a major cause of the Civil War. The war had started in 1861 when 11 states of the South, beginning with South Carolina, seceded from the Union. John Bright was a friend of Frederick Douglass; he had appeared on the platform with him on Douglass's long tour 15 years earlier, and he had contributed to the fund that purchased his freedom from his Maryland owner and allowed him to return home to America in safety. On news of the outbreak of the Civil War in America, many in Britain took the side of the slaveholding landowners in the South, but Bright opposed welcoming the new Confederate States of America into the brotherhood of nation-states. The two lines of verse toward the end of his speech are from English poet Thomas Gray's "Elegy Written in a Country Churchyard."

Is there a man here that doubts for a moment that the object of the war on the part of the South—they began the war—that the object of the war on the part of the South is to maintain in bondage four millions of human beings? That is only a small part of it. The further object is to perpetuate for ever the bondage of all the posterity of those four millions of slaves . . .

The object is, that a handful of white men on that continent shall lord it over many millions of blacks, made black by the very Hand that made us white.

The object is, that they should have the power to breed Negroes, to work Negroes, to lash Negroes, to chain Negroes, to buy and sell Negroes, to deny them the commonest ties of family, or to break their hearts by rending them at their pleasure, to close their mental eye to but a glimpse even of that knowledge which separates us from the brute—for in their laws it is criminal and penal to teach the Negro to read—to seal from their hearts the Book of our religion, and to make chattels and things of men and women and children.

Now I want to ask whether this is to be the foundation, as it is proposed, of a new slave empire, and whether it is intended that on this audacious and infernal basis England's new ally is to be built up.

Now I should have no kind of objection to recognize a country because it was a country that held slaves—to recognize the United States, or to be in amity with it. The question of slavery there, and in Cuba and in Brazil, is, as far as respects the present generation, an accident, and it would be unreasonable that we should object to trade with and have political relations with a country, merely because it happened to have within its borders the institution of slavery, hateful as that institution is.

But in this case it is a new state intending to set itself up on the sole basis of slavery. Slavery is blasphemously declared to be its chief corner-stone. . . .

252

Slavery has been, as we all know, the huge, foul blot upon the fame of the American Republic; it is a hideous outrage against human right and against divine law; but the pride, the passion of man, will not permit its peaceable extinction. . . .

I blame men who are eager to admit into the family of nations a state which offers itself to us, based upon a principle, I will undertake to say, more odious and more blasphemous than was ever heretofore dreamed of in Christian or Pagan, in civilized or in savage times. The leaders of this revolt propose this monstrous thing—that over a territory forty times as large as England, the blight and curse of slavery shall be for ever perpetuated.

I cannot believe, for my part, that such a fate will befall that fair land, stricken though it now is with the ravages of war. I cannot believe that civilization, in its journey with the sun, will sink into endless night in order to gratify the ambition of the leaders of this revolt, who seek to

> Wade through slaughter to a throne,
> And shut the gates of mercy on mankind.

I have another and a far brighter vision before my gaze. It may be but a vision, but I will cherish it.

I see one vast confederation stretching from the frozen North in unbroken line to the glowing South, and from the wild billows of the Atlantic westward to the calmer waters of the Pacific main—and I see one people, and one language, and one law, and one faith, and, over all that wide continent, the home of freedom, and a refuge for the oppressed of every race and of every clime.

Source: Bright, John. *Speeches on the Public Affairs of the Last Twenty Years.* London: Camden Hotten, 1869, p. 138.

ABRAHAM LINCOLN
(1809–1865)
The Gettysburg Address
Gettysburg, Pennsylvania, United States
November 19, 1863

One hundred and fifty years after his death, Abraham Lincoln remains at the center in the pantheon of American presidents. Poor and self-taught, he became a skilled Illinois lawyer and, in 1846, a member of Congress in the U.S. House of Representatives. He drew on his tremendous talent as an orator in 1858 to debate Stephen Douglas for election to the U.S. Senate in the seven Lincoln-Douglas debates. Lincoln's persistent theme was the moral issue of slavery and the need to stop it; Douglas felt each new state had the right to decide the issue. Lincoln lost the election to Douglas, but two years later he ran for president and won. Southern states feared Lincoln would restrict slavery as president, and by the time Lincoln took office in March 1861, seven states had seceded from the Union (Alabama, Florida, Georgia, Louisiana, Mississippi, South Carolina, and Texas) to form the Confederate States of America. The Civil War began in April 1861 at Fort Sumter, South Carolina. The number of Confederate states grew to 11 when Arkansas, North Carolina, Tennessee, and Virginia left the Union. Two years into the war, Union and Confederate forces clashed at the July 1863 Battle of Gettysburg, where 50,000 men were killed or wounded. At the November dedication of the Gettysburg National Cemetery, where the Union dead were buried, Lincoln was not the featured speaker. Edward Everett, a politician famous at that time for his oratory (he had been U.S. senator, governor of Massachusetts, and secretary of state), spoke for more than two hours before the president's turn came to make his few remarks. Today Everett's speech is largely forgotten, while Lincoln's short tribute to those who died and to the future of the Union is considered one of the greatest in the English language. The war ended with the Confederate surrender on April 9, 1865. Just five days later, the angry Confederate spy John Wilkes Booth assassinated Lincoln as he watched a play at Ford's Theater in Washington, D.C.

Four score and seven years ago our fathers brought forth on this continent, a new nation, conceived in liberty, and dedicated to the proposition that all men are created equal.

Now we are engaged in a great civil war, testing whether that nation, or any nation so conceived and so dedicated, can long endure. We are met on a great battlefield of that war. We have come to dedicate a portion of that field, as a final resting place for those who here gave their lives that that nation might live. It is altogether fitting and proper that we should do this.

But in a larger sense, we cannot dedicate—we cannot consecrate—we cannot hallow—this ground. The brave men, living and dead, who struggled here, have consecrated it, far above our poor power to add or detract.

We here highly resolve that these dead shall not have died in vain—
that this nation, under God, shall have a new birth of freedom—
and that government of the people, by the people, for the people,
shall not perish from the earth. —*Abraham Lincoln*

The few photographs that exist of Lincoln at Gettysburg do not show him clearly on the platform. He spoke toward the end of the long program, just before the choir's final song and the benediction. *(Print by Sherwood Lithographic, courtesy of Library of Congress)*

The world will little note, nor long remember, what we say here, but it can never forget what they did here. It is for us the living, rather, to be dedicated here to the unfinished work which they who fought here have thus far so nobly advanced.

It is rather for us to be here dedicated to the great task remaining before us—that from these honored dead we take increased devotion to that cause for which they gave the last full measure of devotion—that we here highly resolve that these dead shall not have died in vain—that this nation, under God, shall have a new birth of freedom—and that government of the people, by the people, for the people, shall not perish from the earth.

Source: Lincoln, Abraham. "The Gettysburg Address." *Speeches and Writings,* 1859–1865. New York: Library of America, 1989, p. 536.

JOHN STUART MILL
(1806–1873)
On the Right of Women to Vote
London, England
July 17, 1866

John Stuart Mill was born in London in 1806, the son of a utilitarian philosopher, James Mill. (Utilitarian belief defines the "goodness" of actions by usefulness to the greatest number of people.) The father brought up his son with exacting demands: Young John learned Greek and Latin and read Plato and Aristotle at a very young age, and he was not allowed the company of children other than his brothers and sisters. While working for the East India Company in London, he studied political economy and wrote compelling essays on philosophy and political theory. One was his 1859 treatise, *On Liberty*, which he had written with his accomplished wife, Harriet Taylor Mill, a philosopher and women's rights activist. He was elected a Member of Parliament in 1865, where he pushed for voting and labor reforms and the emancipation of women. In July the next year, Mill addressed the House of Commons on behalf of "Freeholders, Householders, and others in England and Wales who, fulfilling the conditions of property or rental prescribed by Law as the qualification for the Electoral Franchise, are excluded from the Franchise by reason of their sex." He referred particularly to a petition (listing 1,521 women's signatures) circulated by women requesting they be given the electoral franchise, or right to vote. The mention at the end of "the Throne" refers to Queen Victoria. Mill published an influential essay three years later titled *The Subjection of Women*, arguing that women should be treated with social and legal equality with men. This was in sharp opposition to traditions that said women were weaker physically and mentally and required men to take care of them, first as fathers and brothers, then as husbands. The liberation of women, he believed, would double the minds available to solve humanity's problems, and he put his radical beliefs into action by chairing a women's suffrage (voting) society.

Sir, I rise to make the motion of which I have given notice. After the petition which I had the honor of presenting a few weeks ago, the House would naturally expect that its attention would be called, however briefly, to the claim preferred in that document.

The petition, and the circumstances attendant on its preparation, have, to say the least, greatly weakened the chief practical argument which we have been accustomed to hear against any proposal to admit women to the electoral franchise—namely that few, if any, women desire it.

Originating as that petition did entirely with ladies, without the instigation and, to the best of my belief, without the participation of any person of the male sex in any stage of the proceedings, except the final one of its presentation to Parliament, the amount of response which became manifest, the number of signatures obtained in a very short space of time, not to mention the quality of many of those signatures, may not have been surprising to the ladies who promoted the petition but was certainly quite unexpected by me.

I recognize in it the accustomed sign that the time has arrived when a proposal of a public nature is ripe for being taken into serious consideration—namely when a word spoken on the subject is found to have been the expression of a silent wish pervading a great number of minds, and a signal given in the hope of rallying a few supporters is unexpectedly answered by many.

It is not necessary to offer any justification for the particular motion which I am about to make. When the complaint is made that certain citizens of this nation, fulfilling all the conditions and giving all the guarantees which the Constitution and the law require from those who are admitted to a voice in determining who shall be their rulers, are excluded from that privilege for what appears to them, and for what appears to me, an entirely irrelevant consideration, the least we can do is to ascertain what number of persons are affected by the grievance, and how great an addition would be made to the constituency if this disability were removed.

I should not have attempted more than this in the present session, even if the recent discussions in reference to reform had not been brought to an abrupt close. Even if the late Government had succeeded in its honorable attempt to effect an amicable compromise of the reform question, any understanding or any wish which might have existed as to the finality, for a certain period, of that compromise, could not have effected such a proposal as this, the adoption of which would not be, in any sense of the term, a lowering of the franchise, and is not intended to disturb in any degree the distribution of political power among the different classes of society.

Indeed, honorable gentlemen opposite seem to think, and I suppose they are the best judges, that this concession,

Philosopher and member of the British parliament, John Stuart Mill wrote on personal liberty and human rights and influenced much of modern liberal thought. *(Library of Congress)*

assuming it to be made, if it had any effect on party politics at all, would be favorable to their side; and the right honorable Member for Dublin University, in his humorous manner, advised me on that ground to withdraw this article from my political programme. But I cannot, either in jest or in earnest, adopt his suggestion, for I am bound to consider the permanent benefit of the community before the temporary interest of a party; and I entertain the firmest conviction that whatever holds out an inducement to one-half of the community to exercise their minds on the great social and political questions which are discussed in Parliament, and whatever causes the great influence they already possess to be exerted under the guidance of greater knowledge, and under a sense of responsibility, cannot be ultimately advantageous to the Conservative or any other cause, except so far as that cause is a good one.

And I rejoice in the knowledge that in the estimation of many honorable gentlemen of the party opposite, the proposal made in the petition is, like many of the most valuable Reforms, as truly Conservative, as I am sure it is truly Liberal. I listened with pleasure and gratitude to the right honorable gentleman who is now Chancellor of the Exchequer, when in his speech on the second reading of the Reform Bill, he said he saw no reason why women of independent means should not possess the electoral franchise, in a country where they can preside in manorial courts and fill parish offices—to which let me add, and the Throne.

Source: Mill, John Stuart. "Electoral Franchise for Women." *The Collected Works of John Stuart Mill.* Edited by John M. Robson and Bruce L. Kinzer. Toronto: University of Toronto Press, 1988.

SUSAN B. ANTHONY

(1820–1906)

"Are Women Persons?"

Rochester, New York, United States

June 1873

Susan Brownell Anthony, the daughter of a Massachusetts Quaker abolitionist, labored unflaggingly as a leader of the movement for women's suffrage, or voting rights, for nearly 50 years. Her photographs show a stiff woman in severe dress, belying the dedicated progressive that she was. Like women's rights leader Lucy Stone (SEE her speech, p. 245), Susan Anthony worked as a teacher; she became radicalized by observing that women were paid far less than men for the same work and knowing from experience that girls were regularly denied equal education. Her first efforts at public speaking were for temperance organizations opposed to alcohol and for the American Anti-Slavery Society; she soon became a tireless orator for women's rights. In 1866 she joined with Stone, along with suffragist Elizabeth Cady Stanton and abolitionist Frederick Douglass, to found the American Equal Rights Association, which was to fight for both women's and blacks' equality. After black men received the vote under the Fifteenth Amendment to the Constitution, Anthony and Stanton founded a new group in May 1869, the National Woman Suffrage Association (NWSA), devoted solely to women's rights. In the 1872 presidential election (won by Ulysses Grant), Anthony was arrested and fined $100 for voting illegally on November 5 in Rochester, New York. She pled not guilty of the charge. Although she wasn't allowed to speak in her own defense in court because of her sex, she traveled the county defending her actions in a celebrated speech before numerous audiences in the month before her trial the following year. Her clever argument turned on whether the United States was illegally preventing citizens from voting. The trial's outcome was unfair as the judge, Ward Hunt, was prejudiced and had written his opinion before the trial began and discharged the jury without soliciting their verdict; however, Anthony refused to pay the fine he imposed. (The judge ultimately released her anyway.) Anthony was president of the National American Woman Suffrage Association from 1892 to 1900, but she did not live to see the ratification of the Nineteenth Amendment on August 26, 1920, granting women the right to vote. She died on March 13, 1906.

Friends and fellow citizens: I stand before you tonight under indictment for the alleged crime of having voted at the last presidential election, without having a lawful right to vote. It shall be my work this evening to prove to you that in thus doing, I not only committed no crime, but, instead, simply exercised my citizen's rights, guaranteed to me and all United States citizens by the National Constitution, beyond the power of any State to deny.

Our democratic-republican government is based on the idea of the natural right of every individual member thereof to a voice and a vote in making and executing the laws. We assert the province of government to be to secure the people in the enjoyment of their inalienable right. We throw to the winds the old dogma that government can give rights.

No one denies that before governments were organized each individual possessed the right to protect his own life, liberty and property. When 100 to 1,000,000 people enter into a free government, they do not barter away their natural rights; they simply pledge themselves to protect each other in the enjoyment of them through prescribed judicial and legislative tribunals. They agree to abandon the methods of brute force in the adjustment of their differences and adopt those of civilization. . . . The Declaration of Independence, the United States Constitution, the constitutions of the several states and the organic laws of the territories, all alike propose to protect the people in the exercise of their God-given rights. Not one of them pretends to bestow rights.

"All men are created equal, and endowed by their Creator with certain inalienable rights. Among these are life, liberty and the pursuit of happiness. To secure these, governments are instituted among men, deriving their just powers from the consent of the governed."

It was we, the people; not we, the white male citizens; nor we, the male citizens; but we, the whole people, who formed the Union. —*Susan B. Anthony*

Here is no shadow of government authority over rights, or exclusion of any class from their full and equal enjoyment. Here is pronounced the right of all men, and "consequently," as the Quaker preacher said, "of all women," to a voice in the government. And here, in this first paragraph of the Declaration, is the assertion of the natural right of all to the ballot; for how can "the consent of the governed" be given, if the right to vote be denied? . . .

The preamble of the Federal Constitution says: "We, the people of the United States, in order to form a more perfect union, establish justice, insure domestic tranquility, provide for the common defense, promote the general welfare, and secure the blessings of liberty to ourselves and our posterity, do ordain and establish this Constitution for the United States of America."

It was we, the people; not we, the white male citizens; nor we, the male citizens; but we, the whole people, who formed the Union. And we formed it, not to give the blessings of liberty, but to secure them; not to the half of ourselves and the half of our posterity, but to the whole people—women as well as men. And it is a downright mockery to talk to women of their enjoyment of the blessings of liberty while they are denied the use of the only means of securing them provided by this democratic-republican government—the ballot. . . .

For any state to make sex a qualification, which must ever result in the disfranchisement of one entire half of the people, is to pass a bill of attainder, an ex post facto law, and is therefore a violation of the supreme law of the land. By it the blessings of liberty are forever withheld from women and their female posterity. For them, this government has no just powers derived from the consent of the governed. For them this government is not a democracy; it is not a republic. It is the most odious aristocracy ever established on the face of the globe. An oligarchy of wealth, where the rich govern the poor; an oligarchy of learning, where the educated govern the ignorant; or even an oligarchy of race, where the Saxon rules the African, might be endured; but this oligarchy of sex which makes father, brothers, husband, sons, the oligarchs over the mother and sisters, the wife and daughters of every household; which ordains all men sovereigns, all women subjects—carries discord and rebellion into every home of the nation. . . .

It is urged that the use of the masculine pronouns he, his, and him in all the constitutions and laws is proof that only men were meant to be included in their provisions. If you insist on this version of the letter of the law, we shall insist that you be consistent and accept the other horn of the dilemma, which would compel you to exempt women from taxation for the support of the government and from penalties for the violation of laws. There is no she or her or hers in the tax laws, and this is equally true of all the criminal laws. . . .

Though the words persons, people, inhabitants, electors, citizens, are all used indiscriminately in the national and state constitutions, there was always a conflict of opinion, prior to the war, as to whether they were synonymous terms, but whatever room there was for doubt, under the old regime, the adoption of the Fourteenth Amendment settled that question forever in its first sentence: "All persons born or naturalized in the United States, and subject to the jurisdiction thereof, are citizens of the United Sates, and of the State wherein they reside."

The second settles the equal status of all citizens: "No State shall make or enforce any law which shall abridge the privileges or immunities of citizens of the United States; nor shall any State deprive any person of life, liberty or property without due process of law, or deny to any person within its jurisdiction the equal protection of the laws."

Webster, Worcester, and Bouvier all define a citizen to be a person in the United States, entitled to vote and hold office.

The only question left to be settled now is: Are women persons? I scarcely believe any of our opponents will have the hardihood to say they are not. Being persons, then, women are citizens, and no state has a right to make any new law, or to enforce any old law, which shall abridge their privileges or immunities. Hence, every discrimination against women in the constitutions and laws of the several Sates is today null and void, precisely as is every one against negroes. . . .

We no longer petition Legislature or Congress to give us the right to vote. We appeal to the women everywhere to exercise their too long neglected "citizen's right to vote." We appeal to the inspectors of election everywhere to receive the votes of all United States citizens as it is their duty to do. . . .

And it is on this line that we propose to fight our battle for the ballot—all peaceably, but nevertheless persistently through to complete triumph, when all United States citizens shall be recognized as equals before the law.

Source: Stanton, Elizabeth Cady, and Susan B. Anthony. *Correspondence, Writings, Speeches.* Edited by Ellen C. DuBois. New York: Shocken Books, 1981, pp. 152–165.

WILLIAM GLADSTONE
(1809–1898)
On Empire
West Calder, Midlothian County, Scotland

November 27, 1879

William Gladstone was the "Grand Old Man" of the British parliament, the leader of the Liberal Party who became increasingly liberal with time. He was a Member of Parliament for a remarkable 60 years, and prime minister four times—for 14 years altogether. Recognized as a magnificent orator at Oxford University where he was president of the debating society, he was elected to Parliament in his twenties and later became chancellor of the exchequer (similar to secretary of the Treasury). For a long time he was of the minority in his view that working-class men should have the right to vote as well as the upper classes. But with the Third Reform Act of 1884 (also known as the Representation of the People Act), which granted the vote to all but women, domestic help, bachelors living with their families, and the homeless, he succeeded in measurably increasing the number of voters in the electorate from 3 to 5 million. His Liberal Party principles also included an aversion to war and foreign entanglements. When Gladstone set out on a campaign tour in Scotland—his successful Midlothian Campaign—in late 1879 to talk up the crowds, gathered outdoors, for the 1880 election, the theme was often British foreign policy. The prime minister at that time, Benjamin Disraeli of the Conservative Party, still supported the Ottoman Turks, despite offenses committed by the Turks against Bulgaria during that country's 1876 revolt against the Ottoman Empire. Disraeli supported Turkey, as Britain had during the calamitous Crimean War of 1854, because of British fears of Russian expansion into the eastern Mediterranean. Gladstone's speeches attracted thousand of listeners, and his tour is considered one of the earliest to be conducted like a political campaign is today. On one evening, Gladstone took the prime minister's imperialist foreign policy as his topic.

Gentlemen, the prime minister speaking out—I do not question for a moment his own sincere opinion—has made what I think one of the most unhappy and ominous allusions ever made by a minister of this country. He quoted certain words, easily rendered as "empire and liberty"—words (he said) of a Roman statesman, words descriptive of the State of Rome—and he quoted them as words which were capable of legitimate application to the position and circumstances of England.

I join issue with the prime minister upon that subject, and I affirm that nothing can be more fundamentally unsound, more practically ruinous, than the establishment of Roman analogies for the guidance of British policy.

What, gentlemen, was Rome? Rome was indeed an imperial State, you may tell me—I know not, I cannot read the counsels of Providence—a State having a mission to subdue the world, but a State whose very basis it was to deny the equal rights, to proscribe the independent existence of other nations. That, gentlemen, was the Roman idea. It has been partially and not ill described in three lines of a translation from Virgil by our great poet Dryden, which runs as follows:

O Rome! 'tis thine alone with awful sway
To rule mankind, and make the world obey,
Disposing peace and war thine own majestic way.

We are told to fall back upon this example. No doubt the word "empire" was qualified with the word "liberty." But what did the two words "liberty" and "empire" mean in

RHETORICAL DEVICE

Hypophora: Asking a question, and then providing an answer. (SEE *the related* rhetorical question, *which differs by not providing an answer.*)

But what did the two words "liberty" and "empire" mean in a Roman mouth?
They meant simply this: "Liberty for ourselves, empire over
the rest of mankind." —*William Gladstone*

The only question left to be settled now is: Are women persons? I scarcely believe
any of our opponents will have the hardihood to say they are not.
Being persons, then, women are citizens. —*Susan B. Anthony*

Why ought the slave trade to be abolished?
Because it is incurable injustice. —*William Pitt the Younger*

a Roman mouth? They meant simply this: "Liberty for ourselves, empire over the rest of mankind."

I do not think, gentlemen, that this ministry, or any other ministry, is going to place us in the position of Rome. What I object to is the revival of the idea. I care not how feebly, I care not even how—from a philosophic or historical point of view—how ridiculous the attempt at this revival may be. I say it indicates an intention—I say it indicates a frame of mind, and the frame of mind, unfortunately, I find, has been consistent with the policy of which I have given you some illustrations—the policy of denying to others the rights that we claim ourselves.

No doubt, gentlemen, Rome may have had its work to do, and Rome did its work. But modern times have brought a different state of things. Modern times have established a sisterhood of nations, equal, independent, each of them built up under that legitimate defense which public law affords to every nation, living within its own borders, and seeking to perform its own affairs.

Source: William Gladstone. "Third Midlothian Speech." *Political Speeches in Scotland, November and December 1879.* London: W. Ridgway, 1879, p. 127.

HENRY EDWARD MANNING
(1808–1892)
Condemning Anti-Semitism
London, England
February 1, 1882

Russian czar Alexander II (r. 1855–81) is known most for freeing the serfs (peasant laborers bound to a lord or master) in 1861. He introduced many other relatively liberal reforms to modernize the country, but his assassination by political radicals on March 9, 1881, brought his son Alexander III (r. 1881–94) to the throne. More conservative and nationalistic than his father, the new czar scrapped many planned reforms, such as the development of a Duma, or representative parliament. He imposed Eastern Orthodox Christianity (often known as the Greek rite, rather than Latin) on the entire country and enacted the harsh "May Laws" that restricted where Jews could live, how many could attend university, and which occupations they could follow. Partly also because one of the assassins was rumored to be Jewish, a wave of pogroms—riots and murders—of Jews followed in Russia. At the same time, a vicious revival of anti-Semitism (hostility or

hatred of the Jews) in Germany was pursued by rival groups attempting to gain political advantage there. In London, Roman Catholic cardinal Henry Edward Manning, a longtime supporter of working people and the poor, addressed a demonstration planned by the lord mayor of London condemning the violence and mistreatment of Jews. Manning, the son of a Member of Parliament, was a noted debater in his youth at Oxford University. He had been ordained a Church of England (Protestant) parish priest in 1833 and rose to the position of archdeacon. But in 1851, at age 43, he converted to Catholicism over disagreement with the Anglican Church on the meaning of baptism. He was named cardinal (the highest rank in the Catholic Church under the pope) in 1875. Manning was always concerned with issues of social justice, such as the treatment of prisoners, the living conditions of the poor, and the rights of working men and women.

My Lord Mayor, Ladies and Gentlemen:—It has often fallen to my lot to move a resolution in meetings such as this, but never in my memory have I moved one with more perfect conviction of my reason or more entire concurrence of my heart.

Before I use any further words, it will, perhaps, be better that I should read what that resolution is. It is, "That this meeting, while disclaiming any right or desire to interfere in the internal affairs of another country, and desiring that the most amicable relations between England and Russia should be preserved, feels it a duty to express its opinion that the laws of Russia relating to the Jews tend to degrade them in the eyes of the Christian population, and to expose Russian Jewish subjects to the outbreaks of fanatical ignorance.". . .

While we do not pretend to touch upon any question in the internal legislation of Russia, there are laws larger than any Russian legislation—the laws of humanity and of God, which are the foundation of all other laws, and if in any legislation they be violated, all the nations of Christian Europe, the whole commonwealth of civilized and Christian men would instantly acquire a right to speak out aloud.

And now I must touch upon one point, which I acknowledge has been very painful to me. We have all watched for the last twelve months the anti-Semitic movement in Germany. I look upon it with a twofold feeling—in the first place with horror as tending to disintegrate the foundations of social life, and, secondly, with great fear lest it may light up an animosity, which has already taken flame in Russia and may spread elsewhere.

I have read with great regret an elaborate article, full, no doubt, of minute observations, written from Prussia and published in the *Nineteenth Century,* giving a description of the class animosities, jealousies, and rivalries which are at present so rife in that country. When I read that article, my first feeling was one of infinite sorrow that the power and energy of the Old Testament should be so much greater in Brandenburg than those of the New. I am sorry to see that a society penetrated with rationalism has not so much Christian knowledge, Christian power, Christian character, and Christian virtue as to render it impossible that, cultivated, refined, industrious, and energetic as they are, they should endanger the Christian society of that great kingdom.

I have also read with pain accounts of the condition of the Russian Jews, bringing against them accusations which, if I touch upon them, I must ask my Jewish friends near me to believe I reject with incredulity and horror. Nevertheless, I have read that the cause of what has happened in Russia is that the Jews have been pliers of infamous trades—usurers, immoral, demoralizing, and I know not what. When I read these accusations, I ask, Will they be cured by crime, murder, outrage, abominations of every sort? Are they not learning the lesson from those who ought to teach a higher?

Again, if it be true, which I do not believe, that they are in the condition described are they not under penal laws? Is there anything that can degrade men more than to close against intelligence, energy, and industry all the honorable careers of public life? Is there anything that can debase and irritate the soul of man more than to be told, "You must not pass beyond that boundary; you must not go within eighteen miles of that frontier; you must not dwell in that town; you must live only in that province"? I do not know how anyone can believe that the whole population can fail to be affected in its inmost soul by such laws; and if it be possible to make it worse, this is the mode and the discipline to make it so.

They bring these accusations against the Russian Jews; why do they not bring them against the Jews of Germany? By the acknowledgment of the anti-Semitic movement, the Jews in Germany rise head and shoulders above their fellows. Why do they not bring these accusations against the Jews of France? Is there any career of public utility, any path of honor, civil or military, in which the Jews have not stood side by side with their countrymen?

If the charge is brought against the Jews of Russia, who will bring it against the Jews of England? For uprightness, for refinement, for generosity, for charity, for all the graces and virtues that adorn humanity, where will be found examples brighter or more true of human excellence than in this Hebrew race?

And when we are told that the accounts of those atrocities are not to be trusted, I ask if there were to appear in the newspapers long and minute narratives of murder, rapine, and other atrocities round about the Egyptian hall, in Old Jewry, in Houndsditch, in Shoreditch, if it were alleged that the Lord Mayor was looking on, that the metropolitan police did nothing, that the guards at the Tower were seen mingled with the mob, I believe you would thank any man who gave you an opportunity of exposing and contradicting the statement.

There is a book, my lord, which is common to the race of Israel and to us Christians. That book is a bond between us, and in that book I read that the people of Israel are the eldest people upon the earth. Russia, and Austria, and England are of yesterday compared with the imperishable people which, with an inextinguishable life and immutable traditions, and faith in God and in the laws of God, scattered as it is all over the world, passing through the fires unscathed, trampled into the dust, and yet never combining with the dust into which it is trampled, lives still a witness and a warning to us. We are in the bonds of brotherhood with it. The New Testament rests upon the Old.

They believe in half of that for which we would give our lives. Let us then acknowledge that we unite in a common sympathy. . . .

My lord, I only hope this—that not one man in England who calls himself a civilized or Christian man will have it in his heart to add by a single word to that which this great and ancient and noble people suffer; but that we shall do all we can by labor, by speech, and by prayer to lessen if it be possible, or at least to keep ourselves from sharing in sympathy with these atrocious deeds.

Source: Henry Edward Manning. "Persecution of the Jews." In *Modern Eloquence.* Vol. 9, edited by Thomas Brackett Reed. Chicago: Geo. L. Shuman, 1900, p. 854.

FREDERICK ENGELS
(1820–1895)
Eulogy on Karl Marx
London, England
March 17, 1883

Frederick Engels was born into a manufacturing family in Barmen, Prussia (now part of Germany), in 1820, and enjoyed reading German philosophers as a teenager. In Paris in his early twenties, he met Karl Marx, a political philosopher and author, also from Prussia, and he began to correspond with him—they would maintain a life-long friendship collaborating on socialist theory. Engels formed many of his ideas about the terrible conditions in which working-class people lived while working for a textile firm in Manchester, England, for several years. With Marx, Engels joined the Communist League in Germany, and, for that organization, in 1848 they drew up a document describing the league's purposes and plan of action—*The Communist Manifesto*. The *Manifesto* detailed how oppressed working-class people, the *proletariat*, could overthrow the capitalist ruling classes, or *bourgeoisie*, in a class war to create a communist society: a society without social classes or oppression of the poor. Provisions of the document included abolishing the right to own or inherit property, imposing steep taxes on the rich, and centralizing all industry in the hands of the state. Not surprisingly, most European governments were hostile to the two radicals, and after their participation in revolutionary activities in Prussia in 1849, they lived in exile in England the rest of their lives. Engels, as a successful businessman, supported Marx so that he could continue to write political and economic theory. Their work would heavily influence the Russian communist revolutionary Vladimir Ilyich Lenin, leader of the Russian Revolution. When Karl Marx died in 1883, Engels gave a eulogy, in English, at a small graveside ceremony in London. (He refers to the "militant proletariat of America," but at this time the Socialist Labor Party of America had formed only about six years earlier, and its influence was limited.) Engels continued their work, translating Marx's writings and publishing his own theories on the family and society.

On the 14th of March, at a quarter to three in the afternoon, the greatest living thinker ceased to think. He had been left alone for scarcely two minutes, and when we came back we found him in his armchair, peacefully gone to sleep—but forever.

An immeasurable loss has been sustained both by the militant proletariat of Europe and America, and by historical science, in the death of this man. The gap that has been left by the departure of this mighty spirit will soon enough make itself felt.

Just as Darwin discovered the law of development of organic nature, so Marx discovered the law of development of human history: The simple fact, hitherto concealed by an overgrowth of ideology, that mankind must first of all eat, drink, have shelter and clothing, before it can pursue politics, science, art, religion, etc.; that therefore the production of the immediate material means of subsistence and consequently the degree of economic development attained by a given people or during a given epoch forms the foundation upon which the state institutions, the legal conceptions, art, and even the ideas on religion, of the people concerned have been evolved, and in the light of which they must, therefore, be explained, instead of vice versa, as had hitherto been the case.

But that is not all. Marx also discovered the special law of motion governing the present-day capitalist mode of production, and the bourgeois society that this mode of production has created. The discovery of surplus value suddenly threw light on the problem, in trying to solve which all previous investigations, of both bourgeois economists and socialist critics, had been groping in the dark.

RHETORICAL DEVICE

Euphemism: Using a less offensive expression for one that the audience might find harsh or disagreeable.

Those who established our liberty and our government are daily dropping from among us. —*Daniel Webster, speaking of the deaths of the Founding Fathers*

I assure you, in the name of the Five Nations, that our warriors . . . shall never dig up the hatchet till their brother Yonnondio, or Corlear, shall, either jointly or separately, endeavor to attack the country which the Great Spirit has given to our ancestors. —*Garangula, speaking of war*

On the 14th of March, at a quarter to three in the afternoon, the greatest living thinker ceased to think. —*Frederick Engels, speaking of the death of Karl Marx*

Two such discoveries would be enough for one lifetime. Happy the man to whom it is granted to make even one such discovery. But in every single field which Marx investigated—and he investigated very many fields, none of them superficially—in every field, even in that of mathematics, he made independent discoveries.

Such was the man of science. But this was not even half the man. Science was for Marx a historically dynamic, revolutionary force. However great the joy with which he welcomed a new discovery in some theoretical science whose practical application perhaps it was as yet quite impossible to envisage, he experienced quite another kind of joy when the discovery involved immediate revolutionary changes in industry, and in historical development in general. For example, he followed closely the development of the discoveries made in the field of electricity and recently those of Marcel Deprez.

For Marx was before all else a revolutionist. His real mission in life was to contribute, in one way or another, to the overthrow of capitalist society and of the state institutions which it had brought into being, to contribute to the liberation of the modern proletariat, which he was the first to make conscious of its own position and its needs, conscious of the conditions of its emancipation. Fighting was his element.

And he fought with a passion, a tenacity, and a success such as few could rival. The first *Rheinische Zeitung* in 1842, the Paris *Vorwarts* in 1844, the *Deutsche Brusseler Zeitung* in 1847, the *Neue Rheinische Zeitung* from 1848 to 1849, the *New York Tribune* from 1852 to 1861, and in addition to these a host of militant pamphlets, work in organizations in Paris, Brussels and London, and finally, crowning all, the formation of the great International Working Men's Association—this was indeed an achievement of which its founder might well have been proud even if he had done nothing else.

And consequently, Marx was the best hated and most calumniated man of his time. Governments, both absolutist and republican, deported him from their territories. Bourgeois, whether Conservative or ultra-democratic, vied with one another in heaping slanders upon him. All this he brushed aside as though it were cobweb, ignoring it, answering only when extreme necessity compelled him. And he died beloved, revered and mourned by millions of revolutionary fellow workers—from the mines of Siberia to California, in all parts of Europe and America—and I make bold to say that though he may have had many opponents he had hardly one personal enemy.

His name will endure through the ages, and so also will his work!

Source: Engels, Frederick. "Speech at the Grave of Karl Marx." Marxists Internet Archive. Available online. http://www.marxists.org/archive/marx/works/1883/death/burial.htm. Accessed December 18, 2007.

JOSÉ MARTÍ
(1853–1895)
"Mother America"
New York City
December 19, 1889

Many consider Cuba's finest poet and greatest revolutionary to be the same man, José Martí. The liberation of Latin America had begun in 1810 by Spanish colonial rebel Simón Bolívar, but Cuba (with Puerto Rico) remained among the last colonies of Spain in the Americas. At only 16, Martí was imprisoned and exiled by Spanish colonial authorities for his writings against Spain. He rarely saw Cuba again, living much of his life in exile—14 years of it in New York City. There he published a Spanish-language newspaper and taught classes preparing Cubans for the coming war of independence from Spain. For several years he was diplomatic consul in New York for Argentina, Paraguay, and Uruguay. He gave speeches to rally Cuban tobacco workers living in exile in Florida. He alerted Cubans to U.S. imperialism, urged U.S. policy makers against annexing Cuba, and organized the Cuban Revolutionary Party. In 1889 delegates from nearly every country in the Western Hemisphere met in Washington at the first International Conference of American States to discuss issues of common interest. (In later years, the conference formed the Pan-American Union, which became the Organization of American States, or OAS.) In New York City, Martí was invited to address the delegates at a party hosted by the Spanish-American Literary Society. For Martí, "Mother" America or "Our" America is the Spanish Americas. He paints an astounding picture of the beauty and cruelty of Latin American history, and he refers to many peoples and individuals from colonial times. He mentions Benito Juárez, the first president of Mexico born of Indian parents, and Anacaona, the Taíno queen of Hispaniola, killed by the murderous Spanish governor, Nicolás de Ovando, about 1503. José Martí was killed in battle in 1895 one month after returning to Cuba to lead the revolution he planned. The Cuban people call him "the Apostle."

Our tremulous and exuberant thoughts, in the short time that discretion demands, are hard pressed to put into words the joy that overflows from our souls on this memorable night. What can the imprisoned son say when he sees his mother again from behind the bars of his cell? . . .

Which of us will deny, on this night when no lies are told, that no matter how many roots our faith or affections or habits or business affairs may have in this land of unrestrained hospitality, no matter how lukewarm the faithless magic of ice may have left our souls, we have felt—ever since learning that these noble guests were coming to see us—as if there were more light in our houses, as if we were walking with a livelier step, as if we were younger and more generous, as if our earnings were greater and more certain, and as if in a vase without water there were flowers budding? . . . No matter how great is this land, or how anointed the America of Lincoln may be for the free men of America—for us, in our very heart of hearts where nobody dares to challenge or take issue with our secret feelings, the America of Juárez is greater because it has been more unhappy, and because it is ours. . . .

North America was born of the plow, Spanish America of the bulldog. A fanatical war took from the poetry of his aerial palaces the Moor weakened by his riches; and the remaining soldiers, reared to heresy on hate and sour wine and equipped with suits of armor and arquebuses, rushed upon the Indian protected by his breastplate of cotton. Ships arrived loaded with cavaliers in their half-cuirasses, disinherited second sons, rebellious lieutenants, hungry clergymen, and university students. They brought

269

Cuba celebrated the 150th birthday of José Martí, the Apostle of Cuban Independence, with his portrait on the one peso note. *(Photo by Joel Blit, Shutterstock)*

muskets, shields, lances, thigh-guards, helmets, back-plates, and dogs. They wielded their swords to the four winds, took possession of the land in the name of the King, and plundered the temples of their gold.

Cortés lured Montezuma into the palace he owed to the latter's wisdom or generosity, then held him prisoner there. The simple Anacaona invited Ovando to one of her festivities to show him her country's gardens, its joyful dances, and its virgins, whereupon Ovando's soldiers pulled their swords from beneath their disguises and seized Anacaona's land.

Among the divisions and jealousies of the Indian people, the *conquistador* pushed on in America. Among Aztecs and Tlaxcaltecas, Cortés reached Cuauhtemoc's canoe. Among Quichés and Tzutuhils, Alvarado was victorious in Guatemala. Among the inhabitants of Tunja and Bogota, Quesada marched forward in Colombia. Among the warriors of Atahualpa and Huáscar, Pizarro rode across Peru. By the light of burning temples the red banner of the Inquisition was planted in the breast of the last Indian. The women were carried off.

When the Indian was free his roads were paved with stones, but after the Spaniards came he had nothing but cow paths used by the cow as she went nosing her way to the pasture, or by the Indian deploring how wolves had been turned into men. . . .

What is happening so suddenly to make the whole world pause to listen and marvel and revere? From beneath the cowl of Torquemada comes the redeemed continent, bloody and with sword in hand! All the nations of America declare themselves free at the same time. Bolívar appears with his cohort of luminaries. Even the volcanos acclaim him and publish him to the world, their flanks shaking and thundering. To your horses, all of America! And over plains and mountains, with all the stars aflame, redemptive hoof-beats resound in the night.

The Mexican clergy are now talking to their Indians. With lances held in their teeth, the Venezuelan Indians outdistance the naked runner. The battered Chileans march together, arm in arm with the half-breeds from Peru. Wearing the Phrygian or liberty cap of the emancipated slave, the Negroes go singing behind their blue banner. Squads of *gauchos* in calfskin boots and swinging their *bolas* go galloping in triumph. The revived Pehuenches, hair flying and feathered lances held above their heads, put spurs to their horses. The war-painted Araucanians, carrying their cane lances tipped with colored feathers, come running at full gallop. And when the virgin light of dawn flows over the cliffs, San Martín appears there in the snow crossing the Andes in his battle cape—crest of the mountain and crown of the revolution.

Where is America going, and who will unite her and be her guide? Alone and as one people she is rising. Alone she is fighting. Alone she will win.

And we have transformed all this venom into sap! Never was there such a precocious, persevering, and generous people born out of so much opposition and unhappiness. We were a den of iniquity and we are beginning to be a crucible. We built upon hydras. Our railroads have demolished the pikes of Alvarado. In the public squares where they used to burn heretics, we built libraries. We have as many schools now as we had officers of the Inquisition before. What we have not yet done, we have not had time to do, having been busy cleansing our blood of the impurities bequeathed to us by our ancestors.

The religious and immoral missions have nothing left but their crumbling walls where an occasional owl shows an eye, and where the lizard goes his melancholy way. The new American has cleared the path among the dispirited breeds of men, the ruins of convents, and the horses of barbarians, and he is inviting the youth of the world to pitch their tents in his fields. . . .

Our capable and indefatigable America conquers everything, and each day she plants her banner higher. From sunrise to sunset she conquers everything through the harmonious and artistic spirit of the land that emerged out of the beauty and music of our nature, for she bestows upon our hearts her generosity and upon our minds the loftiness and serenity of her mountains. . . .

That is why we live here with such pride in Our America, to serve and honor her. We certainly do not live here as future slaves or dazzled peasants, but as people able and determined to help a man win esteem for his good qualities and respect for his sacrifices. . . .

We must show our soul as it is to these illustrious messengers who have come here from our nations, so they may see that we consider it faithful and honorable. We must convince these delegates that a just admiration and a usefully sincere study of other nations—a study neither too distant nor myopic—does not weaken the ardent, redemptive, and sacred love for what is our own.

Let us allow them to see that for our personal good—if there is any good in the conscience without peace—we will not be traitors to that which Nature and humanity demand of us. And thus, when each of them, content with our integrity, returns to the shores that we may never see again, he will be able to say to her who is our mistress, hope, and guide: "Mother America, we found brothers there! Mother America, you have sons there!"

Source: Martí, José. "Mother America." Edited by Deborah Shnookal and Mirta Muniz. *José Martí Reader: Writings on the Americas.* New York: Ocean Press, 1999, p. 101.

MACHEMBA

(19th century)

"I Am Sultan in My Land"

German East Africa (now Tanzania)

1890

Between the 1880s and 1910, the years of the great Scramble for Africa, European powers agreed among themselves to divide much of the continent into colonies. Under the encouragement of a German adventurer and explorer named Karl Peters, who formed the German East Africa Company, Germany eventually claimed an area of East Africa (now Rwanda, Burundi, and mainland Tanzania) for cotton and coffee production. In 1888 Germany sent its navy to quash protests from the sultan of Zanzibar (a small archipelago of islands off Tanzania). Several tribal revolts quickly followed. One of these, the Abushiri Revolt, was put down when Major Hermann von Wissmann, the German military commander, hanged the local Arab leader Abushiri ibn Salim al-Harthi in December 1889. In what is now southern Tanzania, a slave trader and chief of the Yao people named Machemba repeatedly defied the authorities of German East Africa. The Germans sent troops against him several times, but he managed to defeat them. He refused to pay taxes they levied. To Major Wissmann, Machemba directed this defiant speech in Kiswahili (the Bantu-based language spoken in eastern Africa). Finally in 1899 the colony seized his stronghold and his followers, but he escaped to safety in Mozambique. Wissman became governor of German East Africa in 1895. After World War I (1914–18), German East Africa ceased to exist as it was divided among Belgium, Britain, and Portugal by the Treaty of Versailles.

I have listened to your words, but I can find no reason why I should obey you. I would rather die. I look for some reason why I should obey you and I find not the smallest.

If it should be friendship that you want, then I am ready for it, today and always. But I will not be your subject.

If it should be war that you desire, then I am also ready.

I do not fall at your feet, for you are God's creature just as I am. I am sultan in my land. You are sultan there in yours.

But listen to me: I do not say that you should obey me, for I know that you are a free man. As for me, I will not come to you, and if you are strong enough, then come and fetch me.

Source: Boahen, A. Adu, ed. *UNESCO General History of Africa Africa.* Vol. 7, *Africa under Colonial Domination, 1880–1935.* Berkeley: University of California Press, 1990, p. 49.

WOBOGO
(19th century)
"Never Come Back"
Ouagadougou, Upper Volta (now Burkina Faso)
1895

With the European powers "scrambling" for possession of African territory, the Berlin Conference of 1884 (attended by Germany, France, Portugal, Britain, Belgium, Russia, Spain, Sweden, Austria-Hungary, Denmark, the United States, and the Ottoman Empire) split up Africa to define areas of influence for many of the participating European nations. Like the others, France was looking to enlarge its claim on that continent. Hoping for continuous, linked possessions across Africa, France's well-armed troops pushed eastward from earlier conquests in Tunisia, Guinea, and Senegal to secure the tiny states on the upper reaches of the Volta River. For hundreds of years, West Africa's powerful Mossi states of Ouagadougou, Yatenga, Tengkodogo, and Gourma had successfully repelled invaders from neighboring kingdoms such as Mali and the Songhai Empire. In 1895 Wobogo, the Morho Naba, or king, of Ouagadougou, rebuffed a French officer named Captain Destenave. But in 1896, with their superior weapons, the French seized Ouagadougou, deposed Wobogo, and installed a ruler of their choosing. This new colony would be known as Upper Volta, and today is the country of Burkina Faso (it received independence from France in 1960). Such colonization by Europeans devastated the natural political order, as enemy tribes often found themselves on the same side of borders imposed by the colonizers; civil war or unrest, even many years later, would be the result. The colonial powers rarely put improvements (such as education, political systems, or hospitals) into the colonies that were in any way equal to the natural resources—such as diamonds, gold, coffee, and cotton—that they took out; this left the young countries weak and vulnerable at independence.

I know that the whites wish to kill me in order to take my country, and yet you claim that they will help me to organize my country. But I find my country good just as it is. I have no need of them.

I know what is necessary for me and what I want; I have my own merchants. Also, consider yourself fortunate that I do not order your head to be cut off.

Go away now, and above all, never come back.

Source: Boahen, A. Adu, ed. *UNESCO General History of Africa, Vol. 7, Africa under Colonial Domination, 1880–1935.* Berkeley: University of California Press, 1990, p. 4.

MÁXIMO GÓMEZ
(1836–1905)
"Respect Our Revolution"
Güira de Melena, Cuba
January 1896

Máximo Gómez was born in the Dominican Republic in 1836. He trained as an officer in the Spanish army and was sent to Cuba, but he soon realized he was serving on the side of slavery and colonialism. He left the Spanish army and joined the newly organizing Cuban patriots' rebel cause. He became commander in chief of the Cuban revolutionary army in the first Cuban war of independence, the Ten Years' War against Spain (1868–78). The war failed to win freedom for Cuba; afterward, he and others of the revolution went into exile (Gómez to Mexico). When Cuban political activist José Martí launched another war of independence in 1895, he appointed the 60-year-old General Gómez chief of the army. Gómez's second in command was Lieutenant-General Antonio Maceo, the black "Bronze Titan" of Cuban liberation. (Together Martí, Gómez, and Maceo are considered the three fathers of Cuban independence.) The larger, better-equipped Spanish forces called Gómez and Maceo "the Fox and the Lion" as a result of their guerrilla-style fighting, which included the dreaded "machete charge." In the west of the island, the two commanders were often generous to wounded enemy soldiers, hoping by a moderate policy to keep the support of the public. When the Cubans defeated a Spanish garrison near Havana in January 1896, Gómez addressed the prisoners. After the U.S. battleship *Maine* was sunk in Havana's harbor on February 15, 1898, (and because of U.S. commercial losses in Cuba and a new-found sense of U.S. importance in Central American affairs), the United States entered the war. On April 19 of that year, the war became the Spanish-American War. Spain surrendered soon after on August 12, and Cuba became an independent republic, under the "protection" of the United States, in 1902. Gómez was encouraged by his compatriots to run for president of Cuba, but he declined and lived in Havana until his death in 1905.

※

Spaniards! If things were the opposite way and you were the victors, not a single one of us would remain alive to tell the tale.

But it is the Cubans who triumphed, and neither Antonio Maceo nor I can find it in our hearts to kill prisoners of war. Both of us respect the vanquished, especially when the enemy, as you were, is courageous.

So then, Spaniards, remain at complete liberty in spite of having shed our blood through a misunderstanding of your own interests. Tell your companions, the Spanish merchants, that the great Cuban Liberating Army will respect the persons and interests of those who obey and respect our Revolution.

But those who oppose it will be crushed.

Source: Foner, Philip S. *Antonio Maceo: The "Bronze Titan" of Cuba's Struggle for Independence.* New York: Monthly Review Press, 1977, p. 209. Copyright © 1977 by Monthly Review Press. Reprinted by permission of Monthly Review Foundation.

MAX SIMON NORDAU
(1849–1923)
Opening Address to the First Zionist Congress
Basel, Switzerland
August 29, 1897

Max Simon Nordau was born in Budapest, Hungary, in 1849. He studied medicine and then took up the pen as a journalist and critic. He married a Protestant Christian woman and became an assimilated European intellectual, writing despairing books about social change and largely leaving his Jewish heritage behind. In Paris he met Theodore Herzl, also a Jewish writer from Budapest corresponding for the same German language newspaper. Both men were deeply affected by the notorious Dreyfus Affair that erupted in Paris in the 1890s. This scandal exposed the wrongful court-martial—as a German spy—of French military officer Alfred Dreyfus, originating in anti-Semitic prejudice within the French army (SEE speech by Émile Zola, page 279). Both witnessed mobs shouting for the death of Jews. Convinced that implacable anti-Semitism remained at the heart of even Europe's most enlightened nations, Herzl envisioned a "Zionist" Jewish homeland where Jews could live free of disabling prejudice; he began traveling and speaking to raise support for the cause. Max Nordau joined him in planning a World Zionist Congress for 1897 in Basel, Switzerland. Nordau's opening address described the miserable condition of the Jews, with special reference to European Jewry. He believed prejudice against Jews remained pervasive because Enlightenment ideas of equality and human rights had been imposed from above, rather than growing out of everyday society. He spoke "with horror" of Marranos (a term for Jews forced under the Spanish Inquisition to conceal their identity), referring to unhappy Jewish converts to Christianity, atheism, even Marxist revolution. (It was from this congress that the forged anti-Semitic documents of the debunked Russian hoax *Protocols of the Elders of Zion* supposedly came.) Nordau spoke again at succeeding Zionist congresses, held every two years with the goal of building a Jewish state in Palestine.

Everywhere, where the Jews have settled in comparatively large numbers among the nations, Jewish misery prevails. It is not the ordinary misery which is probably the unalterable fate of mankind. It is a peculiar misery, which the Jews do not suffer as human beings, but as Jews, and from which they would be free, were they not Jews.

Jewish misery has two forms, the material and the moral. In Eastern Europe, North Africa, and Western Asia—those regions which shelter the vast majority, probably nine-tenths of our race—the misery of the Jews is understood literally. It is the daily distress of the body, anxiety for every following day, the painful fight for the maintenance of a bare existence. In Western Europe, the struggle for existence has been made somewhat lighter for the Jews, although of late the tendency has become visible even there to render it difficult for them again. The question of food and shelter, the question of the security of life, tortures them less; there the misery is moral. . . .

The nations which emancipated the Jews have mistaken their own feelings. In order to produce its full effect, emancipation should first have been completed in sentiment before it was declared by law. But this was not the case. The history of Jewish emancipation is one of the most remarkable pages in the history of European thought. The emancipation of the Jews was not the consequence of the conviction that grave injury had been done to a race, that it had been treated most terribly, and that it was time to atone for the injustice of a thousand years; it was solely the result of the geometrical mode of thought of French rationalism of the 18th century. This rationalism was constructed by the aid of pure logic, without taking into account living sentiments and the principles of the certainty of mathematical action; and it insisted upon trying to introduce these

Max Nordau's democratic ideals impelled the Zionists to form international congresses, rather than elite governing bodies, to discuss Jewish aspirations for a Jewish homeland. *(Library of Congress.)*

creations of pure intellect into the world of reality.

The emancipation of the Jews was an automatic application of the rationalistic method. The philosophy of Rousseau and the encyclopedists had led to the declaration of human rights. Out of this declaration, the strict logic of the men of the Great Revolution deduced Jewish emancipation. They formulated a regular equation: Every man is born with certain rights; the Jews are human beings, consequently the Jews are born to own the rights of man. In this manner, the emancipation of the Jews was pronounced, not through a fraternal feeling for the Jews, but because logic demanded it. Popular sentiment rebelled, but the philosophy of the Revolution decreed that principles must be placed higher than sentiment. Allow me then an expression which implies no ingratitude. The men of 1792 emancipated us only for the sake of principle.

As the French Revolution gave to the world the metric and the decimal systems, so it also created a kind of normal spiritual system which other countries, either willingly or unwillingly, accepted as the normal measure for their state of culture. A country which claimed to be at the height of culture had to possess several institutions created or developed by the Great Revolution; as, for instance, representation of the people, freedom of the press, jury, division of powers, etc. Jewish emancipation was also one of these indispensable articles of a highly cultured state; just as a piano must not be absent from a drawing-room even if not a single member of the family can play it. In this manner Jews were emancipated in Europe not from an inner necessity, but in imitation of a political fashion; not because the people had decided from their hearts to stretch out a brotherly hand to the Jews, but because leading spirits had accepted a certain cultured idea which required that Jewish emancipation should figure also in the Statute book.

Only to one country does this not apply—England. The English people does not allow its progress to be forced upon it from without; it develops progress from its inner self. In England emancipation is a truth. It is not alone written, it is living. It had already been completed in the heart before legislation expressly confirmed it. Out of respect to tradition, one hesitated in England to abolish the legal restrictions of the Nonconformists, at a time when the English had already for more than an age made no difference in society between Christians and Jews. Because a great nation, with a most intense spiritual life, does not allow itself to be guided by any spiritual current or blunder of the time, in England, anti-Semitism is only noticeable in a few instances, and then only it has the importance of an imitation of Continental fashion.

Emancipation has totally changed the nature of the Jew, and made him another being. The Jew without any rights did not love the prescribed yellow Jewish badge on his coat, because it was an official invitation to the mob to commit brutalities, and justified them in anticipation. But voluntarily he did much more to make his separate nature more distinct even than the yellow badge could do. The authorities did not shut him up in a ghetto, he built one for himself. He would dwell with his own, and would have no other relations but those of business with Christians. The word "Ghetto" is today associated with feelings of shame and humiliation. But the Ghetto, whatever may have been the intentions of the people who have created it, was for the Jew of the past not a prison, but a refuge. It is only historical truth if we say that only the Ghetto gave Jews the possibility to survive the terrible persecutions of the Middle Ages.

In the Ghetto, the Jew had his own world; it was to him the sure refuge which had for him the spiritual and moral value of a parental home. Here were associates by whom one wished to be valued, and also could be valued; here was the public opinion to be acknowledged by which was the aim of the Jew's ambition. To be held in low esteem by that public opinion was the punishment for unworthiness. Here all specific Jewish qualities were esteemed, and through their special development that admiration was to be obtained which is the sharpest spur to the human mind. What mattered it that outside the Ghetto was despised that which within it was praised? The opinion of the outside world had no influence, because it was the opinion of ignorant enemies. . . .

Now came Emancipation. The law assured the Jews that they were full citizens of their country. In its honeymoon it evoked also from Christians feelings which warmed and purified the heart. The Jews hastened in a species of intoxication, as it were, to burn their boats. They had now another home; they no longer needed a Ghetto; they had now other connections and were no longer forced to exist only with their co-religionists. Their instinct of self-preservation fitted itself immediately and completely to the new conditions of existence. Formerly this instinct was only directed toward a sharp separation. Now they sought after the closest association and assimilation in place of the distinction, which was their salvation. There followed a true mimicry, and for one or two ages the Jew was allowed to believe that he was only German, French, Italian, and so forth.

All at once, twenty years ago, after a slumber of thirty to sixty years, anti-Semitism once more broke out from the innermost depths of the nations, and revealed to the highest of the mortified Jews his real situation, which he had no longer seen. He was still allowed to vote for members of parliament, but he was himself excluded from the clubs and the meetings of his Christian fellow-countrymen. He was allowed to go wherever he pleased, but everywhere he met with the inscription: "No Jews admitted." He had still the right of discharging all the duties of a citizen, but the nobler rights which are granted to talent and for achievements in those rights were absolutely denied to him. . . .

All the better Jews in Western Europe groan under this, or seek for alleviation. They no longer possess the belief which gives the patience necessary to bear sufferings, because it sees in them the will of a punishing but not loving God. They no longer hope in the advent of the Messiah, who will one day raise them to Glory. Many try to save themselves by flight from Judaism. But racial anti-Semitism denies the power of change by baptism, and this mode of salvation does not seem to have much prospect. It is but a slight recommendation for those concerned, who are mostly without belief (I am not speaking naturally of the minority of true believers) that they enter with a blasphemous lie into the Christian community. In this way there arises a new Marrano. . . .

I think with horror of the future development of this race of new Marranos, who are normally sustained by no tradition and whose soul is poisoned by hostility toward their own and strange blood, and whose self-respect is destroyed through the ever present consciousness of a fundamental lie.

Others hope for the salvation from Zionism, which is for them, not the fulfillment of a mystic promise of the Scripture, but the way to an existence wherein the Jew finds at last the simplest but most elementary conditions of life, that are a matter of course for every Jew of both hemispheres: viz, an assured social existence in a well meaning community, the possibility of employing all his powers for the developments of his real being instead of abusing them for the suppression and falsification of self.

Yet others, who rebel against the lie of the Marranos, and who feel themselves too intimately connected with the land of their birth not to feel what Zionism means, throw themselves into the arms of the wildest revolution, with an indefinite arriere pense that with the destruction of everything in existence, and the construction of a new world, Jew-hatred may not be one of the precious articles transferred from the debris of the old conditions into the new.

This is the history of Israel at the end of the 19th century. To sum it up in a word: The majority of the Jews are a race of accursed beggars. More industrious and more able than the average European, not to speak at all of the inert Asiatic and African, the Jew is condemned to the most extreme pauperism, because he is not allowed to use his powers freely. This poverty grinds down his character, and destroys his body. Fevered by the thirst for higher education, he sees himself repelled from the places where knowledge is attainable—a real intellectual tantalus of our non-mythical times. He dashes his head against the thick ice crusts of hatred and contempt which are formed over his head. Like scarcely any other social being—whom even his belief teaches that it is a meritorious and God-pleasing action for three to take meals together and for ten to pray together—he is excluded from the society of his countrymen and is condemned to a tragic isolation. One complains of Jews intruding everywhere, but they only strive after superiority, because they are denied equality. . . .

To Jewish distress no-one can remain indifferent, neither Christian nor Jew. It is a great sin to let a race to whom even their worst enemies do not deny ability, degenerate in intellectual and physical distress. It is a sin against them and against the work of civilization, in the interest of which Jews have not been useless co-workers.

That Jewish distress cries for help. To find that help will be the great work of this Congress.

Source: Nordau, Max. "Address at the First Zionist Congress." Jewish Virtual Library. Available online. http://www.jewishvirtuallibrary.org/jsource/Zionism/nordau1.html. Accessed November 22, 2007.

ÉMILE ZOLA
(1840–1902)
"Dreyfus Is Innocent!"
Paris, France
February 21, 1898

In 1894 a note found in the trashcan of the German military attaché in Paris tipped off French authorities that there was a spy passing secrets to Germany in the French Army's General Staff. Anti-Semitic individuals (those who hate Jews) in the army (France was largely Catholic) rushed to accuse Captain Alfred Dreyfus, a Jewish artillery officer, of being a traitor, although the investigation turned up little but coincidences to implicate him. The innocent Dreyfus was court-martialed and exiled to a fearsome prison on Devil's Island off French Guiana. Further inquiry suggested a dissipated major named Ferdinand Walsin Esterhazy was the real spy. The army, to save itself from embarrassment, covered up its bungled investigation of Dreyfus and a military court convicted him again. Esterhazy received a cursory military trial and was acquitted on January 11, 1898, after which he wisely left the country. Enraged by the obvious conspiracy within the army, famed novelist and intellectual Émile Zola came to Dreyfus's aid. (Zola had been born in Paris in 1840, the son of an Italian father and French mother. He began writing as a journalist and by 1898 had written dozens of novels, including *Thérèse Raquin* and *Germinal.*) Two days later, on January 13, 1898, Zola published a letter, *J' Accuse* (I Accuse), in a Paris newspaper. In the letter, Zola bravely attacked by name all who had defamed Dreyfus, and he accused the French government of anti-Semitism. The novelist was tried for libel (the writing of damaging falsehoods), as he hoped, which forced the case into open (rather than military) court and set Dreyfus's denial of justice before the world. Zola gave the celebrated appeal to the jury that follows, and he was convicted two days after. He took refuge in England, but he was allowed to return later, "pardoned" by the president. Dreyfus was released in 1899 but he had to wait seven years to be fully exonerated. The scandal surrounding the Dreyfus affair was one reason a law was passed in 1905 to separate church from state in France.

If I am before you, it is because I wished it. I alone decided that this obscure, this abominable affair, should be brought before your jurisdiction, and it is I alone of my free will who chose you, you, the loftiest, the most direct emanation of French justice, in order that France at last may know all, and give her decision. My act had no other object and my person is of no account. I have sacrificed it in order to place in your hands, not only the honor of the army, but the imperiled honor of the nation. . . .

We have had to fight step by step against an extraordinarily obstinate desire for darkness. A battle has been necessary to obtain every atom of truth. Everything has been refused us. Our witnesses have been terrorized in the hope of preventing us from proving our case. And it is on your behalf alone that we have fought, that this proof might be put before you in its entirety, so that you might give your opinion on your consciences without remorse. . . .

Never have I insulted the army. I spoke, on the contrary, of my sympathy, my respect for the nation in arms, for our dear soldiers of France, who would rise at the first menace to defend the soil of France. And it is just as false that I attacked the chiefs, the generals who would lead them to victory. If certain persons at the War Office have compromised the army itself by their acts, is it to insult the whole army to say so? Is it not rather to act as a good citizen to separate it from all that compromises it, to give the alarm, so that the blunders which alone have been the cause of our defeat shall not occur again, and shall not lead us to fresh disaster?

I am not defending myself, moreover. I leave history to judge my act, which was a necessary one; but I affirm that the army is dishonored when gendarmes are allowed to embrace Major Esterhazy after the abominable letters written by him. I affirm that that valiant army is insulted daily by the bandits who, on the plea of defending it, sully it by their degrading championship, who trail in the mud all that France still honors as good and great. I affirm that those who dishonor that great national army are those who mingle cries of *Vive l'armée!* with those of *Á bas les juifs!* and *Vive Esterhazy!*

Dreyfus is innocent! —*Émile Zola*

Grand Dieu! the people of Saint Louis, of Bayard, of Condé, and of Hoche, the people which counts a hundred great victories, the people of the great wars of the Republic and the Empire, the people whose power, grace, and generosity have dazzled the world, crying *Vive Esterhazy!* It is a shame the stain of which our efforts on behalf of truth and justice can alone wipe out! . . .

Do me the honor of believing that I am not defending my liberty. By punishing me you would only magnify me. Whoever suffers for truth and justice becomes august and sacred. Look at me. Have I the look of a hireling, of a liar, and a traitor? Why should I be playing a part? I have behind me neither political ambition nor sectarian passion. I am a free writer, who has given his life to labor; who tomorrow will go back to the ranks and resume his interrupted task.

And how stupid are those who call me an Italian—me, born of a French mother, brought up by grandparents in the Beauce, peasants of that vigorous soil; me, who lost my father at seven years of age, who never went to Italy till I was fifty-four. And yet I am proud that my father was from Venice—the resplendent city whose ancient glory sings in all memories. And even if I were not French, would not the forty volumes in the French language, which I have sent by millions of copies throughout the world, suffice to make me a Frenchman?

So I do not defend myself. But what a blunder would be yours if you were convinced that by striking me you would reestablish order in our unfortunate country! Do you not understand now that what the nation is dying of is the darkness in which there is such an obstinate determination to leave her?

The blunders of those in authority are being heaped upon those of others; one lie necessitates another, so that the mass is becoming formidable. A judicial blunder was committed, and then to hide it, it has been necessary to commit every day fresh crimes against good sense and equity! The condemnation of an innocent man has involved the acquittal of a guilty man, and now today you are asked in turn to condemn me because I have cried out in my anguish on beholding our country embarked on this terrible course. Condemn me, then! But it will be one more error added to the others—a fault the burden of which you will hear in history. And my condemnation, instead of restoring the peace for which you long, and which we all of us desire, will be only a fresh seed of passion and disorder. The cup, I tell you, is full; do not make it run over! . . .

The Dreyfus case, gentlemen, has now become a very small affair. It is lost in view of the formidable questions to which it has given rise. There is no longer a Dreyfus case. The question now is whether France is still the France of the rights of man, the France which gave freedom to the world, and ought to give it justice. Are we still the most noble, the most fraternal, the most generous of nations? Shall we preserve our reputation in Europe for justice and humanity? Are not all the victories that we have won called in question? Open your eyes, and understand that, to be in such confusion, the French soul must have been stirred to its depths in face of a terrible danger. A nation cannot be thus moved without imperiling its moral existence. This is an exceptionally serious hour; the safety of the nation is at stake. . . .

Dreyfus is innocent. I swear it! I stake my life on it—my honor! At this solemn moment, in the presence of this tribunal, which is the representative of human justice, before you, gentlemen, who are the very incarnation of the country, before the whole of France, before the whole world, I swear that Dreyfus is innocent. By my forty years of work, by the authority that this toil may have given me, I swear that Dreyfus is innocent. By all I have now, by the name I have made for myself, by my works which have helped for the expansion of French literature, I swear that Dreyfus is innocent. May all that melt away, may my works perish if Dreyfus be not innocent! He is innocent.

All seems against me—the two Chambers, the civil authority, the most widely circulated journals, the public opinion which they have poisoned. And I have for me only an ideal of truth and justice. But I am quite calm; I shall conquer.

I was determined that my country should not remain the victim of lies and injustice. I may be condemned here. The day will come when France will thank me for having helped to save her honor.

Source: Émile Zola. "Appeal for Dreyfus." Edited by Thomas Brackett Reed. *Modern Eloquence.* Vol. 8. Chicago: Geo. L. Shuman, 1900, p. 1,226.

CRISIS AND ACHIEVEMENT
(1900–1950)

Introduction to Crisis and Achievement

The first half of the 20th century was a time of war and worldwide social upheaval. Two world wars and many smaller ones convulsed the globe. Revolutions shook two of the planet's largest and most conservative countries, Russia and China, along with a host of others. By the end of the period, the European colonial system was unraveling as the cold war between the United States and the Soviet Union got under way in 1945.

WORLD WAR I AND RUSSIAN REVOLUTION

World War I (1914 to 1918) began with the assassination of the heir to the throne of Austria-Hungary, Franz Ferdinand, in the town of Sarajevo. The assassin, Gavrilo Princip, was a Serbian nationalist who wanted the portion of the Austrian monarchy inhabited by Balkan Slavs to become part of Serbia. Austria and Serbia called upon their closest allies, Russia for Serbia and Germany for Austria-Hungary. France and Britain, allies of Russia, were then drawn into the war against Germany. These countries, known collectively as the "Allies" were later joined by Italy and the United States. The Turkish Ottoman Empire and Bulgaria joined Germany and Austria-Hungary to form the "Central powers."

The war produced millions of casualties and put European societies under immense strains, which not all of them could bear. The experience of brutal, static "trench warfare" in the west (in which each side attacked and counterattacked the other from permanent trenches protected by barbed wire) created many alienated soldiers and veterans, who grew to bitterly resent their commanders and who became convinced that civilians could never understand their experiences. Germans faced malnourishment due to the British blockade. Britain confronted

opposition from Irish nationalists, including Patrick Pearse and Roger Casement, who did not see why Irish soldiers should be dying in an English war. The Ottomans carried out a genocidal campaign against their own Armenian Christian population, suspected of sympathy for Christian Russia.

The most dramatic events triggered by World War I occurred in Russia, which after failing to defeat Germany early in the conflict fell back on the defensive. The government of Czar Nicholas II (r. 1894–1917) had already been discredited by its failure in the Russo-Japanese War (1904–05), which had been immediately followed by an unsuccessful revolution. The Russian government was perceived as inept, corrupt, and even treasonous. In 1917 Russia underwent two revolutions. The first, the February Revolution, was led by reformist aristocrats and liberals. They overthrew the monarchy and established a republic, but the new rulers disappointed many by staying in World War I and delaying economic reforms. The second revolution, in October, had as its goals ending the war and instituting socialism (a system that would deny the right to private property ownership and give society as a whole the control of production and distribution of wealth). The October revolution's leader, V. I. Lenin, had been sent home to Russia from his place of exile in Switzerland (Lenin was exiled by the Russians and returned to Russia by the Germans). German leaders hoped that Lenin and his "Bolshevik" party would lead a successful revolution that would knock Russia out of the war. This would allow the German forces fighting the Russians to be shifted to the western front against the British and French.

Although the revolution did take Russia out of the war, the Germans failed in the west. They did so in part because of the entry of the United States into the war, under its idealistic 28th president Woodrow Wilson. After they launched an all-out effort to win on the western front that failed in early 1918, the German leadership had no choice but to surrender. The fact that the Germans surrendered before enemy forces actually set foot on German soil, however, led to the rise of the "stab-in-the-back" legend. This was the myth that German soldiers, undefeated on the battlefield, must have been betrayed by traitors at home.

THE POSTWAR WORLD

War and revolution led to the redrawing of much of the map of central and eastern Europe. The treaty of Brest-Litovsk between Germany and revolutionary Russia had required Russia to abandon vast territories in the west. Germany continued to exist as a state but lost a great deal of territory. Its allies, the Austro-Hungarian and Ottoman Empires, did not fare as well and were dismantled. Several new states in eastern Europe were created out of territories lost by Austria, Russia, and Germany. They included Poland, Czechoslovakia, and the Baltic republics of Latvia, Lithuania, and Estonia. A similar phenomenon occurred in the former Ottoman territories in the Middle East. The empire's successor state was the Republic of Turkey. Turkey's dynamic leader, Mustafa Kemal Atatürk, launched an ambitious nationalist program of modernization, Westernization, and secularization. In the Arab Middle East, the old colonial powers of Britain and France took over much of the territories, sometimes operating through Arab monarchies such as the Hashemite dynasty of Jordan and Iraq. Palestine, where the Jewish Zionist movement (the movement to reestablish a Jewish homeland) had been promised a state, was a special case. Although not directly related to the war, another change was the liberation of much of Ireland from British rule with the creation of a de facto independent Ireland, the Irish Free State.

Another revolutionary change saw the inclusion of women as full citizens in many of the democracies. The cause that suffragists (those seeking the right to vote) such as Emmeline Pankhurst in Britain and Susan B. Anthony in the United States had long fought for began to triumph in the postwar period, with women gaining the vote in both countries. Women's suffrage was also adopted in postwar Germany. Some hoped that women's values would make the country less aggressive and militaristic—a hope doomed to failure.

U.S. president Woodrow Wilson worked to end the era of war by creating international institutions. The new League of Nations, which Wilson strongly supported, would oppose war and aggression. Ironically, powerful political opposition in America kept Wilson's own nation out of the new group. As the new organization also excluded Russia, at this time officially known as the Soviet Union, and Germany, it was never able to fulfill its potential.

DEMOCRACY AND THE CHALLENGES OF FASCISM, COMMUNISM, AND THE DEPRESSION

Fascism was a right-wing political movement emphasizing national unity, strongman leadership, and militarism. Italy's Fascist Party, led by the ex-socialist and war veteran Benito Mussolini, took power in 1923. Mussolini, the inventor of the term "fascism," took power as dictator. Many thought his antidemocratic methods were just what Italy needed. Similar movements arose in other Western countries, but none seemed close to taking power in the 1920s. The German National Socialists (Nazis), under their new leader Adolf Hitler, were defeated when they tried to take over Germay in the "Beer Hall Putsch" on November 8 and 9, 1923.

On the left, democracies faced the challenge of communism, which promoted a classless society based on shared ownership of the means of production. The old socialist parties, many discredited by their support for World War I, split into socialist and communist factions. The new Communist parties were more revolutionary in their ideology, and first and foremost devoted to protecting the Soviet Union and serving Soviet policy. The international organization of Communist parties, the "Comintern," was tightly controlled from Moscow.

The world in the 1930s was hit by one of the biggest economic collapses in history, the "Great Depression." The depression put unemployment on the political agenda in many countries, and it greatly contributed to the strength of both fascist and communist movements. In two of the countries hardest hit, the depression brought great speakers to power—Franklin Delano Roosevelt in the United States and Hitler in Germany. Both fully utilized the new technologies of radio and film to spread their messages in promising to put people back to work.

These new politicians and many of their contemporaries aimed at mass mobilization. Many of the most successful political speechmakers of the early 20th century—Roosevelt, Hitler, and Mohandas K. Gandhi, for example—were known for their effectiveness in addressing mass audiences, not just the elite audiences of parliamentary debate. Fascist movements in particular valued a dramatic, highly emotional style that opponents described as "hysterical" or "strutting." Speechmaking was transformed by new technologies—loudspeakers enabled speakers to address larger crowds than ever before. The radio spread speakers' words over vast areas and for the first time made it possible for them to address a nationwide audience. By bringing speakers into listeners' homes and workplaces, radio permitted the forming of a uniquely intimate bond between leaders and national publics. Politicians in democracies used this feature most effectively, as in Roosevelt's "fireside chats" and Winston Churchill's wartime addresses to the British people.

The conflict between democracy and fascism was not only a rhetorical one, but also one waged militarily. The most important conflict in Europe between the world wars was the Spanish civil war (1936–39), in which the Spanish Republic, supported by a coalition of democratic and leftist forces, fought against Spanish fascists and conservatives under the leadership of General Francisco Franco. Charismatic leaders and spokespeople such as Dolores Ibárruri helped make the cause of the Spanish Republic an international one that attracted volunteers from many countries. However, the failure of the democratic governments of Britain and France to support the republic contributed to the eventual victory of Franco and fascism, a victory that also further demonstrated the ineffectiveness of the League of Nations. The league also proved unable to protect Ethiopia from conquest by Fascist Italy, and China from attack by Japan.

Ironically, the leading democracies of Europe—Britain and France—were also the world's largest imperial powers, facing challenges from an increasingly aware and active colonial world. The best-known anticolonial leader of the interwar period was India's Mohandas K. Gandhi, known as Mahatma, or "Great Soul." Although no anticolonial movement except the Irish was strong enough before the war to gain independence for its country, many people in Europe and the colonies came to gradually realize that the end of empire was just a matter of time.

WORLD WAR II

World War II lasted from 1939 to 1945. It pitted the "Allies" led by Great Britain, the United States of America, and the Soviet Union against the Axis powers led by Nazi Germany, Fascist Italy, and Japan. The war proved to be one of unprecedented destructiveness. Many European cities were partially or wholly destroyed in the conflict, particularly given the wide use of the new tool of strategic bombing. Two Japanese cities, Hiro-

shima and Nagasaki, were destroyed by American atomic bombs in what remains the only use of atomic weapons in war.

The Nazis quickly conquered most of the European continent. Britain, protected by the English Channel and sustained by the inspiring oratory of Winston Churchill, held out. The surprise German attack on the Soviet Union in 1941 proved successful at first, but eventually German troops became bogged down in the vast expanse of Russia, and they grew vulnerable to Soviet counterattacks. Hitler and the Nazis seized upon the opportunity that their early victories in the war presented to carry out their "Final Solution" of the Jewish "problem"—the extermination of the Jews of Europe and North Africa. A total of between 5 and 6 million Jews were murdered. Millions of other Europeans also perished under the Nazi "New Order."

A turning point in the war came with the surprise Japanese attack on the American naval base at Hawaii's Pearl Harbor on December 7, 1941—as Franklin Roosevelt, in a famous speech to the American people, put it, "a date that will live in infamy." The announcement of the war between Japan and America was followed quickly by Nazi Germany's declaration of war on the United States, bringing the Americans into the war in both the Pacific and European theaters. America's unmatched productive capacity was central to the success of the Allies, although by far the bloodiest conflict was that between Germany and the Soviet Union.

THE AFTERMATH OF THE WAR—IRON CURTAIN AND DECOLONIZATION

The aftermath of the war saw the Soviets in control of Eastern Europe and the Americans and their allies in control of Western Europe. Aid from America's Marshall Plan, named after Secretary of State George C. Marshall (also known as the European Recovery Program), was essential for reviving the Western European economies. Despite the hopes inherent in the founding of the United Nations, the two "blocs" hardened. Winston Churchill, in his speech in Fulton, Missouri, provided what became the central metaphor of the Soviet-American division of Europe. He described the European continent as divided by an "Iron Curtain."

The European powers, exhausted after the war, could not hold on to their colonial possessions. Both the United States and the Soviet Union were anticolonial in their ideologies, if not always in practice. Important milestones in the postcolonial era included the independence of India, Britain's largest and most important colony, in 1947. The former British territory was divided into two new independent states, the Muslim state of Pakistan (itself divided into East Pakistan and West Pakistan, two territories geographically divided by India) and the Hindu-majority state of India. In the "partition massacres," millions of Hindus and Muslims were killed, as Pakistan's Hindu population and much of India's Muslim population moved to the other state.

On a somewhat smaller scale, noteworthy struggles accompanied the 1948 independence of the former British mandate territory of Palestine, where many Arabs were driven from the new Jewish state of Israel while many Jews were driven from Arab and Islamic countries to Israel. Both the India/Pakistan conflict and the Israel/Palestine conflict have left painful and dangerous legacies to the present day.

Speeches

MOHANDAS KARAMCHAND GANDHI
(1869–1948)
The Pledge to Resistance
Johannesburg, South Africa

September 11, 1906

Mohandas K. Gandhi was born in 1869 to a Hindu family in Porbandar, a coastal city in Gujarat, western India. He left for England to study law, and in 1893 traveled to the Transvaal, a British colony in southern Africa, to represent an Indian merchant in a legal case. He was dismayed to discover extreme prejudice under the racist regime there, suffering such indignities as being thrown off a train for refusing to move to the third-class coach after buying a first-class ticket. For 20 years he strove to remove barriers to equality for his countrymen in South Africa. In August 1906, a new ordinance, the draft Asiatic Law Amendment Ordinance—known as the Black Act—required Indians to be registered and fingerprinted and to carry a pass under threat of imprisonment and deportation. As secretary of the British Indian Association, Gandhi objected to this degrading law, believing it unfair to free men living under British rule. It was "the first step with a view to hound us out of the country," he said. About 3,000 Indians from all walks of life crowded into the Empire Theatre in Johannesburg that September to hear his first speech calling for civil disobedience. At the close, everyone leaped to their feet to pledge resistance. In the days that followed, Gandhi refined his principle of *satyagraha* ("soul force"), and he developed his tactics of nonviolent resistance. In his view, the enemy was always to be converted by a demonstration of purity and humility and not by use of violence, which would only create anger and brutality. Thousands of Indian protesters refused to register or destroyed their pass cards; they were jailed, some beaten and deported. Many fled the Transvaal. The struggle continued for seven years, until the law was relaxed.

I wish to explain to this meeting that there is a vast difference between this resolution and every other resolution we have passed up to date, and that there is a wide divergence also in the manner of making it. It is a very grave resolution we are making, as our existence in South Africa depends upon our fully observing it. . . .

We all believe in one and the same God, the differences of nomenclature in Hinduism and Islam notwithstanding. To pledge ourselves or to take an oath in the name of that God or with Him as witness is not something to be trifled with. If having taken such an oath we violate our pledge, we are guilty before God and man. Personally I hold that a man who deliberately and intelligently takes a pledge and then breaks it, forfeits his manhood. And just as a copper coin treated with mercury not only becomes valueless when found out but also makes its owner liable to punishment, in the same way a man who lightly pledges his word and then breaks it becomes a man of straw and fits himself for punishment here as well as hereafter. . . .

I know that pledges and vows are, and should be, taken on rare occasions. A man who takes a vow every now and then is sure to stumble. But if I can imagine a crisis in the history of the Indian community of South Africa when it would be in the fitness of things to take pledges, that crisis is surely now.

There is wisdom in taking serious steps with great caution and hesitation. But caution and hesitation have their limits, which we have now passed. The Government has taken leave of all sense of decency. We would only be betraying our unworthiness and cowardice, if we cannot stake our all in the face of the conflagration which envelops us and sit watching it with folded hands.

There is no doubt, therefore, that the present is a proper occasion for taking pledges. But every one of us must think out for himself if he has the will and the ability to pledge himself. Resolutions of this nature cannot be passed by a majority vote. Only those who take a pledge can be bound by it. This pledge must not be taken with a view to produce an effect on outsiders. No one should trouble to consider what impression it might have upon the local government, the Imperial Government, or the Government of India. Each one must only search his own heart, and if the inner voice assures him that he has the requisite strength to carry him through, then only should he pledge himself and then only would his pledge bear fruit.

A few words now as to the consequences. Hoping for the best, we may say that, if a majority of the Indians pledge themselves to resistance and if all who take the pledge prove true to themselves, the Ordinance may not even be passed and, if passed, may be soon repealed. It may be that we may not be called upon to suffer at all.

Mohandas K. Gandhi, center, sits surrounded by staff in Johannesburg, South Africa, four years before he began his civil disobedience campaign against racial prejudice. The year was 1902. *(AP Photo)*

RHETORICAL DEVICE

Paradox: Making a statement that seems opposed to common sense; such statements draw attention to the sentence's meaning.

Non-violence is the first article of my faith.
It is also the last article of my creed. —*Mohandas Gandhi*

Let the veil of silence fall presently over what happened afterwards.
Silence, too, can speak out. —*Lech Wałęsa*

Life springs from death; and from the graves of patriot men and women
spring living nations. —*Patrick Pearse*

All bad precedents have originated in cases which were good. —*Julius Caesar*

But if on the one hand one who takes a pledge must be a robust optimist, on the other hand he must be prepared for the worst. It is therefore that I would give you an idea of the worst that might happen to us in the present struggle.

It is quite possible that in spite of the present warning some or many of those who pledge themselves might weaken at the very first trial. . . . We might have to go to jail, where we might be insulted. We might have to go hungry and suffer extreme heat or cold. Hard labor might be imposed upon us. We might be flogged by rude warders. We might be fined heavily and our property might be attached and held up to auction if there are only a few resisters left. Opulent today, we might be reduced to abject poverty tomorrow. We might be deported. Suffering from starvation and similar hardships in jail, some of us might fall ill and even die. . . .

If someone asks me when and how the struggle may end, I may say that, if the entire community manfully stands the test, the end will be near. If many of us fall back under storm and stress, the struggle will be prolonged. But I can boldly declare, and with certainty, that so long as there is even a handful of men true to their pledge, there can only be one end to the struggle, and that is victory.

Source: Gandhi, M. K. *Satyagraha in South Africa.* Translated by V. G. Desai. Madras: S. Ganesan, Publisher, 1928, p. 164.

MARK TWAIN
(1835–1910)
Farewell to England
Liverpool, England
July 10, 1907

Social events were always more successful when novelist Mark Twain, master of the "dinner talk," was the speaker. Twain was born Samuel Langhorne Clemens in 1835; he lived in Hannibal, Missouri, as a child and later took the pen name Mark Twain from a phrase used by riverboat men to measure river depth. He worked as a Mississippi River steamboat pilot for six years; the setting would inspire two of his greatest stories, *The Adventures of Tom Sawyer* (published in 1876) and *The Adventures of Huckleberry Finn* (in 1884). He was a hardworking author of humor and satire, producing a novel or other work of fiction every year or two (including *The Prince and the Pauper,* in 1882, and *A Connecticut Yankee in King Arthur's Court,* in 1889), but despite his literary success he was often in financial difficulties. His speaking tours were a means of raising money, and they took him as far afield as Australia, India, Mauritius, and South Africa. On June 26, 1907, he was awarded an honorary degree by Oxford University while on a tour of Britain. He had survived the emotionally devastating deaths of his beloved daughter Susy and his wife, Olivia, and was at the zenith of his popularity as a writer and speaker. The British public lionized him, as the Americans had mobbed English author Charles Dickens on his tours of America. The Lord Mayor of Liverpool gave the 72-year-old Twain a farewell banquet, at which several hundred guests ate a 12-course dinner and drank expensive wine. After their toast to "Our Guest," Mark Twain delivered his talk. His conclusion thanking the British for being the kindest of hosts caused a sensation among the audience—a great cheer so lusty that Twain had to wait a long minute to pronounce the last two words.

I don't think I will say anything about the relations of amity existing between our two countries. It is not necessary, it seems to me. The ties between the two nations are so strong that I do not think we need trouble ourselves about them being broken. Anyhow, I am quite sure that in my time, and in yours, my Lord Mayor, those ties will hold good, and please God, they always will. English blood is in our veins, we have a common language, a common religion, a common system of morals, and great commercial interests to hold us together.

Home is dear to us all, and I am now departing for mine on the other side of the ocean. Oxford has conferred upon me the loftiest honor that has ever fallen to my fortune, the one I should have chosen as outranking any and all others within the gift of men or states to bestow upon me. And I have had, in the four weeks that I have been here, another lofty honor, a continuous honor, an honor which has known no interruption in all these twenty-six days, a most moving and pulse-stirring honor: the hearty hand-grip and the cordial welcome which does not descend from the pale gray matter of the brain, but comes up with the red blood out of the heart! It makes me proud, and it makes me humble.

Many and many a year ago I read an anecdote in Dana's book *Two Years Before the Mast.* A frivolous little self-important captain of a coasting-sloop in the dried-apple and kitchen-furniture trade was always hailing every vessel that came in sight, just to hear himself talk and air his small grandeurs.

One day a majestic Indiaman came plowing by, with course on course of canvas towering into the sky, her decks and yards swarming with sailors, with macaws and monkeys and all manner of strange and romantic creatures populating her rigging, her freightage of precious spices lading the breeze with gracious and mysterious odors of the Orient. Of course, the little coaster-captain hopped into the shrouds and squeaked a hail: "Ship ahoy! What ship is that, and whence and whither?"

In a deep and thunderous bass came the answer back, through a speaking-trumpet: "The *Begum of Bengal,* a hundred and twenty-three days out from Canton—homeward bound! What ship is that?"

The little captain's vanity was all crushed out of him, and most humbly he squeaked back: "Only the *Mary Ann,* fourteen hours out from Boston, bound for Kittery Point with—with nothing to speak of!" That eloquent word "only" expressed the deeps of his stricken humbleness.

And what is my case? During perhaps one hour in the twenty-four—not more than that—I stop and reflect. Then I am humble, then I am properly meek, and for that little time I am "only the *Mary Ann,*" fourteen hours out, and cargoed with vegetables and tin-ware; but all the other twenty-three my vain self-satisfaction rides high and I am the stately Indiaman, plowing the great seas under a cloud of sail, and laden with a rich freightage of the kindest words that were ever spoken to a wandering alien, I think; my twenty-six crowded and fortunate days seem multiplied by five; and I am the *Begum of Bengal,* a hundred and twenty-three days out from Canton—homeward bound!

Mark Twain excelled in a long career on the lecture and dinner talk circuit—more than 53 years in public speaking. *(Print by Joseph Keppler, Library of Congress.)*

Source: Twain, Mark. *Mark Twain Speaking.* Edited by Paul Fatout. Iowa City: University of Iowa Press, 1976, p. 577.

EMMELINE PANKHURST
(1858–1928)
"This Women's Civil War"
London, England
February 21, 1913

Emmeline Pankhurst was born Emmeline Goulden in Manchester, England. She was interested in women's rights at a young age, and she attended her first suffrage (voting) meeting at the age of 14. In 1879, along with her husband, Emmeline Pankhurst worked for the Married Women's Property Committee and the Manchester Woman's Suffrage Committee. When she and her daughters, Christabel and Sylvia, formed the Women's Social and Political Union (WSPU) in 1903, only New Zealand and Australia allowed women to vote. In England, women wanted the vote to address social problems such as infant mortality, child abuse, prostitution, and the "sweating" system of poorly paid female work. More than 1,000 women were arrested at WSPU street rallies, some beaten by police. The Black Friday Riot of 1910 occurred when 300 women demonstrating outside the House of Commons were assaulted by police; one hundred of them were arrested. Suffragettes were ridiculed by the press and called "hooligan women." In jail, their hunger strikes were met with forcible feeding—this was a dangerous procedure involving tubes threaded through the mouth to the stomach and occasionally causing pneumonia and death. Two days before this address by Emmeline Pankhurst, WSPU activists bombed the country house of Chancellor of the Exchequer David Lloyd-George. They also broke windows, damaged golf courses, and bombed mailboxes. In April that year, Pankhurst was sentenced to three years in jail in a bombing case, but she was released because of a hunger strike; in July she gave a speech in which she declared, "Give votes to women or kill women!" In November she traveled to the United States to speak. The 55-year-old woman's frail health was damaged by repeated imprisonment and hunger strikes, 12 times in one year alone. Success for Pankhurst came in 1918, when women over 30 years of age who were property holders received the right to vote, and those over 21 could run for election to Parliament. British women finally received equal voting rights with men in 1928.

I am very glad to have this one more opportunity of explaining to an audience in London the meaning of the women's revolution, because it is as much a revolution which is going on in Great Britain as is that series of events taking place in Mexico—a revolution. . . .

Now when the treatment of the Franchise Bill and the Woman Suffrage amendments were under discussion in the House of Commons, Lord Robert Cecil said that had men in this country been treated as women had been in that matter, there would have been insurrection. There was no doubt about it. Well, I think we have convinced the British public that when women arc treated in that way they also take to insurrection. . . .

Well, you know perfectly well that in spite of the alarmist accounts that you see in the Press, so far in our agitation no human being has suffered except the women who are fighting for the liberty of women. As far as we can secure it, even at tremendous risk to ourselves, that self-restraint on the part of women, and that safeguarding of human life will be maintained until we have won, but short of that we mean to do everything and all things that become necessary in order to settle this question of the status of women in this country once and for all.

Now when people take to methods of insurrection, when they proclaim a civil war, they take upon themselves a very serious responsibility. No one recognises that more than the women who are fighting in this women's civil war. I am by nature (and so are all our women) a law-abiding woman. Nothing but extreme provocation leads women to break the law. . . .

Emmeline Pankhurst, activist for women's voting rights, is arrested and carried away by police after trying to deliver a petition to King George V at Buckingham Palace, London, May 1914. *(HIP/Art Resource, NY)*

I was speaking the other night in a hall which is named after a great man who fought in this country against absolute monarchy. Cromwell and his army fought against the divine right of kings. Charles I believed sincerely—and many agreed with him—that kings, because they were kings, had a divine right to rule; they had a divine right to tax the people of this country and spend their money as they pleased without being responsible in any way.

Well, you have abolished the divine right of kings, but you have got the divine right of the man voter substituted for it, and we women to-day are fighting against that divine right. You admire the courage of men like Cromwell. Well, so do we; but it takes a great deal more courage, ladies and gentlemen, to fight against eight million divine rulers that it did to fight against one. . . .

Many of you condemn us, especially if you play golf, or if you sent a very important business letter which did not reach its destination, or if you are a shopkeeper and your windows have been broken. I expect the Chancellor of the Exchequer is coming home post haste to see what has happened to his building. You are all roused and you are all stirred up. Well, you say, "What do you hope to get by that? What is the use of making people angry?" Life-long supporters come to me and say, "You are completely alienating my sympathy." I reply to them: "What did your sympathy do for us, my good friend, when we had it?" . . .

Some of you are writing letters to the papers suggesting all sorts of punishments. That won't stop us. You see, in the way of punishment you cannot go beyond a certain point without reversing the whole progress of civilisation for the last hundred years. You know they thought that when they adopted forcible feeding, which is really a torture worthy of the Middle Ages, that that would put down the agitation, but it has not done so, because you see when you take to torture as punishment you can go as far as life will let you, but your victim will escape you into another life, and then your power over that human being ends, and women in this movement have so made up their minds that there is no other way but the way we have adopted, that we shall go on, and if one falls down by the way a hundred will arise to take her place. . . .

The answer to all the objections which may be made by people who do not like our methods is this: How else than by giving votes to women are you going to govern the women of England!

You cannot govern us if we refuse to be governed. If we withdraw our consent from government no power on earth can govern us. Your police force, your police magistrates, your judges, your army, the navy if you like, all the forces of civilisation, cannot govern one woman if she refuses to be governed. Government rests upon force, you say. Not at all: it rests upon consent, ladies and gentlemen, and women are withdrawing their consent.

Source: Jorgensen-Earp, Cheryl R., ed. *Speeches and Trials of the Militant Suffragettes: The Women's Social and Political Union, 1903–1918.* Madison, N.J.: Fairleigh Dickinson University Press, 1999, p. 286.

PATRICK PEARSE
(1879–1916)
"Ireland Unfree Shall Never Be at Peace"
Dublin, Ireland
August 1, 1915

Patrick Pearse was a Dublin-born instructor in the Gaelic movement, whose members aimed to teach the Irish language, as well as English, to children in Ireland's public schools. He joined the Irish Volunteers, a new volunteer military force to protect the rights of Irishmen, and he also joined the secret, older, and far more radical Irish Republican Brotherhood. The brotherhood had as its aim to overthrow, by force, Britain's rule of Ireland; its members often referred to themselves as "Fenians." Patrick Pearse became commander in chief of Irish forces in the Easter Rebellion uprising in Dublin on April 24, 1916. Respected as an orator, Pearse was chosen to announce the formation of an Irish Republic free of Britain—the dream of Irishmen for centuries. This was the most significant rebellion against the British occupiers since the 1798 Irish rebellion—and the rebellion soon after by Robert Emmet in 1803—that ended the era marked by the rise of the radical group United Irishmen (SEE Emmet's speech, p. 217). The Irish Republican Brotherhood's Easter Rising was doomed from the start, as conflicts among

organizers and a weapons shipment that did not arrive hastened their defeat. Pearse held out for one week before surrendering, and he was executed by the British four days later on May 3, 1916. The year before, he had delivered this magnificent eulogy at the burial of fellow patriot and radical exile Jeremiah O'Donovan Rossa, and thereby confirmed the tradition of great Irish oratory. Rossa was a member of the Fenian Brotherhood, a secret American society related to the Fenians (or Irish Republican Brotherhood) that sent Irish-Americans back to Ireland to participate in uprisings against British rule. In his eulogy, Pearse refers to several Irish republicans and patriots by name, and to the failed Fenian Rising of 1867.

> Life springs from death; and from the graves of patriot men and women spring living nations.
> —*Patrick Pearse*

It has seemed right, before we turn away from this place in which we have laid the mortal remains of O'Donovan Rossa, that one among us should, in the name of all, speak the praise of that valiant man, and endeavor to formulate the thought and the hope that are in us as we stand around his grave. And if there is anything that makes it fitting that I, rather than some other, I rather than one of the grey-haired men who were young with him and shared in his labor and in his suffering, should speak here, it is perhaps that I may be taken as speaking on behalf of a new generation that has been re-baptized in the Fenian faith, and that has accepted the responsibility of carrying out the Fenian programme.

I propose to you then that, here by the grave of this unrepentant Fenian, we renew our baptismal vows; that, here by the grave of this unconquered and unconquerable man, we ask of God, each one for himself, such unshakable purpose, such high and gallant courage, such unbreakable strength of soul as belonged to O'Donovan Rossa.

Deliberately here we avow ourselves, as he avowed himself in the dock, Irishmen of one allegiance only. We of the Irish Volunteers, and you others who are associated with us in today's task and duty, are bound together and must stand together henceforth in brotherly union for the achievement of the freedom of Ireland. And we know only one definition of freedom: it is Tone's definition, it is Mitchel's definition, it is Rossa's definition. Let no man blaspheme the cause that the dead generations of Ireland served by giving it any other name and definition than their name and their definition.

RHETORICAL DEVICE

Epizeuxis: Repeating a single word for emphasis.

It is I alone of my free will who chose you, you, the loftiest,
the most direct emanation of French justice, in order that France at last
may know all, and give her decision. —*Émile Zola*

If I were an American, as I am an Englishman,
while a foreign troop was landed in my country, I never would lay down
my arms—never—never—never! —*William Pitt the Elder*

They think that they have foreseen everything, think that they have
provided against everything; but the fools, the fools, the fools!
They have left us our Fenian dead, and while Ireland holds these graves,
Ireland unfree shall never be at peace. —*Patrick Pearse*

We stand at Rossa's grave not in sadness but rather in exaltation of spirit that it has been given to us to come thus into so close a communion with that brave and splendid Gael. Splendid and holy causes are served by men who are themselves splendid and holy. O'Donovan Rossa was splendid in the proud manhood of him, splendid in the heroic grace of him, splendid in the Gaelic strength and clarity and truth of him. And all that splendor and pride and strength was compatible with a humility and a simplicity of devotion to Ireland, to all that was olden and beautiful and Gaelic in Ireland, the holiness and simplicity of patriotism of a Michael O'Clery or of an Eoghan O'Growney. The clear true eyes of this man almost alone in his day visioned Ireland as we of to-day would surely have her: not free merely, but Gaelic as well; not Gaelic merely, but free as well.

In a closer spiritual communion with him now than ever before or perhaps ever again, in a spiritual communion with those of his day, living and dead, who suffered with him in English prisons, in communion of spirit too with our own dear comrades who suffer in English prisons to-day, and speaking on their behalf as well as our own, we pledge to Ireland our love, and we pledge to English rule in Ireland our hate. This is a place of peace, sacred to the dead, where men should speak with all charity and with all restraint; but I hold it a Christian thing, as O'Donovan Rossa held it, to hate evil, to hate untruth, to hate oppression, and, hating them, to strive to overthrow them.

Our foes are strong and wise and wary. But strong and wise and wary as they are, they cannot undo the miracles of God who ripens in the hearts of young men the seeds sown by the young men of a former generation. And the seeds sown by the young men of '65 and '67 are coming to their miraculous ripening today. Rulers and Defenders of Realms had need to be wary if they would guard against such processes. Life springs from death; and from the graves of patriot men and women spring living nations.

The Defenders of this Realm have worked well in secret and in the open. They think that they have pacified Ireland. They think that they have purchased half of us and intimidated the other half. They think that they have foreseen everything, think that they have provided against everything; but the fools, the fools, the fools! They have left us our Fenian dead, and while Ireland holds these graves, Ireland unfree shall never be at peace.

Source: Padraig Pearse. "Oration at the Graveside of O'Donovan Rossa." Éirígí. Available online. http://www.eirigi.org/archives/padraig_pearse.htm. Accessed December 17, 2007.

ROGER CASEMENT
(1864–1916)
On Loyalty to Ireland
London, England
June 29, 1916

Roger Casement was born in Dublin in 1864 to a Protestant British father and an Irish Catholic mother. He became a British diplomat in Africa, first in Portuguese East Africa and then in Angola and the Congo Free State (today, the Democratic Republic of the Congo). Congo Free State at that time belonged personally to King Leopold II of Belgium. As the British consul in the Congo Free State, Casement witnessed, firsthand, systemic atrocities and murder against the Congolese people. His 1904 report on the scandalous exploitation of the colony for its rubber resources caused the 14 nations that had divided up Africa (at the Berlin Conference of 1884) to review their agreement. Belgium subsequently took over the colony from Leopold in 1908 and renamed it the Belgian Congo. For his contribution in calling attention to abuse, Casement was knighted in 1911. Sent as a consul to South America in 1906, Casement worked on behalf of the exploited Putumayo Indians in Peru; he found himself developing an increasing dislike of the imperial practices of colonizers, Britain included. When World War I began in 1914—he had earlier retired from the diplomatic corps—Casement saw an opportunity, although fraught with danger, to secure assistance from Germany against Britain's repressive rule of Ireland. He traveled to Germany to arrange for a shipment of arms to Ireland for the 1916 Easter Rising and to conclude an agreement of German support for Irish independence. The ship carrying the weapons was intercepted by the British, and the foolhardy Casement, who traveled home to Ireland in a German U-boat, was arrested and charged with treason. His knighthood was taken from him. After his conviction as a traitor, he made this address, or allocution, from the dock before his death sentence was pronounced. He was hanged four days later in London. (His body was taken back to Ireland for reburial in 1965.) Southern Ireland received independence from Britain in 1922.

I may say, my lord, at once, that I protest against the jurisdiction of this court in my case on this charge, and the argument that I am now going to read is addressed not to this court, but to my own countrymen.

There is an objection, possibly not good in law, but surely good on moral grounds, against the application to me here of this old English statute, 565 years old, that seeks to deprive an Irishman today of life and honor, not for "adhering to the King's enemies," but for adhering to his own people.

When this statute was passed, in 1351, what was the state of men's minds on the question of a far higher allegiance—that of a man to God and His kingdom? The law of that day did not permit a man to forsake his Church, or deny his God, save with his life. The "heretic," then, had the same doom as the "traitor".

Today a man may forswear God and His heavenly kingdom, without fear or penalty—all earlier statutes having gone the way of Nero's edicts against the Christians, but that constitutional phantom "the King" can still dig up from the dungeons and torture-chambers of the Dark Ages a law that takes a man's life and limb for an exercise of conscience. . . .

I am being tried, in truth, not by my peers of the live present, but by the fears of the dead past; not by the civilization of the twentieth century, but by the brutality of the fourteenth; not even by a statute framed in the language of the land that tries me, but emitted in the language of an enemy land—so antiquated is the law that must be sought today to slay an Irishman, whose offence is that he puts Ireland first. . . . Judicial assassination today is reserved only for one race of the King's subjects—for Irishmen, for those who cannot forget their allegiance to the realm of Ireland. . . .

What is the fundamental charter of an Englishman's Liberty? That he shall be tried by his peers. With all respect, I assert this court is to me, an Irishman, charged with this offence, a foreign court—this jury is for me, an Irishman, not a jury of my peers to try me on this vital issue, for it is patent to every man of conscience that I have a right, an indefeasible right, if tried at all, under this statute of high treason, to be tried in Ireland, before an Irish court and by an Irish jury. This court, this jury, the public opinion of this country, England, cannot but be prejudiced in varying degrees against me, most of all in time of war. I did not land in England. I landed in Ireland. It was to Ireland I came; to Ireland I wanted to come; and the last place I desired to land was in England. . . .

This is so fundamental a right, so natural a right, so obvious a right, that it is clear that the Crown were aware of it when they brought me by force and by stealth from Ireland to this country. It was not I who landed in England, but the Crown who dragged me here, away from my own country to which I had returned with a price upon my head, away from my own countrymen whose loyalty is not in doubt, and safe from the judgment of my peers whose judgment I do not shrink from. I admit no other judgment but theirs. I accept no verdict save at their hands. . . .

We have been told, we have been asked to hope, that after this war Ireland will get Home Rule, as a reward for the lifeblood shed in a cause which, whomever else its success may benefit, can surely not benefit Ireland.

And what will Home Rule be in return for what its vague promise has taken, and still hopes to take away from Ireland? It is not necessary to climb the painful stairs of Irish history—that treadmill of a nation, whose labors are as vain for her own uplifting as the convict's exertions are for his redemption, to review the long list of British promises made only to be broken—of Irish hopes, raised only to be dashed to the ground.

Home Rule, when it comes, if come it does, will find an Ireland drained of all that is vital to its very existence unless it be that unquenchable hope we build on the graves of the dead. We are told that if Irishmen go by the thousand to die, not for Ireland, but for Flanders, for Belgium, for a patch of sand in the deserts of Mesopotamia, or a rocky trench on the heights of Gallipoli, they are winning self-government for Ireland.

But if they dare to lay down their lives on their native soil, if they dare to dream even that freedom can be won only at home by men resolved to fight for it there, then they are traitors to their country, and their dream and their deaths are phases of a dishonorable fantasy.

But history is not so recorded in other lands. In Ireland alone, in this twentieth century, is loyalty held to be a crime. If loyalty be something less than love and more than law, then we have had enough of such loyalty for Ireland and Irishmen. If we are to be indicted as criminals, to be shot as murderers, to be imprisoned as convicts, because our offence is that we love Ireland more than we value our lives, then I do not know what virtue resides in any offer of self-government held out to brave men on such terms.

Self-government is our right, a thing born in us at birth, a thing no more to be doled out to us, or withheld from us, by another people than the right to life itself—than the right to feel the sun, or smell the flowers, or to love our kind. It is only from the convict these things are withheld, for crime committed and proven and Ireland, that has wronged no man, has injured no land, that has sought no dominion over others—Ireland is being treated today among the nations of the world as if she were a convicted criminal.

If it be treason to fight against such an unnatural fate as this, then I am proud to be a rebel, and shall cling to my "rebellion" with the last drop of my blood. If there be no right of rebellion against the state of things that no savage tribe would endure without resistance, then I am sure that it is better for men to fight and die without right than to live in such a state of right as this.

Where all your rights have become only an accumulated wrong, where men must beg with bated breath for leave to subsist in their own land, to think their own thoughts, to sing their own songs, to gather the fruits of their own labors, and, even while they beg, to see things inexorably withdrawn from them—then, surely, it is a braver, a saner and truer thing to be a rebel, in act and in deed, against such circumstances as these, than to tamely accept it, as the natural lot of men.

My Lord, I have done.

Source: Knott, George H., ed. *Trial of Sir Roger Casement.* Philadelphia: Cromarty Law Book Co., 1917, p. 198.

Woodrow Wilson was for many years a college professor of law and political economy and, after 1902, president of Princeton University. In 1912, after serving two years as the governor of New Jersey, he was elected president of the United States. He was a champion of progressive policies; he instituted the Federal Reserve System of 12 regional banks and signed new antitrust laws to protect consumers. World War I began in Europe in 1914. Germany, Austria-Hungary, Bulgaria, and the Ottoman Empire were the Central Powers, arrayed against the Allied Powers of France, Britain, Belgium, Italy, Serbia, and Russia. Wilson hoped to keep the United States out of the conflict. When a German submarine torpedoed the unarmed British passenger ship *Lusitania* en route from New York City to Britain in May 1915, killing almost 1,200 people, the incident was handled diplomatically by Wilson; in September, Germany ended submarine attacks against passenger ocean liners. Then in March 1917, Germany announced it would resume submarine warfare against even neutral nations, and it began sinking American ships. On April 2 President Wilson reluctantly asked Congress to declare war on Germany, as he believed the war had become a danger to humankind. In his speech Wilson refers to an "intercepted note." This was the "Zimmermann telegram," sent in code to the German ambassador in Mexico City by German foreign secretary Arthur Zimmermann suggesting that Mexico ally itself militarily with Germany against the United States. Mexico's reward was to be the return of Texas, Arizona, and New Mexico. Mexico declined the offer, but the telegram stoked considerable anti-German feeling across the United States and contributed to the decision to go to war.

I have called the Congress into extraordinary session because there are serious, very serious, choices of policy to be made, and made immediately, which it was neither right nor constitutionally permissible that I should assume the responsibility of making.

On the third of February last, I officially laid before you the extraordinary announcement of the Imperial German Government that on and after the first day of February it was its purpose to put aside all restraints of law or of humanity and use its submarines to sink every vessel that sought to approach either the ports of Great Britain and Ireland or the western coasts of Europe or any of the ports controlled by the enemies of Germany within the Mediterranean. . . .

Vessels of every kind, whatever their flag, their character, their cargo, their destination, their errand, have been ruthlessly sent to the bottom without warning and without thought of help or mercy for those on board, the vessels of friendly neutrals along with those of belligerents. Even hospital ships . . . have been sunk with the same reckless lack of compassion or of principle. . . .

The present German submarine warfare against commerce is a warfare against mankind. It is a war against all nations. American ships have been sunk, American lives taken, in ways which it has stirred us very deeply to learn of, but the ships and people of other neutral and friendly nations have been sunk and overwhelmed in the waters in the same way. There has been no discrimination. The challenge is to all mankind. Each nation must decide for itself how it will meet it. The choice we make for ourselves must be made with a moderation of counsel and a temperateness of judgment befitting our character and our motives as a nation. We must put excited feeling away. Our motive will not be revenge or the victorious assertion of the physical might of the

After attacks on American ships by German submarines, U.S. president Woodrow Wilson addresses a joint session of Congress on April 2, 1917, urging it to declare war against Germany. The United States shortly entered World War I. *(AP Photo)*

nation, but only the vindication of right, of human right, of which we are only a single champion. . . .

There is one choice we cannot make, we are incapable of making: we will not choose the path of submission and suffer the most sacred rights of our nation and our people to be ignored or violated. The wrongs against which we now array ourselves are no common wrongs; they cut to the very roots of human life.

With a profound sense of the solemn and even tragical character of the step I am taking and of the grave responsibilities which it involves, but in unhesitating obedience to what I deem my constitutional duty, I advise that the Congress declare the recent course of the Imperial German Government to be in fact nothing less than war against the Government and people of the United States; that it formally accept the status of belligerent which has thus been thrust upon it, and that it take immediate steps not only to put the country in a more thorough state of defense but also to exert all its power and employ all its resources to bring the Government of the German Empire to terms and end the war. . . .

Neutrality is no longer feasible or desirable where the peace of the world is involved and the freedom of its peoples. And the menace to that peace and freedom lies in the existence of autocratic governments backed by organized force which is controlled wholly by their will, not by the will of their people. We have seen the last of neutrality in such circumstances. We are at the beginning of an age in which it will be insisted that the same standards of conduct and of responsibility for wrong done shall be observed among nations and their governments that are observed among the individual citizens of civilized states.

We have no quarrel with the German people. We have no feeling towards them but one of sympathy and friendship. It was not upon their impulse that their Government acted in entering

> The world must be made safe for democracy.
> —*Woodrow Wilson*

this war. It was not with their previous knowledge or approval. It was a war determined upon as wars used to be determined upon in the old, unhappy days when peoples were nowhere consulted by their rulers and wars were provoked and waged in the interest of dynasties or of little groups of ambitious men who were accustomed to use their fellow men as pawns and tools. Self-governed nations do not fill their neighbor states with spies or set the course of intrigue to bring about some critical posture of affairs which will give them an opportunity to strike and make conquest. . . .

One of the things that has served to convince us that the Prussian autocracy was not and could never be our friend is that from the very outset of the present war it has filled our unsuspecting communities and even our offices of government with spies and set criminal intrigues everywhere. . . . That it means to stir up enemies against us at our very doors the intercepted note to the German Minister at Mexico City is eloquent evidence. . . .

We are glad, now that we see the facts with no veil of false pretense about them, to fight thus for the ultimate peace of the world and for the liberation of its peoples, the German peoples included: for the rights of nations great and small and the privilege of men everywhere to choose their way of life and of obedience. The world must be made safe for democracy. Its peace must be planted upon the tested foundations of political liberty. We have no selfish ends to serve. We desire no conquest, no dominion. We seek no indemnities for ourselves, no material compensation for the sacrifices we shall freely make. We are but one of the champions of the rights of mankind. We shall be satisfied when those rights have been made as secure as the faith and the freedom of nations can make them. . . .

It is a distressing and oppressive duty, gentlemen of the Congress, which I have performed in thus addressing you. There are, it may be, many months of fiery trial and sacrifice ahead of us. It is a fearful thing to lead this great peaceful people into war, into the most terrible and disastrous of all wars, civilization itself seeming to be in the balance. But the right is more precious than peace, and we shall fight for the things which we have always carried nearest our hearts—for democracy, for the right of those who submit to authority to have a voice in their own governments, for the rights and liberties of small nations, for a universal dominion of right by such a concert of free peoples as shall bring peace and safety to all nations and make the world itself at last free.

To such a task we can dedicate our lives and our fortunes, everything that we are and everything that we have, with the pride of those who know that the day has come when America is privileged to spend her blood and her might for the principles that gave her birth and happiness and the peace which she has treasured. God helping her, she can do no other.

Source: Wilson, Woodrow. *War Addresses of Woodrow Wilson.* Introduction by Arthur Roy Leonard. Boston: Ginn and Co., 1918, p. 32.

CHARLES E. STANTON
(1859–1933)
"Lafayette, We Are Here"
Paris, France
July 4, 1917

World War I began in 1914, when Austria-Hungary went to war with Serbia after a Serbian nationalist —intent on joining Bosnia, then part of the Austro-Hungarian Empire, to Serbia to form a South Slav kingdom—assassinated Archduke Franz Ferdinand of Austria. Territorial and nationalist tensions had festered in Europe for decades prior. The initial conflict soon became continent-wide as treaties and alliances between individual countries caused a cascade of declarations of war, each country upholding its promises to assist its allies. The United States at first stayed out of the war, but President Woodrow Wilson was forced to end his isolationist policy after German U-boat submarines sank several American merchant vessels. When the United States entered the war, in April 1917, the Allied Powers of Britain, France, Belgium, Italy, and Russia were facing defeat by the Central Powers, primarily Germany and Austria-Hungary. The despairing French were overjoyed by the arrival on July 4, 1917, of General John "Black Jack" Pershing's American troops. They honored the holiday

Lafayette, we are here. —*Charles E. Stanton*

with a parade to the Tomb of Lafayette, the French hero of the American Revolution (1775–83) who had brought money, ships, troops, and valor to assist George Washington's desperate army. Parisians packed the streets shouting, *Vive les Americains!*, throwing flowers, waving flags, and crowding into the ranks of the marching soldiers. Pershing did not speak French, so a member of his staff, Colonel Charles E. Stanton (grandson of Edwin Stanton, Lincoln's secretary of war), made the address. Stanton's short speech in fluent French ended famously, *Lafayette, nous voilà*, or "Lafayette, we are here." This tiny oratorical jewel is often wrongly said to have been delivered by Pershing, who readily admitted that he was not the author of the remarks.

America has joined forces with the Allied Powers, and what we have of blood and treasure are yours. Therefore it is with loving pride we drape the colors in tribute of respect to this citizen of your great republic.

And here and now, in the presence of the illustrious dead, we pledge our hearts and our honor in carrying this war to a successful issue.

Lafayette, we are here.

Source: Stimpson, George William, ed. *Nuggets of Knowledge.* New York: G. Sully and Co., 1928, p. 1.

EMMA GOLDMAN
(1869–1940)
Trial Address
New York, New York, United States

July 9, 1917

Emma Goldman was born in Lithuania to a Jewish family who suffered under the anti-Semitic pogroms (targeted attacks) of the early 1880s. They moved to St. Petersburg, Russia, where young Emma was exposed to ideas of revolution and anarchy and to the use of violence to effect social change. To avoid an arranged marriage, she left for New York City in 1885 at 15 years old; there she lived the harsh life of the working poor. She was radicalized by Chicago's 1886 Haymarket Riot, when workers were striking nationwide for a shorter, eight-hour workday. Anticipating further police violence (strikers had been shot in Wisconsin and Chicago days earlier), a marcher threw a bomb at police; the strike leaders were unjustly condemned to death and hanged. Goldman concluded that revolutionary change was needed. She became a dynamic speaker for the anarchist movement, which espoused extreme individual freedom and the abolition of government. She allied herself with anarchist Alexander Berkman, also an immigrant from Lithuania, who believed political killings were a valuable strategy on behalf of workers. He attempted the murder of a factory manager and was sent to prison; Goldman was widely believed to have been his accomplice. She also was imprisoned in 1893, for "inciting riot" by her street speaking. When an anarchist assassinated President William McKinley in 1901, Goldman was jailed under suspicion. The anarchist movement was becoming increasingly discredited by its identification with violence and many labor groups distanced themselves; Goldman lost her citizenship in 1908. Following the entry of the United States into World War I, she was arrested in 1917 for advocating draft resistance. At her trial (with Alexander Berkman) she explained at length her views against war and the nature of patriotism. In 1919 she was deported to Russia along with other dissenters and antiwar agitators. Quickly disillusioned with the turn to repression in Russia following the revolution, she decamped for Britain where she received citizenship.

〰〰〰

I wish to say that I am a social student. It is my mission in life to ascertain the cause of our social evils and of our social difficulties. As a student of social wrongs it is my aim to diagnose a wrong. . . .

It is organized violence on top which creates individual violence at the bottom. It is the accumulated indignation against organized wrong, organized crime, organized injustice which drives the political offender to his act. To condemn him means to be blind to the causes which make him. I can no more do it, nor have I the right to, than the physician who were to condemn the patient for his disease. You and I and all of us who remain indifferent to the crimes of poverty, of war, of human degradation, are equally responsible for the act committed by the political offender. May I therefore be permitted to say, in the words of a great teacher: "He who is without sin among you, let him cast the first stone." Does that mean advocating violence? You might as well accuse Jesus of advocating prostitution, because He took the part of the prostitute, Mary Magdalene.

Gentlemen of the jury, the meeting of the 18th of May was called primarily for the purpose of voicing the position of the conscientious objector and to point out the evils of conscription. Now, who and what is the conscientious objector? Is he really a shirker, a slacker, or a coward? To call him that is to be guilty of dense ignorance of the forces which impel men and women to stand out against the whole world like a glittering lone star upon a dark horizon. The conscientious objector is impelled by what President Wilson in his speech of Feb. 3, 1917, called "the righteous passion for justice upon which all war, all structure of family, State and of mankind must rest as the ultimate base of our existence and our liberty." The righteous passion for justice which can never express itself in human slaughter—that is the force which makes the conscientious objector. Poor indeed is the country which fails to recognize the importance of that new type of humanity as the "ultimate base of our existence and liberty." It will find itself barren of that which makes for character and quality in its people. . . .

Gentlemen of the jury, most of you, I take it, are believers in the teachings of Jesus. Bear in mind that he was put to death by those who considered his views as being against the law. I also take it that you are proud of your American-ism. Remember that those who fought and bled for your liberties were in their time considered as being against the law, as dangerous disturbers and trou-ble-makers. They not only preached vio-lence, but they carried out their ideas by throwing tea into the Boston harbor. They said that "Resistance to tyranny is obedience to God." They wrote a danger-ous document called the Declaration of Independence. A document which con-tinues to be dangerous to this day, and for the circulation of which a young man was sentenced to ninety days prison in a New York Court, only the other day. They were the Anarchists of their time—they were never within the law. . . .

Lithuanian immigrant "Red Emma," Goldman traveled widely spreading her gospel of anarchy, often speaking on the street and from the running boards of automobiles. Associated with several acts of anarchist violence, she was finally deported for antiwar agitation in 1919. *(Library of Congress)*

If that be crime, we are criminals even like Jesus, Socrates, Galileo, Bruno, John Brown and scores of others. We are in good company, among those whom Havelock Ellis, the greatest living psychologist, describes as the political criminals recognized by the whole civilized world, except America, as men and women who out of deep love for humanity, out of a passionate reverence for liberty and an all-absorbing devotion to an ideal are ready to pay for their faith even with their blood. We cannot do otherwise if we are to be true to ourselves—we know that the political criminal is the precursor of human progress—the political criminal of to-day must needs be the hero, the martyr and the saint of the new age. . . .

Gentlemen of the jury, we respect your patriotism. We would not, if we could, have you change its meaning for yourself. But may there not be different kinds of patriotism as there are different kinds of liberty? I for one cannot believe that love of one's country must needs consist in blindness to its social faults, to deafness to its social discords, of inarticulation to its social wrongs. Neither can I believe that the mere accident of birth in a certain country or the mere scrap of a citizen's paper constitutes the love of country.

I know many people—I am one of them—who were not born here, nor have they applied for citizenship, and who yet love America with deeper passion and greater intensity than many natives whose patriotism manifests itself by pulling, kicking, and insulting those who do not rise when the national anthem is played. Our patriotism is that of the man who loves a woman with open eyes. He is enchanted by her beauty, yet he sees her faults. So we, too, who know America, love her beauty, her richness, her great possibilities; we love her mountains, her canyons, her forests, her Niagara, and her deserts—above all do we love the people that have produced her wealth, her artists who have created beauty, her great apostles who dream and work for liberty—but with the same passionate emotion we hate her superficiality, her cant, her corruption, her mad, unscrupulous worship at the altar of the Golden Calf.

We say that if America has entered the war to make the world safe for democracy, she must first make democracy safe in America. How else is the world to take America seriously, when democracy at home is daily being outraged, free speech suppressed, peaceable assemblies broken up by overbearing and brutal gangsters in uniform; when free press is curtailed and every independent opinion gagged. Verily, poor as we are in democracy, how can we give of it to the world? We further say that a democracy conceived in the military servitude of the masses, in their economic enslavement, and nurtured in their tears and blood, is not democracy at all. It is despotism—the cumulative result of a chain of abuses which, according to that dangerous document, the Declaration of Independence, the people have the right to overthrow.

The District Attorney has dragged in our Manifesto, and he has emphasized the passage, "Resist conscription." Gentlemen of the jury, please remember that that is not the charge against us. But admitting that the Manifesto contains the expression, "Resist conscription," may I ask you, is there only one kind of resistance? Is there only the resistance which means the gun, the bayonet, the bomb or flying machine? Is there not another kind of resistance? May not the people simply fold their hands and declare, "We will not fight when we do not believe in the necessity of war"? May not the people who believe in the repeal of the Conscription Law, because it is unconstitutional, express their opposition in word and by pen, in meetings and in other ways? . . .

Whatever your verdict, gentlemen, it cannot possibly affect the rising tide of discontent in this country against war which, despite all boasts, is a war for conquest and military power. Neither can it affect the ever increasing opposition to conscription which is a military and industrial yoke placed upon the necks of the American people. Least of all will your verdict affect those to whom human life is sacred, and who will not become a party to the world slaughter. Your verdict can only add to the opinion of the world as to whether or not justice and liberty are a living force in this country or a mere shadow of the past. Your verdict may, of course, affect us temporarily, in a physical sense—it can have no effect whatever upon our spirit. For even if we were convicted and found guilty and the penalty were that we be placed against a wall and shot dead, I should nevertheless cry out with the great Luther: "Here I am and here I stand and I cannot do otherwise."

And gentlemen, in conclusion let me tell you that my co-defendant, Mr. Berkman, was right when he said the eyes of America are upon you. They are upon you not because of sympathy for us or agreement with Anarchism. They are upon you because it must be decided sooner or later whether we are justified in telling people that we will give them democracy in Europe, when we have no democracy here? Shall free speech and free assemblage, shall criticism and opinion—which even the espionage bill did not include—be destroyed? Shall it be a shadow of the past, the great historic American past? Shall it be trampled underfoot by any detective, or policeman, anyone who decides upon it? Or shall free speech and free press and free assemblage continue to be the heritage of the American people?

Gentlemen of the jury, whatever your verdict will be, as far as we are concerned, nothing will be changed. I have held ideas all my life. I have publicly held my ideas for twenty-seven years. Nothing on earth would ever make me change my ideas except one thing; and that is, if you will prove to me that our position is wrong, untenable, or lacking in historic fact. But never would I change my ideas because I am found guilty. I may remind you of two great Americans, undoubtedly not unknown to you, gentlemen of the jury, Ralph Waldo Emerson and Henry David Thoreau. When Thoreau was placed in prison for refusing to pay taxes, he was visited by Ralph Waldo Emerson and Emerson said: "David, what are you doing in jail?" and Thoreau replied: "Ralph, what are you doing outside, when honest people are in jail for their ideals?". . . .

But whatever your decision, the struggle must go on. We are but the atoms in the incessant human struggle towards the light that shines in the darkness—the ideal of economic, political and spiritual liberation of mankind!

Source: Emma Goldman. "Address to the Jury." In *Voices of a People's History of the United States,* edited by Howard Zinn and Anthony Arnove, 2004, p. 292. New York: Seven Stories Press.

V. I. LENIN
(1870–1924)
"A Workers' and Peasants' Revolution"
Petrograd, Russia
October 25, 1917

Vladimir Ilyich Lenin was born in 1870 in Ulyanovsk, Russia, east of Moscow on the Volga River. His elder brother was executed for plotting against Czar Alexander III (r. 1881–94) in 1887. Lenin was drawn at the university to Marxism's sympathetic view of the urban lower classes (the *proletariat*, who had no ownership of the means of production and worked only for wages) and their struggle for betterment. He was soon expelled for revolutionary student activities. He became a lawyer but was exiled to Siberia in 1895 for five years for Marxist agitation in promoting class war among St. Petersburg's workers. He was forced to leave Russia to continue his plans for a socialist revolution (with the goal of abolishing economic exploitation), and in London he took control of the Bolshevik wing of the Russian Social Democratic Labor Party in 1906. He spent long years writing Marxist theory. He believed World War I (1914–18) to be an imperialistic war fought by capitalists. As he saw it, capitalism (where goods and services were produced for profit in a free market by private companies and individuals, rather than the state) had aggravated class inequality following the onset of the Industrial Revolution, and workers needed to unite to gain control over production under the leadership of a "vanguard party" of activists. In 1917 the "February Revolution" broke out in Russia while Czar Nicholas II (r. 1894–1917) was away commanding Russian forces, and Lenin returned to his homeland to oppose the Provisional Government. The czar abdicated the next month (he and his family were later murdered). In October, Lenin led the government's overthrow during the "October Revolution," and the next day delivered this speech outlining aims for his planned workers' government, composed of representatives from soviets (local workers' councils). In November he was elected premier of what was to become the Union of Soviet Socialist Republics. Lenin's party became the more radical Communist Party in 1918.

❧

Comrades, the workers' and peasants' revolution, about the necessity of which the Bolsheviks have always spoken, has been accomplished.

What is the significance of this workers' and peasants' revolution? Its significance is, first of all, that we shall have a Soviet government, our own organ of power, in which the bourgeoisie will have no share whatsoever. The oppressed masses will themselves create a power. The old state apparatus will be shattered to its foundations and a new administrative apparatus set up in the form of the Soviet organizations.

From now on, a new phase in the history of Russia begins, and this revolution, the third Russian revolution, should in the end lead to the victory of socialism.

One of our urgent tasks is to put an immediate end to the war. It is clear to everybody that in order to end this war, which is closely bound up with the present capitalist system, capital itself must be fought.

We shall be helped in this by the world working-class movement, which is already beginning to develop in Italy, Britain and Germany.

The proposal we make to international democracy for a just and immediate peace will everywhere awaken an ardent response among the international proletarian masses. All the secret treaties must be immediately published in order to strengthen the confidence of the proletariat.

Within Russia a huge section of the peasantry have said that they have played long enough with the capitalists, and will now march with the workers. A single decree put-

Vladimir Ilyich Lenin addresses the crowd welcoming him in Red Square, Moscow, in October 1917. It was the eve of the Russian Revolution. *(Ablestock)*

ting an end to landed proprietorship will win us the confidence of the peasants. The peasants will understand that the salvation of the peasantry lies only in an alliance with the workers. We shall institute genuine workers' control over production.

We have now learned to make a concerted effort. The revolution that has just been accomplished is evidence of this. We possess the strength of mass organization, which will overcome everything and lead the proletariat to the world revolution.

We must now set about building a proletarian socialist state in Russia.

Long live the world socialist revolution!

Source: Lenin, V. I. "Meeting of the Petrograd Soviet of Workers' and Soldiers' Deputies." Marxists Internet Archive. Available online. http://www.marxists.org/archive/lenin/works/1917/oct/25a.htm. Accessed December 17, 2007.

WOODROW WILSON
(1856–1924)
On Behalf of the League of Nations
Pueblo, Colorado, United States
September 25, 1919

The terrible Great War, now called World War I, ended on November 11, 1918, with the signing of the armistice in France. The war had caused the deaths of 10 million people and devastated wide swaths of the continent of Europe. More than 100,000 American soldiers had died. U.S. president Woodrow Wilson, a peace advocate who had reluctantly sent U.S. troops into the war in 1917, nearly three years after its start, attended the Paris Peace Conference, where victorious leaders wrote the 1919 Treaty of Versailles. Wilson's Fourteen Points, proposed in a speech in January 1918, had formed the basis of much of the deliberation for the treaty; the fourteenth point had been a recommendation for an international association of nations. The completed Treaty of Versailles indeed called for a League of Nations (which was succeeded after World War II [1939–45] by the United Nations). Wilson was an important figure in developing the League of Nations; he won the Nobel Peace Prize in 1919 for his work. In developing the league, the Paris Peace Conference hoped to create international security through disarmament and preventing war, and to provide the means to negotiate conflict between nations peacefully and diplomatically. Forty-two countries, including the victorious nations of World War I, joined the league in its first year, but the U.S. Senate was unwilling to ratify the treaty over concern whether Congress would still have the power to declare war. (The United States ultimately did not become a member.) Desperate to insure world peace, Wilson set out on an exhausting speaking tour from September 3 to September 25 across the United States to convince U.S. citizens to support the League of Nations. This speech in Pueblo, Colorado, often called "The Pueblo Address," was the last before he suffered a stroke that left him incapacitated in office. This is the peroration, or conclusion, of the speech.

〜❦〜

Again and again, my fellow citizens, mothers who lost their sons in France have come to me and, taking my hand, have shed tears upon it not only, but they added, "God bless you, Mr. President!"

Why, my fellow citizens, should they pray God to bless me? I advised the Congress of the United States to create the situation that led to the death of their sons. I ordered their sons overseas. I consented to their sons being put in the most difficult parts of the battle line, where death was certain, as in the impenetrable difficulties of the forest of Argonne.

Why should they weep upon my hand and call down the blessings of God upon me? Because they believe that their boys died for something that vastly transcends any of the immediate and palpable objects of the war. They believe, and they rightly believe, that their sons saved the liberty of the world. They believe that wrapped up with the liberty of the world is the continuous protection of that liberty by the concerted powers of all civilized people.

They believe that this sacrifice was made in order that other sons should not be called upon for a similar gift—the gift of life, the gift of all that died—and if we did not see this thing through, if we fulfilled the dearest present wish of Germany and now dissociated ourselves from those alongside whom we fought in the war, would not something of the halo go away from the gun over the mantelpiece, or the sword? Would not the old uniform lose something of its significance?

These men were crusaders. They were not going forth to prove the might of the United States. They were going forth to prove the might of justice and right, and all the

314

world accepted them as crusaders, and their transcendent achievement has made all the world believe in America as it believes in no other nation organized in the modern world.

There seems to me to stand between us and the rejection or qualification of this treaty the serried ranks of those boys in khaki, not only these boys who came home, but those dear ghosts that still deploy upon the fields of France.

My friends, on last Decoration Day I went on a beautiful hillside near Paris, where was located the cemetery of Suresnes, a cemetery given over to the burial of the American dead. Behind me on the slopes was rank upon rank of living American soldiers, and lying before me upon the levels of the plain was rank upon rank of departed American soldiers.

Right by the side of the stand where I spoke there was a little group of French women who had adopted those graves, had made themselves mothers of those dear ghosts by putting flowers every day upon those graves, taking them as their own sons, their own beloved, because they had died in the same cause—France was free and the world was free because America had come!

I wish some men in public life who are now opposing the settlement for which these men died could visit such a spot as that. I wish that the thought that comes out of those graves could penetrate their consciousness. I wish that they could feel the moral obligation that rests upon us not to go back on those boys, but to see the thing through, to see it through to the end and make good their redemption of the world. For nothing less depends upon this decision, nothing less than liberation and salvation of the world.

You will say, "Is the League an absolute guarantee against war?" No, I do not know any absolute guarantee against the errors of human judgment or the violence of human passion, but I tell you this: With a cooling space of nine months for human passion, not much of it will keep hot.

I had a couple of friends who were in the habit of losing their tempers, and when they lost their tempers they were in the habit of using very unparliamentary language. Some of their friends induced them to make a promise that they never would swear inside the town limits. When the impulse next came upon them, they took a streetcar to go out of town to swear, and by the time they got out of town they did not want to swear. They came back convinced that they were just what they were, a couple of unspeakable fools, and the habit of getting angry and of swearing suffered great inroads upon it by that experience.

Now, illustrating the great by the small, that is true of the passions of nations. It is true of the passions of men however you combine them. Give them space to cool off.

I ask you this: If it is not an absolute insurance against war, do you want no insurance at all? Do you want nothing? Do you want not only no probability that war will not recur, but the probability that it will recur? The arrangements of justice do not stand of themselves, my fellow citizens. The arrangements of this treaty are just, but they need the support of the combined power of the great nations of the world. And they will have that support. Now that the mists of this great question have cleared away, I believe that men will see the truth, eye to eye and face to face.

There is one thing that the American people always rise to and extend their hand to, and that is the truth of justice and of liberty and of peace. We have accepted the truth and we are going to be led by it, and it is going to lead us, and through us the world, out into pastures of quietness and peace such as the world never dreamed of before.

Source: Wilson, Woodrow. *Selected Literary and Political Papers and Addresses of Woodrow Wilson.* Vol. 2. New York: Grosset & Dunlap, 1926, p. 387.

MARIE CURIE
(1867–1934)
On Discovering Radium
Poughkeepsie, New York, United States
May 14, 1921

Usually known as "Madame Curie," Marie Curie was born Marie Skłowdowska in 1867 in Poland. Her father was a physicist and a teacher. She was a brilliant student in high school, but as a woman and a Pole in Russian-controlled Poland, she could not attend university at home; she went to France to study at the Sorbonne University in Paris. There she received advanced degrees in math and science, and she married Pierre Curie, a French physicist and Sorbonne professor. While extracting uranium from ore in the laboratory—radioactivity had only just been discovered in 1896 by Henri Becquerel, a French scientist—she suspected another, but unknown, element's presence. With her husband's and Becquerel's help, she discovered the existence of the far more radioactive radium and polonium, and they announced their find to the world in 1902. The couple shared the Nobel Prize in physics in 1903 with Becquerel for their work on radium and polonium. Pierre Curie died tragically in a traffic accident in 1906. Marie took over his university professorship in physics, and she continued her research in radioactivity. In 1911 she won the Nobel Prize in chemistry for further work isolating radium. She was the first person to win the Nobel twice, and the only winner to receive the prize in two different scientific disciplines. In 1921 Curie left France for a speaking tour of the United States to raise money for her research. Among other stops, her trip took her to Poughkeepsie, New York, to address students at Vassar College, which was then a women's college. Curie was delighted to encourage the young women to continue their studies in science. Curie died in 1934 from a radiation-caused illness; at the time, it was not known that exposure to radiation was a health risk.

❧

I could tell you many things about radium and radioactivity and it would take a long time. But as we cannot do that, I shall only give you a short account of my early work about radium. Radium is no more a baby, it is more than twenty years old, but the conditions of the discovery were somewhat peculiar, and so it is always of interest to remember them and to explain them.

We must go back to the year 1897. Professor Curie and I worked at that time in the laboratory of the school of Physics and Chemistry where Professor Curie held his lectures. I was engaged in some work on uranium rays, which had been discovered two years before by Professor Becquerel.

I spent some time in studying the way of making good measurements of the uranium rays, and then I wanted to know if there were other elements, giving out rays of the same kind. So I took up a work about all known elements, and their compounds and found that uranium compounds are active and also all thorium compounds, but other elements were not found active, nor were their compounds. As for the uranium and thorium compounds, I found that they were active in proportion to their uranium or thorium content. The more uranium or thorium, the greater the activity, the activity being an atomic property of the elements, uranium and thorium.

Then I took up measurements of minerals and I found that several of those which contain uranium or thorium or both were active. But then the activity was not what I could expect, it was greater than for uranium or thorium compounds like the oxides which are almost entirely composed of these elements.

Then I thought that there should be in the minerals some unknown element having a much greater radioactivity than uranium or thorium. And I wanted to find and to separate that element, and I settled to that work with Professor Curie. We thought it would be done in several weeks or months, but it was not so. It took many years of hard work to finish that task. There was not one new element, there were several of them. But the most important is radium, which could be separated in a pure state.

Now, the special interest of radium is in the intensity of its rays which several million times greater than the uranium rays. And the effects of the rays make the radium so important. If we take a practical point of view, then the most important property of the rays is the production of physiological effects on the cells of the human organism. These effects may be used for the cure of several diseases. Good results have been obtained in many cases. What is considered particularly important is the treatment of cancer. The medical utilization of radium makes it necessary to get that element in sufficient quantities. And so a factory of radium was started to begin with in France, and later in America where a big quantity of ore named carnotite is available. America does produce many grams of radium every year, but the price is still very high because the quantity of radium contained in the ore is so small. The radium is more than a hundred thousand times dearer than gold.

But we must not forget that when radium was discovered no one knew that it would prove useful in hospitals. The work was one of pure science. And this is a proof that scientific work must not be considered from the point of view of the direct usefulness of it. It must be done for itself, for the beauty of science, and then there is always the chance that a scientific discovery may become like the radium a benefit for humanity.

The scientific history of radium is beautiful. The properties of the rays have been studied very closely. We know that particles are expelled from radium with a very great velocity near to that of the light. We know that the atoms of radium are destroyed by expulsion of these particles, some of which are atoms of helium. And in that way it has been proved that the radioactive elements are constantly disintegrating and that they produce at the end ordinary elements, principally helium and lead. That is, as you see, a theory of transformation of atoms which are not stable, as was believed before, but may undergo spontaneous changes.

Radium is not alone in having these properties. Many having other radio-elements are known already, the polonium, the mesothorium, the radiothorium, the actinium. We know also radioactive gases, named emanations. There is a great variety of substances and effects in radioactivity. There is always a vast field left to experimentation and I hope that we may have some beautiful progress in the following years.

It is my earnest desire that some of you should carry on this scientific work and keep for your ambition the determination to make a permanent contribution to science.

Source: Curie, Marie. "The Discovery of Radium." Address by Madame M. Curie at Vassar College, May 14, 1921. Ellen S. Richards Monographs No. 2. Poughkeepsie, N.Y.: Vassar College, 1921.

MOHANDAS KARAMCHAND GANDHI
(1869–1948)
"I Want to Avoid Violence"
Ahmedabad, India
March 18, 1922

Mohandas K. Gandhi's campaign of civil disobedience in South Africa succeeded in 1914 with passage of the Indians Relief Bill, which eased repressive laws against Indians. He returned to India, a British colony, determined to achieve self-government for his homeland through a noncooperation movement. He told students at the Madras YMCA in 1915, "It will be your privilege to conquer the conquerors, not by shedding blood but by sheer force of spiritual predominance." In 1919 Britain proclaimed the Rowlatt Act, and other restrictive laws, to curtail people's civil rights and allow authorities extreme powers to detain those engaging in independence activities. The next month, on April 19, riots broke out in the Punjab, culminating in a massacre of hundreds of unarmed Indians celebrating a Sikh festival at Jallianwala Bagh (a public garden in Amritsar) by the British Indian Army. Gandhi became leader of the Indian National Congress in late 1921. He was horrified in February 1922 when demonstrators clashed violently with police in Chauri Chaura, murdering 22 policemen; he temporarily halted his campaign of civil disobedience to rethink it. Shortly after, he was arrested for publishing three articles critical of British rule in his newspaper *Young India,* and he was prosecuted for "bringing contempt and exciting disaffection towards His Majesty's Government." On March 18, at the Great Trial, as it was afterward known, the British prosecutor read excerpts from the articles, paraphrasing Gandhi that, "the duty of a non-cooperator was to preach disaffection towards the existing government and to prepare the country for civil disobedience." Gandhi pleaded guilty, and then he addressed the court. The British judge observed that Gandhi was "in a different category from any person I have ever tried or am likely to have to try, . . . a man of high ideals and of noble and of even saintly life." He had no choice, he said, but to sentence Gandhi according to the law—six years in jail. (He was released after two years.) Gandhi was given the revered title Mahatma by his followers, meaning "great soul."

❧

I would like to state that I entirely endorse the learned Advocate-General's remarks in connection with my humble self. I think that he was entirely fair to me in all the statements that he has made, because it is very true and I have no desire whatsoever to conceal from this Court the fact that to preach disaffection towards the existing system of Government has become almost a passion with me . . .

I want to avoid violence. Non-violence is the first article of my faith. It is also the last article of my creed. But I had to make my choice. I had either to submit to a system which I considered had done an irreparable harm to my country, or incur the risk of the mad fury of my people bursting forth when they understood the truth from my lips. I know that my people have sometimes gone mad; I am deeply sorry for it. I am here to submit not to a light penalty but to the highest penalty. I do not ask for mercy. I do not ask for any extenuating act of clemency. . . .

I owe it perhaps to the Indian public and to the public in England, to placate which this prosecution is mainly taken up, that I should explain why from a staunch loyalist and co-operator I have become an uncompromising disaffectionist and non-co-operator. To the Court, too, I should say why I plead guilty to the charge of promoting disaffection towards the Government established by law in India.

My public life began in 1893 in South Africa in troubled weather. My first contact with British authority in that country was not of a happy character. I discovered that as a man and as an Indian I had no rights. More correctly, I discovered that I had no rights as a man because I was an Indian.

But I was not baffled. I thought that this treatment of Indians was an excrescence upon a system that was intrinsically and mainly good. I gave the Government my voluntary and hearty co-operation, criticizing it fully where I felt it was faulty, but never wishing its destruction.

Consequently when the existence of the Empire was threatened in 1899 by the Boer challenge, I offered my services to it, raised a volunteer ambulance corps and served at several actions that took place for the relief of Ladysmith. Similarly in 1906, at the time of the Zulu revolt, I raised a stretcher-bearer party and served till the end of the "rebellion." On both these occasions I received medals and was even mentioned in dispatches. For my work in South Africa I was given by Lord Hardinge a Kaiser-i-Hind Gold Medal. When the war broke out in 1914 between England and Germany, I raised a volunteer ambulance corps in London consisting of the then resident Indians in London, chiefly students. Its work was acknowledged by the authorities to be valuable. Lastly, in India, when a special appeal was made at the War Conference in Delhi in 1917 by Lord Chelmsford for recruits, I struggled at the cost of my health to raise a corps in Kheda and the response was being made when the hostilities ceased and orders were received that no more recruits were wanted. In all these efforts at service, I was actuated by the belief that it was possible by such services to gain a status of full equality in the Empire for my countrymen.

The first shock came in the shape of the Rowlatt Act, a law designed to rob the people of all real freedom. I felt called upon to lead an intensive agitation against it. Then followed the Punjab horrors beginning with the massacre at Jallianwala Bagh and culminating in crawling orders, public floggings and other indescribable humiliations. I discovered too that the plighted word of the Prime Minister to the Mussalmans of India regarding the integrity of Turkey and the holy places of Islam was not likely to be fulfilled. . . . The Punjab crime was white-washed and most culprits went not only unpunished but remained in service and some continued to draw pensions from the Indian revenue, and in some cases were even rewarded. I saw, too, that not only did the reforms not mark a change of heart, but they were only a method of further draining India of her wealth and of prolonging her servitude.

I came reluctantly to the conclusion that the British connection had made India more helpless than she ever was before, politically and economically. A disarmed India has no power of resistance against any aggressor if she wanted to engage in an armed conflict with him. So much is this the case that some of our best men consider that India must take generations before she can achieve the Dominion status. She has become so poor that she has little power of resisting famines. Before the British advent India spun and

RHETORICAL DEVICE

Distinctio: Explaining a word or expression for the listeners' understanding.

Some of us . . . set ourselves out to prove to our colonial rulers that we had become "civilized;" and by that we meant that we had abandoned everything connected with our own past and learnt to imitate only European ways. —*Julius Nyerere*

Non-violence implies voluntary submission to the penalty for non-co-operation with evil. —*Mohandas Gandhi*

Webster, Worcester, and Bouvier all define a citizen to be a person in the United States, entitled to vote and hold office. —*Susan B. Anthony*

wove in her millions of cottages just the supplement she needed for adding to her meagre agricultural resources. This cottage industry, so vital for India's existence, has been ruined by incredibly heartless and inhuman processes as described by English witnesses.

Little do town-dwellers know how the semi-starved masses of Indians are slowly sinking to lifelessness. Little do they know that their miserable comfort represents the brokerage they get for the work they do for the foreign exploiter, that the profits and the brokerage are sucked from the masses. Little do they realize that the Government established by law in British India is carried on for this exploitation of the masses. No sophistry, no jugglery in figures can explain away the evidence that the skeletons in many villages present to the naked eye. I have no doubt whatsoever that both England and the town dwellers of India will have to answer, if there is a God above, for this crime against humanity which is perhaps unequalled in history.

The law itself in this country has been used to serve the foreign exploiter. My unbiased examination of the Punjab Martial Law cases has led me to believe that at least ninety-five per cent of convictions were wholly bad. My experience of political cases in India leads one to the conclusion that in nine out of every ten cases the condemned men were totally innocent. Their crime consisted in love of their country. In ninety-nine cases out of a hundred, justice has been denied to Indians as against Europeans in the Courts of India. This is not an exaggerated picture. It is the experience of almost every Indian who has had anything to do with such cases. In my opinion, the administration of the law is thus prostituted consciously or unconsciously for the benefit of the exploiter.

The greatest misfortune is that Englishmen and their Indian associates in the administration of the country do not know that they are engaged in the crime I have attempted to describe. I am satisfied that many English and Indian officials honestly believe that they are administering one of the best systems devised in the world and that India is making steady though slow progress. . . .

I have no personal ill will against any single administrator, much less can I have any disaffection towards the King's person. But I hold it to be a virtue to be disaffected towards a Government which in its totality has done more harm to India than any previous system. India is less manly under the British rule than she ever was before. Holding such a belief, I consider it to be a sin to have affection for the system. And it has been a precious privilege for me to be able to write what I have in the various articles tendered in evidence against me.

In fact, I believe that I have rendered a service to India and England by showing in non-co-operation the way out of the unnatural state in which both are living. In my humble opinion, non-co-operation with evil is as much a duty as is co-operation with good. But in the past, non-co-operation has been deliberately expressed in violence to the evildoer. I am endeavoring to show to my countrymen that violent non-co-operation only multiplies evil and that, as evil can only be sustained by violence, withdrawal of support of evil requires complete abstention from violence. Non-violence implies voluntary submission to the penalty for non-co-operation with evil.

I am here, therefore, to invite and submit cheerfully to the highest penalty that can be inflicted upon me for what in law is a deliberate crime and what appears to me to be the highest duty of a citizen. The only course open to you, the Judge, is either to resign your post and thus dissociate yourself from evil, if you feel that the law you are called upon to administer is an evil and that in reality I am innocent; or to inflict on me the severest penalty if you believe that the system and the law you are assisting to administer are good for the people of this country and that my activity is, therefore, injurious to the public weal.

Source: Mahatma Gandhi. "A Plea for the Severest Penalty upon His Conviction for Sedition." In *The Law as Literature,* edited by Louis Blom-Cooper, 96. London: The Bodley Head, Ltd., 1961.

MUSTAFA KEMAL ATATÜRK
(1881–1938)
"Women and Men Will Walk Side by Side"
Izmir, Turkey
January 31, 1923

The end of World War I (1914–18) brought the Ottoman Empire's collapse and the birth of modern Turkey. Military hero Mustafa Kemal (he had commanded troops at the 1915 Battle of Gallipoli) emerged to lead

Mustafa Kemal Atatürk led a radical restructuring of Turkish society, including giving women the right to vote and hold public office. *(Ablestock)*

the Turkish nationalist movement. He organized the first Turkish Grand National Assembly in 1920, and he was its first president. Peace with the Allies (Greece, Britain, France, Italy, Japan, and Romania) finally came at the Treaty of Lausanne in 1923. Kemal was convinced that Turkey should modernize, and that a radical restructuring—Westernizing—of Turkish society and political life would be required; he eventually revolutionized an entire society in rapid time. He abolished the medieval sultanate (hereditary rulers) and caliphate (religious rulers) to create a secular (without an official national religion) state by 1924, with leaders elected by the people. While not renouncing Islam, Islamic courts and schools were replaced with secular ones. In 1923, while running for president, he married a socially prominent, modern, and well-educated young Turkish woman, Latife Uşakligil. Two days afterward, his wife beside him, he gave a campaign speech from which comes this excerpt. He became president of Turkey on October 29, 1923, the day Turkey became a republic. Five years later, he instituted a change from the Arabic alphabet to a simpler Turkish alphabet using modified Roman letters; with the new phonetic system, boys and girls could learn to read easily. In 1934 Turkish women received the right to vote and hold public office—years before women in France or Switzerland. As many as 18 women entered Parliament the next year. (His daughter became an airplane pilot.) In contrast with other Muslim countries, Turkish women now had full rights with men. In 1934 the surname law required all Turks to take a second name. Kemal took the name Atatürk, meaning "father of the Turks," and he is considered the father of the nation by the Turkish people.

If a society contents itself with modernizing only one of the sexes, it will be weakened by more than half. A nation that seeks progress and civilization must accept this. The reason for the lack of success of our society lies in the indifference towards our women.

Man comes into the world to live as long as his destiny allows him. To live is to act. So, if an organ of a society acts while the other lies idle, then it means that society is paralyzed. A society must accept all the conditions and necessities on which its success in life depends. So, if science and technology are necessary for our society, our men and women must equally master them.

As you know, division of labor is necessary in social life as it is in all the other fields. In general division of labor, women should not only carry out their duties, but they should also take part in efforts for the prosperity and welfare of the society. The most important duty of women is motherhood. If we remember that a child's first school is his mother's bosom, we can understand the utmost importance of this duty better.

Our nation has decided to be a powerful one. One of the ways to ensure a powerful nation is to make sure our women are competent in every aspect. For that, our women will acquire scientific and technical information, and complete every phase of education that men complete. Thus women and men will walk side by side in social life helping and protecting each other.

Source: Atatürk, Kemal. "Turkish Women and Their Rights." Republic of Turkey Ministry of Culture. Available online. http://www.kultur.gov.tr/EN/BelgeGoster.aspx?17A16AE30572D 313AC8287D72AD903BED 47E923BC030BA43. Accessed December 18, 2007. Permission of the Ministry of Culture and Tourism, Ankara, Turkey.

ADOLF HITLER
(1889–1945)
"The Drummer of National Germany"
Düsseldorf, Germany
January 27, 1932

Following World War I (1914–18), Imperial Germany was dismantled and its new republican leaders compelled to sign the 1919 Treaty of Versailles. Under the treaty, Germany assumed the blame for the war (the infamous "war guilt clause") and was forced to pay reparations totaling billions of dollars to the victorious allies (France, United States, Italy, Belgium, and Britain). Together, these treaty terms crippled Germany's political and socioeconomic well-being. Onto this desolate stage stepped Adolf Hitler, an Austrian by birth who had fought for the Germans during World War I. Twice wounded, he emerged from the war believing Germany's ills had been brought about not by leadership blunders, but rather by Jews and Communists who had conspired to destroy the German people. To "save" Germany, Hitler joined the German Workers Party (shortly renamed National Socialist German Workers Party), a right-wing organization whose members became mesmerized by Hitler's demagogic oratory and promises of a better life. Although this Nazi Party grew slightly during the 1920s, it was only with the Great Depression (1929–33) that Hitler's vitriolic ideology reached a wider audience—illustrated by this speech to the Düsseldorf Industrial Club—and translated into votes in Germany's parliament, the Reichstag. In addition to promising the German people employment and food, Hitler prophesied the rebirth of Germany as an international superpower, one of pure Aryan (non-Jewish North European) blood that would gain more living space—*Lebensraum*—by conquering lands inhabited by "inferior" races (e.g., Slavs, Jews, and Roma). As World War II (1939–45) was to show, Hitler's theories were translated into reality as millions of people were forcibly relocated or murdered to effect the Führer's plans. (Führer, meaning "the leader," was a title he assumed.) In the end, Hitler himself became a casualty of the violence, committing suicide in Berlin on April 30, 1945, to escape Soviet troops poised to conquer the city.

***

People say to me so often: "You are only the drummer of national Germany." And supposing that I were only the drummer? It would today be a far more statesmanlike achievement to drum once more into this German people a new faith than gradually to squander the only faith they have. . . . The more you bring a people back into the sphere of faith, of ideals, the more will it cease to regard material distress as the one and only thing that counts. And the weightiest evidence for the truth of that statement is our own German people.

We will never forget that the German people waged wars of religion for 150 years with prodigious devotion, that hundreds of thousands of men once left their plot of land, their property, and their belongings simply for an ideal, simply for a conviction. We will never forget that during those 150 years there was no trace of even an ounce of material interest. Then you will understand how mighty is the force of an idea, of an ideal. Only so can you comprehend how it is that in our movement today hundreds of thousands of young men are prepared to risk their lives to withstand our opponents.

I know quite well, gentlemen, that when National Socialists march through the streets and suddenly in the evening there arises a tumult and a commotion, then the bourgeois draws back the window-curtain, looks out, and says: "Once again my night's rest is disturbed: no more sleep for me. Why must these Nazis always be so provocative and run about the place at night?" Gentlemen, if everyone thought like that, then, true enough, no one's sleep at night would be disturbed, but then also the bourgeois today would not be able to venture into the street. If everyone thought in that way, if these young folk had no ideal to move them and drive them forward, then certainly they would gladly be rid of these nightly fights.

But remember that it means sacrifice when today many hundreds of thousands of SA and SS men of the National Socialist movement have every day to mount on their lorries, protect meetings, undertake marches, sacrifice themselves night after night and then come back in the grey dawn to workshop and factory, or as unemployed to take the pittance of the dole: it means sacrifice when from the little they possess they have further to buy their uniforms, their shirts, their badges, yes and even pay their own fares. Believe me, there is already in all this the force of an ideal—a great ideal!

And if the whole German *volk* today had the same faith in its vocation as these hundreds of thousands, if the whole *volk* possessed this idealism, Germany would stand in the eyes of the world otherwise than she stands now! For our situation in the world in its fatal effects is but the result of our own under-estimate of German strength.

Only when we have once more changed this fatal undervaluation of ourselves can Germany take advantage of the political possibilities which, if we look far enough into the future, can place German life once more upon a natural and secure basis—and that means either new living space and the development of a great internal market or protection of German economic life against the world without and utilization of all the concentrated strength of Germany.

The labor resources of our people, the capacities, we have them already; no one can deny that we are industrious. But we must first refashion the political preconditions: without that, industry and capacity, diligence and economy are in the last resort of no avail; an oppressed nation will not be able to spend on its own welfare even the fruits of its own economy but must sacrifice them on the altar of exactions and of tribute.

And so in contrast to our own official Government, I see no hope for the resurrection of Germany if we regard the foreign politics of Germany as the primary factor: our primary need is the restoration of a sound national German body politic armed to strike. In order to realize this end, thirteen years ago I founded the National Socialist Movement: that Movement I have led during the last twelve years and I hope that one day it will accomplish this task and that, as the fairest result of its struggle, it will leave behind it a German body politic completely renewed internally, intolerant of anyone who sins against the *volk* and its interests, intolerant of anyone who will not acknowledge its vital interests or who opposes them, intolerant of and pitiless towards anyone who shall attempt once more to destroy or undermine this body politic, and yet ready for friendship and peace with anyone who has a wish for peace and friendship.

Source: Hitler, Adolf. "Address to the Industry Club." In *The Weimar Republic Sourcebook*, edited by Anton Kaes, Martin Jay, and Edward Dimendberg, 138. Berkeley: University of California Press, 1994.

STEPHEN S. WISE
(1874–1949)
Madison Square Garden Address
March 27, 1933
New York, New York, United States

American Reform Rabbi Stephen Samuel Wise was born in Hungary but lived most of his life in New York City. He helped organize the American Jewish Congress in 1918 (which defended religious and human rights for Jews and others), worked to interest American Jews in Zionism (the movement to reestablish a Jewish homeland in Israel), and served as the first president of the World Jewish Congress. In 1933 reports of atrocities against Jews under Adolf Hitler's Third Reich prompted the American Jewish Congress to organize a rally in New York's immense Madison Square Garden sporting arena. As the main speaker, Wise addressed the huge crowd, asking the German government—Hitler had been named chancellor just two months earlier—to end its anti-Semitic stance and stop scapegoating Jews for the harsh penalties forced on Germany after World War I (1914–18). Hitler only stepped up Nazi attacks against Germany's Jewish citizens. Wise and many Jewish activists grew fearful that agitating on behalf of European Jews might also make American anti-Semitism worse. Wise became excessively cautious, and he has been criticized frequently for letting his close friendship with U.S. president Franklin Delano Roosevelt get in the way of pressuring Roosevelt to do more to save European Jews. In any case, before the United States entered World War II (1939–45) in 1941, the government was more concerned with staying neutral than with granting immigration visas to fleeing Jews, and U.S. officials did not want to accept European refugees. The U.S. State Department kept news of Nazi atrocities quiet for several years, as well. By 1942 approximately 2 million European Jews had been killed by the Nazis. The next year, Wise lost leadership of the American Jewish Congress (to Abba Hillel Silver) because he had agreed to downplay Jewish interest in a homeland in Palestine for the duration of the war. The U.S. government's War Refugee Board (which U.S. secretary of the treasury Henry Morgenthau and U.S. interior secretary Harold Ickes persuaded Roosevelt to establish to assist refugees from European countries under Nazi occupation) was not created until 1944, the year before World War II ended, although it did succeed in rescuing 200,000 Jews, mostly from Hungary.

The American Jewish Congress has called but not caused this protest meeting tonight. The American Jewish Congress has not aroused this protest against anti-Jewish wrongs in Germany but has brought within the bounds of law and order an oceanic tide of indignation against the outrages inflicted upon Jews in these days under the Nazi government.

Not out of the bitterness of anger but out of the deepest of sorrow and the spirit of compassion do we speak tonight. For Germany we have asked and we continue to ask justice and even magnanimity from her erstwhile foes. We demand in the sight of humanity the right for Germany from the nations and the right from Germany for the Jewish people. No wrong under the heavens could be greater than to make German Jews scapegoats because Germany has grievances against the nations. We who would secure justice from the nations for Germany and justice to Jews from Germany affirm tonight that Germany cannot hope to secure justice through injustice to its Jewish people.

This protest of tonight is not against the German people whom we honor and revere and cherish. How could we, of the household of Israel, fail to cherish and honor the German people, one of the great peoples of earth, a people that has made monumental indeed eternal contributions to human well being in the domains of religion, literature, and the arts. How could we fail to cherish and to revere the people of Goethe and Schiller, Immanuel Kant and Hegel, Beethoven and Wagner, Heine and Einstein.

This protest of tonight is not against the political program of Germany, for Germany is master within her own household, but solely against the present anti-Jewish policy of the Nazi government. There is no need for our German-born neighbors in America nor for our fellow Jews in Germany to appeal to us to avoid an anti-Jewish demonstration. We are not against Germany, and it is an unforgivable calumny to declare that we are *"Deutschfeindlich."* We are the friends of and believers in Germany. Germany at its highest, Germany at its truest, the German nation at its noblest. Because we are the friends of Germany, because we have inextinguishable faith in the basic love for righteousness of the German people, we appeal to Germany representing as this meeting does Protestants, Catholics, Jews in the name of America, which has been stirred as rarely before against wrongs perpetrated upon Jews.

We know that it is not easy to cancel the Nazi program of thirteen years, and still we know that it can be done. A dictatorship is omnipotent and above all the German people at its best will support the government in every honest effort to avert the shame on the medievalization of German Jewry. If the Nazi government will use for the suppression of the anti-Semitic campaign in Germany $\frac{1}{100}$ or $\frac{1}{1000}$ part of the vigor and rigor with which it has suppressed differing or, as it believes, dangerous political parties, anti-Semitism will perish in Germany.

We understand the plea and the plaint of our brother Jews in Germany. They are German patriots who love their Fatherland and have had reason to love it. Some of their leaders are under the impact of panic and terror, others under some form of compulsion, in any event the compulsion of a great fear if not actual coercion. Do they appeal to the Nazi Government to bring about a cessation of its anti-Jewish campaign as they have appealed to us to end our protest? We have no quarrel with our Jewish brothers in Germany and their leaders, but their policy of uncomplaining assent and of super-cautious silence has borne evil fruit. They who have virtually been silent through the years of anti-Jewish propaganda cannot be followed by us as the wisest of counselors. And if things are to be worse because of our protest, if there are to be new penalties and new reprisals in Germany, which I cannot bring myself to believe, then humbly and sorrowfully we bow our heads in the presence of the tragic fate that threatens and once again appeal to the public opinion of mankind and to the conscience of Christendom to save civilization from the shame that may be imminent.

To those leaders of German Jewry who declare the present anti-Jewish situation in Germany is a local German question, we call attention to the words of Abraham Lincoln. Defenders of slavery urged and excused slavery on the ground that it was local. Lincoln's answer was SLAVERY IS LOCAL BUT FREEDOM IS NATIONAL. The conscience of humanity has made a world problem of the present situation of the Jews. We lay down no conditions tonight, we make no stipulations, we do not even urge demands. But we do affirm certain elementary axioms of civilization. The Jews of the world, no more than the Jews of Germany, do not demand exceptional treatment or privileged position or favored status for themselves. We do not even ask for rights. We ask only for the right. We demand the right.

What are these elementary maxims of civilization as we call them? The immediate cessation of anti-Semitic activities and propaganda in Germany, including an end to the policy of racial discrimination against and of economic exclusion of Jews from the life of Germany. That is Jewish life, and the human rights of Jews must be safeguarded. One other absolutely reasonable and just axiom rather than demand: The revocation of all special measures already taken against Jewish non-nationals and their equal treatment with all other non-nationals in Germany. Which of these demands shall we abate? Whatever be the threat of reprisal, none of these can be withdrawn or altered or moderated without insult to Germany and without tragic self-stultification on the part of Jews.

But it must be made clear in the hearing of men that even if life and human rights are to be safeguarded, there must not be a substitution of the status of helotry for violence. Such substitution will not satisfy us nor satisfy the aroused conscience of humankind even though Jews in Germany must sink into the horror of seeming acquiescence. Every economic discrimination is a form of violence. Every racial exclusion is violence. To say that there will be no pogroms is not enough. A dry and bloodless economic pogrom remains violence and force.

Hear the word of a great English statesman, of one who did as much as any other Englishman of his day to make England mighty: "Providence would deal good or ill fortune to nations according as they dealt well or ill by the Jews." This is not a warning but a prophecy. May the German people merit the fulfillment of this prophecy of good fortune by dealing well and justly and as a Christian nation by the Jews.

I close as I began. We are not met in the spirit of bitterness, hatred, or revenge. We do not desire that the German people be punished because of the unwisdom of the measures and the injustice of some practices of its government. Whatever nations may ask in the spirit of reparation and reprisal, we who are Jews know that our spirit must be in consonance with the high tradition of Jewish forbearance and Jewish forgiveness. But there must be no further reprisals against our fellow Jews, no penalizing them as German hostages because the conscience of the world utters its mighty protest. God help the German people to be equal to themselves.

Source: Israel, Steve, and Seth Forman, eds. *Great Jewish Speeches throughout History.* Northvale, N.J.: Jason Aronson, 1994, p. 89.

ERNST TOLLER
(1893–1939)
"The Arm of Hitler"
Edinburgh, Scotland
June 19, 1934

On May 10, 1933, the National Socialist German Workers (Nazi) Party, a party steeped in anti-Semitism, held book burnings in several German cities; more than 20,000 books were burned in Berlin alone. Two weeks after the bonfires, the international writers' group, P.E.N. (for Poets, Essayists, Novelists), held their first congress in Dubrovnik, Yugoslavia (present-day Croatia). A German playwright named Ernst Toller planned to speak. Toller had spent six years in jail for communist revolutionary involvement, and he had been exiled. The German delegation, all Nazis, created chaos trying to prevent the Jewish Toller from speaking. P.E.N. president H. G. Wells held a vote and Toller was allowed to continue; the Germans walked out. After the burning of the German Reichstag, or parliament building, the following February 27, 1934, allegedly by communists (but possibly by Nazis themselves), Adolf Hitler, the head of the Nazi Party, arrested many German writers, most especially communists and anarchists. At the P.E.N. congress the next year, Toller delivered an emotional survey of the treatment of writers imprisoned by Hitler, and he implored the audience to agitate on their behalf. Among political prisoners he mentions: Erich Mühsam was a German-Jewish anarchist poet and playwright who ridiculed Hitler; he was arrested in February 1933, sent to concentration camps, and murdered on July 9, 1934. Peace activist Carl von Ossietzky was imprisoned for writing articles exposing Germany's rearming in violation of the 1919 Treaty of Versailles that ended World War I (1914–18); he won the Nobel Peace Prize in 1935. Ernst Thälmann headed the German Communist Party until 1933 when he was thrown in prison, then shot at Buchenwald, one of the largest concentration camps, in 1944. Fritz Gerlich, a journalist who criticized Hitler, was murdered at Dachau, a concentration camp northwest of Munich, on July 1, 1934. Werner Hirsch, a communist newspaper publisher, died in exile in the USSR. Five years later, depressed at hearing of family members sent to concentration camps, Toller committed suicide in New York.

⁂

Permit me first of all to thank you in the name of the writers who have been persecuted and driven from Germany for the kindly welcome that the P.E.N. Club has extended to us.

Although governments may compromise and even conclude alliance with the powers of unrighteousness, the writer obeys only the commands of the spirit of truth and he should never, however much they may threaten, bow down before the powers of violence of the day.

At a time when every day we hear of new outrages, new cruelties, new oppressions, at a time when the misery of millions steadily increases, when tens of thousands of fugitives wander up and down the world without hope and under unjust condemnation, at a time when a new and a terrible war threatens civilization, the conscience of the world becomes dulled and only a few remember the fate of the writers who languish in prison for their faith. These men have already been for seventeen months under arrest. They have never been brought to trial and judged. They have committed no offence against the laws of their land. They are in prison simply because in former years they wrote what displeases the present masters of Germany.

Among these writers are Carl von Ossietzky, Ludwig Renn, Thälmann, Erich Mühsam, Fritz Gerlich, Fritz Küster, Werner Hirsch, Klaus Neudrantz, Carl Mierendorff, Willy Bendel, and several others. And under what conditions—conditions that it is hardly possible for you to realize—do these men live! Abandoned to the hate of tyrants, exposed to the violence of their servile agents, these men live a life of daily physical, intellectual and spiritual privation, often made the victims of brutal ill treatment.

If one asks their oppressors why and for what purpose these men are in prison, the answer is given that they were dangerous elements in society and must be trained to be useful members of it.

And how are they trained? By many hours of military drill, by meaningless manual labour. Men of fifty and sixty years of age are urged and driven up and down the barrack squares, have to do physical drill until they are unable to rise.

No, the motive for their imprisonment is very different. The real cause of it is the desire for revenge on the helpless, the hate of the idea of freedom, the fear of that power which is given to these men (of pillorying the forces that assail the spirit) by the power of the word.

I could read you reports of eyewitnesses on what happens in concentration camps that would overwhelm you with shame that men could so humiliate men. But there is no need to do so. Enough has been written in books and in the press.

Anyone who wanted to hear what was happening has been able to hear; anyone who is willing to know, cannot but know. He who has not heard, has not wanted to hear; he who does not know, has not wanted to know; he who has forgotten has sought to forget.

Many have heard, many know and yet they forget. But to forget is to sin against the spirit. If it were not for the fact that millions have forgotten the war, the danger of a new war would not be so tremendous, the young would not now be taught that war is a glorious thing.

To forget augurs lack of imagination; to forget augurs lack of heart.

We must never forget these men in prison who stood by our side and lived and worked for a common end, who served the cause of peace and sought to make the world a brighter, a happier, a juster place.

The loud exultation of their enemies cannot drown the dull complaint of these suffering men. Let us think of them, those who will not be allowed to know that we think of them as brothers and share their shame and sorrow.

If we really do believe in the power of the word—and as writers we do believe in the power of the word—we ought not to be silent. Even dictatorships bow before public opinion. If world opinion had not made its strong demand, if numberless people had not shown their sympathy, if great newspapers like the *Times*, the *Observer*, and the *Manchester Guardian* had not waged a brave fight, if men who were true to the great traditions of their nations had not lent their aid, would the innocent Dimitroff have been saved from the scaffold?

Jewish playwright Ernst Toller confronted Nazi demands in 1933 that the international writers' organization P.E.N. exclude Jews. Fear was the topic of Toller's speech that year. P.E.N.'s president, H. G. Wells, author of *The Time Machine* and *War of the Worlds,* advised the German chapter to resign "until they should be willing to welcome a member without making his race or politics a bar."
(Library of Congress)

RHETORICAL DEVICE

Praeteritio: The speaker omits, or pretends to omit, material. This may emphasize it as well as allow the speaker to avoid it.

Of the military exploits by which our various possessions were acquired,
or of the energy with which we, or our fathers, drove back
the tide of war, Hellenic or Barbarian, I will not speak,
for the tale would be long and is familiar to you. —*Pericles*

I could read you reports of eyewitnesses on what happens in
concentration camps that would overwhelm you with shame that men
could so humiliate men. But there is no need to do so.
Enough has been written in books and in the press. —*Ernst Toller*

I could tell you many things about radium and radioactivity
and it would take a long time. —*Marie Curie*

I might mention many occasions, Fathers of the Senate, when kings and peoples
under the influence of wrath or pity have made errors of judgment;
but I prefer to remind you of times when our forefathers, resisting
the dictates of passion, have acted justly and in order. —*Julius Caesar*

Often we doubt of the effect, of the value of what we do. Examples such as that ought to give us strength and confidence and prevent us wearying of well doing.

No, we who are now in exile, we must not become weary. If we do, we shamefully surrender: We abandon that Germany of which you will hear nothing in the official press, the Germany that suffers, the Germany that is greater and stronger than you think.

I speak here as a writer to writers. If I did not, I should feel compelled to recall to you those others who are not writers, those workers, pastors, Jews, who have committed no other crime than this, that because of their convictions they could not become National Socialists.

The dictatorship is not content with persecuting writers and suppressing their books in Germany; it persecutes those who have fled from its wrath to foreign countries. The writers and publishers who are exiles from Germany are threatened by special measures taken by the Hitlerite dictatorship. Pressure is brought to bear on every government in the world if it seems weak enough or complacent enough. The chief object of the pressure is to obtain the deportation of the émigré writer to Germany. If that cannot be obtained, then the attempt is made to get him expelled from the land in which he has taken refuge, after he has been condemned *in contumaciam* to imprisonment and his books forbidden.

I recall to your memory the case in Holland of Liepmann, the author of *Murder Made in Germany*. Not long ago another country decided that all printed matter should be banned if it was likely to endanger good relations with other countries. That goes far beyond any of the requirements of international law, which declares that only libels on the heads of foreign states are punishable.

Why this present care for the welfare of a foreign dictatorship? Why is such care shown only now?

Did Italian, Russian, Spanish exiles never write books as the German exiles do? The reason is that neither Spain nor Italy nor Russia possessed a Dr. Goebbels with unlimited funds for the persecution of exiles in the lands in which they have sought refuge.

Today as a result of the pressure exercised by National Socialist officialdom, many non-German papers refuse to mention or review the works of exiled German writers. As a result of pressure from German diplomatic quarters, one of the big bookshops in Madrid refused to display or sell books published by firms that published the works of the exiles.

After the signature of the treaty between Poland and Germany, Polish booksellers ceased to sell the books of the exiles' publishers. Italian booksellers complain that diplomatic pressure is brought to bear upon them to stop selling the works of the exiles. In Greece, at the demand of the German consul, the publisher of the translation of *The Brown Book* was hauled to court and condemned.

At the demand of the German government, the public prosecutor in Argentina issued a summons against an Argentine paper, which had printed an essay by Heinrich Mann. In several lands the production of the new play by Brückner, which has had such a success in Paris, has been forbidden.

Caricatures by famous artists have had to be withdrawn from exhibitions because the representative of the National Socialist government demanded it.

What would happen to Mr. Low or to his editor-in-chief Lord Beaverbrook if the arm of Hitler could reach them? Even in a land so far away as San Salvador, German diplomacy secured the banning of *The Brown Book*.

The Hitlerite dictatorship shrinks from no method of injuring those writers whom it cannot catch. Their books and their manuscripts have been destroyed. Their goods, their furniture, their savings, their houses have been confiscated. Many have been deprived of German citizenship.

Today the world is a very narrow place for those who do not possess a proper passport. If today they are invited to visit another country for urgent business reasons, they cannot go; the frontier is shut to them. They must take endless time and trouble to obtain a piece of paper which permits them to travel from the land in which they live and then it depends whether the other country will make an exception and let them enter.

The German writer Klaus Mann wanted to attend this congress but in spite of all his efforts he was unable to come because he did not possess a passport.

The well-organized persecution of authors, publishers, and booksellers who are obnoxious to the present regime in Germany, a persecution carried on systematically and supported by the immense resources of the state into even the most distant lands, constitutes the most dangerous threat to the freedom of the writer throughout the world.

Will you tolerate this threat? You will perhaps answer me: "What can we do; we are too weak. Our voices will not be heard. The spirit of tyranny and oppression gains ground everywhere." Others again may say: "Isn't it just a piece of quixotry to protest against the crushing of intellectual liberty in Germany when many German writers publicly proclaim themselves enthusiastic supporters of the system and when even if all the rest of the nation revolts from it, its 'intellectual foundations' are still strong."

A casual glance at German papers is enough to let one see with what enthusiasm many German writers describe themselves as pioneers of the national idea. There is no oppression there; this is voluntary service, joyous submission.

A great contemporary writer has said that the writer's talent today plays the part that reason played in the Middle Ages—to disturb faith. And he adds: "Unfortunately there is very little talent today and that explains much."

Be these answers, these opinions, ever so obvious, yet we may not keep silent. The Inquisition too was a power that persecuted and caused men to suffer. Yet those who were persecuted and those who suffered did not renounce their faith.

It is not asked of you that you face death at the stake. It is asked of you only that for the sake of goodness, humanity and justice, for the sake of that day to which—despite the present darkness—mankind will in the future turn, you declare your solidarity with men who are unjustly persecuted, that you do not tolerate the oppression of the spirit by the forces of materialism.

Source: Toller, Ernst. Speech at 1934 P.E.N. conference. Translator unknown. Typescript from P.E.N. International archives, London.

HAILE SELASSIE I
(1892–1975)
Address to the League of Nations
Geneva, Switzerland
June 30, 1936

Emperor Haile Selassie of Ethiopia was named Tafari Makonnen when he was born in 1892. He was descended from Emperor Menelik II (1889–1910), and through him allegedly from 10th century B.C.E. King Solomon of Israel and Queen Makeda (the Queen of Sheba). Makonnen became Haile Selassie—using his childhood baptismal name meaning "instrument in the power of the Trinity" and emperor of Ethiopia in 1930 (he was a Christian Copt). For 40 years, the country had resisted Italy's desire to make Ethiopia—one of the few independent countries of Africa—into a colony. Ethiopia (sometimes called Abyssinia) had defeated an Italian invasion in 1896, in the First Italo-Ethiopian War. Because of Italian aggression at the Walwal oasis in 1934, the emperor appealed to the League of Nations for help, but the league was weak and did not uniformly uphold its own principles. Many countries, such as Britain and France, wanted to keep Italy's friendship as a buttress against Nazi Germany; the United States didn't even belong to the organization. By 1935 Italian fas-

cist dictator Benito Mussolini had readied his plan for conquest. In October, Italy invaded. As Haile Selassie promised his military, he led troops in battle in the province of Tigray (on the present-day border between Ethiopia and Eritrea), warning them, "Soldiers! When it is announced that a respected and beloved leader has died for our freedom in the course of the battle, do not grieve, do not lose hope! Observe that anyone who dies for his country is a fortunate man." After eight months of war, and following many atrocities by Italian troops, Haile Selassie fled, spending five years in exile in England. On May 9, 1936, in Italy, King Victor Emmanuel III (r. 1900–46) declared himself emperor of Ethiopia. The next month Haile Selassie delivered a dignified speech at the League of Nations in Geneva, describing his betrayal by the 52 member countries and the killing mustard gas Italy sprayed from airplanes. British forces assisted Ethiopian troops in driving out the occupying Italians in 1941, and Haile Selassie returned from exile.

***

I, Haile Selassie I, Emperor of Ethiopia, am here today to claim that justice which is due to my people, and the assistance promised to it eight months ago, when fifty nations asserted that aggression had been committed in violation of international treaties.

There is no precedent for a Head of State himself speaking in this assembly. But there is also no precedent for a people being victim of such injustice and being at present threatened by abandonment to its aggressor....

It is my duty to inform the governments assembled in Geneva, responsible as they are for the lives of millions of men, women and children, of the deadly peril which threatens them, by describing to them the fate which has been suffered by Ethiopia. It is not only upon warriors that the Italian Government has made war. It has above all attacked populations far removed from hostilities, in order to terrorize and exterminate them.

At the beginning, towards the end of 1935, Italian aircraft hurled upon my armies bombs of tear-gas.... Men and animals succumbed. The deadly rain that fell from the aircraft made all those whom it touched fly shrieking with pain. All those who drank the poisoned water or ate the infected food also succumbed in dreadful suffering. In tens of thousands, the victims of the Italian mustard gas fell. It is in order to denounce to the civilized world the tortures inflicted upon the Ethiopian people that I resolved to come to Geneva. None other than myself and my brave companions-in-arms could bring the League of Nations the undeniable proof. The appeals of my delegates addressed to the League of Nations had remained without any answer; my delegates had not been witnesses. That is why I decided to come myself to bear witness against the crime perpetrated against my people and give Europe a warning of the doom that awaits it, if it should bow before the accomplished fact. . . .

Indeed the Rome Government, as it has today openly proclaimed, has never ceased to prepare for the conquest of Ethiopia. The Treaties of Friendship it signed with me were not sincere; their only object was to hide its real intention from me. The Italian Government asserts that for 14 years it has been preparing for its present conquest. It therefore recognizes today that when it supported the admission of Ethiopia to the League of Nations in 1923, when it concluded the Treaty of Friendship in 1928, when it signed the Pact of Paris outlawing war, it was deceiving the whole world. . . .

The Walwal incident, in December, 1934, came as a thunderbolt to me. The Italian provocation was obvious and I did not hesitate to appeal to the League of Nations. I invoked the provisions of the treaty of 1928, the principles of the Covenant; I urged the procedure of conciliation and arbitration. Unhappily for Ethiopia this was the time when a certain Government considered that the European situation made it imperative at all costs to obtain the friendship of Italy. The price paid was the abandonment of Ethiopian independence to the greed of the Italian Government. This secret agreement, contrary to the obligations of the Covenant, has exerted a great influence over the course of events. Ethiopia and the whole world have suffered and are still suffering today its disastrous consequences.

This first violation of the Covenant was followed by many others. Feeling itself encouraged in its policy against Ethiopia, the Rome Government feverishly made war preparations, thinking that the concerted pressure which was beginning to be exerted on the Ethiopian Government, might perhaps not overcome the resistance of my people to Italian domination. . . .

The Council and the Assembly unanimously adopted the conclusion that the Italian Government had violated the Covenant and was in a state of aggression. I did not hesitate to declare that I did not wish for war, that it was imposed upon me, and I should struggle solely for the independence and integrity of my people, and that in that struggle I was the defender of the cause of all small States exposed to the greed of a powerful neighbor.

In October 1935, the fifty-two nations who are listening to me today gave me an assurance that the aggressor would not triumph, that the resources of the Covenant would be employed in order to ensure the reign of right and the failure of violence.

I ask the fifty-two nations not to forget today the policy upon which they embarked eight months ago, and on faith of which I directed the resistance of my people against the aggressor whom they had denounced to the world. Despite the inferiority of my weapons, the complete lack of aircraft, artillery, munitions, hospital services, my confidence in the League was absolute. I thought it to be impossible that fifty-two nations, including the most powerful in the world, should be successfully opposed by a single aggressor. Counting on the faith due to treaties, I had made no preparation for war, and that is the case with certain small countries in Europe.

When the danger became more urgent, being aware of my responsibilities towards my people, during the first six months of 1935 I tried to acquire armaments. Many governments proclaimed an embargo to prevent my doing so, whereas the Italian Government through the Suez Canal, was given all facilities for transporting without cessation and without protest, troops, arms, and munitions.

On October 3rd, 1935, the Italian troops invaded my territory. A few hours later only I decreed general mobilization. In my desire to maintain peace I had, following the example of a great country in Europe on the eve of the Great War, caused my troops to withdraw thirty kilometers so as to remove any pretext of provocation.

War then took place in the atrocious conditions which I have laid before the Assembly. In that unequal struggle between a government commanding more than forty-two million inhabitants, having at its disposal financial, industrial and technical means which enabled it to create unlimited quantities of the most death-dealing weapons, and, on the other hand, a small people of twelve million inhabitants, without arms, without resources having on its side only the justice of its own cause and the promise of the League of Nations.

What real assistance was given to Ethiopia by the fifty two nations who had declared the Rome Government guilty of a breach of the Covenant and had undertaken to prevent the triumph of the aggressor? Has each of the States Members, as it was its duty to do in virtue of its signature appended to Article 15 of the Covenant, considered the aggressor as having committed an act of war personally directed against itself? . . .

These are the circumstances in which at the request of the Argentine Government, the Assembly of the League of Nations meets to consider the situation created by Italian aggression. I assert that the problem submitted to the Assembly today is a much wider one. It is not merely a question of the settlement of Italian aggression.

It is collective security: it is the very existence of the League of Nations. It is the confidence that each State is to place in international treaties. It is the value of promises made to small States that their integrity and their independence shall be respected and ensured. It is the principle of the equality of States on the one hand, or otherwise the obligation laid upon small Powers to accept the bonds of vassalship. In a word, it is international morality that is at stake. . . .

Apart from the Kingdom of the Lord there is not on this earth any nation that is superior to any other. Should it happen that a strong government finds it may with impunity destroy a weak people, then the hour strikes for that weak people to appeal to the League of Nations to give its judgment in all freedom. God and history will remember your judgment.

I have heard it asserted that the inadequate sanctions already applied have not achieved their object. At no time, and under no circumstances could sanctions that were intentionally inadequate, intentionally badly applied, stop an aggressor. This is not a case of the impossibility of stopping an aggressor but of the refusal to stop an aggressor. . . .

I ask the fifty-two nations, who have given the Ethiopian people a promise to help them in their resistance to the aggressor, what are they willing to do for Ethiopia? And the great Powers who have promised the guarantee of collective security to small States on whom weighs the threat that they may one day suffer the fate of Ethiopia, I ask what measures do you intend to take?

Representatives of the world, I have come to Geneva to discharge in your midst the most painful of the duties of the head of a State. What reply shall I have to take back to my people?

Source: Haile Selassie. *Haile Selassie I: Silver Jubilee.* Edited by David Abner Talbot. London: W. P. van Stockum, 1955, p. 56.

DOLORES IBÁRRURI
(1895–1989)
"Fascism Is Not Invincible"
Madrid, Spain
January 3, 1937

A fascist government is usually a conservative and militaristic single-party dictatorship that glorifies the nation; it rallies the people around a sense of superiority and often a fear of foreigners or certain ethnic groups. Fascism has an interest in maintaining the position of upper classes relative to lower, and thus it is always anticommunist. In 1936 the Spanish civil war began when General Francisco Franco led a fascist (nationalist) rebellion against the reform-minded (republican) government of Spain. Elections five years earlier had brought in a liberal-leaning government determined to redistribute wealth after the end of the monarchy. But the progressive reforms (and attacks on the Catholic Church) drew the opposition of conservatives; the army, under Franco, carried out a coup d'etat, or sudden overthrow, of the government. Franco's nationalists received aid from fascist dictators Benito Mussolini (of Italy) and Adolf Hitler (of Germany); the republicans received help from the communist Soviet Union. Dolores Ibárruri, a leader of the Spanish Communist Party and a legislator in the Spanish parliament, emerged as the war's legendary orator. She took the name "La Pasionaria" (passion flower), and she coined the republicans' rallying cry, *No pasaran!* (They shall not pass!) She gave this speech after the Battle of Madrid one month before, when 10,000 people had died. With the republicans' defeat in 1939, she escaped to the USSR. Franco installed himself as the head of state; he remained in power for 35 years—until his death in 1975. In exile in the Soviet Union, Ibárruri became secretary general and later, president, of the Communist Party of Spain, while becoming a Soviet citizen. With the death of Franco, she returned to Spain and in 1977 won election, at the age of 82, to the country's new democratic parliament.

❧

People of Madrid! Heroic fighters!

On the threshold of this new year, in which the laurels of victory will one day blossom forth, I address these words to you, full of emotion, love and hope. The traitors who have dyed the soil of our country in blood never believed that our Spain—she belongs to us, and not to those who are selling her piecemeal to alien fascism—would reply to vile treachery and crime by courage, bravery and heroism, and would be able to repulse their frenzied attacks.

The rebels took their own vile souls as a mirror, and depicted our people in their own form and image. They thought that Africa begins at the Pyrenees, that they would encounter no difficulty in subjugating an unarmed people and in establishing a fascist dictatorship at one perfidious blow.

But they did not know our people—our great, heroic and splendid people. They did not know you, militia men; they did not know you, soldiers, sailors and airmen; they did not know that you would vow to defend the Republic, the banner of our fatherland, to defend Spain.

They did not know our women, who are capable of any sacrifice, of any act of self-renunciation, and of sending their sons to the front without a single tear or groan.

Cowards and traitors judge everybody by themselves.

Those who dreamed of seizing the capital of the Republic have learned by bitter experience that it is no easy matter to impose a yoke upon a people which is able, as the defence of Madrid has shown, staunchly and heroically to withstand the savage attacks of fascism.

During the past year the armies of the traitors have learned bow costly it is to impose their domination on a people which wants to be free and to achieve the splendid summits of a new world, the summits of justice.

Those who, while calling themselves patriots, betrayed their country to foreigners, who without a single qualm are destroying monuments of art, and who do not hesitate to murder defenceless women and children, forget that the Spanish people have been firmly steeled in heroic battles, whose immortal history has been written in blood.

The history of our struggle is a most eloquent monument to the valour of the great Spanish people, to their proud contempt of death, and to the undaunted courage with which they enter the lists against all who attempt to enslave them.

Spain will never be fascist! . . .

The clock of history has again struck. Spain is rising, awakening front her age-long sleep and, as in the distant past, is arousing the astonishment of the whole world, which is horrified at the struggle we are obliged to wage.

To the nations which are suffering beneath the bloody yoke of fascism, we are showing the way to smash fascism, to destroy it utterly.

"They shall not pass !"—we exclaimed when the revolt broke out; and this slogan has become part of the flesh and blood of our men and women. This battle cry is piercing the heart of the enemy with the lead of our bullets and the steel of our bayonets.

The year 1937 will be a year of victory. We must now prepare for victory as never before.

It is with feelings of satisfaction that we communists review our activities since the outbreak of the rebellion.

Day by day we point out to the people the path to victory.

We, the organizers of the People's Front, fought for its consolidation with enthusiasm and determination, because only by consolidating the People's Front, only by supporting the government of the People's Front, could the success of our struggle be ensured.

RHETORICAL DEVICE

Amplification: Repeating a term while adding more detail at the same time.

But they did not know our people—our great, heroic,
and splendid people. —*Dolores Ibárruri*

I feel part of a marvelous historical process—the process of the national
revival of Soviet Jewry and its return to the homeland,
to Israel. —*Anatoly Sharansky*

Books are the first victims, the permanent victims, because they are
the primary menace to totalitarian power. —*Jacobo Timerman*

I am talking about genuine peace, the kind of peace that makes life on earth
worth living. —*John F. Kennedy*

We are aided by all who long for economic security—for the security and
abundance that men in free societies can enjoy. —*Harry S. Truman*

> They shall not pass! —*Dolores Ibárruri*

Today we want once more to point out the path of victory. It is this path we are following. We shall impose silence upon those who try to sow confusion and disorganization in our ranks, who are creating a menace to the honest co-operation of the revolutionary forces—the only condition that can ensure victory.

It must not be forgotten that our struggle is a national war for the independence of our country of foreign fascism, a war for the emancipation of the masses of the people from the feudal yoke and from fascist barbarism.

It was not we who started the war.

It was they, the aristocrats, the military caste, the priesthood, the scions of the nobility, the fascists and degenerates, who forced the war upon us. They staked everything on this card—and lost. And we, who had no fatherland, who lived as pariahs in our own country, not possessing a square foot of land because it all belonged to the big landlords, are now fighting for our Spain, a Spain that has arisen on the ruins of the old, feudal, reactionary and slave Spain; we are fighting for the Spain in which a bright life will bloom—liberty, peace and the happiness of the people. In order to win this new Spain, our Spain, we must temper and steel our victorious weapons. . . .

All the means of destruction supplied to the rebels by the German and Italian fascists are now being concentrated against Madrid. The war has converted heroic Madrid, epic Madrid, into a martyr city, whose finest monuments of art have been destroyed, its streets stained with the blood of women and innocent children, and some of its finest people annihilated.

Defenders of Madrid! Heroic fighters on all the fronts! You have proved that you are the worthy offspring of those whom the most powerful armies of the world were unable to defeat.

Let not your energies, your enthusiasm, your determination, flag for a single moment! The eyes of the whole world are turned towards you with hope. We are not alone. On our side are fighting the champions of the European people's front, the heroes of the International Brigades.

The Soviet Union, the great Land of Socialism, which was able to repulse the onslaught of world capitalism, is on our side. Let us follow its example.

To battle and to victory! Let us show the nations which are groaning under fascist tyranny that fascism is not invincible, that fascism can be vanquished.

Forward to victory, to a decisive victory!

Source: Ibárruri, Dolores. *Dolores Ibárruri: Speeches and Articles 1936–1938.* New York: International Publishers, 1938, p. 48.

EDOUARD DALADIER
(1884–1970)
"The Slaves of Nazi Masters"
Paris, France
January 29, 1940

Edouard Daladier was premier of France three times between 1933 and 1940, and also served as secretary of war in 1936. On September 29, 1938, on behalf of France, Daladier signed the Munich Pact (along with Italian dictator Benito Mussolini, British prime minister Neville Chamberlain, and German chancellor Adolf Hitler) appeasing Hitler in his plan to seize the German-speaking Sudetenland, a large part of Czechoslovakia. (Czechoslovakia was given no say in the matter.) Like Chamberlain, Daladier naively thought war with Nazi Germany had been averted. However, Germany soon seized all Czechoslovakia in March 1939, and invaded Poland on September 1 that year. Britain, Australia, New Zealand, France, and Canada declared war on Germany within days, beginning World War II. The following January 1940, a little more than a year after signing the Munich Pact, Daladier—then president and minister of national defense—gave a radio address to the French people describing the horrifying truth he had come to understand about the intentions of Nazi Germany. A month afterward, he was succeeded in office by Paul Reynaud, and then by Philippe Pétain in July of the same year. Germany attacked France on May 10, 1940; after a ruinous campaign in which 200,000 Allied soldiers lost their lives defending France and another 200,000 had to be evacuated to Britain, France was compelled to surrender on June 22. Daladier, who had fled with much of the government to Morocco, a French colony in North Africa, was handed over to Philippe Pétain's collaborationist Vichy government, Germany's puppet regime in France. The Vichy government imprisoned him until 1943, then allowed the Nazis to send him to Buchenwald, a German slave labor concentration camp. He was released in 1945 at the end of World War II, and he rejoined French politics, serving in the National Assembly until 1958.

At the end of five months of war one thing has become more and more clear. It is that Germany seeks to establish a domination over the world completely different from any known in history.

The domination at which the Nazis aim is not limited to the displacement of the balance of power and the imposition of supremacy of one nation. It seeks the systematic and total destruction of those conquered by Hitler, and it does not treat with the nations which he has subdued. He destroys them. He takes from them their whole political and economic existence and seeks even to deprive them of their history and their culture. He wishes to consider them only as vital space and a vacant territory over which he has every right.

The human beings who constitute these nations are for him only cattle. He orders their massacre or their migration. He compels them to make room for their conquerors. He does not even take the trouble to impose any war tribute on them. He just takes all their wealth, and, to prevent any revolt, he wipes out their leaders and scientifically seeks the physical and moral degradation of those whose independence he has taken away.

Under this domination, in thousands of towns and villages in Europe there are millions of human beings now living in misery which, some months ago, they could never have imagined. Austria, Bohemia, Slovakia and Poland are only lands of despair. Their whole peoples have been deprived of the means of moral and material happiness. Subdued by treachery or brutal violence, they have no other recourse than to work for their executioners who grant them scarcely enough to assure the most miserable existence.

There is being created a world of masters and slaves in the image of Germany herself. For, while Germany is crushing beneath her tyranny the men of every race and

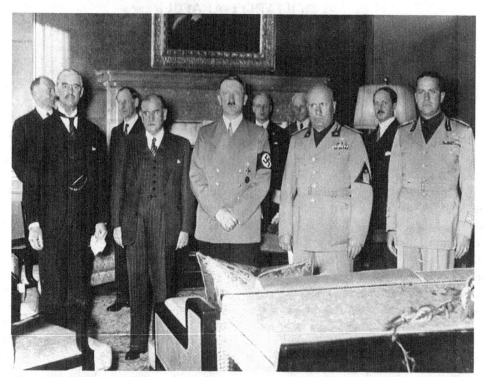

Along with Britain's Neville Chamberlain, Edouard Daladier of France signed the Munich Pact with Hitler in 1938, hoping to end Germany's march to war. In foreground, left to right: Neville Chamberlain, Edouard Daladier, Adolf Hitler, and Benito Mussolini. *(Ablestock)*

language, she is herself being crushed beneath her own servitude and her domination mania. The German worker and peasant are the slaves of their Nazi masters while the worker and peasant of Bohemia and Poland have become in turn slaves of these slaves. Before this first realization of a mad dream, the whole world might shudder.

Nazi propaganda is entirely founded on the exploitation of the weakness of the human heart. It does not address itself to the strong or the heroic. It tells the rich they are going to lose their money. It tells the worker this is a rich man's war. It tells the intellectual and the artist that all he cherished is being destroyed by war. It tells the lover of good things that soon he would have none of them. It says to the Christian believer: "How can you accept this massacre?" It tells the adventurer—"a man like you should profit by the misfortunes of your country."

It is those who speak this way who have destroyed or confiscated all the wealth they could lay their hands on, who have reduced their workers to slavery, who have ruined all intellectual liberty, who have imposed terrible privations on millions of men and women and who have made murder their law. What do contradictions matter to them if they can lower the resistance of those who wish to bar the path of their ambitions to be masters of the world?

For us there is more to do than merely win the war. We shall win it, but we must also win a victory far greater than that of arms. In this world of masters and slaves, which those madmen who rule at Berlin are seeking to forge, we must also save liberty and human dignity.

Source: Edouard Daladier. "Nazis Aim Is Slavery." In *The World's Great Speeches,* edited by Lewis Copeland and Lawrence Lamm, 461. New York: Dover, 1973.

WINSTON CHURCHILL
(1874–1965)
"Blood, Toil, Tears and Sweat"
House of Commons, London, England
May 13, 1940

World War II began in Europe on September 1, 1939, with the German invasion of Poland. By early May 1940, Germany had conquered Denmark and invaded Norway, Belgium, and the Netherlands. In Britain, Prime Minister Neville Chamberlain had lost the confidence of the public—by signing the Munich Pact in 1938, he had allowed himself to be deceived by Hitler's promises of peace. He resigned on May 10, 1940 (the day Hitler's army invaded France). Winston Churchill, often called upon in times of crisis, then was commissioned prime minister by King George VI (r. 1936–52). Churchill came from the aristocracy; his father was Lord Randolph Churchill, chancellor of the exchequer (similar to secretary of the treasury) and a leader in Parliament. Winston Churchill had served in the army—as a soldier and a war correspondent—and was elected to Parliament in 1900. His long career also included World War I (1914–18) stints as first lord of the admiralty and secretary of state for war. Between the world wars he was chancellor of the exchequer for five years. In the 1930s he began to warn Britain of the threat posed by Nazi Germany, but the warnings fell on deaf ears. After accepting his new post as prime minister at the start of World War II (1939–45), Churchill quickly went about selecting the men to take office in his war cabinet. On May 13 he gave his first speech to the House of Commons as prime minister, asking for approval of the new government. (His reference to having nothing to offer but "blood, toil, tears and sweat" is often misquoted as "blood, sweat, and tears.") It was the first of many memorable speeches he gave in 1940 that demonstrated his powers as a statesman and as one of the world's great orators.

> I would say to the House, as I said to those
> who have joined this government:
> I have nothing to offer but blood, toil, tears
> and sweat. —*Winston Churchill*

I beg to move, that this House welcomes the formation of a government representing the united and inflexible resolve of the nation to prosecute the war with Germany to a victorious conclusion.

On Friday evening last I received His Majesty's commission to form a new administration. It as the evident wish and will of Parliament and the nation that this should be conceived on the broadest possible basis and that it should include all parties, both those who supported the late government and also the parties of the opposition. I have completed the most important part of this task.

A War Cabinet has been formed of five Members, representing, with the Opposition Liberals, the unity of the nation. The three party Leaders have agreed to serve, either in the War Cabinet or in high executive office. The three Fighting Services have been filled. It was necessary that this should be done in one single day, on account of the extreme urgency and rigor of events. . . .

I now invite the House, by the motion which stands in my name, to record its approval of the steps taken and to declare its confidence in the new government.

To form an administration of this scale and complexity is a serious undertaking in itself, but it must be remembered that we are in the preliminary stage of one of the greatest battles in history, that we are in action at many other points in Norway and in Holland, that we have to be prepared in the Mediterranean, that the air battle is

On September 9, 1940, Winston Churchill (far right) leads a group of officials inspecting "Blitz" bomb damage inflicted by German aircraft over London. *(AP Photo)*

continuous and that many preparations, such as have been indicated by my honorable friend below the gangway, have to be made here at home.

In this crisis I hope I may be pardoned if I do not address the House at any length today. I hope that any of my friends and colleagues, or former colleagues, who are affected by the political reconstruction, will make allowance, all allowance, for any lack of ceremony with which it has been necessary to act. I would say to the House, as I said to those who have joined this government: "I have nothing to offer but blood, toil, tears and sweat."

We have before us an ordeal of the most grievous kind. We have before us many, many long months of struggle and of suffering.

You ask, what is our policy? I can say: It is to wage war, by sea, land and air, with all our might and with all the strength that God can give us; to wage war against a monstrous tyranny, never surpassed in the dark, lamentable catalogue of human crime. That is our policy.

You ask, what is our aim? I can answer in one word: It is victory, victory at all costs, victory in spite of all terror, victory, however long and hard the road may be; for without victory, there is no survival. Let that be realized; no survival for the British Empire, no survival for all that the British Empire has stood for, no survival for the urge and impulse of the ages, that mankind will move forward towards its goal.

But I take up my task with buoyancy and hope. I feel sure that our cause will not be suffered to fail among men. At this time I feel entitled to claim the aid of all, and I say, "Come then, let us go forward together with our united strength."

Source: Churchill, Winston. "Blood, Toil, Tears and Sweat." Selected Speeches of Winston Churchill. Available online. http://www.winstonchurchill.org/i4a/pages/index.cfm?pageid =389. Accessed December 18, 2007.

WINSTON CHURCHILL
(1874–1965)
"We Shall Fight on the Beaches"
House of Commons, London, England

June 4, 1940

Three weeks after accepting the office of prime minister on May 10, 1940, Winston Churchill returned to the British parliament's House of Commons to report on the disastrous loss of the Netherlands (on May 14) and Belgium (on May 28) to Nazi Germany, and the attack on France. (*SEE* Churchill's May 13 speech, p. 341.) In France the British Expeditionary Force, along with the French army, had been fighting chancellor of Germany Adolf Hitler's army on two fronts, as the German offensive had driven deep into France and split the Allied forces—and their communications—in half. Neither the French, nor the British forces could withstand the rapidly moving German tanks, motorized troops, and continuous aerial bombardment of Hitler's *Blitzkrieg* (in German, the term means "lightning war"). It was a relatively new way of fighting in which ground troops and artillery did not dig into positions and wait out the enemy's defeat, but instead rushed forward as mechanized forces to envelope the enemy and force its collapse. The Germans pushed through France to the English Channel, then swung north up the French coast to trap their victims. In nine anxious days from May 26 to June 4, through mines, bombs, and artillery fire, the Allies' evacuation at Dunkirk (in northern France) proceeded. Using more than 700 ships and boats—many piloted by civilians—the Allies rescued over 330,000 members of the British Expeditionary Force and their French and Belgian allies from Dunkirk. With France falling to German forces, Britain now faced the terrifying prospect of invasion. Through it all Winston Churchill was a tower of determination, refusing to accept defeat—he would not entertain any consideration of negotiating with Hitler. In this excerpt, the resolute climax of one of his greatest speeches, he prepares the populace for invasion and expresses hope for help from the Americas. Indeed, U.S. president Franklin Delano Roosevelt would shortly announce that the United States—although still neutral—would offer "material resources" to the Allies.

Our thankfulness at the escape of our Army and so many men, whose loved ones have passed through an agonizing week, must not blind us to the fact that what has happened in France and Belgium is a colossal military disaster. The French Army has been weakened, the Belgian Army has been lost, a large part of those fortified lines upon which so much faith had been reposed is gone, many valuable mining districts and factories have passed into the enemy's possession, the whole of the Channel ports are in his hands, with all the tragic consequences that follow from that, and we must expect another blow to be struck almost immediately at us or at France.

We are told that Herr Hitler has a plan for invading the British Isles. This has often been thought of before. When Napoleon lay at Boulogne for a year with his flat-bottomed boats and his Grand Army, he was told by someone, "There are bitter weeds in England." There are certainly a great many more of them since the British Expeditionary Force returned.

The whole question of home defense against invasion is, of course, powerfully affected by the fact that we have for the time being in this Island incomparably more powerful military forces than we have ever had at any moment in this war or the last. But this will not continue.

We shall not be content with a defensive war. We have our duty to our ally. We have to reconstitute and build up the British Expeditionary Force once again, under its gallant Commander-in-Chief, Lord Gort. All this is in train; but in the interval we must

---

RHETORICAL DEVICE

Anaphora: Repetition of a word or phrase at the beginning of phrases or sentences that follow. (*See the related* antistrophe)

O'Donovan Rossa was splendid in the proud manhood of him,
splendid in the heroic grace of him, splendid in the Gaelic strength and clarity
and truth of him. —*Patrick Pearse*

We shall fight on the beaches, we shall fight on the landing grounds,
we shall fight in the fields and in the streets . . . —*Winston Churchill*

Give me liberty or give me death! —*Patrick Henry*

And so if we praise him, our words seem rather small and if we praise him,
to some extent we also praise ourselves. —*Jawaharlal Nehru*

---

put our defenses in this Island into such a high state of organization that the fewest possible numbers will be required to give effective security and that the largest possible potential of offensive effort may be realized. On this we are now engaged. . . .

I would observe that there has never been a period in all these long centuries of which we boast when an absolute guarantee against invasion, still less against serious raids, could have been given to our people. In the days of Napoleon the same wind which would have carried his transports across the Channel might have driven away the blockading fleet. There was always the chance, and it is that chance which has excited and befooled the imaginations of many Continental tyrants. Many are the tales that are told.

We are assured that novel methods will be adopted, and when we see the originality of malice, the ingenuity of aggression, which our enemy displays, we may certainly prepare ourselves for every kind of novel stratagem and every kind of brutal and treacherous maneuver. I think that no idea is so outlandish that it should not be considered and viewed with a searching, but at the same time, I hope, with a steady eye. We must never forget the solid assurances of sea power and those which belong to air power if it can be locally exercised.

I have, myself, full confidence that if all do their duty, if nothing is neglected, and if the best arrangements are made, as they are being made, we shall prove ourselves once again able to defend our Island home, to ride out the storm of war, and to outlive the menace of tyranny, if necessary for years, if necessary alone. At any rate, that is what we are going to try to do. That is the resolve of His Majesty's Government—every man of them. That is the will of Parliament and the nation.

The British Empire and the French Republic, linked together in their cause and in their need, will defend to the death their native soil, aiding each other like good comrades to the utmost of their strength. Even though large tracts of Europe and many old and famous states have fallen or may fall into the grip of the Gestapo and all the odious apparatus of Nazi rule, we shall not flag or fail.

We shall go on to the end; we shall fight in France, we shall fight on the seas and oceans, we shall fight with growing confidence and growing strength in the air, we shall defend our Island, whatever the cost may be.

We shall fight on the beaches, we shall fight on the landing grounds, we shall fight in the fields and in the streets, we shall fight in the hills. We shall never surrender, and even if, which I do not for a moment believe, this Island or a large part of it were subjugated and starving, then our Empire beyond the seas, armed and guarded by the British Fleet, would carry on the struggle, until, in God's good time, the New World, with all its power and might, steps forth to the rescue and the liberation of the old.

Source: Churchill, Winston. "We Shall Fight on the Beaches." Selected Speeches of Winston Churchill. Available online. http://www.winstonchurchill.org/i4a/pages/index.cfm?page id=389. Accessed December 18, 2007.

WINSTON CHURCHILL
(1874–1965)
"This Was Their Finest Hour"
House of Commons, London, England
June 18, 1940

French General Maxime Weygand was appointed supreme commander of the Allied forces in France in mid-May, 1940, but the outmatched Allied troops still could not turn the losing Battle of France around. To make matters worse, Italy declared war on France on June 10. By June 14 German dictator Adolf Hitler's army had entered Paris, and by June 18, France had fallen. Britain was now the only Allied power still free (the United States and Soviet Union did not enter World War II until 1941). Poland, Denmark, the Netherlands, Belgium, Luxembourg, and Norway had all succumbed to the "Nazi war machine." On June 23, France officially surrendered to Germany. In this address, Churchill refers to a remarkable "union of common citizenship" with France, forged two days earlier with Undersecretary for War Charles de Gaulle, which would have made Britain and France one country for the purposes of battling Hitler. (French marshall Philippe Pétain preempted this union by deciding to surrender.) (*SEE* speech by de Gaulle, p. 349.) Closing with one of the most moving perorations ever uttered, Churchill anticipates the Battle of Britain, which began on July 10, 1940, and continued through the end of October. It was fought almost entirely by air forces (Hitler's land invasion, scheduled for September, never occurred), and it was won by Britain as Hitler failed to gain a hold on the British Isles, the first important setback to the Nazi onslaught. It was during the long Battle of Britain that Churchill said, about Allied airmen and fighter pilots, "Never was so much owed by so many to so few." His magnificent speeches in that difficult year, broadcast in his instantly recognizable and resonant voice, rallied the beleaguered British people and kept Britain's plight before the world's notice. Churchill is considered one of the great figures of the 20th century.

We must not forget that from the moment when we declared war on the 3rd September it was always possible for Germany to turn all her air force upon this country, together with any other devices of invasion she might conceive, and that France could have done little or nothing to prevent her doing so. We have, therefore, lived under this danger, in principle and in a slightly modified form, during all these months.

In the meanwhile, however, we have enormously improved our methods of defense, and we have learned what we had no right to assume at the beginning, namely, that the individual aircraft and the individual British pilot have a sure and definite superiority. Therefore, in casting up this dread balance sheet and contemplating our dangers with a disillusioned eye, I see great reason for intense vigilance and exertion, but none whatever for panic or despair.

During the first four years of the last war the Allies experienced nothing but disaster and disappointment. That was our constant fear: one blow after another, terrible losses, frightful dangers. Everything miscarried. And yet at the end of those four years the morale of the Allies was higher than that of the Germans, who had moved from one aggressive triumph to another, and who stood everywhere triumphant invaders of the lands into which they had broken.

During that war we repeatedly asked ourselves the question: How are we going to win? and no one was able ever to answer it with much precision, until at the end, quite suddenly, quite unexpectedly, our terrible foe collapsed before us, and we were so glutted with victory that in our folly we threw it away.

347

> Let us therefore brace ourselves to our duties, and so bear ourselves that, if the British Empire and its Commonwealth last for a thousand years, men will still say, "*This* was their finest hour." —*Winston Churchill*

We do not yet know what will happen in France or whether the French resistance will be prolonged, both in France and in the French Empire overseas. The French Government will be throwing away great opportunities and casting adrift their future if they do not continue the war in accordance with their Treaty obligations, from which we have not felt able to release them.

The House will have read the historic declaration in which, at the desire of many Frenchmen—and of our own hearts—we have proclaimed our willingness at the darkest hour in French history to conclude a union of common citizenship in this struggle.

However matters may go in France or with the French Government, or other French Governments, we in this Island and in the British Empire will never lose our sense of comradeship with the French people. If we are now called upon to endure what they have been suffering, we shall emulate their courage, and if final victory rewards our toils they shall share the gains, aye, and freedom shall be restored to all.

We abate nothing of our just demands; not one jot or tittle do we recede. Czechs, Poles, Norwegians, Dutch, Belgians have joined their causes to our own. All these shall be restored.

What General Weygand called the Battle of France is over. I expect that the Battle of Britain is about to begin. Upon this battle depends the survival of Christian civilization. Upon it depends our own British life, and the long continuity of our institutions and our empire.

The whole fury and might of the enemy must very soon be turned on us. Hitler knows that he will have to break us in this island or lose the war. If we can stand up to him, all Europe may be free and the life of the world may move forward into broad, sunlit uplands. But if we fail, then the whole world, including the United States, including all that we have known and cared for, will sink into the abyss of a new Dark Age made more sinister, and perhaps more protracted, by the lights of perverted science.

Let us therefore brace ourselves to our duties, and so bear ourselves that, if the British Empire and its Commonwealth last for a thousand years, men will still say, "*This* was their finest hour."

Source: Churchill, Winston. "Their Finest Hour." Selected Speeches of Winston Churchill. Available online. http://www.winstonchurchill.org/i4a/pages/index.cfm?pageid=389. Accessed December 18, 2007.

CHARLES DE GAULLE
(1890–1970)
"France Is Not Alone!"
London, England
June 18, 1940

The same day Winston Churchill delivered his "Finest Hour" speech (*SEE* Churchill's speech, page 347), a little-known French general named Charles de Gaulle, who had escaped from German-occupied France the day before, broadcast a call to the French people. De Gaulle was a career military officer; as an army captain in World War I (1914–18), he had been held in a German prisoner-of-war camp. In World War II (1939–45), he led a division of French tanks against the Germans in the disastrous Battle of France (May 10–June 22, 1940). As the enemy was poised to seize all France, de Gaulle was appointed brigadier general and French undersecretary of war. He was opposed to surrendering, but French marshall Philippe Pétain had already determined to sign an armistice agreeing to end the fighting. De Gaulle fled to London and received Churchill's permission to make the broadcast to his countrymen, known in France as *L'Appel du 18 juin,* or

Appeal of June 18. He called for France to keep on fighting—like Churchill, he referred to leaning on America for help—despite Marshall Pétain's announcement in France that he would negotiate peace with Germany. The armistice, signed June 23, resulted in the German military occupation of northern France. De Gaulle did not consider Pétain's government legitimate; from abroad, he organized a government in exile—the "Free French" or "Fighting French." (In August, a French court sentenced de Gaulle to death in absentia; the crime was treason—for resisting Pétain's puppet government in Vichy, France.) Free French forces fought successfully in North Africa and landed with the Allies in the August 1944 invasion of southern France. De Gaulle also helped organize the French Resistance. After the ouster of the Germans from Paris, de Gaulle returned as president of the French Provisional Government on August 25, 1944. He became president of France in 1959.

The leaders who, for many years, were at the head of French armies, have formed a government. This government, alleging our armies to be undone, agreed with the enemy to stop fighting.

Of course, we were subdued by the mechanical, ground, and air forces of the enemy. Infinitely more than their number, it was the tanks, the airplanes, the tactics of the Germans which made us retreat. It was the tanks, the airplanes, the tactics of the Germans that surprised our leaders to the point to bring them there where they are today.

But has the last word been said? Must hope disappear? Is defeat final? No!

Believe me, I speak to you with full knowledge of the facts and tell you that nothing is lost for France. The same means that overcame us can bring us to a day of victory.

For France is not alone! She is not alone! She is not alone!

She has a vast Empire behind her. She can align with the British Empire that holds the sea and continues the fight. She can, like England, use without limit the immense industry of the United States.

This war is not limited to the unfortunate territory of our country. This war is not finished by the Battle of France. This war is a worldwide war. All the faults, all the delays, all the suffering, do not prevent there to be, in the world, all the necessary means to one day crush our enemies. Vanquished today by mechanical force, we will be able to overcome in the future by a superior mechanical force.

The destiny of the world is here. I, General de Gaulle, currently in London, invite the officers and the French soldiers who are located in British territory or who would come there, with their weapons or without their weapons, I invite the engineers and the special workers of armament industries who are located in British territory or who would come there, to put themselves in contact with me.

Whatever happens, the flame of the French resistance must not be extinguished and will not be extinguished. Tomorrow, as today, I will speak on Radio London.

Source: Ledwidge, Bernard. *DeGaulle*. New York: St. Martin's Press, 1982, p. 68.

PRINCESS ELIZABETH
(1926–   )
To the Children of the Commonwealth
Windsor Castle, England
October 13, 1940

During World War II (1939–45), Princess Elizabeth (crowned Queen Elizabeth II in 1952) and her younger sister Princess Margaret were sent to the countryside for safety, as were many other British children. Some even took refuge abroad. The two princesses lived five years at Windsor Castle, 20 miles from London. Their parents, King George VI (r. 1936–52) and Queen Elizabeth (r. 1936–52), spent a great deal of the war in London at Buckingham Palace, keeping up a brave front and touring bombing sites in a show of solidarity with public suffering. It was stressful for young children to leave their parents, even for those city children at greatest danger from the bombing. In October 1940, during the Battle of Britain, a confident 14-year-old Elizabeth broadcast a radio address to buoy the spirits of the children of the British Commonwealth. The many Commonwealth nations included Australia, Bermuda, Canada, India, Jamaica, New Zealand, Nigeria, and South Africa; all Britain's crown colonies had declared war on Germany alongside the mother country. Britain's superior navy meant Germany would not invade by sea, so the Battle of Britain (August to October 1940) was fought almost completely by air forces. Germany's prolonged "blitz" bombing (the term came from the German military strategy of *Blitzkrieg,* or "lightning war") at first targeted military and industrial sites, but in September German aircraft began to attack cities; on September 7 an incredible 300 bombers and 600 fighters attacked in one day. Overall, 40,000 people were killed. The Nazis especially targeted London, hit day and night for months. The stalwart population rose to the challenge of defending the capital, defeating Hitler's hope of eroding British morale. In 1945 near the war's end, Princess Elizabeth—no longer the young girl who had listened to the BBC radio show *Children's Hour*—joined the Women's Auxiliary and drove a military vehicle.

⤞⤝

In wishing you all 'good evening' I feel that I am speaking to friends and companions who have shared with my sister and myself many a happy Children's Hour.

Thousands of you in this country have had to leave your homes and be separated from your fathers and mothers. My sister Margaret Rose and I feel so much for you as we know from experience what it means to be away from those we love most of all.

To you, living in new surroundings, we send a message of true sympathy and at the same time we would like to thank the kind people who have welcomed you to their homes in the country.

All of us children who are still at home think continually of our friends and relations who have gone overseas—who have traveled thousands of miles to find a wartime home and a kindly welcome in Canada, Australia, New Zealand, South Africa and the United States of America.

My sister and I feel we know quite a lot about these countries. Our father and mother have so often talked to us of their visits to different parts of the world. So it is not difficult for us to picture the sort of life you are all leading, and to think of all the new sights you must be seeing, and the adventures you must be having.

But I am sure that you, too, are often thinking of the Old Country. I know you won't forget us; it is just because we are not forgetting you that I want, on behalf of all the children at home, to send you our love and best wishes—to you and to your kind hosts as well.

Before I finish I can truthfully say to you all that we children at home are full of cheerfulness and courage. We are trying to do all we can to help our gallant sailors,

Princess Margaret (left) and Princess Elizabeth (right) broadcast to children of the British Commonwealth on the program *The Children's Hour* during World War II. *(AP Photo/PA)*

soldiers and airmen, and we are trying, too, to bear our own share of the danger and sadness of war.

We know, everyone of us, that in the end all will be well; for God will care for us and give us victory and peace. And when peace comes, remember it will be for us, the children of today, to make the world of tomorrow a better and happier place.

My sister is by my side and we are both going to say goodnight to you. Come on, Margaret.

Goodnight, children. Goodnight, and good luck to you all.

Source: The Princess Elizabeth. "Broadcast to the Children of the Commonwealth." British Monarchy Media Centre. Available online. http://www.royal.gov.uk/output/Page4099.asp. Accessed January 4, 2008.

FRANKLIN D. ROOSEVELT
(1882–1945)
"Four Essential Human Freedoms"
Congress, Washington, D.C., United States

January 6, 1941

Franklin Delano Roosevelt was born into wealth and privilege; his fifth cousin, Theodore Roosevelt, was the 26th U.S. president. He entered public service early, becoming a New York state senator in 1910 and assistant secretary of the navy under President Woodrow Wilson during World War I (1914–18). When he was 39 he suffered the great misfortune of his life in falling ill with a disease that paralyzed his legs, but he recovered enough to be elected governor of New York. Roosevelt ran for U.S. president as a Democrat and won in 1932. In his inaugural address, he took the miseries of the Great Depression head-on: "The only thing we have to fear is fear itself," he said. Roosevelt's New Deal—programs and agencies designed to meet the crisis of the Great Depression—quickly put millions of unemployed people back to work and made him extremely popular. U.S. foreign policy was officially neutral during this time, even as World War II raged, but in August 1940 Roosevelt began supplying destroyers to beleaguered Britain. In September the fascist Axis powers of Germany, Italy, and Japan signed the Tripartite Pact of mutual support. In November Roosevelt became the first (and last) U.S. president elected to a third term in office. Much of Europe had been overrun by Nazi Germany and Britain was in serious danger of defeat. In January 1941 Roosevelt made his yearly State of the Union address to Congress, now known as the Four Freedoms speech, preparing American citizens for the conflict he recognized was coming. He did not mention the Axis powers by name, but it was clear whom he meant. The United States would shortly begin supplying food and equipment to Great Britain and its allies under the Lend-Lease plan. It was the Japanese bombing of the naval base and air stations at Pearl Harbor, Hawaii, on December 7, 1941 that would drive the United States headlong into World War II.

Every realist knows that the democratic way of life is at this moment being directly assailed in every part of the world—assailed either by arms, or by secret spreading of poisonous propaganda by those who seek to destroy unity and promote discord in nations that are still at peace.

During sixteen long months this assault has blotted out the whole pattern of democratic life in an appalling number of independent nations, great and small. The assailants are still on the march, threatening other nations, great and small.

Therefore, as your President, performing my constitutional duty to "give to the Congress information of the state of the Union," I find it, unhappily, necessary to report that the future and the safety of our country and of our democracy are overwhelmingly involved in events far beyond our borders.

Armed defense of democratic existence is now being gallantly waged in four continents. If that defense fails, all the population and all the resources of Europe, Asia, Africa and Australasia will be dominated by the conquerors. Let us remember that the total of those populations and their resources in those four continents greatly exceeds the sum total of the population and the resources of the whole of the Western Hemisphere—many times over.

In times like these it is immature—and incidentally, untrue—for anybody to brag that an unprepared America, single-handed, and with one hand tied behind its back, can hold off the whole world.

President Franklin D. Roosevelt signs a declaration of war on Japan after the attack on the United States at Pearl Harbor, Hawaii. *(Library of Congress)*

No realistic American can expect from a dictator's peace international generosity, or return of true independence, or world disarmament, or freedom of expression, or freedom of religion—or even good business. Such a peace would bring no security for us or for our neighbors. "Those, who would give up essential liberty to purchase a little temporary safety, deserve neither liberty nor safety."

As a nation, we may take pride in the fact that we are softhearted; but we cannot afford to be soft-headed. We must always be wary of those who with sounding brass and a tinkling cymbal preach the "ism" of appeasement. We must especially beware of that small group of selfish men who would clip the wings of the American eagle in order to feather their own nests.

I have recently pointed out how quickly the tempo of modern warfare could bring into our very midst the physical attack which we must eventually expect if the dictator nations win this war.

There is much loose talk of our immunity from immediate and direct invasion from across the seas. Obviously, as long as the British Navy retains its power, no such danger exists. Even if there were no British Navy, it is not probable that any enemy would be stupid enough to attack us by landing troops in the United States from across thousands of miles of ocean, until it had acquired strategic bases from which to operate. But we learn much from the lessons of the past years in Europe—particularly the lesson of Norway, whose essential seaports were captured by treachery and surprise built up over a series of years.

The first phase of the invasion of this Hemisphere would not be the landing of regular troops. The necessary strategic points would be occupied by secret agents and their dupes—and great numbers of them are already here, and in Latin America.

As long as the aggressor nations maintain the offensive, they—not we—will choose the time and the place and the method of their attack. That is why the future of all the American Republics is today in serious danger. That is why this Annual Message to the Congress is unique in our history. That is why every member of the Executive Branch of the Government and every member of the Congress faces great responsibility and great accountability.

The need of the moment is that our actions and our policy should be devoted primarily—almost exclusively—to meeting this foreign peril. For all our domestic problems are now a part of the great emergency.

Just as our national policy in internal affairs has been based upon a decent respect for the rights and the dignity of all our fellow men within our gates, so our national policy in foreign affairs has been based on a decent respect for the rights and dignity of all nations, large and small. And the justice of morality must and will win in the end.

Our national policy is this: First, by an impressive expression of the public will and without regard to partisanship, we are committed to all-inclusive national defense.

Second, by an impressive expression of the public will and without regard to partisanship, we are committed to full support of all those resolute peoples, everywhere, who are resisting aggression and are thereby keeping war away from our Hemisphere. By this support, we express our determination that the democratic cause shall prevail; and we strengthen the defense and the security of our own nation.

Third, by an impressive expression of the public will and without regard to partisanship, we are committed to the proposition that principles of morality and considerations for our own security will never permit us to acquiesce in a peace dictated by aggressors and sponsored by appeasers. We know that enduring peace cannot be bought at the cost of other people's freedom. . . .

In the future days, which we seek to make secure, we look forward to a world founded upon four essential human freedoms.

The first is freedom of speech and expression—everywhere in the world.

The second is freedom of every person to worship God in his own way—everywhere in the world.

The third is freedom from want—which, translated into world terms, means economic understandings which will secure to every nation a healthy peacetime life for its inhabitants—everywhere in the world.

The fourth is freedom from fear—which, translated into world terms, means a world-wide reduction of armaments to such a point and in such a thorough fashion that no nation will be in a position to commit an act of physical aggression against any neighbor—anywhere in the world.

That is no vision of a distant millennium. It is a definite basis for a kind of world attainable in our own time and generation. That kind of world is the very antithesis of the so-called new order of tyranny which the dictators seek to create with the crash of a bomb. To that new order we oppose the greater conception—the moral order. A good society is able to face schemes of world domination and foreign revolutions alike without fear.

Since the beginning of our American history, we have been engaged in change—in a perpetual peaceful revolution—a revolution which goes on steadily, quietly adjusting itself to changing conditions—without the concentration camp or the quick-lime in the ditch. The world order which we seek is the cooperation of free countries, working together in a friendly, civilized society.

This nation has placed its destiny in the hands and heads and hearts of its millions of free men and women; and its faith in freedom under the guidance of God. Freedom means the supremacy of human rights everywhere. Our support goes to those who struggle to gain those rights or keep them. Our strength is our unity of purpose. To that high concept there can be no end save victory.

In the future days, which we seek to make secure, we look forward to a world founded upon four essential human freedoms.
—*Franklin Delano Roosevelt*

Source: Roosevelt, Franklin Delano. "Annual Message to Congress." Franklin D. Roosevelt Presidential Library. Available online. http://www.fdrlibrary.marist.edu/4free.html. Accessed December 19, 2007.

Clemens von Galen, a priest who was the son of a German count, was appointed bishop of Münster in 1933, shortly after Adolf Hitler became chancellor of Germany. The devout bishop was vehemently opposed to the "neo-pagan" anti-Christian dogma of the Nazis. The imposing von Galen—he was an extremely tall man—hoped to prevent his flock from being seduced by National Socialist (Nazi) ideology. In July 1941 he preached two sermons against the Nazis, who were expelling priests and nuns and condemning them without trial. But he is most famous—and called "the Lion of Münster"—for forceful opposition to the Nazi program of euthanasia gassings, begun in 1939 and directed at mentally and physically disabled people. In a Sunday sermon at St. Lambert's Church, he courageously condemned the Nazi policy, read out the penal code on murder to the congregation, and described the letter of protest he sent to police and the charges he brought in state court to stop it. The bishop was influential in Westphalia, a heavily Catholic province; although thousands of priests were being imprisoned, even murdered, Nazi authorities did not dare touch him. The euthanasia program was halted, although as many as 100,000 people were already dead. The killings began again in 1942 and later were extended at extermination camps to homosexuals, communists, gypsies, and, with particular malevolence, Jews (with whom von Galen never concerned himself). The sermons were circulated within Germany, even by the Allies, who dropped them as propaganda leaflets from airplanes. After the war, Pope Pius XII (r. 1939–58) made von Galen a cardinal in recognition of his moral and physical courage. A month later the "Lion" died of appendicitis. He was beatified, the first step to becoming a saint, in 2005.

Dearly beloved Christians! The joint pastoral letter of the German bishops, which was read in all Catholic churches in Germany on 26 June, 1941, includes the following words:

"It is true that in Catholic ethics there are certain positive commandments which cease to be obligatory if their observance would be attended by unduly great difficulties; but there are also sacred obligations of conscience from which no one can release us; which we must carry out even if it should cost us our life. Never, under any circumstances, may a man, save in war or in legitimate self-defense, kill an innocent person."

I had occasion on 6th July to add the following comments on this passage in the joint pastoral letter:

"For some months we have been hearing reports that inmates of establishments for the care of the mentally ill who have been ill for a long period and perhaps appear incurable have been forcibly removed from these establishments on orders from Berlin. Regularly the relatives receive soon afterwards an intimation that the patient is dead, that the patient's body has been cremated and that they can collect the ashes. There is a general suspicion, verging on certainty, that these numerous unexpected deaths of the mentally ill do not occur naturally but are intentionally brought about in accordance with the doctrine that it is legitimate to destroy a so-called "worthless life"—in other words to kill innocent men and women, if it is thought that their lives are of no further value to the people and the state. A terrible doctrine which seeks to justify the murder of innocent people, which legitimizes the violent killing of disabled persons who are no longer capable of work, of cripples, the incurably ill and the aged and infirm!"

RHETORICAL DEVICE

Rhetorical question: A question that the speaker asks but does not answer, possibly because the answer is obvious, or because he or she means to provoke the listeners. In a speech they have a powerful effect, as they engage the listener in reflecting what the likely answer is. (*See the related* hypophora.)

What government can possibly be better than that of
the very best man in the whole state? —*Darius*

What happens to a lame horse, an unproductive cow?
—*Cardinal Clemens von Galen*

If you Romans choose to lord it over the world, does it follow
that the world is to accept slavery? —*Caratacus*

For Moses, meek as he was, libeled Cain; and who is it
that has not libeled the Devil? —*Andrew Hamilton*

I am reliably informed that in hospitals and homes in the province of Westphalia lists are being prepared of inmates who are classified as "unproductive members of the national community" and are to be removed from these establishments and shortly thereafter killed. The first party of patients left the mental hospital at Marienthal, near Münster, in the course of this week.

German men and women! Article 211 of the German Penal Code is still in force, in these terms: "Whoever kills a man of deliberate intent is guilty of murder and punishable with death." No doubt in order to protect those who kill with intent these poor men and women, members of our families, from this punishment laid down by law, the patients who have been selected for killing are removed from their home area to some distant place. Some illness or other is then given as the cause of death. Since the body is immediately cremated, the relatives and the criminal police are unable to establish whether the patient had in fact been ill or what the cause of death actually was. I have been assured, however, that in the Ministry of the Interior and the office of the Chief Medical Officer, Dr. Conti, no secret is made of the fact that indeed a large number of mentally ill persons in Germany have already been killed with intent and that this will continue.

Article 139 of the Penal Code provides that "anyone who has knowledge of an intention to commit a crime against the life of any person . . . and fails to inform the authorities or the person whose life is threatened in due time . . . commits a punishable offence." When I learned of the intention to remove patients from Marienthal, I reported the matter on 28th July to the State Prosecutor of Münster Provincial Court and to the Münster chief of police by registered letter, in the following terms:

"According to information I have received, it is planned in the course of this week (the date has been mentioned as 31st July) to move a large number of inmates of the provincial hospital at Marienthal, classified as 'unproductive members of the national community,' to the mental hospital at Eichberg, where, as is generally believed to have happened in the case of patients removed from other establishments, they are to be killed with intent. Since such action is not only contrary to the divine and the natural moral law but under article 211 of the German Penal Code ranks as murder and attracts the death penalty, I hereby report the matter in accordance with my obligation under article 139 of the Penal Code and request that steps should at once be taken to protect the patients concerned by proceedings against the authorities planning their removal and murder, and that I may be informed of the action taken."

I have received no information of any action by the State Prosecutor or the police.

I had already written on 26th July to the Westphalian provincial authorities, who are responsible for the running of the mental hospital and for the patients entrusted to them for care and for cure, protesting in the strongest terms. It had no effect. The first transport of the innocent victims under sentence of death has left Marienthal. And I am now told that 800 patients have already been removed from the hospital at Warstein.

We must expect, therefore, that the poor defenseless patients are, sooner or later, going to be killed. Why? Not because they have committed any offense justifying their death, not because, for example, they have attacked a nurse or attendant, who would be entitled in legitimate self-defense to meet violence with violence. In such a case the use of violence leading to death is permitted and may be called for, as it is in the case of killing an armed enemy.

No, these unfortunate patients are to die, not for some such reason as this but because in the judgment of some official body, on the decision of some committee, they have become "unworthy to live," because they are classed as "unproductive members of the national community."

The judgment is that they can no longer produce any goods; they are like an old piece of machinery which no longer works, like an old horse which has become incurably lame, like a cow which no longer gives any milk. What happens to an old piece of machinery? It is thrown on the scrap heap. What happens to a lame horse, an unproductive cow?

I will not pursue the comparison to the end—so fearful is its appropriateness and its illuminating power.

But we are not here concerned with pieces of machinery; we are not dealing with horses and cows, whose sole function is to serve mankind, to produce goods for mankind. They may be broken up; they may be slaughtered when they no longer perform this function.

No, we are concerned with men and women, our fellow creatures, our brothers and sisters! Poor human beings, ill human beings, they are unproductive, if you will. But does that mean that they have lost the right to live? Have you, have I, the right to live only so long as we are productive, so long as we are recognized by others as productive?

If the principle that man is entitled to kill his unproductive fellow man is established and applied, then woe betide all of us when we become aged and infirm! If it is legitimate to kill unproductive members of the community, woe betide the disabled who have sacrificed their health or their limbs in the productive process! If unproductive men and women can be disposed of by violent means, woe betide our brave soldiers who return home with major disabilities as cripples, as invalids! . . .

Then no man will be safe: some committee or other will be able to put him on the list of "unproductive" persons, who in their judgment have become "unworthy to live." And there will be no police to protect him, no court to avenge his murder and bring his murderers to justice.

Who could then have any confidence in a doctor? He might report a patient as unproductive and then be given instructions to kill him! It does not bear thinking of, the moral depravity, the universal mistrust which will spread even in the bosom of the family, if this terrible doctrine is tolerated, accepted and put into practice.

Woe betide mankind, woe betide our German people, if the divine commandment, "Thou shalt not kill," which the Lord proclaimed on Sinai amid thunder and lightning, which God our Creator wrote into man's conscience from the beginning, if this commandment is not merely violated but the violation is tolerated and remains unpunished!

Source: Von Galen, Clemens August. "Three Sermons in Defiance of the Nazis." Church in History Information Centre. Available online. http://www.churchinhistory.org/pages/booklets/vongalen(n).htm. Accessed December 20, 2007.

FRANKLIN D. ROOSEVELT
(1882–1945)
"A Date Which Will Live in Infamy"
Washington, D.C., United States
December 8, 1941

Before World War II (1939–45) Japan was marked by growing militarism and nationalism. By means of the 1904 Russo-Japanese War (fought over Manchuria and Korea), the annexation of Korea in 1910, the assumption of German island colonies in the Pacific in 1919, and the invasion of Manchuria (northeastern China) in 1931, Japan sought to expand its territory. Population pressures also fueled the interest in empire. Japan had pulled out of the League of Nations (set up as a means to prevent another world war) in 1933, angered by Western disapproval of its expansionist aims, and in 1940—one year into World War II—signed the Tripartite Pact with Italy and Nazi Germany to form the Axis powers. The United States further angered Japan by cutting off shipments of oil in disapproval over the occupation of China and French Indochina (now Cambodia, Laos, and Vietnam). Japan had its eyes on the Dutch East Indies and Malaya, but felt the United States must be neutralized before attempting to gain control there. On December 7, 1941, while Japanese government representatives attended negotiations in Washington, D.C., the U.S. Pearl Harbor naval base in Hawaii was bombed by Japanese aircraft without warning. Nineteen ships were sunk or damaged, nearly 200 planes destroyed, and more than 2,000 people killed; Japan had destroyed almost the entire Pacific fleet. The next day, President Roosevelt asked Congress to declare war on Japan; a memorable line from his address—"a date which will live in infamy"—is known to almost every American. A few days later, Germany and Italy declared war on the United States. The Americans, who had resisted entering World War II, were now drawn into the war headlong. Roosevelt met with British prime minister Winston Churchill, Premier Joseph Stalin of the Soviet Union, and political and military leader Chiang Kai-shek of China to plan the division of battle fronts, and he put the United States in overdrive to produce military hardware. Roosevelt died on April 12, 1945, in the first year of an unprecedented fourth term, knowing war with Germany was nearly over.

***

Yesterday, December 7, 1941—a date which will live in infamy—the United States of America was suddenly and deliberately attacked by naval and air forces of the Empire of Japan.

The United States was at peace with that nation and, at the solicitation of Japan, was still in conversation with its Government and its Emperor looking toward the maintenance of peace in the Pacific. Indeed, one hour after Japanese air squadrons had commenced bombing in Oahu, the Japanese Ambassador to the United States and his colleague delivered to the Secretary of State a formal reply to a recent American message. While this reply stated that it seemed useless to continue the existing diplomatic negotiations, it contained no threat or hint of war or armed attack.

It will be recorded that the distance of Hawaii from Japan makes it obvious that the attack was deliberately planned many days or even weeks ago. During the intervening time the Japanese Government has deliberately sought to deceive the United States by false statements and expressions of hope for continued peace.

The attack yesterday on the Hawaiian Islands has caused severe damage to American naval and military forces. Very many American lives have been lost. In addition American ships have been reported torpedoed on the high seas between San Francisco and Honolulu.

Yesterday the Japanese Government also launched an attack against Malaya.

Last night Japanese forces attacked Hong Kong.

Last night Japanese forces attacked Guam.

Last night Japanese forces attacked the Philippine Islands.

Last night the Japanese attacked Wake Island.

This morning the Japanese attacked Midway Island.

> Yesterday, December 7, 1941—a date which will live in infamy—the United States of America was suddenly and deliberately attacked by naval and air forces of the Empire of Japan.
> —*Franklin D. Roosevelt*

Japan has, therefore, undertaken a surprise offensive extending throughout the Pacific area. The facts of yesterday speak for themselves. The people of the United States have already formed their opinions and well understand the implications to the very life and safety of our nation.

As Commander-in-Chief of the Army and Navy, I have directed that all measures be taken for our defense.

Always will we remember the character of the onslaught against us. No matter how long it may take us to overcome this premeditated invasion, the American people in their righteous might will win through to absolute victory.

I believe I interpret the will of the Congress and of the people when I assert that we will not only defend ourselves to the uttermost but will make very certain that this form of treachery shall never endanger us again.

Hostilities exist. There is no blinking at the fact that our people, our territory and our interests are in grave danger.

With confidence in our armed forces—with the unbounded determination of our people—we will gain the inevitable triumph, so help us God.

I ask that the Congress declare that since the unprovoked and dastardly attack by Japan on Sunday, December seventh, a state of war has existed between the United States and the Japanese Empire.

Source: Roosevelt, Franklin Delano. "Joint Address to Congress." Franklin D. Roosevelt Presidential Library. Available online. http://www.fdrlibrary.marist.edu/dec71941.html. Accessed December 19, 2007.

WENDELL WILLKIE
(1892–1944)
"Lidice Lives . . . in This Little Village in Illinois"
Stern Park Gardens, renamed Lidice, Illinois, United States
July 12, 1942

On May 27, 1942, with Czechoslovakia under Nazi Germany's control, two Czech patriots assassinated Reinhard Heydrich—the "hangman of Europe." Heydrich was a personal favorite of Adolf Hitler, one of his inner circle. He was also the brutal 38-year-old deputy chief of the Gestapo, Hitler's secret police, who had led the Wannsee Conference in Berlin in January that year. Heydrich had outlined for the conference's 15 participants (including Nazi Party leader Adolf Eichmann) the Final Solution to exterminate the Jews of German-occupied Europe. On Hitler's orders, German troops retaliated for Heydrich's death. On June 10, 1942, they executed every man in the Czech village of Lidice, where they believed the two assailants had sheltered. They shipped most of the women to Ravensbrück (a concentration camp), most of the children to Chelmo (an extermination camp) where they died, and razed every building in the town. Hearing of the village's total destruction, the Czech-American citizens of the small town of Stern Park Gardens, Illinois, voted to change the community's name to Lidice (pronounced Li-di-tseh). The address at the renaming ceremony was given by Wendell Willkie, a popular lawyer and businessman from Indiana who had served in the army in World War I (1914–18). He had a talent for oratory that was evident in the courtroom, and he was an early opponent of racial segregation. In 1939 he switched from the Democratic to the Republican Party in order to run for the presidency against Franklin D. Roosevelt in 1940, but he lost the election (Roosevelt was running for his third term in office). Willkie supported Roosevelt's foreign policy—he was not an isolationist—but he opposed his New Deal programs, which were designed to meet the crisis of the Great Depression. When Roosevelt called on him in 1941 and 1942, Willkie put aside politics and became FDR's personal emissary to Britain, the Middle East, China, and the Soviet Union.

Fellow Citizens and all who love freedom everywhere:

Let me tell you a story. Ten miles west of Prague, in Czechoslovakia, there was a little village called Lidice, spelled L I D I C E. It was a mining village, a mile off the main highway, with some lovely old inns, a blacksmith or two, a shoemaker, a wheelwright, a tailor. The village had been there for over six hundred years.

Above the ninety roofs of the town rose the spire of St. Margaret's Church, built in 1736, the home of the faith of the community. This town was remote, peaceful, almost like a village in a fairy tale. But it was not a village in a fairy tale, for its people had tasted the bread and wine of freedom. In this village one of the main streets was named Wilson Street, after an American who had a vision and wanted to share it with the world. And the people of Lidice dreamed the same dream, saw the same vision.

But the Nazis came, and with them, misery and hardship. The altar of St. Margaret's Church was no longer open to the people as it had been for over two hundred years. Men had to watch their words and in their actions; they could no longer be free. But in their hearts, the hearts of the inn-keeper, and the tailor, and the farmer, and the miner, and the priest, was the stubborn independence of their fathers.

Not far from Lidice ran a winding road. On this road on May 27th, six weeks ago, at 10:30 in the morning, a motor car was passing, carrying Hitler's governor of Czechoslovakia, "Hangman" Heydrich—for his cruelties the most hated man in all Europe. The car was held up by two unknown men. Bullets burrowed into the spine of

Reinhard Heydrich. The two patriots disappeared, and one of them, it is said, is now safe in London.

I do not wish to speak of the reign of terror that thereupon swept over all Czechoslovakia. I wish to speak today only of Lidice, and I will give you only the facts. This is not my version of the facts. This is not a version of the facts issued by any of the United Nations as propaganda. These are the facts as officially attested by the German government. They are facts of which the Nazis are proud. They are facts they wish the world to know. They are facts they believe will frighten you and me, and turn our hearts and our knees to water, and make us cry "Truce!"

For Heydrich the Hangman died in agony, just as he had caused thousands of innocent people to die. No proof from that day to this has ever been adduced to show that any of the inhabitants of Lidice had anything to do with the assassination. But the Nazis made their own proof. They were afraid not to, for Heydrich was one of their great men. "One of the best Nazis," Hitler called him, and that, no doubt, is true.

On June 10th an official German statement was issued, not for domestic consumption, but for the world to hear. I quote from it: "It is officially announced that in the course of the search for the murderers of General Heydrich, it has been ascertained that the population of the village of Lidice supported and assisted the perpetrators who came into question ... Because the inhabitants, by their support of the perpetrators, have flagrantly violated the law, all men of the village have been shot. The women have been deported to a concentration camp, and the children sent to appropriate centers of education. All buildings of the village were leveled to the ground, and the name of the village was immediately abolished."

That is the official Nazi report.

They came in the night, men in boots and brown shirts, and they took from their homes the bewildered miners and farmers, the tailor and the priest, the boy of seventeen and the old man of seventy, more than two hundred in all, and they shot them, because they could think of no other way to avenge the death of Heydrich. Fifty-six women they took also and killed, and proudly listed their names. The rest of the women they drove into what they called concentration camps; and these women the world will never see again. They herded the pale, terror-stricken children into trucks and carried them off to correction schools where they would be taught that they must honor the murderers of their fathers and the brutalizers of their mothers. The ninety homes, they burned to the ground, the church of St. Margaret they stamped into the earth. And the name of the little town of Lidice, through which ran the street called after a president of the United States, they rubbed out, they thought, from history.

Why did they do this deed, more terrible than anything that has happened since the Dark Ages, a deed not of passion, but of cold, premeditated, systematic murder and rapine? Why? They did it because they are afraid. They are afraid because the free spirit in men has refused to be conquered. Theirs is a system of force and terror and Lidice is the terrible symbol of that system.

But it is not the only one. Of the five hundred thousand men, women and children who have been shot in Europe by the Nazis, at least twenty-five thousand have perished in mass massacres. Poland, Norway, Belgium, Yugoslavia, all have their Lidices. But this one is a symbol of all we have sworn to remember, if only because the Nazis themselves demand that we forget it. Once more, they have misjudged the human spirit.

Because a hangman was killed, Lidice lives. Because a hangman was killed, Wilson Street must once again be part of a little Bohemian town. Because the lanterns of Lidice have been blacked out, a flame has been lit which can never be extinguished. Each of the wounds of those two hundred men and fifty-six women is a mouth that cries out that other free men and free women must not suffer a like fate. Everywhere, but particularly in our own country, the wave of stubborn, stern resolve rises. Lidice lives. She lives

---

RHETORICAL DEVICE

Hyperbaton: Changing the normal word order for emphasis.

The ninety homes, they burned to the ground, the church of St. Margaret they stamped into the earth. And the name of the little town of Lidice, through which ran the street called after a president of the United States, they rubbed out, they thought, from history. —*Wendell Willkie*

In the Ghetto, the Jew had his own world. . . . What mattered it that outside the Ghetto was despised that which within it was praised? —*Max Nordau*

What was the ruin of Sparta and Athens, but this, that mighty as they were in war, they spurned from them as aliens those whom they had conquered? —*Claudius I*

---

again, thirty-five hundred miles from Wilson Street and St. Margaret's Church, in this little village in Illinois.

I look about me here, and I can see in the distance the black smoke of steel factories, swarming with American workers of all bloods and races. No contrast could be greater than the peaceful Lidice the Nazis thought they had destroyed, and this Illinois country, alive with factories in which the arms of victory are being forged. But I tell you that the two are related. For while such deeds as Lidice are done in another country, we cannot rest until we are sure that they will never be done in our own.

Let us here highly resolve that the memory of this little village of Bohemia, now resurrected by the people of a little village in Illinois, will fire us, now and until the battle is over, with the iron resolution that the madness of tyrants must perish from the earth, so that the earth may return to the people to whom it belongs, and be their village, their home, forever.

Source: Baird, Albert Craig, ed. *Representative American Speeches 1941–1942*. New York: H. W. Wilson, 1942, p. 164.

DOUGLAS MacARTHUR
(1880–1964)
"Today the Guns Are Silent"
Battleship USS *Missouri*, Tokyo Bay, Japan
September 2, 1945

General Douglas MacArthur commanded U.S. forces in the southwest Pacific during World War II (1939–45). He had fought under General "Black Jack" Pershing in World War I (1914–18), and he served as chief of general staff for President Franklin Delano Roosevelt. MacArthur was an emotional, opinionated man, and a born soldier. He was the loyal defender of the Philippines—when the U.S. military was driven from the islands by the Japanese in 1942, he had pledged to return; two years later, he waded ashore with American forces and declared, "People of the Philippines, I have returned!" For Japan, the war was going badly. Germany had surrendered to the Allies on May 8, but Japan still remained grimly determined to fight. The atomic bombings of Hiroshima and Nagasaki (on August 6 and 9, 1945) by the United States and a declaration of war by the Soviet Union caused Japan finally to capitulate. Emperor Hirohito recorded a surrender speech—the *Gyokuon-hoso*, or Imperial Rescript on Surrender. Japanese military officers got wind of the speech and stormed the palace, vainly hoping to destroy the recording before it could get to the public. It was broadcast to the Japanese people on August 15. On September 2, as Supreme Commander for the Allied powers, MacArthur accepted the formal surrender of Japanese forces onboard the battleship USS *Missouri* in Tokyo Bay. MacArthur gave a short speech, and the Japanese foreign minister and army chief of staff stepped forward to sign the articles of surrender. Signing for the Allied powers were representatives from the United States, China, United Kingdom, USSR, Australia, Canada, France, the Netherlands, and New Zealand. The war was officially over. MacArthur then followed with a longer address broadcast to the American people at home. A Japanese representative in the surrender party later reported to the emperor his relief at MacArthur's generous speech.

We are gathered here, representatives of the major warring powers, to conclude a solemn agreement whereby peace may be restored. The issues, involving divergent ideals and ideologies, have been determined on the battlefields of the world and hence are not for our discussion or debate. Nor is it for us here to meet, representing as we do a majority of the peoples of the earth, in a spirit of distrust, malice or hatred.

But rather it is for us, both victors and vanquished, to rise to that higher dignity which alone befits the sacred purposes we are about to serve, committing all our peoples unreservedly to faithful compliance with the undertakings they are here formally to assume.

It is my earnest hope and indeed the hope of all mankind that from this solemn occasion a better world shall emerge out of the blood and carnage of the past—a world founded upon faith and understanding—a world dedicated to the dignity of man and the fulfillment of his most cherished wish—for freedom, tolerance and justice.

The terms and conditions upon which the surrender of the Japanese Imperial Forces is here to be given and accepted are contained in the instrument of surrender now before you.

As Supreme Commander for the Allied Powers, I announce it my firm purpose, in the tradition of the countries I represent, to proceed in the discharge of my responsibilities with justice and tolerance, while taking all necessary dispositions to insure that the terms of surrender are fully, promptly and faithfully complied with.

I now invite the representatives of the Emperor of Japan and the Japanese Government, and the Japanese Imperial General Headquarters, to sign the instrument of surrender at the places indicated.

The Supreme Commander for the Allied Powers will now sign on behalf of the nations at war with Japan. . . .

Let us pray that peace be now restored to the world, and that God will preserve it always.

(after the signing)

My fellow countrymen, today the guns are silent. A great tragedy has ended. A great victory has been won. The skies no longer rain death—the seas bear only commerce—men everywhere walk upright in the sunlight. The entire world is quietly at peace. The holy mission has been completed, and in reporting this to you, the people, I speak for the thousands of silent lips, forever stilled among the jungles and the beaches and in the deep waters of the Pacific which marked the way. I speak for the unnamed brave millions homeward bound to take up the challenge of that future which they did so much to salvage from the brink of disaster.

As I look back on the long tortuous trail from those grim days of Bataan and Corregidor, when an entire world lived in fear, when democracy was on the defensive everywhere, when modern civilization trembled in the balance, I thank a merciful God

Japanese officers and officials face representatives of the Allied powers at the signing of surrender instruments onboard the USS *Missouri* in Tokyo Bay. Admiral Helfrich bends over the table to sign on behalf of the Netherlands, as General Douglas MacArthur stands beside him. MacArthur then made a second speech, broadcast to Americans at home. *(Photo, Naval Historical Center, Number USA C-1189)*

that He has given us the faith, the courage, and the power from which to mold victory. We have known the bitterness of defeat and the exultation of triumph, and from both we have learned there can be no turning back. We must go forward to preserve in peace what we won in war.

A new era is upon us. Even the lesson of victory itself brings with it profound concern, both for our future security and the survival of civilization. The destructiveness of the war potential, through progressive advances in scientific discovery, has in fact now reached a point which revises the traditional concept of war.

Men since the beginning of time have sought peace. Various methods through the ages have attempted to devise an international process to prevent or settle disputes between nations. From the very start workable methods were found insofar as individual citizens were concerned, but the mechanics of an instrumentality of larger international scope have never been successful. Military alliance, balances of power, leagues of nations, all in turn failed, leaving the only path to be by way of the crucible of war.

The utter destructiveness of war now blots out this alternative. We have had our last chance. If we do not now devise some greater and more equitable system Armageddon will be at our door. The problem basically is theological and involves a spiritual recrudescence and improvement of human character that will synchronize with our almost matchless advance in science, art, literature, and all material and cultural developments of the past 2,000 years. It must be of the spirit if we are to save the flesh.

We stand in Tokyo today reminiscent of our countryman, Commodore Perry, 92 years ago. His purpose was to bring to Japan an era of enlightenment and progress by lifting the veil of isolation to the friendship, trade, and commerce of the world. But alas the knowledge thereby gained of western science was forged into an instrument of oppression and human enslavement. Freedom of expression, freedom of action, even freedom of thought were denied through suppression of liberal education, through appeal to superstition, and through the application of force.

We are committed by the Potsdam Declaration of principles to see that the Japanese people are liberated from this condition of slavery. It is my purpose to implement this commitment just as rapidly as the armed forces are demobilized and other essential steps taken to neutralize the war potential. The energy of the Japanese race, if properly directed, will enable expansion vertically rather than horizontally. If the talents of the race are turned into constructive channels, the country can lift itself from its present deplorable state into a position of dignity.

To the Pacific basin has come the vista of a new emancipated world. Today, freedom is on the offensive, democracy is on the march. Today, in Asia as well as in Europe, unshackled peoples are tasting the full sweetness of liberty, the relief from fear.

In the Philippines, America has evolved a model for this new free world of Asia. In the Philippines, America has demonstrated that peoples of the East and peoples of the West may walk side by side in mutual respect and with mutual benefit. The history of our sovereignty there has now the full confidence of the East.

And so, my fellow countrymen, today I report to you that your sons and daughters have served you well and faithfully with the calm, deliberate, determined fighting spirit of the American soldier and sailor, based upon a tradition of historical truth, as against the fanaticism of any enemy supported only by mythological fiction. Their spiritual strength and power has brought us through to victory. They are homeward bound—take care of them.

Source: MacArthur, Douglas. *MacArthur.* Edited by Lawrence Wittner. Englewood Cliffs, N.J.: Prentice Hall, 1971, p. 33.

ROBERT H. JACKSON
(1892–1954)
Opening Address at the Nuremberg Trials
Nuremberg, Germany
November 21, 1945

Nazi Germany leader Adolf Hitler committed suicide on April 30, 1945, near the end of World War II, but 21 of his henchmen were held for trial as war criminals. They included Hermann Göring, Rudolf Hess, Julius Streicher, and Joachim von Ribbentrop. Sickened by Nazi atrocities, the Allied powers—Great Britain, France, Russia, and the United States—formed the International Military Tribunal for prosecution of Nazi war crimes. Each of the four Allies supplied one judge and one chief prosecutor. The defendants were tried for crimes that occurred during the war, not before; the four indictments were conspiracy, waging aggressive war, war crimes, and crimes against humanity. The trial took place at Nuremberg, Germany, the city where the Nuremberg Laws in 1935 had stripped Jews of their rights and where Hitler held his largest Nazi party rallies. U.S. Supreme Court justice Robert Jackson had been in office five years when the war ended. He had been U.S.

attorney general under President Franklin D. Roosevelt, and he was famous for his 1943 Supreme Court opinion that schoolchildren could not be forced to salute the flag. Because Roosevelt had died in office on April 12, 1945, it was President Truman who appointed Jackson to lead the Nuremberg Trials prosecution as chief counsel. Jackson was noted for the brilliance he displayed in his opening and closing speeches of the trials, given before the assembled war criminals, defense lawyers, prosecutors, and judges. He found the prosecution a harder task than courtroom addresses; the cunning Hermann Göring in particular almost bested him in court. The trials lasted eight months, closing on October 1, 1946. Eleven defendants were sentenced to death. (A similar series of trials—the Tokyo Trials—was held in Japan by the International Military Tribunal for the Far East from 1946 to 1948.) After Nuremberg, Robert Jackson returned to the Supreme Court and served until his death in 1954.

The privilege of opening the first trial in history for crimes against the peace of the world imposes a grave responsibility. The wrongs which we seek to condemn and punish have been so calculated, so malignant and so devastating, that civilization cannot tolerate their being ignored because it cannot survive their being repeated. That four great nations, flushed with victory and stung with injury, stay the hand of vengeance and voluntarily submit their captive enemies to the judgment of the law is one of the most significant tributes that Power ever has paid to Reason.

This tribunal, while it is novel and experimental, is not the product of abstract speculations nor is it created to vindicate legalistic theories. This inquest represents the practical effort of four of the most mighty of nations, with the support of seventeen more, to utilize International Law to meet the greatest menace of our times, aggressive war. The common sense of mankind demands that law shall not stop with the punishment of petty crimes by little people. It must also reach men who possess themselves of great power and make deliberate and concerted use of it to set in motion evils which leave no home in the world untouched. It is a cause of this magnitude that the United Nations will lay before Your Honors.

In the prisoners' dock sit twenty-odd broken men. Reproached by the humiliation of those they have led almost as bitterly as by the desolation of those they have attacked, their personal capacity for evil is forever past. It is hard now to perceive in these miserable men, as captives, the power by which, as Nazi leaders, they once dominated much of the world and terrified most of it. Merely as individuals, their fate is of little consequence to the world.

U.S. Supreme Court justice Robert H. Jackson addresses the court at the trials of high-ranking Nazi officials at Nuremberg. *(Photo, Office of U.S. Chief of Counsel, Courtesy Harry S. Truman Library)*

What makes this inquest significant is that those prisoners represent sinister influence that will lurk in the world long after their bodies have returned to dust. They are living symbols of racial hatreds, of terrorism and violence, and of the arrogance and cruelty of power. They are symbols of fierce nationalism and militarism, of intrigue and war-making which have embroiled Europe generation after generation, crushing its manhood, destroying its homes, and impoverishing its life.

They have so identified themselves with the philosophies they conceived and with the forces they directed that any tenderness to them is a victory and an encouragement to all the evils which are attached to their names. Civilization can afford no compromise with the social forces which would gain renewed strength if we deal ambiguously or indecisively with the men in whom those forces now precariously survive.

What these men stand for we will patiently and temperately disclose. We will give you undeniable proofs of incredible events. The catalogue of crimes will omit nothing that could be conceived by a pathological pride, cruelty, and lust for power.

These men created in Germany, under the "Fuehrerprinzip," a National Socialist despotism equaled only by the dynasties of the ancient East. They took from the German people all those dignities and freedoms that we hold natural and inalienable rights in every human being. The people were compensated by inflaming and gratifying hatreds toward those who were marked as "scapegoats."

Against their opponents, including Jews, Catholics, and free labor the Nazis directed such a campaign of arrogance, brutality, and annihilation as the world has not witnessed since the pre-Christian ages. They excited the German ambition to be a "master race," which of course implies serfdom for others. They led their people on a mad gamble for domination. They diverted social energies and resources to the creation of what they thought to be an invincible

> The wrongs which we seek to condemn and punish have been so calculated, so malignant and so devastating, that civilization cannot tolerate their being ignored because it cannot survive their being repeated. —*Robert H. Jackson*

war machine. They overran their neighbors. To sustain the "master race" in its war making, they enslaved millions of human beings and brought them into Germany, where these hapless creatures now wander as "displaced persons."

At length bestiality and bad faith reached such excess that they aroused the sleeping strength of imperiled civilization. Its united efforts have ground the German war machine to fragments. But the struggle has left Europe a liberated yet prostrate land where a demoralized society struggles to survive. These are the fruits of the sinister forces that sit with these defendants in the prisoners' dock. . . .

Unfortunately, the nature of these crimes is such that both prosecution and judgment must be by victor nations over vanquished foes. The worldwide scope of the aggressions carried out by these men has left but few real neutrals. Either the victors must judge the vanquished or we must leave the defeated to judge themselves. After the First World War, we learned the futility of the latter course. The former high station of these defendants, the notoriety of their acts, and the adaptability of their conduct to provoke retaliation make it hard to distinguish between the demand for a just and measured retribution, and the unthinking cry for vengeance which arises from the anguish of war. It is our task, so far as humanly possible, to draw the line between the two. . . .

If these men are the first war leaders of a defeated nation to be prosecuted in the name of the law, they are also the first to be given a chance to plead for their lives in the name of the law. Realistically, the Charter of this Tribunal, which gives them a hearing, is also the source of their only hope. It may be that these men of troubled conscience, whose only wish is that the world forget them, do not regard a trial as a favor. But they do have a fair opportunity to defend themselves, a favor which these men, when in power, rarely extended to their fellow countrymen. Despite the fact that public opinion already condemns their acts, we agree that here they must be given a presumption of innocence, and we accept the burden of proving criminal acts and the responsibility of these defendants for their commission. . . .

We will not ask you to convict these men on the testimony of their foes. There is no count of the Indictment that cannot be proved by books and records. The Germans were always meticulous record keepers, and these defendants had their share of the Teutonic passion for thoroughness in putting things on paper. Nor were they without vanity. They arranged frequently to be photographed in action. We will show you their own films. You will see their own conduct and hear their own voices as these defendants reenact for you, from the screen, some of the events in the course of the conspiracy.

We would also make clear that we have no purpose to incriminate the whole German people. We know that the Nazi Party was not put in power by a majority of the German vote. We know it came to power by an evil alliance between the most extreme of the Nazi revolutionists, the most unrestrained of the German reactionaries, and the most aggressive of the German militarists. If the German populace had willingly accepted the Nazi program, no Storm troopers would have been needed in the early days of the Party and there would have been no need for concentration camps or the Gestapo, both of which institutions were inaugurated as soon as the Nazis gained control of the German state. Only after these lawless innovations proved successful at home were they taken abroad. . . .

In general, our case will disclose these defendants all uniting at some time with the Nazi Party in a plan which they well knew could be accomplished only by an outbreak of war in Europe. Their seizure of the German state, their subjugation of the German people, their terrorism and extermination of dissident elements, their planning and waging of war, their calculated and planned ruthlessness in the conduct of warfare, their deliberate and planned criminality toward conquered peoples, all these are ends for which they acted in concert; and all these are phases of the conspiracy, a conspiracy which reached one goal only to set out for another and more ambitious one.

We shall also trace for you the intricate web of organizations which these men formed and utilized to accomplish these ends. We will show how the entire structure of offices and officials was dedicated to the criminal purposes and committed to use of the criminal methods planned by these defendants and their co-conspirators, many of whom war and suicide have put beyond reach.

It is my purpose to open the case, particularly under Count One of the Indictment, and to deal with the common plan or conspiracy to achieve ends possible only by resort to crimes against peace, war crimes, and crimes against humanity. My emphasis will not be on individual barbarities and perversions which may have occurred independently of any central plan. One of the dangers ever present is that this trial may be protracted by details of particular wrongs and that we will become lost in a "wilderness of single instances." Nor will I now dwell on the activity of individual defendants except as it may contribute to exposition of the common plan.

The case as presented by the United States will be concerned with the brains and authority back of all the crimes. These defendants were men of a station and rank which does not soil its own hands with blood. They were men who knew how to use lesser folk as tools. We want to reach the planners and designers, the inciters and leaders without whose evil architecture the world would not have been for so long scourged with the violence and lawlessness, and wracked with the agonies and convulsions, of this terrible war.

Source: Maser, Werner. *Nuremberg: A Nation on Trial.* New York: Scribner, 1977, p. 85.

WINSTON CHURCHILL
(1874–1965)
Iron Curtain Speech
Fulton, Missouri, United States
March 5, 1946

In 1946, the year after World War II ended, British prime minister Winston Churchill traveled with U.S. president Harry Truman to Westminster College in Fulton, Missouri, to deliver what he considered the most important address of his lengthy career. Churchill, Britain's stalwart prime minister during World War II, had come previously to America to speak—he had addressed Congress three weeks after Japan's attack on Pearl Harbor on December 7, 1941, had catapulted the United States into the war. Churchill titled this new speech in Missouri "The Sinews of Peace," but it has also come to be called "The Iron Curtain Speech." This famous address, given as the Soviet Union was spreading its influence into the countries of Eastern Europe still devastated by World War II, described a menacing communist world lying behind an "iron curtain" dividing Europe in half. The speech succeeded in identifying the earliest days of the coming cold war (1947–91) between the United States and its capitalist allies in the West on one side and the Soviet Union and its communist allies on the other. Churchill named the two evils he saw facing the world: tyranny and fear. A third, poverty, he felt could be overcome in the absence of the other two. As a good friend of President Franklin D. Roosevelt, he stressed the "special relationship" built up during the war between the United States and the British Commonwealth countries. He called for creation of a UN peacekeeping force, and he proposed a permanent alliance (which ultimately became the North Atlantic Treaty Organization, or NATO). He said the know-how to build nuclear weaponry should not be shared with other countries. This wartime spokesman for the British people was chosen prime minister for a third time in 1951. He won the Nobel Prize in literature in 1953 for his histories, biographies, memoirs, and oratory.

The United States stands at this time at the pinnacle of world power. It is a solemn moment for the American Democracy. For with primacy in power is also joined an awe inspiring accountability to the future.

If you look around you, you must feel not only the sense of duty done but also you must feel anxiety lest you fall below the level of achievement. Opportunity is here now, clear and shining for both our countries. To reject it or ignore it or fritter it away will bring upon us all the long reproaches of the after-time. It is necessary that constancy of mind, persistency of purpose, and the grand simplicity of decision shall guide and rule the conduct of the English-speaking peoples in peace as they did in war. We must, and I believe we shall, prove ourselves equal to this severe requirement. . . .

A shadow has fallen upon the scenes so lately lighted by the Allied victory. Nobody knows what Soviet Russia and its Communist international organization intends to do in the immediate future, or what are the limits, if any, to their expansive and proselytizing tendencies. I have a strong admiration and regard for the valiant Russian people and for my wartime comrade, Marshal Stalin. There is deep sympathy and goodwill in Britain—and I doubt not here also—towards the peoples of all the Russias and a resolve to persevere through many differences and rebuffs in establishing lasting friendships.

We understand the Russians need to be secure on her western frontiers by the removal of all possibility of German aggression. We welcome Russia to her rightful place among the leading nations of the world. We welcome her flag upon the seas. Above all, we welcome constant, frequent and growing contacts between the Russian people and our own people on both sides of the Atlantic. It is my duty however, for I am sure you would wish me to state the facts as I see them to you, to place before you certain facts about the present position in Europe.

From Stettin in the Baltic to Trieste in the Adriatic, an iron curtain has descended across the Continent. Behind that line lie all the capitals of the ancient states of Central and Eastern Europe. Warsaw, Berlin, Prague, Vienna, Budapest, Belgrade, Bucharest and Sofia, all these famous cities and the populations around them lie in what I must call the Soviet sphere, and all are subject in one form or another, not only to Soviet influence but to a very high and, in many cases, increasing measure of control from Moscow. Athens alone—Greece with its immortal glories—is free to decide its future at an election under British, American and French observation.

The Russian-dominated Polish Government has been encouraged to make enormous and wrongful inroads upon Germany, and mass expulsions of millions of Germans on a scale grievous and undreamed-of are now taking place. The Communist parties, which were very small in all these Eastern States of Europe, have been raised to pre-eminence and power far beyond their numbers and are seeking everywhere to obtain totalitarian control. Police governments are prevailing in nearly every case, and so far, except in Czechoslovakia, there is no true democracy. . . .

Whatever conclusions may be drawn from these facts—and facts they are—this is certainly not the liberated Europe we fought to build up. Nor is it one which contains the essentials of permanent peace.

The safety of the world requires a new unity in Europe, from which no nation should be permanently outcast. It is from the quarrels of the strong parent races in Europe that the world wars we have witnessed, or which occurred in former times, have sprung. Twice in our own lifetime we have seen the United States—against their wishes and their traditions, against arguments, the force of which it is impossible not to comprehend—drawn by irresistible forces, into these wars in time to secure the victory of the good cause, but only after frightful slaughter and devastation had occurred. Twice the United States has had to send several millions of its young men across the Atlantic to find the war; but now war can find any nation, wherever it may dwell, between dusk and dawn. Surely we should work with conscious purpose for a grand pacification of Europe, within the structure of the United Nations and in accordance with its Charter. . . .

In a great number of countries, far from the Russian frontiers and throughout the world, Communist fifth columns are established and work in complete unity and absolute obedience to the directions they receive from the Communist centre. Except in the British Commonwealth and in the United States where Communism is in its infancy, the Communist parties or fifth columns constitute a growing challenge and peril to Christian civilization. . . .

On the other hand I repulse the idea that a new war is inevitable; still more that it is imminent. It is because I am sure that our fortunes are still in our own hands and that we hold the power to save the future, that I feel the duty to speak out now that I have the occasion and the opportunity to do so.

I do not believe that Soviet Russia desires war. What they desire is the fruits of war and the indefinite expansion of their power and doctrines. But what we have to consider here today while time remains, is the permanent prevention of war and the establishment of conditions of freedom and democracy as rapidly as possible in all countries. Our difficulties and dangers will not be removed by closing our eyes to them. They will not be removed by mere waiting to see what happens; nor will they be removed by a policy of appeasement. What is needed is a settlement, and the longer this is delayed, the more difficult it will be and the greater our dangers will become.

From what I have seen of our Russian friends and Allies during the war, I am convinced that there is nothing they admire so much as strength, and there is nothing for which they have less respect than for weakness, especially military weakness. For that

> From Stettin in the Baltic to Trieste in the Adriatic, an iron curtain has descended across the continent.
> —*Winston Churchill*

reason the old doctrine of a balance of power is unsound. We cannot afford, if we can help it, to work on narrow margins, offering temptations to a trial of strength. If the Western Democracies stand together in strict adherence to the principles of the United Nations Charter, their influence for furthering those principles will be immense and no one is likely to molest them. If however they become divided or falter in their duty and if these all-important years are allowed to slip away then indeed catastrophe may overwhelm us all.

Last time I saw it all coming and cried aloud to my own fellow-countrymen and to the world, but no one paid any attention. Up till the year 1933 or even 1935, Germany might have been saved from the awful fate which has overtaken her and we might all have been spared the miseries Hitler let loose upon mankind. There never was a war in all history easier to prevent by timely action than the one which has just desolated such great areas of the globe. It could have been prevented in my belief without the firing of a single shot, and Germany might be powerful, prosperous and honored today; but no one would listen and one by one we were all sucked into the awful whirlpool. We surely must not let that happen again. This can only be achieved by reaching now, in 1946, a good understanding on all points with Russia under the general authority of the United Nations Organization and by the maintenance of that good understanding through many peaceful years. . . .

If the population of the English-speaking Commonwealths be added to that of the United States with all that such co-operation implies in the air, on the sea, all over the globe and in science and in industry, and in moral force, there will be no quivering, precarious balance of power to offer its temptation to ambition or adventure. On the contrary, there will be an overwhelming assurance of security.

If we adhere faithfully to the Charter of the United Nations and walk forward in sedate and sober strength seeking no one's land or treasure, seeking to lay no arbitrary control upon the thoughts of men; if all British moral and material forces and convictions are joined with your own in fraternal association, the high-roads of the future will be clear, not only for us but for all, not only for our time, but for a century to come.

Source: Churchill, Winston. "Sinews of Peace." Selected Speeches of Winston Churchill. Available online. http://www.winstonchurchill.org/i4a/pages/index.cfm?pageid=389. Accessed December 18, 2007.

BERNARD BARUCH
(1870–1965)
"A Choice between the Quick and the Dead"
New York, New York, United States
June 14, 1946

Bernard Baruch was a self-made millionaire and financier who served as an adviser to U.S. presidents Woodrow Wilson and Franklin Delano Roosevelt during World War I (1914–18) and World War II (1939–45). As a young Wall Street stockbroker, he had earned a fortune speculating in stocks and commodities. During World War I, he served as chairman of the War Industries Board, formed to standardize products and increase manufacturing efficiency in wartime. He accompanied Woodrow Wilson to advise on economics at the Versailles Peace Conference ending World War I. He consulted with President Franklin D. Roosevelt on the nation's recovery from the Great Depression (1929–40) and, during World War II, on taxes and on the shortage of resources such as tin and rubber, essential to war equipment. The war with Germany ended in April 1945, but the war with Japan continued. In an effort to end the war in the Pacific, the United States dropped atomic bombs on the Japanese cities of Hiro-shima and Nagasaki in early August 1945. The resulting devastation—about 120,000 people died instantly and the two cities were largely incinerated—drew concern worldwide about the spread of nuclear weapons. While the United States was the only country with the knowledge and technology to build an atomic bomb, President Truman appointed Baruch to draw up a plan to control nuclear arms. One of the first acts of the United Nations General Assembly—it convened for the first time in January 1946—was to call for an end to nuclear weapons. Bernard Baruch was the U.S. representative to the United Nations Atomic Energy Commission. The 76-year-old elder statesman gave a speech at the opening session, held at Hunter College's gymnasium in New York City, presenting the "Baruch plan." The plan offered to destroy U.S. atomic weapons if the UN enacted controls permitting only peaceful use of nuclear power, but the idea was vetoed by the Soviet Union. Shortly afterward, in 1949, the Soviet Union tested its own bomb.

❧

My fellow members of the United Nations Atomic Energy Commission, and my fellow citizens of the world: We are here to make a choice between the quick and the dead. That is our business.

Behind the black portent of the new atomic age lies a hope which, seized upon with faith, can work our salvation. If we fail, then we have damned every man to be the slave of fear. Let us not deceive ourselves: We must elect world peace or world destruction.

Science has torn from nature a secret so vast in its potentialities that our minds cower from the terror it creates. Yet terror is not enough to inhibit the use of the atomic bomb. The terror created by weapons has never stopped man from employing them. For each new weapon a defense has been produced, in time. But now we face a condition in which adequate defense does not exist.

Science, which gave us this dread power, shows that it can be made a giant help to humanity, but science does not show us how to prevent its baleful use. So we have been appointed to obviate that peril by finding a meeting of the minds and the hearts of our peoples. Only in the will of mankind lies the answer.

It is to express this will and make it effective that we have been assembled. We must provide the mechanism to assure that atomic energy is used for peaceful purposes and preclude its use in war. To that end, we must provide immediate, swift, and sure punishment of those who violate the agreements that are reached by the nations. Penalization is essential if peace is to be more than a feverish interlude between wars. And, too, the United Nations can prescribe individual responsibility and punishment on the principles applied at Nuremberg by the Union of Soviet Socialist Republics, the United Kingdom, France and the United States—a formula certain to benefit the world's future.

In this crisis, we represent not only our governments but, in a larger way, we represent the peoples of the world. We must remember that the peoples do not belong to the governments but that the governments belong to the peoples. We must answer their demands; we must answer the world's longing for peace and security.

In that desire the United States shares ardently and hopefully. The search of science for the absolute weapon has reached fruition in this country. But she stands ready to proscribe and destroy this instrument—to lift its use from death to life—if the world will join in a pact to that end.

In our success lies the promise of a new life, freed from the heart-stopping fears that now beset the world. The beginning of victory for the great ideals for which millions have bled and died lies in building a workable plan. Now we approach fulfillment of the aspirations of mankind. At the end of the road lies the fairer, better, surer life we crave and mean to have.

Only by a lasting peace are liberties and democracies strengthened and deepened. War is their enemy. And it will not do to believe that any of us can escape war's devastation. Victor, vanquished, and neutrals alike are affected physically, economically and morally.

Against the degradation of war we can erect a safeguard. That is the guerdon for which we reach. Within the scope for the formula we outline here, there will be found, to those who seek it, the essential elements of our purpose. Others will see only emptiness. Each of us carries his own mirror in which is reflected hope—or determined desperation—courage or cowardice.

There is a famine throughout the world today. It starves men's bodies. But there is a greater famine—the hunger of men's spirit. That starvation can be cured by the conquest of fear, and the substitution of hope, from which springs faith—faith in each other, faith that we want to work together toward salvation, and determination that those who threaten the peace and safety shall be punished.

The peoples of these democracies gathered here have a particular concern with our answer, for their peoples hate war. They will have a heavy exaction to make of those who fail to provide an escape. They are not afraid of an internationalism that protects; they are unwilling to be fobbed off by mouthings about narrow sovereignty, which is today's phrase for yesterday's isolation.

The basis of a sound foreign policy, in this new age, for all the nations here gathered, is that anything that happens, no matter where or how, which menaces the peace of the world, or the economic stability, concerns each and all of us.

That roughly, may be said to be the central theme of the United Nations. It is with that thought we begin consideration of the most important subject that can engage mankind—life itself. . . .

Now, if ever, is the time to act for the common good. Public opinion supports a world movement toward security. If I read the signs aright, the peoples want a program not composed merely of pious thoughts but of enforceable sanctions—an international law with teeth in it.

We of this nation, desirous of helping to bring peace to the world and realizing the heavy obligations upon us arising from our possession of the means of producing the bomb and from the fact that it is part of our armament, are prepared to make our full contribution toward effective control of atomic energy. . . .

But before a country is ready to relinquish any winning weapons it must have more than words to reassure it. It must have a guarantee of safety, not only against the offenders in the atomic area but against the illegal users of other weapons—bacteriological, biological, gas—perhaps—why not!—against war itself.

In the elimination of war lies our solution, for only then will nations cease to compete with one another in the production and use of dread "secret" weapons which are evaluated solely by their capacity to kill. This devilish program takes us back not merely to the Dark Ages but from cosmos to chaos. If we succeed in finding a suitable way to control atomic weapons, it is reasonable to hope that we may also preclude the use of other weapons adaptable to mass destruction. When a man learns to say "A," he can, if he chooses, learn the rest of the alphabet too.

We are here to make a choice between the quick and the dead. —*Bernard Baruch*

Let this be anchored in our minds: Peace is never long preserved by weight of metal or by an armament race. Peace can be made tranquil and secure only by understanding and agreement fortified by sanctions. We must embrace international cooperation or international disintegration.

Science has taught us how to put the atom to work. But to make it work for good instead of for evil lies in the domain dealing with the principles of human duty. We are now facing a problem more of ethics than of physics.

The solution will require apparent sacrifice in pride and in position, but better pain as the price of peace than death as the price of war.

Source: Trefousse, Hans Louis. *The Cold War: A Book of Documents.* New York: Putnam, 1965, p. 83.

GEORGE C. MARSHALL
(1880–1959)
Announcing the Marshall Plan
Cambridge, Massachusetts, United States
June 5, 1947

George Marshall entered the U.S. Army directly from college. He served as aide to General John Pershing in World War I (1914–18) and, by the start of World War II (1939–45), Marshall had become chief of staff of the U.S. Army. He planned war strategy with President Roosevelt and allies such as British prime minister Winston Churchill, and he presided over an immense expansion and modernization of the unprepared American army. Like Dwight D. Eisenhower and Douglas MacArthur, both commanders of Allied forces in World War II, Marshall achieved the highest possible rank of General of the Army (five stars), a rank equal to Field Marshall in other nation's armies. In 1947, after World War II, Marshall became President Harry Truman's secretary of state. Europe was in dire straits; millions of people were homeless, transportation networks destroyed, heating oil unavailable, and food scarce—people were starving. Recognizing that such economic hardships had helped cause World War I, and might also provide an opportunity for communism to take power in western Europe after World War II, the United States moved to aid Europe. Marshall announced the State Department's plan to revitalize Europe with economic assistance during a graduation address at Harvard University. At first called the European Recovery Program, it came to be called the Marshall Plan; enormously successful, it would eventually extend $13 billion of aid to European countries, including America's erstwhile enemy, Germany, over several years. One outcome of the reconstruction plan was the North Atlantic Treaty Organization (NATO), a mutual defense system that Marshall believed was vital to protect Europe from communist aggression. Twice Marshall was *Time* magazine's Man of the Year. Three years after this address, the 70-year-old Marshall was tapped by President Truman to serve as secretary of defense during the Korean War (1950–51). A professional military man all his life, he won the Nobel Peace Prize in 1953.

I need not tell you that the world situation is very serious. That must be apparent to all intelligent people. I think one difficulty is that the problem is one of such enormous complexity that the very mass of facts presented to the public by press and radio make it exceedingly difficult for the man in the street to reach a clear appraisement of the situation. Furthermore, the people of this country are distant from the troubled areas of the earth and it is hard for them to comprehend the plight and consequent reactions of the long-suffering peoples, and the effect of those reactions on their governments in connection with our efforts to promote peace in the world.

In considering the requirements for the rehabilitation of Europe, the physical loss of life, the visible destruction of cities, factories, mines, and railroads was correctly estimated, but it has become obvious during recent months that this visible destruction was probably less serious than the dislocation of the entire fabric of European economy.

For the past ten years, conditions have been highly abnormal. The feverish preparation for war and the more feverish maintenance of the war effort engulfed all aspects of national economies. Machinery has fallen into disrepair or is entirely obsolete. Under the arbitrary and destructive Nazi rule, virtually every possible enterprise was geared into the German war machine. Long-standing commercial ties, private institutions, banks, insurance companies, and shipping companies disappeared, through loss of capital, absorption through nationalization, or by simple destruction.

In many countries, confidence in the local currency has been severely shaken. The breakdown of the business structure of Europe during the war was complete. Recovery has been seriously retarded by the fact that two years after the close of hostilities a peace settlement with Germany and Austria has not been agreed upon. But even given a more prompt solution of these difficult problems, the rehabilitation of the economic structure of Europe quite evidently will require a much longer time and greater effort than had been foreseen.

There is a phase of this matter which is both interesting and serious. The farmer has always produced the foodstuffs to exchange with the city dweller for the other necessities of life. This division of labor is the basis of modern civilization. At the present time it is threatened with breakdown.

The town and city industries are not producing adequate goods to exchange with the food-producing farmer. Raw materials and fuel are in short supply. Machinery is lacking or worn out. The farmer or the peasant cannot find the goods for sale which he desires to purchase. So the sale of his farm produce for money which he cannot use seems to him an unprofitable transaction. He, therefore, has withdrawn many fields from crop cultivation and is using them for grazing. He feeds more grain to stock and finds for himself and his family an ample supply of food, however short he may be on clothing and the other ordinary gadgets of civilization.

Meanwhile people in the cities are short of food and fuel. So the governments are forced to use their foreign money and credits to procure these necessities abroad. This process exhausts funds which are urgently needed for reconstruction. Thus a very serious situation is rapidly developing which bodes no good for the world. The modern system of the division of labor upon which the exchange of products is based is in danger of breaking down.

The truth of the matter is that Europe's requirements for the next three or four years of foreign food and other essential products—principally from America—are so much greater than her present ability to pay that she must have substantial additional help or face economic, social, and political deterioration of a very grave character.

The remedy lies in breaking the vicious circle and restoring the confidence of the European people in the economic future of their own countries and of Europe as a whole. The manufacturer and the farmer throughout wide areas must be able and willing to exchange their products for currencies the continuing value of which is not open to question.

Aside from the demoralizing effect on the world at large and the possibilities of disturbances arising as a result of the desperation of the people concerned, the consequences to the economy of the United States should be apparent to all. It is logical that the United States should do whatever it is able to do to assist in the return of normal economic health in the world, without which there can be no political stability and no assured peace.

Our policy is directed not against any country or doctrine but against hunger, poverty, desperation, and chaos. Its purpose should be the revival of a working economy in the world so as to permit the emergence of political and social conditions in which free institutions can exist. Such assistance, I am convinced, must not be on a piecemeal basis as various crises develop.

Any assistance that this Government may render in the future should provide a cure rather than a mere palliative. Any government that is willing to assist in the task of recovery will find full cooperation, I am sure, on the part of the United States Government. Any government which maneuvers to block the recovery of other countries cannot expect help from us.

Furthermore, governments, political parties, or groups which seek to perpetuate human misery in order to profit therefrom politically or otherwise will encounter the opposition of the United States.

It is already evident that, before the United States government can proceed much further in its efforts to alleviate the situation and help start the European world on its way to recovery, there must be some agreement among the countries of Europe as to the requirements of the situation and the part those countries themselves will take in order to give proper effect to whatever action might be undertaken by this government. It would be neither fitting nor efficacious for this government to undertake to draw up unilaterally a program designed to place Europe on its feet economically. This is the business of the Europeans. The initiative, I think, must come from Europe.

The role of this country should consist of friendly aid in the drafting of a European program and of later support of such a program so far as it may be practical for us to do so. The program should be a joint one, agreed to by a number, if not all, European nations.

An essential part of any successful action on the part of the United States is an understanding on the part of the people of America of the character of the problem and the remedies to be applied. Political passion and prejudice should have no part. With foresight, and a willingness on the part of our people to face up to the vast responsibility which history has clearly placed upon our country, the difficulties I have outlined can and will be overcome.

I am sorry that on each occasion I have said something publicly in regard to our international situation. I've been forced by the necessities of the case to enter into rather technical discussions. But to my mind, it is of vast importance that our people reach some general understanding of what the complications really are, rather than react from a passion or a prejudice or an emotion of the moment.

As I said more formally a moment ago, we are remote from the scene of these troubles. It is virtually impossible at this distance merely by reading, or listening, or even seeing photographs or motion pictures, to grasp at all the real significance of the situation. And yet the whole world of the future hangs on a proper judgment. It hangs, I think, to a large extent on the realization of the American people, of just what are the various dominant factors. What are the reactions of the people? What are the justifications of those reactions? What are the sufferings? What is needed? What can best be done? What must be done?

Thank you very much.

Source: Marshall, George. "Marshall Plan Speech." George C. Marshall International Center. Available online. http://www.georgecmarshall.org/lt/speeches/marshall_plan.cfm. Accessed September 25, 2007.

JAWAHARLAL NEHRU
(1889–1964)
"A Tryst with Destiny"
New Delhi, India
August 14, 1947

Jawaharlal Nehru was the privileged son of Motilal Nehru, a wealthy Indian nationalist leader. Young Nehru was educated in England and in 1912 became a lawyer in London. At that time, India was a British colony. The British East India Company had begun trading in India as early as 1608, and in 1757 began wresting control from the individual princely states. After the Indian Rebellion of 1857 was crushed, the British government took over rule from the East India Company. India became a full-fledged colony; the "British Raj" was born, with Queen Victoria at its head as empress of India (r. 1876–1901). Reforms in 1909 and 1919 gave Indians participation in local legislatures, but they weren't enough to forestall a vibrant Indian independence movement. With his mentor, Mohandas Gandhi, Nehru led campaigns of civil disobedience against British rule. He was a skilled orator, speaking in support of social reforms and for Muslim-Hindu cooperation. He first became president of the Indian National Congress in 1929, and he spent several years in jail in the independence struggle. At the start of World War II (1939–45), Britain declared war on Germany on behalf of all its colonies, infuriating the Indian National Congress. Nehru and the leaders of the Congress Party were imprisoned three years because of the "Quit India" movement's refusal of aid to Britain unless India was freed. Mutinies within the British Indian Army also compelled Britain to finally realize India's moment had come. The Congress chose Nehru as the country's first prime minister (1947–64), but he was unable to unite Hindus and Muslims and agreed reluctantly to partition the country. At midnight on August 14, 1947, India became independent and was divided into secular (although heavily Hindu) India and Muslim Pakistan—composed of West Pakistan (today's Pakistan), and East Pakistan (today's Bangladesh). The day before independence, Nehru gave this address to India's Constituent Assembly. He refers to Gandhi, calling him the father of the nation.

Long years ago we made a tryst with destiny, and now the time comes when we shall redeem our pledge, not wholly or in full measure, but very substantially. At the stroke of the midnight hour, when the world sleeps, India will awake to life and freedom. A moment comes, which comes but rarely in history, when we step out from the old to the new, when an age ends, and when the soul of a nation, long suppressed, finds utterance. It is fitting that at this solemn moment we take the pledge of dedication to the service of India and her people and to the still larger cause of humanity.

At the dawn of history India started on her unending quest, and trackless centuries are filled with her striving and the grandeur of her success and her failures. Through good and ill fortune alike she has never lost sight of that quest or forgotten the ideals which gave her strength. We end today a period of ill fortune and India discovers herself again. The achievement we celebrate today is but a step, an opening of opportunity, to the greater triumphs and achievements that await us. Are we brave enough and wise enough to grasp this opportunity and accept the challenge of the future?

Freedom and power bring responsibility. The responsibility rests upon this assembly, a sovereign body representing the sovereign people of India. Before the birth of freedom we have endured all the pains of labor and our hearts are heavy with the memory of this sorrow. Some of those pains continue even now. Nevertheless, the past is over and it is the future that beckons to us now.

That future is not one of ease or resting but of incessant striving so that we may fulfill the pledges we have so often taken and the one we shall take today. The service of

Two years before Mahatma Gandhi's assassination by a Hindu fanatic, Jawaharlal Nehru (left) shares a moment with Gandhi (right) during an All-India Congress meeting in Bombay (Mumbai), July 1946. *(AP Photo/Max Desfor)*

India means the service of the millions who suffer. It means the ending of poverty and ignorance and disease and inequality of opportunity. The ambition of the greatest man of our generation has been to wipe every tear from every eye. That may be beyond us, but as long as there are tears and suffering, so long our work will not be over.

And so we have to labor and to work, and work hard, to give reality to our dreams. Those dreams are for India, but they are also for the world, for all the nations and peoples are too closely knit together today for any one of them to imagine that it can live apart. Peace has been said to be indivisible; so is freedom, so is prosperity now, and so also is disaster in this one world that can no longer be split into isolated fragments.

To the people of India, whose representatives we are, we make an appeal to join us with faith and confidence in this great adventure. This is no time for petty and destructive criticism, no time for ill will or blaming others.

We have to build the noble mansion of free India where all her children may dwell. The appointed day has come—the day appointed by destiny—and India stands forth again, after long slumber and struggle, awake, vital, free and independent. The past clings on to us still in some measure and we have to do much before we redeem the pledges we have so often taken. Yet the turning point is past, and history begins anew for us, the history which we shall live and act and others will write about.

It is a fateful moment for us in India, for all Asia and for the world. A new star rises, the star of freedom in the East, a new hope comes into being, a vision long cherished materializes. May the star never set and that hope never be betrayed! We rejoice in that

> A moment comes, which comes but rarely in history, when we step out from the old to the new, when an age ends, and when the soul of a nation, long suppressed, finds utterance. —*Jawaharlal Nehru*

freedom, even though clouds surround us, and many of our people are sorrow stricken and difficult problems encompass us. But freedom brings responsibilities and burdens and we have to face them in the spirit of a free and disciplined people.

On this day our first thoughts go to the architect of this freedom, the Father of our Nation, who, embodying the old spirit of India, held aloft the torch of freedom and lighted up the darkness that surrounded us. We have often been unworthy followers of his and have strayed from his message, but not only we but succeeding generations will remember this message and bear the imprint in their hearts of this great son of India, magnificent in his faith and strength and courage and humility. We shall never allow that torch of freedom to be blown out, however high the wind or stormy the tempest.

Our next thoughts must be of the unknown volunteers and soldiers of freedom who, without praise or reward, have served India even unto death. We think also of our brothers and sisters who have been cut off from us by political boundaries and who unhappily cannot share at present in the freedom that has come. They are of us and will remain of us whatever may happen, and we shall be sharers in their good or ill fortune alike.

The future beckons to us. Whither do we go and what shall be our endeavor? To bring freedom and opportunity to the common man, to the peasants and workers of India; to fight and end poverty and ignorance and disease; to build up a prosperous, democratic and progressive nation; and to create social, economic and political institutions which will ensure justice and fullness of life to every man and woman.

We have hard work ahead. There is no resting for any one of us till we redeem our pledge in full, till we make all the people of India what destiny intended them to be. We are citizens of a great country on the verge of bold advance, and we have to live up to that high standard. All of us, to whatever religion we may belong, are equally the children of India with equal rights, privileges and obligations. We cannot encourage communalism or narrow-mindedness, for no nation can be great whose people are narrow in thought or in action.

To the nations and peoples of the world we send greetings and pledge ourselves to cooperate with them in furthering peace, freedom and democracy. And to India, our much-loved motherland, the ancient, the eternal and the ever new, we pay our reverent homage and we bind ourselves afresh to her service. Jai Hind.

Source: Nehru, Jawaharlal. *Independence and After: A Collection of Speeches.* New York: John Day Co., 1950, p. 3.

JAWAHARLAL NEHRU
(1889–1964)
"A Glory Has Departed"
New Delhi, India

February 2, 1948

Upon receiving independence on August 14, 1947, from Britain, India divided into Muslim Pakistan and Hindu India. Jawaharlal Nehru, a popular and accomplished statesman who had several times been president of the Indian National Congress, became prime minister (1947–64). At the time, a quarter of India's population was Muslim. For decades the Muslim League, a political party representing Indian Muslims, had been unable to find common ground with the mostly Hindu Indian National Congress, even though both parties' platforms favored independence from Britain. Muhammad Ali Jinnah, leader of the league, along with other Muslims felt the Indian National Congress spoke largely for Hindus; they feared Muslim rights and Islamic culture in India would be suppressed. As early as 1940, Jinnah was calling for a separate state at independence. Mohandas Gandhi, the venerable spiritual leader of Indian politics, had been leading a nonviolent resistance movement against British rule for 30 years (SEE his speeches, pp. 291 and 318). Jinnah now organized "Direct Action" strikes promoting an independent Muslim state. Murderous riots between Muslims and Hindus broke out in the east in Bengal (now divided between India and Bangladesh) and in the northwest in the Punjab (now divided between India and Pakistan). With partition in 1947, refugees poured across the borders and intense sectarian violence followed, leaving more than a half million people dead. Seven million Muslim refugees fled to Pakistan, and 10 million Hindus departed for India. During the strife, Mahatma (an honorary title meaning "great soul") Gandhi was shot and killed on January 30, 1948, by a Hindu fanatic who blamed him, wrongly, for the country's partition. The death of Gandhi, the beloved father—"Bapu"—of his country, was a knife in the heart of India. Prime Minister Nehru announced the death by radio broadcast, eloquently appealing for an end to violence. Two days after the 79-year-old holy man's cremation by the Jumna River, Nehru delivered a moving eulogy before the Indian legislature.

(*to the nation*)

Friends and Comrades, the light has gone out of our lives and there is darkness everywhere. I do not know what to tell you and how to say it. Our beloved leader, Bapu as we called him, the Father of the Nation, is no more. Perhaps I am wrong to say that. Nevertheless, we will never see him again as we have seen him for these many years. We will not run to him for advice and seek solace from him, and that is a terrible blow, not to me only, but to millions and millions in this country. And it is a little difficult to soften the blow by any other advice that I or anyone else can give you.

The light has gone out, I said, and yet I was wrong. For the light that shone in this country was no ordinary light. The light that has illumined this country for these many years will illumine this country for many more years, and a thousand years later, that light will be seen in this country and the world will see it and it will give solace to innumerable hearts. For that light represented something more than the immediate past, it represented the living, the eternal truths, reminding us of the right path, drawing us from error, taking this ancient country to freedom.

All this has happened when there was so much more for him to do. We could never think that he was unnecessary or that he had done his task. But now, particularly, when we are faced with so many difficulties, his not being with us is a blow most terrible to bear.

A madman has put an end to his life, for I can only call him mad who did it, and yet there has been enough of poison spread in this country during the past years and

384

months, and this poison has had an effect on people's minds. We must face this poison, we must root out this poison, and we must face all the perils that encompass us, and face them not madly or badly, but rather in the way that our beloved teacher taught us to face them.

The first thing to remember now is that none of us dare misbehave because he is angry. We have to behave like strong and determined people, determined to face all the perils that surround us, determined to carry out the mandate that our great teacher and our great leader has given us, remembering always that if, as I believe, his spirit looks upon us and sees us, nothing would displease his soul so much as to see that we have indulged in any small behavior or any violence.

So we must not do that. But that does not mean that we should be weak, but rather that we should, in strength and in unity, face all the troubles that are in front of us. We must hold together, and all our petty troubles and difficulties and conflicts must be ended in the face of this great disaster. A great disaster is a symbol to us to remember all the big things of life and forget the small things of which we have thought too much. In his death he has reminded us of the big things of life, the living truth, and if we remember that, then it will be well with India. . . .

The greatest prayer that we can offer is to take a pledge to dedicate ourselves to the truth, and to the cause for which this great countryman of ours lived and for which he has died. That is the best prayer that we can offer him and his memory. That is the best prayer we can offer to India and ourselves. Jai Hind.

(to the legislature)
It is customary in the House to pay some tribute to the eminent departed, to say some words of praise and condolence. I am not quite sure in my own mind if it is exactly fitting for me or for any others of this House to say much on this occasion, for I have a sense of utter shame both as an individual and as the head of the government of India that we should have failed to protect the greatest treasure that we possessed.

It is our failure, as it has been our failure in the many months past, to give protection to many an innocent man, woman and child; it may be that the burden and the task was too great for us or for any government. Nevertheless, it is a failure. And today the fact that this mighty person whom we honored and loved beyond measure has gone because we could not give him adequate protection is a shame for all of us. It is a shame to me as an Indian that an Indian should have raised his hand against him; it is a shame to me as a Hindu that a Hindu should have done this deed and done it to the greatest Indian of the day and the greatest Hindu of the age.

We praise people in well-chosen words and we have some kind of a measure for greatness. How shall we praise him and how shall we measure him, because he was not of the common clay that all of us are made of? He came, lived a fairly long span of life and has passed away. No words of praise of ours in this House are needed, for he has had greater praise in his life than any living man in history.

And during these two or three days since his death he has had the homage of the world; what can we add to that? How can we praise him, how can we who have been children of his, and perhaps more intimately his children than the children of his body, for we have all been in some greater or smaller measure the children of his spirit, unworthy as we were?

A glory has departed and the sun that warmed and brightened our lives has set and we shiver in the cold and dark. Yet, he would not have us feel this way. After all, that glory that we saw for all these years, that man with the divine fire, changed us also—and such as we are, we have been molded by him during these years; and out of that divine fire many of us also took a small spark which strengthened and made us work to some extent on the lines that he fashioned. And so if we praise him, our words seem rather small and if we praise him, to some extent we also praise ourselves.

Great men and eminent men have monuments in bronze and marble set up for them, but this man of divine fire managed in his life-time to become enshrined in millions and millions of hearts so that all of us became somewhat of the stuff that he was made of, though to an infinitely lesser degree. He spread out in this way all over India not in palaces only, or in select places or in assemblies but in every hamlet and hut of the lowly and those who suffer. He lives in the hearts of millions and he will live for immemorial ages.

What then can we say about him except to feel humble on this occasion? To praise him we are not worthy—to praise him whom we could not follow adequately and sufficiently. It is almost doing him an injustice just to pass him by with words when he demanded work and labor and sacrifice from us; in a large measure he made this country, during the last thirty years or more, attain to heights of sacrifice which in that particular domain have never been equaled elsewhere. He succeeded in that. Yet ultimately things happened which no doubt made him suffer tremendously though his tender face never lost its smile and he never spoke a harsh word to anyone. Yet, he must have suffered—suffered for the failing of this generation whom he had trained, suffered because we went away from the path that he had shown us. And ultimately the hand of a child of his—for he after all is as much a child of his as any other Indian—a hand of that child of his struck him down.

Long ages afterwards history will judge of this period that we have passed through. It will judge of the successes and the failures—we are too near it to be proper judges and to understand what has happened and what has not happened. All we know is that there was a glory and that it is no more; all we know is that for the moment there is darkness, not so dark certainly because when we look into our hearts we still find the living flame which he lighted there. And if those living flames exist, there will not be darkness in this land and we shall be able, with our effort, remembering him and following his path, to illumine this land again, small as we are, but still with the fire that he instilled into us. . . .

He has gone, and all over India there is a feeling of having been left desolate and forlorn. All of us sense that feeling, and I do not know when we shall be able to get rid of it, and yet together with that feeling there is also a feeling of proud thankfulness that it has been given to us of this generation to be associated with this mighty person. In ages to come, centuries and maybe millennia after us, people will think of this generation when this man of God trod on earth and will think of us who, however small, could also follow his path and tread the holy ground where his feet had been. Let us be worthy of him.

Source: Nehru, Jawaharlal. *Independence and After: A Collection of Speeches.* New York: John Day Co., 1950, p. 17.

ELEANOR ROOSEVELT
(1884–1962)
The Struggles for the Rights of Man
Paris, France
September 28, 1948

Anna Eleanor Roosevelt was born in New York City in 1884 to the wealthy younger brother of President Theodore Roosevelt. She was an awkward, shy child. After her parents' premature deaths, she was sent to school in England to acquire polish and self-confidence; she would ultimately become one of the great humanitarians of the 20th century. When she was 20, she married her fifth cousin, Franklin Delano Roosevelt. He led a vigorous life in politics, first as a U.S. senator, then governor of New York, and finally U.S. president. When he was stricken with paralysis in 1921, Eleanor took on speaking appearances to assist him. As First Lady in the White House (1933–45) she kept a hectic travel schedule, especially to encourage working-class people during the Great Depression and to support the civil rights movement for blacks. After World War II's end (and FDR's death) in 1945, President Truman appointed her U.S. delegate to the fledgling United Nations General Assembly, which replaced the ineffective League of Nations. She became head of the UN Commission on Human Rights the next year. In view of the Nazis' crimes against humanity, the commission was charged with writing a declaration of human rights. Few countries already had a bill of rights; the new declaration—drafted by delegates from Canada, the United States, France, Lebanon, and China—would proclaim rights for citizens of every country. At a meeting of the United Nations in Paris in 1948, Roosevelt addressed UN officials, diplomats, and world leaders at the Sorbonne University on the document she helped write. The Universal Declaration of Human Rights was adopted on December 10, 1948, by 58 nations of the UN General Assembly. The Soviet Union and its satellites, with Saudi Arabia and South Africa, abstained from voting.

I have come this evening to talk with you on one of the greatest issues of our time—that is the preservation of human freedom.

I have chosen to discuss it here in France, at the Sorbonne, because here in this soil the roots of human freedom have long ago struck deep and here they have been richly nourished. It was here the Declaration of the Rights of Man was proclaimed, and the great slogans of the French Revolution—liberty, equality, fraternity—fired the imagination of men. I have chosen to discuss this issue in Europe because this has been the scene of the greatest historic battles between freedom and tyranny. I have chosen to discuss it in the early days of the General Assembly because the issue of human liberty is decisive for the settlement of outstanding political differences and for the future of the United Nations.

The decisive importance of this issue was fully recognized by the founders of the United Nations at San Francisco. Concern for the preservation and promotion of human rights and fundamental freedoms stands at the heart of the United Nations. Its Charter is distinguished by its preoccupation with the rights and welfare of individual men and women. The United Nations has made it clear that it intends to uphold human rights and to protect the dignity of the human personality. In the preamble to the Charter the keynote is set when it declares: "We the people of the United Nations determined . . . to reaffirm faith in fundamental human rights, in the dignity and worth of the human person, in the equal rights of men and women and of nations large and small, and . . . to promote social progress and better standards of life in larger freedom." This reflects the basic premise of the Charter that the peace and security of mankind are dependent on mutual respect for the rights and freedoms of all. . . .

Eleanor Roosevelt speaks at the United Nations in her capacity as a U.S. delegate. After World War II, she served six years in the newly founded United Nations, including as chairperson of the Human Rights Commission drafting the UN Universal Declaration of Human Rights. (*Photo, Franklin D. Roosevelt Library, Hyde Park, New York*)

The Human Rights Commission was given as its first and most important task the preparation of an International Bill of Rights. The General Assembly which opened its third session here in Paris a few days ago will have before it the first fruit of the Commission's labors in this task, that is the International Declaration of Human Rights. . . .

The Declaration has come from the Human Rights Commission with unanimous acceptance except for four abstentions—the U.S.S.R., Yugoslavia, Ukraine, and Byelorussia. The reason for this is a fundamental difference in the conception of human rights as they exist in these states and in certain other Member States in the United Nations.

In the discussion before the Assembly, I think it should be made crystal clear what these differences are and tonight I want to spend a little time making them clear to you. It seems to me there is a valid reason for taking the time today to think carefully and clearly on the subject of human rights, because in the acceptance and observance of these rights lies the root, I believe, of our chance for peace in the future, and for the strengthening of the United Nations organization to the point where it can maintain peace in the future.

We must not be confused about what freedom is. Basic human rights are simple and easily understood: freedom of speech and a free press; freedom of religion and worship; freedom of assembly and the right of petition; the right of men to be secure in their homes and free from unreasonable search and seizure and from arbitrary arrest and punishment.

We must not be deluded by the efforts of the forces of reaction to prostitute the great words of our free tradition and thereby to confuse the struggle. Democracy, freedom, human rights have come to have a definite meaning to the people of the world which we must not allow any nation to so change that they are made synonymous with suppression and dictatorship.

There are basic differences that show up even in the use of words between a democratic and a totalitarian country. For instance "democracy" means one thing to the U.S.S.R. and another to the U.S.A. and, I know, in France. I have served since the first meeting of the nuclear commission on the Human Rights Commission, and I think this point stands out clearly.

The U.S.S.R. Representatives assert that they already have achieved many things which we, in what they call the "bourgeois democracies" cannot achieve because their government controls the accomplishment of these things. Our government seems powerless to them because, in the last analysis, it is controlled by the people. They would not put it that way—they would say that the people in the U.S.S.R. control their government by allowing their government to have certain absolute rights. We, on the other hand, feel that certain rights can never be granted to the government, but must be kept in the hands of the people.

RHETORICAL DEVICE

Alliteration: Repeating the same initial consonant sound of several words in a sentence for emphasis and for appeal to the ear.

These are the signs of reaction, retreat, and retrogression. —*Eleanor Roosevelt*

In the present contest, therefore, you and they will have those feelings that are wont to belong to the victors and the vanquished. —*Publius Cornelius Scipio*

I come not here armed at all points, with law cases and acts of parliament, with the statute book doubled down in dog's-ears, to defend the cause of liberty. —*William Pitt the Elder*

Four score and seven years ago our fathers brought forth on this continent, a new nation, conceived in liberty, and dedicated to the proposition that all men are created equal. —*Abraham Lincoln*

For instance, the U.S.S.R. will assert that their press is free because the state makes it free by providing the machinery, the paper, and even the money for the salaries for the people who work on the paper. They state that there is no control over what is printed in the various papers that they subsidize in this manner, such, for instance, as a trade-union paper. But what would happen if a paper were to print ideas which were critical of the basic policies and beliefs of the Communist government? I am sure some good reason would be found for abolishing that paper....

Long ago in London during a discussion with Mr. Vyshinsky, he told me there was no such thing as freedom for the individual in the world. All freedom of the individual was conditioned by the rights of other individuals. That, of course, I granted. I said: "We approach the question from a different point of view; we here in the United Nations are trying to develop ideals which will be broader in outlook, which will consider first the rights of man, which will consider what makes man more free: not governments, but man."

The totalitarian state typically places the will of the people second to decrees promulgated by a few men at the top....

Sometimes the processes of democracy are slow, and I have known some of our leaders to say that a benevolent dictatorship would accomplish the ends desired in a much shorter time than it takes to go through the democratic processes of discussion and the slow formation of public opinion. But there is no way of insuring that a dictatorship will remain benevolent or that power once in the hands of a few will be returned to the people without struggle or revolution. This we have learned by experience and we accept the slow processes of democracy because we know that shortcuts compromise principles on which no compromise is possible.

The final expression of the opinion of the people with us is through free and honest elections, with valid choices on basic issues and candidates. The secret ballot is an essential to free elections but you must have a choice before you. I have heard my husband say many times that a people need never lose their freedom if they kept their right to a secret ballot and if they used that secret ballot to the full....

In the United States we are old enough not to claim perfection. We recognize that we have some problems of discrimination but we find steady progress being made in the solution of these problems. Through normal democratic processes we are coming to understand our needs and how we can attain full equality for all our people. Free discussion on the subject is permitted. Our Supreme Court has recently rendered decisions to clarify a number of our laws to guarantee the rights of all....

Among free men the end cannot justify the means. We know the patterns of totalitarianism—the single political party, the control of schools, press, radio, the arts, the sciences, and the church to support autocratic authority; these are the age-old patterns against which men have struggled for three thousand years. These are the signs of reaction, retreat, and retrogression.

The United Nations must hold fast to the heritage of freedom won by the struggle of its peoples; it must help us to pass it on to generations to come.

The development of the ideal of freedom and its translation into the everyday life of the people in great areas of the earth is the product of the efforts of many peoples. It is the fruit of a long tradition of vigorous thinking and courageous action. No one race and no one people can claim to have done all the work to achieve greater dignity for human beings and greater freedom to develop human personality. In each generation and in each country there must be a continuation of the struggle and new steps forward must be taken since this is preeminently a field in which to stand still is to retreat.

The field of human rights in not one in which compromise on fundamental principles are possible. The work of the Commission on Human Rights is illustrative. The Declaration of Human Rights provides: "Everyone has the right to leave any country, including his own." The Soviet Representative said he would agree to this right if a single phrase was added to it—"in accordance with the procedure laid down in the laws of that country." It is obvious that to accept this would be not only to compromise but to nullify the right stated. This case forcefully illustrates the importance of the proposition that we must ever be alert not to compromise fundamental human rights merely for the sake of reaching unanimity and thus lose them. . . .

The world at large is aware of the tragic consequences for human beings ruled by totalitarian systems. If we examine Hitler's rise to power, we see how the chains are forged which keep the individual a slave and we can see many similarities in the way things are accomplished in other countries. Politically, men must be free to discuss and to arrive at as many facts as possible and there must be at least a two-party system in a country because when there is only one political party, too many things can be subordinated to the interests of that one party and it becomes a tyrant and not an instrument of democratic government. . . .

The place to discuss the issue of human rights is in the forum of the United Nations. The United Nations has been set up as the common meeting ground for nations, where we can consider together our mutual problems and take advantage of our differences in experience. It is inherent in our firm attachment to democracy and freedom that we stand always ready to use the fundamental democratic procedures of honest discussion and negotiation. It is now as always our hope that despite the wide differences in approach we face in the world today, we can with mutual good faith in the principles of the United Nations Charter, arrive at a common basis of understanding. We are here to join the meetings of this great international Assembly which meets in your beautiful capital city of Paris. Freedom for the individual is an inseparable part of the cherished traditions of France. As one of the Delegates from the United States I pray Almighty God that we may win another victory here for the rights and freedoms of all men.

Source: Roosevelt, Eleanor. "The Struggle for Human Rights." Eleanor Roosevelt Papers Project. George Washington University. Available online. http://www.gwu.edu/~erpapers/documents/speeches/doc026617.cfm. Accessed on August 22, 2007.

HARRY S. TRUMAN

(1884–1972)

The Four Point Speech

Washington, D.C., United States
January 20, 1949

Harry S. Truman first entered national politics in 1935 as a senator from Missouri. His work on the Truman Committee—saving billions of dollars by investigating the poor management of military spending—made him famous. In 1944, as President Franklin D. Roosevelt was running for his fourth term in office, Roosevelt jettisoned his current vice president, Henry Wallace, and added Truman to his ticket. At that time Roosevelt's health was poor; the strain of World War II (1939–45) and his third presidency had left him drained. Only three months into the office of vice president, Truman found himself catapulted to the presidency when Roosevelt died suddenly of a stroke on April 12, 1945. With little prior experience in foreign policy and not even much knowledge of the war's operations, he would shortly learn for the first time of the existence of the new atomic weapon developed by the Manhattan Project. Truman gave the go-ahead for its use after Japan refused to surrender in July 1945.

After World War II came to a close, Truman was kept busy by the new United Nations and North Atlantic Treaty Organization (NATO), and with creating the Marshall Plan (also known as the European Recovery Plan) to bring Europe out of a nightmarish crisis of human misery and economic instability. He used an executive order to desegregate the armed services, and he created the U.S. Air Force in a reorganization of the military. He developed the Truman Doctrine to aid the governments of countries such as Greece and Turkey to prevent communist takeovers and contain the Soviet Union from spreading its influence. In 1948 he was reelected. At his inauguration, he delivered what came to be called the Four Point Speech, emphasizing support for the United Nations, programs to aid postwar world economic recovery, assistance to "freedom-loving nations" against communist aggression, and sharing of scientific and material progress with the world's disadvantaged.

It may be our lot to experience, and in large measure to bring about, a major turning point in the long history of the human race. The first half of this century has been marked by unprecedented and brutal attacks on the rights of man, and by the two most frightful wars in history. The supreme need of our time is for men to learn to live together in peace and harmony.

The peoples of the earth face the future with grave uncertainty, composed almost equally of great hopes and great fears. In this time of doubt, they look to the United States as never before for good will, strength, and wise leadership. It is fitting, therefore, that we take this occasion to proclaim to the world the essential principles of the faith by which we live, and to declare our aims to all peoples.

The American people stand firm in the faith which has inspired this Nation from the beginning. We believe that all men have a right to equal justice under law and equal opportunity to share in the common good. We believe that all men have the right to freedom of thought and expression. We believe that all men are created equal because they are created in the image of God. From this faith we will not be moved.

The American people desire, and are determined to work for, a world in which all nations and all peoples are free to govern themselves as they see fit, and to achieve a decent and satisfying life. Above all else, our people desire, and are determined to work for, peace on earth—a just and lasting peace—based on genuine agreement freely arrived at by equals.

In the pursuit of these aims, the United States and other like-minded nations find themselves directly opposed by a regime with contrary aims and a totally different concept of life. That regime adheres to a false philosophy which purports to offer freedom, security, and greater opportunity to mankind. Misled by this philosophy, many peoples have sacrificed their liberties only to learn to their sorrow that deceit and mockery, poverty and tyranny, are their reward. That false philosophy is communism.

Communism is based on the belief that man is so weak and inadequate that he is unable to govern himself, and therefore requires the rule of strong masters.

Democracy is based on the conviction that man has the moral and intellectual capacity, as well as the inalienable right, to govern himself with reason and justice.

Communism subjects the individual to arrest without lawful cause, punishment without trial, and forced labor as the chattel of the state. It decrees what information he shall receive, what art he shall produce, what leaders he shall follow, and what thoughts he shall think.

Democracy maintains that government is established for the benefit of the individual, and is charged with the responsibility of protecting the rights of the individual and his freedom in the exercise of his abilities.

Communism maintains that social wrongs can be corrected only by violence.

Democracy has proved that social justice can be achieved through peaceful change.

Communism holds that the world is so deeply divided into opposing classes that war is inevitable.

Democracy holds that free nations can settle differences justly and maintain lasting peace.

RHETORICAL DEVICE

Anadiplosis: Repeating a word (or phrase) from the end of a clause or sentence at the beginning of the next, to emphasize the main point. Its relative, *Conduplicatio*, repeats an important word from anywhere in the first clause at the beginning of the next.

To propose the trial of Louis XVI is to question the Revolution. If he may be tried, he may be acquitted; if he may be acquitted, he may be innocent.
—*Maximilien Robespierre*

Our country today is in a bad state for its land is full of fools—
and fools in a country delay the independence of its people. —*Jomo Kenyatta*

I am charged with being an emissary of France!
An emissary of France! —*Robert Emmet*

To those who would claim to speak for Islam, but would deny to our women a place in society, I say the ethos of Islam is equality. Equality between the sexes.
—*Benazir Bhutto*

To conquer we have to dare, to dare again, always to dare!
And France will be saved! —*Georges-Jacques Danton*

These differences between communism and democracy do not concern the United States alone. People everywhere are coming to realize that what is involved is material well-being, human dignity, and the right to believe in and worship God.

I state these differences, not to draw issues of belief as such, but because the actions resulting from the Communist philosophy are a threat to the efforts of free nations to bring about world recovery and lasting peace.

Since the end of hostilities, the United States has invested its substance and its energy in a great constructive effort to restore peace, stability, and freedom to the world. We have sought no territory and we have imposed our will on none. We have asked for no privileges we would not extend to others.

We have constantly and vigorously supported the United Nations and related agencies as a means of applying democratic principles to international relations. We have consistently advocated and relied upon peaceful settlement of disputes among nations. We have made every effort to secure agreement on effective international control of our most powerful weapon, and we have worked steadily for the limitation and control of all armaments. We have encouraged, by precept and example, the expansion of world trade on a sound and fair basis.

Almost a year ago, in company with 16 free nations of Europe, we launched the greatest cooperative economic program in history. The purpose of that unprecedented effort is to invigorate and strengthen democracy in Europe, so that the free people of that continent can resume their rightful place in the forefront of civilization and can contribute once more to the security and welfare of the world.

Our efforts have brought new hope to all mankind. We have beaten back despair and defeatism. We have saved a number of countries from losing their liberty. Hundreds of millions of people all over the world now agree with us, that we need not have war—that we can have peace. . . .

In the coming years, our program for peace and freedom will emphasize four major courses of action.

First, we will continue to give unfaltering support to the United Nations and related agencies, and we will continue to search for ways to strengthen their authority and increase their effectiveness. We believe that the United Nations will be strengthened by the new nations which are being formed in lands now advancing toward self-government under democratic principles.

Second, we will continue our programs for world economic recovery. This means, first of all, that we must keep our full weight behind the European recovery program. We are confident of the success of this major venture in world recovery. We believe that our partners in this effort will achieve the status of self-supporting nations once again. . . .

Third, we will strengthen freedom-loving nations against the dangers of aggression. We are now working out with a number of countries a joint agreement designed to strengthen the security of the North Atlantic area. Such an agreement would take the form of a collective defense arrangement within the terms of the United Nations Charter. We have already established such a defense pact for the Western Hemisphere by the treaty of Rio de Janeiro.

The primary purpose of these agreements is to provide unmistakable proof of the joint determination of the free countries to resist armed attack from any quarter. Each country participating in these arrangements must contribute all it can to the common defense. . . .

Fourth, we must embark on a bold new program for making the benefits of our scientific advances and industrial progress available for the improvement and growth of underdeveloped areas. More than half the people of the world are living in conditions approaching misery. Their food is inadequate. They are victims of disease. Their economic life is primitive and stagnant. Their poverty is a handicap and a threat both to them and to more prosperous areas.

For the first time in history, humanity possesses the knowledge and the skill to relieve the suffering of these people. The United States is pre-eminent among nations in the development of industrial and scientific techniques. The material resources which we can afford to use for the assistance of other peoples are limited. But our imponderable resources in technical knowledge are constantly growing and are inexhaustible.

I believe that we should make available to peace-loving peoples the benefits of our store of technical knowledge in order to help them realize their aspirations for a better life. And, in cooperation with other nations, we should foster capital investment in areas needing development. Our aim should be to help the free peoples of the world, through their own efforts, to produce more food, more clothing, more materials for housing, and more mechanical power to lighten their burdens. . . .

The old imperialism—exploitation for foreign profit—has no place in our plans. What we envisage is a program of development based on the concepts of democratic fair-dealing. . . . Democracy alone can supply the vitalizing force to stir the peoples of the world into triumphant action, not only against their human oppressors, but also against their ancient enemies—hunger, misery, and despair.

On the basis of these four major courses of action we hope to help create the conditions that will lead eventually to personal freedom and happiness for all mankind. . . .

We are aided by all who wish to live in freedom from fear—even by those who live today in fear under their own governments.

We are aided by all who want relief from the lies of propaganda—who desire truth and sincerity.

We are aided by all who desire self-government and a voice in deciding their own affairs.

We are aided by all who long for economic security—for the security and abundance that men in free societies can enjoy.

We are aided by all who desire freedom of speech, freedom of religion, and freedom to live their own lives for useful ends. . . .

To that end we will devote our strength, our resources, and our firmness of resolve. With God's help, the future of mankind will be assured in a world of justice, harmony, and peace.

Source: Truman, Harry. "Inaugural Address." Harry S. Truman Library. Available online. http://www.trumanlibrary.org/publicpapers/index.php?pid=1030&st=&st1=. Accessed December 19, 2007.

THE CONTEMPORARY WORLD
(1950–the Present)

Introduction to the Contemporary World

The second half of the 20th century saw unprecedented advances in the material conditions of human life. Technology and agriculture changed more rapidly and profoundly than ever before in human history. Population also grew quickly, particularly in the poorer nations of the world. Population increases even led to fears of a "population explosion."

Politically, the opening of the period was dominated by two related phenomena, the cold war between the two strongest victorious powers, the United States and the Soviet Union (from 1945 to 1991), and the collapse of the old European colonial empires.

THE COLD WAR

The protagonists of the cold war, the United States and the Soviet Union, remained formally at peace. However, the cold war wasn't simply a clash between the world's two greatest military powers and their respective allies, but between two ideologies—the communism of the Soviet Union, which promoted a classless society based on shared ownership of the means of production, and the democratic capitalism of the United States, which promoted a society based on private or corporate ownership of the means of production. There were numerous conflicts between the two sides, some peaceful and some violent, in the four and a half decades following World War II (1939–45). The Berlin Wall, dividing the German city of Berlin in two, was built in 1961 to prevent residents of communist-controlled East Berlin from fleeing to the richer and freer western part of the city. U.S. president John F. Kennedy made particular use of the wall to contrast the free West and the unfree East in his speech in Berlin, and U.S. president Ronald Reagan would memorably call on Soviet leader Mikhail Gorbachev to "tear down this wall." Outside Europe, the cold war period saw bloody and protracted conflicts in Korea, Vietnam, and Afghanistan, as well as numerous "proxy wars" in which the United States and the Soviet Union backed opposing forces in local disputes.

The greatest fear of the cold war era was that of nuclear destruction. The U.S. nuclear monopoly at the end of World War II proved short-lived as the Soviets quickly developed nuclear bombs of their own. The two sides then went from the atomic bomb, already the most destructive weapon in world history, to develop the far more terrifying hydrogen bomb, or H-Bomb. This bomb would produce a deadly nuclear "fallout," or radiation, that would contaminate or kill hundreds or thousands of miles from the bomb's initial impact. For the first time, it seemed like a great war could mean the end of humanity. Fear of nuclear war waxed and waned with the confrontationalism of cold war politics, peaking in the confrontational era of the 1980s.

Ideology was never the only factor driving the struggle. Both sides were willing to make alliances with states and movements following other philosophies—the United States with conservative authoritarian regimes and the Soviet Union with third world nationalists. Both sides also changed over the period. Nikita Khrushchev, the winner of the power struggle that took place after the death of Joseph Stalin, the general secretary of the Communist Party (1922–53), denounced his predecessor in the "Secret Speech" and somewhat liberalized Soviet policies, while tolerating no challenges to the authority of the Communist Party. Khrushchev's opening proved a false dawn, however, and repression continued. Soviet "dissidents," including Andrei Sakharov and Natan Sharansky, who denounced the communist regime faced repression from their own government, while being treated as heroes by the West. Other dissidents, such as Czechoslovakia's Václav Havel, emerged in the Eastern European Communist regimes supported by Soviet power. The United States moved from confrontation in the 1950s and 1960s to more cooperative relations with the Soviets in the 1970s, only to return to confrontation from the late 1970s through the 1980s. This later confrontational period was epitomized by Reagan's "Evil Empire" speech.

The Soviet Union won a major triumph in the cold war with the establishment of a Soviet-allied Communist regime in Cuba, a Latin American nation the United States had traditionally dominated. The new Cuban leader, revolutionary Fidel Castro, was a particular thorn in the American side for decades. In the Cuban missile crisis of 1963, the presence of Soviet missiles in Cuba, just 90 miles from the Florida coast, led to a terrifying confrontation between the great powers that threatened to bring mankind to the brink of nuclear annihilation. The world breathed a sign of relief when the Soviets withdrew their missiles from Cuba.

DECOLONIZATION AND CIVIL RIGHTS

The dissolution of the colonial empires, which had begun with the independence of India and Pakistan in 1947, continued at an ever-faster pace in the 1950s and 1960s. The decolonization of Africa, under leaders such as Jomo Kenyatta and Kwame Nkrumah, led to the creation of a particularly large number of new nations. Leaders of independent postcolonial countries such as India's Jawaharlal Nehru and the Philippines's Carlos P. Romulo played important roles on the international stage.

The incomplete decolonization of Africa also left lingering problems. Portuguese colonialism in Angola and Mozambique persisted into the 1970s, and the independent regimes of Rhodesia and South Africa were dominated by racist white settler elites that suppressed the black majorities of those countries. South Africa's black leader, Nelson Mandela, was a particularly eloquent and fearless spokesman for his people who attracted international admiration. Another postcolonial problem area has been the Middle East, particularly the relationship between Israel, its Arab neighbors, and the Palestinian people.

As the nations of Asia and Africa freed themselves from white colonial domination, a parallel movement in the United States worked for black people under a different kind of white domination. Overt discrimination against African Americans, both legal and informal, remained the norm nearly a century after the abolition of slavery in 1865. African-American civil rights leaders, such as Martin Luther King, Jr., used the powerful oratorical tradition of the black church to demand their rights from the American government and white society. The effectiveness of this predominantly nonviolent movement in winning political and legal change would help inspire movements elsewhere.

THE UNITED NATIONS AND THE "INTERNATIONAL COMMUNITY"

Much of the drama of the cold war and of postcolonialism played out in the new world political institution founded after World War II, the United Nations. The UN was far more successful than the old League of Nations founded after World War I (1914–18). Its formation expressed the hope for cooperation between the victorious powers to ensure that the world would no longer suffer the scourge of war. Although this dream has never become reality, the UN became an important forum for international disputes as well as the site of important speeches such as American ambassador Adlai Stevenson's statement on the Cuban missile crisis.

The UN and the rise of a truly global media have led speakers to address a new worldwide audience. Dissidents such as Mandela or Poland's anticommunist Lech Wałęsa have addressed themselves not only to their own country, but also to the peoples of the world, hoping to win sympathy for their cause and indirectly to put pressure on their own governments.

By the late 20th century, the United Nations had been joined by a host of international humanitarian and environmental movements. These organizations had precedents in the international movements for abolition of slavery and women's emancipation in the 19th century, but they covered a far greater range of issues. Since these movements had little access to power, they had to persuade, and oratory played a central role in the work of many of them. Humanitarian organizations focus on banning land mines, fighting AIDS, and working for human rights across the globe. Many of the Nobel Peace Prizes issued in the late 20th and early 21st centuries went to such organizations and their leaders.

TELEVISION AND SPEECHMAKING

The most important new technology to affect speechmaking in the late 20th century was television. Television provided a way for not only the orator's words but also the entire presentation to be transmitted to millions. The election of John F. Kennedy to the U.S. presidency in 1960 was one of the first electoral victories to be ascribed to the winner's personal attractiveness and "telegenic" qualities. Kennedy's opponent, Richard M. Nixon, had also made use of televised speechmaking in the famous "Checkers" speech, widely credited with having saved his position as running mate to President Dwight D. Eisenhower. Television has also affected religious oratory. This period in America saw the rise of the "televangelist," the religious orator who primarily addressed a television audience rather than one physically present.

THE POST–COLD WAR WORLD

The end of the cold war and the bipolar U.S.-Soviet world came surprisingly quickly. The most important change leading up to it was a change in the Soviet leadership, when reformer Mikhail Gorbachev came to power as the last general secretary of the Communist Party and head of state in 1985. Gorbachev's policies of glasnost (meaning "openness") and perestroika (reconstruction) partially opened up the Soviet system, allowing Soviet citizens to voice their opposition to government policies more freely. By a process Gorbachev himself did not anticipate but did little to stop, growing freedom led to first the dissolution of the postwar Soviet Empire in Eastern Europe and then the Soviet Union itself. This process was powerfully symbolized in the fall of the Berlin Wall in 1989. After the fall of the Communist regimes in Eastern Europe, the Soviet Union itself dissolved in 1991. The rollback of more than 70 years of Communist history was expressed poignantly in the speech of the new Russian leader, Boris Yeltsin, an ex-communist and first president of the Russian Federation (1991–99), in which he apologized for the murder of the last czar and his family.

The fall of the Soviet Empire was the biggest of several nonviolent (or at least less violent than expected) political transitions that made the late 1980s and early 1990s a time of hope. The period began with the "People Power Revolution" of 1986 in the Philippines, when the government of dictator Ferdinand Marcos was peaceably overthrown. One of the most inspiring of these transitions was the fall of South Africa's apartheid regime and the establishment of a black majority government with Mandela as president.

THE VOICES OF WOMEN AND CHILDREN

One of the greatest revolutions of the time was the emancipation of women in many parts of the world. Those few women who had held positions of political leadership before the 20th century had almost always inherited their power from a husband or a father. Republics where people were elected to power had virtually always excluded women from political leadership. Even when women had won the vote, it often took many years for a woman to rise to the top of the political system. The second half of the 20th century saw many women political leaders, ranging from Israel's Golda Meir to India's Indira Gandhi and Britain's Margaret Thatcher. But not all women whose voices were heard in this period were politicians. Women such as Guatemala's Rigoberta Menchú or Britain's Diana, princess of Wales used their positions of public fame to advance chosen causes.

Another phenomenon of the last few decades of the 20th century was the rise of children as orators. The voices of children expressed an innocence and authenticity that was increasingly valued. The movement against nuclear weapons in the 1980s drew on the power of children such as 14-year-old Susan Hannah Rabin from Vermont. Eleven-year-old South African Nkosi Johnson's speech on AIDS, a "new" disease of the 1980s, derived much of its authority from his own experience as a victim.

NEW CHALLENGES

The optimism of the post-1989 period did not last, as the world moved on to new challenges. One was the rising conflict between radical Islamists and the United States and other Western powers. Although it had roots in the Arab-Israeli and other postcolonial conflicts, radical Islam moved to the center of the world stage on September 11, 2001. Terrorists belonging to the al-Qaeda organization led by Saudi millionaire Osama bin Laden hijacked four jets, flying two into New York's World Trade Center and one into the Pentagon. (The fourth crashed in Pennsylvania after its passengers seized control from the terrorists. It was headed for Washington, D.C.) This horrifying event, leading to the death of nearly 3,000 people, provoked several moving displays of international solidarity from world leaders including Canada's Jean Chrétien and Germany's Johannes Rau. American president George W. Bush won plaudits for his immediate response to the crisis, but the subsequent "war on terror" proved controversial.

Another challenge involved no less than the future of the human race. This was the environmental challenge, and particularly global warming—the gradual increase in the temperature of the Earth caused by the emissions of industrial waste into the atmosphere. American politician Albert Gore, defeated by Bush in a race for the presidency in 2000, found a second career as a prophet of the damage caused by warming and an advocate of measures to deal with it.

Speeches

"I Saw Stalin's Timetable"
Detroit, Michigan, United States
June 9, 1952

Before he escaped to the West in 1948, Nicholas Nyaradi was the Hungarian minister of finance. He had survived World War II (1939–45) with his family in Budapest, the capital city. In early 1945, nearly 1 million Soviet troops had defeated the Nazi occupiers in the ferocious Battle of Budapest (December 29–February 13), in which Nyaradi witnessed the Soviet Red Army's barbarous use of human wave attacks. These two wintry months of siege caused food shortages so severe that Red Army troops ate their own horses. As the devastated city fell in a bloodbath to the Soviets, the desperate population fled; nearly 40,000 had died and many thousands of women and girls were raped. In the first postwar government, Nyaradi negotiated a financial settlement with the Soviets in Moscow regarding German assets in Hungary. This gave him a "ringside seat," as he called it, to observe Russian communism in action in the Soviet Union. But soon Hungarian and then Soviet Communists seized control of Hungary, which became a satellite of the Soviet Union. In exile in America, Nyaradi was frustrated by the attitudes of the majority of Americans, who, he felt, underestimated the threat posed to the West by Joseph Stalin, the general secretary of the Communist Party. Nyaradi traveled the country lecturing on the perils of communism, providing astounding statistics on Stalin's military buildup. The times were jittery in the United States; this was during the Korean War (fought by the United States against communist North Korea from 1950 to 1951) and the Red Scare, a period of intense U.S. fear of infiltrators and homegrown communists. At the beginning of this speech to the Economic Club of Detroit, Nyaradi described how a friendly American truck driver had helped him on the highway with his broken-down car. The truck driver wondered what Nyaradi did for a living; he guessed he was "at least a traveling salesman," rather than the college professor he actually was.

I am a traveling salesman of truth as I learned it—the terrible truth—during the more than four years behind the Iron Curtain while I was fighting a desperate and losing battle against advancing Communism in my own country, and while I was negotiating with top Soviet officials in Moscow.

I am going to tell you the truth. I am going to tell you about a question which is a question of life or death to every single American today, because I am going to tell you that I saw Stalin's timetable. I saw Stalin's timetable not because Stalin showed it to me, but I was in a position to see his plans for coordinating economies, concentrating military powers, preparing his people psychologically, in this dreaded "hate America" campaign for a final showdown.

I am always amazed, gentlemen, to hear some very prominent Americans say that the very last thing Stalin has in mind is a shooting war with your country. Well, I should like to tell you, of course, that Stalin would be happy if he could get around without a shooting war: if he could bleed white your economy; if he could infiltrate your country on the social level; if he could cause disorders here. But I am telling you that a shooting war is not out of the question.

It is a pity that Americans, and sometimes leading American statesmen, don't read books, because I think that the statesmen of the West who sat down at the Conference Table at Teheran, at Yalta and at Potsdam, believing that Russia was a faithful and trustworthy ally of the United States of America, would have eventually changed their opinion, if they had read there in the Lenin Library in Moscow the book of Lenin which I happened to read, and in which Lenin said that there will be a series of conflicts in the world until it will come to the final clash between the forces of Communism and capitalism. And now I am quoting Lenin verbatim: "And at the end of this last showdown, the funeral dirge will be sung either over the tomb of Communism, or over the tomb of capitalism.". . .

Well, gentlemen, I saw Stalin and his henchmen working in order to make this prediction of Lenin come true. I saw that the basic principle of his policy was, is and will be, the destruction of America; the destruction of the last stumbling block on the road leading towards Communist world domination. When I am speaking to you about Stalin's timetable, gentlemen, I am sorry to tell you that we here already are running on borrowed time, because Stalin's timetable is overdue.

I saw his preparations, I saw his plans, and I know that Russia was to have reached its maximum capacity, both in the military and in the economic fields, by the end of last year. . . . The result, gentlemen, that according to statistics which I have seen in the Soviet Ministry of Foreign Trade, five-sixths of Soviet industrial production is going directly or indirectly for war purposes, and only one-sixth of Soviet industrial production serves the purpose of consumer's goods.

You well know, and I don't want to repeat to you, what the military preparations of the Soviet Union are. You well know that they have today under the colors an army which is almost five million men strong, the strongest army in the peacetime history of the world. But what you might not know is that I was able to see little fragments of the plans for a Soviet mobilization, according to which I was able to see that within six months of the start of an eventual war the Soviet Union would be able to send another ten million men into the front lines, which would bring up the total number of the Soviet Army to fifteen million men. If you add to this the five million men of the Chinese Communist Army, and the two million men of the Soviet Eastern European satellites, you will see that in case of a war, you would have to reckon with a twenty-two million-man strong Communist Army on the American defense perimeter. . . .

Today, the whole Soviet orbit is turned into a military camp, and no matter what material you ship into a military camp it becomes of military importance. Wood and glass are certainly not strategic materials, but if you ship them to Russia and the Russians use them to frame Stalin's picture, which they hang up in the barracks to lift the morale of Soviet troops; then, of course, wood and glass become of military importance, too. In my belief, there is only one way to trade with Communist Russia—one safe and secure way—and that is not to trade at all. . . .

Communism as it is now is more than the armed power of a great country. Communism is more than an army. Communism is more than 20,000 jets or 50,000 tanks. Communism is an ideology. It is a philosophy. If I can use this word, it is an evil religion. . . .

I am amazed to see how you Americans take for granted all the wonderful privileges you have here. I am amazed to see how you live without the slightest knowledge of the terrible danger which threatens you. I am amazed to see how you have this most dangerous attitude of "This can't happen to me." I am terribly sorry to tell you gentlemen that Stalin has important allies in your country. I am not speaking only about those fools and criminals in the Communist Party and their fellow travelers who want to undermine your country, but I am speaking about Stalin's allies in the person of those millions and millions of otherwise good, honest Americans whose ignorance and indifference paves the way for Stalin's domination in the world. . . .

I lived once in a city which was just as beautiful, just as happy, just as big and just as colorful as any of your great American cities.

We had 1,500,000 happy men, women and children, working, living and playing in this beautiful city, which was once called "The Queen of the Danube," and then—hell broke loose. First the Nazis marched in and then the Russians came. Those two evil giants, the Nazis and the Communists, battled in our streets, battled in our apartments, in our houses, in our squares and in our gardens for two long months.

One and one-half million civilians lived down in their basements and in the air raid shelters, and for two months we went without food, without water and without medical supplies. Six thousand of our babies died because we didn't have a cup of milk to feed them. If we wanted to drink we had to melt the dirty, filthy snow in our palms because the waterworks was not functioning and we didn't have fuel to warm the snow. If we wanted to eat, at nightfall when the bombing of the city stopped for a minute the population rushed out to the ruined streets and there in the ghostly light of the burning houses we hacked off big chunks of flesh from the carcasses of dead Army horses and ate this meat raw because we didn't have fuel to cook it. . . .

When I am speaking about your privileges, I mean that it is your great privilege to go to bed at night and wake up in the morning in the same bed, because in my part of the world, among 800 million people, the hours between midnight and 4:00 in the morning are hours of anxiety, fear, terror and frustration. That is the time when the Soviet Secret Police go out for their roundups. They round up families, houses, entire cities, or even entire countries. They take the people to jail, to concentration camps or to the gallows. If someone knocks on your door at that time of the night, behind the Iron Curtain, your heart beats up in your throat. . . .

You know, gentlemen, the reason I tell you this is very simple. You of course are very happy that you have a home, that you have a job, that you have a desk, that you have an income and that you have a bank account. You haven't gone through what it means to come to the bank and find a poster on the door saying that the bank is nationalized and your account confiscated. You haven't gone to your farm and seen the Communist Party taking it over for the purpose of a collective farm. You haven't gone to your factory or to your shop and seen the Workers' Council throw you out, in the good case, or arrest you, in the bad case.

But, I went through all this. I lost everything. I was a very wealthy man in my own country, and I have lost not only my job, and not only my belongings, which were all confiscated by the Communists, but what is worse, I have lost my citizenship because my country was enslaved, and I have lost every single relative and friend of mine who remained behind the Iron Curtain. My wife and I were able to flee. The rest of them were arrested. We don't know whether they have been killed, whether they are in Siberia, or what has happened to them.

The reason I am telling you this is because it is a human characteristic that you cannot really appreciate things until you have lost them. I don't want you to lose these things. I want you to appreciate them beforehand. The reason again why I am telling you this, gentlemen, is very simple. We here in this room today have many different things in our backgrounds, but we might have one thing in common: and that is that I, as so many of you here in this audience, am the father of an American citizen. I have a little boy who was born in this country two years ago. His name is Johnny. Today I am telling you this because the only thing that I shall be able to give Johnny is that he will be able to live in a strong and free country, in a country like America always has been.

You see, my little son will never sit in the lap of his grandfather. He will never know how his grandmother would kiss him. He won't have relatives. . . . My wife and I have lost everything that human beings could lose in their lives. I am warning you—warning you very strongly—because the only way that I can preserve my son, the only way that I can make my son happy, is if you people will maintain America as I always knew it and as it always has been, because, believe me gentlemen, the only guarantee for my Johnny, and for the millions of other Johnnys and Marys in this great country is a strong, a powerful, a free and democratic America.

Source: Nyaradi, Nicholas. "I Saw Stalin's Timetable." *Vital Speeches of the Day* 18, no. 21 (August 15, 1952): 667. Permission of John Nyaradi.

JOMO KENYATTA
(1889–1978)
"We Want Self-Government"
Nyeri, Kenya
July 26, 1952

Though African nationalist Jomo Kenyatta is often hailed as the father of the modern nation of Kenya, he is a deeply controversial leader. Born in what was then British East Africa, Kenyatta belonged to the dominant Kikuyu tribe. During his early years he earned an education, first in Britain (where he befriended Ghana's Kwame Nkrumah [SEE Nkrumah's speech, page 411] and helped found the Pan-African Federation) and then in the Soviet Union. In London he lobbied for land and employment opportunities for fellow Kikuyu tribesmen. Following World War II (1939–45), Kenyatta returned to British-ruled Kenya and founded the Kenya African Union (KAU), an organization dedicated to defending African rights against British colonial administrators. It was as president of the KAU that he delivered this speech to an immense gathering of followers, emphasizing democracy, multitribal cooperation, and personal responsibility as the main goals of his organization. He also distanced himself from the recent Mau Mau revolt, an armed insurgency by Kenyan rebels against British authorities that failed militarily but likely hastened Kenyan political independence. Despite Kenyatta's assertion that he took no part in the uprising, a British colonial court months later found him guilty and sentenced him to seven years hard labor. Kenyatta returned to the national spotlight in 1963 by becoming the first prime minister of the independent nation. He remained the leader of Kenya until his death in 1978 through a combination of personal charisma and authoritarian methods. Although lauded for his efforts at reconciliation with white settlers, his commitment to land reforms and aid to the poor, and his pursuit of a pro-democratic, anti-Soviet foreign policy, Kenyatta is also criticized for enriching himself and his family and his alleged involvement in political assassinations.

〜〜〜

I want you to know the purpose of K.A.U. [Kenya African Union]. It is the biggest purpose the African has. It involves every African in Kenya and it is their mouthpiece which asks for freedom. K.A.U. is you and you are the K.A.U. If we unite now, each and every one of us, and each tribe to another, we will cause the implementation in this country of that which the European calls democracy. True democracy has no color distinction. It does not choose between black and white. We are here in this tremendous gathering under the K.A.U. flag to find which road leads us from darkness into democracy. In order to find it we Africans must first achieve the right to elect our own representatives. That is surely the first principle of democracy.

We are the only race in Kenya which does not elect its own representatives in the Legislature, and we are going to set about to rectify this situation. We feel we are dominated by a handful of others who refuse to be just. God said this is our land. The land in which we are to flourish as a people. We are not worried that other races are here with us in our country, but we insist that we are the leaders here, and what we want we insist we get. We want our cattle to get fat on our land so that our children grow up in prosperity; we do not want that fat removed to feed others. He who has ears should now hear that K.A.U. claims this land as its own gift from God, and I wish those who are black, white or brown at this meeting to know this. K.A.U. speaks in daylight. He who calls us the Mau Mau is not truthful. We do not know this thing Mau Mau.

We want to prosper as a nation, and as a nation we demand equality, that is, equal pay for equal work. Whether it is a chief, headman or laborer he needs in these days

Prime Minister of Kenya Jomo Kenyatta receives the Instruments of Independence from Britain's Prince Philip at the independence ceremony in Nairobi, December 12, 1963. *(AP Photo/Dennis Lee Royle)*

increased salary. He needs a salary that compares with a salary of a European who does equal work. We will never get our freedom unless we succeed in this issue. We do not want equal pay for equal work tomorrow—we want it right now. Those who profess to be just must realize that this is the foundation of justice. It has never been known in history that a country prospers without equality. We despise bribery and corruption, those two words that the European repeatedly refers to. Bribery and corruption is prevalent in this country, but I am not surprised. As long as a people are held down, corruption is sure to rise and the only answer to this is a policy of equality. If we work together as one, we must succeed.

Our country today is in a bad state for its land is full of fools—and fools in a country delay the independence of its people. K.A.U. seeks to remedy this situation, and I tell you now it despises thieving, robbery and murder, for these practices ruin our country. I say this because if one man steals, or two men steal, there are people sitting close by lapping up information, who say the whole tribe is bad because a theft has been committed. Those people are wrecking our chances of advancement. They will prevent us getting freedom. If I have my own way, let me tell you I would butcher the criminal, and there are more criminals than one in more senses than one.

The policeman must arrest an offender, a man who is purely an offender, but he must not go about picking up people with a small horn of liquor in their hands and march them in procession with his fellow policemen to Government and say he has got a Mau Mau amongst the Kikuyu people. The plainclothes man who hides in the hedges must, I demand, get the truth of our words before he flies to Government to present them with false information. I ask this of them who are in the meeting to take heed of my words and do their work properly and justly. . . .

Do not be scared of the few policemen under those trees who are holding their rifles high in the air for you to see. Their job is to seize criminals, and we shall save them a duty today. I will never ask you to be subversive but I ask you to be united, for the day of independence is the day of complete unity, and if we unite completely tomorrow, our independence will come tomorrow. This is the day for you to work hard for your country; it is not words but deeds that count and the deeds I ask for come from your pockets. The biggest subscribers to K.A.U. are in this order. First, Thomson's Falls branch, second, Elburgon branch and third Gatundu branch. Do you, in Nyeri branch, want to beat them? Then let us see your deeds come forth.

I want to touch on a number of points, and I ask you for the hundredth time to keep quiet whilst I do this. We want self-government, but this we will never get if we drink beer. It is harming our country and making people fools and encouraging crime. It is also taking all our money. Prosperity is a prerequisite of independence and, more important, the beer we are drinking is harmful to our birthrate. You sleep with a woman for nothing if you drink beer. It causes your bones to weaken, and if you want to increase the population of the Kikuyu you must stop drinking. . . .

K.A.U. is not a fighting union that uses fists and weapons. If any of you here think that force is good, I do not agree with you: remember the old saying that he who is hit with a *rungu* [wooden club] returns, but he who is hit with justice never comes back. I do not want people to accuse us falsely—that we steal and that we are Mau Mau. I pray to you that we join hands for freedom and freedom means abolishing criminality. Beer harms us, and those who drink it do us harm and they may be the so-called Mau Mau. Whatever grievances we have, let us air them here in the open. The criminal does not want freedom and land—he wants to line his own pocket. Let us therefore demand our rights justly. The British Government has discussed the land problem in Kenya and we hope to have a Royal Commission to this country to look into the land problem very shortly. When this Royal Commission comes, let us show it that we are a good peaceful people and not thieves and robbers.

Source: Kenyatta, Jomo. "The Kenya African Union Is Not the Mau Mau." In Sessional Paper No. 5, *The Origins and Growth of Mau Mau*, 1959–1960, edited by F. D. Corfield. Nairobi: Government Printing Office, 1960.

KWAME NKRUMAH
(1909–1972)
The Motion of Destiny
Accra, Ghana
July 10, 1953

Kwame Nkrumah was born in 1909 in Gold Coast, a small territory in West Africa that since 1874 had been a British colony. He was a young Roman Catholic high school teacher and seminary student when he left in 1935 for the United States. He earned degrees in education, theology, and philosophy; and he preached in Philadelphia and New York churches. He went to London in 1945 to study law and became politically active with African nationalists, helping to organize the Fifth Pan-African Congress, which met in Manchester, England. The next year, in 1946, together with Kenya African Union founder and future president Jomo Kenyatta of Kenya, Nkrumah helped form the Pan-African Federation; its goal was independence from colonial powers. At that time, European powers controlled almost all Africa—only Ethiopia and Liberia were free nations. In 1947 Nkrumah was back in the Gold Coast. He drew diverse groups together into the Convention People's Party, and he formed a People's Assembly. The assembly's call for self-government and universal voting rights was rejected by the British colonial government, however. Influenced by Gandhi's movement for self-government, Nkrumah led for several years his own nonviolent "Positive Action" strikes and boycotts, beginning in 1950. Although Nkrumah was jailed for doing so, Britain began the process of giving Gold Coast independence. He won election in 1952 as the first black prime minister. In 1953 he made his Motion of Destiny address to the Legislative Assembly, presenting a motion that Britain grant independence; at the end, he quoted a popular communist credo from Soviet propaganda novelist Nikolai Ostrovsky. Nkrumah changed the country's name to Ghana, after the ancient empire by that name, at independence on March 6, 1957. On that date, Ghana became the 10th independent African nation. Unfortunately, Ghana's promising beginnings shriveled as Nkrumah took increasing control and suppressed the political opposition. He was deposed in 1966 and died in exile.

Mr Speaker, it is with great humility that I stand before my countrymen and before the representatives of Britain, to ask this House to give assent to this Motion. . . .

In seeking your mandate, I am asking you to give my Government the power to bring to fruition the longing hopes, the ardent dreams, the fervent aspirations of the chiefs and people of our country. Throughout a century of alien rule our people have, with ever increasing tendency, looked forward to that bright and glorious day when they shall regain their ancient heritage, and once more take their place rightly as free men in the world.

Mr Speaker, we have frequent examples to show that there comes a time in the history of all colonial peoples when they must, because of their will to throw off the hampering shackles of colonialism, boldly assert their God-given right to be free of a foreign ruler. To-day we are here to claim this right to our independence. . . .

The right of a people to decide their own destiny, to make their way in freedom, is not to be measured by the yardstick of colour or degree of social development. It is an inalienable right of peoples which they are powerless to exercise when forces, stronger than they themselves, by whatever means, for whatever reasons, take this right away from them. If there is to be a criterion of a people's preparedness for self-government, then I say it is their readiness to assume the responsibilities of ruling themselves. For who but a people themselves can say when they are prepared? How can others judge when that moment has arrived in the destiny of a subject people? . . .

I am confident, therefore, that I express the wishes and feelings of the chiefs and people of this country in hoping that the final transfer of power to your Representative Ministers may be done in a spirit of amity and friendship, so that, having peacefully achieved our freedom, the peoples of both countries—Britain and the Gold Coast—may form a new relationship based on mutual respect, trust and friendship. . . .

> Freedom is not something that one people can bestow on another as a gift. They claim it as their own and none can keep it from them. —*Kwame Nkrumah*

In the very early days of the Christian era, long before England had assumed any importance, long even before her people had united into a nation, our ancestors had attained a great empire, which lasted until the eleventh century, when it fell before the attacks of the Moors of the North. At its height that empire stretched from Timbuktu to Bamako, and even as far as to the Atlantic. It is said that lawyers and scholars were much respected in that empire and that the inhabitants of Ghana wore garments of wool, cotton, silk and velvet. There was trade in copper, gold and textile fabrics, and jewels and weapons of gold and silver were carried.

Thus may we take pride in the name of Ghana, not out of romanticism, but as an inspiration for the future. It is right and proper that we should know about our past. For just as the future moves from the present so the present has emerged from the past. Nor need we be ashamed of our past. There was much in it of glory. What our ancestors achieved in the context of their contemporary society gives us confidence that we can create, out of that past, a glorious future, not in terms of war and military pomp, but in terms of social progress and of peace.

For we repudiate war and violence. Our battles shall be against the old ideas that keep men trammelled in their own greed; against the crass stupidities that breed hatred, fear and inhumanity. The heroes of our future will be those who can lead our people out of the stifling fog of disintegration through serfdom, into the valley of light where purpose, endeavour and determination will create that brotherhood which Christ proclaimed two thousand years ago, and about which so much is said, but so little done. . . .

Honourable Members, you are called, here and now, as a result of the relentless tide of history, by Nemesis as it were, to a sacred charge, for you hold the destiny of our country in your hands. The eyes and ears of the world are upon you; yea, our oppressed brothers throughout this vast continent of Africa and the New World are looking to you with desperate hope, as an inspiration to continue their grim fight against cruelties which we in this corner of Africa have never known—cruelties which are a disgrace to humanity, and to the civilisation which the white man has set himself to teach us.

At this time, history is being made; a colonial people in Africa has put forward the first definite claim for independence. An African colonial people proclaim that they are ready to assume the stature of free men and to prove to the world that they are worthy of the trust.

I know that you will not fail those who are listening for the mandate that you will give to your Representative Ministers. For we are ripe for freedom, and our people will not be denied. They are conscious that the right is theirs, and they know that freedom is not something that one people can bestow on another as a gift. They claim it as their own and none can keep it from them.

And while yet we are making our claim for self-government I want to emphasize, Mr Speaker, that self-government is not an end in itself. It is a means to an end, to the building of the good life to the benefit of all, regardless of tribe, creed, colour or station in life. Our aim is to make this country a worthy place for all its citizens, a country that will be a shining light throughout the whole continent of Africa, giving inspiration far beyond its frontiers. And this we can do by dedicating ourselves to unselfish service to humanity. We must learn from the mistakes of others so that we may, in so far as we can, avoid a repetition of those tragedies which have overtaken other human societies.

We must not follow blindly, but must endeavour to create. We must aspire to lead in the arts of peace. The foreign policy of our country must be dedicated to the service of peace and fellowship. We repudiate the evil doctrines of tribal chauvinism, racial prejudice and national hatred. We repudiate these evil ideas because in creating that brotherhood to which we aspire, we hope to make a reality, within the bounds of our small country, of all the grandiose ideologies which are supposed to form the intangible bonds holding together the British Commonwealth of Nations in which we hope to remain. . . .

The strands of history have brought our two countries together. We have provided much material benefit to the British people, and they in turn have taught us many good things. We want to continue to learn from them the best they can give us and we hope that they will find in us qualities worthy of emulation. In our daily lives, we may lack those material comforts regarded as essential by the standards of the modern world, because so much of our wealth is still locked up in our land; but we have the gifts of laughter and joy, a love of music, a lack of malice, an absence of the desire for vengeance for our wrongs, all things of intrinsic worth in a world sick of injustice, revenge, fear and want.

We feel that there is much the world can learn from those of us who belong to what we might term the pretechnological societies. These are values which we must not sacrifice unheedingly in pursuit of material progress. That is why we say that self-government is not an end in itself.

We have to work hard to evolve new patterns, new social customs, new attitudes to life, so that while we seek the material, cultural and economic advancement of our country, while we raise their standards of life, we shall not sacrifice their fundamental happiness. . . .

Mr Speaker, we can only meet the challenge of our age as a free people. Hence our demand for our freedom, for only free men can shape the destinies of their future.

Mr Speaker, Honourable Members, we have great tasks before us. I say, with all seriousness, that it is rarely that human beings have such an opportunity for service to their fellows.

Mr Speaker, for my part, I can only re-echo the words of a great man: "Man's dearest possession is life, and since it is given him to live but once, he must so live as not to be besmeared with the shame of a cowardly existence and trivial past, so live that dying he might say: all my life and all my strength were given to the finest cause in the world—the liberation of mankind."

Mr Speaker, "Now God be thank'd, Who has match'd us with His hour!" I beg to move.

Source: Nkrumah, Kwame. "The Motion of Destiny." In *I Speak of Freedom.* London: Panaf Books, 1973, p. 156.

FIDEL CASTRO
(1926–)
"History Will Absolve Me"
Santiago de Cuba, Cuba
October 16, 1953

Fidel Castro had a disadvantaged childhood in Cuba. He was a good student and entered law school in Havana where he engaged in political action against U.S. involvement in Cuban affairs. As a lawyer he chose to represent the poor, as he was concerned about social injustice. His plans to run for office in the national parliament in 1952 were derailed when General Fulgencio Batista seized power through a coup. On July 26, 1953, Castro led a revolt against Batista's violent dictatorship; it was the beginning of what would later be referred to as the Cuban Revolution (1953–59). His 111 men (including Castro's brother, Raúl) and two women attacked the Moncada military barracks in Santiago de Cuba and the garrison in Bayamo to capture weapons and incite popular revolt. They were quickly routed; 68 were tortured and killed. There was a mass trial for the defendants, while Castro was tried at a secret location. He received a 15-year sentence, but he was freed two years later in an amnesty of political prisoners. Castro's address in his defense (he wrote it down later) brought him fame; he devoted hours to detailing the crimes of the Batista regime, his political philosophy, the misery of the poor, and his plans to redistribute wealth and restore power to the people. He even quoted the U.S. Declaration of Independence—while Castro was a radical, he was not yet the confirmed Marxist he would become. In this excerpt he refers to Antonio Maceo as the "Titan," and to José Martí, the "Apostle" of Cuban independence, the centenary of whose birth was celebrated that year (and was the reason Castro's group took the name Centennial Youth). Castro's "26th of July Movement," named for the date of the Moncada Barracks assault, finally overthrew Batista in 1959 and he took the reins as premier. Six years after the Cuban Revolution he became first secretary of the Cuban Communist Party and led the country into the future as a socialist state aligned with the Soviet Union.

I warn you, I am just beginning! If there is in your hearts a vestige of love for your country, love for humanity, love for justice, listen carefully. I know that I will be silenced for many years; I know that the regime will try to suppress the truth by all possible means; I know that there will be a conspiracy to bury me in oblivion. But my voice will not be stifled—it will rise from my breast even when I feel most alone, and my heart will give it all the fire that callous cowards deny it. . . .

It was never our intention to engage the soldiers of the regiment in combat. We wanted to seize control of them and their weapons in a surprise attack, arouse the people and call the soldiers to abandon the odious flag of the tyranny and to embrace the banner of freedom; to defend the supreme interests of the nation and not the petty interests of a small clique; to turn their guns around and fire on the people's enemies and not on the people, among whom are their own sons and fathers; to unite with the people as the brothers that they are, instead of opposing the people as the enemies the government tries to make of them; to march behind the only beautiful ideal worthy of sacrificing one's life—the greatness and happiness of one's country. To those who doubt that many soldiers would have followed us, I ask: What Cuban does not cherish glory? What heart is not set aflame by the promise of freedom? . . .

Why were we sure of the people's support? When we speak of the people we are not talking about those who live in comfort . . . We're talking about the six hundred thousand Cubans without work, who want to earn their daily bread honestly without having to emigrate from their homeland in search of a livelihood; the five hundred thousand farm laborers who live in miserable shacks, who work four months of the year and starve the rest, sharing their misery with their children . . .

The problem of the land, the problem of industrialization, the problem of housing, the problem of unemployment, the problem of education and the problem of the people's health: these are the six problems we would take immediate steps to solve, along with restoration of civil liberties and political democracy. This exposition may seem cold and theoretical if one does not know the shocking and tragic conditions of the country with regard to these six problems, along with the most humiliating political oppression.

Eighty-five per cent of the small farmers in Cuba pay rent and live under constant threat of being evicted from the land they till. More than half of our most productive land is in the hands of foreigners. In Oriente, the largest province, the lands of the United Fruit Company and the West Indian Company link the northern and southern coasts. There are two hundred thousand peasant families who do not have a single acre of land to till to provide food for their starving children. . . . Only death can liberate one from so much misery. In this respect, however, the State is most helpful—in providing early death for the people. Ninety per cent of the children in the countryside are consumed by parasites which filter

Cuban prime minister Fidel Castro speaks to reporters on arrival in Washington, D.C., April 15, 1959. Three months after his rebel forces overthrew Fulgencio Batista's dictatorship, he visited Washington at the invitation of the press. Although Castro claimed he was not a communist, U.S. president Dwight D. Eisenhower would not meet with him, as Castro's regime had already begun seizing American property in Cuba. *(Photo, Library of Congress)*

through their bare feet from the ground they walk on. . . . They will grow up with rickets, with not a single good tooth in their mouths. By the time they reach thirty, they will have heard ten million speeches and will finally die of misery and deception . . .

Chronicles of our history, down through four and a half centuries, tell us of many acts of cruelty: the slaughter of defenseless Indians by the Spaniards; the plundering and atrocities of pirates along the coast; the barbarities of the Spanish soldiers during our War of Independence; the shooting of prisoners of the Cuban Army by the forces of Weyler; the horrors of the Machado regime, and so on through the bloody crimes of March, 1935. But never has such a sad and bloody page been written in numbers of victims and in the viciousness of the victimizers, as in Santiago de Cuba. . . .

In every society there are men of base instincts. The sadists, brutes, conveyors of all the ancestral atavisms go about in the guise of human beings, but they are monsters, only more or less restrained by discipline and social habit. If they are offered a drink from a river of blood, they will not be satisfied until they drink the river dry. All these men needed was the order. At their hands the best and noblest Cubans perished: the most valiant, the most honest, the most idealistic. The tyrant called them mercenaries. There they were dying as heroes at the hands of men who collect a salary from the Republic and who, with the arms the Republic gave them to defend her, serve the interests of a clique and murder her best citizens.

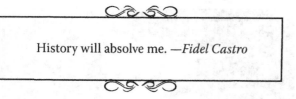

History will absolve me. —*Fidel Castro*

Throughout their torturing of our comrades, the Army offered them the chance to save their lives by betraying their ideology and falsely declaring that Prío had given them money. When they indignantly rejected that proposition, the Army continued with its horrible tortures. They crushed their testicles and they tore out their eyes. But no one yielded. No complaint was heard nor a favor asked. Even when they had been deprived of their vital organs, our men were still a thousand times more men than all their tormentors together. Photographs, which do not lie, show the bodies torn to pieces.

Other methods were used. Frustrated by the valor of the men, they tried to break the spirit of our women. With a bleeding eye in their hands, a sergeant and several other men went to the cell where our comrades Melba Hernández and Haydée Santamaría were held. Addressing the latter, and showing her the eye, they said: "This eye belonged to your brother. If you will not tell us what he refused to say, we will tear out the other." She, who loved her valiant brother above all things, replied full of dignity: "If you tore out an eye and he did not speak, much less will I."

Later they came back and burned their arms with lit cigarettes until at last, filled with spite, they told the young Haydée Santamaría: "You no longer have a fiancé because we have killed him too." But still imperturbable, she answered: "He is not dead, because to die for one's country is to live forever." Never had the heroism and the dignity of Cuban womanhood reached such heights. . . .

For my dead comrades, I claim no vengeance. Since their lives were priceless, the murderers could not pay for them even with their own lives. It is not by blood that we may redeem the lives of those who died for their country. The happiness of their people is the only tribute worthy of them.

What is more, my comrades are neither dead nor forgotten; they live today, more than ever, and their murderers will view with dismay the victorious spirit of their ideas rise from their corpses. Let the Apostle speak for me: "There is a limit to the tears we can shed at the graveside of the dead. Such limit is the infinite love for the homeland and its glory, a love that never falters, loses hope nor grows dim. For the graves of the martyrs are the highest altars of our reverence.". . .

We are Cubans and to be Cuban implies a duty; not to fulfill that duty is a crime, is treason. We are proud of the history of our country; we learned it in school and have grown up hearing of freedom, justice and human rights. We were taught to venerate the glorious example of our heroes and martyrs. Céspedes, Agramonte, Maceo, Gómez and Martí were the first names engraved in our minds. We were taught that the Titan once said that liberty is not begged for but won with the blade of a machete.

We were taught that for the guidance of Cuba's free citizens, the Apostle wrote in his book The Golden Age: "The man who abides by unjust laws and permits any man to trample and mistreat the country in which he was born is not an honorable man . . . In the world there must be a certain degree of honor just as there must be a certain amount of light. When there are many men without honor, there are always others who bear in themselves the honor of many men. These are the men who rebel with great force against those who steal the people's freedom, that is to say, against those who steal honor itself. In those men thousands more are contained, an entire people is contained, human dignity is contained. . . ."

We were taught that the 10th of October and the 24th of February are glorious anniversaries of national rejoicing because they mark days on which Cubans rebelled against the yoke of infamous tyranny. We were taught to cherish and defend the beloved flag of the lone star, and to sing every afternoon the verses of our National Anthem: "To live in chains is to live in disgrace and in opprobrium," and "to die for one's homeland is to live forever!" All this we learned and will never forget, even though today in our land there is murder and prison for the men who practice the ideas taught to them since the cradle. We were born in a free country that our parents bequeathed to us, and the Island will first sink into the sea before we consent to be the slaves of anyone.

It seemed that the Apostle would die during his Centennial. It seemed that his memory would be extinguished forever. So great was the affront! But he is alive; he has not died. His people are rebellious. His people are worthy. His people are faithful to his memory. There are Cubans who have fallen defending his doctrines. There are young men who in magnificent selflessness came to die beside his tomb, giving their blood and their lives so that he could keep on living in the heart of his nation. Cuba, what would have become of you had you let your Apostle die?

I come to the close of my defense plea but I will not end it as lawyers usually do, asking that the accused be freed. I cannot ask freedom for myself while my comrades are already suffering in the ignominious prison of the Isle of Pines. Send me there to join them and to share their fate. It is understandable that honest men should be dead or in prison in a Republic where the President is a criminal and a thief. . . .

I know that imprisonment will be harder for me than it has ever been for anyone, filled with cowardly threats and hideous cruelty. But I do not fear prison, as I do not fear the fury of the miserable tyrant who took the lives of 70 of my comrades.

Condemn me. It does not matter. History will absolve me.

Source: Castro, Fidel. "History Will Absolve Me." Fidel Castro History Archive. Marxists Internet Archive. Available online. http://www.marxists.org/history/cuba/archive/castro/index. htm. Accessed May 14, 2007.

CARLOS PEÑA ROMULO
(1899–1985)
"Changing the Face of the World"
Bandung, Indonesia
April 19, 1955

Building on the success of Kwame Nkrumah's Fifth Pan-African Congress 10 years earlier, the Bandung Conference of 1955 brought together leaders of 23 Asian and six African countries to Bandung, Indonesia, in peaceful solidarity to discuss issues of national sovereignty, colonialism, racism, and political freedom. Sponsored by Burma (Myanmar), Ceylon (Sri Lanka), India, Indonesia, and Pakistan, the conference celebrated the growing membership of the young Third World movement. ("Third World" refers to poorer less-advanced countries, many just throwing off colonialism; the First and Second Worlds are Western and communist nations, respectively. The terms are no longer favored.) A noted speaker at Bandung was statesman Carlos P. Romulo of the Philippines, formerly an American colony. Romulo had been a teenage newspaper reporter and was captain of his debate team in high school and college. After receiving several advanced degrees from colleges and universities in the United States, he worked his way up to editor-in-chief for a Manila newspaper conglomerate. When the United States entered World War II in 1941, he signed on as aide to U.S. Army general Douglas MacArthur, who then was assigned to defend the Philippines from Japanese aggression. When Japan seized the islands in 1942, Romulo joined the exile government of Philippines president Manuel Quezon. In the army, Romulo attained the rank of brigadier general by 1944. After independence in 1946, he became the first Filipino delegate to the new United Nations, was elected president of the U.N. General Assembly in 1949, and chaired the UN Security Council. In his masterful address at Bandung, Romulo nimbly defended democracy against communism, which he refrained from naming because of the sensitivity of communist heads of state (such as Zhou Enlai, premier of China) in the audience. The Non-Aligned Movement (a loose association of South American, African, and Asian countries) grew out of this conference; its members attempted to remain aloof from the two cold war power blocs (centered around the United States and the Soviet Union).

<hr>

We of the Philippines have a profound sense of the great historic events dramatized by this unique gathering. We were, may I remind you, the first of the new nations to emerge in the great rearrangement of the world which began after the end of the Second World War. Our Republic came to being, freely and peacefully, on July 4, 1946. Since that time we have watched with proud solidarity and a feeling of oneness the establishment of the other independent nations of a free Asia, so old and yet so new. We have in these nine years taken our stand firmly behind the struggle of every people to become master of its own fate, to enjoy its own identity, to be responsible for its own acts, to join in the immense task of building a new structure of human well-being and free institutions, the task, indeed, of changing the face of the world. . . .

The majority of independent nations represented here won their independence only within the last decade. Who would have been bold enough, twenty years ago, to predict that this would be so? Who will be bold enough now to say how soon or how slowly those peoples in Africa strong enough to win it will acquire the right to face their own problems in their own way on their own responsibility?

The handwriting of history is spread on the wall; but not everybody reads it the same way or interprets similarly what he reads there. We know the age of European empire is at an end; not all Europeans know that yet. Not all Asians or Africans have been or are still aware that they must make themselves the conscious instruments of historic decision. . . .

It is perilously easy in this world for national independence to be more fiction than fact. . . . Is political freedom achieved when the national banner rises over the seat of government, the foreign ruler goes, and the power passes into the hands of our own leaders? Is the struggle for national independence the struggle to substitute a local oligarchy for the foreign oligarchy? Or is it just the beginning of the conquest of real freedom by the people of the land? Is there political freedom where only one political party may rule? Is there political freedom where dissent from the policy of the government means imprisonment or worse? It strikes me that autocratic rule, control of the press, and the police state are exactly the worst features of some colonialist systems against which we have fought all our lives and against which so many of us are still fighting. Is this really the model of the freedom we seek? Or is it the free interplay of contending parties, the open competition of ideas and political views in the market place, the freedom of a man to speak up as he chooses, be he right or wrong? . . .

Besides the issues of colonialism and political freedom, all of us here are concerned with the matter of racial equality. This is a touchstone, I think, for most of us assembled here and the peoples we represent. The systems and the manners of it have varied, but there has not been . . . a Western colonial regime which has not imposed, to a greater or lesser degree, on the people it ruled the doctrine of their own racial inferiority. We have known, and some of us still know, the searing experience of being demeaned in our lands, of being systematically relegated to subject status not only politically and economically and militarily—but racially as well. . . . Today this type of Western racism survives in virulent form only in certain parts of Africa, notably in the Union of South Africa, but certainly in many other places as well on that vast continent. Against this every decent man on earth has to set his face. . . .

But there is something more too. It is one of our heaviest responsibilities, we of Asia and Africa, not to fall ourselves into the racist trap. We will do this if we let ourselves be drawn insensibly—or deliberately—into any kind of counter-racism, if we respond to the white man's prejudice against us as non-white with prejudice against whites simply because they are white. What a triumph this would be for racism if it should come about. How completely we would defeat ourselves and all who have ever struggled in our countries to be free! . . .

It is our task to rise above this noxious nonsense. We have the responsibility to remain aware that this kind of racist attitude has been the practice not of all white men, but only of some, that it flies in the face of their own profoundest religious beliefs and political goals and aspirations, that in almost all Western lands, and especially in the United States, the internal struggle against racism and all its manifestations has been going on steadily and victoriously. . . .

But we must also soberly ask ourselves: is there a single society or culture represented in this Conference which does not in some degree have its counterpart of this kind of prejudice and ignorance? Where is the society in which men have not in some manner divided themselves for political, social and economic purposes, by wholly irrational and indefensible categories of status, birth, and yes, even skin color? It was a major part of the greatness of India's immortal leader, Mahatma Gandhi, that he devoted so much of his fruitful life of selflessness and sacrifice to a struggle against precisely this kind of thing in Indian life. . . .

I ask you to remember that just as Western political thought has given us all so many of our basic ideas of political freedom, justice and equity, it is Western science which in this generation has exploded the mythology of race. Let us not preserve stupid racial superstitions, which belong to the past. Let us work to remove this ugly disease wherever it is rooted, whether it be among Western men or among ourselves.

Lastly, I have said that all of us here are concerned with peaceful economic growth. . . . I think the shape of the world is going to be determined in large measure by the way in which the peoples of Asia and Africa go about the business of transforming their lives and their societies. . . .

There is one road to change which some countries have adopted and which offers itself to the rest of us as a possible choice. This is the road which proposes total change through total power, through avowed dictatorship and the forcible manipulation of men and means to achieve certain ends, the rigid control of all thought and expression, the ruthless suppression of all opposition, the pervasive control of human life in all spheres by a single, tightly-run self-selected organization of elite individuals. I know that an elaborate series of phrases and rationalization are often used to describe this system. But I am concerned not with propaganda myths. I am concerned with realities. I think we all have to be concerned with what this system offers and what it means.

Does the road to greater freedom really lie through an indefinite period of less freedom? Is it for this that we have in this generation raised our heads and taken up the struggle against foreign tyrannies?

Has all the sacrifice, struggle and devotion, all been, then, for the purpose of replacing foreign tyranny by domestic tyranny?

Do we fight to regain our manhood from Western colonial rulers only to surrender it to rulers among ourselves who seize the power to keep us enslaved?

Is it true, can it be true, in this vastly developed 20th Century, that national progress must be paid for with the individual well-being and freedom of millions of people? Can we really believe that this price will, in some dim and undefined future time, be redeemed by the well-being and freedom of the yet unborn?

The philosophers of this system have answered this question through their doctrine of the so-called withering away of the state. But the rulers who have established their power in real life and not in the realm of bookish dreams have abandoned this tenet of their faith. We have had ample opportunity to witness over more than a generation now that this kind of power, once established, roots itself more and more deeply, gets more and more committed to perpetuating itself. Moreover—and the whole logic of human experience throws its weight into the scale—this system of power becomes inherently expansionist. It can not accept the premise of peace with opponents outside its borders any more than it can make peace with opponents inside its borders. It seeks and must seek to crush all opposition, wherever it exists. . . .

No, my friends, I don't think we have come to where we are, only to surrender blindly to a new super-barbarism, a new super-imperialism, a new super-power. We do not want leaderships in our countries subservient to foreign rulers, be they in London or Paris, The Hague or Washington, or, we must add, Moscow. I think our peoples want to worship the Almighty and live in accordance with His laws, to better their lot, to educate themselves and their children, raise themselves from the degradation of want and disease and misery, by holding up their own heads and acting freely to achieve these great and difficult aims by their own free means in partnership with similarly dedicated people everywhere in the world.

That is the freedom of the democratic way of life. That is the freedom we want all the peoples of Asia and Africa to enjoy. . . . This is the time for Asia and Africa to reassert this principle and serve notice to the world that only by its unqualified acceptance by everyone can there be peace and justice for all mankind.

Source: Romulo, Carlos P. *Vital Speeches of the Day* 21, no. 16 (June 1, 1955): 1,270.

NIKITA KHRUSHCHEV
(1894–1971)
The Secret Speech
Moscow, USSR
February 25, 1956

Joseph Stalin succeeded Vladimir Lenin as leader of the Soviet Union (USSR) in 1924. Although Stalin transformed a backward agrarian nation into a great world power, his rule was disgraced by show trials, savage political purges, and the Great Terror (or Great Purge) of 1937–38. Using torture and forced confessions, an estimated 8 million Soviet citizens were denounced as "enemies of the people" and forced into the Gulag system of brutal concentration camps; several hundred thousand were executed. The Soviet secret police threw a wide net for their victims—they came from the high ranks of the Communist Party, all levels of the state bureaucracy, the educated and professional elites, and well-off farmers from the countryside. Stalin encouraged the public to adore him: he was awarded pompous, adulatory titles, towns were named after him, and statues of Stalin appeared everywhere. Three years after Stalin's death in 1953, Nikita Khrushchev, as first secretary of the Communist Party, broke with party mythology to denounce Stalin and the "cult of the individual" (or "cult of personality") at the 20th Party Congress in Moscow. The hours-long "Secret Speech" was given to a closed session on the last day of the Congress; among other revelations, Khrushchev reported on what had befallen party members elected at the 17th Party Congress of 1934—that 70 percent had been executed in the Great Purge. This news created consternation among the spellbound audience of party delegates. News of the repudiation of Stalin escaped to the West and confirmed long-held views of the cruel and paranoid dictator. The Russian public, brought up on pro-Stalin propaganda, heard of the speech in shock about a month later. In 1958 Khrushchev became premier of the USSR and set about a reform program of de-Stalinization.

Comrades! In the report of the Central Committee of the Party at the Twentieth Congress, in a number of speeches by delegates to the Congress, quite a lot has been said about the cult of the individual and about its harmful consequences.

After Stalin's death the Central Committee of the Party began to implement a policy of explaining concisely and consistently that it is impermissible and foreign to the spirit of Marxism-Leninism to elevate one person, to transform him into a superman possessing supernatural characteristics akin to those of a god. Such a man supposedly knows everything, sees everything, thinks for everyone, can do anything, is infallible in his behavior.

Such a belief about a man, and specifically about Stalin, was cultivated among us for many years. . . .

Allow me first of all to remind you how severely the classics of Marxism-Leninism denounced every manifestation of the cult of the individual. . . . Engels wrote: "Both Marx and I have always been against any public manifestation with regard to individuals, with the exception of cases when it had an important purpose; and we most strongly opposed such manifestations which during our lifetime concerned us personally."

The great modesty of the genius of the revolution, Vladimir Ilyich Lenin, is known. Lenin had always stressed the role of the people as the creator of history, the directing and organizational role of the Party as a living and creative organism, and also the role of the Central Committee. . . . Being a militant Marxist-revolutionist, always unyielding in matters of principle, Lenin never imposed by force his views upon his co-workers. He tried to convince; he patiently explained his opinions to others. . . .

Stalin acted not through persuasion, explanation, and patient cooperation with people, but by imposing his concepts and demanding absolute submission to his opinion. Whoever opposed this concept or tried to prove his viewpoint, and the correctness of his position, was doomed to removal from the leading collective and to subsequent moral and physical annihilation. . . .

> Comrades! We must abolish the cult of the individual decisively, once and for all.
> —*Nikita Khrushchev*

Stalin originated the concept "enemy of the people." This term automatically rendered it unnecessary that the ideological errors of a man or men engaged in controversy be proven; this term made possible the usage of the most cruel repression, violating all norms of revolutionary legality, against anyone who in any way disagreed with Stalin, against those who were only suspected of hostile intent, against those who had bad reputations. . . . Mass arrests and deportations of many thousands of people, execution without trial and without normal investigation created conditions of insecurity, fear and even desperation.

This, of course, did not contribute toward unity of the Party ranks and of all strata of working people, but on the contrary brought about annihilation and the expulsion from the Party of workers who were loyal but inconvenient to Stalin. . . .

It was determined that of the 139 members and candidates of the Party's Central Committee who were elected at the Seventeenth Congress, 98 persons, 70 percent, were arrested and shot (mostly in 1937–1938). . . . The same fate met not only the Central Committee members but also the majority of the delegates to the Seventeenth Party Congress. Of 1,966 delegates with either voting or advisory rights, 1,108 persons were arrested on charges of anti-revolutionary crimes, decidedly more than a majority. . . . This was the result of the abuse of power by Stalin, who began to use mass terror against the Party cadres. . . .

Stalin was a very distrustful man, sickly suspicious. . . . Everywhere and in everything he saw "enemies," "two-facers" and "spies." . . . When Stalin said that one or another should be arrested, it was necessary to accept on faith that he was an "enemy of the people." Meanwhile, Beria's gang, which ran the organs of state security, outdid itself in proving the guilt of the arrested and the truth of materials which it falsified. And what proofs were offered? The confessions of the arrested, and the investigative judges accepted these "confessions." And how is it possible that a person confesses to crimes which he has not committed? Only in one way—because of application of physical methods of pressuring him, tortures, bringing him to a state of unconsciousness, deprivation of his judgment, taking away of his human dignity. . . .

All the more monstrous are the acts whose initiator was Stalin and which are rude violations of the basic Leninist principles of the nationality policy of the Soviet state. We refer to the mass deportations from their native places of whole nations. . . . A decision was taken and executed concerning the deportation of all the Karachai from the lands on which they lived. . . . The same lot befell the whole population of the Autonomous Kalmyk Republic. . . . All the Chechen and Ingush peoples were deported and the Chechen-Ingush Autonomous Republic was liquidated. . . . All Balkars were deported to faraway places. . . . No man of common sense can grasp how it is possible to make whole nations responsible for inimical activity, including women, children, old people. . . .

Comrades! The cult of the individual acquired such monstrous size chiefly because Stalin himself, using all conceivable methods, supported the glorification of his own person. This is supported by numerous facts. One of the most characteristic examples of Stalin's self-glorification and of his lack of even elementary modesty is the edition of his *Short Biography*, which was published in 1948.

This book is an expression of the most dissolute flattery, an example of making a man into a godhead, of transforming him into an infallible sage, "the greatest leader," "sublime strategist of all times and nations." Finally no other words could be found with which to lift Stalin up to the heavens.

We need not give here examples of the loathsome adulation filling this book. All we need to add is that they all were approved and edited by Stalin personally. . . . Where and when could a leader so praise himself? Is this worthy of a leader of the Marxist-Leninist type? No. . . .

You remember well the wise words of Lenin that the Soviet state is strong because of the awareness of the masses that history is created by the millions and tens of millions of people. Our historical victories were attained thanks to the organizational work of the Party, to the many provincial organizations, and to the self-sacrificing work of our great nation. These victories are the result of the great drive and activity of the nation and of the Party as a whole; they are not at all the fruit of the leadership of Stalin, as the situation was pictured during the period of the cult of the individual. . . .

Comrades: We must abolish the cult of the individual decisively, once and for all. . . . The Twentieth Congress of the Communist Party of the Soviet Union has manifested with a new strength the unshakable unity of our Party, its cohesiveness around the Central Committee, its resolute will to accomplish the great task of building Communism. . . .

We are absolutely certain that our Party, armed with the historical resolutions of the Twentieth Congress, will lead the Soviet people along the Leninist path to new successes, to new victories. Long live the victorious banner of our Party—Leninism!

Source: Talbott, Strobe, ed. "Khrushchev's Secret Speech." *Khrushchev Remembers.* Boston: Little, Brown, 1970, p. 559.

LUIS MUÑOZ MARÍN
(1898–1980)
"An America to Serve the World"
Coral Gables, Florida, United States

April 7, 1956

Luis Muñoz Marín was the son of Luis Muñoz Rivera, a nationalist descended from a politically active Puerto Rican family. Muñoz Rivera had championed independence from Spain, and later negotiated for self-government under the U.S. occupation that began in 1898; he represented Puerto Rico in the U.S. Congress and acquired U.S. citizenship for his countrymen. He founded a San Juan newspaper, *El Liberal*, that his son, Muñoz Marín, later edited. Luis Muñoz Marín served a term in the Puerto Rican senate beginning in 1933. Originally a socialist who pursued independence, he founded the powerful Popular Democratic Party in 1938, advocating social and economic reform and later supporting the island's status as an associated state, or commonwealth, of the United States. Until 1948 Puerto Rican governors had been chosen by U.S. presidents; that year, on a platform championing the rural and working poor, Muñoz Marín became the first governor of Puerto Rico to be democratically elected; he was reelected three times, serving 16 years altogether. Under his watch, Puerto Rico drafted its first constitution and officially became an Associated Free State of the United States in 1952. His "Operation Bootstrap" succeeded in bringing greater industrialization and freed the island from dependence on low-wage sugarcane farming. In 1956 he addressed an association of Harvard University alumni clubs at their convention in Coral Gables, Florida, speaking on the important common ground the United States and Puerto Rico must forge in defeating communism and furthering understanding among the peoples of the Americas. It was a taut cold war moment—three years after Marxist Fidel Castro overthrew the Cuban dictatorship of Fulgencio Batista and six years before the Cuban missile crisis brought Russian nuclear weapons to the Western Hemisphere. Although criticized by nationalists for accepting colonial status under the United States, Muñoz Marín is often called the "Father of Modern Puerto Rico."

❧

Since July 25, 1952, Puerto Rico is a self-governing Commonwealth, associated with the American Union through a voluntary compact. It represents a novel, flexible, imaginative relationship within the American constitutional tradition. . . . It is as well an experiment in non-nationalistic political freedom for a Latin American people. Puerto Rico, we know, is not a republic. Neither is it, under its new status, a U.S. possession or territory, nor is it in any way a colony. It is a new kind of state, both in the sense of the U.S. Federal System and in the general sense of people organized to govern themselves. . . .

What is the meaning of this constitutional process, and of the economic and social effort that runs parallel with it, in terms of inter-American relations? What contribution to U.S. policies and U.S. prestige in this vital area of the world is being thus made? I think the answer to these questions can be better understood if placed within the context of the great problems which the United States is facing in its unavoidable and dramatic responsibility to champion the cause of free government and democratic values in this tense, war-weary world.

The Western world, with the American Union in the leadership, is facing the military challenge of communism. It is facing it by preparedness and vigilance and by a constant and sincere search for agreement on disarmament. But we know that the conflict with communist totalitarianism is not just an attempt to guarantee survival by military means, or even by disarmament. In a way, the armament race, gigantic and ominous as it is, gives one a feeling of anachronism, that it is a symbol of a world ailing because of its own physical strength and seeking for its cure a great wisdom that constantly eludes it.

Disarmament, if it comes, will not by itself stop the challenge to freedom. It would, however, make it a creative challenge. The struggle would then increasingly shape itself, I believe, as the ideological clash between the attempt to defeat economic poverty by political slavery and the purpose to enhance political and human freedom by economic productivity and social justice.

As it stands today, both struggles are going on, the military and the ideological. Within recent months we have witnessed an intensification of the ideological fight. We have all observed the moves of the Soviet Union into the field of technical assistance and economic aid to the underdeveloped areas, as well as of Russian support for old grievances against Western powers. In a world still bedeviled by undernourishment, evil housing conditions, scant protection against disease, little economic security, the Soviet thrust is more challenging to the Western world, that believes in fighting these evils through freedom, than a stockpile of hydrogen bombs.

The Soviet Prime Minister has announced Russia's intention of offering technical assistance to Latin America and to find better trade channels for its commerce. One of the top men of the Soviet is about to initiate a tour through Latin America offering manna. No doubt a vigorous offensive shall follow by the communists and their friends in Latin America to picture the Soviet pattern of life as most enticing to the underdeveloped economies in the Western Hemisphere and to unfold before their eyes a vision of a swift Industrial Revolution that may bring, in a generation, the abolition of poverty. They will speak of freedom as well as of economic salvation.

They will probably not be believed as to freedom; but they need not be, because many of the peoples are living under governments that are not democratic. The peoples are unfree and miserably poor. Even if only half of the Russian picture is accepted, the vision would be one of the unfamiliar surcease of extreme poverty even if under the familiar absence of democratic freedom. All such governments in Latin America claim to be anti-communist, and there is no reason to believe that they are not. There is, however, no doubt that in practice, in relation to the lives of their own peoples, they are also anti-democratic. The dealings of the U.S. with such regimes present a most delicate problem. There is no question that the U.S. must assure the peoples of the hemisphere of its genuine concern for their political freedom and human rights. And it is called upon to do this difficult feat while keeping its skirts clear of any suspicion of intervention in the internal affairs of other countries. It is a dilemma. But I believe there are ways for the U.S. to make a sufficiently clear distinction between its friends who are democrats and anti-communist and its friends who are only anti-communists.

In this respect, we should convince ourselves, and so become strongly convincing, that the answer to the communist challenge lies in the ability of the Western powers, and especially the United States, to show to the less fortunate countries of the world that a greater transformation can be achieved, at an even faster rate and on sounder economic foundations, without shattering, or ignoring, as the Russians and the Red Chinese have done, the fabric of political and individual liberties. . . .

It is in this connection that the Puerto Rican experience can be clarifying. For it demonstrates a joint political creativeness of the U.S. and a people of Latin-American origin. In the economic, social and cultural field, it reveals the U.S. at its undogmatic best: the helping hand guided by the undoctrinaire spirit, so forgetful of its bigness that it fully reveals its greatness. For if the Commonwealth idea is a tangible proof of the possibility of original political thinking in the Americas, a dramatic refutation of the communist claim that the United States position is narrow, colonialist and reactionary, the social and economic surge in Puerto Rico clearly demonstrates that a people of different historical background can find a way out of their former anguish and despair, in close association with the United States.

We have called this surge "Operation Bootstrap"—an effort to lead the people out of extreme poverty, if possible, not into extreme wealth; and to do this—"Operation Commonwealth"—in an association with the American Union so close as that of common citizenship. We have been healthily undoctrinaire, with no fixed taboos, no immutable sacred cows, in the use of instruments to achieve a better standard of living, caring only that all instruments used conformed to the democratic process and could be tested periodically by approval of the public will at the polls.

The Commonwealth Government pioneered in building and operating factories when there was need to do so, because private capital was hesitant to do it. It socialistically established and managed industries, and then capitalistically sold them to private enterprise and used the money in further stimulation of economic development by some more private enterprise. It has pioneered in attracting United States and foreign capital, in stimulating private initiative and investment, to promote prompt and effective industrialization. It has used United States techniques and ideas, adapting and rejecting them with a frank experimental temper. It has engaged in land reform without destroying the basic unit of production and without unfair expropriation. It has launched an educational program—"Operation Serenity"—for young and adults which consumes nearly one third of our budget. . . .

Because the people of our Commonwealth are fired with a vision of what human energies can do to overcome man-created or nature-created misery, we have insisted in making Puerto Rico a training center for technical assistance, a laboratory for visitors from the New World and even Africa and Asia, so that they may see for themselves our unrelenting and peaceful war on colonialism, poverty, disease, ignorance, and hopelessness—carried out in terms of a deep sense of friendship, of brotherhood with the U.S.

Even before Congress appropriated money for the Point Four program, our government established an office and offered its services and cooperation. We have received over 2,700 visitors and trainees—the vast majority from Latin America, who have acquired first hand knowledge of how the two great cultures of America can work together in terms of freedom, respect, and economic achievement. We have had of late in Puerto Rico eminent visitors like the wise President of Haiti, Paul Magloire, and that staunch defender of hemispheric solidarity through freedom, President José Figueres of Costa Rica. We have held numerous inter-American conferences, seminars, workshops, and meetings, always aiming at making our island a place where people of good faith from this Hemisphere can meet to discuss their common problems and aspirations in an atmosphere of freedom and mutual trust.

We are a Latin American country composed of citizens of the United States. But that does not quite express it. It is not only that the citizenship is U.S. period, and the culture Latin American period. It is more than just the addition of those two concepts. It is an emerging new manner in the Americas, an example, perhaps a still dimly realized preview, of what a grand hemispheric union might look like to our children. In saying this, I am not referring to political institutions. Democratic peoples have to be constantly creative, and the Commonwealth of Puerto Rico, the people of it, are naturally by no means pretending to offer a pattern of political union. They believe that their experience may be a stimulant to imaginative search—political, cultural, social, economic. We are seeking serenity through an efficiency placed at the service of understanding.

This is a job in which we want to participate more and more. As we scan the social, economic, and political horizon, as we shape the course of the future generation in terms of a fuller and richer society, conducted with freedom and order, with more education than conspicuous consumption, with more imagination than acquisitiveness, we feel the deep spiritual urge to link our experience and hope to the wider search for hemispheric unity. The dream we dream is a realistic dream. Hard study, cool reasoning, unremitting labor and unfailing dedication, can make it possible.

Let us urgently devise the basic objectives in housing, in health, in education, in economic productivity, in communications, which may be attainable by different areas of the Hemisphere, according to their human and material resources. Let us solemnly declare that our essential goal—the goal of all Americans, North and South—is the abolition of extreme poverty, in the areas of misery remaining in regions of the U.S. and in the altiplano of Bolivia, the plains of Venezuela, the coffee lands of Puerto Rico and Central America, the sierras of Mexico—to wipe out extreme poverty in this Hemisphere within the lifetime of children already born.

Let us encourage government and private initiative to share in a good partnership with a view to better distributive justice for all; and let's not be doctrinaire about it. Let us not be doctrinaire either as to socialism or capitalism, but only as to freedom and human dignity. Let us give friendly support to all groups thinking in terms of a greater, truly hemispheric America, not merely Latin, not merely Anglo-Saxon, and not merely temporary while a Russian danger lasts. An America to serve the world.

Source: Muñoz Marín, Luis. "An America to Serve the World." Fundación Luis Muñoz Marín. Available online. http://www.munoz-marin.org/pags_nuevas_folder/discursos_folder/discursos_menu.html. Accessed December 18, 2007.

GOLDA MEIR
(1898–1978)
"Peace with Our Arab Neighbors"
United Nations, New York City

October 7, 1957

European anti-Semitism and the millennia-long homelessness of the Jewish people gave birth around 1896 to the Zionist movement. The aim was to

Golda Meir was appointed Israeli minister of foreign affairs in 1956 and became prime minister of Israel in 1969. (AP Photo)

reestablish a national homeland for Jews in the land of Israel, in Palestine. From the 16th century until World War I (1914–18), Palestine had been a part of the Ottoman Empire. After the defeat of Germany and its ally, the Ottoman Empire, by Britain and the Allied powers (including the United States), the League of Nations—set up to oppose war and aggression—divided up the defeated aggressors' territories and gave Britain a mandate to govern Palestine. The Balfour Declaration, issued by the British government in 1917, stated Britain's support for a Jewish homeland in Palestine. After the murder of six million Jews by Nazi Germany in World War II (1939–45), the United Nations (replacing the League of Nations) agreed to the establishment of a Jewish nation in Palestine in 1947, dividing Palestine into separate Jewish and Arab states. Arab nations, however, furious at the move, refused to recognize Israel. Israel went ahead and declared itself an independent nation on May 14, 1948; neighboring Arab states (Egypt, Syria, Lebanon, Iraq, and Transjordan) declared war on Israel the next day. War occurred again in 1956. In October the following year, Israel's foreign minister, Golda Meir, addressed the United Nations General Assembly on Arab refusal to acknowledge Israel, regional cold war tensions, the problems of refugees, and discrimination against Israeli ships in the Egyptian-held Suez Canal; at the end of her speech she directed a special appeal to the Arab states. Meir had grown up as an immigrant child in the United States. Active in the Zionist movement, she married and moved to Israel in 1921. She emerged as a Zionist labor leader, and she was one of the signers of the declaration establishing Israel as a state. She became an ambassador, then a member of the Israeli parliament, and, in 1969, prime minister.

I should like from this rostrum to address to the Arab States of the Middle East a solemn appeal: Israel is approaching its tenth anniversary. You did not want it to be born; you fought against the decision in the United Nations. You then attacked us by military force. We have all been witnesses to sorrow, destruction and spilling of blood and tears.

428

RHETORICAL DEVICE

Analogy: Comparing two things in an extended fashion to highlight meaning and strengthen the point. (*See the related* metaphor *and* simile.)

Power may justly be compared to a great river. While kept within its due bounds it is both beautiful and useful. But when it overflows its banks, it . . . brings destruction and desolation wherever it comes. —*Andrew Hamilton*

If you kill me you will not easily find another like me, who, if I may use such a ludicrous figure of speech, am a sort of gadfly, given to the state by the God; and the state is like a great and noble steed who is tardy in his motions owing to his very size, and requires to be stirred into life. —*Socrates*

The spokes of the wheel are the rules of pure conduct: Justice is the uniformity of their length, wisdom is the tire; modesty and thoughtfulness are the hub in which the immovable axle of truth is fixed. —*Gautama Buddha*

Yet Israel is here, growing, developing and progressing. It has gained many friends, and their number is steadily increasing.

We are an old, tenacious people and, as our history has proved, not easily destroyed. Like you we have regained our national independence and, as with you so with us, nothing will cause us to give it up. We are here to stay. History has decreed that the Middle East consists of independent Israel and the independent Arab States. This verdict will never be reversed.

In the light of these facts, what is the use or realism or justice of policies and attitudes based on the fiction that Israel is not there or will somehow disappear? Would it not be better for all to build a future for the Middle East based on cooperation? Israel will exist and flourish even without peace, but surely a future of peace would be better both for Israel and for its neighbors.

The Arab world, with its twelve sovereignties and four million square miles, can well afford to accommodate itself to peaceful cooperation with Israel. Does hate for Israel and the aspiration for its destruction make one child in your countries happier? Does it convert one hovel into a house? Does culture thrive on the soil of hatred?

The deserts of the Middle East are in need of water, not bombers. Tens of millions of its inhabitants are craving for the means of life and not for implements of death. I ask all of you, old and new members of the United Nations, to use your influence not to deepen the abyss of misunderstanding but to bridge it.—*Golda Meir*

We have not the slightest doubt that eventually there will be peace and cooperation between us. We are prepared and anxious to bring it about now.

I should also like to address myself to all delegates in this Assembly, and especially to the powers directly involved in the problems of the Middle East. The deserts of the Middle East are in need of water, not bombers. Tens of millions of its inhabitants are craving for the means of life and not for implements of death. I ask all of you, old and new members of the United Nations, to use your influence not to deepen the abyss of misunderstanding but to bridge it.

I conclude with a word of deepest appreciation to those countries, member states of the United Nations, who ten years ago helped to lay the foundation for Israel's statehood, and whose continued understanding, assistance and friendship have enabled us to weather the storms which beset our path.

Many of these countries are without direct interest of any kind in our area. But their appreciation of the moral, social, historic and religious factors involved has led them to profoundly held convictions which they have maintained with staunchness and courage. Their friendship and help will never be forgotten by the people of Israel and the Jewish people as a whole. It is also a source of satisfaction and joy that with many of the new countries that have in the meantime joined the U.N. we are linked in bonds of friendship, of understanding and of mutual aid.

In celebrating the tenth anniversary of Israel's independence, we look back on a decade of struggle, of achievement in some areas and of failure in others. Our greatest grief has been the lack of progress towards peace with our Arab neighbors. It is our profoundest hope that the coming period may make a decisive step forward in this regard, to the inestimable benefit of all the peoples of the Middle East and perhaps of the whole world.

Source: Meir, Golda. "Israel Committed to Peace." October 7, 1957. Israel Ministry of Foreign Affairs. Available online. http://www.mfa.gov.il/MFA/Foreign+Relations/Israels+Foreign+R elations+since+1947/1947-1974/1+Israel+Committed+to+Peace+-+Address+to+the+Gener. htm. Accessed September 10, 2008.

RICHARD M. NIXON
(1913–1994)
To the Russian People
Moscow, USSR
August 1, 1959

Richard Nixon is best known for the Watergate scandal (illegal political activities he authorized) that brought his resignation as U.S. president in 1974. He successfully used his time in office, however, to improve dangerous cold war relations with communist behemoths China and the Soviet Union. Early in his career, he had been vice president in President Dwight D. Eisenhower's administration (1952–60), and he had journeyed to the Soviet Union for a nine-day visit. It was the tense cold war year of 1959, although the visit came during the Khrushchev thaw, when Soviet premier (and first secretary of the Communist Party) Nikita Khrushchev (1958–64) was attempting within Russia to repair some of Stalin's "excesses." In Moscow, Nixon was scheduled to open the traveling American National Exhibition on its first day. He took Khrushchev to tour the exhibit of American life and technology before it officially opened. It was then that the testy "Kitchen Debate" occurred, as the pair stood before the display kitchen in the model American home, debating communism versus capitalism through their interpreters. The day before leaving to return home, in an unusual gesture of openness from the Soviets, Nixon was permitted to give a televised and radio address to the Russian people. He complimented them on their hard work and sense of humor, offered a brief history of the arms buildup and American proposals promoting peace, and, in closing, mentioned a conversation with Khrushchev—who had predicted Nixon's grandchildren would live under communism. In later years as president, Nixon opened the Strategic Arms Limitation Talks with the Soviet Union in 1969 to limit the escalating arms race. Relations with China at that time were so tense that an American ping-pong team's 1971 visit was a major breakthrough. Nixon followed with a startling visit in 1972 to Mao Zedong, leader of the government and party of the People's Republic of China (1949–76); Nixon was said to have "opened" China.

What we need today is not two worlds but one world where different peoples choose the economic and political systems which they want, but where there is free communication among all the peoples living on this earth.

Let us expand the concept of open skies. What the world also needs are open cities, open minds and open hearts.

Let us have peaceful competition not only in producing the best factories but in producing better lives for our people.

Let us cooperate in our exploration of outer space. As a worker told me in Novosibirsk, let us go to the moon together.

Let our aim be not victory over other peoples but the victory of all mankind over hunger, want, misery and disease, wherever it exists in the world.

I realize that this era of peaceful competition and even cooperation seems like an impossible dream when we consider the present differences we have between us. But the leaders of our countries can help make this dream come true. So far as the leader of our country is concerned, I can assure you that President Eisenhower has no objective to which he is more dedicated.

As far as Mr. Khrushchev is concerned, as I am sure you know, we disagree sharply on political and economic philosophy and on many world problems. But these characteristics are evident to anyone who meets him—He is a self-made man who worked his way up from the bottom; he is an articulate spokesman for the economic system in which he believes; he has immense drive; in sum, he is one of those individuals who,

Soviet premier Nikita Khrushchev, left, and U.S. vice president Richard Nixon, right, spar in the Kitchen Debate. Moscow, July 24, 1959 *(Courtesy Richard Nixon Presidential Library)*

whether you agree with him or disagree with him, is a born leader of men. Because he has these unique qualities and because the decisions he makes will affect not only the 200 million people of the USSR but the 3 billion people on this earth, he carries a tremendous responsibility on his shoulders.

I would not be so presumptuous as to try to give him advice on how he should fulfill that responsibility. But could I relate something that I noted on the trip I have just completed? In every factory and on hundreds of billboards I saw this slogan, "Let us work for the victory of Communism."

If Mr. Khrushchev means by this slogan working for a better life for the people within the Soviet Union that is one thing. If, on the other hand, he means the victory of Communism over the United States and other countries, this is a horse of a different color. For we have our own ideas as to what system is best for us.

If he devotes his immense energies and talents to building a better life for the people of his own country, Mr. Khrushchev can go down in history as one of the greatest leaders the Soviet people have ever produced. But if he diverts the resources and talents of his people to the objective of promoting the communization of countries outside the Soviet Union, he will only assure that both he and his people will continue to live in an era of fear, suspicion and tension.

The Geneva conference is a case in point. It would not be proper for me to comment on the specific proposals that are pending before that conference at this time. But agreements between great powers cannot be reached unless they take into account the views and interests of all parties concerned. I was encouraged to note in my conversations with Mr. Khrushchev that he recognizes this fact and agrees that a successful outcome of this conference could be a great step forward in settling some of the problems I have discussed tonight.

I have one final thought to add. Mr. Khrushchev predicted that our grandchildren would live under Communism. He reiterated this to me in our talks last Sunday.

Let me say that we do not object to his saying this will happen. We only object if he tries to bring it about.

And this is my answer to him. I do not say that your grandchildren will live under capitalism. We prefer our system. But the very essence of our belief is that we do not and will not try to impose our system on anybody else. We believe that you and all other peoples on this earth should have the right to choose the kind of economic or political system which best fits your particular problems without any foreign intervention.

As I leave your country, I shall never forget an incident that occurred as I was driving through your beautiful Ural mountains. A group of children on the side of the road threw wildflowers into my car and cried in English the words "friendship, friendship." Mr. Zhukov told me that the first word children who study English are taught is the word "friendship." There could be no more eloquent expression of the attitude of the Soviet people, an attitude which we share in common with you.

Finally, may I express on behalf of my wife and I, and all the members of our party, our deep appreciation for the warm friendship and boundless hospitality we have found everywhere we have gone in the Soviet Union. I pledge to you that in the years to come I shall devote my best efforts to the cause of peace with justice for all the peoples of the world.

Source: Nixon, Richard. "Address to the Russian People." In *The Speaker's Resource Book*, edited by Carroll Arnold, Douglas Ehninger, and John Gerber, 241. Chicago: Scott, Foresman, 1961.

HAROLD MACMILLAN
(1894–1986)
"The Wind of Change"
Cape Town, South Africa
February 3, 1960

Harold Macmillan became British prime minister in 1957, as anticolonial unrest (including the Suez crisis, in which Britain tried to reestablish control over the Egyptian-held Suez Canal) was speeding up Britain's evolving policy of decolonization and majority rule in Africa. A month into a tour of six African nations in 1960, he made his last stop in South Africa (a Commonwealth realm), which would be the most challenging of his visit. He had worked on his speech for weeks with advisers, and he was so nervous beforehand he was physically sick. This important speech—hard truths to the all-white South African parliament—signaled to the world that Britain recognized that black Africans' aspirations for self-government were natural and right, that such ambitions followed a course of events as old as the breakup of the Roman Empire and as recent as the wave of nationalism that crossed Asia just a few years earlier. "The wind of change is blowing through this continent, and whether we like it or not, this growth of national consciousness is a political fact," Macmillan said, ". . . and our national policies must take account of it." Macmillan called attention to Britain's dissatisfaction with South Africa's doctrine of white superiority and its policy of forced racial separation, or apartheid. The speech did not sit well with South African prime minister (and apartheid architect) Henrik Verwoerd, who answered bitterly that the rights of whites in Africa should not be forgotten. Six weeks later the Sharpeville Massacre occurred—69 peaceful black antiapartheid protesters were shot to death by white South African police. Because of international condemnation and opposition from other British Commonwealth nations, the Union of South Africa left the Commonwealth the next year, in 1961, to become the Republic of South Africa. The United Nations passed a resolution condemning South Africa for its racist treatment of black and coloured (mixed race) citizens in 1962. But in 1960 alone, 16 new African states joined the United Nations.

As I've traveled around the Union I have found everywhere, as I expected, a deep preoccupation with what is happening in the rest of the African continent. I understand and sympathize with your interests in these events and your anxiety about them.

Ever since the break-up of the Roman Empire one of the constant facts of political life in Europe has been the emergence of independent nations. They have come into existence over the centuries in different forms, with different kinds of Government, but all have been inspired by a deep, keen feeling of nationalism, which has grown as the nations have grown.

In the twentieth century, and especially since the end of the war, the processes which gave birth to the nation states of Europe have been repeated all over the world. We have seen the awakening of national consciousness in peoples who have for centuries lived in dependence upon some other power. Fifteen years ago this movement spread through Asia. Many countries there of different races and civilizations pressed their claim to an independent national life.

Today the same thing is happening in Africa, and the most striking of all the impressions I have formed is of the strength of this African national consciousness. In different places it takes different forms, but it is happening everywhere.

The wind of change is blowing through this continent, and, whether we like it or not, this growth of national consciousness is a political fact. We must all accept it as a fact, and our national policies must take account of it.

Of course, you understand this better than anyone. You are sprung from Europe, the home of nationalism, and here in Africa you have yourselves created a new nation. Indeed, in the history of our times yours will be recorded as the first of the African nationalisms, and this tide of national consciousness which is now rising in Africa is a fact for which you and we and the other nations of the Western World are ultimately responsible.

> The wind of change is blowing through this continent, and, whether we like it or not, this growth of national consciousness is a political fact. —*Harold Macmillan*

For its causes are to be found in the achievements of Western civilization, in the pushing forward of the frontiers of knowledge, in the applying of science in the service of human needs, in the expanding of food production, in the speeding and multiplying of the means of communication, and perhaps, above all, the spread of education . . .

As I see it the great issue in this second half of the twentieth century is whether the uncommitted peoples of Asia and Africa will swing to the East or to the West. Will they be drawn into the Communist camp? Or will the great experiments in self-government that are now being made in Asia and Africa, especially within the Commonwealth, prove so successful, and by their example so compelling, that the balance will come down in favour of freedom and order and justice?

The struggle is joined, and it is a struggle for the minds of men. What is now on trial is much more than our military strength or our diplomatic and administrative skill. It is our way of life. The uncommitted nations want to see before they choose.

What can we show them to help them choose right? Each of the independent members of the Commonwealth must answer that question for itself. It is a basic principle of our modern Commonwealth that we respect each other's sovereignty in matters of internal policy. At the same time we must recognize that in this shrinking world in which we live today the internal policies of one nation may have effects outside it. We may sometimes be tempted to say to each other, "Mind your own business," but in these days I would myself expand the old saying so that it runs: "Mind your own business, but mind how it affects my business, too."

Let me be very frank with you, my friends. What Governments and Parliaments in the United Kingdom have done since the war in according independence to India, Pakistan, Ceylon, Malaya and Ghana, and what they will do for Nigeria and other countries now nearing independence, all this, though we take full and sole responsibility for it, we do in the belief that it is the only way to establish the future of the Commonwealth and of the Free World on sound foundations.

All this of course is also of deep and close concern to you for nothing we do in this small world can be done in a corner or remain hidden. What we do today in West, Central and East Africa becomes known tomorrow to everyone in the Union, whatever his language, colour or traditions. Let me assure you, in all friendliness, that we are well aware of this and that we have acted and will act with full knowledge of the responsibility we have to all our friends.

Nevertheless I am sure you will agree that in our own areas of responsibility we must each do what we think right. What we think right derives from a long experience both of failure and success in the management of our own affairs. We have tried to learn and apply the lessons of our judgement of right and wrong. Our justice is rooted in the same soil as yours—in Christianity and in the rule of law as the basis of a free society.

This experience of our own explains why it has been our aim in the countries for which we have borne responsibility, not only to raise the material standards of living, but also to create a society which respects the rights of individuals, a society in which men are given the opportunity to grow to their full stature—and that must in our view include the opportunity to have an increasing share in political power and responsibility, a society in which individual merit and individual merit alone is the criterion for a man's advancement, whether political or economic . . .

The attitude of the United Kingdom towards this problem was clearly expressed by the Foreign Secretary, Mr Selwyn Lloyd, speaking at the United Nations General Assembly on 17 September 1959. These were his words:

> In those territories where different races or tribes live side by side the task is to ensure that all the people may enjoy security and freedom and the chance to contribute as individuals to the progress and well being of these countries. We reject the idea of any inherent superiority of one race over another. Our policy therefore is non-racial. It offers a future in which Africans, Europeans, Asians, the peoples of the Pacific and others with whom we are concerned, will all play their full part as citizens in the countries where they live, and in which feelings of race will be submerged in loyalty to new nations.

I have thought you would wish me to state plainly and with full candour the policy for which we in Britain stand. It may well be that in trying to do our duty as we see it we shall sometimes make difficulties for you. If this proves to be so we shall regret it. But I know that even so you would not ask us to flinch from doing our duty.

As a fellow member of the Commonwealth it is our earnest desire to give South Africa our support and encouragement, but I hope you won't mind my saying frankly that there are some aspects of your policies which make it impossible for us to do this without being false to our own deep convictions about the political destinies of free men to which in our own territories we are trying to give effect. I think we ought, as friends, to face together, without seeking to apportion credit or blame, the fact that in the world of today this difference of outlook lies between us . . .

The fact is that in this modern world no country, not even the greatest, can live for itself alone. Nearly two thousand years ago, when the whole of the civilized world was comprised within the confines of the Roman Empire, St Paul proclaimed one of the great truths of history—we are all members one of another. During this twentieth century that eternal truth has taken on a new and exciting significance.

It has always been impossible for the individual man to live in isolation from his fellows, in the home, the tribe, the village, or the city. Today it is impossible for nations to live in isolation from one another. What Dr John Donne said of individual men three hundred years ago is true today of my country, your country, and all the countries of the world:

> Any man's death diminishes me, because I am involved in Mankind. And therefore never send to know for whom the bell tolls; it tolls for thee.

All nations now are interdependent one upon another, and this is generally realized throughout the Western World . . . Those of us who by grace of the electorate are temporarily in charge of affairs in your country and in mine, we fleeting transient phantoms on the great stage of history, we have no right to sweep aside on this account the friendship that exists between our countries, for that is the legacy of history. It is not ours alone to deal with as we wish. To adapt a famous phrase, it belongs to those who are living, but it also belongs to those who are dead and to those who are yet unborn. We must face the differences, but let us try to see beyond them down the long vista of the future.

I hope—indeed, I am confident—that in another fifty years we shall look back on the differences that exist between us now as matters of historical interest, for as time passes and one generation yields to another, human problems change and fade. Let us remember these truths. Let us resolve to build, not to destroy, and let us remember always that weakness comes from division, strength from unity.

Source: Macmillan, Harold. "The Wind of Change." *Pointing the Way 1959–1961.* London: Macmillan, 1972, p. 473. Reproduced under the terms of the Click-Use Licence.

PATRICE LUMUMBA
(1925–1961)
Independence Day Address
Kinshasa, Democratic Republic of the Congo
June 30, 1960

Born in 1925 in the Belgian Congo (today the Democratic Republic of the Congo), Patrice Lumumba came of age in a region riven by tribal conflict and subject to the faraway Belgian government. Educated at Protestant schools near his village, as a young man Lumumba moved to the capital city of Léopoldville (now Kinshasa), where he worked as a post office clerk and accountant. He became active in politics by writing articles for Congolese independence journals. Lumumba's commitment to independence from Belgium led him in 1958 to create the Congolese National Movement (MNC), the first nationwide Congolese political party dedicated to national liberation. When the Belgian government announced in 1959 that it would initiate a five-year program leading to Congolese independence, Lumumba and other militant nationalists were outraged—they believed the plan was a ruse to install pro-Belgian leaders through rigged elections. Determined to achieve freedom, Lumumba's MNC entered the elections. Their overwhelming victory brought independence in 1960 and the appointment of Lumumba as the first prime minister of the Democratic Republic of the Congo. At the independence ceremony, Lumumba undiplomatically delivered this forthright address (in French, the official language) to celebrate his people's liberation from colonial rule. In the audience was King Baudouin of Belgium, present to officially hand over his former colony to its new republican government; the embarrassed king was incensed. Belgium and the West were leery of Lumumba; they saw him as communist-influenced. Six months later, following an international crisis over a secessionist province, the American CIA-supported Congolese president Joseph Kasavubu removed Lumumba as prime minister, imprisoned him, and then handed him over to Lumumba's Belgium-supported Congolese enemies. On January 17, 1961, Lumumba was secretly executed by firing squad. Later, between 1971 and 1997, the Republic of Congo was named Zaire.

***

Men and women of the Congo, victorious fighters for independence, today victorious, I greet you in the name of the Congolese government. All of you, my friends, who have fought tirelessly at our sides, I ask you to make this June 30, 1960, an illustrious date that you will keep indelibly engraved in your hearts, a date of significance of which you will teach to your children, so that they will make known to their sons and to their grandchildren the glorious history of our fight for liberty.

For this independence of the Congo, even as it is celebrated today with Belgium, a friendly country with whom we deal as equal to equal, no Congolese worthy of the name will ever be able to forget that it was by fighting that it has been won, a day-to-day fight, an ardent and idealistic fight, a fight in which we were spared neither privation nor suffering, and for which we gave our strength and our blood.

We are proud of this struggle, of tears, of fire, and of blood, to the depths of our being, for it was a noble and just struggle, and indispensable to put an end to the humiliating slavery which was imposed upon us by force.

This was our fate for eighty years of a colonial regime; our wounds are too fresh and too painful still for us to drive them from our memory. We have known harassing work, exacted in exchange for salaries which did not permit us to eat enough to drive away hunger, or to clothe ourselves, or to house ourselves decently, or to raise our children as creatures dear to us.

438

We have known ironies, insults, blows that we endured morning, noon, and evening, because we are Negroes. Who will forget that to a black one said *tu*, certainly not as to a friend, but because the more honorable *vous* was reserved for whites alone?

We have seen our lands seized in the name of allegedly legal laws which in fact recognized only that might is right.

We have seen that the law was not the same for a white and for a black, accommodating for the first, cruel and inhuman for the other.

We have witnessed atrocious sufferings of those condemned for their political opinions or religious beliefs; exiled in their own country, their fate truly worse than death itself.

We have seen that in the towns there were magnificent houses for the whites and crumbling shanties for the blacks, that a black was not admitted in the motion-picture houses, in the restaurants, in the stores of the Europeans; that a black traveled in the holds, at the feet of the whites in their luxury cabins.

Who will ever forget the massacres where so many of our brothers perished, the cells into which those who refused to submit to a regime of oppression and exploitation were thrown?

All that, my brothers, we have endured. But we, whom the vote of your elected representatives have given the right to direct our dear country, we who have suffered in our body and in our heart from colonial oppression, we tell you very loud, all that is henceforth ended.

The Republic of the Congo has been proclaimed, and our country is now in the hands of its own children. Together, my brothers, my sisters, we are going to begin a new struggle, a sublime struggle, which will lead our country to peace, prosperity, and greatness. Together, we are going to establish social justice and make sure everyone has just remuneration for his labor.

We are going to show the world what the black man can do when he works in freedom, and we are going to make of the Congo the center of the sun's radiance for all of Africa.

We are going to keep watch over the lands of our country so that they truly profit her children. We are going to restore ancient laws and make new ones which will be just and noble.

We are going to put an end to suppression of free thought and see to it that all our citizens enjoy to the full the fundamental liberties foreseen in the Declaration of the Rights of Man.

We are going to do away with all discrimination of every variety and assure for each and all the position to which human dignity, work, and dedication entitles him.

We are going to rule not by the peace of guns and bayonets but by a peace of the heart and the will.

And for all that, dear fellow countrymen, be sure that we will count not only on our enormous strength and immense riches but on the assistance of numerous foreign countries whose collaboration we will accept if it is offered freely and with no attempt to impose on us an alien culture of no matter what nature.

In this domain, Belgium, at last accepting the flow of history, has not tried to oppose our independence and is ready to give us their aid and their friendship, and a treaty has just been signed between our two countries, equal and independent. On our side, while we stay vigilant, we shall respect our obligations, given freely.

Thus, in the interior and the exterior, the new Congo, our dear Republic that my government will create, will be a rich, free, and prosperous country. But so that we will reach this aim without delay, I ask all of you, legislators and citizens, to help me with all your strength.

I ask all of you to forget your tribal quarrels. They exhaust us. They risk making us despised abroad.

I ask the parliamentary minority to help my Government through a constructive opposition and to limit themselves strictly to legal and democratic channels.

I ask all of you not to shrink before any sacrifice in order to achieve the success of our huge undertaking.

In conclusion, I ask you unconditionally to respect the life and the property of your fellow citizens and of foreigners living in our country. If the conduct of these foreigners leaves something to be desired, our justice will be prompt in expelling them from the territory of the Republic; if, on the contrary, their conduct is good, they must be left in peace, for they also are working for our country's prosperity.

The Congo's independence marks a decisive step towards the liberation of the entire African continent.

Sire, Excellencies, Mesdames, Messieurs, my dear fellow countrymen, my brothers of race, my brothers of struggle—this is what I wanted to tell you in the name of the government on this magnificent day of our complete independence. Our government—strong, national, popular—will be the health of our country.

I call on all Congolese citizens, men, women and children, to set themselves resolutely to the task of creating a prosperous national economy which will assure our economic independence.

Glory to the fighters for national liberation! Long live independence and African unity! Long live the independent and sovereign Congo!

Source: Lumumba, Patrice. "Independence Day Address." Africa Within. Available online. http://africawithin.com/lumumba/independence_speech.htm. Accessed January 2, 2008.

PATRICK DUNCAN
(1918–1967)
"An Unjust Law Is No True Law"
Cape Town, South Africa
November 17, 1960

Patrick Duncan was born into wealth and privilege in the apartheid world of forced racial separation in the Union of South Africa. His father was Sir Patrick Duncan, a Briton appointed by King George VI (r. 1936–52) as governor-general of South Africa (a British Commonwealth realm until 1961). The younger Duncan worked in various jobs as a colonial administrator, but by 1952 he had come to reject the automatic privilege that came with being born white. He joined the antiapartheid movement against the racist regime, was jailed for participating in the African National Congress's nonviolent Defiance Campaign of 1952, and founded the liberal journal *Contact*. His disillusionment with Gandhian nonviolence was complete by March 21, 1960, when peaceful black protestors marching at Sharpeville, near Johannesburg, were attacked by South African police. The police shot and killed 69 and wounded 176 others. In the turbulent aftermath of the Sharpeville Massacre, the government proclaimed a state of emergency, banning the African National Congress and detaining 20,000 people. Duncan was arrested for publishing articles in *Contact* that were critical of the government's racist policies and which revealed atrocities committed against innocent blacks. He was put on trial for "issuing subversive statements." Duncan addressed the court in a brilliant self-defense, decrying the unjust laws under which he was prosecuted and citing classical thinkers and philosophers to support his position. He was banned by the government for a second time and had to flee the country to continue his work. In Algeria in 1964, he became the only white member of the Pan-Africanist Congress. Duncan never returned to South Africa; he died in exile in 1967, one of a number of intrepid white South Africans who fought apartheid, but who remain largely forgotten.

I WAS astonished when the summons in this case was served on me, for I had thought that the government would have hesitated, from a sense of shame, to revive the painful memories of what it did to the people of South Africa in March and April of this year.

The prosecution has alleged that eight articles, published on 2nd and 16th April this year in *Contact*, were 'subversive statements', and that I have broken the law by having distributed them. These articles describe, and comment on, certain acts done by the government. These acts include large-scale murder by the police, and two treacherous breaches of faith.

Other articles in the issues which are before the court include reports of barbaric floggings of innocent people by the Cape Town police. These criminal acts, perpetrated by and in the name of the government, achieved world notoriety, and shocked the conscience of the whole human race.

Now that the clamour of world publicity has somewhat abated I should have thought that a government of guilty men, such as is the South African government, would have left these horrors alone, to be forgotten. I thought that these guilty men at least had shame. I now see that I was mistaken.

These words that I have used of the government are hard. I have not used them lightly. I have pondered long the question of whether to use them or not. I have decided to use them, and I am prepared to prove that my use of them is justified. . . .

I do not wish to waste the time of the court. I did distribute the articles in question. *I am solely and wholly responsible for what they say.* With this heavy charge hanging over me I should like the court to know precisely why I did distribute them, well knowing that material of this kind might be held to conflict with government policy and regulations.

The principal reason for my decision to go ahead and publish them in these circumstances was that I deny that the emergency regulations ever were or are law in the true sense of the word, or that they were or are in any way binding on the conscience.

I maintain that the regulations are lacking in two essential ingredients of true law, and that they are not, therefore, true law.

The missing ingredients are, firstly, the legitimacy of parliament, and, secondly, the morality of the law. . . .

Some people who have been charged under these regulations have contended that all the institutions of government, and therefore all the laws passed since Union, have no legitimacy because the non-Whites had no part in establishing the state.

A case could, I believe, be made in support of their contention. There are, after all, many rules in life that want the full force of law. Children playing in their sand-pits make rules; bandits make and can often enforce rules; usurper kings and governments purport to make rules. But only governments which are, and which are believed to be, legitimate can make laws in the fullest sense of that word, laws which are binding on the people that are governed.

It is obvious that not all who exercise power can bind the consciences of the ruled. During the Nazi occupation of Europe, Hitler's gauleiters made rules, and often succeeded in enforcing obedience to them, because they had a victorious army behind them. These rules did not, however, have the character of law. A case could be made in support of the contention that the government in South Africa is as illegitimate as that of Hitler's occupying armies. It is, however, not necessary for me to enter too deeply into this question, nor to pursue this line of argument, for I rest my case on the simple statement that these regulations are fatally defective by reason of their injustice.

The civilizations of Greece and of Rome, the traditions of Christianity, both Catholic and Reformed, on which our whole culture is based, proclaim unanimously that an

---

RHETORICAL DEVICE

Metabasis: Using a sentence to refer to material already covered, perhaps even summarizing, and outlining what is now coming.

As I have now replied to my calumniators, as far as my own character required, though not so fully as their villainy deserved, I shall add a few more words on the state of public affairs. —*Gaius Marius*

Why do I mention this? Because I am going to explain to you why I have such an evil name. —*Socrates*

I did distribute the articles in question. . . . With this heavy charge hanging over me I should like the court to know precisely why I did distribute them. —*Patrick Duncan*

In view of this, we must first make it clear what is meant by such terms as "reactionary," "counterrevolutionary," and "revolutionary." —*Wei Jingsheng*

unjust law is no true law and cannot bind the conscience of the subject, and that the subject has no duty to obey such a law. . . .

Apartheid legislation was condemned by anticipation in the pages of both Locke and St Thomas Aquinas. Locke, as quoted above, said that for a decree to be a law, and for it not to be merely arbitrary, there must be 'one rule for rich and poor, for the favourite at court and the countryman at plough'. If he had lived in modern South Africa he would no doubt have added the words 'and one law for Black and White'.

St Thomas Aquinas cuts even nearer the bone when he says that a law is unjust 'when burdens are imposed unequally on the community'.

Some apartheid laws impose such unequal burdens on the community that I have stigmatized them as 'anti-life' because they appear hostile to the non-Whites.

How else can one explain the cruel cancellation of the African school-feeding scheme, while White children continue to be fed by the State? How else can one explain the mean attempt to abridge and constrict, by administrative action, the pension scheme for non-Whites which this government inherited from its predecessors? How else can one explain the present intention of this government to institute family allowances—for Whites only?

Some laws then, actually seek to deny life to non-Whites. Others, while not exhibiting hostility to this extent, yet shamelessly deny justice. . . .

The making of these hostile and unjust regulations is consistent only with a state of mind in the legislator of deep and inveterate enmity borne towards the majority of the people of South Africa.

They are not law. Law, as we have seen, to be true law must nurture life, must promote the common good, must be imposed equally on the community.

It may, however, be argued that however violent, unjust, or antilife these regulations were, they were necessary for the preserving of law and order.

I admit immediately that this is superficially the most plausible argument against me. I am confident, however, that what I have said remains valid despite this allegation. For one has to consider what law, what order, is being preserved at such cost. It is clear from everything that I have said that the law to be preserved is the law of greedy race supremacy, and the order to be preserved is the order of apartheid.

I would remind this court that Himmler and Hitler did little that was not legal. Like this government, they took the trouble to pass regulations to give the appearance of legality to their dark deeds. Before their genocidal attack on the Jewish communities of Europe they passed the Nuremburg race laws.

Mere order, mere law, I say, are not ends in themselves. They must be related to life, to morality, and to justice.

It might also be argued that it was my patriotic duty to obey, at a time of difficulty and danger to the State, the State's regulations, and that it was my duty to do nothing that could draw on my country the opprobrium of the world.

I say that the opposite was my duty. I am unquestioningly loyal to South Africa, to the fifteen millions of people of all races who are my fellow citizens, and to the lovely land which is ours. I have therefore a duty to protect my people and my country against any group which is hostile to the majority of our people, even though by a series of historic swindles, such a group has been able temporarily to arrogate to itself the name of government.

The anger of the world is not against South Africa. The anger of the world is against this greedy oligarchy that battens on the people that it hates. So far from trying to diminish the world's anger, I believe that it was my patriotic duty to do all in my power to increase it.

I also believe that it was my patriotic duty to speak up for another reason. The injustices done in March and April purported to have been done in the name of all South Africans. For the whole of South Africa to have kept silence then would have been for the whole country to stand arraigned before the highest tribunal of the human race, the Security Council of the United Nations, as steeped in a uniform guilt. I spoke up because I wished to protect the majority of my fifteen million fellow-citizens from the righteous detestation of the whole human race.

It was also, as I see it, my duty to speak the truth then, for no other newspaper in the country felt free to do so. These regulations had dealt an intentional blow against the press of South Africa, whose freedom was thereby curtailed, and curtailed more completely than at any time since the governorship of Lord Charles Somerset. I knew that if only one newspaper were to continue to publish the truth and to comment without fear, other newspapers might follow suit. I acted in the interests of the freedom of the press, which is the most precious freedom left to us in South Africa, though even this freedom has been whittled away and is now finally menaced by a new Bill. . . .

To summarize: I decided to publish all the articles in the heat of the crisis of April. Looking back from this somewhat calmer period I would omit nothing, add nothing, and change nothing. I leave it to a future South Africa to justify or to condemn what I did.

Source: Duncan, Patrick. "Statement in Answer to the Charge of Seditious Libel." In *The Law as Literature*, edited by Louis Blom-Cooper, 102. London: The Bodley Head, Ltd., 1961. From "Statement made in the Regional Court, Cape Town," printed in *Contact*, copyright © December 1960. Permission of Lady Bryan, Patrick Duncan's widow.

DWIGHT D. EISENHOWER
(1890–1969)
"The Military-Industrial Complex"
Washington, D.C., United States
January 17, 1961

Three days before John F. Kennedy took office, outgoing President Dwight D. Eisenhower gave a televised farewell address from the White House. General Eisenhower had planned strategy against Axis enemies Germany and Japan at the Pentagon during the early months of World War II (1939–45). In London in 1942 and 1943, he commanded the North African and Mediterranean theaters of operation. By then a four-star general, he became supreme commander of the Allied Expeditionary Force, an immense armada that invaded Nazi-occupied France to liberate Europe on June 6, 1944, known as D-day. A five-star general at the end of the war, Eisenhower became U.S. Army chief of staff, and in 1950 he was chosen to head the newly formed military alliance, the North Atlantic Treaty Organization (NATO). The enormously popular general left NATO in 1952 to run for U.S. president. He served two terms, and at the end delivered his most historically important address, one that made a byword of "military-industrial complex." Eisenhower did not originate the term, but he made it famous. (Eisenhower had originally drafted "military-industrial-*congressional* complex," but he altered it to please congressmen who objected.) A military-industrial complex is the close reciprocal relationship that develops between a country's military and the industry (corporations) that supply the military's machinery and other goods. These corporations—also called defense contractors—are dependent on the military for their continued operation; in addition, politicians and lobbyists grease this complex relationship. All these parties are looking to profit in some manner, and they may ultimately undermine the public's interest in peace. Historically, rivalries between the military-industrial complexes of unfriendly nations have contributed to exacerbating tensions between nations, rather than simply arising in response to them. Eisenhower warned the American people and Congress to beware the powerful influence of military and industrial forces working together, but under successive presidents the arms industry continued to grow.

We now stand ten years past the midpoint of a century that has witnessed four major wars among great nations. Three of these involved our own country. Despite these holocausts, America is today the strongest, the most influential, and most productive nation in the world.

Understandably proud of this preeminence, we yet realize that America's leadership and prestige depend not merely upon our unmatched material progress, riches, and military strength but on how we use our power in the interests of world peace and human betterment. . . .

A vital element in keeping the peace is our military establishment. Our arms must be mighty, ready for instant action, so that no potential aggressor may be tempted to risk his own destruction.

Our military organization today bears little relation to that known by any of my predecessors in peacetime, or indeed by the fighting men of World War II or Korea.

Until the latest of our world conflicts, the United States had no armaments industry. American makers of plowshares could, with time and as required, make swords as well. But now we can no longer risk emergency improvisation of national defense; we have been compelled to create a permanent armaments industry of vast proportions. Added to this, 3½ million men and women are directly engaged in the defense establishment. We annually spend on military security more than the net income of all United States corporations.

Departing president Dwight D. Eisenhower sits with in-coming president John F. Kennedy at Kennedy's inauguration, January 20, 1961. Eisenhower had delivered his farewell speech, warning of the "military-industrial complex," just days before, and Kennedy would momentarily deliver his celebrated Inaugural Address. *(AP Photo)*

This conjunction of an immense military establishment and a large arms industry is new in the American experience. The total influence—economic, political, even spiritual—is felt in every city, every statehouse, every office of the Federal Government. We recognize the imperative need for this development. Yet we must not fail to comprehend its grave implications. Our toil, resources, and livelihood are all involved; so is the very structure of our society.

In the councils of government we must guard against the acquisition of unwarranted influence, whether sought or unsought, by the military-industrial complex. The potential for the disastrous rise of misplaced power exists and will persist.

We must never let the weight of this combination endanger our liberties or democratic processes. We should take nothing for granted. Only an alert and knowledgeable citizenry can compel the proper meshing of the huge industrial and military machinery of defense with our peaceful methods and goals so that security and liberty may prosper together.

Akin to and largely responsible for the sweeping changes in our industrial-military posture has been the technological revolution during recent decades. In this revolution research has become central; it also becomes more formalized, complex, and costly. A steadily increasing share is conducted for, by, or at the direction of the Federal Government.

Today the solitary inventor, tinkering in his shop, has been overshadowed by task-forces of scientists in laboratories and testing fields. In the same fashion the free university, historically the fountainhead of free ideas and scientific discovery, has experienced a revolution in the conduct of research.

We must guard against the acquisition of unwarranted influence, whether sought or unsought, by the military-industrial complex. —*Dwight D. Eisenhower*

Partly because of the huge costs involved, a government contract becomes virtually a substitute for intellectual curiosity. For every old blackboard there are now hundreds of new electronic computers. The prospect of domination of the nation's scholars by Federal employment, project allocations, and the power of money is ever present and is gravely to be regarded. Yet, in holding scientific research and discovery in respect, as we should, we must also be alert to the equal and opposite danger that public policy could itself become the captive of a scientific-technological elite.

It is the task of statesmanship to mold, to balance, and to integrate these and other forces, new and old, within the principles of our democratic system—ever aiming toward the supreme goals of our free society.

Source: Eisenhower, Dwight D. "Farewell Address." Eisenhower Presidential Library. Available online. http://www.eisenhower.archives.gov/speeches/farewell_address.html. Accessed December 20, 2007.

JOHN F. KENNEDY
(1917–1963)
Inaugural Address
Washington, D.C., United States
January 20, 1961

At 43, John Fitzgerald Kennedy, popularly known by his initials, "J.F.K.," was the youngest president ever elected. He was the first born in the 20th century as well as the first Roman Catholic president. He came from a wealthy, politically active Boston family; his father, Joseph P. Kennedy, was U.S. ambassador to London; two brothers became U.S. senators. The U.S. Navy accepted Kennedy into the service during World War II (1939–45), despite sometimes poor health; he received a medal for heroism when a Japanese destroyer sank his patrol boat. After the war, Kennedy was elected to the U.S. House of Representatives, and, in 1952, to the U.S. Senate. He ran for election to the presidency in 1960 and won, adroitly handling anti-Catholic bias by assuring the public that he kept religion separate from his political life. He had a flair for words—he had already won a Pulitzer Prize in 1957 for his book *Profiles in Courage*—and employed a superb speechwriter, Ted Sorensen,

for the address he gave at the outdoor inauguration ceremony installing him in office. Kennedy's exciting and idealistic inaugural speech stands near the top in American political oratory. He called on Americans to serve their country, pledged to commit his administration to the pursuit of peace and human rights and assistance to the world's poor, and warned aggressors (the Soviet Union) that the United States would not tolerate interference in the Americas. The many memorable passages make the speech instantly recognizable, the most famous being "Ask not what your country can do for you—ask what you can do for your country." Kennedy's short tenure was troubled by the Cuban missile crisis of 1963 (the presence of Soviet missiles in Cuba) and the war in Vietnam (1954–75); he signed important civil rights legislation and test ban treaties, and he began the Apollo Project to put a man on the Moon. He was assassinated on November 22, 1963, in Dallas, Texas.

We observe today not a victory of party but a celebration of freedom—symbolizing an end as well as a beginning—signifying renewal as well as change. For I have sworn before you and Almighty God the same solemn oath our forbears prescribed nearly a century and three-quarters ago.

The world is very different now. For man holds in his mortal hands the power to abolish all forms of human poverty and all forms of human life. And yet the same revolutionary beliefs for which our forebears fought are still at issue around the globe—the belief that the rights of man come not from the generosity of the state but from the hand of God.

We dare not forget today that we are the heirs of that first revolution. Let the word go forth from this time and place, to friend and foe alike, that the torch has been passed to a new generation of Americans—born in this century, tempered by war, disciplined by a hard and bitter peace, proud of our ancient heritage—and unwilling to witness or permit the slow undoing of those human rights to which this nation has always been committed, and to which we are committed today at home and around the world.

Let every nation know, whether it wishes us well or ill, that we shall pay any price, bear any burden, meet any hardship, support any friend, oppose any foe to assure the survival and the success of liberty.

This much we pledge—and more.

To those old allies whose cultural and spiritual origins we share, we pledge the loyalty of faithful friends. United there is little we cannot do in a host of cooperative ventures. Divided there is little we can do—for we dare not meet a powerful challenge at odds and split asunder.

To those new states whom we welcome to the ranks of the free, we pledge our word that one form of colonial control shall not have passed away merely to be replaced by a far more iron tyranny. We shall not always expect to find them supporting our view. But we shall always hope to find them strongly supporting their own freedom—and to remember that, in the past, those who foolishly sought power by riding the back of the tiger ended up inside.

To those people in the huts and villages of half the globe struggling to break the bonds of mass misery, we pledge our best efforts to help them help themselves, for whatever period is required—not because the communists may be doing it, not because we seek their votes, but because it is right. If a free society cannot help the many who are poor, it cannot save the few who are rich.

To our sister republics south of our border, we offer a special pledge—to convert our good words into good deeds—in a new alliance for progress—to assist free men and free governments in casting off the chains of poverty. But this peaceful revolution of hope cannot become the prey of hostile powers. Let all our neighbors know that we shall join with them to oppose aggression or subversion anywhere in the Americas. And let every other power know that this Hemisphere intends to remain the master of its own house.

To that world assembly of sovereign states, the United Nations, our last best hope in an age where the instruments of war have far outpaced the instruments of peace, we renew our pledge of support—to prevent it from becoming merely a forum for invective—to strengthen its shield of the new and the weak—and to enlarge the area in which its writ may run.

Finally, to those nations who would make themselves our adversary, we offer not a pledge but a request: that both sides begin anew the quest for peace, before the dark powers of destruction unleashed by science engulf all humanity in planned or accidental self-destruction.

We dare not tempt them with weakness. For only when our arms are sufficient beyond doubt can we be certain beyond doubt that they will never be employed.

But neither can two great and powerful groups of nations take comfort from our present course—both sides overburdened by the cost of modern weapons, both rightly alarmed by the steady spread of the deadly atom, yet both racing to alter that uncertain

RHETORICAL DEVICE

Asyndeton: Leaving out the conjunctions between phrases or words, giving a sense of flowing speech.

Let every nation know, whether it wishes us well or ill, that we shall pay any price, bear any burden, meet any hardship, support any friend, oppose any foe to assure the survival and the success of liberty. —*John F. Kennedy*

In education, in marriage, in religion, in everything, disappointment is the lot of woman. —*Lucy Stone*

The battle, sir, is not to the strong alone; it is to the vigilant, the active, the brave. —*Patrick Henry*

We learned not to believe in anything, to ignore one another, to care only about ourselves. —*Václav Havel*

> And so, my fellow Americans, ask not what your country can do for you—ask what you can do for your country. —*John F. Kennedy*

balance of terror that stays the hand of mankind's final war.

So let us begin anew—remembering on both sides that civility is not a sign of weakness, and sincerity is always subject to proof. Let us never negotiate out of fear. But let us never fear to negotiate.

Let both sides explore what problems unite us instead of belaboring those problems which divide us.

Let both sides, for the first time, formulate serious and precise proposals for the inspection and control of arms—and bring the absolute power to destroy other nations under the absolute control of all nations.

Let both sides seek to invoke the wonders of science instead of its terrors. Together let us explore the stars, conquer the deserts, eradicate disease, tap the ocean depths and encourage the arts and commerce.

Let both sides unite to heed in all corners of the earth the command of Isaiah—to "undo the heavy burdens and let the oppressed go free."

And if a beachhead of cooperation may push back the jungle of suspicion, let both sides join in creating a new endeavor, not a new balance of power, but a new world of law, where the strong are just and the weak secure and the peace preserved.

All this will not be finished in the first one hundred days. Nor will it be finished in the first one thousand days, nor in the life of this Administration, nor even perhaps in our lifetime on this planet. But let us begin.

In your hands, my fellow citizens, more than mine, will rest the final success or failure of our course. Since this country was founded, each generation of Americans has been summoned to give testimony to its national loyalty. The graves of young Americans who answered the call to service surround the globe.

Now the trumpet summons us again—not as a call to bear arms, though arms we need—not as a call to battle, though embattled we are—but a call to bear the burden of a long twilight struggle, year in and year out, "rejoicing in hope, patient in tribulation"—a struggle against the common enemies of man: tyranny, poverty, disease and war itself.

Can we forge against these enemies a grand and global alliance, North and South, East and West, that can assure a more fruitful life for all mankind? Will you join in that historic effort?

In the long history of the world, only a few generations have been granted the role of defending freedom in its hour of maximum danger. I do not shrink from this responsibility—I welcome it. I do not believe that any of us would exchange places with any other people or any other generation. The energy, the faith, the devotion which we bring to this endeavor will light our country and all who serve it—and the glow from that fire can truly light the world.

And so, my fellow Americans: ask not what your country can do for you—ask what you can do for your country.

My fellow citizens of the world: ask not what America will do for you, but what together we can do for the freedom of man.

Finally, whether you are citizens of America or citizens of the world, ask of us here the same high standards of strength and sacrifice which we ask of you. With a good conscience our only sure reward, with history the final judge of our deeds, let us go forth to lead the land we love, asking His blessing and His help, but knowing that here on earth God's work must truly be our own.

Source: Kennedy, John F. "Inaugural Address." John F. Kennedy Presidential Library. Available online. http://www.jfklibrary.org/Historical+Resources/Archives/Reference+Desk/Speeches/Speeches+of+John+F.+Kennedy.htm. Accessed December 20, 2007.

GIDEON HAUSNER
(1915–1990)
"Six Million Accusers"
Jerusalem, Israel
April 17, 1961

It was zealous Nazi bureaucrat Adolf Eichmann who oversaw the deportation of European Jewry to death camps during World War II (1939–45). As chief of the Gestapo (Nazi secret police) section concerning Jews, he assisted Hitler in planning the Final Solution for exterminating Jews, 6 million of whom died. In one year and from one country alone—Hungary in 1944—400,000 Jews were murdered in accordance with Eichmann's plans. He was not brought to justice at the Nuremberg Trials of 1945–46, as he had escaped from U.S. custody (using a false name, his identity was not immediately recognized). With the help of an Austrian-born Catholic bishop in Italy (an honorary member of the Nazi Party), he obtained a false passport and escaped in 1950 to Argentina. Eichmann assumed a phony identity, Riccardo Klement, and worked a series of low-level jobs for a factory and water company; he lived with his family in Buenos Aires for 10 years. But in May 1960 after years of patient detective work, agents of Mossad, the Israeli intelligence service, kidnapped him as he was on his way home from work. Eichmann was smuggled out of Argentina and brought to Jerusalem to stand trial on 15 criminal charges, including crimes against humanity. The trial began in Jerusalem in April 1961. Gideon Hausner, attorney-general of Israel from 1960 to 1963, was the chief prosecutor who delivered the trial's opening speech, an address that lasted eight hours. Eichmann never disputed the charges; his defense rested on having "only followed orders." The court rejected this defense, as similar defenses by Nazi war criminals had been rejected at the Nuremberg Trials. Eichmann was found guilty, condemned to death, and hanged. Hausner was later elected to the Israeli parliament, the Knesset, in 1965, where he served four terms in office.

When I stand before you here, Judges of Israel, to lead the Prosecution of Adolf Eichmann, I am not standing alone. With me are six million accusers. But they cannot rise to their feet and point an accusing finger towards him who sits in the dock and cry: "I accuse." For their ashes are piled up on the hills of Auschwitz and the fields of Treblinka, and are strewn in the forests of Poland. Their graves are scattered throughout the length and breadth of Europe. Their blood cries out, but their voice is not heard. Therefore I will be their spokesman and in their name I will unfold the awesome indictment.

The history of the Jewish people is steeped in suffering and tears. . . . Yet never, down in the entire blood-stained road traveled by this people, never since the first days of its nationhood, has any man arisen who succeeded in dealing it such grievous blows as did Hitler's iniquitous regime, and Adolf Eichmann as its executive arm for the extermination of the Jewish people. In all human history there is no other example of a man against whom it would be possible to draw up such a bill of indictment as has been read here. The most terrible crimes of those fearful figures of barbarism and bloodlust, Genghis Khan, Attila, or Ivan the Terrible, the telling of which curdles our blood and makes our hair stand on end with horror, deeds, that have become "a proverb and a taunt" and an "everlasting abhorrence" to the nations—these almost seem to pale into insignificance when contrasted with the abominations, the murderous horrors, which will be presented to you in this trial.

At the dawn of history, there were examples of wars of extermination, when one nation assaulted another with intent to destroy, when, in the storm of passion and battle, peoples were slaughtered, massacred or exiled. But only in our generation has a nation attacked an entire defenseless and peaceful population, men and women, greybeards, children and infants, incarcerated them behind electrified fences, imprisoned them in concentration camps, and resolved to destroy them utterly.

In this trial, we shall also encounter a new kind of killer, the kind that exercises his bloody craft behind a desk, and only occasionally does the deed with his own hands. True, we have certain knowledge of only one incident in which Adolf Eichmann actually beat to death a Jewish boy, who had dared to steal fruit from a peach tree in the yard of his Budapest home. But it was his word that put gas chambers into action; he lifted the telephone, and railroad cars left for the extermination centers; his signature it was that sealed the doom of thousands and tens of thousands. He had but to give the order, and at his command the troopers took the field to rout Jews out of their neighborhoods, to beat and torture them and chase them into ghettoes, to pin the badges of shame on their breasts, to steal their property—till finally, after torture and pillage, after everything had been wrung out of them, when even their hair had been taken, they were transported, en masse to the slaughter. Even the corpses were still of value: the gold teeth were extracted and the wedding rings removed.

We shall find Eichmann describing himself as a fastidious person, a "white-collar" worker. To him, the decree of extermination was just another written order to be executed; yet he was the one who planned, initiated and organized, who instructed others to spill this ocean of blood, and to use all the means of murder, theft, and torture.

He must bear the responsibility therefore, as if it was he who with his own hands knotted the hangman's noose, who lashed the victims into the gas-chambers, who shot in the back and pushed into the open pit every single one of the millions who were slaughtered. Such is his responsibility in the eyes of the law, and such is his responsibility according to every standard of conscience and morality.

Adolf Eichmann will tell you that he carried out the orders of his superiors. But the conscience of the world, speaking with the voice of the International Military Tribunal, has declared that orders contrary to the principles of conscience and morality, orders that violate the essential imperatives on which human society is based and negate the basic rules without which men cannot live together—such orders constitute no defense, legal or moral. Therefore, in the light of this ruling, our own law in Israel has denied the Accused the right to submit such a defense.

But that is by no means all. We shall prove to the Court that he went far beyond his actual orders, that he took the initiative in extermination operations for which he had been given no orders whatsoever, and carried them out only because of his devotion to his task in which he saw his life's mission. When, in the summer of 1944, Horthy in Hungary did not want to cooperate with the exterminators, Eichmann managed by stealth to push through another death-train from Kistarcsa to Auschwitz. . . .

We shall see how Eichmann contended with German diplomats themselves, and with various authorities in the occupied zones, who did not cooperate or do everything he wanted. We shall see his anger at Italian officials, who on many occasions frustrated his plans; his wrath at the fact that Denmark, through a noble and dangerous operation, had smuggled her Jews to Sweden; his struggles with all the governments of the occupied countries to make them cooperate in his work. When the Pope himself interceded for the Jews of Rome, who were arrested "practically underneath the Vatican windows" (in the words of the German Foreign Ministry), and Eichmann was asked to leave them in Italian labor camps instead of deporting them, the request was turned down—the Jews were sent to Auschwitz.

But no part of all this bloody work is so shocking and terrible as that of the million Jewish children whose blood was spilt like water throughout Europe. How they were separated by force from their mothers who tried to hide them, murdered and thrown out of trucks in the camps, torn to pieces before their mothers' eyes, their little heads smashed on the ground—these are the most terrible passages of the tale of slaughter. You will hear evidence of actions which the mind of man does not want to believe. . . .

Nor can we say who suffered the more terrible fate: those who died or those who concealed themselves in every conceivable hiding place and crevice, who lived in perpetual terror of expulsion, who survived by grace of Christian neighbors who agreed to hide them. Children would come home from the schools and centers organized by the community to find their parents' home was empty, for they had been sent by some "Aktion" or "operation" to their deaths; and that the apartment had in the meantime been occupied by others.

You will hear evidence of tender infants pressed by their mothers to their bodies in the gas chambers so that they were not immediately poisoned, until the executioners came and threw them alive into the furnaces or the ready graves.

Those unhappy children who lived for years in fear of the beating of a rifle butt on their door; who had been sent by their parents to the woods in an attempt to save them, who had been taught to choke their tears and sighs because a weeping child would be shot on the spot; who had been ordered to deny their origins and pretend to be Christian; who saw their fathers being lashed with whips before their eyes; in front of whom "discussions" would be carried on by the German executioners as to who should be killed first—the father or the son; who went to the open graves with "Hear, O Israel" on their lips—these children and youths, who despite all the desperate measures and concealments would finally fall into the hands of their hunters, they are the very soul and innermost core of the indictment. Those Anne Franks and Justine Draengers and a million others, those unplumbed treasures of radiant youth and hope for life and achievement—they were the future of the Jewish people. He that destroyed them was seeking to destroy the Jewish people.

We shall present the pictures of some of those children, swollen with hunger, frightened and crushed, with eyes frozen with terror. We shall show you the photographs of their starved bodies thrown into manure wagons, of the helpless little ones on the threshold of the extermination chambers. . . .

Eichmann was in Auschwitz and saw what was being done there. He directed the operations and gave instructions which transports were to be sent to immediate extermination and which were to be kept for extermination later on. . . . The killings in Auschwitz were carried out by every method: shooting, hanging and beating, but mainly in the massive gas chambers. Here, once again, we are confronted with the signboards: "Wasch- und Desinfektionsraum" (Washing and Disinfection Room). The "shower" was a flow of poison gas which the SS introduced with their own hands. The death factory operated unceasingly. The extermination of 2,000 people lasted twenty-five minutes, after which the bodies were taken to one of the five giant furnaces. When there was no room in the furnaces the bodies were burned in the open.

Here, too, hair was shorn, teeth extracted and rings removed. About forty people were employed to handle the teeth alone, and day by day kilograms of gold were melted down, at times as much as 12 kilograms a day. At first the victims' ashes were buried in pits, but later they were thrown into the Vistula.

At Auschwitz, medical experiments were made on human beings as if they were guinea pigs. . . . The methods of punishment at Auschwitz would not have shamed the most cruel barbarians in history. Beating on the naked body was a comparatively light punishment. Water was poured into people's ears, fingernails extracted and prisoners starved until they went out of their minds. In the bunker of those sentenced for punishment by starvation a dead prisoner was found, bent over whom was a second prisoner, also dead, grasping the liver from the corpse of the first. He had died while tearing at the liver of a fellow human being. The Nazi contribution to European culture was the reintroduction of cannibalism. . . .

We shall prove that the accused performed all these deeds with the set purpose of destroying the Jewish people, wholly or in part. Adolf Eichmann will enjoy a privilege which he did not accord to a single one of his victims. He will be able to defend himself before the court. His fate will be decided according to law and according to the evidence, with the burden of proof resting upon the prosecution. And the judges of Israel will pronounce true and righteous judgment.

Source: Hausner, Gideon. "Trial Address." The Nizkor Project—The Trial of Adolf Eichmann. Available online. http://www.nizkor.org/hweb/people/e/eichmann-adolf/transcripts/. Accessed December 20, 2007.

ADLAI STEVENSON
(1900–1965)
Speech at the United Nations
United Nations, New York City
October 25, 1962

The "thirteen days" of the Cuban missile crisis brought the world's two superpowers, the United States and the Soviet Union (USSR), terrifyingly close to nuclear engagement during the cold war (1947–91). On October 16, 1962, President John F. Kennedy learned from aerial photos that the Soviet Union had installed offensive nuclear ballistic missiles in nearby Communist Cuba, just 90 miles from the Florida coast. Partly in response to the foolish U.S. attempt at overthrowing Cuban dictator Fidel Castro in 1961—the Bay of Pigs invasion—Castro had formalized ties with the USSR and permitted the missile bases built. Such interference in the Western Hemisphere was precisely what Kennedy had warned the Soviets against in his inaugural address of January 1961 (*SEE* Kennedy's speech, page 448). On October 22 the president publicly announced the discovery, blockaded Soviet shipping to Cuban ports, and gave Premier Khrushchev an ultimatum to remove the

weapons. Three days later at an emergency meeting of the United Nations Security Council, U.S. ambassador Adlai Stevenson contended sharply with Soviet ambassador Valerian Zorin over the existence of the missiles. It was a diplomatic success for Stevenson, and ultimately for Kennedy. On October 28 Soviet general secretary Nikita Khrushchev agreed to withdraw the missiles (the United States later agreed to close bases in Turkey). Stevenson was a lawyer who had served on the U.S. delegation to the United Nations for three years before being elected governor of Illinois in 1948. A stirring public speaker, he twice won the Democratic nomination to run for president, in 1952 and again in 1956, but he lost to Dwight D. Eisenhower. President Kennedy sent him to the United Nations as U.S. ambassador in 1961. With a quick intelligence and a keen skill at public speaking, Stevenson's wit made him a formidable adversary for the Soviet ambassador.

Stevenson: I want to say to you, Mr. Zorin, that I do not have your talent for obfuscation, for distortion, for confusing language, and for doubletalk. And I must confess to you that I am glad that I do not!

But if I understood what you said, you said that my position had changed, that today I was defensive because we did not have the evidence to prove our assertions, that your Government had installed long-range missiles in Cuba.

Well, let me say something to you, Mr. Ambassador—we do have the evidence. We have it, and it is clear and it is incontrovertible. And let me say something else—those weapons must be taken out of Cuba.

Next, let me say to you that, if I understood you, with a trespass on credulity that excels your best, you said that our position had changed since I spoke here the other day because of the pressures of world opinion and the majority of the United Nations. Well, let me say to you, sir, you are wrong again. We have had no pressure from anyone whatsoever. We came here today to indicate our willingness to discuss [U.N. Secretary General] Mr. U Thant's proposals, and that is the only change that has taken place.

But let me also say to you, sir, that there has been a change. You—the Soviet Union—have sent these weapons to Cuba. You—the Soviet Union—have upset the balance of power in the world. You—the Soviet Union—have created this new danger, not the United States.

And you asked, with a fine show of indignation, why the President did not tell Mr. Gromyko last Thursday about our evidence, at the very time that Mr. Gromyko was blandly denying to the President that the U.S.S.R. was placing such weapons on sites in the new world.

Well, I will tell you why—because we were assembling the evidence, and perhaps it would be instructive to the world to see how far a Soviet official would go in perfidy. Perhaps we wanted to know if this country faced another example of nuclear deceit like that one a year ago, when in stealth the Soviet Union broke the nuclear test moratorium.

And while we are asking questions, let me ask you why your Government—your Foreign Minister—deliberately, cynically deceived us about the nuclear build-up in Cuba.

And, finally, Mr. Zorin, I remind you that the other day you did not deny the existence of these weapons. Instead, we heard that they had suddenly become defensive weapons. But today, again if I heard you correctly, you now say that they do not exist, or that we haven't proved they exist, with another fine flood of rhetorical scorn.

All right, sir, let me ask you one simple question: Do you, Ambassador Zorin, deny that the U.S.S.R. has placed and is placing medium- and intermediate-range missiles and sites in Cuba? Yes or no—don't wait for the translation—yes or no?

Zorin: I am not in an American court of law, and therefore do not answer a question put to me in the manner of a prosecuting counsel. You will receive the answer in due course. . .

Stevenson: You are in the courtroom of world opinion right now, and you can answer yes or no. You have denied they exist. And I want to know if I understood you correctly.

Zorin: Please continue your statement, Mr. Stevenson. You will receive my answer in due course.

Stevenson: I am prepared to wait for my answer until hell freezes over, if that's your decision. And I am also prepared to present the evidence in this room. . . .

I have had no reply to the question, and I will now proceed, if I may, to finish my statement.

I doubt if anyone in this room, except possibly the representative of the Soviet Union, has any doubt about the facts. But in view of his statements and the statements of the Soviet Government up until last Thursday, when Mr. Gromyko denied the existence or any intention of installing such weapons in Cuba, I am going to make a portion of the evidence available right now. If you will indulge me for a moment, we will set up an easel here in the back of the room where I hope it will be visible to everyone. . . .

[Stevenson comments on numerous aerial photographs in detail.]

Stevenson: I won't detain you but one minute. I have not had a direct answer to my question. The representative of the Soviet Union says that the official answer of the U.S.S.R. was the Tass statement that they don't need to locate missiles in Cuba. Well, I agree—they don't need to. But the question is, have they missiles in Cuba? And that question remains unanswered. I knew it would be.

As to the authenticity of the photographs, which Mr. Zorin has spoken about with such scorn, I wonder if the Soviet Union would ask its Cuban colleague to permit a U.N. team to go to these sites. If so, I can assure you that we can direct them to the proper places very quickly.

And now I hope that we can get down to business, that we can stop this sparring. We know the facts, and so do you, sir, and we are ready to talk about them. Our job here is not to score debating points. Our job, Mr. Zorin, is to save the peace. And if you are ready to try, we are.

Source: Stevenson, Adlai, and Valerian Zorin. "Has the U.S.S.R. Missiles in Cuba?" *Vital Speeches of the Day* 29, no. 3 (November 15, 1962): 77.

On Dancing the *Gombe Sugu*

Dar es Salaam, Tanganyika, now Tanzania

December 10, 1962

Germany's largest colony in Africa, held from 1885 to 1918, was German East Africa. After the Allied powers defeated Germany in World War I (1914–18), Britain received a mandate to administer a large portion of German East Africa and in 1921 changed its name to Tanganyika. The next year Julius Kambarage Nyerere was born in northern Tanganyika. He became a teacher, and he received advanced degrees from Makerere University in Uganda and the University of Edinburgh, Scotland. After his return home, he organized the Tanganyika African National Union (TANU) in 1954. TANU became the pro-independence political party, as Nyerere spoke out for independence from Britain, even taking his case to the United Nations. Nyerere obtained a seat in the colonial legislative council in 1958; Africans increasingly found representation in the council as TANU began to dominate the elections. From there, change came quickly. Tanganyika received freedom from Britain in 1961 and Nyerere became the first prime minister. The next year, June 1962, he was elected president when the country became a British Commonwealth republic. His inauguration took place in the capital city of Dar es Salaam. In this excerpt from his inaugural address, he laments the loss of African culture to colonialism. In 1964 Tanganyika joined with the island of Zanzibar to create Tanzania, with Nyerere as its first president. Like many African nationalists who wished to break with the capitalist systems of their European oppressors, Nyerere was long interested in creating an African socialist state in his homeland, under a new kind of African socialism. He promoted self-reliance and equality and the development of rural areas, but his efforts to force collective farming were unsuccessful and the country faced economic decline. He left office peacefully in 1985.

❧

I want to tell you about two of the changes which I have made in the Ministries. One is a major change, the other a minor one. . . .

The major change I have made is to get up an entirely new Ministry: the Ministry of National Culture and Youth. I have done this because I believe that its culture is the essence and spirit of any nation. A country which lacks its own culture is no more than a collection of people without the spirit which makes them a nation. Of all the crimes of colonialism there is none worse than the attempt to make us believe we had no indigenous culture of our own; or that what we did have was worthless—something of which we should be ashamed, instead of a source of pride.

Some of us, particularly those of us who acquired a European type of education, set ourselves out to prove to our colonial rulers that we had become 'civilized'; and by that we meant that we had abandoned everything connected with our own past and learnt to imitate only European ways. Our young men's ambition was not to become well educated Africans, but to become Black Europeans! Indeed, at one time it was a compliment rather than an insult to call a man who imitated the Europeans a 'Black European'.

When we were at school we were taught to sing the songs of the Europeans. How many of us were taught the songs of the Wanyamwezi or of the Wahehe? Many of us have learnt to dance the 'rumba', or the 'chachacha,' to 'rock'n'roll' and to 'twist' and even to dance the 'waltz' and the 'foxtrot'. But how many of us can dance, or have even heard of, the *Gombe Sugu*, the *Mangala*, the *Konge, Nyang'umumi, Kiduo* or *Lele Mama?*

Lots of us can play the guitar, the piano, or other European musical instruments. How many Africans in Tanganyika, particularly among the educated, can play the African drums? How many can play the *nanga*, or the *zeze* or the *marimba*, the *kilanzi*, *ligombo* or the *imangala*? And even though we dance and play the piano, how often does that dancing—even if it is 'rock'n'roll' or 'twist'—how often does it really give us the sort of thrill we get from dancing the *mganda* or the *gombe sugu*—even though the music may be no more than the shaking of pebbles in a tin? It is hard for any man to get much real excitement from dances and music which are not in his own blood.

So I have set up this new Ministry to help us regain our pride in our own culture. I want it to seek out the best of the traditions and customs of all our tribes and make them a part of our national culture. I hope that everybody will do what he can to help the work of this new Ministry. But I don't want anybody to imagine that to revive our own culture means at the same time to reject that of any other country. A nation which refuses to learn from foreign cultures is nothing but a nation of idiots and lunatics. Mankind could not progress at all if we all refused to learn from each other. But to learn from other cultures does not mean we should abandon our own. The sort of learning from which we can benefit is the kind which can help us to perfect and broaden our own culture.

Yesterday 1 took an oath. I swore that as President of the Republic of Tanganyika I would do my duty and carry out my work without fear or favour, affection or ill-will towards anyone. That was no hollow formula, to be spoken and forgotten. It was a most solemn promise, made before Almighty God, that with His help I shall prove myself worthy of the responsibility which you—the people of Tanganyika—have entrusted to me; that I shall strive to fulfil the task laid upon me, without permitting myself to be influenced by any personal likes or dislikes, nor by consideration of my own comfort or convenience.

Julius Nyerere, president of Tanzania, greets Ugandan president Milton Obote (right) in Kampala, Uganda, in July 1969. *(AP Photo)*

I say 'I' swore. But in actual fact it is true to say that 'WE' swore; for I took that oath on your behalf. Every citizen of Tanganyika, whether he be the President, a politician, a civil servant, a farmer, a teacher, or the lowest-paid worker in the land, every single one of us has an equal duty to give of his best. Every one of us has an equal duty to do the work entrusted to him—whatever that work may be—as if he too had taken a solemn oath to devote himself, without thought for his own advantage, to building our new Republic of Tanganyika.

Source: Nyerere, Julius K. *Freedom and Unity: A Selection from Writings and Speeches 1952–1965.* Dar es Salaam, Tanzania: Oxford, 1967, p. 176. Reproduced under the terms of the Click-Use Licence.

JOHN F. KENNEDY
(1917–1963)
American University Address
Washington, D.C., United States
June 10, 1963

After the use by the United States of the first nuclear bombs on Japan, ending World War II (1939–45), a race to develop atomic weapons began among world powers. By 1960 four nations were testing atomic bombs: the United States, Soviet Union, United Kingdom, and France. Around this time, food in the United States was discovered to contain radioactive deposits, which added to existing fears of nuclear annihilation. In June 1963, just months after the presence of Soviet missiles in Cuba ignited the Cuban missile crisis, President John F. Kennedy gave the graduation address at American University in Washington, D.C. This important address announced cold war treaty talks in Moscow between the United States, Great Britain, and the Soviet Union to outlaw nuclear tests; and Kennedy pledged the United States would not resume atmospheric testing of atomic weapons if other nations refrained too. (For his American audience, Kennedy also observed that peace begins at home, referring indirectly to civil rights disorder in American cities.) The Partial Test Ban Treaty (or Limited Nuclear Test Ban Treaty) was signed on August 6, 1963, by the three negotiating countries, and by the vast majority of nations in the next months. It banned testing nuclear weapons in the atmosphere, outer space, or underwater, to slow the arms race and prevent radioactive contamination of the planet. This was the first treaty attempting to halt proliferation of nuclear weapons. Following in later years were the 1968 Nuclear Non-Proliferation Treaty and the 1996 Comprehensive Test Ban Treaty. Kennedy's speech was noted seriously by the leaders of the Soviet Union. Forty years later Russia's Mikhail Gorbachev, secretary general of the Communist Party (1985–91), would quote Kennedy in gently rebuking the United States for its 2003 invasion of Iraq under President George W. Bush—"peace is a process, peace is a way of solving problems," he said. (*SEE* Gorbachev's speech, p. 582). Just months after signing the treaty, Kennedy was killed by an assassin in Dallas, Texas, on November 22, 1963.

❧

I have chosen this time and this place to discuss a topic on which ignorance too often abounds and the truth is too rarely perceived—yet it is the most important topic on earth: world peace.

What kind of peace do I mean? What kind of peace do we seek? Not a Pax Americana enforced on the world by American weapons of war. Not the peace of the grave or the security of the slave. I am talking about genuine peace, the kind of peace that makes life on earth worth living, the kind that enables men and nations to grow and to hope and to build a better life for their children—not merely peace for Americans but peace for all men and women—not merely peace in our time but peace for all time.

I speak of peace because of the new face of war. Total war makes no sense in an age when great powers can maintain large and relatively invulnerable nuclear forces and refuse to surrender without resort to those forces. It makes no sense in an age when a single nuclear weapon contains almost ten times the explosive force delivered by all the allied air forces in the Second World War. It makes no sense in an age when the deadly poisons produced by a nuclear exchange would be carried by wind and water and soil and seed to the far corners of the globe and to generations yet unborn. . . .

Let us focus instead on a more practical, more attainable peace—based not on a sudden revolution in human nature but on a gradual evolution in human institutions—on a series of concrete actions and effective agreements which are in the interest of all concerned. There is no single, simple key to this peace—no grand or magic formula to be adopted by one or two powers. Genuine peace must be the product of many nations, the sum of many acts. It must be dynamic, not static, changing to meet the challenge of each new generation. For peace is a process—a way of solving problems. . . .

Let us reexamine our attitude toward the Soviet Union. It is discouraging to think that their leaders may actually believe what their propagandists write. It is discouraging to read a recent authoritative Soviet text on Military Strategy and find, on page after page, wholly baseless and incredible claims—such as the allegation that "American imperialist circles are preparing to unleash different types of wars . . . that there is a very real threat of a preventive war being unleashed by American imperialists against the Soviet Union . . . [and that] the political aims of the American imperialists are to enslave economically and politically the European and other capitalist countries . . . [and] to achieve world domination . . . by means of aggressive wars."

Truly, as it was written long ago: "The wicked flee when no man pursueth." Yet it is sad to read these Soviet statements—to realize the extent of the gulf between us. But it is also a warning—a warning to the American people not to fall into the same trap as the Soviets, not to see only a distorted and desperate view of the other side, not to see conflict as inevitable, accommodation as impossible, and communication as nothing more than an exchange of threats.

No government or social system is so evil that its people must be considered as lacking in virtue. As Americans, we find communism profoundly repugnant as a negation of personal freedom and dignity. But we can still hail the Russian people for their many achievements—in science and space, in economic and industrial growth, in culture and in acts of courage.

Among the many traits the peoples of our two countries have in common, none is stronger than our mutual abhorrence of war. Almost unique among the major world powers, we have never been at war with each other. And no nation in the history of battle ever suffered more than the Soviet Union suffered in the course of the Second World War. At least 20 million lost their lives. Countless millions of homes and farms were burned or sacked. A third of the nation's territory, including nearly two thirds of its industrial base, was turned into a wasteland—a loss equivalent to the devastation of this country east of Chicago.

Today, should total war ever break out again—no matter how—our two countries would become the primary targets. It is an ironic but accurate fact that the two strongest powers are the two in the most danger of devastation. All we have built, all we have worked for, would be destroyed in the first 24 hours. And even in the cold war, which brings burdens and dangers to so many nations, including this Nation's closest allies—our two countries bear the heaviest burdens. For we are both devoting massive sums of money to weapons that could be better devoted to combating ignorance, poverty, and disease. We are both caught up in a vicious and dangerous cycle in which suspicion on one side breeds suspicion on the other, and new weapons beget counter-weapons. . . .

Let us reexamine our attitude toward the cold war, remembering that we are not engaged in a debate, seeking to pile up debating points. We are not here distributing blame or pointing the finger of judgment. We must deal with the world as it is, and not as it might have been had the history of the last 18 years been different.

We must, therefore, persevere in the search for peace in the hope that constructive changes within the Communist bloc might bring within reach solutions which now seem beyond us. We must conduct our affairs in such a way that it becomes in the Communists' interest to agree on a genuine peace. Above all, while defending our own vital interests, nuclear powers must avert those confrontations which bring an adversary to a choice of either a humiliating retreat or a nuclear war. To adopt that kind of course in the nuclear age would be evidence only of the bankruptcy of our policy—or of a collective death-wish for the world.

To secure these ends, America's weapons are non-provocative, carefully controlled, designed to deter, and capable of selective use. Our military forces are committed to peace and disciplined in self-restraint. Our diplomats are instructed to avoid unnecessary irritants and purely rhetorical hostility. . . .

It is our hope—and the purpose of allied policies—to convince the Soviet Union that she, too, should let each nation choose its own future, so long as that choice does not interfere with the choices of others. The Communist drive to impose their political and economic system on others is the primary cause of world tension today. For there can be no doubt that, if all nations could refrain from interfering in the self-determination of others, the peace would be much more assured. . . .

We have also been talking in Geneva about the other first-step measures of arms control designed to limit the intensity of the arms race and to reduce the risks of accidental war. Our primary long range interest in Geneva, however, is general and complete disarmament—designed to take place by stages, permitting parallel political developments to build the new institutions of peace which would take the place of arms. The pursuit of disarmament has been an effort of this Government since the 1920s. It has been urgently sought by the past three administrations. And however dim the prospects may be today, we intend to continue this effort—to continue it in order that all countries, including our own, can better grasp what the problems and possibilities of disarmament are.

The one major area of these negotiations where the end is in sight, yet where a fresh start is badly needed, is in a treaty to outlaw nuclear tests. The conclusion of such a treaty, so near and yet so far, would check the spiraling arms race in one of its most dangerous areas. It would place the nuclear powers in a position to deal more effectively with one of the greatest hazards which man faces in 1963, the further spread of nuclear arms. It would increase our security—it would decrease the prospects of war. Surely this goal is sufficiently important to require our steady pursuit, yielding neither to the temptation to give up the whole effort nor the temptation to give up our insistence on vital and responsible safeguards.

I am taking this opportunity, therefore, to announce two important decisions in this regard.

First: Chairman Khrushchev, Prime Minister Macmillan, and I have agreed that high-level discussions will shortly begin in Moscow looking toward early agreement on a comprehensive test ban treaty. Our hopes must be tempered with the caution of history—but with our hopes go the hopes of all mankind.

Second: To make clear our good faith and solemn convictions on the matter, I now declare that the United States does not propose to conduct nuclear tests in the atmosphere so long as other states do not do so. We will not be the first to resume. Such a declaration is no substitute for a formal binding treaty, but I hope it will help us achieve it.

Finally, my fellow Americans, let us examine our attitude toward peace and freedom here at home. The quality and spirit of our own society must justify and support our efforts abroad. We must show it in the dedication of our own lives—as many of you who are graduating today will have a unique opportunity to do, by serving without pay in the Peace Corps abroad or in the proposed National Service Corps here at home.

But wherever we are, we must all, in our daily lives, live up to the age-old faith that peace and freedom walk together. In too many of our cities today, the peace is not secure because the freedom is incomplete.

It is the responsibility of the executive branch at all levels of government—local, State, and National—to provide and protect that freedom for all of our citizens by all means within their authority. It is the responsibility of the legislative branch at all levels, wherever that authority is not now adequate, to make it adequate. And it is the responsibility of all citizens in all sections of this country to respect the rights of all others and to respect the law of the land.

All this is not unrelated to world peace. "When a man's ways please the Lord," the Scriptures tell us, "he maketh even his enemies to be at peace with him." And is not peace, in the last analysis, basically a matter of human rights—the right to live out our lives without fear of devastation—the right to breathe air as nature provided it—the right of future generations to a healthy existence? . . .

The United States, as the world knows, will never start a war. We do not want a war. We do not now expect a war. This generation of Americans has already had enough—more than enough—of war and hate and oppression. We shall be prepared if others wish it. We shall be alert to try to stop it. But we shall also do our part to build a world of peace where the weak are safe and the strong are just. We are not helpless before that task or hopeless of its success. Confident and unafraid, we labor on—not toward a strategy of annihilation but toward a strategy of peace.

Source: Kennedy, John F. "Commencement Address at American University." John F. Kennedy Presidential Library. Available online. http://www.jfklibrary.org/Historical+Resources/ Archives/Reference+Desk/Speeches/Speeches+ of+John+F.+Kennedy.htm. Accessed December 20, 2007.

JOHN F. KENNEDY
(1917–1963)
"Ich bin ein Berliner"
Berlin, West Germany
June 26, 1963

President John F. Kennedy visited the Berlin Wall in June 1963, two years after the communist East German government built the wall to keep their citizens from fleeing to West Germany. After the defeat of Nazi Germany in World War II (1939–45), the four major Allied powers—France, Britain, the United States, and the Soviet Union—had divided Germany into four zones for temporary governing purposes. The capital city of Berlin, located within the larger Soviet zone, also was divided. Each occupying power administered a zone. By 1949 the British, French, and American zones were joined to form the Federal Republic of Germany, along with the corresponding three zones of Berlin, while the Soviets retained their zones and renamed them the German Democratic Republic, or East Germany. This left West Berlin as a capitalist island inside communist East Germany. Trapped within Soviet-controlled territory, many East Germans tried to defect to the West through Berlin, until the wall—snipers posted along its length—stopped the exodus. The wall divided Berlin in half, and it remained in place for 28 years until it came down in 1989. Kennedy's visit in 1963 drew a million West Berliners, most of the city's population; he spoke from a raised platform before the wall. He began by observing that a boast in ancient times had been, "I am a Roman citizen," and received thunderous approving roars from the audience to his repeated declaration "I am a Berliner," spoken in German, a stroke of genius that came to him shortly before. (Contrary to myth, "Berliner" did not signify a jelly donut to his hearers.) The defiant speech was clearly directed at the Soviet occupiers of East Germany, not just West Berliners. In 1989, with communist governments falling throughout Eastern Europe, East Germany dismantled the wall and the country was absorbed into the German Federal Republic.

Two thousand years ago the proudest boast was *Civis Romanus sum*. Today, in the world of freedom, the proudest boast is *Ich bin ein Berliner*.

There are many people in the world who really don't understand, or say they don't, what is the great issue between the free world and the Communist world. Let them come to Berlin.

There are some who say that communism is the wave of the future. Let them come to Berlin.

And there are some who say in Europe and elsewhere we can work with the Communists. Let them come to Berlin.

And there are even a few who say that it is true that communism is an evil system, but it permits us to make economic progress. *Lasst sie nach Berlin kommen*. Let them come to Berlin.

Freedom has many difficulties and democracy is not perfect, but we have never had to put a wall up to keep our people in, to prevent them from leaving us. I want to say, on behalf of my countrymen, who live many miles away on the other side of the Atlantic, who are far distant from you, that they take the greatest pride that they have been able to share with you, even from a distance, the story of the last eighteen years. I know of no town, no city, that has been besieged for eighteen years that still lives with the vitality and the force, and the hope and the determination of the city of West Berlin.

While the wall is the most obvious and vivid demonstration of the failures of the Communist system, for all the world to see, we take no satisfaction in it, for it is, as your Mayor has said, an offense not only against history but an offense against humanity, separating families, dividing husbands and wives and brothers and sisters, and dividing a people who wish to be joined together.

President John F. Kennedy addresses the people of Berlin in the Rudolph Wilde Platz, West Berlin, Federal Republic of Germany. *(Photo: Robert Knudsen, White House/John F. Kennedy Presidential Library and Museum, Boston)*

What is true of this city is true of Germany—real, lasting peace in Europe can never be assured as long as one German out of four is denied the elementary right of free men, and that is to make a free choice. In eighteen years of peace and good faith, this generation of Germans has earned the right to be free, including the right to unite their families and their nation in lasting peace, with good will to all people. You live in a defended island of freedom, but your life is part of the main.

So let me ask you as I close, to lift your eyes beyond the dangers of today, to the hopes of tomorrow, beyond the freedom merely of this city of Berlin, or your country of Germany, to the advance of freedom everywhere, beyond the wall to the day of peace with justice, beyond yourselves and ourselves to all mankind.

Freedom is indivisible, and when one man is enslaved, all are not free. When all are free, then we can look forward to that day when this city will be joined as one and this country and this great Continent of Europe in a peaceful and hopeful globe. When that day finally comes, as it will, the people of West Berlin can take sober satisfaction in the fact that they were in the front lines for almost two decades.

All free men, wherever they may live, are citizens of Berlin, and, therefore, as a free man, I take pride in the words *Ich bin ein Berliner.*

Source: Kennedy, John F. "Remarks at the Rudolph Wilde Platz." John F. Kennedy Presidential Library. Available online. http://www.jfklibrary.org/Historical+Resources/Archives/Reference+Desk/ Speeches/Speeches+of+John+F.+Kennedy.htm. Accessed December 20, 2007.

NELSON MANDELA
(1918–)
The Rivonia Trial Address
Pretoria, South Africa

April 20, 1964

Like his father, Nelson Mandela was brought up to be a leader and an adviser to the future king of his Thembu tribe. He was born in the Transkei, a tribal area on the south coast of South Africa, from which many men migrated north to work in the gold mines. Mandela moved north to Johannesburg also, but he found clerical work and began to study law. South Africa had a long tradition of pass laws and color bars that controlled where blacks and other persons of color, such as Indians could live and work (*SEE* Mohandas Gandhi's speech, p. 291). The government elected in 1948 took the system to unprecedented levels, however, developing new laws to prevent race mixing, and requiring separate facilities—schools, beaches, hospitals—for the different racial groups. Nonwhites lost voting rights, and blacks (75 percent of the population) were not permitted to enter "white" areas unless they worked there. In

this setting, Mandela became a lawyer and a member of the African National Congress (ANC). He helped lead the nonviolent Defiance Campaign, modeled after the teachings of Gandhi, until it was shut down by the government. Mandela was arrested in 1962 after the police discovered the headquarters in Rivonia (a Johannesburg suburb) of the ANC's guerrilla warfare branch, Umkhonto we Sizwe (Spear of the Nation). He and eight others were put on trial for treason and sabotage, and also accused of being communists, with the likelihood of the death sentence. Mandela chose to speak for himself at length in court. He was sentenced to life in the maximum security prison on Robben Island, near Cape Town, where the government held political prisoners. When he was released 26 years later, in February 1990, Mandela addressed the waiting press, quoting at the end the last paragraph of his courtroom speech.

At the outset, I want to say that the suggestion made by the State in its opening that the struggle in South Africa is under the influence of foreigners or communists is wholly incorrect. I have done whatever I did, both as an individual and as a leader of my people, because of my experience in South Africa and my own proudly felt African background, and not because of what any outsider might have said.

In my youth in the Transkei I listened to the elders of my tribe telling stories of the old days. Amongst the tales they related to me were those of wars fought by our ancestors in defense of the fatherland. The names of Dingane and Bambata, Hintsa and Makana, Squngthi and Dalasile, Moshoeshoe and Sekhukhuni, were praised as the glory of the entire African nation. I hoped then that life might offer me the opportunity to serve my people and make my own humble contribution to their freedom struggle. This is what has motivated me in all that I have done in relation to the charges made against me in this case.

Having said this, I must deal immediately and at some length with the question of violence. Some of the things so far told to the Court are true and some are untrue. I do not, however, deny that I planned sabotage. I did not plan it in a spirit of recklessness, nor because I have any love of violence. I planned it as a result of a calm and sober assessment of the political situation that had arisen after many years of tyranny, exploitation, and oppression of my people by the Whites.

I admit immediately that I was one of the persons who helped to form Umkhonto we Sizwe, and that I played a prominent role in its affairs until I was arrested in August 1962. . . . I, and the others who started the organization, did so for two reasons.

Firstly, we believed that as a result of Government policy, violence by the African people had become inevitable, and that unless responsible leadership was given to canalize and control the feelings of our people, there would be outbreaks of terrorism which would produce an intensity of bitterness and hostility between the various races of this country which is not produced even by war.

Secondly, we felt that without violence there would be no way open to the African people to succeed in their struggle against the principle of white supremacy. All lawful modes of expressing opposition to this principle had been closed by legislation, and we were placed in a position in which we had either to accept a permanent state of inferiority, or to defy the Government. We chose to defy the law. We first broke the law in a way which avoided any recourse to violence; when this form was legislated against, and then the Government resorted to a show of force to crush opposition to its policies, only then did we decide to answer violence with violence.

But the violence which we chose to adopt was not terrorism. We who formed Umkhonto were all members of the African National Congress, and had behind us the ANC tradition of non-violence and negotiation as a means of solving political disputes. We believe that South Africa belongs to all the people who live in it, and not to one group, be it black or white. We did not want an interracial war, and tried to avoid it to the last minute. . . .

We of the ANC had always stood for a non-racial democracy, and we shrank from any action which might drive the races further apart than they already were. But the hard facts were that fifty years of non-violence had brought the African people nothing but more and more repressive legislation, and fewer and fewer rights. It may not be easy for this Court to understand, but it is a fact that for a long time the people had been talking of violence—of the day when they would fight the White man and win back their country—and we, the leaders of the ANC, had nevertheless always prevailed upon them to avoid violence and to pursue peaceful methods.

When some of us discussed this in May and June of 1961, it could not be denied that our policy to achieve a nonracial State by non-violence had achieved nothing, and that our followers were beginning to lose confidence in this policy and were developing disturbing ideas of terrorism. . . . This then was the plan. Umkhonto was to perform sabotage, and strict instructions were given to its members right from the start, that on no account were they to injure or kill people in planning or carrying out operations. . . .

I have denied that I am a communist, and I think that in the circumstances I am obliged to state exactly what my political beliefs are.

I have always regarded myself, in the first place, as an African patriot. After all, I was born in Umtata, forty-six years ago. My guardian was my cousin, who was the acting paramount chief of Tembuland, and I am related both to the present paramount

I have fought against white domination, and I have fought against black domination. I have cherished the ideal of a democratic and free society in which all persons live together in harmony and with equal opportunities. It is an ideal which I hope to live for and to achieve. But if needs be, it is an ideal for which I am prepared to die. —*Nelson Mandela*

The 1964 Rivonia Trial of Nelson Mandela and African National Congress leaders was preceded by an earlier mass trial of 156 antiapartheid activists, including Mandela, known as the Treason Trial (1956–61). Nelson Mandela (right) leaves the day's proceedings in August 1958 in Pretoria, South Africa. *(AP Photo/Schadeberg)*

chief of Tembuland, Sabata Dalindyebo, and to Kaizer Matanzima, the Chief Minister of the Transkei.

Today I am attracted by the idea of a classless society, an attraction which springs in part from Marxist reading and, in part, from my admiration of the structure and organization of early African societies in this country. The land, then the main means of production, belonged to the tribe. There were no rich or poor and there was no exploitation.

It is true, as I have already stated, that I have been influenced by Marxist thought. But this is also true of many of the leaders of the new independent States. Such widely different persons as Gandhi, Nehru, Nkrumah, and Nasser all acknowledge this fact.

We all accept the need for some form of socialism to enable our people to catch up with the advanced countries of this world and to overcome their legacy of extreme poverty. But this does not mean we are Marxists.

Indeed, for my own part, I believe that it is open to debate whether the Communist Party has any specific role to play at this particular stage of our political struggle. The basic task at the present moment is the removal of race discrimination and the attainment of democratic rights on the basis of the Freedom Charter. In so far as that Party furthers this task, I welcome its assistance. I realize that it is one of the means by which people of all races can be drawn into our struggle.

From my reading of Marxist literature and from conversations with Marxists, I have gained the impression that communists regard the parliamentary system of the West as undemocratic and reactionary. But, on the contrary, I am an admirer of such a system.

The Magna Carta, the Petition of Rights, and the Bill of Rights are documents which are held in veneration by democrats throughout the world.

I have great respect for British political institutions, and for the country's system of justice. I regard the British Parliament as the most democratic institution in the world, and the independence and impartiality of its judiciary never fail to arouse my admiration.

The American Congress, that country's doctrine of separation of powers, as well as the independence of its judiciary, arouses in me similar sentiments.

I have been influenced in my thinking by both West and East. All this has led me to feel that in my search for a political formula, I should be absolutely impartial and objective. I should tie myself to no particular system of society other than of socialism. I must leave myself free to borrow the best from the West and from the East. . . .

The Government often answers its critics by saying that Africans in South Africa are economically better off than the inhabitants of the other countries in Africa. I do not know whether this statement is true and doubt whether any comparison can be made without having regard to the cost-of-living index in such countries. But even if it is true, as far as the African people are concerned it is irrelevant. Our complaint is not that we are poor by comparison with people in other countries, but that we are poor by comparison with the white people in our own country, and that we are prevented by legislation from altering this imbalance. . . .

Africans want to be paid a living wage. Africans want to perform work which they are capable of doing, and not work which the Government declares them to be capable of. Africans want to be allowed to live where they obtain work, and not be endorsed out of an area because they were not born there. Africans want to be allowed to own land in places where they work, and not to be obliged to live in rented houses which they can never call their own. Africans want to be part of the general population, and not confined to living in their own ghettoes.

African men want to have their wives and children to live with them where they work, and not be forced into an unnatural existence in men's hostels. African women want to be with their menfolk and not be left permanently widowed in the Reserves. Africans want to be allowed out after eleven o'clock at night and not to be confined to their rooms like little children. Africans want to be allowed to travel in their own country and to seek work where they want to and not where the Labor Bureau tells them to. Africans want a just share in the whole of South Africa; they want security and a stake in society.

Above all, we want equal political rights, because without them our disabilities will be permanent. I know this sounds revolutionary to the whites in this country, because the majority of voters will be Africans. This makes the white man fear democracy.

But this fear cannot be allowed to stand in the way of the only solution which will guarantee racial harmony and freedom for all. It is not true that the enfranchisement of all will result in racial domination. Political division, based on color, is entirely artificial and, when it disappears, so will the domination of one color group by another. The ANC has spent half a century fighting against racialism. When it triumphs it will not change that policy.

This then is what the ANC is fighting. Their struggle is a truly national one. It is a struggle of the African people, inspired by their own suffering and their own experience. It is a struggle for the right to live.

During my lifetime I have dedicated myself to this struggle of the African people. I have fought against white domination, and I have fought against black domination. I have cherished the ideal of a democratic and free society in which all persons live together in harmony and with equal opportunities. It is an ideal which I hope to live for and to achieve. But if needs be, it is an ideal for which I am prepared to die.

Source: Mandela, Nelson. "Second Court Statement." *The Struggle Is My Life.* New York: Pathfinder Press, 1990, p. 161. Permission of Nelson Mandela Foundation.

MARTIN LUTHER KING, JR.
(1929–1968)
Nobel Peace Prize Address
Oslo, Norway
December 10, 1964

Martin Luther King, Jr., was the son of an Atlanta, Georgia, Baptist preacher. He became pastor of his own church in Montgomery, Alabama, in 1953, a time when racial prejudice and "Jim Crow" laws prevented black children from attending school with whites, when blacks could not vote or get equal treatment with whites under the law. When Rosa Parks, an African-American seamstress, was arrested for refusing to give up her seat on a Montgomery bus to a white man, black community leaders organized a successful boycott of city buses. On December 5, 1955, the boycott's first day, King was elected president of the Montgomery Improvement Association, set up to direct the boycott and negotiate the hiring of black drivers and equal treatment of black and white riders. At a mass meeting that evening, he gave his first civil rights speech; he was only 26 years old but already had the oratorical power that would make him the nation's preeminent civil rights leader. He was arrested and his house bombed, but he persisted, applying the moral authority of Mahatma Gandhi's principles of nonviolent resistance and civil disobedience (SEE Gandhi's speeches, pages 291 and 318) to the struggle of American blacks for the full rights of American citizenship. The federal government and many whites were suspicious and resentful, not wanting to give up privilege but also fearing, wrongly, that his movement was communist influenced. On August 28, 1963, two months before President John F. Kennedy was to introduce new civil rights legislation in Congress, King, with other black leaders and Christian and Jewish religious leaders, led the great March on Washington. On the steps of the Lincoln Memorial, he delivered his matchless "I have a dream" speech. The next year, he was awarded the Nobel Peace Prize, and he gave this address. He was assassinated in Memphis, Tennessee, on April 4, 1968, by a white segregationist. He was just 39 years old.

I accept the Nobel Prize for Peace at a moment when 22 million Negroes of the United States of America are engaged in a creative battle to end the long night of racial injustice. I accept this award on behalf of a civil rights movement which is moving with determination and a majestic scorn for risk and danger to establish a reign of freedom and a rule of justice.

I am mindful that only yesterday in Birmingham, Alabama, our children, crying out for brotherhood, were answered with fire hoses, snarling dogs and even death. I am mindful that only yesterday in Philadelphia, Mississippi, young people seeking to secure the right to vote were brutalized and murdered. And only yesterday more than forty houses of worship in the state of Mississippi alone were bombed or burned because they offered a sanctuary to those who would not accept segregation. I am mindful that debilitating and grinding poverty afflicts my people and chains them to the lowest rung of the economic ladder.

Therefore, I must ask why this prize is awarded to a movement which is beleaguered and committed to unrelenting struggle; to a movement which has not won the very peace and brotherhood which is the essence of the Nobel Prize.

After contemplation, I conclude that this award which I receive on behalf of that movement is a profound recognition that nonviolence is the answer to the crucial political and moral question of our time—the need for man to overcome oppression and violence without resorting to violence and oppression.

Civilization and violence are antithetical concepts. Negroes of the United States, following the people of India, have demonstrated that nonviolence is not sterile passivity, but a powerful moral force which makes for social transformation. Sooner or later all the people of the world will have to discover a way to live together in peace, and thereby transform this pending cosmic elegy into a creative psalm of brotherhood. If this is to be achieved, man must evolve for all human conflict a method which rejects revenge, aggression and retaliation. The foundation of such a method is love.

The tortuous road which has led from Montgomery, Alabama to Oslo bears witness to this truth. This is a road over which millions of Negroes are traveling to find a new sense of dignity. This same road has opened for all Americans a new era of progress and hope. It has led to a new Civil Rights Bill, and it will, I am convinced, be widened and lengthened into a super highway of justice as Negro and white men in increasing numbers create alliances to overcome their common problems.

I accept this award today with an abiding faith in America and an audacious faith in the future of mankind. I refuse to accept despair as the final response to the ambiguities of history. I refuse to accept the idea that the "isness" of man's present nature makes him morally incapable of reaching up for the eternal "oughtness" that forever confronts him. I refuse to accept the idea that man is mere flotsam and jetsam in the river of life, unable to influence the unfolding events which surround him. I refuse to accept the view that mankind is so tragically bound to the starless midnight of racism and war that the bright daybreak of peace and brotherhood can never become a reality.

I refuse to accept the cynical notion that nation after nation must spiral down a militaristic stairway into the hell of thermonuclear destruction. I believe that unarmed truth and unconditional love will have the final word in reality. This is why right temporarily defeated is stronger than evil triumphant. I believe that even amid today's motor bursts and whining bullets, there is still hope for a brighter tomorrow. I believe that wounded justice, lying prostrate on the blood-flowing streets of our nations, can be lifted from this dust of shame to reign supreme among the children of men. I have the audacity to believe that peoples everywhere can have three meals a day for their bodies, education and culture for their minds, and dignity, equality and freedom for their spirits. I believe that what self-centered men have torn down, men other-centered can build up.

I still believe that one day mankind will bow before the altars of God and be crowned triumphant over war and bloodshed, and nonviolent redemptive good will proclaim the rule of the land. "And the lion and the lamb shall lie down together and every man shall sit under his own vine and fig tree and none shall be afraid." I still believe that We Shall Overcome!

This faith can give us courage to face the uncertainties of the future. It will give our tired feet new strength as we continue our forward stride toward the city of freedom. When our days become dreary with low-hovering clouds and our nights become darker than a thousand midnights, we will know that we are living in the creative turmoil of a genuine civilization struggling to be born.

Today I come to Oslo as a trustee, inspired and with renewed dedication to humanity. I accept this prize on behalf of all men who love peace and brotherhood. I say I come as a trustee, for in the depths of my heart I am aware that this prize is much more than an honor to me personally.

Every time I take a flight, I am always mindful of the many people who make a successful journey possible—the known pilots and the unknown ground crew.

So you honor the dedicated pilots of our struggle who have sat at the controls as the freedom movement soared into orbit. You honor, once again, Chief Lutuli of South Africa, whose struggles with and for his people, are still met with the most brutal expression of man's inhumanity to man. You honor the ground crew without whose labor and sacrifices the jet flights to freedom could never have left the earth. Most of these people will never make the headline and their names will not appear in *Who's Who*. Yet when years have rolled past and when the blazing light of truth is focused on this marvelous age in which we live—men and women will know and children will be taught that we have a finer land, a better people, a more noble civilization—because these humble children of God were willing to suffer for righteousness' sake.

I think Alfred Nobel would know what I mean when I say that I accept this award in the spirit of a curator of some precious heirloom which he holds in trust for its true owners—all those to whom beauty is truth and truth beauty—and in whose eyes the beauty of genuine brotherhood and peace is more precious than diamonds or silver or gold.

Source: King, Martin Luther, Jr. Acceptance Speech. The Nobel Foundation. Available online. http://nobelprize.org/nobel_prizes/peace/laureates/1964/king-acceptance.html. Accessed December 20, 2007. © The Nobel Foundation 1964.

ROBERT F. KENNEDY
(1925–1968)
"A Desert of Our Own Creation"
Manhattan, Kansas, United States
March 18, 1968

As U.S. Attorney General, Robert F. Kennedy advised his brother, President John F. Kennedy, during his time in office. After JFK's assassination, "Bobby" Kennedy was elected U.S. senator from New York. He worked diligently for civil rights for black Americans, and he disagreed bitterly with President Johnson's expansion of the Vietnam War. What had begun as civil war in Vietnam became a wider conflict as the United States dispatched hundreds of thousands of soldiers in an attempt to prevent communist North Vietnam from taking over South Vietnam. With the war going badly and tens of thousands of American soldiers dying, antiwar protesters marched on the Pentagon and Washington, burned draft cards, and staged sit-ins and other acts of civil disobedience. There was widespread draft resistance. In 1968, two days after Robert Kennedy announced he was running for president, he stopped at Kansas State University and gave one of his most noted speeches. He opened by saying the campaign was about more than who would be elected; it was also about solving the nation's three crises, the first being the "failed promise of America," seen in poverty and unemployment. The second was "inaction in the face of danger," especially civil rights violence (Martin Luther King, Jr., would be assassinated two weeks later). The third was the tragedy in Vietnam. Kennedy quoted a speech the Roman historian Tacitus put in the mouth of Calgacus, a British chieftain in 84 C.E. As Calgacus is about to fight General Agricola's troops, he says of the Romans, "To robbery, slaughter, plunder they give the false name of 'empire' and where they make a desert, they call it peace." Robert Kennedy was assassinated two months later in Los Angeles, after making another campaign address. The United States finally called it quits in Vietnam in 1973.

❧

Today I would speak to you of the third of those great crises: of the war in Vietnam. I come here, to this serious forum in the heart of the nation to discuss with you why I regard our policy there as bankrupt: not on the basis of emotion, but fact; not, I hope, in clichés—but with a clear and discriminating sense of where the national interest really lies.

I do not want—as I believe most Americans do not want—to sell out American interests, to simply withdraw, to raise the white flag of surrender. That would be unacceptable to us as a country and as a people. But I am concerned—as I believe most Americans are concerned—that the course we are following at the present time is deeply wrong. I am concerned—as I believe most Americans are concerned—that we are acting as if no other nations existed, against the judgment and desires of neutrals and our historic allies alike. I am concerned—as I believe most Americans are concerned—that our present course will not bring victory; will not bring peace; will not stop the bloodshed; and will not advance the interests of the United States or the cause of peace in the world.

I am concerned that, at the end of it all, there will only be more Americans killed; more of our treasure spilled out; and because of the bitterness and hatred on every side of this war, more hundreds of thousands of Vietnamese slaughtered; so that they may say, as Tacitus said of Rome: "They made a desert, and called it peace."

And I do not think that is what the American spirit is really all about.

Let me begin this discussion with a note both personal and public. I was involved in many of the early decisions on Vietnam, decisions which helped set us on our present path. It may be that the effort was doomed from the start; that it was never really possible to bring all the people of South Vietnam under the rule of the successive governments we supported—governments, one after another, riddled with corruption, inefficiency, and greed; governments which did not and could not successfully capture and energize the national feeling of their people. If that is the case, as it well may be, then I am willing to bear my share of the responsibility, before history and before my fellow-citizens.

But past error is no excuse for its own perpetuation. Tragedy is a tool for the living to gain wisdom, not a guide by which to live. Now as ever, we do ourselves best justice when we measure ourselves against ancient tests, as in the Antigone of Sophocles: "All men make mistakes, but a good man yields when he knows his course is wrong, and repairs the evil. The only sin is pride.". . .

As the scale of the fighting has increased, South Vietnamese society has become less and less capable of organizing or defending itself, and we have more and more assumed the whole burden of the war. In just three years, we have gone from 16,000 advisors to over 500,000 troops; from no American bombing North or South, to an air campaign against both, greater than that waged in all the European theater in World War II; from less than 300 American dead in all the years prior to 1965, to more than 500 dead in a single week of combat in 1968.

And once again the President tells us, as we have been told for twenty years, that "we are going to win;" "victory" is coming. . . .

An American commander said of the town of Ben Tre, "It became necessary to destroy the town in order to save it." It is difficult to quarrel with the decision of American commanders to use air power and artillery to save the lives of their men; if American troops are to fight for Vietnamese cities, they deserve protection. What I cannot understand is why the responsibility for the recapture and attendant destruction of Hue, and Ben Tre and the others, should fall to American troops in the first place. . . .

We must ask our government—we must ask ourselves: where does such logic end? If it becomes "necessary" to destroy all of South Vietnam in order to "save it", will we do that too? And if we care so little about South Vietnam that we are willing to see the land destroyed and its people dead, then why are we there in the first place?

Can we ordain to ourselves the awful majesty of God—to decide what cities and villages are to be destroyed, who will live and who will die, and who will join the refugees wandering in a desert of our own creation? If it is true that we have a commitment to the South Vietnamese people, we must ask, are they being consulted—in Hue, or Ben Tre, or in the villages from which the 3 million refugees have fled? . . .

Will it be said of us, as Tacitus said of Rome: "They made a desert and called it peace?"

It is also said that we are protecting Thailand—or perhaps Hawaii—from the legions of the Communists. Are we really protecting the rest of Southeast Asia by this spreading conflict? And in any case, is the destruction of South Vietnam and its people a permissible means of defense?

Let us have no misunderstanding. The Viet Cong are a brutal enemy indeed. Time and time again, they have shown their willingness to sacrifice innocent civilians, to engage in torture and murder and despicable terror to achieve their ends. . . .

We set out to prove our willingness to keep our commitments everywhere in the world. What we are ensuring instead is that it is most unlikely that the American people would ever again be willing to again engage in this kind of struggle. Meanwhile our oldest and strongest allies pull back to their own shores, leaving us alone to police all of Asia. . . .

All this bears directly and heavily on the question of whether more troops should now be sent to Vietnam—and if more are sent, what their mission will be. We are entitled to ask—we are required to ask—how many more men, how many more lives, how much more destruction will be asked, to provide the military victory that is always just around the corner, to pour into this bottomless pit of our dreams?

But this question the Administration does not and cannot answer. It has no answer—none but the ever-expanding use of military force and the lives of our brave soldiers, in a conflict where military force has failed to solve anything in the past. The President has offered to negotiate—yet this weekend he told us again that he seeks not compromise but victory, "at the negotiating table if possible, on the battlefield if necessary." But at a real negotiating table, there can be no "victory" for either side, only a painful and difficult compromise. To seek victory at the conference table is to ensure that you will never reach it. Instead, the war will go on, year after terrible year—until those who sit in the seats of high policy are men who seek another path. And that must be done this year.

For it is long past time to ask: what is this war doing to us? Of course it is costing us money—fully one-fourth of our federal budget—but that is the smallest price we pay. The cost is in our young men, the tens of thousands of their lives cut off forever. The cost is in our world position—in neutrals and allies alike, every day more baffled by and estranged from a policy they cannot understand.

Higher yet is the price we pay in our own innermost lives, and in the spirit of our country. For the first time in a century, we have open resistance to service in the cause of the nation. For the first time perhaps in our history, we have desertions from our army on political and moral grounds. The front pages of our newspapers show photographs of American soldiers torturing prisoners. Every night we watch horror on the evening news. Violence spreads inexorably across the nation, filling our streets and crippling our lives. And whatever the costs to us, let us think of the young men we have sent there: not just the killed, but those who have to kill; not just the maimed, but also those who must look upon the results of what they do.

It may be asked, is not such degradation the cost of all wars? Of course it is. That is why war is not an enterprise lightly to be undertaken, nor prolonged one moment past its absolute necessity. All this—the destruction of Vietnam, the cost to ourselves, the danger to the world—a all this we would stand willingly, if it seemed to serve some worthwhile end.

But the costs of the war's present course far outweigh anything we can reasonably hope to gain by it, for ourselves or for the people of Vietnam. It must be ended, and it can be ended, in a peace of brave men who have fought each other with a terrible fury, each believing he and he alone was right. We have prayed to different gods, and the prayers of neither have been answered fully. Now, while there is still time for some of them to be partly answered, now is the time to stop.

And the fact is that much can be done. We can—as I have urged for two years, but as we have never done—negotiate with the National Liberation Front. We can—as we have never done—assure the Front a genuine place in the political life of South Vietnam. We can—as we are refusing to do today—begin to deescalate the war, concentrate on protecting populated areas, and thus save American lives and slow down the destruction of the countryside. We can—as we have never done—insist that the government of South Vietnam broaden its base, institute real reforms, and seek an honorable settlement with their fellow countrymen.

This is no radical program of surrender. This is no sell-out of American interests. This is a modest and reasonable program, designed to advance the interests of this country and save something from the wreckage for the people of Vietnam. . . .

Our country is in danger: not just from foreign enemies; but above all, from our own misguided policies—and what they can do to the nation that Thomas Jefferson once told us was the last, best, hope of man. There is a contest on, not for the rule of

America, but for the heart of America. In these next eight months, we are going to decide what this country will stand for—and what kind of men we are.

So I ask for your help, in the cities and homes of this state, into the towns and farms: contributing your concern and action, warning of the danger of what we are doing—and the promise of what we can do. I ask you, as tens of thousands of young men and women are doing all over this land, to organize yourselves, and then to go forth and work for new policies—work to change our direction—and thus restore our place at the point of moral leadership, in our country, in our own hearts, and all around the world.

Source: Kennedy, Robert F. "Conflict in Vietnam and at Home." Kansas State University. Available online. http://ome.ksu.edu/lectures/landon/trans/Kennedy68.html. Accessed December 20, 2007. Used by permission of the Landon Lecture Series at Kansas State University.

CHAIM HERZOG
(1918–1997)
"The Aim of Zionism"
United Nations, New York City
November 10, 1975

Four wars fought between 1948 and 1973 destroyed almost all goodwill between Israel and Arab nations. In 1975, 19 Arab states (allied with many communist and third world nations), accused Israel of racism and imperialism. They sponsored a resolution in the United Nations equating Zionism (support for reestablishing a national homeland for Jews in Israel [Palestine]) with South Africa's apartheid system of forced racial segregation, stating, "Zionism is a form of racism and racial discrimination." Seventy-two nations voted in agreement. Two months earlier, the Organization of African Unity had declared, "The racist regime in occupied Palestine and the racist regime in Zimbabwe and South Africa have a common imperialist origin." Chaim Herzog, Israel's ambassador to the United Nations from 1975 to 1978, was an Irish Jew whose father had been the chief rabbi of Ireland. The family emigrated to Palestine in 1935 when Herzog

was 17; the Holy Land received many European Jews as new residents at this time—some fleeing anti-Semitic persecution and others following the Zionist dream of a Jewish homeland. As a British intelligence officer in World War II (1939–45), Herzog witnessed the horrors of Nazi death camps. He fought in both the Arab Revolt of 1936 and the 1948 Arab-Israeli War. Now addressing the UN General Assembly, Herzog noted the irony that the insulting resolution should be approved on the anniversary of Kristallnacht, one of the most notorious dates in Nazi history, when Jews were attacked violently and synagogues burned across Germany. He laid out a short history of Zionism and deplored what he called the two great evils menacing the world: ignorance and hatred. Then, denouncing the resolution, he tore the text in two. Herzog became president of Israel in 1983. On December 16, 1991, the resolution was overwhelming revoked.

❦

It is symbolic that this debate, which may well prove to be a turning point in the fortunes of the United Nations and a decisive factor as to the possible continued existence of this organization, should take place on November 10. Tonight, thirty-seven years ago, has gone down in history as Kristallnacht, the Night of the Crystals. This was the night in 1938 when Hitler's Nazi storm-troopers launched a coordinated attack on the Jewish community in Germany, burned the synagogues in all its cities, and made bonfires in the streets of the Holy Books and the Scrolls of the Holy Law and Bible. It was the night when Jewish homes were attacked and heads of families taken away, many of them never to return. It was the night when the windows of all Jewish businesses and stores were smashed, covering the streets in the cities of Germany with a film of broken glass which dissolved into the millions of crystals which gave that night its name. It was the night which led eventually to the crematoria and the gas chambers, Auschwitz, Birkenau, Dachau, Buchenwald, Theresienstadt and others. . . .

I do not come to this rostrum to defend the moral and historical values of the Jewish people. They do not need to be defended. They speak for themselves. They have given to mankind much of what is great and eternal. They have done for the spirit of man more than can readily be appreciated by a forum such as this one.

I come here to denounce the two great evils which menace society in general and a society of nations in particular. These two evils are hatred and ignorance. These two evils are the motivating force behind the proponents of this resolution and their supporters. These two evils characterize those who would drag this world organization, the ideals of which were first conceived by the prophets of Israel, to the depths to which it has been dragged today.

The key to understanding Zionism is in its name. The easternmost of the two hills of ancient Jerusalem during the tenth century B.C.E. was called Zion. In fact, the name Zion, referring to Jerusalem, appears 152 times in the Old Testament.... "Mount Zion" is the place where God dwells. Jerusalem, or Zion, is a place where the Lord is King, and where He has installed His king, David.

King David made Jerusalem the capital of Israel almost 3,000 years ago, and Jerusalem has remained the capital ever since. During the centuries the term "Zion" grew and expanded to mean the whole of Israel. The Israelites in exile could not forget Zion. The Hebrew Psalmist sat by the waters of Babylon and swore: "If I forget thee, O Jerusalem, let my right hand forget her cunning." This oath has been repeated for thousands of years by Jews throughout the world. It is an oath which was made over 700 years before the advent of Christianity and over 1,200 years before the advent of Islam. Zion came to mean the Jewish homeland, symbolic of Judaism, of Jewish national aspirations.

At the podium in the UN General Assembly, Chaim Herzog, Israel's ambassador to the United Nations, tears in half a copy of the 1975 UN resolution declaring that Zionism is a form of racism. *(AP Photo)*

While praying to his God, every Jew, wherever he is in the world, faces towards Jerusalem. For over 2,000 years of exile these prayers have expressed the yearning of the Jewish people to return to their ancient homeland, Israel. In fact, a continuous Jewish presence, in larger or smaller numbers, has been maintained in the country over the centuries.... Zionism is to the Jewish people what the liberation movements of Africa and Asia have been to their own people....

In modern times, in the late nineteenth century, spurred by the twin forces of anti-Semitic persecution and of nationalism, the Jewish people organized the Zionist movement in order to transform their dream into reality. Zionism as a political movement was the revolt of an oppressed nation against the depredation and wicked discrimination and oppression of the countries in which anti-Semitism flourished. It is no coincidence that the co-sponsors and supporters of this resolution include countries who are guilty of the horrible crimes of anti-Semitism and discrimination to this very day.

Support for the aim of Zionism was written into the League of Nations Mandate for Palestine and was again endorsed by the United Nations in 1947, when the General Assembly voted by overwhelming majority for the restoration of Jewish independence in our ancient land.

The re-establishment of Jewish independence in Israel, after centuries of struggle to overcome foreign conquest and exile, is a vindication of the fundamental concepts of the equality of nations and of self-determination. To question the Jewish people's right to national existence and freedom is not only to deny to the Jewish people the right accorded to every other people on this globe, but it is also to deny the central precepts of the United Nations.... How sad it is to see here a group of nations, many of whom have but recently freed themselves of colonial rule, deriding one of the most noble liberation movements of this century....

The Arab delegates talk of racism. What has happened to the 800,000 Jews who lived for over two thousand years in the Arab lands, who formed some of the most ancient communities long before the advent of Islam. Where are they now?

The Jews were once one of the important communities in the countries of the Middle East, the leaders of thought, of commerce, of medical science. Where are they in Arab society today? You dare talk of racism when I can point with pride to the Arab ministers who have served in my government; to the Arab deputy speaker of my Parliament; . . . to the fact that it is as natural for an Arab to serve in public office in Israel as it is incongruous to think of a Jew serving in any public office in an Arab country, indeed being admitted to many of them. Is that racism? It is not! That, Mr. President, is Zionism. . . .

Over the centuries it has fallen to the lot of my people to be the testing agent of human decency, the touchstone of civilization, the crucible in which enduring human values are to be tested. A nation's level of humanity could invariably be judged by its behavior towards its Jewish population. Persecution and oppression have often enough begun with the Jews, but it has never ended with them. The anti-Jewish pogroms in Czarist Russia were but the tip of the iceberg which revealed the inherent rottenness of a regime that was soon to disappear in the storm of revolution. The anti-Semitic excesses of the Nazis merely foreshadowed the catastrophe which was to befall mankind in Europe. . . .

On the issue before us, the world has divided itself into good and bad, decent and evil, human and debased. We, the Jewish people, will recall in history our gratitude to those nations who stood up and were counted and who refused to support this wicked proposition. I know that this episode will have strengthened the forces of freedom and decency in this world and will have fortified the free world in their resolve to strengthen the ideals they so cherish. I know that this episode will have strengthened Zionism as it has weakened the United Nations. . . .

For us, the Jewish people, this is but a passing episode in a rich and event-filled history. We put our trust in our Providence, in our faith and beliefs, in our time-hallowed tradition, in our striving for social advance and human values, and in our people wherever they may be. For us, the Jewish people, this resolution based on hatred, falsehood and arrogance, is devoid of any moral or legal value. For us, the Jewish people, this is no more than a piece of paper and we shall treat it as such.

Source: Herzog, Chaim. "Statement in the General Assembly." Israel Ministry of Foreign Affairs. Available online. http://www.mfa.gov.il/mfa/foreign%20relations/israels%20foreign%20relations%20since%201 947/1974–1977/. Accessed December 20, 2007.

ANWAR SADAT
(1918–1981)
To the Israeli Knesset
Jerusalem, Israel
November 20, 1977

Anwar Sadat grew up in a poor family in the Egyptian Nile Delta. He joined Egypt's army and took part in the revolution of 1952, a military coup d'état initiated by Gamal Abdel Nasser that unseated the corrupt pro-British monarchy of King Farouk. When Nasser took power as president in 1954, Sadat served as minister of state, president of the National Assembly, and, in 1964, vice president. Nasser's death in 1970 left Sadat with the presidency. He limited Soviet influence in Egypt, and he launched the 1973 Yom Kippur War (or October War) against Israel to demonstrate Egyptian military strength and regain territory lost in the 1967 Six-Day War (Egypt was defeated). He had been president seven years when he surprised and incensed Arab states in 1977 by approaching Israel for peace talks. He accepted an invitation from Israeli prime minister Menachem Begin (1977–83) to address Israel's legislature, the Knesset, in Jerusalem. This brave and historic overture extended Egypt's hand in friendship; he also shared, candidly but diplomatically, hard truths about changes Israel must implement to end hostilities. The next year, Sadat and Begin won the Nobel Peace Prize for their historic agreement, the Camp David Accords, worked out in March 1978, with U.S. president Jimmy Carter, at the country retreat for American presidents in Camp David, Maryland. As part of the agreement, Israel returned the Sinai Peninsula to Egypt. But many Arab nations harbored deep bitterness toward Sadat; his separate peace with their common enemy deprived them of the support of the largest Arab nation in their quest to eliminate Israel and solve the problem of homeless Palestinian refugees sheltering in their countries. Egypt was voted out of the Arab League for 10 years. Sadat's suppression of dissidents also made him unpopular at home. On October 6, 1981, Egyptian extremists opposed to negotiating with Israel assassinated him. In his speech, Sadat refers to the "Big Five," who are the five nations of the UN Security Council: China, France, Russia, the United Kingdom, and the United States.

I come to you today on solid ground, to shape a new life, to establish peace. We all love this land, the land of God. We all—Muslims, Christians and Jews—worship God and no one but God. God's teachings and commandments are love, sincerity, purity and peace.

I do not blame all those who received my decision, when I announced it to the entire world before the Egyptian People's Assembly, with surprise and amazement.... No one would have ever conceived that the President of the biggest Arab State, which bears the heaviest burden and the top responsibility pertaining to the cause of war and peace in the Middle East, could declare his readiness to go to the land of the adversary while we were still in a state of war....

After long thinking, I was convinced that the obligation of responsibility before God, and before the people, make it incumbent on me that I should go to the farthest corner of the world, even to Jerusalem, to address Members of the Knesset, the representatives of the People of Israel....

Frankness makes it incumbent upon me to tell you the following:

First: I have not come here for a separate agreement between Egypt and Israel. This is not part of the policy of Egypt. The problem is not that of Egypt and Israel. Any separate peace between Egypt and Israel, or between any Arab confrontation State and Israel, will not bring permanent peace based on justice in the entire region. Rather, even if peace between all the confrontation States and Israel were achieved, in the absence

481

On November 21, 1977, the day after his unprecedented address to the Knesset, Israel's legislature, Egyptian president Anwar Sadat (right) and Israeli prime minister Menachem Begin (left) hold a press conference. *(AP Photo)*

of a just solution to the Palestinian problem, never will there be that durable and just peace upon which the entire world insists today.

Second: I have not come to you to seek a partial peace, namely to terminate the state of belligerency at this stage, and put off the entire problem to a subsequent stage. This is not the radical solution that would steer us to permanent peace. Equally, I have not come to you for a third disengagement agreement in Sinai, or in the Golan and the West Bank. For this would mean that we are merely delaying the ignition of the fuse; it would mean that we are lacking the courage to confront peace, that we are too weak to shoulder the burdens and responsibilities of a durable peace based on justice.

I have come to you so that together we might build a durable peace based on justice, to avoid the shedding of one single drop of blood from an Arab or an Israeli. It is for this reason that I have proclaimed my readiness to go to the farthest corner of the world.

Here, I would go back to the answer to the big question: how can we achieve a durable peace based on justice?

In my opinion, and I declare it to the whole world from this forum, the answer is neither difficult nor impossible, despite long years of feud, blood vengeance, spite and hatred, and breeding generations on concepts of total rift and deep-rooted animosity. The answer is not difficult, nor is it impossible, if we sincerely and faithfully follow a straight line.

You want to live with us in this part of the world. In all sincerity, I tell you, we welcome you among us, with full security and safety. This, in itself, is a tremendous turning point, one of the landmarks of a decisive historical change.

We used to reject you. We had our reasons and our fears, yes. We used to brand you as "so-called" Israel, yes. We were together in international conferences and organizations and our representatives did not, and still do not, exchange greetings, yes. . . .

Yet, today I tell you, and declare it to the whole world, that we accept to live with you in permanent peace based on justice. We do not want to encircle you or be encircled ourselves by destructive missiles ready for launching, nor by the shells of grudges and hatred. I have announced on more than one occasion that Israel has become a fait accompli, recognized by the world, and that the two super powers have undertaken the responsibility of its security and the defense of its existence.

As we really and truly seek peace, we really and truly welcome you to live among us in peace and security.

There was a huge wall between us which you tried to build up over a quarter of a century. . . . It was a wall that warned us against extermination and annihilation if we tried to use our legitimate right to liberate the occupied territories. Together we have to admit that that wall fell and collapsed in 1973.

Yet, there remained another wall. This wall constitutes a psychological barrier between us. A barrier of suspicion. A barrier of rejection. A barrier of fear of deception. A barrier of hallucinations around any action, deed or decision. A barrier of cautious and erroneous interpretations of all and every event or statement. It is this psychological barrier which I described in official statements as representing 70 percent of the whole problem.

Today, through my visit to you, I ask you: why don't we stretch our hands with faith and sincerity so that, together, we might destroy this barrier? . . .

To tell you the truth, peace cannot be worth its name unless it is based on justice, and not on the occupation of the land of others. It would not be appropriate for you to demand for yourselves what you deny others. With all frankness, and with the spirit that has prompted me to come to you today, I tell you: you have to give up, once and for all, the dreams of conquest, and give up the belief that force is the best method for dealing with the Arabs. You should clearly understand and assimilate the lesson of confrontation between you and us.

Expansion does not pay. To speak frankly, our land does not yield itself to bargaining. It is not even open to argument. To us, the national soil is equal to the holy valley where God Almighty spoke to Moses—peace be upon him. None of us can, or accept to, cede one inch of it, or accept the principle of debating or bargaining over it.

I sincerely tell you that before us today lies the appropriate chance for peace, if we are really serious in our endeavors for peace. It is a chance that time cannot afford once again. It is a chance that, if lost or wasted, the plotter against it will bear the curse of humanity and the curse of history.

RHETORICAL DEVICE

Parenthesis: Placing an aside within another sentence, to provide pertinent information in a fresh, dramatic fashion.

Yesterday, December 7, 1941—a date which will live in infamy—
the United States of America was suddenly and deliberately attacked by
naval and air forces of the Empire of Japan. —*Franklin Delano Roosevelt*

I am by nature (and so are all our women) a law-abiding woman. Nothing but extreme provocation leads women to break the law. —*Emmeline Pankhurst*

We all—Muslims, Christians and Jews—worship God
and no one but God. —*Anwar Sadat*

What is peace for Israel? It means that Israel lives in the region with her Arab neighbors, in security and safety. To such logic, I say yes. It means that Israel lives within her borders, secure against any aggression. To such logic, I say yes. It means that Israel obtains all kinds of guarantees that ensure those two factors. To this demand, I say yes. More than that: we declare that we accept all the international guarantees you envisage and accept. We declare that we accept all the guarantees you want from the two super powers or from either of them, or from the Big Five, or some of them.

Once again, I declare clearly and unequivocally that we agree to any guarantees you accept because, in return, we shall obtain the same guarantees.

In short, then, when we ask: what is peace for Israel, the answer would be that Israel live within her borders with her Arab neighbors, in safety and security within the framework of all the guarantees she accepts and which are offered to the other party. But how can this be achieved? How can we reach this conclusion which would lead us to permanent peace based on justice?

There are facts that should be faced with all courage and clarity. There are Arab territories that Israel has occupied by armed force. We insist on complete withdrawal from these territories, including Arab Jerusalem.

I have come to Jerusalem, as the City of Peace, which will always remain as a living embodiment of coexistence among believers of the three religions. It is inadmissible that anyone should conceive the special status of the City of Jerusalem within the framework of annexation or expansionism, but it should be a free and open city for all believers.

Above all, the city should not be severed from those who have made it their abode for centuries. Instead of awakening the prejudices of the Crusaders, we should revive the spirit of Ornar ibn el-Khattab and Saladdin, namely the spirit of tolerance and respect for rights. The holy shrines of Islam and Christianity are not only places of worship, but a living testimony of our uninterrupted presence here politically, spiritually and intellectually. Let us make no mistake about the importance and reverence we Christians and Muslims attach to Jerusalem. . . .

As for the Palestinians' cause, nobody could deny that it is the crux of the entire problem. Nobody in the world could accept, today, slogans propagated here in Israel, ignoring the existence of the Palestinian People, and questioning their whereabouts. The cause of the Palestinian People and their legitimate rights are no longer ignored or denied today by anybody. Rather, nobody who has the ability of judgment can deny or ignore it.

It is an acknowledged fact received by the world community, both in the East and in the West, with support and recognition in international documents and official statements. It is of no use to anybody to turn deaf ears to its resounding voice, which is being heard day and night, or to overlook its historical reality. Even the United States, your first ally which is absolutely committed to safeguard Israel's security and existence, and which offered and still offers Israel every moral, material and military support—I say, even the United States has opted to face up to reality and facts, and admit that the Palestinian People are entitled to legitimate rights and that the Palestinian problem is the core and essence of the conflict and that, so long as it continues to be unresolved, the conflict will continue to aggravate, reaching new dimensions. In all sincerity, I tell you that there can be no peace without the Palestinians. It is a grave error of unpredictable consequences to overlook or brush aside this cause.

I shall not indulge in past events since the Balfour Declaration sixty years ago. You are well acquainted with the relevant facts. If you have found the legal and moral justification to set up a national home on a land that did not all belong to you, it is incumbent upon you to show understanding of the insistence of the People of Palestine on establishing, once again a state on their land. When some extremists ask the Palestinians to give up this sublime objective, this, in fact, means asking them to renounce their identity and every hope for the future. I hail the Israeli voices that called for the recognition of the Palestinian People's rights to achieve and safeguard peace. . . .

Ladies and Gentlemen, peace is not the mere endorsement of written lines; rather, it is a rewriting of history. Peace is not a game of calling for peace to defend certain whims or hide certain ambitions. Peace is a giant struggle against all and every ambition and whim. Perhaps the examples taken from ancient and modern history teach us all that missiles, warships and nuclear weapons cannot establish security. Rather, they destroy what peace and security build. For the sake of our peoples, and for the sake of the civilizations made by man, we have to defend man everywhere against the rule of the force of arms, so that we may endow the rule of humanity with all the power of the values and principles that promote the sublime position of mankind.

Allow me to address my call from this rostrum to the People of Israel. I address myself with true and sincere words to every man, woman and child in Israel.

From the Egyptian People who bless this sacred mission of peace, I convey to you the message of peace, the message of the Egyptian People who do not know fanaticism, and whose sons, Muslims, Christians, and Jews, live together in a spirit of cordiality, love and tolerance. This is Egypt whose people have entrusted me with that sacred message, the message of security, safety and peace. To every man, woman and child in Israel, I say: encourage your leadership to struggle for peace. . . .

I have come here to deliver a message. I have delivered the message, and may God be my witness.

I repeat with Zechariah, "Love right and justice."

I quote the following verses from the holy Koran: "We believe in God and in what has been revealed to us and what was revealed to Abraham, Ismail, Isaac, Jacob, and the tribes and in the books given to Moses, Jesus, and the prophets from their lord. We make no distinction between one and another among them and to God we submit."

Source: Sadat, Anwar. "Statement to the Knesset by President Sadat." Israel Ministry of Foreign Affairs. Available online. http://www.mfa.gov.il/mfa/foreign%20relations/israels%20foreign %20relations%20since%201 947/1977–1979/. Accessed December 20, 2007.

NATAN SHARANSKY
(1948–)
"At Peace with My Conscience"
Moscow, USSR
July 14, 1978

During the cold war (1947–91), few people who wished to leave the Soviet Union or other Soviet bloc countries, even temporarily, were allowed to do so. Determined individuals often had to resort to defection, risking arrest and execution, as the government regarded escapees as traitors renouncing allegiance to the state. Jewish citizens who applied to emigrate to Israel were rarely permitted to leave, and they were often persecuted and lost their jobs for making the request. Jewish computer scientist and mathematician Anatoly Sharansky, called Natan (his great-grandfather's name) by his activist friends, was a Zionist "refusenik" whose case became known around the world. After requesting permission to emigrate to Israel in 1973, the Soviet government denied him the necessary exit visa that would permit him to travel. The excuse was "national security," a common claim that the refusenik was in possession of state secrets learned on the job. Sharansky (sometimes spelled Shcharansky) subsequently worked with human rights groups, supporting other refuseniks and internally exiled intellectuals such as nuclear physicists Yuri Orlov and Andrei Sakharov; as a defiant anticommunist he drew embarrassing international attention. In 1977 Sharansky was arrested. The "show trial" for treason in 1978 rested on false charges of spying and could have carried the death sentence. Before his conviction he courageously addressed the courtroom, turning only at the end to the officers of the court, to whom he had "nothing to say." His brother Leonid secretly recorded the speech. The sentence was "light"—13 years in a labor camp; he spent eight in the Siberian gulag (prison labor camp system) before he was freed in exchange for Soviet spies arrested in the West. He joined his wife Avital in Jerusalem in 1986, and he entered politics a few years later. Sharansky became a member of the Israeli parliament, the Knesset, from 2003 to 2006.

~~~

From the start of my investigation, the heads of the KGB told me often that given my position with regard to this case, I would receive either capital punishment or, at best, fifteen years of imprisonment. They promised that if I changed my mind and cooperated with them in their struggle against Jewish activists and dissidents, I would receive a short, symbolic sentence and the opportunity to join my wife in Israel. But I did not change my position either during the investigation or at the trial, and yesterday the prosecution demanded that I be sentenced to a term of fifteen years.

Five years ago I applied for an exit visa to emigrate from the USSR to Israel. Today I am further than ever from my goal. This would seem to be a cause for regret, but that is not the case. These five years were the best of my life. I am happy that I have been able to live them honestly and at peace with my conscience. I have said only what I believed, and have not violated my conscience even when my life was in danger.

I am also happy to have been able to help many people who needed help and who turned to me. I am proud that I came to know and work with such people as Andrei Sakharov, Yuri Orlov, and Alexander Ginzburg, who are carrying on the best traditions of the Russian intelligentsia. But most of all, I feel part of a marvelous historical process—the process of the national revival of Soviet Jewry and its return to the homeland, to Israel. I hope that the false and absurd but terribly serious charges made today against me—and the entire Jewish people—will not impede the process of the national revival of the Jews of Russia, as the KGB has assured me they would, but will actually provide a new impulse, as has often happened in our history.

My relatives and friends know how strong was my desire to join my wife in Israel, and with what joy at any moment I would have exchanged my so-called fame as a Jewish activist—for which the charge asserts I was striving—for a visa to Israel. For two thousand years the Jewish people, my people, have been dispersed all over the world and seemingly deprived of any hope of returning. But still, each year Jews have stubbornly, and apparently without reason, said to each other, *Leshana haba'a b'Yerushalayim* (Next year in Jerusalem)! And today, when I am further than ever from my dream, from my people, and from my Avital, and when many difficult years of prisons and camps lie ahead of me, I say to my wife and to my people, *Leshana haba'a b'Yerushalayim.*

And to the court, which has only to read a sentence that was prepared long ago—to you I have nothing to say.

Source: Sharansky, Natan. *Fear No Evil.* New York: Random House, 1988, p. 223. From *Fear No Evil* by Natan Sharansky, copyright ©1988 by Random House, Inc. Used by permission of Random House, Inc.

WEI JINGSHENG

(1950–   )

"These Leaders Are Not Gods"

Beijing, China
October 16, 1979

From simple origins as an electrician for the Beijing Zoo, Wei Jingsheng became the father of the democracy movement in Communist China, and China's most famous political prisoner. Like citizens of the Soviet Union, the Chinese people were not free to protest the government's policies or demand such civil liberties as freedom of speech. Imprisonment, even execution, could be the fate of dissidents. However, during a short-lived period of relative political freedom in 1978 and 1979—the Beijing Spring—thousands of pro-democracy advocates dared to post messages of dissent on a stretch of brick masonry in Beijing called the Democracy Wall. In March 1979, Wei pasted on an essay, "Democracy: The Fifth Modernization." The title was a reference to the government's "Four Modernizations" policy, largely about economic development, announced the previous year. Wei's essay countered communist propaganda, making the case that China would never be able to modernize without turning to democracy. Courageously, he signed it with his own name and address. Wei also published a dissident magazine, *Exploration*, in which he described China's leader from 1956 to 1966, Deng Xiaoping, as a dictator. The authorities arrested him for "counterrevolutionary crimes" and, falsely, with passing secret information to foreigners. He spoke in his own defense at his trial, and the speech was smuggled out to the press. In his address, he refers to such Marxist concepts as the proletariat, or working class people. Sentenced to 15 years in prison, he was tortured and kept in solitary confinement. Released in 1993, he was quickly jailed again. China finally expelled him in 1997, after 18 years in prison. He gave a press conference in New York on November 21, saying, "I have waited decades for this chance to exercise my right to free speech, but the Chinese people have been waiting for centuries."

❧

I see as unfounded and unsubstantiated the charges in the indictment brought by the People's Procuratorate of Peking's [Beijing's] Municipality. My editing of publications and my writing of posters were both in accordance with Article 45 of the constitution: "Citizens enjoy freedom of speech, correspondence, the press, assembly, association, procession, demonstration and the freedom to strike, and have the right to 'speak out freely, air their views fully, hold great debates and write big-character posters.'"

Our reasons for producing our publication were simply to attempt a tentative exploration of the path along which China could advance this objective. Our activities, motivated by the principles I have just mentioned, are described as counterrevolutionary by the Public Security Department and the Procuratorate. We cannot accept such a description.

The indictment states that I carried out counterrevolutionary propaganda and agitation, and describes my essays, "Democracy: The Fifth Modernization," etc., as reactionary articles. Likewise our publication *Exploration* is referred to as reactionary. In view of this, we must first make it clear what is meant by such terms as "reactionary," "counterrevolutionary" and "revolutionary."

As a result of the influence of all those years of cultural autocracy, and the obscurantist policy of keeping the people in a state of blind ignorance in the "Gang of Four" era, there are even now people whose outlook is that if one does things exactly in accordance with the will of the leadership currently in power, this is what is meant by being "revolutionary" whereas to run counter to the will of those currently in power is counterrevolutionary.

Pro-democracy demonstrators in Hong Kong hold signs with the photo of Chinese activist Wei Jingsheng during a visit by Chinese premier Li Peng on September 22, 1997. The protestors demanded that Wei, still in prison, be released. *(AP Photo/Vincent Yu)*

I cannot agree with such a vulgar debasement of the concept of revolution. The term "revolutionary" entails following a course of action whereby one moves with the current of historical development, and strives to remove all that is old and conservative, blocking and impeding the onward flow of history. Revolution is the struggle of new phenomena against old phenomena. To attach the label of perpetual revolution to the will and ambition of those currently in power is tantamount to stifling all diversity of thought. . . .

The present historical trend or current is a democratic one. . . . Thus, the democratic trend is this age's revolutionary current, while those autocratic conservatives who stand in opposition to the democratic trend are the real counterrevolutionaries of the age.

The central argument of those articles of mine, such as "Democracy: The Fifth Modernization," is that without democracy there will be no Four Modernizations; without the *fifth* modernization, or democracy, any talk of modernization will remain an empty lie. How does such an argument constitute counterrevolution? Surely it is those very people who oppose democracy who should be included in the counterrevolutionary category? . . .

The Marxism I attacked in my essays is in no way the Marxism of more than a hundred or so years ago, but rather the form of Marxism favored by that school of political con men such as Lin Biao and the "Gang of Four." I recognize nothing in this world as constantly immutable, nor any theory as absolutely correct. All ideological theory is relative, for within its existing context it contains elements of relative truth and, conversely, elements of relative absurdity. . . .

Marxism, over a hundred years of development, has been successively transformed into a number of divergent schools—Kautskyism, Leninism, Trotskyism, Stalinism, Mao Zedong Thought, Eurocommunism, etc. While these different theories all abide by the basic tenets of Marxism, or do so in part, they have also carried out partial modifications and revisions of Marxism as a system. Thus, though they are called Marxist, none of them is the original Marxist system. . . .

Following a hundred years of actual practice, those governments which have emerged from this method of dictatorship, where power has been concentrated—such as those of the Soviet Union, Vietnam, and China before smashing of the "Gang of Four"—have without exception deteriorated into fascist regimes, where a small leading faction imposes its autocracy over the large mass of ordinary laboring people.

Moreover, the fascist dictators, in whose grasp the government has come to rest, have long since ceased to use the dictatorship of the proletariat as a tool of implementing the old ideals of Communism itself. Precisely the opposite is the case. For without exception these rulers have used the ideals of Communism to reinforce the so-called dictatorship of the proletariat so that it may function as a tool for the benefit of those in power.

Thus, Marxism's fate is common to that of several religions. After the second or third generation of transmission, its revolutionary substance is quietly removed, while its doctrinal ideals are partially taken over by the rulers, to be used as an excuse to enslave the people and as a tool to deceive and fool them. . . . Those who forbid the critical treatment of Marxism are engaged in the very process of transforming Marxism into a religious faith. Any man has the right to believe and adhere to the theories he holds to be correct, but he should not use legally binding stipulations to impose on others the theories he has faith in, otherwise he is interfering with the liberties of his fellow men. . . .

The indictment claims that, by flaunting the banner of so-called free speech for democracy and human rights, I incited the overthrow of the socialist system and the political power of the dictatorship of the proletariat.

First of all, allow me to point out there is nothing whatsoever "so-called" about free speech. On the contrary, it is stipulated by the constitution as a right to be enjoyed by all citizens. The Public Prosecutor's choice of such a term in discussing rights granted citizens by the constitution not only shows his prejudice when thinking on such matters, but further illustrates that he has forgotten his responsibility to protect the rights of his fellow citizens. He makes the rights of the citizens in this country of ours the object of ridicule. . . .

The public prosecutor's accusation that I wanted to overthrow the socialist system is even more at odds with the facts. . . . Of course in the eyes of the prosecutor, his interpretation of a socialist system may possibly differ enormously from my conception of that system. I recognize that in reality the socialist system may take many different forms and not be one stereotype.

In the light of their most obvious distinction, I would classify socialist systems into two large categories. The first is the Soviet-style of dictatorial socialism, with its chief characteristic of having its power concentrated in the hands of the minority in authority. The second category is democratic socialism, with the power reinvested in the whole people organized on a democratic footing. The majority of people in our nation all wish for the implementation of this kind of socialism. The aim of our exploratory inquiry was to seek the way to attain such a socialist system. . . .

I consider that without carrying out a reform of the social system, without a true establishment of popular democratic power, and if there is no democratic system of government to act as a guarantee, then our nation's economic modernization cannot be attained. Perhaps the members of the Office of the Procuratorate do not agree with my theory, but their disagreement with my theories does not brand me as someone wanting to overthrow the socialist system. . . .

I would only point out two things. First, the constitution grants citizens the right to criticize their leaders, because these leaders are not gods. It is only through the people's criticism and supervision that those leaders will make fewer mistakes, and only in this way that the people will avoid the misfortune of having their lords and masters ride roughshod over them. Then, and only then, will the people be able to breathe freely.

Secondly, . . . it is the people's prerogative, when faced by unreasonable people and unacceptable matters, to make criticisms. Indeed, it is also their unshirkable duty so to do and this is a sovereign right with which no individual or government organization has a right to interfere. . . .

Naturally, criticism should have substantial factual basis, nor should we tolerate personal attacks and malicious slandering. This taboo was one of the principles adhered to by our publication, as our introductory opening statement to our readers demonstrates. If the prosecution feels that in this respect I did not do enough, I am willing to accept the criticism put forward by the prosecution or anyone else.

That concludes my defense address.

Source: Wei Jingsheng. "Trial of Wei Jingsheng." In *The Democracy Reader,* edited by Diane Ravitch and Abigail Thernstrom. New York: HarperCollins, 1992, p. 163. Permission of Wei Jingsheng.

JACOBO TIMERMAN
(1923–1999)
"The Books Were the First Victims"
Key Biscayne, Florida, United States
May 5, 1981

Jacobo Timerman and his family emigrated to Argentina from the Ukraine in 1928, to escape anti-Jewish pogroms there. As practicing Jews and Zionists (supporters of the reestablishment of a Jewish homeland), the Timermans faced hostility among Argentina's staunchly Catholic and anti-Semitic population. Despite an impoverished childhood, by the 1970s Timerman had established himself as a successful journalist in Buenos Aires. Not only had he started a publishing house, Timerman Editores, but he had also founded a liberal daily newspaper called *La Opinión*. It was his role as editor of *La Opinión* that resulted in his abduction on April 15, 1977, and his torture by the Argentine government. The year before, because of activity by Marxist guerrillas and widespread labor unrest, the Argentine military had taken control of the government and established a right-wing dictatorship under General Jorge Rafael Videla (1976–81). To silence the opposition, the military dictatorship abducted, tortured, and killed an estimated 20,000 Argentinian citizens deemed dangerous to the government; more than 100 journalists perished in the state-sponsored terror, which became known as the "Dirty War" (1976–83). Because he defied censorship laws in printing information about human rights violations, Timerman spent nearly two years brutally tortured and interrogated in Argentine jails. On his release, he was exiled to Israel with his family, where in 1981 he published his book *Prisoner without a Name, Cell without a Number,* a detailed account of his persecution. For his humanitarian ideals and courage in defending the right to free speech, Timerman was awarded the Golden Pen of Freedom by the World Association of Newspapers and delivered this address at the 1981 convention of the Association of American Publishers. Argentina regained a democratic government in 1983, and Timerman was able to return to testify against leaders of the dictatorship.

A little less than half a century ago, my mother pasted on the wall of our home a photograph that had appeared in a Buenos Aires newspaper. The PEN Club was holding its conference, and the photo showed Emil Ludwig giving a report on the persecution of Jews in Germany. In the first row, the French Catholic writer and philosopher Jacques Maritain was sobbing, his head bent, his hands covering his face; Stefan Zweig was comforting him, with one arm around his shoulders.

That image has stayed with me all my life, taking on different meanings, assuming different symbols or roles. I always had it within reach, and when I needed it I used it. I never needed it more than in the secret prisons where I was tortured and interrogated by the Argentine army, four years ago.

Those interrogations were numerous and varied. Some of them were organized with great legal protocol, and directed by a general in full uniform. Some were conducted by teams of torturers. Between the two extremes there were many variations: the questioner who was sympathetic; the shouter; the one who took advantage of a moment when he was alone to whisper that he was not in agreement with what was happening; the generous man who offered to take a message to my family. All of the variations of which state terrorism is capable.

A military intelligence officer was in charge of the investigation, but the experts alternated. One session might be devoted to the Jewish conspiracy, and to my surprise, I would discover that the expert was fluent in Hebrew. Another might be devoted to international politics, and to my contacts abroad, especially with the United States government. There were specialists in finance, mass communications media, regional geopolitics of Latin America, Middle East politics. Almost all of them were of the same type: they had each accumulated a great mass of facts, dates, figures and names in their particular subject. The relationship they would establish between those facts and reality was one of total paranoia.

Every exercise in violence and repression requires its own semantics. Even petty thieves and the great gentlemen of the Cosa Nostra have created a language of their own. Perhaps the most perfect example is the way in which the Nazis referred to the most horrible crime in memory, describing the extermination of the Jewish people as "the final solution to the Jewish problem."

When I read today of a Soviet citizen denied work for being a dissident, arrested because he has no job, and accused of "hooliganism," it reminds me of Hermann Goering's statement during the first year of the Nazi regime, in 1933, when the Jews complained that police were protecting the mobs that vandalized their shops. Goering said: "I refuse to make the police the guardians of Jewish department stores." The Jews were not asking for the police to protect them, just to stop protecting their attackers. I am reminded too of the current President of Argentina, General Roberto Viola, who refers to the 20,000 men, women and children who have disappeared in the past four years after arrest by security forces as "forever absent," as though they had simply left without saying goodbye.

There could be several explanations for this peculiar use of language: the need to disguise violence in order to make it psychically more bearable for the murderers themselves; or the need to hide their crimes from others. But from my own experience, I believe it would be a mistake to suppose that these semantics are meant to disguise reality for psychological or political reasons. I believe they are the honest expression of reality as it is lived by the totalitarians of right or left, the terrorists of the opposition or the terrorists of the State, the religious fanatics of the Judeo-Christian tradition or the fundamentalists of the oriental faiths. At no time do they intend to lie....

Those who examined and tortured me believed, and still believe, seriously and honestly, in the Zionist-Marxist conspiracy, in the same way that the Soviet experts who questioned Anatoly Scharansky in Moscow believed, and still believe, in the Zionist-capitalist conspiracy. These two inquiries took place at the same time, April 1977, thousands of miles apart, and in the framework of two apparently very different regimes, the Soviet Union and Argentina.

At one of the interrogations to which I was submitted in a clandestine prison, a new specialist appeared. The look of an intellectual, the attitudes of an intellectual; a great reader.... But although there was no torture at that interrogation, there was an enormous sense of repressed violence. This new specialist's mission was to discover the significance, the objectives, of a small company I had founded a year earlier, which had been surprisingly successful: it was a publishing firm called Timerman Editores.... This company could not have been compared, in importance, to my newspaper, *La Opinion*. But it became clear—from the level of the interrogation, from the importance they gave to it, from its duration, and especially from the verbal violence and the accusations they framed—that they saw in that publishing company an even greater danger, an even greater threat than in the newspaper, to that society they were defending, that species of Argentine Thousand Year Reich that they wanted to build.

The questioner was convinced that the books could become, or that they already were, something more dangerous than a daily newspaper. And this fact, together with the image of that photograph placed on the wall by my mother, led me to a conclusion. A newspaper may be silenced, confiscated, pressured or won over with threats. If the journalists' articles are not published, their writing has no importance. Furthermore, if they are not going to be published, they won't get written in the first place. But books are written, whether or not they are published at the moment or in the place they are written. They have a secure destiny. A manifest destiny. A lasting existence.

I came to another conclusion as well. The man who interrogated me about books was more worried than those who questioned me about my newspaper, because my paper was already in their hands, directed by a general of the Argentine army. But the books I had published might be issued again someday, in Argentina or abroad. . . . The new President of Argentina, General Roberto Viola, once explained that although I was innocent, I could not be set free because the military government would be judged by the book I would surely write.

Looking back we can see that it was not the international press, nor the politicians, nor the diplomats, who first understood, defined and described the Nazi madness. It was the books. Books which one way or another found their way to publication.

And it was books that explained and defined—with more serenity, objectivity and intelligence than the press, the politicians, the diplomats—the paranoia of the Soviet leaders, from *Darkness at Noon* to *A Day in the Life of Ivan Denisovich*.

From the moment of the military coup in Argentina until the time of my arrest, twelve months passed. I devoted myself to trying to save lives, the few that could be rescued from a regime that felt itself omnipotent and exercised omnipotence with total impunity. There were writers whose lives we tried to save, but I didn't pay much attention to what was happening with books. The Argentine government never imposed preventive censorship, except during the first twenty-four hours after taking power. It practiced censorship in another way. On the press, it inflicted a kind of biological censorship. One hundred journalists have disappeared in five years of military government. In a field with so few professionals, this was a true form of genocide.

But now I remember, reconstructing the facts, the conversations, the period as well as possible, that even before the disappearance of the journalists, and before some of the newspapers began to have problems (mine was closed for several days for having published an article by a Jesuit priest criticizing state terrorism), even before all that, there were books that vanished. They were the first victims. They could no longer be found in the bookshops; the publishers didn't have them; they were removed from the public libraries; they were denounced in the Nazi Argentine press, the magazine *Cabildo*; or in the pro-Nazi press, the newspaper *La Nueva Provincia* and the magazine *Somos.*

So, in the Argentina of 1976–77, the books were the first victims. It was the same in Hitler's Germany and Stalin's Russia. Books are the first victims, the permanent victims, because they are the primary menace to totalitarian power. At the same time, the persistence and permanence of books makes them the most critical factor in the creation of forces that can and will struggle against irrationalism, paranoia, and state and private terrorism of both right and left.

When the KGB began its campaign of psychological destruction against the dissident writer Vladimir Voinovich, they took advantage of his absence to inform his mother that he had died—and this provoked the old woman's death. Voinovich wrote directly to Andropov, chief of the KGB: "It is time that you understood that the more you torment a writer, the longer his books will live; they will survive him and survive his persecutors."

His books will survive and they will be our ultimate hope. It is true that the suffocation of totalitarianism drove to suicide such beloved writers as Sergei Esenin, Vladimir Mayakovsky, and then Ernst Toller, Walter Benjamin, Stefan Zweig. And it is true as well that their books still live, and will continue to live, as Voinovich said. . . .

It is true that in the 1930s Nazism revealed greater imagination in the fields of repression and assassination than democracy did in comprehending the phenomenon of Nazism. It is true that the same thing happened in the thirties and forties with the crimes of Stalinism. And it is true that since World War II the criminal imagination of private and state terrorism has shown itself superior to the democratic imagination.

But now everything has changed. Although the totalitarians and the terrorists may have more imagination a new world movement has arisen, that of human rights. What began as a humanitarian, almost philanthropic activity has turned into a powerful ideology. What was believed to be an activity for sensitive spirits, which would cease without government support has turned into an avalanche of private action.

The Helsinki Accords, designed by governments to dissolve certain blockages in international politics, were immediately taken up by civil organizations, by brave and conscientious individuals, who made them into the first great instrument in the modification of the most hermetic totalitarian society of the twentieth century, Communist society. . . .

We should take heart from what has happened in the United States in recent weeks. The inauguration of President Reagan was greeted by the Argentine military with champagne toasts, and their wives adorned themselves with orchids for the numerous celebrations. In their euphoria over the election of a hard-line Republican, the Argentine military once again began kidnapping human rights activists. But there was such a strong reaction from the American press, the human rights organizations, individuals and legislators, that they were forced to retreat within a few hours—something that no government had been able to achieve. The underlying principle has been proven by Andrei Sakharov and his friends, and by countless others: the value of democratic ideology is infinitely more powerful in the hands of private organizations than in those of official diplomacy.

American publishers, indeed all artists, writers and thinkers, should be emblems of the role of the creative imagination in the continuing struggle for human rights. We have a singular power, one of the few that have survived so much violence: our relationship with the world of ideas. That is what totalitarianism and terrorism fear the most. We must be fully conscious of the trembling we can cause in some, and the respect we can inspire in others. It is true that those who are part of our world are the first victims. But they are also the last hope.

Source: Timerman, Jacobo. "First Victims, Last Hope." *Boston Review.* August 1981. Available online. http://bostonreview.net/BR06.4/timerman.html. Accessed December 20, 2007. Permission of Hector Timerman.

RONALD REAGAN
(1911–2004)
The "Evil Empire" Speech
Orlando, Florida, United States
March 8, 1983

There are two addresses often called the "Evil Empire" speech, but President Ronald Reagan gave that name only to his remarks at the National Association of Evangelicals convention in Florida in 1983. In an important earlier address in London to the British House of Commons on June 8, 1982, he referred to the "totalitarian evil" of communism, which he said would be left on the "ash heap of history." In this he was breaking with the previous U.S. policy of détente, or easing of relations, with the Soviet Union; his feeling was that Soviet aggression needed to be met head-on. Nine months later in Orlando, after addressing the usual conservative concerns over abortion and prayer in schools, he took the ideas of his London speech further, alluding to "aggressive impulses of an evil empire." "Peace through strength," he told his hearers, arguing that a nuclear weapons freeze would only benefit the Soviet Union.

Many critics, at home and abroad, found these hard-line speeches and his "Star Wars" address unnecessarily provocative to the Soviet Union during the dangerous years of the cold war (1947–91), when Reagan had also expanded the U.S. military and when the United States was developing new weapons. But others credit Reagan's forthright denunciations for hastening the demise of communism and the birth in 1985 of Soviet premier Mikhail Gorbachev's *perestroika* (meaning "restructuring") policy of economic and social reform. The Soviet Union finally broke up in 1991. Reagan had entered the presidency in 1981, after serving eight years as a Republican governor of California. He had earlier been a Hollywood movie actor and president of the Screen Actors Guild, and he was always comfortable in front of the camera or speaking publicly. He was regarded as a gifted orator, with impeccable timing and a talent for humor.

There are a great many God-fearing, dedicated, noble men and women in public life, present company included. And yes, we need your help to keep us ever mindful of the ideas and the principles that brought us into the public arena in the first place. The basis of those ideals and principles is a commitment to freedom and personal liberty that, itself, is grounded in the much deeper realization that freedom prospers only where the blessings of God are avidly sought and humbly accepted.

The American experiment in democracy rests on this insight. Its discovery was the great triumph of our Founding Fathers, voiced by William Penn when he said: "If we will not be governed by God, we must be governed by tyrants." Explaining the inalienable rights of men, Jefferson said, "The God who gave us life, gave us liberty at the same time." And it was George Washington who said that "of all the disposition and habits which lead to political prosperity, religion and morality are indispensable supporters."

And finally, that shrewdest of all observers of American democracy, Alexis de Tocqueville, put it eloquently after he had gone on a search for the secret of America's greatness and genius, and he said: "Not until I went into the churches of America and heard her pulpits aflame with righteousness did I understand the greatness and the genius of America. . . . America is good. And if America ever ceases to be good, America will cease to be great."

Well, I'm pleased to be here today with you who are keeping America great by keeping her good. Only through your work and prayers and those of millions of others cans we hope to survive this perilous century and keep alive this experiment in liberty, this last, best hope of man.

496

I want you to know that this administration is motivated by a political philosophy that sees the greatness of America in you, her people, and in your families, churches, neighborhoods, communities—the institutions that foster and nourish values like concern for others and respect for the rule of law under God. . . .

There is sin and evil in the world, and we're enjoined by Scripture and the Lord Jesus to oppose it with all our might. Our nation, too, has a legacy of evil with which it must deal. The glory of this land has been its capacity for transcending the moral evils of our past. For example, the long struggle of minority citizens for equal rights, once a source of disunity and civil war, is now a point of pride for all Americans. We must never go back. There is no room for racism, anti-Semitism, or other forms of ethnic and racial hatred in this country.

I know that you've been horrified, as have I, by the resurgence of some hate groups preaching bigotry and prejudice. Use the mighty voice of your pulpits and the powerful standing of your churches to denounce and isolate these hate groups in our midst. The commandment given us is clear and simple: "Thou shalt love thy neighbor as thyself."

But whatever sad episodes exist in our past, any objective observer must hold a positive view of American history, a history that has been the story of hopes fulfilled and dreams made into reality. Especially in this century, America has kept alight the torch of freedom, but not just for ourselves but for millions of others around the world.

And this brings me to my final point today. During my first press conference as president, in answer to a direct question, I pointed out that, as good Marxist-Leninists,

U.S. president Ronald Reagan delivers the "Evil Empire" speech to the National Association of Evangelicals, meeting in Orlando, Florida, on March 8, 1983. *(Photo courtesy Ronald Reagan)*

> I urge you to beware the temptation of pride—the temptation of blithely declaring yourselves above it all and label both sides equally at fault, to ignore the facts of history and the aggressive impulses of an evil empire, to simply call the arms race a giant misunderstanding and thereby remove yourself from the struggle between right and wrong and good and evil. —*Ronald Reagan*

the Soviet leaders have openly and publicly declared that the only morality they recognize is that which will further their cause, which is world revolution. I think I should point out I was only quoting Lenin, their guiding spirit, who said in 1920 that they repudiate all morality that proceeds from supernatural ideas—that's their name for religion—or ideas that are outside class conceptions. Morality is entirely subordinate to the interests of class war. And everything is moral that is necessary for the annihilation of the old, exploiting social order and for uniting the proletariat.

Well, I think the refusal of many influential people to accept this elementary fact of Soviet doctrine illustrates a historical reluctance to see totalitarian powers for what they are. We saw this phenomenon in the 1930s. We see it too often today.

This doesn't mean we should isolate ourselves and refuse to seek an understanding with them. I intend to do everything I can to persuade them of our peaceful intent, to remind them that it was the West that refused to use its nuclear monopoly in the forties and fifties for territorial gain and which now proposes a 50 percent cut in strategic ballistic missiles and the elimination of an entire class of land-based, intermediate-range nuclear missiles.

At the same time, however, they must be made to understand we will never compromise our principles and standards. We will never give away our freedom. We will never abandon our belief in God. And we will never stop searching for a genuine peace. But we can assure none of these things America stands for through the so-called nuclear freeze solutions proposed by some. . . .

Yes, let us pray for the salvation of all of those who live in that totalitarian darkness—pray they will discover the joy of knowing God. But until they do, let us be aware that while they preach the supremacy of the state, declare its omnipotence over individual man, and predict its eventual domination of all peoples on the earth, they are the focus of evil in the modern world. . . .

Because they sometimes speak in soothing tones of brotherhood and peace, because, like other dictators before them, they're always making "their final territorial demand," some would have us accept them as their word and accommodate ourselves to their aggressive impulses. But if history teaches anything, it teaches that simpleminded appeasement or wishful thinking about our adversaries is folly. It means the betrayal of our past, the squandering of our freedom.

So, I urge you to speak our against those who would place the United States in a position of military and moral inferiority. . . . In your discussions of the nuclear freeze proposals, I urge you to beware the temptation of pride—the temptation of blithely declaring yourselves above it all and label both sides equally at fault, to ignore the facts of history and the aggressive impulses of an evil empire, to simply call the arms race a giant misunderstanding and thereby remove yourself from the struggle between right and wrong and good and evil.

I ask you to resist the attempts of those who would have you withhold your support for our efforts, this administration's efforts, to keep America strong and free, while we negotiate real and verifiable reductions in the world's nuclear arsenals and one day, with God's help, their total elimination.

While America's military strength is important, let me add here that I've always maintained that the struggle now going on for the world will never be decided by bombs or rockets, by armies or military might. The real crisis we face today is a spiritual one; at root, it is a test of moral will and faith. . . .

I believe we shall rise to the challenge. I believe that communism is another sad, bizarre chapter in human history whose last pages even now are being written. I believe this because the source of our strength in the quest for human freedom is not material, but spiritual. And because it knows no limitation, it must terrify and ultimately triumph over those who would enslave their fellow man. For in the words of Isaiah: "He giveth power to the faint; and to them that have no might He increased strength. . . . But they that wait upon the Lord shall renew their strength; they shall mount up with wings as eagles; they shall run, and not be weary."

Yes, change your world. One of our Founding Fathers, Thomas Paine, said, "We have it within our power to begin the world over again." We can do it, doing together what no one church could do by itself.

Source: Reagan, Ronald. "Address to the National Association of Evangelicals." Ronald Reagan Presidential Library. Available online. http://www.reagan.utexas.edu/archives/speeches/ major.html. Accessed December 20, 2007.

Susan Hannah Rabin was 14 in May 1981, when she and sister Nessa with friends Susie and Becky Dennison, and Schumann siblings Maria, Max, and Solveig—all from Plainfield, Vermont—organized the Children's Campaign for Nuclear Disarmament. Talking about nuclear war terrified them; getting involved to prevent it seemed like a good idea. They participated in the national Nuclear Weapons Freeze Campaign's symbolic peace march from Washington, Vermont, to Moscow, Vermont. They also started a letter-writing campaign; children could send letters to be forwarded to President Ronald Reagan, and the Children's Campaign would first read them at the White House. They hoped they might get 2,000; they eventually got more than 7,000. That October they held the letter-reading outside the White House fence. More letters arrived. In June 1982, the group sent out another handwritten press release: "The Children's Campaign for Nuclear Disarmament will read aloud letters written to President Reagan from children around the country Saturday, June 19 beginning at 8:00 AM in front of the White House. Press conference at 1:30 PM." They took turns reading on the sidewalk outside the White House that summer day, but the president, who had taken a tough stance against communism and a hostile Soviet Union, and devoted millions of dollars to the armed forces in an unprecedented military buildup in peacetime, still declined to meet with them. (Three months earlier, Reagan had delivered his "Evil Empire" speech castigating the Soviet Union [SEE Reagan's speech, page 496].) Local chapters of the Children's Campaign opened across the United States and Europe. In June 1983, Rabin traveled to Siunto Bath, Finland, to read the group's address to the International Conference on Children and War, jointly sponsored by the Swiss-based International Peace Bureau, the Peace Union of Finland, and the Geneva International Peace Research Institute.

❧

The Children's Campaign for Nuclear Disarmament was formed in May 1981 by a group of friends. We are children who fear for our lives and the lives of all the children on earth. We decided to start the Children's Campaign because we felt scared and hopeless about the threat of nuclear war. At first we weren't sure about how to start a group, but we felt that we had to do something that would have some effect, instead of just talking about the issue among ourselves.

We wanted to involve as many kids as possible in an action that would allow them to express their fears of nuclear war and have their opinions heard.

At our first meeting we decided to undertake a children's letter-writing campaign. We asked kids all over the country to write letters to President Reagan opposing the nuclear arms race. The letters were sent to the Children's Campaign office, and on October 17, 1981 a group of thirty children took the letters to the White House. All day outside the White House fence we read each of the 2,832 letters aloud to people passing by. The letters were mostly short, simple, and very powerful.

Dear President Reagan,

My name is David Hayes. I am 10 years old. I think nuclear war is bad because many innocent people will die. The world could even be destroyed. I don't want to die. I don't want my family to die. I want to live and grow up.

Please stop nuclear bombs. Please work to bring nuclear disarmament to the world.

Sincerely,
David Hayes
Groveland, Massachusetts

Dear President Reagan,

Will you please stop making nuclear bombs?

Thank you.

Damian Trevor Age 7
Philadelphia, Pennsylvania

We had tried to make an appointment with President Reagan, but the White House refused to acknowledge us. There were newspaper, radio, and TV reporters at the letter-reading, so many people all over the country heard that we children are afraid for our future.

The Children's Campaign for Nuclear Disarmament has evolved into a chapter organization. There are more than 50 local groups in towns and cities in the U.S. and several in Europe. These chapters are run by kids in schools, churches, and neighborhoods. The groups have held peace walks, rallies, letter-writings to the governments and newspapers. They show films and makes speeches about the danger of nuclear bombs. Most of the groups are trying to educate kids about the nuclear threat and involve these kids in the growing movement to end the nuclear arms race. The work is sometimes frustrating, but working to help prevent the destruction of our future gives us hope.

All the work the Children's Campaign is involved with strengthens our feeling that the arms race must be stopped. Nuclear war is closer with each new bomb made, and the world will not be safe until production of nuclear weapons is stopped in both the U.S. and U.S.S.R. and all the bombs are taken apart. The Children's Campaign is trying to make people aware of the threat of nuclear war, and we are pleading for a safe future.

Source: Rabin, Susan Hannah. *The Children's Campaign for Nuclear Disarmament.* Children's Campaign for Nuclear Disarmament. Edited by Guido Grünewald. Helsinki, Finland: International Peace Bureau/Peace Union of Finland, 1985, pp. 33–35. Permission of Susan Hannah Rabin.

"The Value of Human Solidarity"

Oslo, Norway

December 11, 1983

Behind the communist Iron Curtain in 1970, an electrician and budding human rights activist named Lech Wałęsa participated in a strike (work stoppage) at the Lenin Shipyards in Gdańsk, Poland, a port city on the Baltic Sea with a long tradition of shipbuilding. Eighty strikers were killed by police; the government's violent repression recalled a similar event in 1956 in Poznań, when about 75 strikers demanding more pay and better working conditions were killed, among them Romek Strzalkowski, a 13-year-old boy. Wałęsa lost his job in 1976 for illegal political agitation and could not find work for some time afterward. He was arrested in 1979 for organizing an independent (noncommunist) trade union, a group of people with a common bond of employment—such as ship carpenters—joining to improve wages and working conditions. (Most Communist governments, such as Poland's, banned independent trade unions as being "antistate.") Back at the shipyard in 1980, Wałęsa led a new trade union, dubbed Solidarity, in a peaceful strike with thousands of fellow shipyard workers. His success at negotiating the Gdańsk Agreement with the government, the approving attention the Solidarity movement was getting in the world press, and the spread of strikes across Poland caused the new Soviet-backed prime minister Wojciech Jaruzelski (1981–90) to declare martial law on December 13, 1981, and suppress the popular union. Wałęsa spent a year in jail. He was awarded the Nobel Peace Prize for 1983. Unable to appear in person (he was afraid the government would prevent his return to Poland), his wife Danuta accepted the prize for him; a Solidarity adviser read his Nobel lecture to the audience. The Solidarity movement eventually grew to 10 million Poles. Poland's Communist government fell in 1989 after the Soviet Union dropped its support, and Wałęsa was elected president of Poland the next year.

I belong to a nation which over the past centuries has experienced many hardships and reverses. The world reacted with silence or with mere sympathy when Polish frontiers were crossed by invading armies.... My youth passed at the time of the country's reconstruction from the ruins and ashes of the [second world] war in which my nation never bowed to the enemy, paying the highest price in the struggle....

I was barely thirteen years old when, in June 1956, the desperate struggle of the workers of Poznan for bread and freedom was suppressed in blood. Thirteen also was the boy—Romek Strzalkowski—who was killed in the struggle. It was the "Solidarity" union which 25 years later demanded that tribute be paid to his memory. In December 1970, when workers' protest demonstrations engulfed the towns of the Baltic coast, I was a worker in the Gdansk Shipyard and one of the organizers of the strikes. The memory of my fellow workers who then lost their lives, the bitter memory of violence and despair has become for me a lesson never to be forgotten.

A few years later, in June 1976, the strike of the workers at Ursus and Radom was a new experience which not only strengthened my belief in the justness of the working people's demands and aspirations, but has also indicated the urgent need for their solidarity. This conviction brought me, in the summer of 1978, to the Free Trade Unions—formed by a group of courageous and dedicated people who came out in the defense of the workers' rights and dignity.

In July and August of 1980 a wave of strikes swept throughout Poland. The issue at stake was then something much bigger than only material conditions of existence. My road of life has, at the time of the struggle, brought me back to the shipyard in Gdansk.

The whole country has joined forces with the workers of Gdansk and Szczecin. The agreements of Gdansk, Szczecin and Jastrzebie were eventually signed and the Solidarity union has thus come into being.

The great Polish strikes, of which I have just spoken, were events of a special nature. Their character was determined on the one hand by the menacing circumstances in which they were held and, on the other, by their objectives. The Polish workers who participated in the strike actions, in fact represented the nation.

Fellow workers at the Lenin Shipyards cheer Solidarity labor leader Lech Wałęsa as he leaves work in Communist-controlled Gdańsk, Poland, on June 17, 1983. He would receive the Nobel Prize later that year. *(AP Photo/Langevin)*

When I recall my own path of life I cannot but speak of the violence, hatred and lies. A lesson drawn from such experiences, however, was that we can effectively oppose violence only if we ourselves do not resort to it.

In the brief history of those eventful years, the Gdansk Agreement stands out as a great charter of the rights of the working people which nothing can ever destroy. Lying at the root of the social agreements of 1980 are the courage, sense of responsibility, and the solidarity of the working people. Both sides have then recognized that an accord must be reached if bloodshed is to be prevented. The agreement then signed has been and shall remain the model and the only method to follow, the only one that gives a chance of finding a middle course between the use of force and a hopeless struggle.

Our firm conviction that ours is a just cause and that we must find a peaceful way to attain our goals gave us the strength and the awareness of the limits beyond which we must not go. What until then seemed impossible to achieve has become a fact of life. We have won the right to association in trade unions independent from the authorities, founded and shaped by the working people themselves.

Our union—the Solidarity—has grown into a powerful movement for social and moral liberation. The people, freed from the bondage of fear and apathy, called for reforms and improvements. We fought a difficult struggle for our existence. That was and still is a great opportunity for the whole country. I think that it marked also the road to be taken by the authorities, if they thought of a state governed in cooperation and participation of all citizens.

Solidarity, as a trade union movement, did not reach for power, nor did it turn against the established constitutional order. During the fifteen months of Solidarity's legal existence nobody was killed or wounded as a result of its activities. Our movement expanded by leaps and bounds. But we were compelled to conduct an uninterrupted struggle for our rights and freedom of activity while at the same time imposing upon ourselves the unavoidable self-limitations. The program of our movement stems from the fundamental moral laws and order. The sole and basic source of our strength is the solidarity of workers, peasants and the intelligentsia, the solidarity of the nation, the solidarity of people who seek to live in dignity, truth, and in harmony with their conscience.

Let the veil of silence fall presently over what happened afterwards. Silence, too, can speak out.

One thing, however, must be said here and now on this solemn occasion: the Polish people have not been subjugated nor have they chosen the road of violence and fratricidal bloodshed.

We shall not yield to violence. We shall not be deprived of union freedoms. We shall never agree with sending people to prison for their convictions. The gates of prisons must be thrown open and persons sentenced for defending union and civic rights must be set free. The announced trials of eleven leading members of our movement must never be held. All those already sentenced, or still awaiting trials for their union activities or their convictions, should return to their homes and be allowed to live and work in their country.

The defense of our rights and our dignity, as well as efforts never to let ourselves to be overcome by the feeling of hatred—this is the road we have chosen.

The Polish experience, which the Nobel Peace Prize has put into limelight, has been a difficult, a dramatic one. Yet, I believe that it looks to the future. The things that have taken place in human conscience and re-shaped human attitudes cannot be obliterated or destroyed. They exist and will remain.

We are the heirs of those national aspirations thanks to which our people could never be made into an inert mass with no will of their own. We want to live with the belief that law means law and justice means justice, that our toil has a meaning and is not wasted, that our culture grows and develops in freedom.

As a nation we have the right to decide our own affairs, to mould our own future. This does not pose any danger to anybody. Our nation is fully aware of the responsibility for its own fate in the complicated situation of the contemporary world.

Despite everything that has been going on in my country during the past two years, I am still convinced that we have no alternative but to come to an agreement, and that the difficult problems which Poland is now facing can be resolved only through a real dialogue between state authorities and the people. . . .

He who once became aware of the power of solidarity and who breathed the air of freedom will not be crushed. The dialogue is possible and we have the right to it. The wall raised by the course of events must not become an insurmountable obstacle. My most ardent desire is that my country will recapture its historic opportunity for a peaceful evolution and that Poland will prove to the world that even the most complex situations can be solved by a dialogue and not by force.

We are ready for the dialogue. We are also prepared, at any time, to put our reasons and demands to the judgment of the people. We have no doubts as to what verdict would be returned.

I think that all nations of the world have the right to life in dignity. I believe that, sooner or later, the rights of individuals, of families, and of entire communities will be respected in every corner of the world. Respect for civic and human rights in Poland and for our national identity is in the best interest of all Europe. For, in the interest of Europe is a peaceful Poland, and the Polish aspirations to freedom will never be stifled.

Source: Wałęsa, Lech. "Nobel Lecture." The Nobel Foundation. Available online. http://nobel prize.org/nobel_prizes/peace/laureates/1983/walesa-lecture.html. Accessed December 20, 2007. © The Nobel Foundation 1983.

"Your Freedom and Mine Cannot Be Separated"

Soweto, South Africa

February 10, 1985

Nelson Mandela spent most of his life struggling to free fellow black South Africans from the racist laws of apartheid, a system that relegated blacks to second-class citizenship. He opened a law office with colleague Oliver Tambo and, working with the African Nation Congress (ANC), led mass protests following Indian nationalist and social reformer Mohandas Gandhi's idea of satyagraha, that is, nonviolent struggle. Government repression made even nonviolent protest impossible; in 1960 the Sharpeville Massacre occurred when white police shot and killed 69 blacks peacefully protesting racist laws. The ANC turned to terrorism, and it was banned by the government as a subversive group. Mandela was tried for treason in 1964 as a member of the ANC's guerrilla wing (SEE his trial speech, page 466) and sentenced to life in prison. When his wife, Winnie, was also imprisoned for political protests, their children had to be sent away to boarding school. In 1985 he had been in prison for more than 20 years when P. W. Botha, president of South Africa (1984–89), offered Mandela release on the condition he renounce violence as a political weapon. Mandela refused; at a mass meeting in Jabulani Stadium in Soweto, his daughter Zinzi read to his followers his answer, brought from Cape Town's Pollsmoor Prison. Mandela refers in the speech to three past prime ministers, architects of the brutal "modern" apartheid. Extreme political violence followed, as the government put down antiapartheid resistance, and radical black nationalists wreaked havoc with bombings. In 1990 new South African president Frederik de Klerk released Mandela without conditions; in total he had endured 27 years in prison. Bans were lifted from groups such as the African National Congress, and the government began negotiations with the ANC to end apartheid. Three years later Mandela won the Nobel Peace Prize, and in 1994 he was elected president of South Africa.

Speech by Mandela's daughter Zinzi

On Friday my mother and our attorney saw my father at Pollsmoor Prison to obtain his answer to Botha's offer of conditional release. The prison authorities attempted to stop this statement being made but he would have none of this and made it clear that he would make the statement to you, the people. . . .

My father and his comrades at Pollsmoor Prison send their greetings to you, the freedom-loving people of this our tragic land, in the full confidence that you will carry on the struggle for freedom. He and his comrades at Pollsmoor Prison send their very warmest greetings to Bishop Desmond Tutu. Bishop Tutu has made it clear to the world that the Nobel Peace Prize belongs to you who are the people. We salute him.

My father and his comrades at Pollsmoor Prison are grateful to the United Democratic Front who without hesitation made this venue available to them so that they could speak to you today. My father and his comrades wish to make this statement to you, the people, first. They are clear that they are accountable to you and to you alone. And that you should hear their views directly and not through others.

My father speaks not only for himself and for his comrades at Pollsmoor Prison, but he hopes he also speaks for all those in jail for their opposition to apartheid, for all those who are banished, for all those who are in exile, for all those who suffer under apartheid, for all those who are opponents of apartheid and for all those who are oppressed and exploited.

Throughout our struggle there have been puppets who have claimed to speak for you. They have made this claim, both here and abroad. They are of no consequence. My father and his colleagues will not be like them. My father says:

Zinzi reads her father's address

I am a member of the African National Congress. I have always been a member of the African National Congress and I will remain a member of the African National Congress until the day I die. Oliver Tambo is much more than a brother to me. He is my greatest friend and comrade for nearly fifty years. If there is any one amongst you who cherishes my freedom, Oliver Tambo cherishes it more, and I know that he would give his life to see me free. There is no difference between his views and mine.

I am surprised at the conditions that the government wants to impose on me. I am not a violent man. My colleagues and I wrote in 1952 to Malan asking for a round table conference to find a solution to the problems of our country, but that was ignored. When Strijdom was in power, we made the same offer. Again it was ignored. When Verwoerd was in power we asked for a national convention for all the people in South Africa to decide on their future. This, too, was in vain.

It was only then, when all other forms of resistance were no longer open to us, that we turned to armed struggle. Let Botha show that he is different to Malan, Strijdom and Verwoerd. Let him renounce violence. Let him say that he will dismantle apartheid. Let him unban the people's organization, the African National Congress. Let him free all who have been imprisoned, banished or exiled for their opposition to apartheid. Let him guarantee free political activity so that people may decide who will govern them.

I cherish my own freedom dearly, but I care even more for your freedom. Too many have died since I went to prison. Too many have suffered for the love of freedom. I owe it to their widows, to their orphans, to their mothers and to their fathers who have grieved and wept for them. Not only I have suffered during these long, lonely, wasted years. I am not less life-loving than you are. But I cannot sell my birthright, nor am I prepared to sell the birthright of the people to be free. I am in prison as the representative of the people and of your organization, the African National Congress, which was banned.

RHETORICAL DEVICE

Antistrophe: Repeating a word or phrase at the end of the phrases or sentences that follow (sometimes also called epiphora). (*See the related* anaphora)

This is so fundamental a right, so natural a right, so obvious a right,
that it is clear that the Crown were aware of it when they brought me by force
and by stealth from Ireland to this country. —*Roger Casement*

I have fought against white domination,
and I have fought against black domination. —*Nelson Mandela*

For France is not alone! She is not alone! She is not alone! —*Charles de Gaulle*

Let our object be our country, our whole country,
and nothing but our country. —*Daniel Webster*

What freedom am I being offered while the organization of the people remains banned?

What freedom am I being offered when I may be arrested on a pass offence?

What freedom am I being offered to live my life as a family with my dear wife who remains in banishment in Brandfort?

What freedom am I being offered when I must ask for permission to live in an urban area?

What freedom am I being offered when I need a stamp in my pass to seek work?

What freedom am I being offered when my very South African citizenship is not respected?

Only free men can negotiate. Prisoners cannot enter into contracts. Herman Toivo ja Toivo, when freed, never gave any undertaking, nor was he called upon to do so. I cannot and will not give any undertaking at a time when I and you, the people, are not free.

Your freedom and mine cannot be separated. I will return.

Source: Mandela, Nelson. "I Am Not Prepared to Sell the Birthright of the People to Be Free." *The Struggle Is My Life.* New York: Pathfinder Press, 1990, p. 194. Permission of Nelson Mandela Foundation.

In 1983 World War II Nazi war criminal Klaus Barbie was discovered hiding in Bolivia and extradited to France. He was 70 years old and living under a false name to prevent Nazi hunters from finding him. The notorious "butcher of Lyon" had already been sentenced to death in absentia for war crimes committed in Nazi-occupied France. As head of the Gestapo (Nazi secret police) in Lyon from 1942 to the war's end, he was responsible for the death of Jean Moulin, famed French Resistance leader, and for the deportation of thousands of French Jews to death camps. Among those deportees were 44 children who had been hiding in a children's refuge in Izieu, a village near Lyon. In April 1944, they were sent with their seven adult caretakers to their deaths, mostly at Auschwitz-Birkenau, a death camp in the south of Poland. With his capture, France planned a trial for Barbie's "crimes against humanity." Elie Wiesel, the 1986 Nobel Peace Prize winner, testified at Barbie's trial on his own experience as a child at Auschwitz-Birkenau. Wiesel was 15 and living in the village of Sighet, then in Hungary, when his family and nearby communities of Jews, almost 33,000 people, were deported to Auschwitz. It was April 1944—the same month the children of Izieu arrived in Auschwitz—and it would be a year before he was liberated by the U.S. Army (after being marched by the retreating Nazis to Buchenwald concentration camp in central Germany). He had lost his grandparents, parents, and little sister to the crematoria. At the war's end he found himself in France, then New York, where he obtained U.S. citizenship. He published *Night,* the story of his Holocaust experience, in 1958, and has since lectured widely against violence and racism. Klaus Barbie received a sentence of life imprisonment, and he died in 1991.

Mr. President, gentlemen of the bench, gentlemen of the jury, I thank you for inviting me to appear before you today....

May I say immediately that I feel no hatred toward the accused? I have never met him; our paths never crossed. But I have met killers who, like him, along with him, chose to be enemies of my people and of humanity. I may have known one or another of his victims....

No, there is no hatred in me; there never was any. There is no question of hatred here—only justice. And memory. We are trying to do justice to our memory.

Here is one memory: the spring of 1944. A few days before the Jewish Pentecostal holiday—Shavuot. This was 43 years ago, almost to the day. I was 15 1/2 years old....

The Germans invaded Hungary on March 19, 1944. Starting then, events moved at a headlong pace that gave us no respite. A succession of anti-Semitic decrees and measures were passed: the prohibition of travel, confiscation of goods, wearing of yellow stars, ghettoes, transports.

We watched as our world was systematically narrowed. For the Jews, the country was limited to one town, the town to one neighborhood, the neighborhood to one street, the street to one room, the room to a sealed boxcar crossing the Polish countryside at night.

Like the Jewish children of Izieu, the Jewish adolescents from my town arrived at the Auschwitz station one afternoon. What is this? we wondered. I remember the silence in the car. As I remember the rest. The barbed wire fences stretching away to infinity. The yelling of the prisoners whose duty it was to "welcome" us, the gunshots fired by the SS, the barking of their dogs. And up above us all, above the planet itself, immense flames rising toward the sky as though to consume it....

509

On January 17, 1988, Nobel Peace Prize winners Elie Wiesel (right) and Lech Wałęsa (left) pray on a visit to Poland's Auschwitz-Birkenau Nazi death camp, where during World War II 1 million people were murdered, most of them Jews. *(AP Photo/Sokolowski)*

An order rang out: "Line up by family." That's good, I thought, we will stay together. Only for a few minutes, however: "Men to the right, women to the left." The blows rained down on all sides. I was not able to say goodbye to my mother. Nor to my grandmother. I could not kiss my little sister. With my two older sisters, she was moving away, borne by the crazed black tide.

This was a separation that cut my life in half. I rarely speak of it, almost never. I cannot recall my mother or my little sister. With my eyes, I still look for them, I will always look for them. And yet, I know. I know everything. No, not everything. One cannot know everything. I could imagine it, but I do not allow myself to. . . .

What I saw is enough for me. In a small woods somewhere in Birkenau I saw children being thrown into the flames alive by the SS. Sometimes I curse my ability to see. It should have left me without ever returning. I should have remained with those little charred bodies. Since that night, I have felt a profound, immense love for old people and children. Every old person recalls my grandfather, my grandmother, every child brings me closer to my little sister, the sister of the Jewish children of Izieu.

Night after night, I kept asking myself: What does this all mean? What is the sense of this murderous enterprise? It functioned perfectly. The killers killed, the victims died, the fire burned and an entire people thirsting for eternity turned to ash, annihilated by a nation which, until then, was considered to be the best educated, the most cultivated in the world.

If anyone claims to have found an answer, it can only be a false one. . . . One cannot understand Auschwitz either without God or with God. One cannot conceive of it in terms of man or of heaven. Why was there so much hatred in the enemy toward Jewish children and old people? Why this relentlessness against a people whose memory of suffering is the oldest in the world?. . .

It is for the dead, but also for the survivors, and even more for their children—and yours—that this trial is important: It will weigh on the future. In the name of justice? In the name of memory. Justice without memory is an incomplete justice, false and unjust. To forget would be an absolute injustice in the same way that Auschwitz was the absolute crime. To forget would be the enemy's final triumph. . . . "Even if you survive, even if you tell, no one will believe you," an SS told a young Jew somewhere in Galicia.

This trial has already contradicted that killer. The witnesses have spoken; their truth has entered the awareness of humanity. Thanks to them, the Jewish children of Izieu will never be forgotten.

Source: Wiesel, Elie. "Wiesel Testimony." *Historic Documents of 1987.* Washington, D.C.: Congressional Quarterly Inc., p. 518. Permission of Elie Wiesel.

RONALD REAGAN
(1911–2004)
"Mr. Gorbachev, Tear Down This Wall!"
West Berlin, Germany
June 12, 1987

In 1987, the cold war (1947–91) still in force, President Ronald Reagan stood on a platform in West Berlin with the Berlin Wall and the Brandenburg Gate behind him. Almost 25 years earlier, President John F. Kennedy had come to Germany to speak at the Berlin Wall, marking the second anniversary of its building in 1961. "Ich bin ein Berliner" (I am a Berliner), Kennedy had declared in support of the beleaguered West Berliners, as the million-deep crowd went wild with excitement (*SEE* Kennedy's speech, page 464). The wall separating East and West Berlin had been erected by the Soviets to keep the East German people from fleeing to the West from their Communist-controlled country. The Soviet authorities claimed it was for protection against fascists (defeated Nazi Germany had been a fascist government). But as the barbed wire and other defenses were on the inside, and East Germans attempting to climb it were shot by snipers, it was clear that the intent was to keep people in. And as the wall passed in front of the Brandenburg Gate (a ceremonial arrangement of columns and pediment that straddled a boulevard into the city), the gate was rendered impassible. In 1983 Reagan delivered his provocative "Evil Empire" speech in Orlando, Florida, referring to the "aggressive impulses of an evil empire" (*SEE* page 496), and in a hard-line speech to the British parliament he had described communism as "totalitarian evil." Believing that soft-pedaling U.S. differences with the USSR only emboldened the Soviets, Reagan visited Berlin to offer a new challenge. Reagan's catchy call ("Mr. Gorbachev, open this gate! Mr. Gorbachev, tear down this wall!") was meant to be heard by Soviet leader Mikhail Gorbachev, who had been in power since 1985. Gorbachev, facing economic collapse at home, allowed the wall to be dismantled in 1989. The Soviet Union dissolved in 1991. In his speech, Reagan refers to the U.S. Marshall Plan, which sent extensive post-war reconstruction aid to Europe.

❧◦❧

Twenty four years ago, President John F. Kennedy visited Berlin, speaking to the people of this city and the world at the city hall. Well, since then two other presidents have come, each in his turn, to Berlin. And today I, myself, make my second visit to your city. We come to Berlin, we American Presidents, because it's our duty to speak, in this place, of freedom. . . .

Our gathering today is being broadcast throughout Western Europe and North America. I understand that it is being seen and heard as well in the East. To those listening throughout Eastern Europe, I extend my warmest greetings and the good will of the American people. To those listening in East Berlin, a special word: Although I cannot be with you, I address my remarks to you just as surely as to those standing here before me. For I join you, as I join your fellow countrymen in the West, in this firm, this unalterable belief: *Es gibt nur ein Berlin.* [There is only one Berlin.]

Behind me stands a wall that encircles the free sectors of this city, part of a vast system of barriers that divides the entire continent of Europe. From the Baltic, south, those barriers cut across Germany in a gash of barbed wire, concrete, dog runs, and guard towers. Farther south, there may be no visible, no obvious wall. But there remain armed guards and checkpoints all the same—still a restriction on the right to travel, still an instrument to impose upon ordinary men and women the will of a totalitarian state. Yet it is here in Berlin where the wall emerges most clearly; here, cutting across your city, where the news photo and the television screen have imprinted this brutal division of a continent upon the mind of the world. Standing before the Brandenburg

511

>
>
> Mr. Gorbachev, open this gate! Mr. Gorbachev, tear down this wall! —*Ronald Reagan*

Gate, every man is a German, separated from his fellow men. Every man is a Berliner, forced to look upon a scar.

President von Weizsacker has said: "The German question is open as long as the Brandenburg Gate is closed." Today I say: As long as this gate is closed, as long as this scar of a wall is permitted to stand, it is not the German question alone that remains open, but the question of freedom for all mankind. Yet I do not come here to lament. For I find in Berlin a message of hope, even in the shadow of this wall, a message of triumph.

In this season of spring in 1945, the people of Berlin emerged from their air raid shelters to find devastation. Thousands of miles away, the people of the United States reached out to help. And in 1947 Secretary of State—as you've been told—George Marshall announced the creation of what would become known as the Marshall plan. Speaking precisely forty years ago this month, he said: "Our policy is directed not against any country or doctrine, but against hunger, poverty, desperation, and chaos.". . .

In the 1950s, Khrushchev predicted: "We will bury you." But in the West today, we see a free world that has achieved a level of prosperity and wellbeing unprecedented in all human history. In the Communist world, we see failure, technological backwardness, declining standards of health, even want of the most basic kind—too little food. Even today, the Soviet Union still cannot feed itself. After these four decades, then, there stands before the entire world one great and inescapable conclusion: Freedom leads to prosperity. Freedom replaces the ancient hatreds among the nations with comity and peace. Freedom is the victor.

And now the Soviets themselves may, in a limited way, be coming to understand the importance of freedom. We hear much from Moscow about a new policy of reform and openness. Some political prisoners have been released. Certain foreign news broadcasts are no longer being jammed. Some economic enterprises have been permitted to operate with greater freedom from state control. Are these the beginnings of profound changes in the Soviet state? Or are they token gestures, intended to raise false hopes in the West, or to strengthen the Soviet system without changing it? We welcome change and openness; for we believe that freedom and security go together, that the advance of human liberty can only strengthen the cause of world peace.

There is one sign the Soviets can make that would be unmistakable, that would advance dramatically the cause of freedom and peace. General Secretary Gorbachev, if you seek peace, if you seek prosperity for the Soviet Union and Eastern Europe, if you seek liberalization: Come here to this gate! Mr. Gorbachev, open this gate! Mr. Gorbachev, tear down this wall!

I understand the fear of war and the pain of division that afflict this continent—and I pledge to you my country's efforts to help overcome these burdens. To be sure, we in the West must resist Soviet expansion. So we must maintain defenses of unassailable strength. Yet we seek peace; so we must strive to reduce arms on both sides.

Beginning ten years ago, the Soviets challenged the Western alliance with a grave new threat, hundreds of new and more deadly SS-20 nuclear missiles, capable of striking every capital in Europe. The Western alliance responded by committing itself to a counter-deployment unless the Soviets agreed to negotiate a better solution; namely, the elimination of such weapons on both sides. For many months, the Soviets refused to bargain in earnestness. As the alliance, in turn, prepared to go forward with its counter-deployment, there were difficult days—days of protests like those during my 1982 visit to this city—and the Soviets later walked away from the table.

But through it all, the alliance held firm. And I invite those who protested then—I invite those who protest today—to mark this fact: Because we remained strong, the

Soviets came back to the table. And because we remained strong, today we have within reach the possibility, not merely of limiting the growth of arms, but of eliminating, for the first time, an entire class of nuclear weapons from the face of the Earth. As I speak, NATO ministers are meeting in Iceland to review the progress of our proposals for eliminating these weapons. At the talks in Geneva, we have also proposed deep cuts in strategic offensive weapons. And the Western allies have likewise made far-reaching proposals to reduce the danger of conventional war and to place a total ban on chemical weapons.

While we pursue these arms reductions, I pledge to you that we will maintain the capacity to deter Soviet aggression at any level at which it might occur. And in cooperation with many of our allies, the United States is pursuing the Strategic Defense Initiative—research to base deterrence not on the threat of offensive retaliation, but on defenses that truly defend; on systems, in short, that will not target populations, but shield them. By these means we seek to increase the safety of Europe and all the world. But we must remember a crucial fact: East and West do not mistrust each other because we are armed; we are armed because we mistrust each other. And our differences are not about weapons but about liberty. When President Kennedy spoke at the City Hall those 24 years ago, freedom was encircled, Berlin was under siege. And today, despite all the pressures upon this city, Berlin stands secure in its liberty. And freedom itself is transforming the globe. . . .

In Europe, only one nation and those it controls refuse to join the community of freedom. Yet in this age of redoubled economic growth, of information and innovation, the Soviet Union faces a choice: It must make fundamental changes, or it will become obsolete. Today thus represents a moment of hope. We in the West stand ready to cooperate with the East to promote true openness, to break down barriers that separate people, to create a safer, freer world.

And surely there is no better place than Berlin, the meeting place of East and West, to make a start. . . .

As I looked out a moment ago from the Reichstag, that embodiment of German unity, I noticed words crudely spray-painted upon the wall, perhaps by a young Berliner: "This wall will fall. Beliefs become reality." Yes, across Europe, this wall will fall. For it cannot withstand faith; it cannot withstand truth. The wall cannot withstand freedom.

Source: Reagan, Ronald. "Address at the Brandenburg Gate." Ronald Reagan Presidential Library. Available online. http://www.reagan.utexas.edu/archives/speeches/major.html. Accessed December 20, 2007.

SALAH KHALAF
(1933–1991)
"No Peace without the Palestinians"
Jerusalem, Israel
February 22, 1989

Prompted in part by European anti-Semitism, the Zionist movement formed in the late 1800s with the aim of creating a Jewish homeland in Palestine. Britain gained control of Palestine from Turkey in World War I (1914–18), and with the approval of the League of Nations and the United Nations, Britain agreed to the establishment of a homeland for the Jews. Continuing Jewish immigration into Palestine angered Arabs, who demanded an Arab Palestinian state. The day Israel came into being, May 14, 1948, Arab League states launched an attack. Israel handily won that war, the 1948 Arab-Israeli War. The war and Israeli forces displaced about three-quarters of a million Palestinians, who fled to Arab countries, and a similar number of Jews from Arab nations who resettled in Israel and elsewhere. The Palestinians remained refugees, however, as Arab nations withheld citizenship. Further wars with Israel followed in 1956, 1967, and 1973. In 1964 the Palestine Liberation Organization (PLO) was formed to represent the Palestinian people; it called for Israel's violent destruction and the right of Palestinian refugees to return. Salah Khalaf (known also as Abu Iyad), a Palestinian from Jaffa, was a founder of the PLO; he was chief deputy to chairman Yasir Arafat and a member of the murderous Black September terrorist wing. Over time, angering many Palestinians and radical Arabs, the hard-line PLO leadership became more moderate. After the 1987 intifada (Palestinian uprising in Israeli-occupied territories) in the Gaza Strip and West Bank, leaving 1,000 people dead, Arafat and Khalaf (through the Algiers Resolution) claimed to disavow terrorism and accept Israel's existence. In 1989 Khalaf videotaped an overture to peace that was smuggled into Israel and shown at the International Center for Peace in the Middle East. He spoke in Arabic to disprove Israeli accusations that he spoke in conciliatory terms in English to Israelis but used militant words in Arabic to Arabs. Palestinian extremists assassinated him in 1991.

I look forward to a future in which our meetings will be face to face, and we can discuss directly the future of our two peoples as well as the future of real peace. Although circumstances have prevented this on this occasion, I hope that in the near future we will address each other neither via the newspapers nor through video but through such personal contacts.

When I say these words, I say them on the basis of a fixed strategy according to which we now work after painful experience, and so that we may not deceive you. In the past we believed that this land is ours alone. We did not believe in the idea of coexistence between two states, although we used to believe in the idea of coexistence as religions, or rather as people belonging to different religions. This kind of co-existence between Muslims, Christians, and Jews has been practiced by our people in this land. However, the idea of coexistence between two states was, in the past, remote.

Everything that has happened to the Palestinian people and to the Israeli people—the blood which has been spilled, the victims, the maimed—all this has moved us to react naturally to the call of every Palestinian and Israeli child, so that we can take a serious step toward peace. Thus came the resolutions adopted in Algiers. These resolutions were not passed just by a leadership. They proceeded from a legislative council which represents the Palestinian people in its entirety. The council passed these resolutions after an arduous process of dialogue and discussion, and everybody was convinced that there is no path but the path of peace.

What is important is that our Palestinian people and the Israeli people feel that the Palestinian leadership has responded to the widely supported call by our people for peace.

Some people asked us whether the Israeli leadership would respond to our call for peace and to our resolutions. We replied that this is not what is most important. What is important is that our Palestinian people and the Israeli people feel that the Palestinian leadership has responded to the widely supported call by our people for peace. What is important is that this call touch the heart and mind of every Israeli child, woman, and man, because it is inevitable that peace will prevail, and that the two-state solution will be achieved.

So why the agony and the procrastination? The disagreement really is over the price. Are we prepared to pay the price of proceeding with courage and strength, inspired by the agony and suffering of our people? Or, would we rather drag our feet until there are more killed, more children who are subjected to terror, and until there are more disfigured and crippled victims, in this useless war?

It is on this basis that I address you, and say to you that the Algiers resolutions, and Arafat's statements at the press conference in Geneva, reflect the heartfelt convictions of every Palestinian. We would remind you, however, that just as you have some extremists, we also have many such people. The test of courage is when such extremism is countered head on, rather than surrendered to.

Does any Israeli really believe in his heart that it is possible to destroy five million Palestinians? We have asked a similar question of ourselves and have concluded that we cannot destroy the Israeli people. The realistic solution, therefore, is that we live side by side, and that we walk the path of peace.

Some people wonder whether this coexistence is only a first stage. We answer, no. We want a definitive settlement. But a definitive settlement will only come if its peace is just. Peace is not a piece of paper. All questions connected with peace and security have to be discussed in negotiations. The important thing is that the two peoples, the Palestinians and the Israelis, come to believe in the necessity of coexistence between two states. We are ready to reach any security arrangements through meetings but, believe me, real security lies only in the real belief in peace.

The real issue is not negotiations in which Israel seeks this piece of land or in which we seek that piece of land. This is a small geographic area, without much elbowroom. We do not seek to have a Berlin Wall or any other wall separating us. We want there to be openness. The only thing we seek is that there be real—as opposed to verbal—normalization. I am confident that peace has now come to settle in the heart and conscience of every Palestinian. I am confident that if we search deeply in the hearts and minds of Israelis, we shall find peace there, too.

However, it is important to take stock at some point and to admit that the ill-feelings that have accumulated in the past cannot be destroyed over night. We must live with the idea of peace ourselves first if we are to transmit it to others. Without accepting it ourselves, and living with it, we cannot transmit these ideas and beliefs to others.

I say truly that the Palestinian leadership and the Palestinian people want peace. The steps taken in Algiers and in Geneva reflect this conviction of the need for peace. So that peace may be achieved, however, it is necessary that the Israeli leadership change its mentality of rejectionism, obduracy, the constant addition of further conditions, and seeking to win time.

I do not know why time should be won. Is it so that yet more conditions may be imposed on the Palestinians? This is absurd and will lead to nothing.

It is important that we capitalize on this historic opportunity. Each time our people hear of martyrs and of more wounded, the chances for peace will inevitably be pushed further away. This now is the opportunity that we must take. Let us be courageous and grasp it firmly. Let us put all the issues on the table. We believe in direct meetings; we are ready for such meetings, and we say it publicly, on any level. Let the Israelis come and meet us secretly, openly, or any other way.

We are anxious for such meetings, not because we are in despair. Quite the contrary, it is because we are strong, because we have confidence in ourselves and in the need for peace, because we seek this peace and have every faith in it, that we have arrived at a truth that we hope the Israeli leaders will also arrive at before it is too late. This is the truth which says that two peoples and two states must coexist on this land.

All other matters are open to discussion. Our covenant and yours can be discussed. All security arrangements and guarantees can be discussed in direct meetings. Then, if we reach an agreement, as I am sure we shall, we can take this agreement to an international conference where the entire world can be a witness to these security arrangements, and so that not a single loophole will be left to spoil it.

Thus, we do not see the international conference as an end in itself, but as a means to guarantee the safety of the two states in the context of an international agreement. And what is important for us is that these meetings and contacts and dialogues take place in advance of the conference, so that the conference itself becomes the forum in which to bring our agreement to fruition. Those who stand in the way of peace want the river of blood to continue to flow. Instead of seeking to achieve peace in order to avoid more victims, they seek more victims in order to achieve peace. I don't know what kind of peace it would be which is built on a mountain of corpses and skulls, and crippled, wounded, and killed. It would be a peace that is useless.

There are many peace movements, large and small, in Israel. To those I say, in the name of the Palestinian people, the PLO, and the Palestinian leadership: to every child in Israel, to every woman and every man, through you, that we are genuine in our desire for a strategic peace. A peace through which we shall bring security and stability to this region. A peace in which people can begin to devote their time and energy to making their lives prosperous and genuinely peaceful.

Why do the Palestinians and Israelis have to live in fear? How can we put an end to this fear, this state of mutual terror in which both Israelis and Palestinians live? There is no way out except through peace with the Palestinian people, whose suffering is the root of the problem.

Perhaps I need not mention the peace agreement with Egypt or any other attempts at agreements with others. Perhaps all these agreements were good from the Israeli leadership's point of view. But you should ask yourselves, why do these agreements not produce real peace? The answer is that the basic element required for such a peace was missing, namely, the Palestinian people.

As I said earlier, everything can be discussed with complete reassurance. We say this because, as I also said earlier, we are confident that our call for peace is a strategic call, and not just a call for useless talks. But we must note that a real peace is a just peace. When peace is just, it can be lasting. And a just peace, now that we live in an age of rockets and long-distance artillery, cannot be tied to technicalities and armaments. Rather, the condition for real peace is that there be a genuine desire to coexist. We must work on our people to develop this desire, and you must equally work on yours. This is the road to real security and real peace.

The final question I wish to raise at this symposium in this context is, if this historic opportunity following the Algiers resolutions is missed, then what will the alternative be? Israel may be able to survive this situation for one more year, or two, or even ten. But believe me, after these ten years, and after hundreds and maybe thousands of other victims, we shall find ourselves back at this point: There can be no peace without the Palestinians. There can be no peace without coexistence with the Palestinians. There can be no peace without two states which will coexist side by side, and which will be able to say to the entire world: The war in the Middle East has ended, and the tragedy is over.

Source: Khalaf, Salah. "Address by Salah Khalaf to the International Center for Peace in the Middle East." In *The Israeli-Palestinian Conflict: A Documentary Record,* edited by Yehuda Lukacs, p. 438. Cambridge: Cambridge University Press, 1992. Translated by the Foundation for Middle East Peace. Reprinted by permission.

VIKTOR ORBÁN
(1963–)
On the Reburial of Imre Nagy
Budapest, Hungary
June 16, 1989

Imre Nagy was a former Hungarian premier (1953–55) who led the 1956 revolution against Hungary's Communist government. During World War I (1914–18), Nagy had served in the Austro-Hungarian army, and afterward he joined the Communist Party. An agriculture expert, he became minister of agriculture in Hungary's post–World War II (1939–45) Communist government. He was promoted to prime minister in 1953. While in office he developed his reformist "New Course" policy, cutting back on the Soviet-influenced reliance on heavy industry, collectivization of farming, and use of police state bullying methods. This was not acceptable to Soviet leaders, and in 1955 he lost his positions both in government and in the Communist Party. The next year on October 23, the Hungarian Revolution erupted when university students in Budapest, encouraged by an uprising in Communist-controlled Poland a few months earlier, revolted against the Soviet-backed Hungarian government. As the revolution mushroomed, the government fell and Nagy was reinstated. His movement pledged international political neutrality and moved to disassociate itself from the USSR. Within days, Soviet troops and tanks swarmed in to crush the revolution, and 2,500 Hungarian people lost their lives. The Soviet-backed new government executed Nagy in 1958 and buried him in an unmarked grave in Budapest. In 1989 the Hungarian government, in recognition of the patriotic nature of the uprising, "rehabilitated" Nagy and reburied him and four others with full honors. A sixth coffin represented young and unknown victims of the crushed rebellion. With Soviet troops still in Hungary, Victor Orbán was the courageous 26-year-old student spokesman for Fidesz, the Federation of Young Democrats, who spoke at the ceremony in Budapest's Heroes' Square. Orbán became a member of the Hungarian parliament in 1990, served as president of Fidesz, and was prime minister from 1998 to 2002.

Citizens!

In the forty years since the beginning of the communist dictatorship and the Soviet occupation, Hungary has only once had the chance, only once had the strength and the courage, to attain her ambitions of 1848: national independence and political liberty. Our aims haven't changed; we will not renounce any of the goals of 1848, as we cannot renounce 1956, either.

The young Hungarians now struggling for democracy bow their heads before the communist Imre Nagy and his companions for two reasons.

We appreciate that these statesmen identified themselves with the wishes of the Hungarian nation, that they broke with the sacred tenets of communism—that is, with blind obedience to the Russian empire and with the dictatorship of a single party.

In 1956, the Hungarian Socialist Workers' Party (MSZMP) seized our future. Thus, there in the sixth coffin, alongside the massacred youth, lay our prospects for years to come.

Friends! We young people fail to understand many things that are obvious to the older generations. We are puzzled that those who were so eager to slander the Revolution and Imre Nagy have suddenly become the greatest supporters of the former prime minister's policies. Nor do we understand why the party leaders who saw to it that we were taught from books that falsified the Revolution are now rushing to touch the coffins as if they were good-luck charms.

We need not be grateful for their permission to bury our martyrs after thirty-one years; nor do we have to thank them for allowing our political organizations to function. Hungary's leaders are not to be praised because they have refrained from using weapons against those striving for democracy and free elections, because they have not adopted, as well they could, the methods of Li Peing, Pol Pot, Jaruzelski, and Rákosi.

Citizens! Thirty-three years after the Hungarian Revolution was crushed and thirty-one years after the execution of the last legitimate prime minister, we may now have a chance to achieve peacefully the goals that the revolutionaries briefly attained through bloody combat.

If we trust our souls and our strength, we can put an end to the communist dictatorship; if we are determined enough, we can force the party to submit to free elections; and if we do not lose sight of the ideals of 1956, then we will be able to elect a government that will immediately begin negotiations on the swift withdrawal of the Russian troops. We can fulfill the will of the Revolution if—and only if—we are brave enough.

We cannot trust the party-state to change of its own accord. Remember: on October 6, 1956, on the very day Lászlo Rajk was reburied, the party's daily declared in bold letters: "Never Again!" Three weeks later, the communist party ordered its security forces to shoot and kill defenseless people. Before two years had passed, the MSZMP had hundreds of innocent people, even party members, sentenced to death on trumped-up charges.

We will never accept the empty promises of communist leaders; our goal is to prevent the ruling party from ever using force against us again. This is the only way to avoid new coffins—new burials like today's.

Imre Nagy, Miklós Gimes, Géza Losonczy, Pál Maléter, and József Szilágyi gave their lives for Hungarian independence and liberty. These values are still cherished by Hungary's youth: we bow to your memory.

Requiseat in pacem!

Source: Orbán, Viktor. "The Reburial of Imre Nagy." In *The Democracy Reader*, edited by Diane Ravitch and Abigail Thernstrom, p. 249. New York: HarperCollins, 1992. Reprinted by permission of the Institute for Democracy in Eastern Europe, Washington, D.C.

FANG LIZHI
(1936–   )
"The Terror That Has Filled Beijing"
Beijing, China
November 15, 1989

As a university vice president and professor, leading astrophysicist Fang Lizhi encouraged students to question the lack of democracy, human rights, and academic freedom in Communist China. Fearless in resisting warnings he should curb his public comments, Fang was arrested several times and had his right to travel abroad curtailed. He was denounced and then dismissed from the university, and the Chinese Communist Party stripped him of membership. He became known as "China's Andrei Sakharov" after the famous dissident (also a physicist) who campaigned for human rights within the Soviet Union. When the Chinese government massacred hundreds of pro-democracy demonstrators, mostly students, in the April to June 1989 uprising in Beijing's Tiananmen Square, Fang and his wife received asylum in the U.S. embassy. Encouraged by the ongoing liberalization in Mikhail Gorbachev's Soviet Union (1985–91) and by their memories of the "Beijing Spring"

of 1978–79, as many as 100,000 students had gathered in Tiananmen Square to protest the Communist Party's demotion of Hu Yaobang, a popular reformer who had just died. As days passed, the students began demonstrating for political reform and free speech and against corruption, and they were joined by city workers. Students went on strike within universities across China, and a hunger strike began in Tiananmen Square. After six weeks, the government declared martial law; soon after, tanks and troops armed with bayonets entered the square and began firing. Estimates of the number killed average about 5,000 people, although the government claimed no students died. Fang remained a full year in the U.S. embassy; while there he received the Robert F. Kennedy Human Rights Award, and he sent a speech to be read for him at the award ceremony in Washington, D.C. A year later he was allowed to leave for the United States, where he now teaches physics and astronomy.

I am moved because you have chosen to honor me with the 1989 Robert F. Kennedy Human Rights Award, for it attests to the fact that I have not been, and am not now alone. But I am filled with sorrow, to see that in this land of my birth, human dignity has once again been trampled upon. What is more, having had my own basic human rights stripped away, I am now more acutely aware than ever how far we are from accomplishing what we must in the cause of advancing respect for all human beings.

The values underlying human dignity are common to all people. They are comprised of universally applicable standards of human rights that hold no regard for race, language, religion or other beliefs. Symbolized by the United Nations Declaration of Human Rights, these universal standards have increasingly earned the acceptance and respect of the world at large. When a commemorative gathering was held last November in Beijing to honor the fortieth anniversary of the Declaration, many of us were delighted, because it seemed to us at the time that the principles of human rights were finally starting to take root in our ancient land.

However, time after time such fond dreams have been shattered by a harsh reality. In the face of the bloody tragedy of last June, we now must admit to having been far too optimistic. Some of those who were responsible for this repression have recently attempted to defend their behavior by declaring that "China has its own standard of human rights," and have completely rejected the world's censure by refusing to acknowledge the universal nature of human rights. They appear to think that by simply labelling something a "household affair" to be dealt with internally, they can ignore the laws of human decency and do as they please. . . .

Nowadays, a growing number of Chinese believe that for China to catch up with the modern world, we must change our own society by absorbing those aspects of more modern civilizations, especially science and democracy, that have proven both progressive and universal. From the Movement for Science and Democracy of 1919 to the rising tide of demand for intellectual freedom in 1957, and from the protest marches of 1926 that were confronted with swords and guns to the demonstrations of 1989 that were confronted by tanks, we can see how passionately the Chinese people have wanted a just, rational and prosperous society. Although China has some very deep-seated problems that have caused it to lag behind developed countries, our history shows that Chinese have long sought the same kind of progress and development as people everywhere regardless of their race or nationality, that when it comes to such common aspirations, Chinese are no different from any other people. Like all other members of the human race, Chinese are born with a body and a brain, and with passions and a soul, and they ought to be able to enjoy the same inalienable rights, dignity, and liberty as other human beings.

Allow me to draw an historical analogy: Recent propaganda to the effect that "China has its own standard of human rights" bears an uncanny resemblance to pronouncements made by our 18th century rulers when they declared that "China has its own astronomy." The feudal aristocracy of 200 years ago opposed the notion of an astronomy based on science, and refused to acknowledge the universal applicability of modern astronomy, even that it might be of some use in formulating the Chinese calendar. The reason they opposed modern astronomy was that its laws, which pertain everywhere, made it apparent that the "divine right of rule" claimed by these people was a fiction. By the same token, the principles of human rights, which are also universal, make it clear that the "right to rule" claimed by their successors today is just as baseless. This is why in every era rulers buoyed up by special privilege have opposed the idea of equality that is inherent in such universal ideas.

The advance of civilization has largely followed from the discovery and development of just such universally applicable concepts and laws. Those who rejected the idea that science had universal application were, in fact, doing nothing more than demonstrating their fear of modern culture. The feudal aristocrats of two centuries past saw astronomy as a bearer of this modern culture, and as a result, ruthlessly persecuted those who engaged in its study and practice. Indeed, in one instance of such oppression during the early Qing Dynasty, five astronomers from the Beijing Observatory were even put to death. But far from demonstrating might, such brutality only demonstrated fear. Equally terrified by the implications of universal human rights, modern-day dictators may also resort to murder. But no more than in the case of their predecessors should we construe their actions as an indication of strength.

Some people say that the terror that has filled Beijing since June can not but help make one pessimistic. And, I must admit to such feelings myself. But, I would also like to offer up a small bit of encouragement. Remember, that in this current climate of terror, it may well be those who have just killed their fellow human beings who are most terrified. *We* must be forced to live in terror today, but *we* have no fear of tomorrow, whereas the murderers are not only fearful of the present, but are even more fearful of the future. Thus, we actually have no reason to lose faith. Ignorance may dominate in the short run through the use of violence, but just as surely as the earth turns it will eventually be unable to resist the advance of universal laws.

Of course, it takes time for the earth to turn, and for China things may take even longer to right themselves. With this in mind, I would like to say a few things to the young Chinese in the audience. I know that many of you have dedicated your lives to building our country anew. Since the road to rebirth will be a long one, I fervently hope that you will not break off your education, but, instead, will work harder than ever to deepen and enrich your knowledge. We are all disciples of non-violence. And, what power can non-violence summon up by way of resistance against the armed violence of the world? Although there are many forms of non-violence, perhaps most basic is the force of knowledge. Without knowledge, non-violence can degenerate into pleading for mercy, and history is unmoved by such pleading. To paraphrase Albert Einstein, it is only when we stand on the shoulders of the giant, which is knowledge, that we are truly able to change the course of history. . . .

In my field of modern cosmology, the first principle is called the "Cosmological Principle." It says that the universe has no center, that it has the same properties throughout. Every place in the universe has, in this sense, equal rights. How can the human race that has evolved in a universe of such fundamental equality, fail to strive for a society without violence or terror? And, how, then, can *we* fail to build a world in which the rights due every human being from birth are respected?

May the blessings of the universe be upon us.

Source: Fang Lizhi. "Professor Fang Lizhi's Acceptance Speech." *Failure of the Democracy Movement: Human Rights in the People's Republic of China 1988/89.* Contemporary Asian Studies Series. Baltimore, Md.: School of Law, University of Maryland, 1991, p. 135. Robert F. Kennedy Award Address, reprinted by permission of Fang Lizhi.

VÁCLAV HAVEL
(1936–   )
"A Contaminated Moral Environment"
Prague, Czechoslovakia
January 1, 1990

While living under Czechoslovakia's Communist regime, playwright Václav Havel was a prominent critic of totalitarian society. His plays, such as *The Garden Party*—which parodied life under communism—were banned by the Communist authorities following the Prague Spring of 1968. This was a nine-month period under Czechoslovak leader Alexander Dubček, when citizens were permitted more freedom of speech and to travel, among other reforms. New political parties began to emerge. Worried that the relaxation of controls was going too far, Soviet premier Leonid Brezhnev (1964–82) and the leaders of Warsaw Pact nations (communist states of eastern Europe) declared they would intervene if noncommunist ideology got the upper hand in Czechoslovakia. In August 1968, the Soviet Union followed through, invading Czechoslovakia with thousands of tanks and hundreds of thousands of troops drawn from Warsaw Pact nations, ending the brief interlude. His plays banned,

Havel took to political action. He was imprisoned in 1979 for more than four years for leading the dissident group Charter 77, whose approximately 250 signers criticized the government's human rights failures. In 1989, as democratic reform was sweeping communism from eastern Europe and the Berlin Wall had fallen, Czech citizens took to the streets with peaceful strikes and massive demonstrations. Members of Charter 77, including Havel, helped Czechoslovakia transition to democracy through a new political party, Civic Forum. Led by Havel, a champion of nonviolent resistance, the "Velvet Revolution" obtained the resignation of the Communist leadership in November 1989. Havel was elected president of Czechoslovakia in the last days of the year. On New Year's Day, 1990, he addressed the country with his hopes for a new moral order. Three years later he won the presidency again, this time of the Czech Republic, which had split away from the new Slovak Republic.

For forty years you heard from my predecessors on this day different variations on the same theme: how our country was flourishing, how many million tons of steel we produced, how happy we all were, how we trusted our government, and what bright perspectives were unfolding in front of us.

I assume you did not propose me for this office so that I, too, would lie to you.

Our country is not flourishing. The enormous creative and spiritual potential of our nations is not being used sensibly. Entire branches of industry are producing goods that are of no interest to anyone, while we are lacking the things we need. The state, which calls itself a workers' state, humiliates and exploits workers. Our obsolete economy is wasting the little energy we have available. A country that once could be proud of the educational level of its citizens spends so little on education that it ranks today as seventy-second in the world. We have polluted the soil, rivers and forests bequeathed to us by our ancestors, and we have today the most contaminated environment in Europe. Adults in our country die earlier than in most other European countries.

Allow me a small personal observation. When I flew recently to Bratislava, I found some time during discussions to look out of the plane window. I saw the industrial complex of Slovnaft chemical factory and the giant Petr'alka housing estate right behind it. The view was enough for me to understand that for decades our statesmen and political leaders did not look or did not want to look out of the windows of their planes. No study of statistics available to me would enable me to understand faster and better the situation in which we find ourselves.

But all this is still not the main problem. The worst thing is that we live in a contaminated moral environment. We have fallen morally ill because we became used to saying something different from what we thought. We learned not to believe in anything, to ignore one another, to care only about ourselves. Concepts such as love, friendship, compassion, humility or forgiveness lost their depth and dimension, and for many of us they represented only psychological peculiarities, or they resembled gone-astray greetings from ancient times, a little ridiculous in the era of computers and spaceships. Only a few of us were able to cry out loudly that the powers that be should not be all-powerful and that the special farms, which produced ecologically pure and top-quality food just for them, should send their produce to schools, children's homes and hospitals if our agriculture was unable to offer them to all.

The previous regime—armed with its arrogant and intolerant ideology—reduced man to a force of production, and nature to a tool of production. In this it attacked both their very substance and their mutual relationship. It reduced gifted and autonomous people, skillfully working in their own country, to the nuts and bolts of some monstrously huge, noisy and stinking machine, whose real meaning was not clear to anyone. It could not do more than slowly but inexorably wear out itself and all its nuts and bolts.

When I talk about the contaminated moral atmosphere, I am not talking just about the gentlemen who eat organic vegetables and do not look out of the plane windows. I am talking about all of us. We have all become used to the totalitarian system and accepted it as an unchangeable fact and thus helped to perpetuate it. In other words, we are all—though naturally to differing extents—responsible for the operation of the totalitarian machinery. None of us is just its victim. We are all also its co-creators.

Why do I say this? It would be very unreasonable to understand the sad legacy of the last forty years as something alien, which some distant relative bequeathed to us. On the contrary, we have to accept this legacy as a sin we committed against ourselves. If we accept it as such, we will understand that it is up to us all, and up to us alone to do something about it. We cannot blame the previous rulers for everything, not only because it would be untrue, but also because it would blunt the duty that each of us faces today: namely, the obligation to act independently, freely, reasonably and quickly. Let us not be mistaken: the best government in the world, the best parliament and the best president, cannot achieve much on their own. And it would be wrong to expect a general remedy from them alone. Freedom and democracy include participation and therefore responsibility from us all.

If we realize this, then all the horrors that the new Czechoslovak democracy inherited will cease to appear so terrible. If we realize this, hope will return to our hearts. . . .

Everywhere in the world people wonder where those meek, humiliated, skeptical and seemingly cynical citizens of Czechoslovakia found the marvelous strength to shake the totalitarian yoke from their shoulders in several weeks, and in a decent and peaceful way. And let us ask: Where did the young people who never knew another system get their desire for truth, their love of free thought, their political ideas, their civic courage and civic prudence? . . .

Humanistic and democratic traditions, about which there had been so much idle talk, did after all slumber in the unconsciousness of our nations and ethnic minorities, and were inconspicuously passed from one generation to another, so that each of us could discover them at the right time and transform them into deeds.

We had to pay, however, for our present freedom. Many citizens perished in jails in the 1950s, many were executed; thousands of human lives were destroyed, hundreds of thousands of talented people were forced to leave the country. Those who defended the honor of our nations during the Second World War, those who rebelled against totalitarian rule and those who simply managed to remain themselves and think freely, were all persecuted. We should not forget any of those who paid for our present freedom in one way or another. Independent courts should impartially consider the possible guilt of those who were responsible for the persecutions, so that the truth about our recent past might be fully revealed.

We must also bear in mind that other nations have paid even more dearly for their present freedom, and that indirectly they have also paid for ours. The rivers of blood that have flowed in Hungary, Poland, Germany and recently in such a horrific manner in Romania, as well as the sea of blood shed by the nations of the Soviet Union, must not be forgotten. First of all because all human suffering concerns every other human being. But more than this, they must also not be forgotten because it is these great sacrifices that form the tragic background of today's freedom or the gradual emancipation of the nations of the Soviet Bloc, and thus the background of our own newfound freedom. Without the changes in the Soviet Union, Poland, Hungary, and the German Democratic Republic, what has happened in our country would have scarcely happened. And if it did, it certainly would not have followed such a peaceful course. . . .

Our state should never again be an appendage or a poor relative of anyone else. It is true that we must accept and learn many things from others, but we must do this in the future as their equal partners, who also have something to offer.

Our first president, T. G. Masaryk,

On the day of the resignation of Czechoslovakia's Communist leadership—and just days before his election as president—pro-democracy "Velvet Revolution" leader Václav Havel (right) celebrates with Alexander Dubček (left), leader of the brief Prague Spring of 1968. *(AP Photo/ Dusan Vranic)*

wrote: "Jesus, not Caesar." In this he followed our philosophers Chelcicky and Comenius. I dare to say that we may even have an opportunity to spread this idea further and introduce a new element into European and global politics. Our country, if that is what we want, can now permanently radiate love, understanding, the power of the spirit and of ideas. It is precisely this glow that we can offer as our specific contribution to international politics. . . .

There are free elections and an election campaign ahead of us. Let us not allow this struggle to dirty the so-far clean face of our gentle revolution. Let us not allow the sympathies of the world, which we have won so fast, to be equally rapidly lost through our becoming entangled in the jungle of skirmishes for power. Let us not allow the desire to serve oneself to bloom once again under the noble veil of the desire to serve the common good. It is not really important now which party, club or group prevails in the elections. The important thing is that the winners will be the best of us, in the moral, civic, political and professional sense, regardless of their political affiliations. The future policies and prestige of our state will depend on the personalities we select, and later, elect to our representative bodies.

My dear fellow citizens! . . . The most distinguished of my predecessors opened his first speech with a quotation from the great Czech educator Comenius. Allow me to conclude my first speech with my own paraphrase of the same statement:

People, your government has returned to you!

Source: Havel, Václav. "New Year's Address to the Nation." Office of President of the Czech Republic. Available online. http://old.hrad.cz/president/Havel/speeches/index_uk.html. Accessed December 20, 2007.

SEVERN CULLIS-SUZUKI
(1979–   )
Address to the Earth Summit
Rio de Janeiro, Brazil
June 11, 1992

The last decades of the 20th century witnessed a new willingness by world leaders to consider the hopes and views of often marginalized people: indigenous people, people of color, women, the poor, and even children. In June 1992, a 12-year-old girl named Severn Cullis-Suzuki stepped to the podium to address a session of the United Nations's "Earth Summit," calling on adults to take responsibility for the decline in biodiversity and the destruction of the Earth's environment. Cullis-Suzuki's father is environmental activist David Suzuki, host of a popular Canadian science television series. As a Japanese-Canadian child during World War II (1939–45), David Suzuki was interned in a prison camp in British Columbia amid anti-Japanese hysteria, and the young girl said her father taught her to always fight against injustice. "You have to stand up for what you believe," she observed. She visited the Amazon when she was eight years old and was dismayed to see slash burning being used to clear the rain forest. Back home in Vancouver, British Columbia, she founded an environmental club, ECO—Environmental Children's Organization—with classmates, and she was determined to speak out on preserving the natural environment. The children raised the money themselves to attend the UN Conference on Environment and Development—the Earth Summit—held in Rio de Janeiro, Brazil, in June 1992. Cullis-Suzuki addressed the plenary session using a speech composed by the group. Her commanding presence and strong voice drew rapt attention from the audience of world delegates. The next year in Beijing, she received the UN Environment Program's Global 500 Award. In college, she studied ecology, evolutionary biology, and ethnobotany. Today she continues to work for environmental quality around the world.

Hello, I'm Severn Suzuki speaking for E.C.O.—The Environmental Children's organization.

We are a group of twelve- and thirteen-year-olds from Canada trying to make a difference: Vanessa Suttie, Morgan Geisler, Michelle Quigg and me. We raised all the money ourselves to come 6,000 miles to tell you adults you must change your ways. Coming here today, I have no hidden agenda. I am fighting for my future.

Losing my future is not like losing an election or a few points on the stock market. I am here to speak for all generations to come. I am here to speak on behalf of the starving children around the world whose cries go unheard. I am here to speak for the countless animals dying across this planet because they have nowhere left to go. We cannot afford to not be heard.

I am afraid to go out in the sun now because of the holes in the ozone. I am afraid to breathe the air because I don't know what chemicals are in it. I used to go fishing in Vancouver with my dad until just a few years ago we found the fish full of cancers. And now we hear about animals and plants going extinct every day—vanishing forever.

In my life, I have dreamt of seeing the great herds of wild animals, jungles and rainforests full of birds and butterflies, but now I wonder if they will even exist for my children to see. Did you have to worry about these little things when you were my age?

All this is happening before our eyes and yet we act as if we have all the time we want and all the solutions. I'm only a child and I don't have all the solutions, but I want you to realize, neither do you! You don't know how to fix the holes in our ozone layer. You don't know how to bring salmon back up a dead stream. You don't know how to bring back an animal now extinct. And you can't bring back forests that once grew where there is now desert.

If you don't know how to fix it, please stop breaking it!

Here, you may be delegates of your governments, business people, organizers, reporters or politicians—but really you are mothers and fathers, brothers and sisters, aunts and uncles—and all of you are somebody's child.

I'm only a child, yet I know we are all part of a family, five billion strong—in fact, 30 million species strong—and we all share the same air, water and soil. Borders and governments will never change that. I'm only a child, yet I know we are all in this together and should act as one single world towards one single goal.

In my anger, I am not blind, and in my fear, I am not afraid to tell the world how I feel.

In my country, we make so much waste, we buy and throw away, buy and throw away, and yet northern countries will not share with the needy. Even when we have more than enough, we are afraid to lose some of our wealth, afraid to share.

In Canada, we live the privileged life, with plenty of food, water and shelter—we have watches, bicycles, computers and television sets. Two days ago here in Brazil, we were shocked when we spent some time with some children living on the streets. And this is what one child told us: "I wish I was rich and if I were, I would give all the street children food, clothes, medicine, shelter and love and affection."

If a child on the street who has nothing, is willing to share, why are we who have everything still so greedy?

I can't stop thinking that these children are my age, that it makes a tremendous difference where you are born, that I could be one of those children living in the Favellas of Rio. I could be a child starving in Somalia, a victim of war in the Middle East or a beggar in India. I'm only a child, yet I know if all the money spent on war was spent on ending poverty and finding environmental answers, what a wonderful place this earth would be!

At school, even in kindergarten, you teach us to behave in the world. You teach us not to fight with others, to work things out, to respect others, to clean up our mess, not to hurt other creatures to share—not be greedy. Then why do you go out and do the things you tell us not to do?

Do not forget why you're attending these conferences, who you're doing this for—we are your own children. You are deciding what kind of world we will grow up in. Parents should be able to comfort their children by saying "everything's going to be alright," "we're doing the best we can," and "it's not the end of the world."

But I don't think you can say that to us anymore. Are we even on your list of priorities? My father always says, "You are what you do, not what you say." Well, what you do makes me cry at night. You grownups say you love us. I challenge you, please make your actions reflect your words. Thank you for listening.

Source: Cullis-Suzuki, Severn. *Tell the World.* Toronto, Ontario: Doubleday Canada, 1993. Permission of Severn Cullis-Suzuki.

RIGOBERTA MENCHÚ TUM
(1959–)
"Freedom for the Indians"
Oslo, Norway
December 10, 1992

For decades, from 1960 through the 1980s, Guatemala suffered through unrest, military rule, and the political violence of civil war, with thousands of people dead and missing. The war was fought on one side by leftist rebel guerrillas, interested in winning land and human rights for the indigenous poor. On the other side stood the Guatemalan military (supported by the United States) and right-wing vigilante groups, hoping to preserve power and profit for big business and the military. While tens of thousands of the government's political opponents ended up dead, the poor peasantry and indigenous people in their villages suffered the worst of the army's atrocities. Rigoberta Menchú Tum, a poor Quiché Mayan Indian of Guatemala, devoted herself to political activity and social work for the oppressed poor. She participated in strikes and demonstrations in Guatemala City, advocating for Indian rights and an end to violence. When family members (her parents plus six other close relatives) were killed by right-wing death squads, she went into hiding in fear for her life. In exile in Mexico, she continued her work for freedom and justice, helping to found and eventually lead an opposition party in exile, United Representation of Guatemalan Opposition. She dictated her story for an influential book, *I, Rigoberta Menchú*, published in 1983 (the book, while largely true, was later found to contain exaggerations); her engrossing story brought her attention around the world. In 1992 she won the Nobel Peace Prize, delivering her Nobel lecture on the customary date of December 10, the anniversary of the death of Alfred Nobel, the pacifist Swedish inventor of dynamite who established the prize. The Guatemalan civil war came to an end in 1996, after some 200,000 people had died.

I feel a deep emotion and pride for the honor of having been awarded the Nobel Peace Prize for 1992. A deep personal feeling and pride for my country and its very ancient culture. . . .

There is no doubt whatsoever that it constitutes a sign of hope in the struggle of the indigenous people in the entire continent. It is also a tribute to the Centro-American people who still search for their stability, for the structuring of their future, and the path for their development and integration, based on civil democracy and mutual respect. . . .

Paradoxically, it was actually in my own country where I met, on the part of some people, the strongest objections, reserve and indifference, for the award of the Nobel Prize to this Quiché Indian. Perhaps because in Latin America, it is precisely in Guatemala where the discrimination towards natives, towards women, and the repression of the longing for justice and peace, are more deeply rooted. . . .

With deep pain, on one side, but with satisfaction on the other, I have to inform you that the Nobel Peace Prize 1992 will have to remain temporarily in Mexico City . . . waiting for peace in Guatemala. Because there are no political conditions in my country that would indicate or make me foresee a prompt and just solution. The satisfaction and gratitude are due to the fact that Mexico, our wonderful neighbor country, that has been so dedicated and interested, that has made such great efforts in respect of the negotiations that are being conducted to achieve peace, that has received and admitted so many refugees and exiled Guatemalans, has given us a place in the Museo del Templo Mayor (the cradle of the ancient Aztecas) so that the Nobel Prize may remain

Standing before a Mayan ruin crowded with celebrants in Guatemala City, Rigoberta Menchú Tum addresses supporters on October 17, 1992, the day after her award of the Nobel Peace Prize was announced. *(AP Photo/Dan Hernandez)*

there, until peaceful and safe conditions are established in Guatemala to place it there, the land of the Quetzal....

Please allow me, ladies and gentlemen, to say some words about my country and the civilization of the Mayas. The Maya people developed and spread geographically through some 300,000 square kilometers; they occupied parts of the south of Mexico, Belize, Guatemala, as well as Honduras and El Salvador. They developed a very rich civilization in the area of political organization, as well as in social and economic fields. They were great scientists in the fields of mathematics, astronomy, agriculture, architecture and engineering. They were great artists in the fields of sculpture, painting, weaving and carving.

The Mayas discovered the mathematic zero value, at about the same time that it was discovered in India and later passed on to the Arabs. Their astronomic forecasts based on mathematic calculations and scientific observations were amazing, and still are. They prepared a calendar more accurate than the Gregorian, and in the field of medicine they performed intra-cranial surgical operations....

Who can predict what other great scientific conquests and developments these people could have achieved, if they had not been conquered in blood and fire, and subjected to an ethnocide that affected nearly 50 million people in the course of 500 years.... Let there be freedom for the Indians, wherever they may be in the American continent....

The expressions of great happiness by the Indian organizations in the entire continent, and the worldwide congratulations received for the award of the Nobel Peace Prize, clearly indicate the great importance of this decision. It is the recognition of the European debt to the American indigenous people. It is an appeal to the conscience of humanity so that those conditions of marginalization that condemned them to colonialism and exploitation may be eradicated. It is a cry for life, peace, justice, equality and fraternity between human beings. . . .

Today in the 47th period of sessions of the General Assembly, the United Nations will institute 1993 as the International Year of the Indian People, in the presence of well-known chiefs of the organizations of the Indian people and the Continental Resistance Movement of Indians, blacks and other people. . . .

In the attempt to crush rebellion, dictatorships have committed the greatest atrocities. They have leveled villages, and murdered thousands of farmers, particularly Indians, hundreds of trade union workers and students, outstanding intellectuals and politicians, priests and nuns. Through this systematic persecution in the name of the safety of the nation, one million farmers were removed by force from their lands; 100,000 had to seek refuge in neighboring countries. In Guatemala there are today almost 100,000 orphans and more than 40,000 widows. The practice of "missing" politicians was invented in Guatemala, as a government policy. As you know, I am myself a survivor of a massacred family. . . .

Democracy in Guatemala must be built up as soon as at all possible. It is necessary that the human rights be fully complied with: put an end to racism, guarantee freedom to organize and to move within all sectors of the country. In short, it is imperative to open the fields to the multi-ethnic civil society with all its rights, to demilitarize the country and establish the basis for its development, so that it can be pulled out of today's underdevelopment and poverty. . . .

Today we must fight for a better world, without poverty, without racism. . . . The people of Guatemala will mobilize and be aware of their strength in building up a worthy future. They are preparing themselves to sow the future, to free themselves from atavisms, to rediscover their heritage. To build a country with a genuine national identity, to start a new life. By combining all the shades and nuances of the "ladinos", the "Garífunas," and Indians in the Guatemalan ethnic mosaic, we . . . give them brightness and a superior quality, just the way our weavers weave. A typical "güipil" shirt brilliantly composed, a gift to humanity.

Source: Menchú Tum, Rigoberta. "Nobel Lecture." The Nobel Foundation. Available online. http://nobelprize.org/nobel_prizes/peace/laureates/1992/tum-lecture.html. Accessed December 20, 2007. © The Nobel Foundation 1992.

PAUL KEATING
(1944–   )
The Redfern Address
Sydney, Australia
December 10, 1992

Some 40,000 to 50,000 years before the European discovery of the Australian continent, natives of what is now Indonesia embarked on a journey that resulted in the peopling of Australia. Modern descendants of these early people now call themselves indigenous Australians (this includes both Torres Strait islanders and the aboriginal people of mainland Australia). These men and women make up less than 2.5 percent of Australia's population; however, the controversy surrounding their treatment by British settlers has plagued the Australian government for many years. While aboriginal Australians have chronically suffered from shorter life expectancy, higher rates of unemployment, and lower levels of education than have their nonindigenous peers, only in the last few decades has the Australian government publicly recognized these problems and passed laws to aid indigenous citizens. A landmark court case—the 1992 Mabo judgment—declared that land owned by Aborigines prior to the European colonization of Australia may be acknowledged under common law. This ruling overturned centuries of legal prejudice against indigenous claims and finally recognized ancient tribal ownership of land as equal to the common law practices of Australian settlers. The Australian government and its citizens have also taken strides to heal the emotional rift between indigenous people and white Australians. A "National Sorry Day," for instance, has been celebrated annually since 1998 to atone for past mistreatment. Paul Keating, Australian prime minister from 1991 to 1996, was particularly energetic in his support of aboriginal rights, as this speech given in Redfern, a Sydney suburb with a large aboriginal population, reveals. Keating committed himself to combating their problems, and he acknowledged that, if conditions were to improve, both indigenous and nonindigenous Australians must work together.

I am very pleased to be here today at the launch of Australia's celebration of the 1993 International Year of the World's Indigenous People. It will be a year of great significance for Australia.

It comes at a time when we have committed ourselves to succeeding in the test which so far we have always failed. Because, in truth, we cannot confidently say that we have succeeded as we would like to have succeeded if we have not managed to extend opportunity and care, dignity and hope to the indigenous people of Australia—the Aboriginal and Torres Strait Island people.

This is a fundamental test of our social goals and our national will: our ability to say to ourselves and the rest of the world that Australia is a first rate social democracy, that we are what we should be—truly the land of the fair go and the better chance. There is no more basic test of how seriously we mean these things. It is a test of our self-knowledge. Of how well we know the land we live in. How well we know our history. How well we recognize the fact that, complex as our contemporary identity is, it cannot be separated from Aboriginal Australia. How well we know what Aboriginal Australians know about Australia.

Redfern is a good place to contemplate these things. Just a mile or two from the place where the first European settlers landed, in too many ways it tells us that their failure to bring much more than devastation and demoralization to Aboriginal Australia continues to be our failure.

More I think than most Australians recognize, the plight of Aboriginal Australians affects us all. In Redfern it might be tempting to think that the reality Aboriginal Aus-

531

tralians face is somehow contained here, and that the rest of us are insulated from it. But of course, while all the dilemmas may exist here, they are far from contained. We know the same dilemmas and more are faced all over Australia.

This is perhaps the point of this Year of the World's Indigenous People: to bring the dispossessed out of the shadows, to recognize that they are part of us, and that we cannot give indigenous Australians up without giving up many of our own most deeply held values, much of our own identity—and our own humanity.

Nowhere in the world, I would venture, is the message more stark than in Australia. We simply cannot sweep injustice aside. Even if our own conscience allowed us to, I am sure, that in due course, the world and the people of our region would not. There should be no mistake about this—our success in resolving these issues will have a significant bearing on our standing in the world.

However intractable the problems may seem, we cannot resign ourselves to failure—any more than we can hide behind the contemporary version of Social Darwinism which says that to reach back for the poor and dispossessed is to risk being dragged down. That seems to me not only morally indefensible, but bad history.

We non-Aboriginal Australians should perhaps remind ourselves that Australia once reached out for us. Didn't Australia provide opportunity and care for the dispossessed Irish? The poor of Britain? The refugees from war and famine and persecution in the countries of Europe and Asia? Isn't it reasonable to say that if we can build a prosperous and remarkably harmonious multicultural society in Australia, surely we can find just solutions to the problems which beset the first Australians—the people to whom the most injustice has been done.

And, as I say, the starting point might be to recognize that the problem starts with us non-Aboriginal Australians. It begins, I think, with the act of recognition. Recognition that it was we who did the dispossessing. We took the traditional lands and smashed the traditional way of life. We brought the disasters. The alcohol. We committed the murders. We took the children from their mothers. We practiced discrimination and exclusion.

It was our ignorance and our prejudice. And our failure to imagine these things being done to us. With some noble exceptions, we failed to make the most basic human response and enter into their hearts and minds. We failed to ask—how would I feel

RHETORICAL DEVICE

Assonance: Repeating similar vowel sounds (joined to different consonants) within a sentence.

What kind of peace do I mean? . . . Not the peace of the grave
or the security of the slave. —*John F. Kennedy*

It seems to me that if we can imagine the injustice,
then we can imagine its opposite. —*Paul Keating*

If there is any one amongst you who cherishes my freedom,
Oliver Tambo cherishes it more, and I know that
he would give his life to see me free. —*Nelson Mandela*

if this were done to me? As a consequence, we failed to see that what we were doing degraded all of us.

If we needed a reminder of this, we received it this year. The Report of the Royal Commission into Aboriginal Deaths in Custody showed with devastating clarity that the past lives on in inequality, racism and injustice in the prejudice and ignorance of non-Aboriginal Australians, and in the demoralization and desperation, the fractured identity, of so many Aborigines and Torres Strait Islanders.

For all this, I do not believe that the Report should fill us with guilt. Down the years, there has been no shortage of guilt, but it has not produced the responses we need. Guilt is not a very constructive emotion. I think what we need to do is open our hearts a bit. All of us. Perhaps when we recognize what we have in common we will see the things which must be done—the practical things. . . .

If we improve the living conditions in one town, they will improve in another. And another. If we raise the standard of health by 20 per cent one year, it will be raised more the next. If we open one door others will follow. When we see improvement, when we see more dignity, more confidence, more happiness—we will know we are going to win. We need these practical building blocks of change.

The Mabo judgment should be seen as one of these. By doing away with the bizarre conceit that this continent had no owners prior to the settlement of Europeans, Mabo establishes a fundamental truth and lays the basis for justice. It will be much easier to work from that basis than has ever been the case in the past. For this reason alone we should ignore the isolated outbreaks of hysteria and hostility of the past few months. Mabo is an historic decision—we can make it an historic turning point, the basis of a new relationship between indigenous and non-Aboriginal Australians.

The message should be that there is nothing to fear or to lose in the recognition of historical truth, or the extension of social justice, or the deepening of Australian social democracy to include indigenous Australians. There is everything to gain.

Even the unhappy past speaks for this. Where Aboriginal Australians have been included in the life of Australia they have made remarkable contributions. Economic contributions, particularly in the pastoral and agricultural industry. They are there in the frontier and exploration history of Australia. They are there in sport to an extraordinary degree. In literature and art and music.

In all these things they have shaped our knowledge of this continent and of ourselves. They have shaped our identity. They are there in the Australian legend. We should never forget—they helped build this nation. And if we have a sense of justice, as well as common sense, we will forge a new partnership.

As I said, it might help us if we non-Aboriginal Australians imagine ourselves dispossessed of land we have lived on for 50,000 years—and then imagine ourselves told that it had never been ours.

Imagine if ours was the oldest culture in the world and we were told that it was worthless. Imagine if we had resisted this settlement, suffered and died in the defense of our land, and then were told in history books that we had given up without a fight. Imagine if non-Aboriginal Australians had served their country in peace and war and were then ignored in history books. Imagine if our feats on sporting fields had inspired admiration and patriotism and yet did nothing to diminish prejudice. Imagine if our spiritual life was denied and ridiculed.

Imagine if we had suffered the injustice and then were blamed for it. It seems to me that if we can imagine the injustice then we can imagine its opposite. And we can have justice. . . .

From their music and art and dance we are beginning to recognize how much richer our national life and identity will be for the participation of Aboriginals and Torres Strait Islanders. We are beginning to learn what the indigenous people have known for many thousands of years—how to live with our physical environment.

Ever so gradually we are learning how to see Australia through Aboriginal eyes, beginning to recognize the wisdom contained in their epic story. I think we are beginning to see how much we owe the indigenous Australians and how much we have lost by living so apart.

I said we non-indigenous Australians should try to imagine the Aboriginal view. . . . There is one thing today we cannot imagine. We cannot imagine that the descendants of people whose genius and resilience maintained a culture here through 50,000 years or more, through cataclysmic changes to the climate and environment, and who then survived two centuries of dispossession and abuse, will be denied their place in the modern Australian nation.

We cannot imagine that. We cannot imagine that we will fail. And with the spirit that is here today I am confident that we won't. I am confident that we will succeed in this decade.

Source: Keating, Paul. "Redfern Speech." The Hon. Paul Keating Official Website. Available online. http://www.keating.org.au/main.cfm. Accessed December 21, 2007.

AUNG SAN SUU KYI
(1945–   )
On the Rightful Place of Women
Beijing, China
August 31, 1995

Born at the end of World War II (1939–45), Aung San Suu Kyi was the daughter of Aung San, Burma's most celebrated nationalist of the 20th century and the founder of the Burma Independence Army. General Aung San was assassinated in 1947, when his daughter was only two. She studied at Oxford University, took a United Nations post, and twice was a visiting scholar abroad. In 1988 she assumed her role as the most influential modern-day proponent of Burmese democracy, human rights, and nonviolence. Following popular protests against the repressive military dictatorship (in power since 1962), violently quelled by military forces, Aung San Suu Kyi founded her own political party, the National League for Democracy. She courageously traveled the country promoting her democratic agenda and championing the rights of fellow citizens. In the subsequent 1990 elections to the national parliament, her party won a landslide victory, only to have the military leadership ignore the results and place Aung San Suu Kyi and hundreds of her supporters in jail. Even when she was awarded the Nobel Peace Prize in 1991, her young son Alexander Aris had to accept the prize on her behalf. "By her own dedication and personal sacrifice she has come to be a worthy symbol through whom the plight of all the people of Burma may be recognized. And no one must underestimate that plight. Nor should we forget the many senior and highly respected leaders besides my mother who are all incarcerated," he said, in accepting. Her first imprisonment ended in 1995, just prior to this speech, sent by videotape to the Non-Governmental Organization Forum on Women, held in Beijing. Soon after, Aung San Suu Kyi was returned to house arrest for her continued opposition to the despotic military regime in Myanmar (Burma's official name since 1989).

⁓⁓⁓

It is a wonderful but daunting task that has fallen on me to say a few words by way of opening this Forum, the greatest concourse of women (joined by a few brave men!) that has ever gathered on our planet. I want to try and voice some of the common hopes which firmly unite us in all our splendid diversity.

But first I would like to explain why I cannot be with you in person today. Last month I was released from almost six years of house arrest. The regaining of my freedom has in turn imposed a duty on me to work for the freedom of other women and men in my country who have suffered far more—and who continue to suffer far more—than I have. It is this duty which prevents me from joining you today. Even sending this message to you has not been without difficulties. But the help of those who believe in international cooperation and freedom of expression has enabled me to overcome the obstacles. They made it possible for me to make a small contribution to this great celebration of the struggle of women to mold their own destiny and to influence the fate of our global village.

The opening plenary of this Forum will be presenting an overview of the global forces affecting the quality of life of the human community and the challenges they pose for the global community as a whole and for women in particular as we approach the twenty-first century. However, with true womanly understanding, the Convener of this Forum suggested that among these global forces and challenges, I might wish to concentrate on those matters which occupy all my waking thoughts these days: peace, security, human rights and democracy. I would like to discuss these issues particularly in the context of the participation of women in politics and governance.

Nobel Prize winner and pro–democracy leader Aung San Suu Kyi speaks to a large crowd of supporters outside her Rangoon (Yangon) home in June 1996. Since her party won the 1990 elections that would have made her prime minister, she has been either jailed or under house arrest by the repressive Burmese military. *(AP Photo)*

For millennia women have dedicated themselves almost exclusively to the task of nurturing, protecting and caring for the young and the old, striving for the conditions of peace that favor life as a whole. To this can be added the fact that, to the best of my knowledge, no war was ever started by women. But it is women and children who have always suffered most in situations of conflict. Now that we are gaining control of the primary historical role imposed on us of sustaining life in the context of the home and family, it is time to apply in the arena of the world the wisdom and experience thus gained in activities of peace over so many thousands of years. The education and empowerment of women throughout the world cannot fail to result in a more caring, tolerant, just and peaceful life for all. . . .

This year is the International Year for Tolerance. The United Nations has recognized that "tolerance, human rights, democracy and peace are closely related. Without tolerance, the foundations form democracy and respect for human rights cannot be strengthened, and the achievement of peace will remain elusive." My own experience during the years I have been engaged in the democracy movement of Burma has convinced me of the need to emphasize the positive aspect of tolerance. It is not enough simply to "live and let live": genuine tolerance requires an active effort to try to understand the point of view of others; it implies broadmindedness and vision, as well as confidence in one's own ability to meet new challenges without resorting to intransigence or violence. In societies where men are truly confident of their own worth women are not merely "tolerated," they are valued. Their opinions are listened to with respect, and they are given their rightful place in shaping the society in which they live.

There is an outmoded Burmese proverb still recited by men who wish to deny that women too can play a part in bringing necessary change and progress to their society: "The dawn rises only when the rooster crows." But Burmese people today are well aware of the scientific reasons behind the rising of dawn and the falling of dusk. And the intelligent rooster surely realizes that it is because dawn comes that it crows and not the other way round. It crows to welcome the light that has come to relieve the darkness of night.

It is not the prerogative of men alone to bring light to this world: women with their capacity for compassion and self-sacrifice, their courage and perseverance, have done much to dissipate the darkness of intolerance and hate, suffering and despair. . . . Traditionally the home is the domain of the woman. But there has never been a guarantee that she can live out her life there safe and unmolested. There are countless women who are subjected to severe cruelty within the heart of the family which should be their haven. And in times of crisis when their menfolk are unable to give them protection, women have to face the harsh challenges of the world outside while continuing to discharge their duties within the home....

In my country at present, women have no participation in the higher levels of government and none whatsoever in the judiciary. Even within the democratic movement only 14 out of the 485 MPs elected in 1990 were women—all from my own party, the National League for Democracy. These 14 women represent less than three percent of the total number of successful candidates. They, like their male colleagues, have not been permitted to take office since the outcome of those elections has been totally ignored. Yet the very high performance of women in our educational system and in the management of commercial enterprises proves their enormous potential to contribute to the betterment of society in general. Meanwhile our women have yet to achieve those fundamental rights of free expression, association and security of life denied also to their menfolk.

The adversities that we have had to face together have taught all of us involved in the struggle to build a truly democratic political system in Burma that there are no gender barriers that cannot be overcome. The relationship between men and women should, and can be, characterized not by patronizing behavior or exploitation, but by *metta* (that is to say loving kindness), partnership and trust. We need mutual respect and understanding between men and women, instead of patriarchal domination and degradation, which are expressions of violence and engender counter-violence. We can learn from each other and help one another to moderate the "gender weaknesses" imposed upon us by traditional or biological factors....

This forum of non-governmental organizations represents the belief in the ability of intelligent human beings to resolve conflicting interests through exchange and dialogue. It also represents the conviction that governments alone cannot resolve all the problems of their countries. The watchfulness and active cooperation of organizations outside the spheres of officialdom are necessary to ensure the four essential components of the human development paradigm ... productivity, equity, sustainability and empowerment. The last is particularly relevant: It requires that "development must be *by* people, not only *for* them. People must participate fully in the decisions and processes that shape their lives." In other words people must be allowed to play a significant role in the governance of their country. And "people" include women, who make up at least half of the world's population.

The last six years afforded me much time and food for thought. I came to the conclusion that the human race is not divided into two opposing camps of good and evil. It is made up of those who are capable of learning and those who are incapable of doing so. Here I am not talking of learning in the narrow sense of acquiring an academic education, but of learning as the process of absorbing those lessons of life that enable us to increase peace and happiness in our world. Women in their role as mothers have traditionally assumed the responsibility of teaching children values that will guide them throughout their lives. It is time we were given the full opportunity to use our natural teaching skills to contribute towards building a modern world that can withstand the tremendous challenges of the technological revolution which has in turn brought revolutionary changes in social values.

As we strive to teach others we must have the humility to acknowledge that we too still have much to learn. And we must have the flexibility to adapt to the changing needs of the world around us. Women who have been taught that modesty and pliancy are among the prized virtues of our gender are marvelously equipped for the learning process. But they must be given the opportunity to turn these often merely passive virtues into positive assets for the society in which they live.

These, then, are our common hopes that unite us—that as the shackles of prejudice and intolerance fall from our own limbs we can together strive to identify and remove the impediments to human development everywhere. The mechanisms by which this great task is to be achieved provide the proper focus of this great forum. I feel sure that women throughout the world who, like me, cannot be with you join me now in sending you all our prayers and good wishes for a joyful and productive meeting.

Source: Aung San Suu Kyi. "Words of Freedom." U.S. Department of State Bureau of International Information Programs. Available online. http://usinfo.state.gov/dd/eng_democracy_dialogues/womens_rights/womens_rights_aung_san_suu_kyi.html. Accessed December 20, 2007.

KING HUSSEIN OF JORDAN
(1935–1999)
Eulogy to Yitzhak Rabin
Jerusalem, Israel
November 6, 1995

King Hussein became the third king of Jordan when he was only 17, on the abdication of his sick father in 1952. Hussein was a member of the Hashemite dynasty, an ancient family—descended from Muhammad's daughter—who had ruled Mecca since the 10th century. He was educated in Jordan and England. He was a pro-Western moderate and a fun-loving man—he brought his motorcycle with him on state visits to the United States—and he eventually married four times. Bordered by more radical Arab states, Iraq and Syria, Jordan also shared a long border with Israel and was subject to conflicting pressures. In 1967 Jordan suffered serious military defeat in the Six-Day War (Arab-Israeli War), losing the West Bank to Israel and being forced to accommodate a huge influx of Palestinian refugees. A pragmatist, Hussein approached the United States and European countries, trying to build better relations between the Arab world and the West, and he attempted to bring reluctant Arab nations around to the idea of recognizing Israel's right to exist. In 1993, while Yitzhak Rabin was prime minister of Israel, the Palestine Liberation Organization signed the Oslo Accords with Israel; the agreement withdrew Israeli troops from the West Bank and created a Palestinian Authority. The next year Hussein concluded the Israel-Jordan Treaty of Peace with Yitzhak Rabin; the only other Arab country to have made peace with Israel was Egypt (in 1978). Hussein and Rabin became friends in the process. Two years later, on November 4, 1995, a right-wing Israeli radical opposed to the Oslo Accords assassinated Rabin in Tel Aviv, Israel. Hussein spoke at Rabin's funeral—he mentions a previous visit to Jerusalem, made when he was only 16 with his grandfather, King Abdullah I (r. 1946–51). A Palestinian assassin had shot at them both; Abdullah died, while Hussein escaped injury.

My sister, Mrs. Leah Rabin, my friends, I had never thought that the moment would come like this when I would grieve the loss of a brother, a colleague and a friend—a man, a soldier who met us on the opposite side of a divide, whom we respected as he respected us. A man I came to know because I realized, as he did, that we have to cross over the divide, establish a dialogue, get to know each other and strive to leave for those who follow us a legacy that is worthy of them. And so we did. And so we became brethren and friends.

I've never been used to standing, except with you next to me, speaking of peace, speaking about dreams and hopes for generations to come that must live in peace, enjoy human dignity, come together, work together, to build a better future which is their right. Never in all my thoughts would it have occurred to me that my first visit to Jerusalem and response to your invitation, the invitation of the Speaker of the Knesset, the invitation of the president of Israel, would be on such an occasion.

You lived as a soldier, you died as a soldier for peace and I believe it is time for all of us to come out, openly, and to speak our piece, but here today, but for all the times to come. We belong to the camp of peace. We believe in peace. We believe that our one God wishes us to live in peace and wishes peace upon us, for these are His teachings to all the followers of the three great monotheistic religions, the children of Abraham.

Let's not keep silent. Let our voices rise high to speak of our commitment to peace for all times to come, and let us tell those who live in darkness who are the enemies of life, and through faith and religion and the teachings of our one God, this is where we stand. This is our camp. May God bless you with the realization that you must join it and we pray that He will, but otherwise we are not ashamed, nor are we afraid, nor are we anything but determined to fulfill the legacy for which my friend fell, as did my grandfather in this very city when I was with him and but a young boy.

He was a man of courage, a man of vision and he was endowed with one of the greatest virtues that any man can have. He was endowed with humility. He felt with those around him and in a position of responsibility, he placed himself, as I do and have done, often, in the place of the other partner to achieve a worthy goal. And we achieved peace, an honorable peace and a lasting peace. He had courage, he had vision, and he had a commitment to peace, and standing here, I commit before you, before my people in Jordan, before the world, myself to continue with our utmost, to ensure that we leave a similar legacy. And when my time comes, I hope it will be like my grandfather's and like Yitzhak Rabin's.

May your spirit rise high and may it sense how the people of Jordan, my family, the people of Israel, decent people throughout the world feel today. So many live and so many inevitably die. This is the will of God. This is the way of all, but those who are fortunate and lucky in life, those who are greater, those who leave something behind, and you are such a man, my friend.

The faces in my country amongst the majority of my people and our armed forces and people who once were your enemies are somber today and their hearts are heavy. Let's hope and pray that God will give us all guidance, each in his respective position to do what he can for the better future that Yitzhak Rabin sought with determination and courage. As long as I live, I'll be proud to have known him, to have worked with him, as a brother and as a friend, and as a man, and the relationship of friendship that we had is something unique and I am proud of that.

On behalf of the people of Jordan, my large Jordanian family, my Hashemite family, all those who belong to the camp of peace, to all those who belong to the camp of peace, our deepest sympathies, our deepest condolences as we share together this moment of remembrance and commitment, to continue our struggle for the future of generations to come, as did Yitzhak Rabin, and to fulfill his legacy.

Source: King Hussein. "Eulogy at the Funeral of Prime Minister Rabin." Israel Ministry of Foreign Affairs. Available online. http://www.mfa.gov.il/mfa/foreign%20relations/israels%20foreign%20relations%20since%201947/1995–1996/. Accessed December 21, 2007. Permission of Jordan Information Bureau.

KIM PHÚC
(1963–   )
At the Vietnam War Memorial
Washington, D.C., United States
November 11, 1996

Napalm is a flammable sticky jelly, made of gasoline and a thickener; it is the 20th century's "improvement" on the ancient Greek fire that Byzantine forces launched so successfully, often by catapult, against enemy ships during sieges of Constantinople. Thinned down, napalm is used in flame-throwers; but far more lethally, during the Vietnam War, the United States and South Vietnam dropped napalm in bombs against the communist enemy: the Vietcong (insurgents within South Vietnam fighting against the South Vietnamese government) and the North Vietnamese. As intended, the resulting fires destroyed foliage in the countryside, ridding areas of insurgent hideouts and leaving terrain clear for helicopters to land. As of 1981, the United Nations outlawed use of napalm against civilians, but even so that would not have helped Kim Phúc. Tragically, the nine-year-old girl was burned accidentally in a misdirected napalm strike by South Vietnamese pilots over her village of Trang Bang (near Saigon) in 1972. She suffered third-degree burns over half her body, requiring 17 operations to restore her health. Her Pulitzer Prize–winning picture, taken moments after the bombing by Associated Press photographer Nick Ut, captured the horror of the war and delivered it worldwide. (He then rushed her to the hospital.) At the war's end, South Vietnam fell under communist North Vietnamese control. Phúc went to Cuba for her university studies and met her future husband there. They defected to Canada when an opportunity arose in 1992 and have since become Canadian citizens. UNESCO recruited her as a Goodwill Ambassador in 1994, and, as a peace activist, she founded an organization to provide assistance to child victims of war. On Veterans' Day in 1996, she spoke at the U.S. Vietnam War Memorial in Washington, D.C.

Dear Friends: I am very happy to be with you today. I thank you for giving me the opportunity to talk and meet with you on this Veterans' Day.

As you know I am the little girl who was running to escape from the napalm fire. I do not want to talk about the war because I cannot change history.

I only want you to remember the tragedy of war in order to do things to stop fighting and killing around the world.

I have suffered a lot from both physical and emotional pain. Sometimes I thought I could not live, but God saved me and gave me faith and hope.

Even if I could talk face to face with the pilot who dropped the bombs, I would tell him we cannot change history but we should try to do good things for the present and for the future to promote peace.

I did not think that I could marry nor have any children because of my burns, but now I have a wonderful husband and lovely son and a happy family.

Dear friends, I just dream one day people all over the world can live in real peace—no fighting, and no hostility. We should work together to build peace and happiness for all people in all nations.

Thank you so much for letting me be a part of this important day.

Source: Phúc, Kim. Veterans' Day Speech. Vietnam War Memorial, Washington, D.C. Photocopy of typescript. November 11, 1996. Permission of Kim Phúc.

DIANA, PRINCESS OF WALES
(1961–1997)
"This Terrible Legacy of Mines"
London, England
June 12, 1997

In at least 70 nations around the globe, antipersonnel land mines pose a problem for societies long after conflict is over. Years later, land mines turn unsuspecting civilians into "collateral damage." They kill, rip off legs or hands, and leave behind millions of disabled people, many of them children, whom poor nations cannot afford to care for. In many regions, people cannot farm their land because of mines, and refugees cannot return to their homes. Countries with severe problems with land mines include Cambodia, Afghanistan, Angola, Bosnia, Somalia, and Mozambique. Many organizations, including the International Campaign to Ban Land Mines (ICBL), Human Rights Watch, and the International Red Cross have brought pressure to bear on national governments to ban land mines. The Treaty on Conventional Weapons in 1980 tried unsuccessfully to restrict land mine use. Canada led the way in 1997 by adopting the UN's Mine Ban Treaty (or Ottawa Treaty) to ban stockpiling or use of antipersonnel mines. That year, the ICBL won the Nobel Peace Prize. Jody Williams, an American from Vermont, accepted the prize as head of ICBL; in her Nobel address she spoke of land mines having "contaminated the globe in epidemic proportion." Many public personalities have also rallied around a ban, Archbishop Desmond Tutu of South Africa, Queen Noor of Jordan, and Princess Diana of Britain among them. Diana's celebrity drew needed attention to the maimed victims of mines. This speech, made just three months before she died in a car crash on August 31, 1997, describes her visit to Angola. Her influence proved substantial in passing the Mine Ban Treaty. More than 150 nations had signed the treaty by 2007; among the exceptions are the United States, Russia, and China.

❧

I must begin by saying how warmly I welcome this conference on landmines convened by the Mines Advisory Group and the Landmines Survivors' Network. It is so welcome because the world is too little aware of the waste of life, limb and land which anti-personnel landmines are causing among some of the poorest people on earth. Indeed, until my journey to Angola early this year I was largely unaware of it too.

For the mine is a stealthy killer. Long after conflict is ended, its innocent victims die or are wounded singly, in countries of which we hear little. Their lonely fate is never reported. The world, with its many other preoccupations, remains largely unmoved by a death roll of something like 800 people every month—many of them women and children. Those who are not killed outright—and they number another 1,200 a month—suffer terrible injuries and are handicapped for life. I was in Angola in January with the British Red Cross—a country where there are 15 million landmines in a population, Ladies and Gentlemen, of 10 million—with the desire of drawing world attention to this vital, but hitherto largely neglected issue.

Some people chose to interpret my visit as a political statement. But it was not. I am not a political figure. As I said at the time, and I'd like to reiterate now, my interests are humanitarian. That is why I felt drawn to this human tragedy. This is why I wanted to play down my part in working towards a worldwide ban on these weapons.

During my days in Angola, I saw at first hand three aspects of this scourge. In the hospitals of Luanda, the capital, and Huambo, scene of bitter fighting not long ago, I visited some of the mine victims who had survived, and saw their injuries. I am not going to describe them, because in my experience it turns too many people away from the subject. Suffice to say, that when you look at the mangled bodies, some of them children, caught by these mines, you marvel at their survival. What is so cruel about these injuries, is that they are almost invariably suffered where medical resources are scarce.

I observed for myself some of the obstacles to improving medical care in most of these hospitals. Often there is a chronic shortage of medicine, of pain-killers, even of anesthetics. Surgeons constantly engaged in amputating shattered limbs never have all the facilities we would expect to see here. So the human pain that has to be borne is often beyond imagining. This emergency medical care, moreover, is only the first step back to a sort of life. For those whose living is the land, loss of an arm or leg, is an overwhelming handicap which lasts for life. I saw the fine work being done by the Red Cross and other agencies to replace lost limbs. But making prostheses is a costly as well as a complicated business. For example, a young child will need several different fittings as it grows older. Sometimes, the severity of the injury makes the fitting of an artificial limb impossible. There are never enough resources to replace all the limbs that are lost.

As the Red Cross have expressed it: "Each victim who survives, will incur lifetime expenses for surgery and prosthetic care totaling between 2,000 and 3,000 pounds."

That is an intolerable load for a handicapped person in a poor country. That is something to which the world should urgently turn its conscience.

In Angola, one in every 334 members of the population is an amputee! Angola has the highest rate of amputees in the world. How can countries which manufacture and trade in these weapons square their conscience with such human devastation?

My third main experience was to see what has been done, slowly and perilously, to get these mines out of the earth. In the Kuito and Huambo region I spent a morning with our small team from Halo Trust, which is training Angolans to work on the pervasive minefields and supervising their work. I speak of "our team" because men of the Mines Advisory group—or, in this instance, the Halo Trust—who volunteer for this hazardous work are usually former members of our own Services. I take this opportunity to pay my tribute to the work these men do on our behalf—the perils they encounter are not just confined to mines. Two members of the Mines Advisory Group team in Cambodia, Chris Howes and Houn Horth, were kidnapped by the Khmer Rouge a year ago and their fate is uncertain. We can only pray for their safe return.

Much ingenuity has gone into making some of these mines. Many are designed to trap an unwary de-miner. Whenever such tricky mines appear, the de-miner will call in one of the supervising team, who will then take over. That is what keeps their lives perpetually at risk. It might be less hazardous, I reflected, after my visit to Angola, if some of the technical skills used in making mines had been applied to better methods of removing them. Many of these mines are relatively cheap—they can be bought for five pounds apiece, or less. Tracing them, lifting them, and disposing of them, costs far more—sometimes as much as a hundred times more.

Angola is full of refugees returning after a long war. They present another aspect of this tragedy. The refugee turns towards home, often ignorant of conditions in his homeland. He knows of mines, but homeward bound, eagerness to complete the journey gets the better of him. Or he finds mines on what was once his land, and attempts to clear them. There were many examples of that in Angola. These mines inflict most of their casualties on people who are trying to meet the elementary needs of life. They strike the wife, or the grandmother, gathering firewood for cooking. They ambush the child sent to collect water for the family.

I was impressed to see the work being done by many of the world's agencies on "Mine Awareness." If children can be taught at school, if adults can be helped to learn what to do, and what not to do in regions that have been mined, then lives can be saved and injuries reduced.

There are said to be around 110 million mines lurking somewhere in the world—and over a third of them are to be found in Africa! Angola is probably more heavily mined than anywhere else, because the war went on for such a long time, and it invaded so much of the country. So that country is going to be infested with mines, and will suffer many more victims. And this brings me to one of the main conclusions I reached after this experience.

Even if the world decided tomorrow to ban these weapons, this terrible legacy of mines already in the earth would continue to plague the poor nations of the Globe. "The evil that men do, lives after them."

And so, it seems to me, there rests a certain obligation upon the rest of us.

One of my objectives in visiting Angola was to forward the cause of those, like the Red Cross, striving in the name of humanity to secure an international ban on these weapons. Since then, we are glad to see, some real progress has been made. There are signs of a change of heart—at least in some parts of the world. For that we should be cautiously grateful. If an international ban on mines can be secured it means, looking far ahead, that the world may be a safer place for this generation's grandchildren. . . .

The more expeditiously we can end this plague on earth caused by the landmine, the more readily can we set about the constructive tasks to which so many give their hand in the cause of humanity.

Source: Diana, Princess of Wales. "Responding to Land Mines: A Modern Tragedy and Its Solutions." Landmine Survivors Network. Available online. http://www.landminesurvivors.org/news_feature.php?id=38. Accessed December 21, 2007. Permission of Landmine Survivors Network.

BENAZIR BHUTTO
(1953–2007)
"One Billion Muslims Are at the Crossroads"
Cambridge, Massachusetts, United States
November 7, 1997

Benazir Bhutto was born in Karachi, Pakistan, to an active political dynasty. Her father, Zulfikar Ali Bhutto, founded the comparatively liberal—it advocated democracy and supported the rights of women—Pakistan Peoples Party, or PPP, in 1967, and he became president in 1971. He was a secular nationalist who declared Pakistan an Islamic Republic and nationalized private industries, but charges of corruption and murder of a political rival dogged his regime; he was overthrown by a military coup in 1977. Ordered to stand trial for murder by General Muhammad Zia-ul-Haq, the new ruler, Zulfikar Bhutto was sentenced to death and hanged in 1979. Between 1969 and 1977, Benazir Bhutto had been studying at Harvard and Oxford Universities; a powerful speaker, she was president of the elite debating society, the Oxford Union. Although exiled from Pakistan after her father's death, she became the official head of the PPP in 1984. Four years later, after Zia's death, she returned to Pakistan. Her party won a majority in elections, and she was named prime minister. She became prime minister again in 1993, but both times she was removed from office (and her husband tried and imprisoned) under multiple charges of taking kickbacks, money laundering, and bribery. She went into exile in 1998, protesting that the charges were politically motivated. In October 2007 she returned to Pakistan to run for president and contest the repressive policies of President Pervez Musharraf, who had taken power in 1999 in another military coup. But before the elections could take place, she was killed in an attack at a political rally in Rawalpindi on December 27, 2007, blamed by many on Islamic extremists, although some charged Musharraf's government with complicity. Ten years earlier, she had delivered this speech at Harvard University, arguing that Islam was naturally democratic—that it was communism that had driven Muslim states to dictatorships—and offering her experience heading a Muslim state as proof that it is not Islam that makes women second-class citizens.

Our generation stands at the doorway of history. Not only the doorway of a new century, but the doorway of a new millennium. And as we prepare ourselves to meet this new century, this new millennium, I believe we need to clearly understand the challenges that still await us and await the new century.

I believe there are four simultaneous challenges that the world faces today. First, the rise of ethnic and religious hatred, prejudice and intolerance.

Second, the gulf of wealth and health emerging between the developed and developing countries, and within nations themselves.

Third, the growing sense of alienation by the people in a complex and fast-moving world and the ability of their governments to resolve the problem that the new technology era faces.

And fourth, the continuing gender inequity in all societies, west as well as east, that creates social division in the society as we move towards a new century. . . .

This is an era where we see an increasing focus on Islam and the West. The entire world community, and specifically the United States, have a fundamental strategic interest in events in the Muslim world. All across the world, in the Middle East, in Southwest Asia and Southeast Asia and Africa, one billion Muslims are at the crossroads. They must choose between progress and extremism. They must choose between education and ignorance. They must choose between the force of new technologies and

Former Pakistan prime minister Benazir Bhutto returned to Pakistan from exile in October 2007. In this photo, taken on Nov. 10, 2007, six weeks before her assassination, she shouts, "Freedom, freedom!" at a protest against President Pervez Musharraf's suppression of the media. *(AP Photo/Tom Hanson)*

the forces of old repression. Thus, one billion Muslims must choose between the past and the future.

The United States must do everything within its power to ensure that progressive, pluralistic Muslim countries like Pakistan are in a position to serve as role models to the entire Islamic world. And Pakistan is also an important Asian country at the cross-roads to the strategic oil reserves of the Gulf and Central Asia. And to the markets of South Asia and East Asia. In terms of demographics, in terms of production, in terms of consumption, in terms of markets, in terms of an expanding capital-intensive middle class, the Asian continent will surely set the tone, set the pace, and dominate the economic and geopolitical exigencies of the coming era.

I wonder how many people realize that Pakistan is the second largest Muslim state on earth. A state, as I've said, at the crossroads of the oil-rich Gulf and Central Asia. A state, as I've said, at the crossroads to the markets of South Asia and East Asia. A state that can serve as a model of moderation and modality to one billion Muslims across the planet. As a Pakistani, I wish to explore with you today the West's relationship with the Islamic world and the role that we can play to create a civil, political, economic and religious dialogue between the East and the West at this critical moment.

I believe it was only four years ago, when Harvard Professor Samuel Huntington, shocked the world with his provocative essay entitled "The Clash of Civilizations." As a Muslim woman, who had been educated and lived extensively in the United States and the United Kingdom, I was initially taken aback by the negative conclusion and the specter of inevitable conflict that he outlined. I particularly disagreed with Professor Huntington's unshakable pessimism about the emerging clash between the West and an increasingly self-confident and economically independent Islamic world.

But, four years later, my assessment of Professor Huntington's thesis has moderated. At the very least, I believe that his article has served a very useful purpose in bringing to the forefront of intellectual opinion significant issues that do warrant exploration, that do warrant debate. For whether we like it or not, whether it must be so or not, the world seems to be increasingly looking at the values and mores of the West and the values and traditions of Islam as mutually exclusive and confrontational.

Let's explore some of these issues today. The world is certainly a different place now than it was just ten short years ago. At that point, the nuclear threat was omnipresent. The Cold War raged on between the West and the Soviet bloc, reaching a boiling point in the battle for the self-determination of Afghanistan. It was the alliance between the West and the Islamic world, through the fifties and the sixties, through the seventies and the eighties, that was central to the containment of communism on the Asian continent. For communism, Afghanistan became an overheated pressure cooker that manifested the inevitable doom of a system that could not realistically address its people's political and economic needs.

Muslim resistance to the Soviets in Afghanistan proved once and for all that the Soviet Union could not, with all its military might, suppress the forces of history and the forces of justice. Afghanistan proved that might does not make right. It was the victory of the Mujahideen, the Islamic freedom fighters supported by the Western Muslim Alliance, that proved to extinguish the fading embers of a dying system. This alliance, that of the Western Muslim Alliance, broke the back of the Soviet Union. It was our joint stand against the Soviet occupiers of Afghanistan that secured for all mankind the final victory of democracy and market-based economics.

I remember vividly my own feelings on February 15, 1989, when, as Prime Minister of Pakistan, I celebrated the final withdrawal of Soviet forces from our frontiers in Afghanistan. Little did I realize at that glorious moment that the victory in Afghanistan would be a catalyst to a curious consequence. The West's interest in, indeed need for, alliance with the Islamic world has steadily deteriorated over the last eight years. Interdependence during the Cold War period gave way to indifference in the post Cold War period. Indifference has now, in many ways, been replaced with apprehension.

There are some in the West who would like to think of Muslims as terrorists and fanatics. I would like to assure you that Muslims are neither. Muslims, on the other hand, who benefited from economic and military assistance from the West for a half a century, are bewildered by the sudden turn of events where aid has totally ceased with the end of the communist threat. Muslims who consider themselves allies of the West do not comprehend the distancing of the West. For instance, a country like Pakistan was receiving $4.6 billion of military and economic assistance from the United States. . . . Suddenly, the aid dried up. And it coincided with the resurgence of democracy. And, instead of being better off, people were worse off, because now we had less resources and less income. And many could not understand why, at a time when the old resources were diminishing, the West was beginning to perceive the Muslims with a certain degree of apprehension. Because Islam is a religion that sanctifies Abraham, Moses and Jesus as prophets, it was even more bewildering for Muslims to find that the West suddenly was suspicious of them. And Islam is, in fact, an integral part of the Judeo-Christian civilization. So, being an integral part of the Judeo-Christian civilization, it was a sudden shock for Muslims to find that the world was being perceived as being two blocs: that is, the West and Islam. . . .

While many in the West believe that there is no place for democracy in Islam, given the few number of democratic Muslim states, Muslims, on the other hand, believe that democracy is inherent in our faith. In Islam, dictatorship is never condoned. Dictatorship is considered a usurpation of the power of the people. Muslims are exalted to fight tyranny wherever they see it; and indeed, Muslims are told that if you do not have the strength to fight tyranny when you see it, go into exile. But do not stand silent in the face of tyranny. For to be silent in the face of tyranny is to condone tyranny.

There are four democratic principles at the heart of Islam. The first is consultation, or Shura; then, consensus, or Ijma; and finally independent judgment, or Ijdaha. Instead of Islam being incompatible with democracy, our holy book makes it clear that the principle operations of the democratic process—consultation between the elected officials and the people, accountability of leaders to the people they serve—are fundamental to Islam. The holy book says that Islamic society is contingent on mutual advice, through mutual discussions, on an equal footing. Let me repeat that now: Equal footing. Ladies and gentleman, the Holy Koran is as committed to equality as it is to democracy. As committed to pluralism and tolerance as it is to order and doctrine. I know this is inconsistent with Western stereotypes. But, nevertheless, it is true. Consultation under the Holy Koran demands that public decisions are made by representative personalities. By men and by women who enjoy the confidence of the people and the integrity of their own character. . . . Islamic law rests on the consent of and the consultation with the people as fundamentally as British Parliamentary democracy or American separation of powers is founded on the people's will.

Western political scientists, these days, hypothesize populist strategies to create more effective forms of participatory democracy. But Muslims do not believe they have to go back to the drawing board to conceptualize democratic order. It is right there in the holy book. Under Islam, we do not have to create a sense of community and individual responsibility. It is there in the holy book itself. Enlightened Muslims find Western lectures on democracy condescending. Muslims need the West to acknowledge that dictatorship came about because of the strategic need to contain communism. Dictatorship did not come about because it was a part of Muslim faith or culture.

That is why, for decades, not only Muslim Asia but Spain and Portugal were governed by Fascism. Greece was ruled by military Junta. Argentina, Brazil, Paraguay, and Chile faced social and political repression. On October 21, 1997, in a lecture in Cyprus, Professor Huntington ruefully noted that non-democratic regimes, more often than not, were pro-American. The future of democracy in the post-Cold War world will remain contingent on the strategic interests of Pax Americana. The strategic interests have changed. They are no longer of an ideological nature. They are of an economic nature. Market politics, global trade and energy reserves remain the strategic interests of the West in the new political era in the post-Cold War period.

There is much that Islam and the West can do together to build a new economic and social order, as we approach the new millennium. But, the twenty-first century must be a century of moral universality, not selectivity. It is time for the West to understand that colonialism and exploitation, both of a material and spiritual kind, are over. It is also time for the Islamic world to begin to rely on ourselves and each other to address the lingering problems of the twentieth century and the unlimited opportunities of the twenty-first century. . . .

And we Muslims must live by the true spirit of Islam. Not just by its rituals. To those who would claim to speak for Islam, but would deny to our women a place in society, I say the ethos of Islam is equality. Equality between the sexes. There is no religion that, in its writings and its teachings, is more respectful for the role of women in society than Islam.

To those in the West who would condemn Islam for being anti-women, let me as the first Muslim woman elected Prime Minister of her country recall that three Muslim countries—Pakistan, Bangladesh, and Turkey—have all had democratically elected women as head of their government. In other words, my friends, there is much that we can learn from each other. Islam and the West; the West and Islam, as we cross into a new century and into a new millennium.

There are many problems that we confront simultaneously. The Islamic extremists who burn books and keep young women in purdha are really not that different from the Christian fundamentalists who attack clinics in America or the Jewish extremists who massacre worshippers in Hebron. So, let us decide to cast aside myths and stereotypes about each other. For Islam and for the West, it is time to attack the common and real enemies of our respective societies. These enemies are not people; they are ignorance and hatred. These enemies are not ethnic minorities; they are starvation and intolerance. Myopia and prejudice, whether it be religious, political, ethnic, gender or intellectual, are the common enemies of our hope for the twenty-first century. They are the fuel of the clash of civilization. . . .

In less than 800 days we will witness, for only the third time in recorded history, the momentous turning of the millennium. Where and what will we be at that extraordinary moment, when the huge ball drops and the year 2000 lights up the sky? Will we be prisoners of the mindset of the past? Or, will we be liberated to the endless possibilities of an historic future?

Source: Bhutto, Benazir. "Speech to the John F. Kennedy School of Government." Gifts of Speech, Sweet Briar College. Available online. http://gos.sbc.edu/b/bhutto2.html. Accessed January 18, 2008. Permission of the John F. Kennedy School of Government, Harvard University.

CRAIG KIELBURGER
(1982–)
"Free the Children"
Toronto, Canada
November 28, 1997

At age 12, Craig Kielburger attracted global attention when he first addressed the annual convention of the Ontario Federation of Labor. He had discovered in the *Toronto Star* the story of Iqbal Masih, a young boy in Pakistan who had worked long hours in a carpet factory since he was sold into bonded labor at four years old. Iqbal had escaped. With the help of an activist labor group in Pakistan, he was giving speeches against child labor and aiding other children in freeing themselves from bonded labor when he was killed by unknown assassins. He was 12 years old. Indelibly impressed with Iqbal's story, Kielburger founded Free The Children with 11 young Canadian friends in his hometown of Thornhill, Canada. Within minutes of addressing the Ontario labor convention-goers, he raised $130,000 for a program to help children in India freed from forced labor. Two years later, at 14, Kielburger returned to the same hall to address the 1997 convention. The young children's rights activist reported on his travels to India, Brazil, and Thailand, and on success in making child labor an issue for national governments. School-building has been an important part of Free The Children's work—450 new schools have been the result. By 2005, Free The Children had one million child participants in 45 countries, and in many places brought about government action on the neglected issue of child labor. Kielburger obtained a degree in peace and conflict studies from the University of Toronto, and he continues to lead Free The Children. Even in the year 2002, the UN International Labor Organization estimated that 250 million of the world's children ages five to 14 years old were working.

Two years ago I stood before you and I told you the story of a young boy from Pakistan named Iqbal Masi, who at the age of four was sold into bondage. Now, I was a lot shorter then; in fact I was almost a foot shorter, and I remember I had to use a stool just to reach the microphones. And my voice was a few octaves higher. But that day something magical happened in this very room, because that day your desire and your spirit to help working and abused children made news around the world. . . .

In the past two years I've had the opportunity to travel to many countries throughout this world and to meet many children who are suffering. I've met children living on the streets of some of the world's largest cities, sleeping on cement, in the gutters, and in the cold. I've met children in Haiti sold as domestic servants as young as five and six years old, where they often face physical and sexual abuse. [In India] I've accompanied freed children, after raids on their carpet factories, back to their homes. And as we rode in the cars, they clapped their hands and chanted, "We are free, we are free!" And one boy who I'll never forget was Megashir. He showed me the scars which ran all down his body—his hands, his arms, his legs, even his throat—where he had been branded with red hot irons when he helped his youngest brother escape from bondage.

In Brazil, I've gone into the sugar cane fields and met children who wield the huge machetes, razor sharp, in order to cut the sugar cane which ends up on our tables—in our sugar bowls and in our breakfast cereals—every morning. And in the Philippines I've met with children who live and work in garbage dumps, scrambling to survive as they compete with maggots and rats for their daily meal. I've even walked the streets of Patpong, a notorious red light district in Bangkok, Thailand, with an undercover police officer who was offered, in my presence, an eight-year-old boy for his sexual pleasure.

These are children. They are all children.

And I've also learned that it is not only in Third World countries where children are suffering. Even here in Canada, a country which has been named by the United Nations as one of the best places in the world to live, . . . 40% of those who use food banks are under the age of 18, and 25% of Canadian homeless are children.

Two years ago your support and generosity breathed life into Free the Children. Your moral support gave us strength. We knew we were doing the right thing. We knew the time had come for a children's organization to work and to speak on behalf of children. . . . We've grown from a fledgling youth group with only ten boys and girls in Thornhill, Ontario, to an international youth movement with young people around the world. We have groups not only in Canada and the United States, but also in Australia, in Europe, in South America, in Singapore—young people who are standing up to end the abuse and to end the exploitation of children, and who are standing up to give other youth a voice on issues which affect them.

Craig Kielburger, child activist founder of the children's labor organization Free The Children, addresses a news conference in February 1996 in Ottawa, Canada. He was 13 at the time. *(AP Photo/Tom Hanson)*

And over the past two years we've tried to make child labor an issue which politicians can no longer ignore. Because since the age of Charles Dickens and Oliver Twist, politicians have been saying child labor is a necessary evil. But what they have not told you is that their governments spend, on average, thirty times more on the military than on primary education. These governments should be building schools, not army tanks. And we simply do not believe, we simply do not believe, that the adults of this world can put a man on the moon or invent a nuclear bomb, but they cannot feed and protect the world's children. We simply do not believe it.

And that is why we have been encouraging other young people to write letters to world leaders and to multinational corporations to demand that they put the protection of children as a priority. In Fort McMurray, Alberta, Alicia Laureson, a 12-year-old member of Free the Children, convinced her school board and city council to pass a resolution stating that they will not buy sporting equipment such as soccer balls, or other items, made by the exploitation of children. . . .

I've come here to tell you that change is coming about. Child labor has become one of the most talked-about issues, not only in Canada but around the world. South Asian governments recently met together and they promised by the year 2000 to eliminate the most exploitive forms of child labor, and by 2010 eliminate all child labor. The Pakistani government announced they will be raising the amount they spend on primary education from 1% now to 3% of their national budget, and they will be building over 1,000 literacy centers. Brazil has now introduced a labeling system, and they have labeled 500 products "child labor free.". . . Last month I returned to the same [sugar cane] plantation and children came up to me waving their arms and saying "Remember me?" They said, "We now go to school.". . .

There is still much work that has to be done. We realize that often children are working because they are poor and they are helping their families survive. We are opening two schools in rural India to help take children out of the dangerous fireworks factories and gem-cutting industry. Because these families are so poor, we are buying 40 cows and milking animals to give to these families so they can earn alternate sources of income while they are sending their children to school. While in Kenya, I visited schools which did not have the most basic of supplies . . . And so upon my return to Canada, we've organized schools in Ontario to collect school supplies for these children, because education is the most important way to break the cycle of poverty.

Free the Children now has two main goals. Our first goal is to free children from abuse and exploitation. And our second goal is to train youth leaders to free children from the idea that they are powerless, that we have no role to play in today's society, that we cannot become involved in social issues . . .

Through my travels I've had the opportunity to meet many street children. And with street children, loyalty is everything—because they don't have much in the name of material possessions, but they do have their friends. And if a street child in India is crippled or has no legs, his friends will carry him place to place. Or if you hand an orange to a street girl in Brazil, she will automatically take that orange, peel it, break it, and divide it among her friends. There is no question about the matter.

And over the past two years, the Ontario Federation of Labor has been loyal to us, and for that we thank you. We want you to know that we count you among our very best friends. And we thank you for not only believing in us, but for believing in young people across Canada and around the world. And we hope that we can continue to walk side by side in the journey to making this world a better place, a place where all children have the same rights, the same opportunities, and have a greater hope for the future.

Source: Kielburger, Craig. Address. Ontario Federation of Labor Conference 1997. VHS videocassette tape. 28 November 1997. Courtesy of Free The Children, www.freethechildren. com.

BORIS YELTSIN
(1931–2007)
Apology for the Murder of the Romanovs
St. Petersburg, Russia
July 17, 1998

Russian czar Nicholas II, the last of the Romanov emperors, was forced to abdicate in 1917 in the early days of the Russian Revolution. A year after his abdication, fearful that the czar might escape and return to the throne, the revolutionary council in Yekaterinburg ordered the murder of Nicholas along with his wife Alexandra, their five children, and four servants. Their bodies were secretly buried in a forest near the site of their massacre. Eighty years later to the day, in what became a moment of national repentance for abuses during the Soviet era, the recovered bones were moved to St. Petersburg, the traditional burial place of the czars. (The bodies of two children were not found at that time, but in 2007 anthropologists announced they had found the children's remains.) At the funeral service in St. Peter and Paul Cathedral, Russian president Boris Yeltsin spoke before the nine small coffins. Before he became president, Yeltsin was a high-ranking Communist Party officer in and out of favor with the party and Mikhail Gorbachev, the party general secretary. Although he had a conspicuous problem with alcoholism, Yeltsin was popular with the public and was elected the first president of the Russian Federation in 1991. That same year a coup was attempted against Gorbachev, president of the Soviet Union, and Yeltsin rushed to Moscow to defend him. At the year's end, Yeltsin closed down the Communist Party within Russia, helped force out Gorbachev, peacefully dissolved the Soviet Union, and became head of the country. Yeltsin's attempts at the difficult transition to a free market economy suffered, as prices rose and the country experienced severe corruption and a widespread economic downturn. He resigned his office in 1999 to Vladimir Putin.

Today is an historic day for Russia. Eighty years have passed since the murder of the last Russian emperor and his family.

For many years we were silent about this terrible crime, but the truth must be told. The massacre in Yekaterinburg has become one of the most shameful pages in our history. By burying the remains of the innocent victims, we want to atone for the sins of our ancestors. Those who committed this crime are guilty, as well as those who justified it for decades. We are all guilty.

We cannot lie to ourselves by justifying this senseless cruelty on political grounds. The execution of the Romanov family was the result of an irreconcilable split in Russian society between "us" and "them." The results are felt even now.

Burying the remains of the victims is an act of human justice, a symbol of unity, and atonement for common guilt. Before the historical memory of the nation, we all have responsibilities, and that is why I could not fail to come here today. I must be here, as a human being and as president.

I bow my head before the victims of the merciless killing.

While building a new Russia we must rely on historical experience. Many glorious pages of our country's history are linked with the Romanovs. But with this name is connected one of its bitterest lessons—that attempts to change life by violence are doomed to failure.

We must end this century, which for Russia became a century of blood and lawlessness, with repentance and reconciliation, regardless of political views, religion, or ethnic origin. This is our historic chance. On the threshold of the third millennium, we must do this for those living now and the generations to come.

Let us remember those who became innocent victims of hatred and violence. May they rest in peace.

Source: Yeltsin, Boris. "Yeltsin's Speech at Burial." Associated Press, trans. Center for Defense Information. Available online. http://www.cdi.org/russia/johnson/2270.html##2. Accessed December 20, 2007.

NKOSI JOHNSON

(1989–2001)

At the 13th International AIDS Conference

Durban, South Africa

July 9, 2000

Although AIDS (Acquired Immune Deficiency Syndrome) was first identified in France and the United States in the early 1980s, the epidemic began in Africa in the mid-20th century. HIV, the virus causing AIDS, had crossed into humans from wild chimpanzees. In some areas of sub-Saharan Africa, such as South Africa, the epidemic exploded; large segments of the population became infected. Mother-to-child transmission at birth was discovered to be an unfortunate source of new victims. As researchers in the United States developed anti-retroviral AIDS drugs (such as AZT), they found that the drugs could drastically reduce the number of babies acquiring AIDS from their mothers. Although South African doctors approved the new drugs, President Thabo Mbeki of South Africa (1999–   ) would not agree to a national drug treatment program, not even for pregnant women. Mbeki was a former member of the South African Communist Party; he had a lingering mistrust of the West and allowed himself to be influenced by a fringe element among researchers who claimed HIV did not cause AIDS. He promoted herbal remedies and poverty-reduction to treat the disease, while South Africa developed the world's highest per capita number of AIDS sufferers. As the 13th International Conference on AIDS opened in Durban, anger swelled against Mbeki's policies. Immediately after Mbeki addressed the conference, 11-year-old Nkosi Johnson took the platform. He described his own struggle with the disease and called for drug treatment for pregnant women. His speech, which he wrote himself, was broadcast around the globe, and the young boy was widely cheered for his bravery and good sense. Nkosi had been born HIV-positive in a Johannesburg suburb in 1989. Because his mother was dying of AIDS, the care center's director, Gail Johnson, had adopted him. Nkosi lived only another year after his address.

We are all the same! —*Nkosi Johnson*

Hi, my name is Nkosi Johnson. I live in Melville, Johannesburg, South Africa. I am 11 years old and I have full-blown AIDS. I was born HIV-positive.

When I was two years old, I was living in a care centre for HIV/AIDS-infected people. My mommy was obviously also infected and could not afford to keep me because she was very scared that the community she lived in would find out that we were both infected and chase us away.

I know she loved me very much and would visit me when she could. And then the care centre had to close down because they didn't have any funds. So my foster mother, Gail Johnson, who was a director of the care centre and had taken me home for weekends, said at a board meeting she would take me home. She took me home with her and I have been living with her for eight years now.

She has taught me all about being infected and how I must be careful with my blood. If I fall and cut myself and bleed, then I must make sure that I cover my own wound and go to an adult to help me clean it and put a plaster on it. I know that my blood is only dangerous to other people if they also have an open wound and my blood goes into it. That is the only time that people need to be careful when touching me.

In 1997 mommy Gail went to the school, Melpark Primary, and she had to fill in a form for my admission and it said "does your child suffer from anything" so she said "yes, AIDS."

Nkosi Johnson—at 11 years old likely the youngest prominent AIDS activist—takes the microphone to address the 13th International AIDS Conference in Durban, South Africa. *(AP Photo/Themba Hadebe)*

My mommy Gail and I have always been open about me having AIDS. And then my mommy Gail was waiting to hear if I was admitted to school. Then she phoned the school, who said "we will call you" and then they had a meeting about me. Of the parents and the teachers at the meeting 50% said "yes" and 50% said "no.". . .

The media found out that there was a problem about me going to school. No one seemed to know what to do with me because I am infected. The AIDS workshops were done at the school for parents and teachers to teach them not to be scared of a child with AIDS. I am very proud to say that there is now a policy for all HIV-infected children to be allowed to go into schools and not be discriminated against.

And in the same year, just before I started school, my mommy Daphne died. She went on holiday to Newcastle—she died in her sleep. And mommy Gail got a phone call and I answered and my aunty said, "please can I speak to Gail?"

Mommy Gail told me almost immediately my mommy had died and I burst into tears. My mommy Gail took me to my mommy's funeral. I saw my mommy in the coffin and I saw her eyes were closed and then I saw them lowering it into the ground and then they covered her up. My granny was very sad that her daughter had died. . . .

I hate having AIDS because I get very sick and I get very sad when I think of all the other children and babies that are sick with AIDS.

I just wish that the government can start giving AZT to pregnant HIV mothers to help stop the virus being passed on to their babies. Babies are dying very quickly and I know one little abandoned baby who came to stay with us and his name was Micky. He couldn't breathe, he couldn't eat and he was so sick and mommy Gail had to phone welfare to have him admitted to a hospital and he died. But he was such a cute little baby and I think the government must start doing it because I don't want babies to die.

Because I was separated from my mother at an early age, because we were both HIV positive, my mommy Gail and I have always wanted to start a care centre for HIV/AIDS mothers and their children. I am very happy and proud to say that the first Nkosi's Haven was opened last year. And we look after 10 mommies and 15 children.

My mommy Gail and I want to open five Nkosi's Havens by the end of next year because I want more infected mothers to stay together with their children—they mustn't be separated from their children so they can be together and live longer with the love that they need.

When I grow up, I want to lecture to more and more people about AIDS, and if mommy Gail will let me, around the whole country. I want people to understand about AIDS, to be careful and respect AIDS—you can't get AIDS if you touch, hug, kiss, hold hands with someone who is infected.

Care for us and accept us—we are all human beings. We are normal. We have hands. We have feet. We can walk, we can talk, we have needs just like everyone else. Don't be afraid of us—we are all the same!

Source: Johnson, Nkosi. "Nkosi's Speech." Nkosi Johnson AIDS Foundation. Available online. http://www.nkosi.iafrica.com/contentPage.asp?pageID=7. Accessed December 20, 2007. Permission of Gail Johnson.

VOJISLAV KOŠTUNICA
(1944–   )
"Dear Liberated Serbia!"
Belgrade, Yugoslavia
October 5, 2000

The Socialist Federal Republic of Yugoslavia (SFRY) succeeded the Kingdom of Yugoslavia in 1943; it included Bosnia-Herzegovina, Serbia, Croatia, Macedonia, Montenegro, and Slovenia. During bloody independence wars between 1991 and 2001, the republic disintegrated into its several parts while the horror of genocide and ethnic cleansing directed at national and religious minorities filled the television news. The North Atlantic Treaty Organization (NATO) eventually intervened in 1995 to stop the conflict, first in Bosnia and then in Kosovo (a part of Serbia), but it was unable to prevent the movement of millions of refugees displaced among the new republics. In 1992 the Federal Republic of Yugoslavia (FRY) was formed from Serbia and Montenegro, with ex-communist Slobodan Milošević as president. In Yugoslavia (FRY), Vojislav Koštunica was a lawyer and politician who had earlier run afoul of the communist Yugoslav (SFRY) government for criticizing the policies of President Marshal

Tito (1945–80). Koštunica had never belonged to the Communist Party, and he was not allied with President Milošević. As the first free elections loomed, parties in opposition to Milošević threw their weight behind Koštunica and he won the September 2000 election for president of Yugoslavia (FRY). Milošević refused to acknowledge his loss to Koštunica, and he called for a new election. The country erupted in strikes and violence. On October 5 the parliament building was stormed, and Koštunica installed in office. That night he spoke warmly and passionately to the hundreds of thousands who filled Belgrade's city center to cheer his election. Chants of "Victory!" and "Arrest Slobo!" punctuated his speech. At the mention of Milošević, the boos were deafening. The next year Milošević was extradited to the Hague Tribunal for prosecution of genocide and crimes against humanity. In 2003 Yugoslavia (FRY) broke into Serbia and Montenegro, and Koštunica became prime minister of Serbia.

Dear, liberated Serbia! Belgrade! Belgrade is Serbia today, not Serbia in miniature but a big Serbia. Our great and beautiful Serbia has risen to get rid of one man, Slobodan Milošević. Serbia is at a standstill until one man leaves. When he leaves, Serbia will be on the move again, the Serbs will be on the move again.

But Serbia is not using violence to force him out as he has been claiming and pushing our people for years; we are forcing him out because he has lost the elections.

And for this reason, because of your vote at the elections on 24th September, I am very proud. I am proud that I am a citizen of Serbia and Yugoslavia, I am proud that I belong to our sacred church, I am proud because you have placed your trust in me.

Of course, I am proud that you have elected me President of the Federal Republic of Yugoslavia!

I feel like the president, I am the president thanks to your votes, thanks to the basic rule of democracy: the people decide, a majority of people decide.

This is what happened at the 24th September elections. The entire population of Serbia and I took part in these elections with one word on our lips, the most commonly heard word at all our rallies, the word I have repeated numerous times from Kosovska Mitrovica to Subotica and that word is peace, peace between us, peace between Serbia, Yugoslavia and the entire world, peace between Serbia and Montenegro.

But there is a man who has for years been sowing discord, disquiet, fear, who has been installing fear, insecurity into people, a man who has dragged Serbia into unnec-

Vojislav Koštunica is surrounded by the press during Serbia's contentious elections on September 24, 2000. When President Slobodan Milošević refused to acknowledge the results giving Koštunica the presidency, citizens took to the streets to install Koštunica in office. *(AP Photo/Darko Vojinovic)*

essary wars and now wants to wage a war against with his own people just because he lost the elections.

But I am asking you who stole these elections, who violated the constitution, who amended the constitution like a bandit, who has provoked conflict with Montenegro, who wanted elections if not Slobodan Milošević.

He wanted the elections, so let him have them. He set the rules for these elections. He lies to the people, he gives the most insulting statements about his own people via his own deceitful TV.

We have said let him chose what he wants, let him chose the rules, let him chose weapons. His weapons are lies and violence, our weapons are truth and non-violence, and that is how we took part in the elections.

But at the same time we said that only until that day, 24th September, you can lie, you can deceive, you can say whatever you like, but from that day our rules apply: Not a single vote can be lost, not a single vote can be stolen. And this is what we have done.

He does not need to be arrested, he put himself under arrest a long time ago, he fled from the people a long time ago, he who does not live among the people, who does not dare to be with the people, who does not know his people, so he has condemned himself to captivity.

We know what freedom is. We have fought for freedom at these elections.

Source: Koštunica, Vojislav. "Dear Liberated Serbia." BBC News. Available online. http://news.bbc.co.uk/2/hi/europe/959312.stm. Accessed December 20, 2007.

JOHN PAUL II
(1920–2005)
Apology for the Sack of Constantinople
Athens, Greece
May 4, 2001

Roman Catholic pope John Paul II was born Karol Jósef Wojtyła in 1920 in the south of Poland. Because the Nazi occupiers of Poland in World War II (1939–45) had closed all higher education to Poles, young Wojtyla had to attend a secret seminary school to become a priest. He became a bishop in 1958 under Poland's communist government, and, in 1978, he was elected pope by the Vatican's papal conclave. He took the name John Paul II. An internationalist in outlook, John Paul traveled widely; for many of his destinations, such as South Korea, Japan, and England, he was the first pope ever to visit. His appearances sometimes drew crowds of several million people. Synagogues and Islamic mosques hosted him; he was credited with doing much to improve Catholicism's relationships with other faiths. He also attempted to heal divisions within Christianity. As a part of his vigorous schedule, he journeyed in 1999 to Romania to meet the patriarch of the Eastern Orthodox Church, which broke from the Roman church in 1054 in the Great Schism. Similarly, he visited Athens in 2001, where he met with Archbishop Christodoulos of the Greek Orthodox Church. With clerics of both divisions of Christianity looking on, he delivered a long-awaited apology for the sacking of Constantinople 800 years earlier. This event in 1204 was the climax of the disastrous Fourth Crusade, which sailed from Venice in 1202 to reclaim Jerusalem from Muslim rule, but which never reached the Holy Land. Instead, the crusaders were persuaded by Alexius IV, exiled heir to the Byzantine throne, to help install him as emperor in Constantinople. On the failure of that scheme, they stripped the city of its treasures, installed Latin (Roman Catholic) priests in place of Orthodox, and one of their nobles, Baldwin I, as emperor.

I wish first of all to express to you the affection and regard of the Church of Rome. Together we share the apostolic faith in Jesus Christ as Lord and Savior; we have in common the apostolic heritage and the sacramental bond of Baptism; and therefore we are all members of God's family, called to serve the one Lord and to proclaim his Gospel to the world. The Second Vatican Council called on Catholics to regard the members of the other Churches "as brothers and sisters in the Lord," and this supernatural bond of brotherhood between the Church of Rome and the Church of Greece is strong and abiding.

Certainly, we are burdened by past and present controversies and by enduring misunderstandings. But in a spirit of mutual charity these can and must be overcome, for that is what the Lord asks of us. Clearly there is a need for a liberating process of purification of memory. For the occasions past and present, when sons and daughters of the Catholic Church have sinned by action or omission against their Orthodox brothers and sisters, may the Lord grant us the forgiveness we beg of him.

Some memories are especially painful, and some events of the distant past have left deep wounds in the minds and hearts of people to this day. I am thinking of the disastrous sack of the imperial city of Constantinople, which was for so long the bastion of Christianity in the East. It is tragic that the assailants, who had set out to secure free access for Christians to the Holy Land, turned against their own brothers in the faith. The fact that they were Latin Christians fills Catholics with deep regret. How can we fail to see here the inexplicable wickedness at work in the human heart? To God alone belongs judgment, and therefore we entrust the heavy burden of the past to his endless mercy, imploring him to heal the wounds which still cause suffering to the spirit of the Greek people. Together we must work for this healing if the Europe now emerging is to be true to its identity, which is inseparable from the Christian humanism shared by East and West.

At this meeting, I also wish to assure Your Beatitude that the Church of Rome looks with unaffected admiration to the Orthodox Church of Greece for the way in which she has preserved her heritage of faith and Christian life. The name of Greece resounds wherever the Gospel is preached. The names of her cities are known to Christians everywhere from the reading of the Acts of the Apostles and the Letters of Saint Paul. From the Apostolic era until now, the Orthodox Church of Greece has been a rich source from which the Church of the West too has drawn for her liturgy, spirituality and jurisprudence. A patrimony of the whole Church are the Fathers, privileged interpreters of the apostolic tradition, and the Councils, whose teachings are a binding element of all Christian faith. The universal Church can never forget what Greek Christianity has given her, nor cease to give thanks for the enduring influence of the Greek tradition. . . .

Finally, Your Beatitude, I wish to express the hope that we may walk together in the ways of the Kingdom of God. In 1965, the Ecumenical Patriarch Athenagoras and Pope Paul VI by a mutual act removed and cancelled from the Church's memory and life the sentence of excommunication between Rome and Constantinople. This historic gesture stands as a summons for us to work ever more fervently for the unity which is Christ's will. Division between Christians is a sin before God and a scandal before the world. It is a hindrance to the spread of the Gospel, because it makes our proclamation less credible. The Catholic Church is convinced that she must do all in her power to "prepare the way of the Lord" and to "make straight his paths;" and she understands that this must be done in company with other Christians—in fraternal dialogue, in cooperation and in prayer. . . .

In a spirit of fraternal charity and lively hope, I wish to assure you that the Catholic Church is irrevocably committed to the path of unity with all the Churches. Only in this way will the one People of God shine forth in the world as the sign and instrument of intimate union with God and of the unity of the entire human race.

Source: John Paul II. "Address to Holy Synod." *L'Osservatore Romano,* Weekly Edition in English. No. 19, May 9, 2001, pp. 3, 5. Reprinted courtesy L'Osservatore Romano, Weekly Edition in English, May 9, 2001.

JEAN CHRÉTIEN

(1934–   )

"With the United States Every Step of the Way"

Ottawa, Canada
September 14, 2001

On September 11, 2001, 19 Islamist terrorists sent by al-Qaeda founder Osama bin Laden simultaneously hijacked four passenger jets in the United States on long-planned suicide missions. They flew one plane into each of the two towers of the World Trade Center in New York City, and one into the Pentagon in Arlington, Virginia, near Washington, D.C. The fourth jet crashed in rural Shanksville, Pennsylvania, as the passengers struggled to prevent the terrorists from completing their mission (unknown to the passengers, the hijackers' destination was the U.S. Capitol in Washington, D.C.). In New York, the twin 110-story office towers burned and fell within two hours, killing 2,603 people, including more than 300 firemen. The skyscrapers' collapse caused massive destruction in lower Manhattan. In the Pentagon, 125 people died in the impact and fire. Altogether, 246 passengers on the four airplanes, not including the hijackers, were killed. Al-Qaeda's nearly 3,000 victims were largely civilians, and from more than 90 different countries. It was not immediately clear who had directed the attacks, and out of fear that more might follow, air traffic across the country was shut down for days, causing widespread chaos. Canada also shut down its airspace to permit flights to the United States that were still in the air to land, and the nation accommodated 44,000 stranded passengers, many of whom were made welcome in Canadian homes. The United Nations met to condemn the attacks, and from around the world messages of condolence flowed to the United States. Canadian prime minister Jean Chrétien (1993–2003) declared a national day of mourning, and addressed the U.S. ambassador, Paul Cellucci, at an outdoor ceremony on Parliament Hill attended by more than 100,000 people. Canada lost 24 citizens in the tragedy.

❧

Mr. Ambassador, you have assembled before you, here on Parliament Hill and right across Canada, a people united in outrage, in grief, in compassion, and in resolve. A people of every faith and nationality to be found on earth.

A people who, as a result of the atrocity committed against the United States on September 11, 2001, feel not only like neighbors, but like family.

At a time like this, words fail us. We reel before the blunt and terrible reality of the evil we have just witnessed. We cannot stop the tears of grief. We cannot bring back lost wives and husbands. Sons and daughters. American citizens, Canadian citizens, citizens from all over the world. We cannot restore futures that have been cut terribly short.

At a time like this, the only saving grace is our common humanity and decency. At a time like this, it is our feelings, our prayers and our actions that count.

By their outpouring of concern, sympathy and help, the feelings and actions of Canadians have been clear. And, even as we grieve our own losses, the message they send to the American people is equally clear.

Do not despair. You are not alone. We are with you. The whole world is with you.

The great Martin Luther King, in describing times of trial and tribulation, once said that, "In the end, it is not the words of your enemies that you remember, it is the silence of your friends." Mr. Ambassador, as your fellow Americans grieve and rebuild, there will be no silence from Canada.

Our friendship has no limit. Generation after generation, we have traveled many difficult miles together. Side by side, we have lived through many dark times. Always

RHETORICAL DEVICE

Rule of three: Using three examples, or three clauses, three statements, and so on, is a time-honored way to provide balance that hearers will recognize.

Our Union is now complete; our constitution composed, established, and approved. —*Samuel Adams*

Why should you take by force that from us which you can have by love? Why should you destroy us, who have provided you with food? What can you get by war? —*Powhatan*

Mr. Ambassador, we will be with the United States every step of the way. As friends. As neighbors. As family. —*Jean Chrétien*

firm in our shared resolve to vanquish any threat to freedom and justice. And together, with our allies, we will defy and defeat the threat that terrorism poses to all civilized nations.

Mr. Ambassador, we will be with the United States every step of the way. As friends. As neighbors. As family.

Source: Chrétien, Jean. "On the Occasion of the National Day of Mourning." Office of the Prime Minister of Canada. Available online. http://epe.lac-bac.gc.ca/100/205/301/ prime_minister-ef/jean_chretien/2003-12-08/stagingpm_3a8080/newsroom.asp@ language=e&page=newsroom.htm. Accessed December 22, 2007. Address by Prime Minister Jean Chrétien on the occasion of the National Day of Mourning in Canada in memory of the victims of the terrorist attacks in the United States, September 14, 2001. Reproduced with the permission of the Minister of Public Works and Government Services Canada, and courtesy of the Privy Council Office, 2008.

JOHANNES RAU
(1931–2006)
"America Does Not Stand Alone"
Berlin, Germany
September 14, 2001

One day after al-Qaeda mastermind Osama bin Laden's lethal terrorist attacks against the United States on September 11, 2001, the North Atlantic Treaty Organization (NATO) met in Brussels, Belgium, to declare solidarity with the United States. The 19 member states invoked Article 5, which declares that an attack against one member country is an attack against all. They devised Operation Eagle Assist, in which 13 NATO countries would send aircraft to patrol the United States for almost eight months. The European Union proclaimed September 14 a day of mourning, and many countries observed a three-minute silence at noon to express sympathy for the nearly 3,000 dead. In Germany, Chancellor Gerhard Schröder (1998–2005) announced that Germany, a NATO member, would provide assistance to the United States. At the Bundestag (German parliament), Majority Leader Peter Struck declared, "Today we are all Americans." Speaking at a demonstration of support at the Brandenburg Gate in Berlin, German president Johannes Rau (1999–2004) quoted U.S. president John F. Kennedy's statement of friendship in his 1961 inaugural address (*SEE* Kennedy's speech, page 448). Rau recalled American support for Berlin—a free market Western city located deep within communist East Germany—during the cold war (1947–91). With assistance from Britain, the United States had airlifted food, medicine, and supplies, even heating coal, into West Berlin for eight months during the Soviet Union's blockade of 1948–49. During some weeks more than 1,000 airplanes arrived per day, totaling over a quarter million flights. The Berlin Airlift was most famous for bringing candy to Berlin's children.

No one knows better than the people of Berlin what America has done for freedom and democracy in Germany. We would not be able to stand here at the Brandenburg Gate this evening had America not supported us over many years and in difficult times.

Thus today from Berlin we say to all Americans: America does not stand alone. The whole world stands at this time at the side of the great American nation. The German people stands at the side of the American people. We are bound by friendship, we are bound by the same values, we are bound by our love of freedom.

Here in Berlin we remember American aid after the war, the defense of the freedom of Berlin and America's great contribution to German unity.

I particularly welcome all Americans who live with us in Berlin and all over Germany or who are visiting. In these difficult days their thoughts are at home.

As Germans our thoughts and our feelings also go out to America. We all still have the dreadful pictures in our heads. We cannot get them out of our minds. We have all become witnesses to murderous acts of violence such as the world has never before experienced outside times of war.

We think of the mothers and fathers who have lost their children.

We think of the children who will never see their parents again.

We think of all those who have lost friends and colleagues.

We think of the immeasurable suffering that hatred and terror has brought to many thousands of families all across the country.

The murderers' targets were in New York and Washington. But all people all over the world have been stricken. The victims include people from Asia, from Australia and from Europe, from Africa and from America. The attack targeted the entire world community. We stand united here in solidarity. We stand together against hatred and violence.

Particularly in Berlin, John F. Kennedy is unforgotten. In his first speech as American President, he described America's solidarity with us Europeans thus:

America does not stand alone.
—*Johannes Rau*

"To those old allies whose cultural and spiritual origins we share, we pledge the loyalty of faithful friends. United there is little we cannot do in a host of cooperative ventures. Divided there is little we can do—for we dare not meet a powerful challenge at odds and split asunder."

Today I say as German Federal President and today we all say: America, too, can rely upon this loyalty of a faithful friend.

Many people are afraid at this time. I understand that. This fear must not cripple us. The rage which many feel, the powerlessness which is so difficult to bear, must not make us descend into panic.

The murderers and those who incited them are difficult to find and yet more difficult to combat. But no matter who they are, they are murderers, nothing else—and therefore they must be punished. They do not stand for a people, they do not stand for a religion, they do not stand for a culture. Fanaticism destroys every culture. Fundamentalism does not bear witness to faith, rather is its arch-enemy.

We will not and must not allow ourselves to be led by anyone into condemning entire religions or entire peoples or entire cultures as guilty. But those who sink to associate with the murderers—for whatever reason—those who offer them protection and assistance make themselves as culpable as the murderers.

We will not react to the challenge with powerlessness or with weakness, rather with strength and determination. And with circumspection. Hatred must not lead us into hatred. Hatred blinds. Nothing is so difficult to build and nothing so easy to destroy as peace.

We have to combat terrorism and we will defeat it. We need great staying power to do so. Whoever wants to truly overcome terrorism must ensure through political action that the ground is cut from below the feet of the prophets of violence. Poverty and exploitation, misery and lack of rights drive people to despair. The disregard of religious feelings and cultural traditions robs people of hope and dignity. This leads some to violence and terror. This sows hatred even in the hearts of children.

All people have the right to respect and dignity. Those who experience respect in their lives and love their lives will not want to throw it away. Those who live in dignity and confidence will hardly become a suicide attacker.

Determined action is the order of the day. Because we know and demonstrate that, because we leave no doubt about it, we say the best protection against terror, violence and war is a just international order. Peace will be the fruit of justice. That is a laborious process. It takes a long time and costs more than just time. But for us a more peaceful, secure world has to be worth it. For us and the children of our world.

We have seen apocalyptic pictures. They must rouse us so that peace can make new ground. Freedom needs the strong power of peace and freedom is part of peace.

We have all reason to be vigilant, but no reason to panic. Above all else we need carefully considered action. Our common goal is peace and security, justice and freedom for all people, no matter where they live.

John F. Kennedy remarked in his day, "Our goal is not the victory of might, but the vindication of right". If we, the nations of the world, stand united, terror will not triumph.

Source: Rau, Johannes. "Standing against Terror—Standing with the United States of America." U.S. Diplomatic Mission to Germany. Available online. http://usa.usembassy.de/gemeinsam/rau091401e.htm. Accessed December 21, 2007.

To the United Nations on the Terrorist Attacks

New York City

November 10, 2001

Two months after the deadly September 11, 2001, terrorist attacks on the World Trade Center and Pentagon that killed nearly 3,000 people, President George W. Bush addressed the General Assembly at United Nations headquarters in New York City. By then, investigators had determined that 19 fanatical jihadists, mostly Saudis, from Saudi fugitive Osama bin Laden's al-Qaeda terrorist network had carried out the attacks. Their mission was to foment "holy war" to destroy the United States and to establish their fanatical vision of Islamic faith and law in their own countries. Their reasons for attacking the United States included American support for Israel and the stationing of American troops in Muslim lands. On October 7, 2001, the United States and a small coalition of international forces began military operations to find bin Laden and his followers in their Afghan hideout; a second goal was to eradicate the extremist Taliban regime that gave al-Qaeda refuge in Afghanistan. Bush announced a "War on Terror" in 2002 and the right to declare "preventive war." Thus, in the erroneous belief that Saddam Hussein's Iraq possessed nuclear weapons and was behind al-Qaeda, President Bush launched an invasion of Iraq in 2003; he had already determined to oust Hussein at the time of this speech. No weapons of mass destruction were located, nor did investigators find any connection between Iraq and al-Qaeda. Other than Great Britain, few U.S. allies sent more than token contributions to the Iraq invasion; it had no UN approval and little support among people abroad. The Iraq War (begun in 2003) squandered the global good will toward the United States after the al-Qaeda attacks. And after six years of searching, the United States was still unable to locate bin Laden in his hideouts in Afghanistan and Pakistan.

<hr />

We meet in a hall devoted to peace, in a city scarred by violence, in a nation awakened to danger, in a world uniting for a long struggle. Every civilized nation here today is resolved to keep the most basic commitment of civilization: We will defend ourselves and our future against terror and lawless violence.

The United Nations was founded in this cause. In a second world war, we learned there is no isolation from evil. We affirmed that some crimes are so terrible they offend humanity itself. And we resolved that the aggressions and ambitions of the wicked must be opposed early, decisively, and collectively, before they threaten us all. That evil has returned, and that cause is renewed.

A few miles from here, many thousands still lie in a tomb of rubble. Tomorrow, the Secretary General, the President of the General Assembly, and I will visit that site, where the names of every nation and region that lost citizens will be read aloud. If we were to read the names of every person who died, it would take more than three hours.

Those names include a citizen of Gambia, whose wife spent their fourth wedding anniversary, September the 12th, searching in vain for her husband. Those names include a man who supported his wife in Mexico, sending home money every week. Those names include a young Pakistani who prayed toward Mecca five times a day, and died that day trying to save others.

The suffering of September the 11th was inflicted on people of many faiths and many nations. All of the victims, including Muslims, were killed with equal indifference and equal satisfaction by the terrorist leaders. The terrorists are violating the tenets of every religion, including the one they invoke.

Last week, the Sheikh of Al-Azhar University, the world's oldest Islamic institution of higher learning, declared that terrorism is a disease, and that Islam prohibits killing innocent civilians. The terrorists call their cause holy, yet, they fund it with drug dealing; they encourage murder and suicide in the name of a great faith that forbids both. They dare to ask God's blessing as they set out to kill innocent men, women and children. But the God of Isaac and Ishmael would never answer such a prayer. And a murderer is not a martyr; he is just a murderer.

Time is passing. Yet, for the United States of America, there will be no forgetting September the 11th. We will remember every rescuer who died in honor. We will remember every family that lives in grief. We will remember the fire and ash, the last phone calls, the funerals of the children.

And the people of my country will remember those who have plotted against us. We are learning their names. We are coming to know their faces. There is no corner of the Earth distant or dark enough to protect them. However long it takes, their hour of justice will come.

Every nation has a stake in this cause. As we meet, the terrorists are planning more murder—perhaps in my country, or perhaps in yours. They kill because they aspire to dominate. They seek to overthrow governments and destabilize entire regions. Last week, anticipating this meeting of the General Assembly, they denounced the United Nations. They called our Secretary General a criminal and condemned all Arab nations here as traitors to Islam.

Few countries meet their exacting standards of brutality and oppression. Every other country is a potential target. And all the world faces the most horrifying prospect of all: These same terrorists are searching for weapons of mass destruction, the tools to turn their hatred into holocaust. They can be expected to use chemical, biological and nuclear weapons the moment they are capable of doing so. No hint of conscience would prevent it.

This threat cannot be ignored. This threat cannot be appeased. Civilization, itself, the civilization we share, is threatened. History will record our response, and judge or justify every nation in this hall.

The civilized world is now responding. We act to defend ourselves and deliver our children from a future of fear. We choose the dignity of life over a culture of death. We choose lawful change and civil disagreement over coercion, subversion, and chaos. These commitments—hope and order, law and life—unite people across cultures and continents. Upon these commitments depend all peace and progress. For these commitments, we are determined to fight.

The United Nations has risen to this responsibility. On the 12th of September, these buildings opened for emergency meetings of the General Assembly and the Security Council. Before the sun had set, these attacks on the world stood condemned by the world. And I want to thank you for this strong and principled stand.

I also thank the Arab Islamic countries that have condemned terrorist murder. Many of you have seen the destruction of terror in your own lands. The terrorists are increasingly isolated by their own hatred and extremism. They cannot hide behind Islam. The authors of mass murder and their allies have no place in any culture, and no home in any faith. . . .

For every regime that sponsors terror, there is a price to be paid. And it will be paid. The allies of terror are equally guilty of murder and equally accountable to justice.

The Taliban are now learning this lesson—that regime and the terrorists who support it are now virtually indistinguishable. Together they promote terror abroad and impose a reign of terror on the Afghan people. . . . I make this promise to all the victims of that regime: The Taliban's days of harboring terrorists and dealing in heroin and brutalizing women are drawing to a close. And when that regime is gone, the people of Afghanistan will say with the rest of the world: good riddance. . . .

The most basic obligations in this new conflict have already been defined by the United Nations. On September the 28th, the Security Council adopted Resolution 1373. Its requirements are clear: Every United Nations member has a responsibility to crack down on terrorist financing. We must pass all necessary laws in our own countries to allow the confiscation of terrorist assets. We must apply those laws to every financial institution in every nation.

We have a responsibility to share intelligence and coordinate the efforts of law enforcement. If you know something, tell us. If we know something, we'll tell you. And when we find the terrorists, we must work together to bring them to justice. We have a responsibility to deny any sanctuary, safe haven or transit to terrorists. Every known terrorist camp must be shut down, its operators apprehended, and evidence of their arrest presented to the United Nations. We have a responsibility to deny weapons to terrorists and to actively prevent private citizens from providing them. . . .

The war against terror must not serve as an excuse to persecute ethnic and religious minorities in any country. Innocent people must be allowed to live their own lives, by their own customs, under their own religion. And every nation must have avenues for the peaceful expression of opinion and dissent. When these avenues are closed, the temptation to speak through violence grows.

We must press on with our agenda for peace and prosperity in every land. My country is pledged to encouraging development and expanding trade. My country is pledged to investing in education and combating AIDS and other infectious diseases around the world. Following September 11th, these pledges are even more important. In our struggle against hateful groups that exploit poverty and despair, we must offer an alternative of opportunity and hope.

The American government also stands by its commitment to a just peace in the Middle East. We are working toward a day when two states, Israel and Palestine, live peacefully together within secure and recognized borders as called for by the Security Council resolutions. We will do all in our power to bring both parties back into negotiations. But peace will only come when all have sworn off, forever, incitement, violence and terror. . . .

It is our task—the task of this generation—to provide the response to aggression and terror. We have no other choice, because there is no other peace. We did not ask for this mission, yet there is honor in history's call. We have a chance to write the story of our times, a story of courage defeating cruelty and light overcoming darkness. This calling is worthy of any life, and worthy of every nation. So let us go forward, confident, determined, and unafraid.

Source: Bush, George W. "Address to the United Nations General Assembly." American Presidency Project, University of California–Santa Barbara. Available online. http://www.presidency.ucsb.edu/ws/index.php?pid=58802. Accessed December 22, 2007.

KOFI ANNAN
(1938–   )
"Two States, Israel and Palestine"
Beirut, Lebanon
March 27, 2002

Since Israel was formed, most Palestinian leaders have not acknowledged Israel's right to exist; Palestinians instead experience Israel's presence as a force occupying their homeland. Two major uprisings against Israel—intifada—have occurred. In Arabic, intifada means "shaking off." The first Palestinian intifada ran from 1987 to 1993. The 1993 Oslo peace process, negotiated with hopes by the Palestine Liberation Organization's Yasir Arafat and Israeli prime minister Yitzhak Rabin (1992–95), ultimately failed; it had committed Palestinians to reducing violence and Israelis to withdrawing from the West Bank and Gaza. In July 2000, seven years later, U.S. president Bill Clinton attempted unsuccessfully to broker peace between Arafat (at that time president of the Palestinian Authority) and Israeli prime minister Ehud Barak (1999–2001) at Camp David, the American presidents' country retreat in Maryland. Despite what Israel considered a generous offer from Barak, Arafat would not agree to negotiate. The second intifada began two months afterward, in September 2000. That uprising reached epic levels of bloodshed in 18 months. More than 5,000 people died; one-quarter of those were Israelis, the rest Palestinian. In March 2002, Crown Prince Abdullah of Saudi Arabia offered a "land for peace" proposal for discussion at the 22-nation Arab League summit in Beirut. The proposal traded peace and recognition of Israel (which previously only Egypt and Jordan recognized) in exchange for return of occupied Palestinian land. But disputes among leaders and Palestinian suicide bombings in Israel caused the summit to flounder. UN Secretary-General Kofi Annan of Ghana addressed the summit, chiding both sides—Israel's prime minister Ariel Sharon (2001–06) and Palestine's president Arafat (1996–2004)—for their failure to make peace. A diplomat from Ghana, Annan had been educated in the United States and Switzerland. He worked for 20 years at the United Nations, becoming Secretary-General in 1997. Annan and the United Nations together won the 2001 Nobel Peace Prize for their efforts.

There is no conflict in the world today whose solution is so clear, so widely agreed upon, and so necessary to world peace as the Israeli-Palestinian conflict. Tragically, however, there is no conflict whose path to resolution seems so thickly entangled with hatred and mistrust, or so vulnerable to the acts of extremists. This paradox must not be allowed to persist. Through political courage and leadership, we must bridge the gap between our vision of peace and the present reality of conflict.

There is a solution to the paradox. The leaders on both sides, specifically Prime Minister Sharon and Chairman Arafat, must reaffirm the strategic choice for peace, based on a just, lasting and comprehensive settlement. It is their role, and their duty, to lead their peoples back from the brink. History, and their peoples, will remember them kindly if they rise to the challenge. History, and their peoples, will judge them harshly if they do not.

We all yearn to see a new era of peace and security for all. This yearning is reflected in Security Council resolution 1397, passed earlier this month, which affirms a vision of the Middle East as a region "where two States, Israel and Palestine, live side by side within secure and recognized borders." Building on the bedrock of its earlier resolutions 242 and 338, the Security Council has thus established a firm framework for a just and viable solution of the problem of Palestine.

We are no less united in our grave concern for the regional dimension of this conflict, and in calling for a comprehensive peace between Israel and all its neighbors,

United Nations secretary-general Kofi Annan (right) prepares to speak at the opening of the Arab League summit in Beirut on March 27, 2002. Seated with him are European Union foreign policy chief Javier Solana (left) and Spanish prime minister José Maria Aznar (center). *(AP Photo/Santiago Lyon)*

including Syria and Lebanon. The world as a whole yearns, with your peoples and the people of Israel, for an end to the bloodshed and suffering.

The people of the Arab world are not alone in believing that the Palestinians have a right to their own State in peace and security; that the long occupation must end; that there must be an immediate improvement in the unbearable living conditions of the Palestinians; and that Israel must immediately abandon such indefensible methods as targeted assassinations, and the use of heavy weaponry in densely populated areas.

But the people of Israel are not alone, either, in believing that they have a right to live in peace and security, free from terror; that suicide attacks against Israeli civilians are morally repugnant, and should not be glorified but denounced as such by all Arab leaders; and that the Arab world as a whole must come to terms—once and for all, in public and in private—with the right of Israel to exist.

These beliefs of both sides are shared by people all over the world.

The Palestinians are right to call for a horizon of peace. All of us want to see an end to the occupation, the withdrawal of Israeli settlements, and the establishment of a sovereign Palestinian State. And the Israelis are equally entitled to expect a horizon of peace. All of us want to hear a firm and credible assurance from you—the leaders of the Arab League—that, once Israel concludes a just and comprehensive peace and withdraws from Arab lands, it can look forward to peace and full normal relations with all the Arab world. That assurance can—and I say must—be your contribution to peace between Palestinians and Israelis.

The important proposal put forward by His Royal Highness Crown Prince Abdullah of Saudi Arabia can be the foundation. Based on the principle of "land for peace", it provides a clear and compelling vision. The search for peace and stability has never been more urgent. I appeal to you today to unite in support of this vision, showing the world—and the parties—that you are ready to help them in making the crucial choices for peace. . . .

The Arab world has for too long been prevented from realizing its potential by the persistence of conflict, mistrust and instability. Though we meet at a time of crisis and tension, I urge you to look towards a future of peace and prosperity, and to take steps within your own societies to bring it closer. I appeal to you to confront the menace of extremism, hatred and intolerance, and to ensure that they find no place in your school curricula, or in the minds of your young people.

Your peoples, like all peoples—and particularly the youth, the under-twenties who represent nearly 50 per cent of your population—yearn for the opportunities of free and open societies characterized by good governance, human rights, freedom of expression and the rule of law. Only in this context will they be able to make the most of their abilities and bequeath a better future to their children. Only in this way can poverty, illiteracy and extremism be replaced by peace, stability and prosperity—to the benefit of all the peoples of this region.

I wish you all success in your deliberations, and thank you for the honour of being invited to address you today. *Shoukran jazeelan wa as-Salaam aleikum.* [Thank you very much, and Peace be with you.]

Source: Annan, Kofi. "Leading Their Peoples Back from the Brink Is the Duty of Israeli, Palestinian Leaders, Secretary-General Tells Arab League Summit." United Nations Press release [SG/SM/8177]. Available online. http://www.un.org/News/Press/docs/2002/sgsm8177.doc.htm. Accessed December 20, 2007.

MAHATHIR BIN MOHAMAD
(1925–   )
"Muslims Everywhere Must Condemn Terrorism"
Kuala Lumpur, Malaysia
April 1, 2002

After the September 11, 2001, terrorist attacks in the United States by al-Qaeda, attacks (and foiled plots) continued worldwide by Muslim extremists: in Paris in September, in India and Singapore in December, in Pakistan in January 2002. That April, the 57 countries of the Organization of the Islamic Conference met in Kuala Lumpur, Malaysia, to discuss terrorism at an extraordinary session of the Islamic Conference of Foreign Ministers on Terrorism. Meanwhile, violence in the Middle East exploded. Suicide bombings of Israeli civilians, including 30 deaths in an attack on Jews celebrating Passover, were met by counterstrikes and an Israeli military siege of Palestinian cities. Four days later, on March 31, 2002, a Palestinian suicide bomber killed 15 people in a restaurant in Haifa, Israel. In Kuala Lumpur, Prime Minister Mahathir bin Mohamad of Malaysia appealed to the attendees at the Islamic Conference to condemn attacks on civilians as terrorism. But most nations at the conference rejected assertions that the Palestinians employed terror in their struggle for an independent state. While Israel, and many countries of the West, saw Palestinian violence as terrorism, Arab states and many Muslim nations viewed it as a legitimate liberation struggle by martyrs and freedom fighters against foreign occupiers. Finally, only Malaysia and Bosnia voted to define suicide bombers as terrorists. Despite his position at the conference, Mahathir bin Mohamad was not in favor of actions taken by the West—he was critical of the United States's Iraq War (begun in 2003), and he condemned Israel for provoking much of the terrorist violence. He was an outspoken doctor elected to the Malaysian parliament in 1964; he served as minister of education and became prime minister in 1981, remaining in that position for more than 20 years. He resigned in June 2002.

Terrorism we all know has always been with us. It is not a new phenomenon. What is new is that newer and more diabolical ways have been used in order to kill and injure more people and achieve more spectacular damage.

But we have always been ambiguous, regarding terrorism in other countries as not really terrorism but as the legitimate struggles of people against their oppressive Governments or alien rule. As long as it happens to other people we do not believe we should do anything.

Certainly we do not feel a need for a universal effort to fight against terrorism.

But we know now that no country is safe, no one is safe.

We recognize now that terrorism is a crime, a heinous crime against humanity as a whole. It is a crime against the whole world no matter who or what or which country is being targeted. The attack on September 11, we know, affects the whole world and damaged not just buildings in a particular country and the people in them but it has struck at the very foundation of the world's economy. And it has resulted in death and destruction for the country and people believed to be the base of the attacks. It has shattered the confidence of the world and has left an atmosphere of fear. . . .

We must all fight against terrorists and terrorism, for none of us are really safe. But we cannot fight an enemy we cannot identify.

Fighting terrorists is not like fighting another country. We can flatten the enemy country until nothing is left of that country. It is entirely possible to do that now, and it has been done. But we can still miss the terrorists, for we do not know who they are and where they are. They may not be in the country we have destroyed. They may be elsewhere; they may even be in our own country. . . .

We have a need to agree on the way to identify the terrorist, to agree on what constitutes an act of terror. Discriminating against people who are ethnically or religiously similar to the terrorists only angers more people and perhaps contributes to the breeding of new terrorists. It is counter productive.

We already know that it is entirely possible for freedom fighters struggling against oppression to be mistaken for and to be deliberately labeled as terrorists by their oppressors. Thus Jomo Kenyatta, Robert Mugabe, Nelson Mandela, Sam Nujoma were all labeled as terrorists, were hunted and faced jail sentences if they were captured. But we know that today they are accepted as respected leaders of their countries. . . .

So how do we identify terrorists? How do we distinguish freedom fighters from terrorists, how do we determine which government should be condemned for acts of terrorism or harboring terrorists?

War is about killing people. Why should it matter how people are killed? Yet today, in war, poison gas is outlawed by international convention. In the struggles waged by oppressed people, can there be weapons or forms of attacks that should be proscribed by international convention? Can there be aggressive acts by those in authority that should be condemned and punished?. . .

I would like to suggest here that armed attacks or other forms of attack against civilians must be regarded as acts of terror and the perpetrators regarded as terrorists. Whether the attackers are acting on their own or on the orders of their governments, whether they are regulars or irregulars, if the attack is against civilians then they must be considered as terrorists.

Groups or governments that support attacks on civilians must be regarded as terrorists, irrespective of the justification of the operations carried out, irrespective of the nobility of the struggle. However, if civilians are accidentally caught in the crossfire, the attackers should not be labeled as terrorists.

According to this definition of terrorism, the attack on the World Trade Center on September 11, the human bomb attacks by Palestinians and the Tamil Tigers, the attacks against civilians by Israeli forces, the killings of Bosnian Muslims and others must be considered acts of terror, and the perpetrators must be condemned as terrorists. And anyone supporting them must be considered terrorists. Where states are behind the acts of terrorism, the whole government must stand condemned. But no race or religion should be condemned or discriminated against simply because people of the same race or their co-religionists have been involved in terrorist activities. . . .

While we should identify terrorists everywhere and act in whatever way prescribed we must also find ways and means to prevent as much as possible the tendency of certain people or governments to resort to terrorism. We must identify the causes of their bitterness and anger and we must remove these causes. These are acts of the desperate, acts of people who see no way to redress their grievances, to alleviate their sufferings. . . .

For the Muslims the grievances are real and truly unbearable, beyond mere understanding and tolerance. For the past five decades the Palestinians, for example, have not only had their lands confiscated but they have also been expelled from their own land by the Israelis. . . . Because they throw stones at the Israelis they are shot at and killed, children included. For the Israelis it is not an eye for an eye; it is a life for being hit by a stone. They believe that by terrorizing the terrorists they can stop the carnage. The suicide bombers consider themselves already dead and are on the way to heaven. They are not likely to be deterred by the threat of death. Killing their leader is not going to help either. More violent leaders will replace the fallen leader and the terror attacks will go on. The Holocaust did not defeat the Jews. A second Holocaust with Arabs for victims will not defeat the Arabs either. Israelis must come to their senses and opt for de-escalation of terror rather than escalating it.

If the Israelis won't, then the world must forcibly stop them. If we are serious about stopping terrorists then we must stop both the Palestinians and the Israelis from mutual massacre. . . .

Because of all this there is a great deal of bitterness and anger among Muslims. The impotence of Muslim countries to do anything to remedy the situation adds to this frustration and anger. While the majority of them are resigned to their fate, a small number cannot help but feel a need to vent their anger in some way.

These people may be misguided. They may be wrong in believing they are fighting a jihad, a holy war. They may achieve nothing to put an end to their grievances. Indeed they may actually be doing a lot of harm to their cause, to their co-religionists, to Islam itself. But the fact remains that they are very angry and bitter and willing to commit terrible acts of terror, even if they lose their lives in the process. . . .

But Muslims everywhere must condemn terrorism once it is clearly defined. Terrorizing people is not the way of Islam. Certainly, killing innocent people is not Islamic. Bitter and angry though we may be, we must demonstrate to the world that Muslims are rational people when fighting for our rights and we do not resort to acts of terror. We must object strongly to the linking of Muslims with terror just because a few Muslims have resorted to acts of terror. We must point out that Christians, Buddhists, Hindus, Jews and others are equally guilty of terrorism. Terrorists must be identified by their acts, and nothing else. And we as responsible Muslims must contribute to the fight against terrorism by helping to define what constitutes terrorism and who are the terrorists. . . .

We have a duty here to the Muslim ummah, to Islam, and to Allah. Let us put aside other considerations and strive for consensus in our fight against the blight of blind anger and frustration, and prove that Islam is indeed a way of life that will bring about wellbeing and glory, to Muslims and to mankind as a whole.

Source: Mahathir bin Mohamad. "Extraordinary Session of the Islamic Conference of Foreign Ministers on Terrorism." Studien von Zeitfragen. Available online. http://www.jahr buch2002.studien-von-zeitfragen.net/Zeitfragen/Mahathir_OIC/mahathir_oic.html. Accessed December 22, 2007.

MUHAMMAD YUNUS
(1940–   )
"Poverty Was All around Me"
London, England
March 11, 2003

In 2006 Bangladeshi economics professor Muhammad Yunus and his Grameen Bank received the Nobel Peace Prize for bringing economic development to the poorest of the world's poor. Yunus believes peace is inextricably linked to poverty. "Poverty is the absence of all human rights," Yunus said in his Nobel acceptance speech. He explained that 40 percent of the world's people are living on 94 percent of the world's income. The other 60 out of every 100 people are living on only 6 percent of that income. "Over one billion people live on less than a dollar a day. This is no formula for peace." Yunus developed the idea of microcredit to give the poor in Bangladesh the chance of small-scale entrepreneurship. The Grameen Bank he founded in 1976 makes tiny loans—as small as $12—to people (usually women) who are too poor to be considered for loans by standard banks con-

cerned with customer creditworthiness. He found to his delight that the poor made excellent borrowers, reliably paying back loans to their sewing or weaving businesses, and putting profits into helping their families. Many could send children to school for the first time, and the Grameen Bank, as it grew, was able to offer a significant number of scholarships. Importantly, hereditary poverty could be broken. The bank invested in a yogurt factory to produce affordable food, and in an eye hospital to offer cataract surgery, examples of what Yunus describes as "social businesses." Microcredit proved to be such a powerful force that it has been reproduced in more than 100 countries; in many places it constitutes the first significant opportunity women have had for bettering their lives. In London in 1973, he described the discovery that led to the bank's development.

For the last two decades I have been talking about creating a world free from poverty. I talk about it not because it is unjust to have a world with poverty, which is, of course, true. I talk about it simply because I am totally convinced from my experience of working with poor people that they can get themselves out of poverty if we give them the same or similar opportunities as we give to others. The poor themselves can create a poverty-free world—all we have to do is to free them from the chains that we have put around them. . . .

Poverty is not created by the poor people. So we shouldn't give them an accusing look. They are the victims. Poverty has been created by the economic and social system that we have designed for the world. It is the institutions that we have built, and feel so proud of, which created poverty. It is the concepts we developed to understand the reality around us, made us see things wrongly. They took us down a wrong path, and caused misery for people. It is our policies borne out of our reasonings and theoretical framework, with which we explain interactions among institutions and people, that caused this problem for so many human beings. It is the failure at the top—rather than lack of capability at the bottom—which is the root cause of poverty. . . .

I became involved in the poverty issue not as a policymaker or a researcher. I became involved because poverty was all around me. I could not turn my eyes away from it. In 1974, I found it difficult to teach elegant theories of economics in the classroom in the backdrop of a terrible famine in Bangladesh. Suddenly I felt the emptiness of those theories in the face of crushing hunger and poverty. I wanted to do something immediate to help people around me. Not knowing what I could do, I decided to find a way to make myself useful to others on a one-on-one basis. I wanted to find something

---

RHETORICAL DEVICE

Simile: Comparing two dissimilar things, often—but not always—introduced by the words "like," "than," "so," or "as." Similes provide rich images. (*See* the related metaphor.)

Take care not to be taken and butchered like cattle, rather than, fighting like men, to leave to your enemies a bloody and mournful victory. —*Catiline*

We shall regard you, therefore, as a brother; and you may sleep tranquilly, without fear of the Chippewas. —*Minavavana*

Poor people are like bonsai trees. —*Muhammad Yunus*

I do not think of myself as a saint. —*Martin Luther*

---

specific to do to help another human being just to get by another day with a little more ease than the previous day. That brought me to the issue of poor people's struggle and helplessness in finding microscopic amounts of money in support of their efforts to eke out a living.

I was shocked to discover a woman borrowing US $0.25 with the condition that the lender will have the exclusive right to buy all she produces at the price the lender decides! What a way to recruit slave labor. I decided to make a list of the victims of this money-lending "business" in the village next door to our campus. When my list was done it had the names of 42 victims. Total amount they borrowed was US $27! What a lesson for an economics professor who was teaching his students the Five Year Development Plan of the country with billions of dollars in investments to help the poor. I could not think of anything better than offering this US $27 from my own pocket to get the victims out of the clutches of the moneylenders. The excitement that was created by this action got me further involved in it. The question that arose in my mind was, if you can make so many people so happy with such a tiny amount of money, why shouldn't you do more of it?

I have been trying to do just that ever since. First thing I did was to try to connect the poor people with the bank located in the campus. It did not work. The bank said that the poor are not creditworthy. After all my efforts over several months failed I offered to become a guarantor for the loans to the poor. I was stunned by the result. The poor paid back their loans every single time! But I kept confronting difficulties in expanding the program through the existing banks. Several years later I decided to create a separate bank for the poor, to give loans without collateral. Finally in 1983 I succeeded in doing that. I named it Grameen Bank or Village Bank. It now works all over Bangladesh, giving loans to 2.5 million poor people, 95 per cent women.

The bank is owned by the borrowers. In a cumulative way the bank has given total loans of about US $3.75 billion. Generally the repayment rate has been over 98 per cent. It makes profit. Financially, it is self-reliant—it has stopped taking donor money since 1995, stopped taking loans from domestic market since 1998. It has enough deposits to carry out its lending program. It gives income-generating loans, housing loans, and student loans to the poor families. More than half a million houses have been built with loans from Grameen Bank. Impact studies done on Grameen Bank by independent researchers find that 5 per cent of borrowers come out of poverty every year, children are healthier, education and nutrition level is higher, housing condition is better, child mortality declined by 37 per cent, status of women has been enhanced, ownership of assets by poor women, including housing, has improved dramatically. Now the obvious question that anybody will ask—if poor people can achieve all this through their own efforts within a market environment, why isn't the world doing more of this? Some progress has been made. But much more could have been achieved. . . .

Grameen-type microcredit has spread around the world over the last two decades. Nearly 100 countries have Grameen-type microcredit programs. In 1997, a Microcredit Summit was held in Washington DC, which adopted a goal to reach 100 million poorest families with microcredit and other financial services, preferably through the women in those families, by 2005. At that time number of families reached with microcredit was only 7.5 million globally, of which 5 million was in Bangladesh. Today, I am guessing, this outreach has crossed 35 million. I am hoping it will cross half way mark, i.e., 50 million mark, by the end of this year. . .

The most important step to end poverty is to create employment and income opportunity for the poor. But orthodox economics recognizes only wage-employment. It has no room for self-employment. But self-employment is the quickest and easiest way to create employment for the poor. I have been arguing that credit should be accepted as a human right, because it is so important for a person who is looking for an income. Credit can create self-employment instantaneously. Why wait for others to create a job for you when a person can create his or her own job. And this is so much more convenient for women who would prefer to work out of their homes. We are so much influenced by orthodox economics that we forget that our forefathers did not wait for someone else to create jobs for them. They just went ahead in a routine manner to create their own jobs and income. . . .

Try to imagine how the economists would have built their theory if they had started out with an axiom that all men and women are created equal, that each of them is endowed with unlimited creativity, and each of them is a potential entrepreneur. I am sure you'll agree with me, with this as a starting point, they would have built a very different economic theory, and we would have created a very different, and definitely much better, world as a result.

It will be an uphill task to end poverty in the world unless we create new economic thinking and get rid of the biases in our concepts, institutions, policies, and above all, our mindsets created by the existing orthodoxy. Unless we change our mindsets, we cannot change our world. . . .

By restricting the driving force of the market to narrow self-interest, economics also missed the greatest opportunity to become a truly social science and escape from being a cut and dry dollar-and-cent science. Nobody doubts that an entrepreneur can set up a pharmaceutical company to make a big profit for himself or herself. But it can be equally plausible that a person sets up a pharmaceutical company to bring quality medicine at the lowest price possible so that even the poorest family can afford it. If economics could envisage two types of entrepreneurs, personal-gain driven and social-objective-driven, it would not only be more realistic, but it would have helped the world solve many of the problems that profit-driven market doesn't solve today. . . .

I don't think I need to work hard to convince anyone that there are millions of investors right now who would gladly put their money into a social enterprise if they can be assured that their investment will at least retain its original value, while making a significant impact on the lives of the poor people, deprived people, or any group of disadvantaged people. I receive many letters from people around the world asking me if they can invest in Grameen Bank. Obviously none of them are looking for an opportunity to make money by investing in Grameen Bank. Why has our business world failed to offer opportunities to people who want to invest for the benefit of the people?. . .

Poor people are like bonsai trees. They could have grown into giant trees if they had been supported by the right environment for growth. It is the size of the pots on which they were made to grow that turned them into sad replicas of the real trees. . . . Grameen Bank not only focuses on giving financial services, but it also promotes a strong social agenda. The "Sixteen Decisions" adopted by Grameen Bank borrowers commit them to bring many non-economic changes in their lives, such as, keeping families small, sending children to school and making sure they stay in school, breaking away from the custom of giving dowry to the bride-groom's family, making sure they drink clean drinking water, etc. Because of Sixteen Decisions, Grameen borrowers have taken great care to send their children to school. Today not only are all of them in school, but some of them are also in colleges, universities, and professional schools. Grameen Bank hopes to see that the second generation of the borrowers will grow up to take advantage of the knowledge economy and permanently shift away from poverty. Grameen Bank offers nearly 4,000 scholarships every year to leading students of Grameen families, gives student loans to 100 per cent of students who are in the institutions of higher education. . . .

Can we really reduce extreme poverty by half by 2015? My emphatic, unequivocal answer is, yes, we can. We can do more than that. We can set ourselves on a course to eliminate poverty from the world for all time to come. We can get ready to put poverty in the museum, where it belongs.

Source: Yunus, Muhammad. "Halving Poverty by 2015." Commonwealth Secretariat. Available online. http://www.thecommonwealth.org/speech/34293/35178/152062/152039/37474/commonwealth_lecture_2003.htm. Accessed December 22, 2007. Permission of the Commonwealth Foundation. The Commonwealth Lecture is organized by the Commonwealth Foundation, London.

GERHARD SCHRÖDER
(1944–)
"I Bow My Head before the Victims"
Berlin, Germany
January 25, 2005

On January 27, 1945, the Soviet army liberated a few thousand prisoners left behind by the retreating Nazis at the immense concentration-extermination camp complex of Auschwitz-Birkenau in Poland; the Italian writer Primo Levi was among those liberated. Ten days earlier, in the middle of winter, the Germans had forced about 60,000 of the most able-bodied among the sick and starved Auschwitz prisoners to depart west into Germany on a death march that a quarter of them did not survive; among these were the renowned author Elie Wiesel (SEE his speech, page 509) and his father. In its five years in operation, Auschwitz sent between one and two million people to their deaths; the exact number will never be known. Ninety percent were Jews, shipped to the camp from all over Europe; the rest were Poles and Roma (gypsies). Other Jews were processed administratively at Auschwitz but died or survived elsewhere; young German-Jewish diarist Anne Frank was one who was shipped from Auschwitz to die in Bergen-Belsen, a concentration camp in northwest Germany. In January 2005, 60 years after the liberation of this terrible place, the International Auschwitz Committee held a commemoration in Berlin. Since World War II (1939–45), Germany had made great effort to repudiate Nazism; the provisional German constitution written immediately after the war affirmed a commitment to human rights and a rejection of Nazi supremacist ideology. Yet, as years passed and memory faded, young Germans born after the war wondered why they should feel guilt for the actions of the previous generations. Gerhard Schröder, Germany's chancellor from 1998 to 2005, spoke to the audience of Holocaust survivors and, over them, to all Germany. Schröder had courageously extended himself in a similar manner the previous year in apologizing to Poland for the wholesale slaughter of Polish civilians during the 1944 Warsaw Uprising against Nazi occupiers.

Survivors of Auschwitz-Birkenau, Ladies and gentlemen, I would like to thank the International Auschwitz Committee for the invitation to speak to you here today.

In my estimation an invitation of this kind is still not something that can be taken for granted. It would be fitting for us Germans to remain silent in the face of what was the greatest crime in the history of mankind. Words by government leaders are inadequate when confronted with the absolute immorality and senselessness of the murder of millions.

We look for rational understanding of something that is beyond human comprehension. We seek definitive answers, but in vain.

What is left is the testimony of those few who survived and their descendants.

What is left are the remains of the sites of these murders and the historical record.

What is left also is the certainty that these extermination camps were a manifestation of absolute evil.

Evil is not a political or scientific category. But, after Auschwitz, who could doubt that it exists, and that it manifested itself in the hate-driven genocide carried out by the Nazi regime?

However, noting this fact does not permit us to circumvent our responsibility by blaming everything on a demonic Hitler. The evil manifested in the Nazi ideology was not without its precursors. There was a tradition behind the rise of this brutal ideology and the accompanying loss of moral inhibition. Above all, it needs to be said that the

Nazi ideology was something that people supported at the time and that they took part in putting into effect.

Now, sixty years after the liberation of Auschwitz by the Red Army, I stand before you as the representative of a democratic Germany. I express my shame for the deaths of those who were murdered and for the fact that you, the survivors, were forced to go through the hell of a concentration camp.

Chelmno, Belzec, Sobibor, Treblinka, Maidanek, and Auschwitz-Birkenau are names that will forever be associated with the history of the victims as well as with German and European history. We know that.

We bear this burden with sadness, but also with a serious sense of responsibility.

Millions of men, women, and children were gassed, starved, or shot by German SS troops and their helpers. Jews, gypsies, homosexuals, political prisoners, POWs, and resistance fighters from across Europe were exterminated with cold industrial perfection or were enslaved and worked to death.

Never before had there been a worse breakdown of thousands of years of European culture and civilization. After the war it took some time before the full extent of this breakdown was realized. We are aware of it, but I doubt that we will ever be able to understand it. The past cannot be "overcome." It is the past. But its traces and, above all, the lessons to be learned from it extend to the present.

There will never be anything that can make up for the horror, the torment, and the agony that took place in the concentration camps. It is only possible to provide the families of those who died and the survivors a certain amount of compensation. Germany has faced this responsibility for a long period of time now with its government policies and court decisions, supported by a sense of justice on the part of the people.

The young men and women in the photo we see here were freed in the summer of 1945. Most survivors went in different directions after their liberation: to Israel, to North and South America, to neighboring European countries, or back to their countries of origin. However, some of them stayed in or returned to Germany, the country where the so-called 'Final Solution' originated. It was an extraordinarily difficult decision for them, and often enough it was not a voluntary decision, but rather the result of total desperation. However, hope did return to their disrupted lives, and many did remain in Germany, and we are grateful for that.

Today the Jewish community in Germany is the third-largest in Europe. It is full of vitality and growing rapidly. New synagogues are being built. The Jewish community is and will remain an irreplaceable part of our society and culture. Its brilliant as well as painful history will continue to be both an obligation and a promise for the future.

We will use the powers of government to protect it against the anti-Semitism of those who refuse to learn the lessons of the past. There is no denying that anti-Semitism continues to exist. It is the task of society as a whole to fight it. It must never again become possible for anti-Semites to attack and cause injury to Jewish citizens in our country or any other country and in doing so bring disgrace upon our nation.

Right-wing extremists, with their spray-painted slogans, have the special attention of our law enforcement and justice authorities. But the process of dealing politically with neo-Nazis and former Nazis is something we all need to do together. It is the duty of all democrats to provide a strong response to neo-Nazi incitement and recurrent attempts on their part to play down the importance of the crimes perpetrated by the Nazi regime. For the enemies of democracy and tolerance there can be no tolerance.

The survivors of Auschwitz have called upon us to be vigilant, not to look away, and not to pretend we don't hear things. They have called upon us to acknowledge human rights violations and to do something about them. They are being heard, particularly by young people, for instance by those who are looking at the Auschwitz memorial today with their own eyes. They are speaking with former prisoners. They are helping to maintain and preserve the memorial. They will also help to inform future generations of the crimes committed by the Nazi regime.

The vast majority of the Germans living today bear no guilt for the Holocaust. But they do bear a special responsibility. Remembrance of the war and the genocide perpetrated by the Nazi regime has become part of our living constitution. For some this is a difficult burden to bear.

Nonetheless this remembrance is part of our national identity. Remembrance of the Nazi era and its crimes is a moral obligation. We owe it to the victims, we owe it to the survivors and their families, and we owe it to ourselves.

It is true, the temptation to forget is very great. But we will not succumb to this temptation. The Holocaust memorial in the center of Berlin cannot restore the lives or the dignity of the victims. It can perhaps serve survivors and their descendants as a symbol of their suffering. It serves us all as a reminder of the past.

We know one thing for sure. There would be no freedom, no human dignity, and no justice if we were to forget what happened when freedom, justice, and human dignity were desecrated by government power. Exemplary efforts are being undertaken in many German schools, in companies, in labor unions, and in the churches. Germany is facing up to its past.

From the Shoa and Nazi terror a certainty has arisen for us all that can best be expressed by the words "never again." We want to preserve this certainty. All Germans, but also all Europeans, and the entire international community need to continue to learn to live together with respect, humanity, and in peace.

The Convention on the Prevention and Punishment of the Crime of Genocide was a direct effect of the Holocaust on international law. It requires people of different cultural, religious, and racial origins to respect and protect life and human dignity throughout the world. You in the International Auschwitz Committee support this with the exemplary work you are doing in the interest of all people.

Together with you I bow my head before the victims of the death camps. Even if one day the names of the victims should fade in the memory of mankind, their fate will not be forgotten. They will remain in the heart of history.

Source: Schröder, Gerhard. "Nazi Ideology Was Something People Supported at the Time." Germany Info, German Embassy Washington, D.C. Available online. http://www.germany. info/relaunch/politics/speeches/012505.html. Accessed January 9, 2008.

MIKHAIL GORBACHEV
(1931–   )
"The Historical Achievement of Perestroika"
Manhattan, Kansas, United States
October 28, 2005

Mikhail Gorbachev was born in 1931 in southwestern Russia, then the largest of the 15 republics of the Union of Soviet Socialist Republics (USSR or Soviet Union). He grew up on a collective farm, studied law, and worked in Communist Party positions beginning in 1955. Brilliant and effective, he rose rapidly through party ranks; by 1974 he was appointed to the Supreme Soviet, the USSR's legislative assembly. He was appointed to the Soviet Politburo (highest level of the Communist Party) in 1979; as top Communist Party positions held more power than those in government (such as president), this was an important post. Gorbachev traveled abroad more than most party leaders ever had; he saw firsthand that the West was pulling ahead of the Soviet Union. In 1985 he became general secretary of the Communist Party. Now head of the Soviet Union, he could introduce reform. Glasnost, or "openness," attempted to increase public debate, even press freedom, and reduce secrecy. Perestroika, "restructuring," permitted private businesses and shifted control of industry from the state to workers. Gorbachev's bold reforms resulted in increasing the power of the individual republics—they began using democratic methods to reawaken nationalist identities. The complex party connections between the republics and the central government frayed and left the Soviet Union without the strong central control needed to hold the federation together. While freedom and democracy grew, the economy floundered and severe food shortages gripped the country. In 1990 and 1991 the Baltic states of Lithuania, Estonia, and Latvia declared independence. After an attempted coup in 1991, Gorbachev resigned and Boris Yeltsin took over. The Soviet Union collapsed that year and the republics became independent nations. Years later, Gorbachev reflected in English on the birth of perestroika, also quoting John F. Kennedy's noted 1963 speech on peace at American University (SEE Kennedy's speech, page 460).

※

In the history of Russia there were three events in the 20th Century that had a tremendous impact on the lives of people in my country and throughout the world. It is the 1917 revolution, the victory over Nazism in the great patriotic war in World War II, and finally Perestroika.

Starting in 1982, one after another, three general secretaries of the Communist party died, and this was perceived in rather dramatic terms under the question of generational change at the very top of government in the USSR. Our society was demanding change. This was, so to say, in the air at all times then. The main theme in the evaluation of the situation in our society was that we could no longer live as before, because a country that was extremely rich and intellectual, [with] natural resources, was not able to provide a decent living for its citizens. The economy was stagnant. The bureaucracy had a stranglehold over the entire country. There was one ideology, one form of property. All of this impeded growth and impeded necessary change.

Our country was being stifled because of the absence of freedom. Stalinism and the system that had generated was being rejected at the popular level, at the cultural level. Add to this the fact that the economy was stagnating and was more and more lacking behind the developed world. The rate of growth was getting lower and lower. The productivity was one-third of what it was in the west, and in agriculture, just one-fifth of what it was in the developed countries. . . .

If you recall the period of the beginning of the 1980s, the main thing that strikes you is that all of us were passengers on this deadly train that was called the nuclear arms

U.S. President Ronald Reagan (left) shares a toast with general secretary of the Communist Party and leader of the Soviet Union Mikhail Gorbachev (right) in Washington, D.C., on December 9, 1987. *(AP Photo/Ron Edmonds)*

race. This train had the kind of speed and momentum such that many people believed that it could not be stopped, that it could not even be slowed down. This was extremely dangerous, because of the nuclear conflict which [could have] started, perhaps not because of a political decision, but also because of a failure in command and control systems of these powerful weapons.

The ideological and political confrontation, the confrontation of the different social models, all of this played together. The domestic and the external factors dictated to us a need for change: the policy of Perestroika. The philosophical opinions of Perestroika, the political thinkings were a response not only to the problems that we were facing in the USSR, but also to the problems of the world.

On March the 11th, [1985,] after the death of my predecessor, Constantine Chernenko. . . . I was elected unanimously the general secretary of the central committee. At that time in the beginning of Perestroika we were getting tremendous support from the people and that was of great importance for me. . . .

For the USSR, Perestroika meant overcoming totalitarianism and moving toward democracy, toward freedom. But this did not happen overnight. As we were moving forward, as we were taking steps in domestic policy, we saw increasing resistance particularly among bureaucracy, the party bureaucracy, the state bureaucracy and the military bureaucracy. And among some people too, among part of our society Perestroika was seen as some kind of gift from the heavens that something—that things will change for the better overnight. We were saying that change is something that everyone needs to do. All of us, from an ordinary worker to the general secretary of the Communist Party, needed to change.

We had initial illusions, the illusion of being able to improve the old system, that we could give second wind to the old system without really changing it. But that failed and, therefore, toward the end of 1986 we began to contemplate political reforms. That was the first step. Along the path of reforming, replacing the system we proposed a step-by-step approach to reforming Soviet society, moving gradually toward freedom and democracy and market economics.

This ideology of this philosophy of Perestroika would result in bringing together the interests of individuals on the one hand and of the whole of society on the other hand. The most important thing, of course, was to place the individual, the human being, at the center of this change.

So let me now very quickly describe some aspects of that period, because I would like to give more time to the current situation. In August 1991 the attempt was made to organize a coup d'etat. The coup d'etat weakened my position and as a result the leaders of Russia, Ukraine, and Belarus agreed to dismantle the Soviet Union. They did that behind my back. So Perestroika is the period that started on March 11, 1985, and ended on December 25, 1991. What happened afterwards was a different history, was a different course.

Boris Yeltsin had a different strategy. That strategy included breaking up the country, for Russia to abandon the other republics and, as he hoped, to move forward more rapidly, without the burden of the other republics. That was an illusion, illusion in public policy means misadventure, a reckless adventure that ended badly. The country disintegrated, the wealth of our nation was plundered, and the economy was opened up while it was not ready to compete with the more advanced economies. That virtually destroyed the economy, the savings of the people and the economic situation, [and] as a result of those policies brought the country to the brink of catastrophe. It is only because of the enormous resources and also because of the efforts of the local and regional level that that blow was to some extent softened, but it was a heavy blow and we are still living the consequences of those policies.

And, therefore, I'm often asked whether Perestroika was defeated or it was victorious. Well, it is true that Perestroika was interrupted; it is true that we were not able

---

RHETORICAL DEVICE

Pleonasm: Using redundancy, or more words than necessary, can emphasize a point.

The bureaucracy had a stranglehold over the entire country.
—*Mikhail Gorbachev*

Not a single vote can be lost, not a single vote can be stolen. —*Vojislav Koštunica*

Everywhere, where the Jews have settled in comparatively large numbers among the nations, Jewish misery prevails. —*Max Nordau*

to achieve all the goals that we had planned. However, we were able to do something fundamental, and that is ending the totalitarianism system, implementing a pluralistic economy, and creating opportunities for people to benefit from freedom of speech, freedom of religion, freedom of assembly. The country opened up the world and the world opened to us. We also adopted a law on the freedom of movement, the freedom of integration, and finally we prepared a union treaty for a new union of the republics. And what we were able to do, up until August 1991, is what enabled us, what enabled the country, to continue to move forward. Our country will not return to the past. This is not just a political statement, this is the view, this is the position, the opinion of our entire society and that is the greatest historical achievement of Perestroika. . . .

Let's go back to not only the domestic policy, but the important changes that Perestroika produced in international affairs. We were able to establish dialogue and normal relations with the United States of America, and I would like to pay tribute to President Ronald Reagan and Secretary of State Schultz. They did a great deal. They also had to overcome some resistance, including resistance among their own people, to meet us halfway. I believe that President Reagan was a great president and I pay tribute for his contribution. . . .

After the revolution in central and eastern Europe, those nations too were given a right to choose. We never interfered. On the very first day of my leadership I said to my colleagues, "You should develop your own policies, we will not interfere in your affairs because it is your responsibility." . . . It is sometimes said that I gave away Poland, I gave away Hungary, I gave away the Czech Republic. Well, I gave it to their people, I gave Hungary to the Hungarians, Poland to the Polish. That's how it should be. . . .

Today the interdependence and the interconnectedness of the world, what we call globalization, has increased more than ever before. Globalization is pushing the world toward the future, but nevertheless we see that globalization does not include billions of people. Finally, we see in the world today the emergence of new giants, China, India, Brazil, the world feels that those countries are making an increasing impact on all economic and political processes. They are becoming important decision makers and we each should rethink the world in view of these new trends in the world today. And, of course, solutions are not military solutions, solutions are intellectual, solutions are political, solutions are that we should build a new relationship that would include, integrate, those new giants into the global processes. . . .

If globalization is only meant from increased profits without paying attention to the social problems, ethnic problems and environmental problems, globalization is dangerous. And let's bear this in mind when we think about this global world.

Let me also speak about the role of the United States. America has a right to reclaim leadership because of its power, because of its democratic traditions, because of its cultural and economic influences, but this leadership should be exercised not through domination but through partnership with other nations.

The past few years have shown that people in the world do not accept attempts to dictate to them, or attempts by any country to be a world policeman. And I think that it's very important that after the recent very difficult years, we have seen that in the administration, in the American political community, there is a growing understanding of this, and I believe this is very important and I think that this will move this great country to get a better understanding of its role and responsibility in the world. . . .

So let me quote from a very interesting speech that was made on June 10, 1963, by the President of the United States, John F. Kennedy. This is what he said speaking at American University in Washington. I quote, "The most important subject is peace. What kind of peace am I speaking about? What kind of peace should we strive for? It's not a Pax Americana imposed by American weapons of war. It's not the peace of the grave, and not the safety of a slave. I'm speaking of a true peace, a peace for which one wants to live, a peace that enables every nation, every person, to grow, to hope and to build a better life for their children.

It is a peace not just for Americans, but a peace for all people. It is a peace not only for today but also for tomorrow. A true peace should be the result of the efforts of many nations, a sum of many actions. It should be dynamic, not static; it should be changing in order to respond to challenges of every new generation, because peace is a process, peace is a way of addressing problems."

Today we are facing a situation that is as important for mankind as the situation when these prophetic words of President Kennedy were spoken. I believe that perhaps he died for those words.

So a new vision, a new policy, we need a political will and responsibility that he mentioned at that time and I very much share this view of John F. Kennedy. We need that approach today more than yesterday. Thank you.

Source: Gorbachev, Mikhail. "Landon Lecture." Kansas State University. Available online. http://www.mediarelations.k-state.edu/WEB/News/NewsReleases/Gorbachevtext102805.html. Accessed December 22, 2007. Used by permission of the Landon Lecture Series at Kansas State University.

ALBERTO J. MORA
(1951–)
"Cruelty Disfigures Our National Character"
Boston, United States
May 22, 2006

Alberto Mora was born into a family that had experienced the lack of the rule of law: His maternal grandparents escaped Communist Hungary, and, as a child, Mora was forced to flee Cuba with his family after Castro's violent overthrow of the Batista regime during the Cuban Revolution (1956–59). Mora worked for the U.S. Information Agency and the U.S. State Department's Foreign Service, before becoming the U.S. Navy general counsel, or chief lawyer, during President George W. Bush's administration (2001–08). He was a civilian with the equivalent rank of a four-star admiral. In 2002 he discovered that high government officials, including the secretary of defense, had authorized policies permitting cruelty, or "coercive interrogation techniques," toward combatants captured in the nation's "war on terror." These policies during the Iraq War (begun in 2003) circumvented the usual interpretations of what consti-

tuted torture, and Mora believed them to be illegal and a violation of human rights. For several years he warned Pentagon leaders against defying the Geneva Convention against prisoner abuse as well as the U.S. Constitution's prohibition against cruel punishments. Later, abuses by U.S. interrogators at Iraq's Abu Ghraib prison and at the military's detention camp at Guantánamo Bay in Cuba surfaced, just as he had feared. Photos of these abuses became public; they caused a firestorm of criticism around the world and cost the United States support in the war in Iraq. As Mora saw it, torture lost the United States its moral authority in a shaky world order. For his bravery in opposing civilian and military leaders to uphold a moral and political position against torture, Mora was awarded the 2006 John F. Kennedy Profile in Courage Award at the JFK Presidential Library in Boston. He gave this speech after receiving the award.

There have been times in our nation's history when, in our quest for security, our fear momentarily overcomes our judgment and our power slips the discipline of the law and our national values.

One such moment occurred in 1942 following the Japanese attack on Pearl Harbor. In what will always be regarded as an act of national shame, military authorities rounded up 120,000 American citizens of Japanese ancestry and incarcerated them on the presumption of disloyalty. These citizens were stripped of their rights and held in detention camps for the duration of the war. Many lost businesses and property. When we recall this event—and it is relevant to our current situation—we also recall with shame the Supreme Court's abdication of its judicial responsibilities in the notorious *Korematsu* decision, where it endorsed the legality of the patently unconstitutional detention.

Korematsu reminds us that when threats and fear converge, our laws and principles can become fragile. They are fragile today. In the summer of 2002—sixty years after *Korematsu* and only four years ago—at Guantanamo and elsewhere, U.S. authorities held in detention individuals thought to have information on other impending attacks against the United States. Unless this information was obtained, it was believed, more Americans—perhaps many more—would die. In this context, our government issued legal and policy documents providing, in effect, that for some detainees labeled as "unlawful combatants," interrogation methods constituting cruel, inhuman, and degrading treatment could be applied under the president's constitutional commander-in-chief authorities.

587

Although there is continuing debate as to the details of how, when, and why, we know such cruel treatment was applied at Abu Ghraib, Guantanamo, and other locations. We know the treatment may have reached the level of torture in some instances. And there are still questions as to whether these policies were related, if at all, to the deaths of several dozen detainees in custody.

It is astonishing to me, still, that I should be here today addressing the issue of American cruelty—or that anyone would ever have to. Our forefathers, who permanently defined our civic values, drafted our Constitution inspired by the belief that law could not create, but only recognize, certain inalienable rights granted by God—to every person, not just citizens, and not just here, but everywhere. Those rights form a shield that protects core human dignity. Because this is so, the Eighth Amendment prohibits cruel punishment. The constitutional jurisprudence of the Fifth and Fourteenth Amendments outlaws cruel treatment that shocks the conscience. The Nuremberg Trials—that triumph of American justice and statesmanship that launched the modern era of human rights and international criminal law—treated prisoner abuse as an indictable crime. The Geneva Conventions forbid the application of cruel, inhuman, and degrading treatment to all captives, as do all of the major human rights treaties adopted and ratified by our country during the last century. There should have been no doubt or ambiguity about the standard of conduct that our laws require of us. And even if laws have jurisdictional limits, there could have been no doubt about what our values forbade.

Despite this, there was abuse. Not all were mistreated, but some were. For those mistreated, history will ultimately judge what the precise quantum of abuse inflicted was—whether it was torture or some lesser cruelty—and whether it resulted from official commission, omission, or whether it occurred despite every reasonable effort to prevent the abuse. Whatever the ultimate historical judgment, it is established fact that documents justifying and authorizing the abusive treatment of detainees during interrogation were approved and distributed.

These authorizations rested on the three beliefs: that no law prohibited the application of cruelty; that no law should be adopted that would do so; and that our government could choose to apply the cruelty—or not—as a matter of policy depending on the dictates of perceived military necessity. Some officials may also have believed that, if this abuse were disclosed or discovered, virtually no one would care. The resulting, inescapable truth is that—no matter how circumscribed these policies were, or how short their duration, or how few the victims—for as long as these policies were in effect our government had adopted what only can be labeled as a policy of cruelty.

The fact that we adopted this policy demonstrates that this war has tested more than our nation's ability to defend ourselves. It has tested our response to our fears, and the measure of our courage. It has tested our commitment to our most fundamental values and our constitutional principles. It has tested the depth of our commitment to those certain truths that our forefathers held to be self-evident. It has tested our understanding of what the terms "justice," "the law," "the rule of law," and "human rights" are. It has tested our vision of what the relationship should be between the individual and the government. And, no less important, this war has tested our definition of human dignity.

In this war, we have come to a crossroads—much as we did in the events that led to *Korematsu:* Will we continue to regard the protection and promotion of human dignity as the essence of our national character and purpose, or will we bargain away human and national dignity in return for an additional possible measure of physical security?

We need to be clear. Cruelty disfigures our national character. It is incompatible with our constitutional order, with our laws, and with our most prized values. Cruelty can be as effective as torture in destroying human dignity, and there is no moral distinction between one and the other. To adopt and apply a policy of cruelty anywhere within this world is to say that our forefathers were wrong about their belief in the rights of man, because there is no more fundamental right than to be safe from cruel and inhumane treatment. Where cruelty exists, law does not.

Why should we still care about these issues? The Abu Ghraib abuses have been exposed; Justice Department memoranda justifying cruelty and even torture have been ridiculed and rescinded; the authorizations for the application of extreme interrogation techniques have been withdrawn; and, perhaps most critically, the Detainee Treatment Act of 2005, which prohibits cruel, inhuman, and degrading treatment, has been enacted, thanks to the courage and leadership of Senator John McCain.

We should care because the issues raised by a policy of cruelty are too fundamental to be left unaddressed, unanswered, or ambiguous. We should care because a tolerance of cruelty will corrode our values and our rights and degrade the world in which we live. It will corrupt our heritage, cheapen the valor of the soldiers upon whose past and present sacrifices our freedoms depend, and debase the legacy we will leave to our sons and daughters. We should care because it is intolerable to us that anyone should believe for a second that our nation is tolerant of cruelty. And we should care because each of us knows that this issue has not gone away.

The years ahead will continue to test our national security. We again will be tempted to violate our values in the mistaken belief that we will be made more secure by doing so. When that test comes again—and it certainly will—we must muster the courage to defend our principles more firmly. We will have to be prepared—as President Kennedy said in his inaugural speech of his own, "new generation" of Americans—to be, also, a generation "unwilling to witness or permit the slow undoing of those human rights to which this nation has always been committed, and to which we are committed today at home and around the world."

Source: Mora, Alberto J. Acceptance Speech. John F. Kennedy Presidential Library. Available online. http://www.jfklibrary.org/Education+and+Public+Programs/Profile+in+Courage+Award/ Award+Recipients/Alberto+Mora/. Accessed December 22, 2007. Permission of John F. Kennedy Library Foundation/Alberto Mora.

AKBAR GANJI

(1960–)

"The Struggle against Violence"

Moscow, Russia

June 6, 2006

Born in the Iranian provincial capital of Qazvin, as a young man Akbar Ganji welcomed the 1979 Iranian Revolution, believing it to be a positive step for his country following years of oppressive rule under the CIA-backed monarch Mohammad Reza Pahlavi (r. 1941–79). Ganji's initial enthusiasm even led him to join the Islamic Revolutionary Guards and later to accept a position at the Ministry of Culture and Islamic Guidance. His close contact with Ayatollah Khomeini's regime (1979–89), however, soon led to his disillusionment, and Ganji turned to journalism as a way to protest the Iranian government's human rights abuses. He embarked upon a career as an investigative journalist that would earn him accolades abroad and imprisonment—and allegedly torture—at home. His most famous work is a collection of articles published in 2000, under the name *Dungeon of Ghosts,* which accused then-president Akbar Hashemi Rafsanjani (1989–97) and his associates of murdering five prominent Iranian intellectuals

and dissidents. Due to this book and his participation in a high-profile international conference in Berlin at which Iranian social and political reform was debated, Iranian officials arrested Ganji and charged him with "damaging national security" by "lies" and "propaganda." Found guilty, he was eventually sentenced to six years in prison. Ganji's incarceration made international headlines when he released a 2002 manifesto detailing his vision for a democratic Iran, and later when he went on a hunger strike to protest his torture. Finally released from prison in 2006, Ganji has since embarked on a world tour to meet with leading intellectuals in an effort to bring democracy to Iran. His journalistic work has been recognized with many eminent awards. In receiving the World Association of Newspapers' Golden Pen Award, he delivered the following address, ironically in Moscow, where many journalists under the presidency of Vladimir Putin (1999–2008) have been murdered or have died under suspicious circumstances.

※

In the presence of representatives from the world media gathered here, let me begin by thanking the World Association of Newspapers for giving me the Golden Pen Award. I am humbled by the honor. I think the prize should in fact go to all Iranian dissidents and freedom fighters.

What will follow are the views of only one Iranian dissident about the current world conditions. They are no more than an effort to "think out loud," an attempt to offer problems for a dialogue, for an exchange of views and finally for critical but reasoned discussion. What I offer here is a synopsis of a lengthier piece whose text has been made available in both Persian and English.

Our ideal is the creation of a humane world, but in fact we live in a world steeped in reckless and widespread violence, a world of genocides and civil wars, of ethnic cleansing and gross violations of citizens' rights in many corners of the globe. These instances of moral depravity have deprived all of us of the chance to live in a secure world of enduring peace. But in our world today, there are also bright lights of hope. Today, more than ever in human history, thanks to improved means of communication, people, free from their ethnic, racial, and religious identities—or more specifically, free from any secondary identity—simply as human beings, are concerned about the fate of other human beings.

Today we are witnessing the birth of a new moral concept in the world: Global citizenship. Today vast numbers of people no longer consider themselves merely the citizen of a state, no longer feel compassion only for their compatriots, but rather consider themselves also citizens of the world. They feel compassion with other global citizens. Our gathering here today is the best example of solidarity among citizens of the world. But we must accept that we are only at the beginning of the road. There are still too many calamities around us, calamities like terrorism, coercion, dictatorship, discrimination, and war.

These are indications that we need to still find ways to expand this solidarity, and give reality to the concept of world citizenship. In my mind, Kant is the philosopher who can be most helpful to us on this path. According to Kant, humans have rights by the mere fact of their humanity, and in that sense, humans are all equal, and laws are just only if they treat everyone without exception, equally, and they can safeguard the liberty of all. Kant invites us to be humble and benevolent. Such benevolence and humility require us to always put ourselves in the place of the other, and do unto others as we do unto ourselves.

Only in this way can human solidarity be strengthened. Only through this perspective will we consider our gifts and privileges, as well as our needs, things we must share with others. According to Kant, humans are ends in themselves, and must never be used as means to other ends. An authentic life is one wherein every individual has the right to pursue his or her own goals, and is not deemed merely a tool to be used by others to achieve their goals. If we can create equality for everyone, then this authentic life can become a reality, and people can, in cooperation and competition with one another, pursue their goals successfully, and have a chance to offer their values for scrutiny and discussion in the public domain.

Today we need to help create and strengthen a truly viable, clever, and vital public domain, and we ourselves must move in that arena, and use it to control and curtail power and criticize those politicians who have turned human beings into tools and means. Only through such a public sphere can we stand up to ideological and intellectual totalitarianism that wishes to impose its vision of a perfect world forcefully on everyone. As Kant has written, the principle of human freedom is the foundation of a democratic state and for him, freedom is when no one can coerce me to pursue my happiness according to their vision. Everyone must be free in their pursuit of their own happiness.

Central to this idea of freedom and democracy is that women must have equal rights with men, and must be allowed free and equal access to the public sphere. The worst kind of despotism is a patriarchal system wherein men define everyone's norms of happiness. But we can go one step further than Kant, and declare that if we are to have a world where each individual is free to pursue his or her own goals and idea of happiness, we must cement a solidarity against violence and those who promote it.

The foundation of this solidarity can be Jesus Christ's famous aphorism, "Love Thy Neighbor." But we must have an expanded view of what neighbor means: My neighbor is not just my "brother in faith;" any human being anywhere in the world, regardless of their dress, their color, their gender, and their faith is my neighbor. I must respect their dignity. Citizens of the world under every name are my neighbors. A violent act against any citizen of the world is a violent act against all of us.

Defending the rights of these neighbors can create the kind of solidarity we need, the kind that deters violent forces from treading on the rights of even the most unknown citizen of our world. The other principle we must cultivate is the notion of publicity and transparency in politics. These characteristics were amongst Kant's ideals as well.

Every decision in the public domain, particularly every political decision, must be made publicly and transparently. It must be open to the scrutiny of everyone. We must shed the light of enquiry into the dark house of politics. Only this way can we criticize, analyze, and deconstruct the decisions that are intertwined with our fate. Only this way can we approve, improve, or reject these decisions.

Today the role of the media particularly is to focus this light into these dark houses.

Our world today suffers from violence; this violence has many facets. It creates different forms of pain and suffering. Terror, oppression, imprisonment, and solitary confinement are only the more obvious facets of this violence. They are the tools of despots and dogmatists, who use them to force their ideas and ideals on the citizenry. Human rights know no boundaries, and accept no exceptions. The idea that this religious tenet or those local cultural norms render certain human rights obsolete or impractical must not be allowed to be used by despots to legitimize their despotism.

Today we must struggle against violence in every one of its facets. Today the kind of revolutionary violence referred to by people like Sartre, Fanon, and Marcuse are no longer legitimate. We have seen how violence only begets violence; how revolutionary violence destroys both the bad and the good. We must no longer use violence as a weapon to fight violence. Peaceful resistance, peaceful civic resistance, must replace revolutionary violence.

My slogan for fighting against oppression and violence is simple: Forgive, but never forget. Forgiveness is a virtue that overcomes even legitimate anger and hatred. Forgiveness foregoes revenge. But forgiving injustice does not mean forgetting it. It does not mean foregoing the struggle against it. Forgiveness only implies giving up hatred and vengeance. Forgiveness leaves hatred to the hateful, ill-wishing to evildoers, and revenge to the vengeful. But forgiveness does not condone forgetting the crime. Nor does it condone our duty to resist bravely the criminal rulers or the dogmatic defenders of past crimes. We must always remember that the crime and the injustice did occur. We must always remember the conditions that led to the creation of fascism, totalitarianism, and other forms of dictatorship that have been the source of injustice.

And we must inculcate this knowledge into our individual and collective memory, so that we can ensure that they shall never happen again. Paul Ricceur said it best when he declared that moral and committed humans hear constantly in their memory the voices of all the oppressed, from behind prison walls, concentration camps, and torture chambers. They hear these cries and never allow these voices of conscience to be drowned out.

The principle of "Forgive but never forget" is the *sine qua non* of a democracy, free from violence. After discovering the truth, after shining the light of truth into the dark houses in which violent decisions have been made, after exposing injustice, we will forgive the despots and the criminals, so that the vicious cycle of violence does not continue. Anger, hatred, and hostility cannot create a democratic society free from the scourge of violence. That is why we need to forgive, but never forget. Forgiveness does not wash away the crime, or mangle our memories; it only does away with the need for hatred and revenge; it does not obviate struggle, but only the need for hatred. Those who forgive go on with their fight against evil with a heart filled with joy and free of hate.

War is the other scourge of our time, and our citizens of the world have as their goal an end to all wars, and the achievement of an enduring peace; the kind of enduring peace first advocated by Kant. According to Kant, enduring peace can come only if democracy spreads around the world. Democracies usually don't enter into wars with one another. Today, only citizens of the world can, through the requisite sense of responsibility that comes with such citizenship, stop the *khodsar* [illegal] decisions of *khodsar* governments in fanning the flames of war.

Now that I have said these few words, I can with a more deliberate consciousness accept, on behalf of all the citizens of the world, and as a humble member of this great community that fights every facet of violence, the Golden Pen Award.

Source: Ganji, Akbar. Acceptance speech. Iran Press Service. Available online. http://www.iran-press-service.com/ips/articles-2006/june2006/ganji_awarded_6606.shtml. Accessed December 20, 2007. Permission of World Association of Newspapers.

ALBERT GORE, JR.
(1948–   )
"A Planetary Emergency"
New York, New York, United States
September 18, 2006

The son of a Tennessee senator, Albert Gore, Jr., grew up between Tennessee and Washington, D.C. After service as a military journalist in the Vietnam War (1954–75) and a job reporting for a Tennessee newspaper, in 1976 he won a seat in the U.S. House of Representatives. In 1984 he was elected to the U.S. Senate, and from 1993 to 2001 he was vice president under President Bill Clinton. Gore ran for president in 2000; in an unusually close election, the Supreme Court handed the victory to the Republican candidate, George W. Bush, son of President George H. W. Bush (1989–93). Gore had won the popular vote but lost the vote in the Electoral College. Gore, who had supported the Kyoto Protocol in 1998 to reduce greenhouse emissions but which Congress never ratified, then returned to a long-standing interest—pollution and the environment. He joined the chorus of scientists warning of danger in the buildup of atmospheric carbon dioxide. His 2006 film on climate change, *An Inconvenient Truth* (in which he also starred), won an Academy Award for Documentary Feature for the director. On stage at the awards ceremony, Gore called solving the climate crisis "a moral issue." In New York in September 2006, he spoke at New York University's School of Law. He went to Congress on March 21, 2007, to speak at hearings on global warming, where some members were still skeptical that global climate change was caused by human activity. Solutions that Gore offered at various times included increasing the required automobile mileage efficiency of car manufacturers and requiring coal-fired power plants to capture their carbon emissions. Six months later he won the 2007 Nobel Peace Prize for his work in raising awareness of climate change.

A few days ago, scientists announced alarming new evidence of the rapid melting of the perennial ice of the north polar cap, continuing a trend of the past several years that now confronts us with the prospect that human activities, if unchecked in the next decade, could destroy one of the earth's principle mechanisms for cooling itself. Another group of scientists presented evidence that human activities are responsible for the dramatic warming of sea surface temperatures in the areas of the ocean where hurricanes form. A few weeks earlier, new information from yet another team showed dramatic increases in the burning of forests throughout the American West, a trend that has increased decade by decade, as warmer temperatures have dried out soils and vegetation. All these findings come at the end of a summer with record breaking temperatures and the hottest twelve month period ever measured in the U.S., with persistent drought in vast areas of our country. *Scientific American* introduces the lead article in its special issue this month with the following sentence: "The debate on global warming is over."

Many scientists are now warning that we are moving closer to several "tipping points" that could—within as little as 10 years—make it impossible for us to avoid irretrievable damage to the planet's habitability for human civilization. In this regard, just a few weeks ago, another group of scientists reported on the unexpectedly rapid increases in the release of carbon and methane emissions from frozen tundra in Siberia, now beginning to thaw because of human caused increases in global temperature. The scientists tell us that the tundra in danger of thawing contains an amount of additional global warming pollution that is equal to the total amount that is already in the earth's atmosphere. Similarly, earlier this year, yet another team of scientists reported that the previous twelve months saw 32 glacial earthquakes on Greenland between 4.6 and

5.1 on the Richter scale—a disturbing sign that a massive destabilization may now be underway deep within the second largest accumulation of ice on the planet, enough ice to raise sea level 20 feet worldwide if it broke up and slipped into the sea. Each passing day brings yet more evidence that we are now facing a planetary emergency—a climate crisis that demands immediate action to sharply reduce carbon dioxide emissions worldwide in order to turn down the earth's thermostat and avert catastrophe.

The serious debate over the climate crisis has now moved on to the question of how we can craft emergency solutions in order to avoid this catastrophic damage. . . .

Two weeks ago, Democrats and Republicans joined together in our largest state, California, to pass legally binding sharp reductions in CO2 emissions. 295 American cities have now independently "ratified" and embraced CO2 reductions called for in the Kyoto Treaty. 85 conservative evangelical ministers publicly broke with the Bush-Cheney administration to call for bold action to solve the climate crisis. Business leaders in both political parties have taken significant steps to position their companies as leaders in this struggle and have adopted a policy that not only reduces CO2 but makes their companies zero carbon companies. Many of them have discovered a way to increase profits and productivity by eliminating their contributions to global warming pollution. . . .

Our children have a right to hold us to a higher standard when their future—indeed the future of all human civilization—is hanging in the balance. They deserve better than the spectacle of censorship of the best scientific evidence about the truth of our situation and harassment of honest scientists who are trying to warn us about the looming catastrophe. They deserve better than politicians who sit on their hands and do nothing to confront the greatest challenge that humankind has ever faced—even as the danger bears down on us.

We in the United States of America have a particularly important responsibility, after all, because the world still regards us—in spite of our recent moral lapses—as the natural leader of the community of nations. Simply put, in order for the world to respond urgently to the climate crisis, the United States must lead the way. . . .

At present, the global system for carbon emissions trading is embodied in the Kyoto Treaty. It drives reductions in CO2 and helps many countries that are a part of the treaty to find the most efficient ways to meet their targets for reductions. It is true that not all countries are yet on track to meet their targets, but the first targets don't have to be met until 2008 and the largest and most important reductions typically take longer than the near term in any case.

The absence of the United States from the treaty means that 25% of the world economy is now missing. It is like filling a bucket with a large hole in the bottom. When the United States eventually joins the rest of the world community in making this system operate well, the global market for carbon emissions will become a highly efficient closed system and every corporate board of directors on earth will have a fiduciary duty to manage and reduce CO2 emissions in order to protect shareholder value.

Many American businesses that operate in other countries already have to abide by the Kyoto Treaty anyway, and unsurprisingly, they are the companies that have been most eager to adopt these new principles here at home as well. The United States and Australia are the only two countries in the developed world that have not yet ratified the Kyoto Treaty. . . .

I look forward to the deep discussion and debate that lies ahead. But there are already some solutions that seem to stand out as particularly promising:

First, dramatic improvements in the efficiency with which we generate, transport and use energy will almost certainly prove to be the single biggest source of sharp reductions in global warming pollution. Because pollution has been systematically ignored in the old rules of America's marketplace, there are lots of relatively easy ways to use new and more efficient options to cheaply eliminate it. Since pollution is, after all, waste, business and industry usually become more productive and efficient when they systematically go about reducing pollution. After all, many of the technologies on which we depend are actually so old that they are inherently far less efficient than newer technologies that we haven't started using. One of the best examples is the internal combustion engine. When scientists calculate the energy content in BTUs of each gallon of gasoline used in a typical car, and then measure the amounts wasted in the car's routine operation, they find that an incredible 90% of that energy is completely wasted. . . .

A second group of building blocks to solve the climate crisis involves America's transportation infrastructure. We could further increase the value and efficiency of a distributed energy network by retooling our failing auto giants—GM and Ford—to require and assist them in switching to the manufacture of flex-fuel, plug-in, hybrid vehicles. The owners of such vehicles would have the ability to use electricity as a principle source of power and to supplement it by switching from gasoline to ethanol or biodiesel. This flexibility would give them incredible power in the marketplace for energy to push the entire system to much higher levels of efficiency and in the process sharply reduce global warming pollution.

This shift would also offer the hope of saving tens of thousands of good jobs in American companies that are presently fighting a losing battle selling cars and trucks that are less efficient than the ones made by their competitors in countries where they were forced to reduce their pollution and thus become more efficient.

It is, in other words, time for a national oil change. That is apparent to anyone who has looked at our national dipstick.

Our current ridiculous dependence on oil endangers not only our national security, but also our economic security. Anyone who believes that the international market for oil is a "free market" is seriously deluded. It has many characteristics of a free market, but it is also subject to periodic manipulation by the small group of nations controlling the largest recoverable reserves, sometimes in concert with companies that have great influence over the global production, refining, and distribution network. . . .

Buildings—both commercial and residential—represent a larger source of global warming pollution than cars and trucks. But new architecture and design techniques are creating dramatic new opportunities for huge savings in energy use and global warming pollution. As an example of their potential, the American Institute of Architecture and the National Conference of Mayors have endorsed the "2030 Challenge," asking the global architecture and building community to immediately transform building design to require that all new buildings and developments be designed to use one half the fossil fuel energy they would typically consume for each building type, and that all new buildings be carbon neutral by 2030, using zero fossil fuels to operate. . . .

Many believe that a responsible approach to sharply reducing global warming pollution would involve a significant increase in the use of nuclear power plants as a substitute for coal-fired generators. While I am not opposed to nuclear power and expect to see some modest increased use of nuclear reactors, I doubt that they will play a significant role in most countries as a new source of electricity. The main reason for my skepticism about nuclear power playing a much larger role in the world's energy future is not the problem of waste disposal or the danger of reactor operator error, or the vulnerability to terrorist attack. Let's assume for the moment that all three of these problems can be solved. That still leaves two serious issues that are more difficult constraints. The first is economics; the current generation of reactors is expensive, take a long time to build, and only come in one size—extra large. . . . Secondly, if the world as a whole chose nuclear power as the option of choice to replace coal-fired generating plants, we would face a dramatic increase in the likelihood of nuclear weapons proliferation. During my eight years in the White House, every nuclear weapons proliferation issue we dealt with was connected to a nuclear reactor program. Today, the dangerous weapons programs in both Iran and North Korea are linked to their civilian reactor programs. Moreover, proposals to separate the ownership of reactors from the ownership of the fuel supply process have met with stiff resistance from developing countries who want reactors. As a result of all these problems, I believe that nuclear reactors will only play a limited role.

The most important set of problems by that must be solved in charting solutions for the climate crisis have to do with coal, one of the dirtiest sources of energy that produces far more CO2 for each unit of energy output than oil or gas. Yet, coal is found in abundance in the United States, China, and many other places. Because the pollution from the burning of coal is currently excluded from the market calculations of what it costs, coal is presently the cheapest source of abundant energy. And its relative role is growing rapidly day by day.

Fortunately, there may be a way to capture the CO2 produced as coal is burned and sequester it safely to prevent it from adding to the climate crisis. It is not easy. This technique, known as carbon capture and sequestration (CCS) is expensive and most users of coal have resisted the investments necessary to use it. However, when the cost of *not* using it is calculated, it becomes obvious that CCS will play a significant and growing role as one of the major building blocks of a solution to the climate crisis. . . .

Individual Americans of all ages are becoming a part of a movement, asking what they can do as individuals and what they can do as consumers and as citizens and voters. Many individuals and businesses have decided to take an approach known as "Zero Carbon." They are reducing their CO2 as much as possible and then offsetting the rest with reductions elsewhere including by the planting of trees. At least one entire community—Ballard, a city of 18,000 people in Washington State—is embarking on a goal of making the entire community zero carbon.

This is not a political issue. This is a moral issue. It affects the survival of human civilization. It is not a question of left vs. right; it is a question of right vs. wrong. Put simply, it is wrong to destroy the habitability of our planet and ruin the prospects of every generation that follows ours.

What is motivating millions of Americans to think differently about solutions to the climate crisis is the growing realization that this challenge is bringing us unprecedented opportunity . . . an opportunity to experience something that few generations ever have the privilege of knowing: a common moral purpose compelling enough to lift us above our limitations and motivate us to set aside some of the bickering to which we as human beings are naturally vulnerable.

America's so-called "greatest generation" found such a purpose when they confronted the crisis of global fascism and won a war in Europe and in the Pacific simultaneously. In the process of achieving their historic victory, they found that they had gained new moral authority and a new capacity for vision. . . . This is an opportunity for bipartisanship and transcendence, an opportunity to find our better selves and in rising to meet this challenge, create a better brighter future—a future worthy of the generations who come after us and who have a right to be able to depend on us.

Source: Gore, Al. "Finding Solutions to the Climate Crisis." Luxorion. Available online. http://www.astrosurf.com/luxorion/climate-crisis-al-gore.htm. Accessed December 22, 2007. Permission of former Vice President Al Gore.

"Our Future Is in Our Environment"

Chicago, Illinois, United States

May 17, 2007

Born in Nyeri, Kenya, Wangari Maathai struggled to obtain an education at a time when, as a native African and a woman, most doors were closed to her. With persistence, however, she received a biology degree in the United States, then returned to Kenya to pursue a doctorate from the University of Nairobi. She became the first woman in all of East and Central Africa to earn a Ph.D. Maathai became the chairperson of the Department of Veterinary Anatomy in Nairobi, a position that allowed her to reach fellow science students as well as other women striving for education. It was during her 1981 to 1987 tenure as chairperson of the National Council of Women that she conceived of a project that would empower African women while promoting environmental renewal and responsibility: the planting of trees. Known as the Green Belt Movement, in the past quarter century this grassroots organization has planted more than 30 million trees, opened more than 3,000 nurseries, and created more than 80,000 job opportunities for rural men and women. Maathai came to understand the crucial connection between environmental destruction and the outbreak of war, as people fought over dwindling reserves of food, arable land, and clean water. As a spokeswoman for environmentalism and human rights, Maathai's activism increasingly turned to the extension of democracy in her own country, governed by narrow one-party rule for most of her life, and toward the promotion of democracy in neighboring African nations. This marriage of democratic principles with conservationism earned Maathai the Nobel Peace Prize in 2004. Several years later, she addressed the 2007 Rotarian Conference in Chicago on the link between peace and the wise management of environmental resources.

I wish to emphasize the importance of sustainable management of the environment and how failure to do so eventually makes people not only poorer, but also at conflict with each other.

Responsible and accountable management of resources is closely linked to peace and security. Indeed, many conflicts are caused by competition over national resources. This is partly because as resources become more scarce and there is not enough to go around, or as people become selfish, greedy and corrupt, there is a drive by the powerful and the privileged to control those resources at the exclusion of others.

Unfortunately, those who feel excluded marginalized and unfairly treated look for any means available to seek justice and dignity. That is how dissatisfactions are born and nurtured until they become conflicts, clashes and wars.

There is therefore, need to educate ourselves about the linkage between the way the environment is managed vis à vis, peace and security. If the linkage between the way we manage our resources and peace were adequately understood and appreciated by all types of leaders, and if there were the will, many conflicts would be preempted. With that understanding, the environment would be prioritized in our national budgets and in our development plans.

As it is now, this linkage is poorly understood and many people are unwilling to consider it. The environment is still treated as a luxury item drawing attention only when it is to be exploited to provide timber or land for agriculture. People look at forests, for example, and see land and shambas [agricultural fields], rather than an essen-

Wangari Maathai (center in patterned dress), Nobel Peace Prize winner and founder of Kenya's Green Belt Movement, plants a tree with Kenyan children. *(Photo courtesy of Green Belt Movement International)*

tial resource that provides primary services like water, regulates climate and rainfall, cleans the air we breathe and is an essential habitat for wildlife.

Because the environment is not adequately appreciated, governments would rather prioritize the Ministry of Internal Security so that guns and bullets can be bought. In many of our countries those are used to kill each other within our own borders.

Even though many organizations and individuals, and especially in the environmental movement, had been drawing attention to this linkage between governance and the environment for many years, it was not until the Norwegian Nobel Committee brought it to the attention of the world in 2004, that people paid special attention.

In Kenya we had been using tree planting as a vehicle to deliver this message for over 30 years. But it took the Norwegian Nobel Committee to challenge the propaganda spread by those in power to the effect that those in the Green Belt Movement, who are standing up for the environment, were anti-government and anti-development. On the contrary, the recognition asserted that by planting trees and resisting destruction of the environment, environmentalists were acting like responsible patriots, who deserved praise, not jail.

In its one hundred year history, the Norwegian Nobel Committee has challenged the world to focus on issues that are important to peace by honoring individuals and organizations whose work contribute to peace and security or towards understanding the causes of conflicts and wars.

Initially, the Committee honored people who expressed great human compassion and dared to walk to the battlefields to pick the dead and wounded soldiers. These would give decent burials to the dead and nursing care to the wounded. The other groups honored were those who brought warring parties together for dialogue and reconciliation so that they could end their conflicts. In more recent times, by honoring crusaders of human rights and justice, the Committee recognized the fact that it is impossible to have peace without respecting human rights, the dignity of human beings and the rule of law.

Then came 2004, and the Norwegian Nobel Committee decided to make a historic shift again and recognize a new area, which it felt must be addressed if the world is to enjoy peace and security: The sustainable management of the environment. For the first time it also linked that to good governance, respect for human rights and the rule of law.

I had the honor and the privilege to be named the winner and become the flag bearer, but what was being recognized was a huge constituency of individuals and organizations who continuously and persistently had demonstrated that peace cannot be found where there are violation of rights, disrespect for the rule of law, where there are injustices, unfairness and inequities. Peace cannot be found where the voice of the minorities, the poor and the powerless are ignored and marginalized; where there is poverty in the midst of wealth.

This is because these ills in our societies are not accidents. They are allowed and tolerated by leaders who refuse to be fair and just to those they govern. They refuse to manage national resources sustainably and distribute them equitably. . . .

Sooner or later those who feel unfairly treated and denied justice will seek that justice using whatever means is available to them. Indeed there are hardly any wars being fought anywhere in the world today that are not wars over the need to expand borders, access and control water, minerals, grazing land, agricultural land or access forests or coastlines. . . .

Here in the Africa region there are many conflicts. Which of them are being fought by people whose environment is responsibly, accountably and sustainably managed? Where people feel included and participating in the affairs of their nation? Where people feel that their voices are listened to? Where people feel that they sit at the national table sharing resources in a fair and just way? None! Therefore, until leaders take care of the environment and the resources therein, until they promote justice and fairness, there will be no peace and security.

One of the resources we should particularly care about is the forest. Not only because forests provide humanity with many services, but mostly because without them the long-term life of the nation is undermined. This is especially now when the looming crisis of climate change is becoming a national threat.

In Africa, many investors prefer to clear cut indigenous forests and replace them with farms of commercial plantations of imported species of trees or crops. This is partly because forests are wetter, more fertile, and therefore investors can make quick profits for the shortest time. We often justify this destruction by promising jobs and wealth. But at what cost? Countries must weigh the short term benefits of quick profits and few jobs against the long term interests of both the present and the future generations. Can destruction of forests make us richer or reduce our poverty?

Before answering that question in the affirmative, let us consider the fact that the African people are among the poorest in the world. Yet Africa is one of the richest continents in the world, richly endowed with expansive lands, oceans, abundant fish, rivers, extraordinary wildlife and biodiversity, oil, precious stones and a huge population. So why are the majority of Africans poorer than most? Why do the majority of Africans continue to live in extreme poverty? Why are they not achieving the Millennium Development Goals (MDGs)? Why are deserts threatening many of our countries?

I believe that the answer lies in the way we misgovern and mismanage our various resources. Sometimes this is due to ignorance but it also due to bad leadership, greed and corruption. While it is said that people get leaders they deserve, perhaps it is also true that countries are as good as their leaders.

Otherwise, how do we explain that so many people are able to come to Africa and manage our resources for their benefit and leave the continent as happy, healthy and wealthy investors? Yet Africans hardly benefit? The leaders of Africa, including the business community, need to access our style of self-governance, resource management and pattern of distribution.

We have no future in a degraded environment and the more the environment is degraded the more we shall fight over what is left. That is until we become environmental refugees, running to foreign countries where people govern themselves responsibly, accountably, share their resources a bit more equitably and take care of their environment and development.

In conclusion I wish to draw your attention to the issue of global warming. . . . We already experience signs that could partly be attributed to global warming: melting snow in mountains like Mt. Kenya, Kilimanjaro, Ruwenzori; change in rainfall patterns, rivers drying up, prolonged drought, crop failure, accelerated processes of desertification, starvation and death of people and livestock.

Whatever the cause of this phenomenon, it would be very unwise to destroy resources, like forests, that mitigate against changes that will have great impact on the lives of millions of our people. So, let us do the little we can do and be proactive rather than passive victims of environmental degradation and negative impacts of climate change. . . .

Understanding the linkage between sustainable management of the environment and peace and security, indeed our very survival, is essential. That is the message the Norwegian Nobel Peace Committee wanted to pass to the world. That is the message I wanted to share with you at this time.

Our future is in our environment.

Source: Maathai, Wangari. "Our Environment, Our Future." The Greenbelt Movement. Available online. http://www.greenbeltmovement.org/a.php?id=238. Accessed December 20, 2007. Permission of Wangari Maathai.

Appendix 1

Writing a Persuasive Speech

All good writing intends in some way to persuade the reader or hearer. Even fiction attempts to convince the reader to believe in the world the author has imagined. Some writing is particularly intended to persuade: newspaper editorials, business advertising, a letter requesting a job, but most especially the composing of speeches.

Usually the reason for giving a speech is to persuade an audience of certain views or to suggest that something ought to be done. A good topic often has some aspect of disagreement or argument or necessary change, perhaps pointing out something that needs fixing or promoting some other way of looking at a problem. The speaker's aim is to induce other people to think the same way about this issue.

Speeches are most effective when the topic is limited to a specific idea or issue rather than a wide-ranging one. Consider the Gettysburg Address—Lincoln limited himself to the narrow theme of honoring the battlefield dead, and composed one of the most beautiful American speeches ever given. Politician Edward Everett, the featured speaker that day, held forth for two hours, touching on many ideas yet failing to leave behind a clear statement.

Speakers are almost always more successful when addressing a familiar subject. That may mean choosing a topic, or an "argument," you already know well. Or it may mean doing research to become informed on another question. For instance, on a local issue, contact individuals involved to get their opinions, and read newspaper stories with facts about the case. The more familiar a speaker is with the subject matter, the greater likelihood of producing evidence to persuade the audience.

Before beginning to write, make a simple list of your position's strong points. Try to anticipate what the "opposition" might say. There will be the opportunity, within the speech, to disarm opponents by stating their possible objections and then defending your position.

Early in the speech, state your assertion or main opinion in a manner sure to get the audience's attention. Patrick Henry does this in the opening two paragraphs of his famous "Give me liberty or give me death" speech, delivered in 1775 as the Second Virginia Convention debated whether to arm the colony against the British. Henry first applauds the patriotism and ability of the other speakers, then says he has another view of the colony's situation. "The question before the House," he says, is "nothing less than a question of freedom or slavery." Notice that his main point is not a fact—it is an opinion, an assertion, a position statement.

In the main body of the speech, the speaker presents the evidence to support the assertion. Evidence can be examples, facts, expert opinions, anecdotes, even statistics. In Charles de Gaulle's Appeal of June 18 (given in 1940 as Nazi Germany had nearly conquered France and General de Gaulle had fled to London), he gives his reasons why Frenchmen everywhere should not give up: France still has her friends and empire; France is not the only country attacked; France can use war materials supplied by the United States. He says this, of course, not in a list but in beautifully written short paragraphs that use several "tricks" of the orator's art. Many of these tricks are known as rhetorical devices, or figures of speech.

For instance, de Gaulle did not say, "France still has her friends." He took advantage of the marvelous powers of understatement and repetition and said instead, "For France is not alone! She is not alone! She is not alone!"

In this way, rhetorical devices make speeches lively and the style attractive and beautiful to the ear. (Examples of rhetorical devices have been placed in sidebars throughout this book.) With these devices, speakers can appeal to the emotions of audiences in subtle ways, not unlike the ways that music appeals to people's emotions. Another of the important uses of rhetorical devices is to emphasize the significant points of a speech, helping the audience to focus where the speaker intended and to fully understand the meaning.

Many of these devices will be familiar already, even come naturally as you write and speak. Some are liberating to use as they seem to flaunt the advice English teachers give about grammar and style—for instance, in using repetition and redundancy, even incomplete sentences. Learn to recognize them, to gain a sense of what using rhetorical devices can contribute to a speech. (Do not be put off by the Greek and Roman names they were given!) For example, asking a rhetorical question (a question for which the speaker does not supply an answer) gives an audience the impression they are involved, as the question stimulates possible answers in their minds. Repeating words and phrases in particular ways can be extremely effective in drawing the audience's attention to key points.

An emotional appeal or digression can be extremely effective after developing your case. Is there a personal experience to share, an anecdote that will arrest the audience? Provoking emotion in listeners can make a speech unforgettable. For example, in South Africa in 1985 Nelson Mandela declined the offer of release from prison if he would renounce his anti-apartheid activism. He smuggled out from his cell a speech, delivered by his daughter, which included this passage: "I cherish my own freedom dearly, but I care even more for your freedom. Too many have died since I went to prison. Too many have suffered for the love of freedom. I owe it to their widows, to their orphans, to their mothers and to their fathers who have grieved and wept for them. . . . But I cannot sell my birthright, nor am I prepared to sell the birthright of the people to be free." Who could hear that and fail to be stirred? Most people will not be delivering an address of that sort, of course, but on even the smallest of occasions it is possible to rouse the listeners.

For your speech's conclusion, the "peroration," it is important to restate your position to remind the audience, and sum up evidence in a compelling way. Listen to Emmeline Pankhurst, English activist for women's voting rights in 1913: She says in her last paragraph, "How else than by giving votes to women are you going to govern the women of England!" To present a compelling ending, she next uses a rhetorical device (*procatalepsis*) to disarm her foes' argument: "You cannot govern us if we refuse to be governed. . . . Government rests upon force, you say. Not at all; it rests upon consent, ladies and gentlemen, and women are withdrawing their consent."

In her closing sentence, Pankhurst has announced her conclusion about what women will be doing. Indian nationalist and social reformer Mohandas Gandhi similarly closed a speech in 1906 by predicting, "So long as there is even a handful of men true to their pledge, there can be only one end to the struggle, and that is victory." A closing sentence can be a recommendation—let listeners know what you want them to do. Here is Powhatan finishing his speech to Virginia colonist Captain John Smith: "And, above all, I insist that the guns and swords, the cause of all our jealousy and uneasiness, be removed and sent away."

The last line of the speech may also be a challenge, a call to action. Presidential adviser Bernard Baruch's 1946 address to the United Nations advocated the control of nuclear weapons. He concluded: "The solution will require apparent sacrifice in pride and in position, but better pain as the price of peace than death as the price of war."

Once the draft of the speech is written, put it aside for a day and then revise. Revisiting the speech later will reveal many more areas to improve than if you had finished the speech in one sitting. Then, read the speech out loud a number of times, altering the text in little ways to make it flow naturally. A good speaker becomes so familiar with the speech that there will be little need to refer to the written text when delivering it. But bring the written text to the lectern anyway, even if it seems to be no longer needed!

Appendix 2

Delivering a Great Speech

Studying rhetoric or oratory—the art of public speaking—was an important part of schooling for the elite two thousand years ago, and in many centuries since that time. As recently as the 19th century, children regularly practiced declamation at school, delivering an address previously given by another person. Often it was the speech of a master orator such as the Greek Demosthenes or Cicero of Rome. Students of oratory then graduated to writing and delivering their own speeches.

Today in school there is little time for rhetoric except as an extracurricular activity—debate. Yet addressing the public is something almost everyone has to do at some point in life. Anyone can step into public speaking simply by giving readings at church or making announcements at school assemblies, or by joining a debate club.

This book collects a great number of speeches that can be used for declamation, including many from present-day orators. You can learn from these men and women by practicing delivering their speeches, in the same way that painters sometimes learn from the masters by copying their paintings. Audio recordings and the Internet make it possible to listen to recent orators delivering their own speeches as well.

A speech almost always begins as a written piece; few people can deliver a good speech without first writing it out and practicing the delivery. Speakers can diverge from written speeches, of course, but writing the speech down first will make certain that important arguments and main points will not be forgotten.

In ancient times (and more recently in those cultures without written language) an orator was expected to memorize his speech, to be able to deliver it without paper (or teleprompter). Today, audiences are not surprised to see a written text on the lectern. They *are* unhappy, though, when speakers keep their faces in the text during the entire delivery! To avoid this, print out the speech in a large font size, perhaps 16-point, so you can look up at the audience and then find your place again easily. (If looking into their faces brings on anxiety, find other focus points within the group.) Separate the text into many short paragraphs to make it easy to read, and even leave a line space between paragraphs.

Successful speakers take their time with their words. Try to avoid that common problem of beginning speakers—speaking too fast. It is a natural reaction; when people feel nervous, they want to get the job over with. Getting it over with, however, makes for a poor performance. Take pity on the audience and take time with them; they are not as familiar with the material, and need a little extra time to process the information. Think of the audience as friends; they want the speaker to succeed with an interesting speech as much as the speaker does. To get a sense of good pacing, listen to a speech by U.S. president Ronald Reagan or Britain's Prime Minister Winston Churchill—easily found on the Internet.

The nature of the audience will greatly affect the approach of a speech and choice of words. Use a tone of voice and demeanor appropriate to the setting. Are you speaking to classmates about to elect the class president? Addressing a school Parents' Night? Giving a pep talk to the baseball team? Perhaps saying a few words at the funeral for a grandparent? Very different styles of address might come from those scenarios.

It is important for speakers to know their audience. Respecting the audience means understanding what their beliefs are and what they already know, especially if they are young or uninformed. One occasional pitfall of public speaking is to underestimate listeners' experience or intelligence by addressing them in an oversimplified manner—"talking down" to them—which they will resent as superior and condescending. Take care not to offend the audience—no one can persuade anyone using rude words or calling names; jokes that demean or poke fun at other groups almost always backfire. And it is particularly disrespectful to use off-color words with an audience that is either older or younger than you are, or when the opposite sex is present.

Steer clear of expressing too much anger at people who disagree, whether they are present or not. A convincing speaker must appear fair and honest—make the audience trust you. Be well informed. Show them that you know what you are talking about by providing evidence to support your opinions. Speakers sound more authoritative when they do not preface statements with "I think" or "I believe" and these phrases are unnecessary as the audience expects speakers to give their own opinions.

Speakers should always avoid the appearance of bragging in anything they have to say about themselves. Modesty and understatement go a long way with an audience whenever speakers refer to their own accomplishments.

The day before delivering the speech, practice. Read and reread the speech out loud until it is intimately familiar. Time yourself delivering it—does its length fit into the space allotted, or is it too short or too long?

Lastly, will the audience ask questions afterward? Anticipating what those questions might be, and having a few answers jotted down at the end of the speech in preparation, can really help a speaker feel in control of the situation.

Appendix 3

Working with Speeches as Primary Sources

Quoting the words of a historical figure can be an essential part of a biographical sketch or an essay on an historic event. Such quotes are easily found in the speeches and other public utterances—such as sermons or trial addresses—that an individual may have made. Speeches make excellent sources for the authentic words and ideas of people throughout history.

Like letters, journals, and photographs, speeches are primary source documents. They are historical artifacts created by people who participated in events of the past. (A secondary source is an account written about events after they took place.) In this book, the speeches are primary sources. The introductions to the speeches, and the historical introductions beginning each chapter, are secondary sources. Individuals in the past may have left both primary and secondary sources if, say, they composed letters to friends (primary), gave campaign speeches (primary), and wrote histories of their towns or states (secondary).

There are many issues to consider when using a particular speech as a primary source.

What is known about how the speech was preserved? Perhaps soldiers recounted the exact words of their commander—or maybe an ancient historian "recorded" what he thought the general had likely said. Accurate records of many old speeches have been preserved, even those made by the ancient Greeks and Romans, but sometimes a speech was recounted orally by several hearers so that a number of versions came to exist. In the past few hundred years, a speaker's written or printed text is much more likely to have been preserved or reprinted than in older times.

Who was the speaker? Consider not just the speaker's biographical details but also his or her point of view. Was she an old sage with many years of political skill behind her words, or a young girl filled with idealism? Was he an aristocrat, born to privilege, or poor and self-taught, the subject of a colonial power? And importantly, were they speaking for themselves or for an organization or political party? For female orators, what might it have been like to give a speech at a time when women were commonly relegated to sitting in the balcony? What about a black orator alone on the stage, braving a sea of white faces?

Consider who the orator was addressing, and where the speech was delivered—the audience (and even the place) may have affected the choice of words or theme. Was the orator speaking to a large public group or to a small private audience? Was the audience young or old, and were they a mixed group of men and women, or a gathering of one gender? Did the speaker address a legislative assembly, or the faithful in a house of worship? Or was the speech made to jurors in a hostile court, to party followers under a tent in the outback, or to soldiers suited up for battle? The answers may help reveal how courageous, biased, cunning, earnest, naïve, impatient, wise, even crazed the speaker may have been, and how the speech may have been tailored to fit the audience and the occasion.

Consider what genre the speech fits into. It could be a eulogy (appreciation for the dead), sermon, patriotic address, farewell speech, or part of a debate. Was the text likely to have been composed carefully ahead of time, for a special occasion, or was it the result of a sudden event? Is the speaker discussing matters that he knows about personally? Is she offering information to persuade the audience? What is the speech's most important message?

Sometimes speeches contain memorable phrases. It might be a phrase that captures the message or one that expresses the speaker's outlook or passion, and perhaps is even used to identify the speech—such as Ronald Reagan's "Tear down this wall!" or Lucy Stone's "A disappointed woman."

The speaker's language may be formal and stilted, casual and conversational, even excitable, bombastic, or inflammatory. The speaker may have used big words, or the speech of everyday people. Notice that in some speeches the text proceeds on an even pace; in others, passion builds. Is the speech funny, does it produce tears, or does the hair rise on the back of your neck as you read? You can get more sense of the speech by reading it out loud.

If possible, listen to an audio recording of the speech as it was given. You should be able to hear the speaker's pacing or demeanor—how well he told a joke or how much passion was in her voice. Was the speech likely to have kept the audience's attention? Is it known how the crowd responded to the speech?

Not all of these questions need answering, of course, only those that are relevant to evaluating a particular speech. If there are references to unfamiliar places or things, you must research them to have a full understanding of the text. Once you understand the speech fully, how does it help unravel the events of the time?

Finally, speeches may be biased like any other primary document. They are the words of individuals, who bring to their speeches all the limitations of education and experience, and all the prejudices of their time and place. Because a speech is so often an instrument for persuasion, the speaker has a decided point of view. A good researcher might ask: Did the speaker have reason to lie or distort the truth? Do the speaker's statements fit with other evidence about this event or issue? Historians—and *Webster's Dictionary* says anyone is a historian who studies, writes, or chronicles history—must be skeptical of every piece of evidence from the past, and must consider and compare all other related evidence before drawing conclusions.

Remember, it is often easier to detect bias in the speeches of people from previous times, or from another point of view, than our own. Researchers have to consider carefully to detect bias. But even a biased speech can reveal information about the speaker's time. If the source raises questions, you may be able to answer them with further research.

General Bibliography

General Speech Treasuries

Baird, Albert Craig, ed. *American Public Addresses 1740–1952.* New York: McGraw Hill, 1956.

Brewer, David J., ed. *World's Best Orations from the Earliest Period to the Present Time.* Chicago: Ferd. P. Kaiser, 1899.

Bryan, William Jennings, ed. *The World's Famous Orations.* New York: Funk & Wagnall, 1906.

Copeland, Lewis, and Lawrence Lamm, eds. *The World's Great Speeches.* New York: Dover, 1973.

Crosscup, Richard, ed. *Classic Speeches: Words That Shook the World.* New York: Philosophical Library, 1965.

Goodrich, Chauncey A., ed. *Select British Eloquence.* New York: Harper & Bros., 1853.

Hazeltine, Mayo, ed. *Famous Orations.* New York: Collier & Son, 1903.

Hurd, Charles, ed. *A Treasury of Great American Speeches.* New York: Hawthorn Books, 1959.

Israel, Steve, and Seth Forman, eds. *Great Jewish Speeches throughout History.* Northvale, N.J.: Jason Aronson, 1994.

Lee, Guy Carleton, ed. *The World's Orators.* New York: Putnam, 1900.

MacArthur, Brian, ed. *Penguin Book of 20th Century Speeches.* London: Viking, 1992.

———. *The Penguin Book of Historic Speeches.* London: Penguin, 1996.

McIntire, Suzanne. *American Heritage Book of Great American Speeches for Young People.* New York: John Wiley & Sons, 2001.

Moore, Frank. *American Eloquence: A Collection of Speeches and Addresses.* New York: D. Appleton Co., 1857.

Nix, Michele S. *Women at the Podium: Memorable Speeches in History.* New York: HarperCollins, 2000.

Peterson, Houston, ed. *A Treasury of the World's Great Speeches.* New York: Simon & Schuster, 1954.

Platz, Mabel, ed. *Anthology of Public Speeches.* New York: H. W. Wilson, 1940.

Reed, Thomas Brackett, ed. *Modern Eloquence.* Chicago: Geo. L. Shuman, 1900.

Safire, William, ed. *Lend Me Your Ears.* New York: W. W. Norton, 1992.

Scotland, Andrew, ed. *The Power of Eloquence: A Treasury of British Speech.* London: Cassell, 1961.

Suriano, Gregory, ed. *Great American Speeches.* New York: Gramercy Books, 1993.

Vital Speeches of the Day. City News Pub. Co., New York. Published semi-monthly since 1934.

Collected Speeches and Biographies, A Selection

Augustine. *Selected Sermons of St. Augustine.* Translated by Quincy Howe, Jr. New York: Holt, Rinehart Winston, 1966.

Bolívar, Simón. *Selected Writings of Bolivar.* Edited by Harold Bierck. New York: Banco de Venezuela with Colonial Press, 1951.

Bright, John. *Speeches on the Public Affairs of the Last Twenty Years.* London: Camden Hotten, 1869.

Churchill, Winston. *Blood, Toil, Tears and Sweat: The Speeches of Winston Churchill.* Edited by David Cannadine. Boston: Houghton Mifflin, 1989.

Douglass, Frederick. *The Frederick Douglass Papers.* Edited by John Blassingame. New Haven, Conn.: Yale University Press, 1979.

Emory, John. *The Works of the Reverend John Wesley.* New York: Mason & Lane, 1840.

Gandhi, M. K. *Speeches and Writings of Mahatma Gandhi.* Madras: G. A. Natesan & Co., 1933.

Gladstone, William. *Political Speeches in Scotland, November and December 1879.* London: W. Ridgway, 1879.

Guthman, Edwin, and C. Richard Allen, eds. *RFK: Collected Speeches.* New York: Viking, 1993.

Haile Selassie. *Haile Selassie I: Silver Jubilee.* Edited by David Abner Talbot. London: W.P. van Stockum, 1955.

Huxley, Leonard. *Life and Letters of Thomas Henry Huxley.* New York: D. Appleton, 1916.

Ibárruri, Dolores. *Dolores Ibarruri: Speeches and Articles 1936–1938.* New York: International Publishers, 1938.

Ledwidge, Bernard. *DeGaulle.* New York: St. Martin's Press, 1982.

Lincoln, Abraham. *Speeches and Writings, 1859–1865.* New York: Library of America, 1989.

Livingstone, David. *Dr. Livingstone's Cambridge Lectures.* Edited by Rev. William Monk. Cambridge: Deighton, Bell and Co., 1858.

MacArthur, Douglas. *MacArthur.* Edited by Lawrence Wittner. Englewood Cliffs, N.J.: Prentice Hall, 1971.

Mandela, Nelson. *The Struggle Is My Life.* New York: Pathfinder Press, 1990.

Martí, José. *Our America: Writings on Latin America and the Struggle for Cuban Independence.* Edited by Philip S. Foner. New York: Monthly Review Press, 1977.

Mill, John Stuart. *The Collected Works of John Stuart Mill.* Edited by John M. Robson and Bruce L. Kinzer. Toronto: University of Toronto Press, 1988.

Nehru, Jawaharlal. *Independence and After: A Collection of Speeches.* New York: John Day Co., 1950.

Nyerere, Julius K. *Freedom and Unity: A Selection from Writings and Speeches 1952–1965.* Dar es Salaam, Tanzania: Oxford, 1967.

Reagan, Ronald. *Speaking My Mind.* New York: Simon & Schuster, 1989.

Shnookal, Deborah, and Mirta Muniz, eds. *José Martí Reader: Writings on the Americas.* New York: Ocean Press, 1999.

Talbott, Strobe, ed. *Khrushchev Remembers.* Boston: Little, Brown, 1970.

Timmons, Wilbert, H. *Morelos of Mexico.* El Paso: Texas Western College Press, 1963.

Twain, Mark. *Mark Twain Speaking.* Edited by Paul Fatout. Iowa City: University of Iowa Press, 1976.

Villari, Pasquale. *The Life and Times of Girolamo Savonarola.* Translated by Linda Villari. New York: Scribner's, 1888.

Wells, William V. *The Life and Public Services of Samuel Adams.* Boston: Little, Brown, 1875.

Whipple, Edwin Percy, ed. *The Great Speeches and Orations of Daniel Webster.* New York: Little, Brown, 1914.

Wilson, Woodrow. *Selected Literary and Political Papers and Addresses of Woodrow Wilson.* New York: Grosset & Dunlap, 1926.

Documentary Histories and Sourcebooks

Arnold, Carroll, Douglas Ehninger, and John Gerber, eds. *The Speaker's Resource Book.* Chicago: Scott, Foresman, 1961.

Blom-Cooper, Louis, ed. *The Law as Literature.* London: The Bodley Head, Ltd., 1961.

Boahen, A. Adu, ed. *Africa under Colonial Domination, 1880–1935. (UNESCO General History of Africa, Vol. 7).* Berkeley: University of California Press, 1990.

Burns, E. Bradford, ed. *A Documentary History of Brazil.* New York: Knopf, 1966.

Chandler, Peleg Whitman. *American Criminal Trials.* Boston: Charles Little & James Brown, 1841.

De Bary, William Theodore, and Irene Bloom, eds. *Sources of Chinese Tradition.* New York: Columbia University Press, 1999.

Drake, Samuel. *Book of the Indians.* New York: AMS Press, 1976.

Horne, Charles F., ed. *Sacred Books and Early Literature of the East.* New York: Parke, Austin, Lipscomb, 1917.

Jorgensen-Earp, Cheryl R., ed. *Speeches and Trials of the Militant Suffragettes: The Women's Social and Political Union, 1903–1918.* Madison, N.J.: Fairleigh Dickinson University Press, 1999.

Kaes, Anton, Martin Jay, and Edward Dimendberg, eds. *The Weimar Republic Sourcebook.* Berkeley: University of California Press, 1994.

Keen, Benjamin, ed. *Readings in Latin American Civilization.* Cambridge: Riverside Press, 1955.

Laqueur, Walter, and Barry Rubin, eds. *The Israel-Arab Reader: A Documentary History of the Middle East Conflict.* New York: Penguin, 1984.

Lee, Peter H., and William Theodore de Bary. *Sources of Korean Tradition.* New York: Columbia University Press, 1997.

Lieberman, Leo, and Arthur Beringause, eds. *Classics of Jewish Literature.* New York: Philosophical Library, 1987.

Lukacs, Yehuda, ed. *Israeli-Palestinian Conflict: A Documentary Record.* Cambridge: Cambridge University Press, 1992.

Maser, Werner. *Nuremberg: A Nation on Trial.* New York: Scribner, 1977.

Mazrui, Ali A., and C. Wondji, eds. *Africa since 1935. (UNESCO General History of Africa, Vol. 8).* London: Heineman, 1993.

Moquin, Wayne, ed. *Great Documents in American Indian History.* New York: Da Capo Press, 1973.

Ogg, Frederic Austin, ed. *Source Book of Medieval History.* New York: American Book Co., 1908.

Ravitch, Diane. *The American Reader: Words That Moved a Nation.* New York: HarperCollins, 1990.

Ravitch, Diane, and Abigail Thernstrom, eds. *The Democracy Reader: Classic and Modern Speeches, Essays, Poems, Declarations, and Documents on Freedom and Human Rights Worldwide.* New York: HarperCollins, 1992.

Stanton, Elizabeth Cady, and Susan B. Anthony. *Correspondence, Writings, Speeches.* Edited by Ellen C. DuBois. New York: Shocken Books, 1981, pp. 152–165.

Stanton, Elizabeth Cady, Susan B. Anthony, and Matilda Joslyn Gage. *History of Woman Suffrage.* Rochester, N.Y.: Charles Mann, 1889.

Trefousse, Hans Louis. *The Cold War: A Book of Documents.* New York: Putnam, 1965.

Tsunoda, Ryusaku, William Theodore de Bary, and Donald Keene, eds. *Sources of Japanese Tradition.* New York: Columbia University Press, 1958.

Warner, Michael, ed. *American Sermons: The Pilgrims to Martin Luther King.* New York: Library of America, 1999.

Zinn, Howard, and Anthony Arnove, eds. *Voices of a People's History of the United States.* New York: Seven Stories Press, 2004.

On Writing and Delivering Speeches

Humes, James C. *Speak Like Churchill, Stand Like Lincoln: 21 Powerful Secrets of History's Greatest Speakers.* New York: Three Rivers Press, 2002.
A presidential speechwriter describes the skills used by great orators in history.

Noonan, Peggy. *On Speaking Well: How to Give a Speech with Style, Substance, and Clarity.* New York: ReganBooks, 1999.
Written by the celebrated speechwriter for President Ronald Reagan.

Valenti, Jack. *Speak Up with Confidence: How to Prepare, Learn, and Deliver Effective Speeches.* New York: Morrow, 1982.
Written by the speechwriter for Lyndon Johnson who went on to be president of the Motion Picture Association.

Selected Web sites

American Rhetoric Online Speechbank
URL:http://www.americanrhetoric.com/speechbank.htm.
Indexed database of more than 5,000 American speeches, many in full text, audio, and video versions. Includes a special section, "The Rhetoric of 9-11."

Churchill Centre
URL: http://www.winstonchurchill.org/i4a/pages/index.cfm?pageid=1.
Speeches, quotations, facts (and falsehoods debunked), and much more at this excellent site on all things Churchill.

Collected Works of Mahatma Gandhi Online. *Mahatma Gandhi Research and Media Service,* GandhiServe Foundation, Berlin
URL: http://www.gandhiserve.org.
Extensive material on Gandhi, including photographs and downloadable files of his writings, correspondence, and speeches.

Dwight D. Eisenhower Presidential Library
URL:http://www.eisenhower.archives.gov/speeches/Eisenhower_speeches.html.
Presidential library site contains numerous speeches by Eisenhower, including pre- and post-presidential addresses.

Eleanor Roosevelt Papers Project. George Washington University
URL:http://www.gwu.edu/~erpapers/documents/speeches/doc026617.cfm.
University project to place Eleanor Roosevelt's letters, articles, book excerpts, speeches, and broadcast appearances in a comprehensive website.

Franklin D. Roosevelt Presidential Library
URL: http://www.fdrlibrary.marist.edu/dec71941.html.
Presidential library site offers full text of Roosevelt's "fireside chats," selected speeches, and thousands of photographs.

Gifts of Speech: Women's Speeches from Around the World. Sweet Briar College
URL: http://gos.sbc.edu/.
A collection of speeches by prominent contemporary women from around the world, many not seen elsewhere, with some historical speeches.

Jewish Virtual Library
URL: http://www.jewishvirtuallibrary.org.
Extensive site covering issues, events, biography, and documents related to Jewish history (including the Arab-Israeli conflict).

John F. Kennedy Presidential Library
URL:http://www.jfklibrary.org/Historical+Resources/Archives/Reference+Desk/Speeches/Speeches+of+John+F.+Kennedy.htm.
Numerous selected speeches and press conferences from Kennedy's career, including pre-presidential speeches beginning in 1946. Also speeches by his brothers, Robert F. Kennedy and Edward M. Kennedy.

Marxists Internet Archive
URL: http://www.marxists.org/archive.
Extensive collection of material on Marxist adherents of every stripe from all over the world. Many speeches, including some by revolutionaries who

died before Marx was born, and by other unconventional thinkers.

Miller Center of Public Affairs, Scripps Library and Multimedia Archive.
URL: http://millercenter.org/scripps/archive/speeches.
This University of Virginia site offers text and (where possible) audio recordings of speeches of all U.S. presidents.

Papers of Benjamin Franklin. American Philosophical Society/Yale University
URL: http://www.franklinpapers.org/franklin/framed Volumes.jsp.
Major project to place online all Franklin's correspondence, speeches, and other papers.

Papers of George Washington. University of Virginia
URL: http://gwpapers.virginia.edu/documents/farewell/transcript.html.
Extensive collection of all George Washington's papers, including annual and inaugural addresses with background information.

Ronald Reagan Presidential Library
URL: http://www.reagan.utexas.edu/archives/speeches/major.html.
Presidential library site has Reagan's pre-presidential and presidential speeches from 1964 through 1989, with links to audio recordings.

Silva Rhetoricae—*The Forest of Rhetoric*
URL: http://humanities.byu.edu/rhetoric/silva.htm.
Excellent in-depth discussion of classical rhetoric and collection of rhetorical devices, with textual examples, from Brigham Young University.

Speeches by Title

Speeches by Orator

Speeches by Nationality

Vatican

Venezuela

Vietnam

List of Rhetorical Devices

Comprehensive Index

Locators in *italic* indicate illustrations.

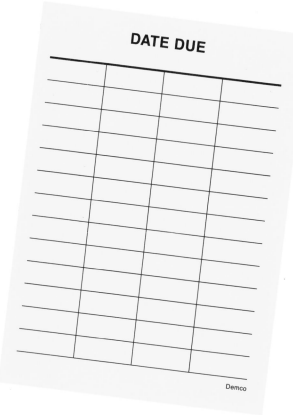

DATE DUE

Demco